THE GREEN GUIDE

Châteaux of the Loire

While every effort is made to ensure
that all information printed in this guide is correct
and up-to-date, Michelin Travel Publications
(a trading division of Michelin Tyre PLC)
accepts no liability for any direct, indirect
or consequential losses howsoever caused
so far as such can be excluded by law.

Travel Publications

Hannay House, 39 Clarendon Road
Watford, Herts WD17 1JA, UK
☎ 01923 205 240 - Fax 01923 205 241
www.ViaMichelin.com
TheGreenGuide-uk@uk.michelin.com

Manufacture française des pneumatiques Michelin
Société en commandite par actions au capital de 304 000 000 EUR
Place des Carmes-Déchaux – 63 Clermont-Ferrand (France)
R.C.S. Clermont-Fd B 855 200 507

No part of this publication may be reproduced in any form
without the prior permission of the publisher

© Michelin et Cie, Propriétaires-éditeurs, 2000
Dépôt légal août 2000 – ISBN 2-06-000123-4 – ISSN 0763-1383
Printed in France 01-03/6.4

Typesetting: LE SANGLIER, Charleville-Mézières
Printing - binding : I.M.E., Baume-les-Dames

Cover design: Carré Noir, Paris 17ᵉ arr.

THE GREEN GUIDE:
The Spirit of Discovery

The exhilaration of new horizons,
the fun of seeing the world,
the excitement of discovery:
this is what we seek to share with you.
To help you make the most
of your travel experience,
we offer first-hand knowledge and turn
a discerning eye on places to visit.
This wealth of information
gives you the expertise to plan
your own enriching adventure.
With THE GREEN GUIDE
showing you the way, you can explore
new destinations with confidence
or rediscover old ones.
Leisure time spent with THE GREEN
GUIDE is also a time for refreshing
your spirit, enjoying yourself,
and taking advantage of our selection
of fine restaurants, hotels
and other places for relaxing.
So turn the page and open a window
on the world. Join THE GREEN GUIDE
in the spirit of discovery.

Contents

Practical information   16

Planning your trip   18
Formalities   21
Budget   22
Getting there   24
Motoring in France   25
Where to stay, Where to eat   26
Basic information   30
Shopping   33
Discovering the region   33
Sports and outdoor activities   41
Suggested reading   45
Calendar of events   47
Useful French words and phrases   50

Introduction   52

The Loire Valley   54
Historical table and notes   60
A long and eventful history   63
Châteaux and castle life   67
The finest French in France   72
Art and architecture   74
Food and wine   84

Sights   88

In alphabetical order

Admission times and charges   312

Index   332

Dormer window, Amboise Château

B. Kaufmann/MICHELIN

Wildlife in Sologne

S. Cordier/JACANA

Maps and plans

In addition to the Map of principal sights and the Map of regional driving tours at the beginning of this guide, there are a number of useful maps and plans in the guide, listed here:

Thematic maps

Map of places to stay	28
Landscapes	54
Local specialities and wines	84
Parc naturel régional Loire-Anjou-Touraine	174
Le Mans racing circuits	222
Campaign of Joan of Arc	235
Siege of Orléans	236

Town plans

Amboise	94
Angers	104
Baugé	114
Beaugency	118
Blois	128
Châteaudun	147
Château-Gontier	149
Château-Renault	155
Chinon	167
La Ferté-Bernard	185
La Flèche	188
Lavardin	201
Loches	205
Le vieux Mans	218
Le Mans	219
Orléans	240
Romorantin-Lanthenay	254
Saumur	268
Sully-sur-Loire	282
Tours	290
Vendôme	303

Monuments

Angers: St-Maurice Cathedral	100
Château de Châteaudun	147
Château de Chinon	169
Fontevraud Abbey	191
Le Mans: St-Julien Cathedral	220
Vendôme: Trinity Abbey	304

Local maps for touring

From Angers: La Loire Maugeoise	110
The Baugeois	115
From Blois: La Loire Tourangelle	131
Upper reaches of the Loir	134
Around Brou: Le Perche-Gouet	139
Vallée de la Mayenne	151
Around Chinon	170
Around Cholet	179
Vallée de la Manse	198
Vallée du Layon	203
Down the Sarthe Valley	225
Around Mondoubleau	227
From Orléans: La Loire Blésoise	244
Ste-Maure Plateau	263
From Saumur: La Loire Angevine	272
Lakes and moors of the Sologne	279
From Tours: Downstream to Chinon	297
Middle reaches of the Loir	306

Villandry gardens

Rosé wine from the Loire Valley

Studio 3bis/MICHELIN

J.-D. Sudres/PHOTONONSTOP

Michelin maps

COMPANION PUBLICATIONS

Regional and local maps

To make the most of your journey, travel with Michelin maps at a scale of 1:200 000: Regional maps nos 232, 237 and 238 and the new local maps, which are illustrated on the map of France below.

Maps of France

And remember to travel with the latest edition of the map of France no 721, which gives an overall view of the region of the Châteaux of the Loire, and the main access roads which connect it to the rest of France. The entire country is mapped at a 1:1 000 000 scale and clearly shows the main road network. Convenient Atlas formats (spiral, hard cover and "mini") are also available.

Internet

Michelin is pleased to offer a route-planning service on the Internet: www.ViaMichelin.com. Choose the shortest route, a route without tolls, or the Michelin recommended route to your destination; you can also access information about hotels and restaurants from The Red Guide, and tourists sites from The Green Guide.

There are a number of useful maps and plans in the guide, listed in the table of contents.

Bon voyage!

Using this guide

● The summary maps on the following pages are designed to assist you in planning your trip: the **Map of principal sights** identifies major sights and attractions, the Map of regional driving tours proposes regional driving itineraries.

● The **Practical information** section offers useful addresses for planning your trip, seeking accommodation, indulging in outdoor activities and more; festival and carnival dates; suggestions for thematic tours on scenic railways and through nature reserves etc. The **Map of places to stay** points out pleasant holiday spots. We have selected **hotels and restaurants**, and other places for **entertainment and going out** for many of the towns in this guide. Turn to the pages bordered in blue.

● We recommend that you read the **Introduction** before setting out on your trip. The background information It contains on history, the arts and traditional culture will prove most instructive and make your visit more meaningful.

● The main towns and attractions are presented in alphabetical order in the Sights section. In order to ensure quick, easy identification, original place names have been used throughout the guide. The clock symbol ⊙, placed after monuments or other sights, refers to the **Admission times and charges** section at the end of the guide, in which the names appear in the same order as in the Sights section.

● The **Index** lists attractions, famous people and events, and other subjects covered in the guide.

Let us hear from you. We are interested in your reaction to our guide, in any ideas you have to offer or good addresses you would like to share. Send your comments to Michelin Travel Publications, Hannay House, 39 Clarendon Road, Watford, Herts WD17 15A, U.K. or by e-mail to thegreenguide-uk@uk.michelin.com.

Château de Chenonceau

Key

Selected monuments and sights

◉ ⇒ Tour - Departure point

⛪ ⚰ Catholic church

⛪ ✝ Protestant church, other temple

▨ ▣ 🕌 Synagogue - Mosque

▧ Building

■ Statue, small building

✝ Calvary, wayside cross

◎ Fountain

●━■▪ Rampart - Tower - Gate

✕ Château, castle, historic house

∴ Ruins

⌣ Dam

☼ Factory, power plant

☆ Fort

∩ Cave

🐗 Prehistoric site

▼ Viewing table

\// Viewpoint

▲ Other place of interest

Sports and recreation

🏇 Racecourse

⛸ Skating rink

≈ 🏊 Outdoor, indoor swimming pool

🎥 Multiplex Cinema

⛵ Marina, sailing centre

🏠 Trail refuge hut

□━■━■━□ Cable cars, gondolas

□━┼┼┼┼━□ Funicular, rack railway

🚂 Tourist train

◆ Recreation area, park

🧜 Theme, amusement park

🦌 Wildlife park, zoo

❀ Gardens, park, arboretum

🕊 Bird sanctuary, aviary

🚶 Walking tour, footpath

😊 Of special interest to children

Abbreviations

A Agricultural office (Chambre d'agriculture)

C Chamber of Commerce (Chambre de commerce)

H Town hall (Hôtel de ville)

J Law courts (Palais de justice)

M Museum (Musée)

P Local authority offices (Préfecture, sous-préfecture)

POL. Police station (Police)

🛡 Police station (Gendarmerie)

T Theatre (Théatre)

U University (Université)

	Sight	Seaside resort	Winter sports resort	Spa
Highly recommended	★★★	�	✻✻✻	♰♰♰
Recommended	★★	☝☝	✻✻	♰♰
Interesting	★	☝	✻	♰

Additional symbols

🛈		Tourist information
══	══	Motorway or other primary route
❶	❶	Junction: complete, limited
⊨══⊨	══	Pedestrian street
ⲭ═══ⲭ		Unsuitable for traffic, street subject to restrictions
⊞⊞⊞	- - - -	Steps - Footpath
🚂	🚘	Train station - Auto-train station
🚌	S.N.C.F.	Coach (bus) station
⊷		Tram
⬛		Metro, underground
P/R		Park-and-Ride
♿		Access for the disabled
✉		Post office
☎		Telephone
✉		Covered market
⁎⤫⁎		Barracks
△		Drawbridge
⋃		Quarry
✕		Mine
Ⓑ	Ⓕ	Car ferry (river or lake)
⛴		Ferry service: cars and passengers
⛴		Foot passengers only
③		Access route number common to Michelin maps and town plans
Bert (R.)…		Main shopping street
AZ B		Map co-ordinates

Hotels and restaurants

20 rooms: Number of rooms:
38,57/57,17€ price for one person/ double room

half-board or full board: Price per person, based
42,62€ on double occupancy

🍽 *6,85€* Price of breakfast; when not given, it is included in the price of the room (i.e., for bed-and-breakfasts)

120 sites: Number of camp sites and cost
12,18€ for 2 people with a car

12,18€ lunch- Restaurant: fixed-price menus
16,74/38,05€ served at lunch only-mini/maxi price fixed menu (lunch and dinner) or à la carte

rest. Lodging where meals are served
16,74/38,05€ mini/maxi price fixed menu or à la carte

meal 15,22€ "Family style" meal

reserv Reservation recommended

🚫 No credit cards accepted

P Reserved parking for hotel patrons

The prices correspond to the higher rates of the tourist season

Principal sights

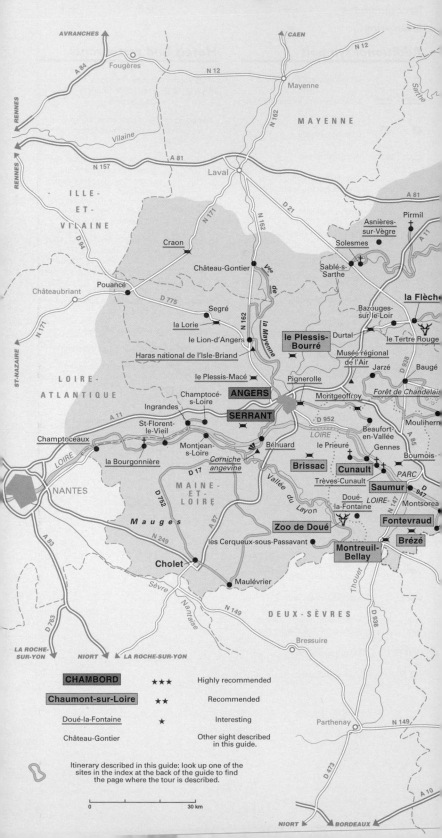

CHAMBORD	★★★	Highly recommended
Chaumont-sur-Loire	★★	Recommended
Doué-la-Fontaine	★	Interesting
Château-Gontier		Other sight described in this guide.

Itinerary described in this guide: look up one of the sites in the index at the back of the guide to find the page where the tour is described.

0   30 km

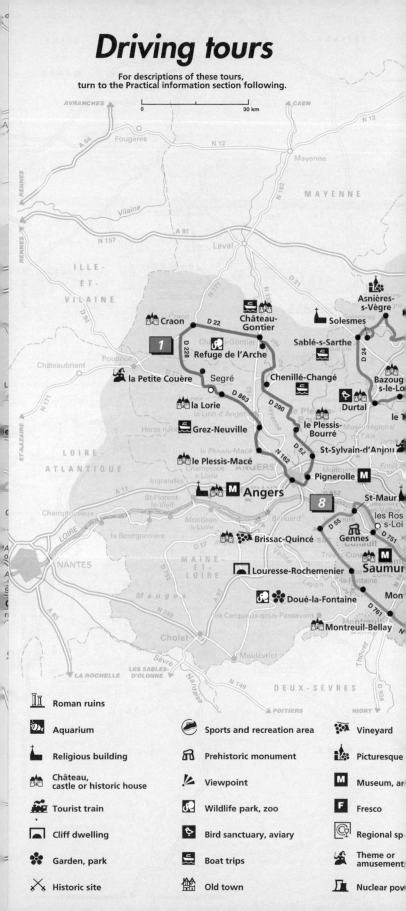

Driving tours

For descriptions of these tours,
turn to the Practical information section following.

0 ——— 30 km

Map labels:

AVRANCHES
CAEN
N 12
N 12
Fougères
A 84
Mayenne
MAYENNE
N 162
RENNES
Vilaine
A 81
Laval
N 157
D 21
ILLE-
ET-
VILAINE
D 94
Châteaubriant
Pouancé
N 171
Craon
D 22
Château-
Gontier
Solesmes
Asnières-
s-Vègre
Sablé-s-Sarthe
1
D 228
Refuge de l'Arche
D 24
Bazoug
s-le-Loi
la Petite Couère
Segré
Chenillé-Changé
la Lorie
D 863
D 290
Durtal
le P
Haras natio
Grez-Neuville
le Plessis-
Bourré
D 52
le Plessis-Macé
N 162
St-Sylvain-d'Anjou
LOIRE-
ATLANTIQUE
A 11
ANGERS
Pignerolle
M
St-Florent-
le-Vieil
M
Angers
Champtoceaux
8
St-Maur
les Ros
s-Loi
NANTES
la Bourgonnière
Brissac-Quincé
Gennes
D 751
D 17
MAINE-
ET-
LOIRE
Louresse-Rochemenier
M
Saumu
A 81
Doué-la-Fontaine
Mon
N 249
D 761
Cholet
Montreuil-Bellay
LA ROCHELLE
LES SABLES-
D'OLONNE
N 149
DEUX-SÈVRES
POITIERS
NIORT

Legend

Roman ruins	
Aquarium	**Sports and recreation area** — **Vineyard**
Religious building	**Prehistoric monument** — **Picturesque**
Château, castle or historic house	**Viewpoint** — **Museum, ar**
Tourist train	**Wildlife park, zoo** — **Fresco**
Cliff dwelling	**Bird sanctuary, aviary** — **Regional sp**
Garden, park	**Boat trips** — **Theme or amusement**
Historic site	**Old town** — **Nuclear pow**

PARIS

YVELINES

SEINE-ET-MARNE

N 104

ESSONNE

EURE-ET-LOIR

Chartres

Fontainebleau

SEINE

Melun

N 8

AUXERRE

SENS

Pithiviers

Yèvre-le-Châtel

Puiseaux

Boësse

Beaune-la-Rolande

Chamerolles

Boiscommun

Bellegarde

Montargis

LOIRET

Étang de la Vallée

Orléans **M**

Meung-sur-Loire

Châteauneuf-sur-Loire **M**

Germigny-des-Prés **F**

la Source

St-Benoît-sur-Loire

Beaugency

Cléry-St-André

4

LOIRE

Sully-sur-Loire

la Ferté-St-Aubin

Domaine du Ciran

Dampierre

St-Dyé-s-Loire

D 952

Gien **M**

Chambord

D 51

Souvigny-en-Sologne

Pont-Canal

Bracieux

Lamotte-Beuvron

Cerdon

Villesavin

LA SOLOGNE

Lassay-sur-Croisne

Aliotis

Salbris

le Moulin

Romorantin-Lanthenay

Selles-sur-Cher

Mennetou-sur-Cher

Vierzon

CHER

NEVERS

VALENÇAY

BOURGES

INDRE

châteauroux

1	Haut-Anjou
2	Le Mans, Sarthe and Loir
3	The Loir Valley and the Vendôme region
4	Orléans and Sologne
5	Blois and the great châteaux of the Renaissance
6	Val de Touraine: drink in the beauty
7	The most beautiful châteaux in Touraine
8	The Saumur region and the Layon Valley

The gardens at Château de Villandry

Practical
information

Planning your trip

USEFUL ADDRESSES

Internet

www.ambafrance-us.org
The French Embassy in the USA has a Web site providing basic information (geography, demographics, history), a news digest and business-related information. It offers special pages for children, and pages devoted to culture, language study and travel, and you can reach other selected French sites (regions, cities, ministries) with a hypertext link.

www.franceguide.com
The French Government Tourist Office / Maison de la France site is packed with practical information and tips for those travelling to France. The home page has a number of links to more specific guidance, for American or Canadian travellers for example, or to the FGTO's London pages.

www.FranceKeys.com
This sight has plenty of practical information for visiting France. It covers all the regions, with links to tourist offices and related sites. Very useful for planning the details of your tour in France!

www.fr-holidaystore.co.uk
The French Travel Centre in London has gone on-line with this service, providing information on all of the regions of France, including updated special travel offers and details on available accommodation.

www.visiteurope.com
The European Travel Commission provides useful information on travelling to and around 27 European countries, and includes links to some commercial booking services (ie vehicle hire), rail schedules, weather reports and more.

French tourist offices

For information, brochures, maps and assistance in planning a trip to France travellers should apply to the official French Tourist Office in their own country:

Australia – New Zealand

Sydney – BNP Building, 12 Castlereagh Street, Sydney, New South Wales 2000
☏ (02) 9231 5244 – Fax: (02) 9221 8682.

Canada

Montreal – 1981 Avenue McGill College, Suite 490, Montreal PQ H3A 2W9
☏ (514) 288-4264 – Fax: (514) 845 4868.

Toronto – 30 St Patrick's Street, Suite 700, Toronto, Ontario
☏ (416) 979 7587.

Eire

Dublin – 10 Suffolk Street, Dublin 2
☏ (01) 679 0813 – Fax: (01) 679 0814.

South Africa

P.O. Box 41022, Craig Hall 2024,
☏ (011) 880 8062.

United Kingdom

London Maison de France – 178 Piccadilly, London WIV OAL
☏ (09068) 244 123 – Fax: 020 793 6594.

United States

East Coast – New York – 444 Madison Avenue, 16th Floor, NY 10022-6903,
☏ (212) 838-7800 – Fax: (212) 838-7855.

Mid West – Chicago – 676 North Michigan Avenue, Suite 3360, Chicago, IL 60611-2819.
☏ (312) 751-7800 – Fax: (312) 337-6339.

West Coast – Los Angeles – 9454 Wilshire Boulevard, Suite 715, Beverly Hills, CA 90212-2967.
☏ (310) 271-6665 – Fax: (310) 276-2835.
Information can also be requested from **France on Call**,
☏ (202) 659-7779.

Local tourist offices

Visitors may also contact local tourist offices for more precise information, to receive brochures and maps. The addresses and telephone numbers of tourist offices in the larger towns are listed after the symbol ▣, in the *Admission times and charges* section at the end of the guide. Below, the addresses are given for local tourist offices of the *départements* and *régions* covered in this guide. The index lists the *département* after each town.

At regional level, address inquiries to:

Maison des Pays de la Loire, 6 rue Cassette, 75006 Paris, ☏ 01 53 63 02 50.

Comité Régional du Tourisme des Pays de la Loire, (Loire-Atlantique, Maine-et-Loire, Mayenne, Sarthe, Vendée); 2 rue de la Loire, BP 20411, 44204 Nantes Cedex 02, ☏ 02 40 48 24 20; www.cr-pays-de-la-loire.fr

Comité Régional du Tourisme du Centre-Val de Loire, (Cher, Eure-et-Loir, Indre, Indre-et-Loire, Loir-et-Cher, Loiret); 37 avenue de Paris, 45000 Orléans, ☏ 02 38 79 95 00, www.loirevalleytourism.com

For each *département* within the region, address inquires to the **Comité Départemental du Tourisme (CDT)**:

Cher, 5 rue de Séraucourt, 18000 Bourges, ☏ 02 48 67 00 10, www.berrylecher.com

Eure-et-Loir, 10 rue du Docteur Maunoury, BP 67, 28002 Chartres Cedex, ☏ 02 37 84 01 00, www.chartrescountry.com
Reservations (Gîtes and Clévacances): www.resinfrance.com

Indre, 1 rue St-Martin, BP 141, 36003 Châteauroux Cedex, ☏ 02 54 07 36 36, www.berrylindre.com

Touraine-Val de Loire (**Indre-et-Loire** *Département*), 9 rue Buffon, BP 3217, 37032 Tours Cedex, ☏ 02 47 31 47 48, www.tourisme-touraine.com

Loir-et-Cher, 5 rue de la Voûte-du-Château, BP 149, 41005 Blois Cedex, ☏ 02 54 57 00 41, www.tourismeloir-et-cher.com

Loiret, 8 rue d'Escures, 45000 Orléans, ☏ 02 38 78 04 04, www.TourismLoiret.com

Anjou (**Maine-et-Loire** *Département*), place du Président-Kennedy, BP 32147, 49021 Angers Cedex 02, ☏ 02 41 23 51 51.

Mayenne, 84 avenue Robert-Buron, BP 1429, 53014 Laval Cedex, ☏ 02 43 53 18 18.

Sarthe, 40 rue Joinville, 72000 Le Mans, ☏ 02 43 40 22 50, www.sarthe.com

Tourist Information Centres (▣) – See the *Admission times and charges* for the addresses and telephone numbers of the local tourist offices *(Syndicats d'Initiative)*; they provide information on craft courses and itineraries with special themes – wine tours, history tours, artistic tours.

Seven towns and areas, labelled "Villes et Pays d'Art et d'Histoire" by the Ministry of Culture, are mentioned in this guide (Angers, Blois, Chinon, Loches, Le Mans, Tours and Vendôme). They are particularly active in promoting their architectural and cultural heritage and offer guided tours by highly qualified guides as well as activities for 6-12 year olds. More information is available from local tourist offices and from www.vpah.culture.fr.

Embassies and consulates in France

Australia	Embassy	4 rue Jean-Rey, 75015 Paris ☏ 01 40 59 33 00 – Fax: 01 40 59 33 10.
Canada	Embassy	35 avenue Montaigne, 75008 Paris ☏ 01 44 43 29 00 – Fax: 01 44 43 29 99.
Eire	Embassy	4 rue Rude, 75016 Paris ☏ 01 44 17 67 00 – Fax: 01 44 17 67 60.
New Zealand	Embassy	7 ter rue Léonard-de-Vinci, 75016 Paris ☏ 01 45 01 43 43 – Fax: 01 45 01 43 44.
South Africa	Embassy	59 quai d'Orsay, 75007 Paris ☏ 01 53 59 23 23 – Fax: 01 53 59 23 33.
UK	Embassy	35 rue du Faubourg St-Honoré, 75008 Paris ☏ 01 44 51 31 00 – Fax: 01 44 51 31 27.
	Consulate	16 rue d'Anjou, 75008 Paris ☏ 01 44 51 31 01 (visas).
USA	Embassy	2 avenue Gabriel, 75008 Paris ☏ 01 43 12 22 22 – Fax: 01 42 66 97 83.
	Consulate	2 rue St-Florentin, 75001 Paris ☏ 01 42 96 14 88.
	Consulate	15 avenue d'Alsace, 67082 Strasbourg ☏ 03 88 35 31 04 – Fax: 03 88 24 06 95.

TRAVELLERS WITH SPECIAL NEEDS

The sights described in this guide which are easily accessible to people of reduced mobility are indicated in the *Admission times and charges* by the symbol &.
On TGV and Corail trains, operated by the national railway (SNCF), there are special wheelchair slots in 1st class carriages available to holders of 2nd-class tickets. On Eurostar and Thalys special rates are available for accompanying adults. All airports are equipped to receive physically disabled passengers.
Web-surfers can find information for slow walkers, mature travellers and others with special needs at www.access-able.com. For information on museum access for the disabled contact La Direction, Les Musées de France, Service Accueil des Publics Spécifiques, 6 rue des Pyramides, 75041 Paris Cedex 1, ☎ 01 40 15 35 88.

The Red Guide France and the **Michelin Camping Caravaning France** indicate hotels and camp sites with facilities suitable for physically handicapped people.

SEASONS AND WEATHER

Visitors to the Loire Valley will be impressed by the beauty and variety of the landscape all year round. When planning your visit, it is worth noting that the weather can be very hot and the various places of interest draw large crowds of visitors at the height of the summer (July-August).
Spring comes early to the Loire Valley, especially in the western Loire which seems to enjoy its own microclimate, creating a pocket of mild weather conditions. Trees burst into blossom as early as the beginning of April in the Angers region and local plant life thrives in May and June, with green fields and orchards stretching away on either side of the roads. The River Loire is at its most scenic during this period.
By July, the river is reduced to a narrow stream in places, winding between golden sandbanks. Tempting as it is to go for a swim, bathers should first check that the river bed is safe, as the sandbanks can be quite treacherous in some places.
The month of September, characteristically mild, heralds the wine harvest, in honour of which there are lively traditional harvest processions held throughout the Loire Valley.

Weather forecast

Météo-France offers recorded information at national, regional and local level. This information is updated three times a day and is valid for five days.

National forecast: ☎ 08 36 68 01 01.

Regional forecast: ☎ 08 36 68 00 00.

Local forecast: ☎ 08 36 68 02 followed by the number of the *département* (Cher: 18; Eure-et-Loir: 28; Indre: 36; Indre-et-Loire: 37; Loir-et-Cher: 41; Loiret: 45; Maine-et-Loire: 49; Mayenne: 53; Sarthe: 72).

What to pack

As little as possible! Cleaning and laundry services are available everywhere. Most personal items can be replaced at reasonable cost. Try to pack everything into one suitcase and a tote bag. Porter help may be in short supply, and new purchases will add to the original weight. Take an extra tote bag for packing new purchases, shopping at the open-air market, carrying a picnic etc. Be sure luggage is clearly labelled and old travel tags removed. Do not pack medication in checked luggage, but keep it with you.

Formalities

Documents

Passport – Nationals of countries within the European Union entering France need only a national identity card. Nationals of other countries must be in possession of a valid national **passport**. In case of loss or theft, report to your embassy or consulate and the local police.

Visa – No **entry visa** is required for Canadian, US or Australian citizens travelling as tourists and staying less than 90 days, except for students planning to study in France. If you think you may need a visa, apply to your local French Consulate.
US citizens should obtain the booklet *Safe Trip Abroad* (US$1), which provides useful information on visa requirements, customs regulations, medical care etc for international travellers. Published by the Government Printing Office, it can be ordered by phone (☎ (202) 512-1800) or consulted on-line (www.access.gpo.gov). General passport information is available by phone toll-free from the Federal Information Center (item 5 on the automated menu), ☎ 800-688-9889. US passport application forms can be downloaded from http://travel.state.gov.

Customs

Apply to the Customs Office (UK) for a leaflet on customs regulations and the full range of duty-free allowances; available from HM Customs and Excise, Dorset House, Stamford Street, London SE1 9PS, ☎ 0207 928 3344. The US Customs Service offers a publication *Know before you go* for US citizens: for the office nearest you, consult the phone book, Federal Government, US Treasury (www.customs.ustreas.gov).
There are no customs formalities for holidaymakers bringing their caravans into France for a stay of less than six months. No customs document is necessary for pleasure boats and outboard motors for a stay of less than six months but the registration certificate should be kept on board.
Americans can bring home, tax-free, up to US$400 worth of goods (limited quantities of alcohol and tobacco products); Canadians up to CND$300; Australians up to AUS$400 and New Zealanders up to NZ$700.
Persons living in a member state of the European Union are not restricted with regard to purchasing goods for private use, but the recommended allowances for alcoholic beverages and tobacco are as follows:

Spirits (whisky, gin, vodka etc)	10 litres	Cigarettes	800
Fortified wines (vermouth, port etc)	20 litres	Cigarillos	400
Wine (not more than 60 sparkling)	90 litres	Cigars	200
Beer	110 litres	Smoking tobacco	1kg

Health

First aid, medical advice and chemists' night service rota are available from chemists/drugstores *(pharmacie)* identified by the green cross sign.
It is advisable to take out comprehensive insurance coverage as the recipient of medical treatment in French hospitals or clinics must pay the bill. **Nationals of non-EU countries** should check with their insurance companies about policy limitations. Reimbursement can then be negotiated with the insurance company according to the policy held.
All prescription drugs should be clearly labelled; it is recommended that you carry a copy of the prescription.
British and Irish citizens should apply to the Department of Health and Social Security for Form E 111, which entitles the holder to urgent treatment for accident or unexpected illness in EU countries. A refund of part of the costs of treatment can be obtained on application in person or by post to the local Social Security Offices *(Caisse Primaire d'Assurance Maladie)*. **Americans** concerned about travel and health can contact the International Association for Medical Assistance to Travelers, which can also provide details of English-speaking doctors in different parts of France: ☎ (716) 754-4883.
The American Hospital of Paris is open 24hr for emergencies as well as consultations, with English-speaking staff, at 63 boulevard Victor-Hugo, 92200 Neuilly-sur-Seine, ☎ 01 46 41 25 25. Accredited by major insurance companies.
The British Hospital is just outside Paris in Levallois-Perret, 3 rue Barbès.

Budget

CURRENCY

There are no restrictions on the amount of currency visitors can take into France. Visitors carrying a lot of cash are advised to complete a currency declaration form on arrival, because there are restrictions on currency export.

Notes and coins

Since 17 February 2002, the **euro** has been the only currency accepted as a means of payment in France, as in the 11 other European countries participating in the monetary union. It is divided into 100 cents or centimes. Since June 2002, notes and coins in French francs can only be exchanged at the Banque de France (3 years for coins and 10 years for notes).

Banks

Although business hours vary from branch to branch, banks are generally open from 9am to noon and 2pm to 4pm and are closed either on Monday or on Saturday. Banks close early on the day before a bank holiday. A passport is necessary as identification when cashing travellers' cheques in banks. Commission charges vary and hotels usually charge more than banks for cashing cheques.

One of the most economical ways to obtain money in France is by using **ATM machines** to get cash directly from your bank account (with a debit card) or to use your credit card to get a cash advance. Be sure to remember your PIN number, you will need it to use cash dispensers and to pay with your card in shops, restaurants etc. Code pads are numeric; use a telephone pad to translate a letter code into numbers. PIN numbers have 4 digits in France; inquire with the issuing company or bank if the code you usually use is longer. Visa is the most widely accepted credit card, followed by MasterCard; other cards, credit and debit (Diners Club, Plus, Cirrus etc) are also accepted in some cash machines. American Express is more often accepted in premium establishments. Most places post signs indicating which cards they accept; if you don't see such a sign, and want to pay with a card, ask before ordering or making a selection. Cards are widely accepted in shops, hypermarkets, hotels and restaurants, at tollbooths and in petrol stations.

Before you leave home, check with the bank that issued your card for emergency replacement procedures. Carry your card number and emergency phone numbers separate from your wallet and handbag; leave a copy of this information with someone you can easily reach. If your card is lost or stolen while you are in France, call one of the following 24-hour hotlines:

American Express	☎ 01 47 77 72 00	**Visa**	☎ 08 36 69 08 80
Mastercard/Eurocard	☎ 01 45 67 84 84	**Diners Club**	☎ 01 49 06 17 50

You must report any loss or theft of credit cards or travellers' cheques to the local police who will issue you with a certificate (useful proof to show the issuing company). It may be a good idea to carry some travellers' cheques in addition to your cards, and to keep them in a safe place in case of emergency.

PRICES AND TIPS

Since a service charge is automatically included in the price of meals and accommodation in France, any additional tipping is up to the visitor, generally small change, and generally not more than 5%. Taxi drivers and hairdressers are usually tipped 10-15%.

As a rule, the cost of staying in a hotel, eating in a restaurant or buying goods and services is significantly lower in the French regions than in Paris.

Here are a few indicative prices, based on surveys conducted by French authorities in 2001. Exchange rates change regularly, so you will have to check before you leave for an exact calculation. At press time, the exchange rate for 1€ was: USD 0.98; GBP 0.63; CAD 1.56; AUD 1.82.

Restaurants usually charge for meals in two ways: a *menu*, that is a fixed price menu with 2 or 3 courses, sometimes with a small pitcher of wine, all for a stated price, or *à la carte*, the more expensive way, with each course ordered separately.

Cafés have very different prices, depending on where they are located. The price of a drink or a coffee is cheaper if you stand at the counter *(comptoir)* than if you sit down *(salle)* and sometimes it is even more expensive if you sit outdoors *(terrace)*.

Hotel rooms (based on double occupancy) in a city	Euros
1 star (French Tourist board standards)	27.44 – 53.36
2 star	53.36 – 76.22
3 star	76.23 – 121.97
4 star	137.21 – 228.69
4 star (luxury)	228.69 – 381.15

Food and entertainment	Euros
Movie ticket	7.62
River cruise	6.1 – 9.91
Dinner cruise	68.61 – 76.23
In a café: Expresso coffee	1.83
Café au lait	3.35
Soda	3.35
Beer	3.05
Mineral water	3.05
Ice cream	4.88
Ham sandwich	3.20
Baguette of bread	0.69
Soda (1 litre in a shop)	2.13
Restaurant meal (3 courses, no wine)	22.87
Big Mac menu meal	5.34
French daily newspaper	0.91
Foreign newspaper	1.52 – 2.29
Compact disc	12.00 – 21.00
Telephone card – 50 units	7.47
Telephone card – 120 units	14.86
Cigarettes (pack of 20)	2.44 – 3.25

Public transportation	Euros
Bus, street car, metro ticket	1.30
Book of ten tickets	9.30
Taxi (5km + tip)	10.00
TGV ticket Paris-Angers 2nd class	40.40

Discounts

Tourist Pass: 100 sights for 42.69 €

This pass gives unrestricted access to more than 100 historic buildings managed by the *Centre des Monuments Nationaux*. It is valid for one year throughout France as of the date of purchase and is for sale at the entrance to major historic buildings, monuments and museums. With the pass, you can save time by skipping the wait at the ticket window. For a list of all the monuments, plus details on their history, information on travel, and other entertaining features to help you plan your trip, visit the lively web site: www.monuments-france.fr.

Significant discounts are available for senior citizens, students, youth under age 25, teachers, and groups for public transportation, museums and monuments and for some leisure activities such as movies (at certain times of the day). Bring student or senior cards with you, and bring along some extra passport-size photos for discount travel cards.

The **International Student Travel Conference** (www.istc.org), global administrator of the International Student and Teacher Identity Cards, is an association of student travel organizations around the world. ISTC members collectively negotiate benefits with airlines, governments, and providers of other goods and services for the student and teacher community, both in their own country and around the world. The non-profit association sells international ID cards for students, youth under age 25 and teachers (who may get discounts on museum entrances, for example). The ISTC is also active in a network of international education and work exchange programmes. The corporate headquarters address is Herengracht 479, 1017 BS Amsterdam, The Netherlands, ☎ 31 20 421 28 00; Fax 31 20 421 28 10.

See the section below on travelling by rail in France for other discounts on transportation.

Getting there

By air

The various international and other independent airlines operate services to **Paris** (Roissy-Charles de Gaulle and Orly airports) and **Nantes**. Check with your travel agent, however, before booking direct flights, as it is sometimes cheaper to travel via Paris. Air France (☎ 0820 820 820), the national airline, links Paris to Nantes several times a day.

Contact airline companies and travel agents for details of package tour flights with a rail or coach link-up as well as fly-drive schemes.

By sea (from the UK or Ireland)

There are numerous **cross-Channel services** (passenger and car ferries, hovercraft) from the United Kingdom and Ireland, as well as the rail Shuttle through the Channel Tunnel (**Le Shuttle-Eurotunnel**, ☎ 0990 353-535). To choose the most suitable route between your port of arrival and your destination use the Michelin Tourist and Motoring Atlas France, Michelin map 911 (which gives travel times and mileages) or Michelin maps from the 1:200 000 series (with the yellow cover). For details apply to travel agencies or to:

P & O Stena Line Ferries	Channel House, Channel View Road, Dover CT17 9JT, ☎ 0990 980 980 or 01304 863 000 (Switchboard), www.p-and-o.com
Hoverspeed	International Hoverport, Marine Parade, Dover, Kent CT17 9TG, ☎ 0990 240 241, Fax 01304 240088, www.hoverspeed.co.uk
Brittany Ferries	Millbay Docks, Plymouth, Devon, PL1 3EW, ☎ 0990 360 360, www.brittany-ferries.com
Portsmouth Commercial Port (and ferry information)	George Byng Way, Portsmouth, Hampshire PO2 8SP, ☎ 01705 297391, Fax 01705 861165
Irish Ferries	50 West Norland Street, Dublin 2, ☎ (353) 16 610 511, www.irishferries.com
Seafrance	Eastern Docks, Dover, Kent, CT16 1JA, ☎ 01304 212696, Fax 01304 240033, www.seafrance.fr

By rail

Eurostar runs via the Channel Tunnel between **London** (Waterloo) and **Paris** (Gare du Nord) in 3hr (bookings and information ☎ 0345 303 030 in the UK; ☎ 1-888-EUROSTAR in the US). In Paris it links to the high-speed rail network (TGV) which covers most of France. There is fast inter-city service from **Paris** (Gare Montparnasse) to **Vendôme** *(45min)*, **Le Mans** *(50min)*, **Tours** *(1hr)* and **Angers** *(1hr 30min)* on the TGV. **Eurailpass, Flexipass, Eurailpass Youth, EurailDrive Pass** and **Saverpass** are travel passes which may be purchased by residents of countries outside the European Union. In the US, contact your travel agent or **Rail Europe** 2100 Central Ave. Boulder, CO, 80301, ☎ 1 800-4-EURAIL or **Europrail International** ☎ 1 888 667 9731. If you are a European resident, you can buy an individual country pass, if you are not a resident of the country you where you plan to use it. In the UK, contact Europrail at 179 Piccadilly London W1V 0BA ☎ 0990 848 848. Information on schedules can be obtained on web sites for these agencies and the **SNCF**, respectively: www.raileurop.com.us, www.eurail.on.ca, www.sncf.fr. At the SNCF site, you can book ahead, pay with a credit card, and receive your ticket in the mail at home.

There are numerous **discounts** available when you purchase your tickets in France, from 25-50% below the regular rate. These include discounts for using senior cards and youth cards (the nominative cards with a photograph must be purchased – 45 and 41€, respectively), and lower rates for 2-9 people travelling together (no card required, advance purchase necessary). There are a limited number of discount seats available during peak travel times, and the best discounts are available for travel during off-peak periods.

Tickets bought in France must be validated *(composter)* by using the orange automatic date-stamping machines at the platform entrance (failure to do so may result in a fine).

The French railway company SNCF operates a telephone information, reservation and prepayment service in English from 7am to 10pm (French time). In France call ☏ 08 36 35 35 39 (when calling from outside France, drop the initial 0).

By coach

Regular coach services between **London** and **Tours** or **Nantes**:

Eurolines (London), 52 Grosvenor Gardens, Victoria, London SW1W 0AU, ☏ 0171 730 8235, Fax 0171 730 8721.

Eurolines (Paris), 28 avenue du Général-de-Gaulle, 93541 Bagnolet, ☏ 01 49 72 51 51.

Motoring in France

The area covered in this guide is easily reached by main motorways and national roads. **Michelin map 911** indicates the main itineraries as well as alternate routes for avoiding heavy traffic during busy holiday periods, and gives estimated travel times. **Michelin map 914** is a detailed atlas of French motorways, indicating tolls, rest areas and services along the route; it includes a table for calculating distances and times. The latest Michelin route-planning service is available on Internet, **www.ViaMichelin.com**. Travellers can calculate a precise route using such options as shortest route, route avoiding toll roads or the Michelin-recommended route. In addition to tourist information (hotels, restaurants, attractions), you will find a magazine featuring articles with up-to-the-minute reports on holiday destinations.

The roads are very busy during the holiday period (particularly weekends in July and August) and, to avoid traffic congestion it is advisable to follow the recommended secondary routes (signposted as *Bison Futé – itinéraires bis*). The motorway network includes rest areas *(aires)* and petrol stations, usually with restaurant and shopping complexes attached, about every 40km/25mi, so that long-distance drivers have no excuse not to stop for a rest every now and then.

Documents

Travellers from other European Union countries and North America can drive in France with a valid national or home-state **driving licence**. An **international driving licence** is useful because the information on it appears in nine languages (keep in mind that traffic officers are empowered to fine motorists). A permit is available (US$10) from the National Automobile Club, 1151 East Hillsdale Blvd., Foster City, CA 94404, ☏ 650-294-7000 or www.nationalautoclub.com; or contact your local branch of the American Automobile Association. For the vehicle, it is necessary to have the registration papers (logbook) and a nationality plate of the approved size.

Certain motoring organisations (AAA, AA, RAC) offer accident **insurance** and breakdown service schemes for members. Check with your current insurance company in regard to coverage while abroad. If you plan to hire a car using your credit card, check with the company, which may provide liability insurance automatically (and thus save you having to pay the cost for optimum coverage).

Highway code

The minimum driving age is 18. Traffic drives on the right. All passengers must wear **seat belts**. Children under the age of 10 must ride in the back seat. Headlights must be switched on in poor visibility and at night; use sidelights only when the vehicle is stationary.

In the case of a **breakdown**, a red warning triangle or hazard warning lights are obligatory. In the absence of stop signs at intersections, cars must **yield to the right**. Traffic on main roads outside built-up areas (priority indicated by a yellow diamond sign) and on roundabouts has right of way. There are many **roundabouts** (traffic circles) located just on the edge of towns; they are designed to reduce the speed of the traffic entering the built-up area and you must slow down when you approach one and yield to the cars in the circle. Vehicles must stop when the lights turn red at road junctions and may filter to the right only when indicated by an amber arrow.

The regulations on **drinking and driving** (limited to 0.50g/l) and **speeding** are strictly enforced – usually by an on-the-spot fine and/or confiscation of the vehicle.

Speed limits – Although liable to modification, these are as follows:
– toll motorways *(autoroutes)* 130kph/80mph (110kph/68mph when raining):
– dual carriageways and motorways without tolls 110kph/68mph (100kph/62mph when raining):
– other roads 90kph/56mph (80kph/50mph when raining) and in towns 50kph/31mph:
– outside lane on motorways during daylight, on level ground and with good visibility
– minimum speed limit of 80kph/50mph.

Parking Regulations – In town there are zones where parking is either restricted or subject to a fee; tickets should be obtained from the ticket machines (*horodateurs* – small change necessary) and displayed inside the windscreen on the driver's side; failure to display may result in a fine, or towing and impoundment. Other parking areas in town may require you to take a ticket when passing through a barrier. To exit, you must pay the parking fee (usually there is a machine located by the exit – *sortie*) and insert the paid-up card in another machine which will lift the exit gate.

Tolls – In France, most motorway sections are subject to a toll *(péage)*. You can pay in cash or with a credit card (Visa, Mastercard).

Car rental

There are car rental agencies at airports, railway stations and in all large towns throughout France. European cars have manual transmission; automatic cars are available in larger cities only if an advance reservation is made. Drivers must be over 21; between ages 21-25, drivers are required to pay an extra daily fee; some companies allow drivers under 23 only if the reservation has been made through a travel agent. It is relatively expensive to hire a car in France; Americans in particular will notice the difference and should make arrangements before leaving, take advantage of fly-drive offers, or seek advice from a travel agent, specifying requirements.

Central Reservation numbers in France:

Avis: 08 02 05 05 05
Budget France: 08 00 10 00 01
SIXT-Eurorent: 01 40 65 01 00
A Baron's Limousine: 01 45 30 21 21

Europcar: 08 03 35 23 52
Hertz France: 01 39 38 38 38
National-CITER: 01 45 22 88 40

Worldwide Motorhome Rentals offers fully equipped campervans for rent. You can view them on the company's web pages (mhrww.com) or call (US toll-free) US ☎ 888- 519-8969; outside the US ☎ 530-389-8316 or Fax 530-389-8316.

Overseas Motorhome Tours Inc. organises escorted tours and individual rental of recreational vehicles: in the US ☎ 800-322-2127; outside the US ☎ 1-310-543-2590; Internet www.omtinc.com.

Petrol (US: gas) – French service stations dispense: *sans plomb 98* (super unleaded 98), *sans plomb 95* (super unleaded 95), *diesel/gazole* (diesel) and *GPL* (LPG). Petrol is considerably more expensive in France than in the USA. Prices are listed on signboards on the motorways; it is usually cheaper to fill up after leaving the motorway; check the large hypermarkets on the outskirts of town.

Where to stay, Where to eat

Places to stay

This map illustrates a selection of holiday destinations which are particularly to be recommended for the accommodation and leisure facilities they offer, and for their pleasant setting. It shows **overnight stops**, fairly large towns which should be visited and which have good accommodation facilities as well as traditional destinations for a **short break**, which combine accommodation, charm and a peaceful setting. As far as Angers, Le Mans, Orléans and Tours are concerned, the influence they exert in the region and the wealth of monuments, museums and other sights to which they are home make them the ideal setting for a **weekend break**.

Finding a hotel

The Green Guide is pleased to offer a new feature: lists of selected hotels and restaurants for this region. Turn to the sections bordered in blue for descriptions and prices of typical places to stay and eat with local flair. The key on page 8-9 explains the symbols and abbreviations used in these sections. We have reported the prices and conditions as we observed them, but of course changes in management and other factors may mean that you will find some discrepancies. Please feel free to keep us informed of any major differences you encounter.

Use the **Map of places to stay** below to identify recommended places for overnight stops. For an even greater selection, use **The Red Guide France**, with its famously reliable star-rating system and hundreds of establishments all over France. Book ahead to ensure that you get the accommodation you want, not only in the tourist season (the Loire valley is a very popular holiday destination!), but year round, as many towns fill up during trade fairs, arts festivals etc. Some places require an advance deposit or a reconfirmation. Reconfirming is especially important if you plan to arrive after 6pm.

For further assistance, **Loisirs Accueil** is a booking service that has offices in some French *départements* – contact the tourist offices listed above for further information.
A guide to good-value, family-run hotels, **Logis et Auberges de France**, is available from the French Tourist Office, as are lists of other kinds of accommodation such as hotel-châteaux, bed-and-breakfasts etc.
Relais et châteaux provides information on booking in luxury hotels with character: 15 rue Galvani, 75017 Paris, ☎ 01 45 72 90 00.

Economy Chain Hotels – If you need a place to stop en route, these can be useful, as they are inexpensive (30-45€ for a double room) and generally located near the main road. While breakfast is available, there may not be a restaurant; rooms are small, with a television and bathroom. Central reservation numbers:
– **Akena** ☎ 01 69 84 85 17
– **B&B** ☎ 0 803 00 29 29 (inside France); 33-2 98 33 75 00 (from outside France)
– **Mister Bed** ☎ 01 46 14 38 00
– **Villages Hôtel** ☎ 03 80 60 92 70

The hotels listed below are slightly more expensive (from 45€), and offer a few more amenities and services. Central reservation number:
– **Campanile, Climat de France, Kyriad** ☎ 01 64 62 46 46

Many chains have on-line reservations: www.etaphotel.com; www.ibishotel.com.

Renting a cottage, Bed and Breakfast

The **Maison des Gîtes de France** is an information service on self-catering accommodation in the Loire Valley (and the rest of France). *Gîtes* usually take the form of a cottage or apartment decorated in the local style where visitors can make themselves at home, or bed and breakfast accommodation *(chambres d'hôtes)* which consists of a room and breakfast at a reasonable price.
Contact the Gîtes de France office in Paris: 59 rue St-Lazare, 75439 Paris Cedex 09, ☎ 01 49 70 75 75, or their representative in the UK, **Brittany Ferries** *(address above)*. The Internet site, **www.gites-de-france.fr**, has a good English version. From the site, you can order catalogues for different regions illustrated with photographs of the properties, as well as specialised catalogues (bed and breakfasts, farm stays etc). You can also surf on **www.loire-valley-holidays.com** to view and book cottages in Touraine and contact the local tourist offices which may have lists of available properties and local bed and breakfast establishments.

WWW.enpaysdelaloire.com is currently being translated into English and is due to be up and running come December 2002. The site comprises thousands of short descriptive texts on accommodation etc. The site is already active in French.

Hostels, Camping

To obtain an International Youth Hostel Federation card (there is no age requirement, and there is a senior card available too) you should contact the IYHF in your own country for information and membership applications (US ☎ 202 783 6161; UK ☎ 1727 855215. There is a new booking service on the internet (iyhf.org), which you may use to reserve rooms as far as six months in advance.
There are two main youth hostel associations *(auberges de jeunesse)* in France, the **Ligue Française pour les Auberges de la Jeunesse** (67 rue Vergniaud, 75013 Paris, ☎ 01 44 16 78 78; www.auberges-de-jeunesse.com) and the **Fédération Unie des Auberges de Jeunesse** (4 boulevard Jules-Ferry, 75011 Paris, ☎ 01 43 57 02 60, Fax 01 43 57 53 90).

There are numerous officially graded **camp sites** with varying standards of facilities throughout the Loire Valley. The **Michelin Camping Caravaning France** guide lists a selection of camp sites. The area is very popular with campers in the summer months, so it is wise to reserve in advance.

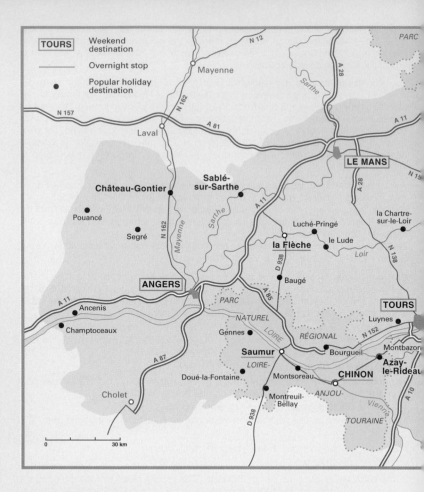

Finding a restaurant

Turn to the pages bordered in blue for descriptions and prices of selected places to eat in the different locations covered in this guide. The key on page 9 explains the symbols and abbreviations used in these sections. Use **The Red Guide France**, with its famously reliable star-rating system and hundreds of establishments all over France, for an even greater choice. If you would like to experience a meal in a highly rated restaurant from The Red Guide, be sure to book ahead! In the countryside, restaurants usually serve lunch between noon and 2pm and dinner between 7.30-10pm. It is not always easy to find something in-between those two meal times, as the non-stop restaurant is still a rarity in the provinces. However, a hungry traveller can usually get a sandwich in a café, and ordinary hot dishes may be available in a *brasserie*.

La Carte	The Menu
ENTREES	STARTERS
Crudités	Raw vegetable salad
Terrine de lapin	Rabbit terrine (pâté)
Frisée aux lardons	Curly lettuce with bacon bits
Escargots	Snails
Salade au crottin de Chavignol	Goat cheese on a bed of lettuce
PLATS (VIANDES)	MAIN COURSES (MEAT)
Bavette à l'échalote	Sirloin with shallots
Faux filet au poivre	Sirloin with pepper sauce
Pavé de rumsteck	Thick rump steak
Côtes d'agneau	Lamb chops
Filet mignon de porc	Pork filet
Blanquette de veau	Veal in cream sauce
Nos viandes sont garnies	Our meat dishes are served with vegetables

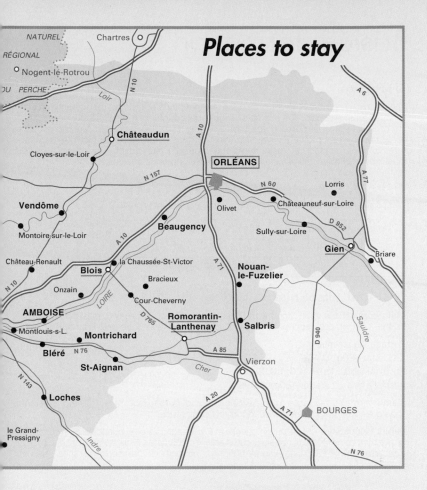

Places to stay

PLATS (POISSONS, VOLAILLE)	MAIN COURSES (FISH, FOWL)
Filets de sole	Sole fillets
Dorade aux herbes	Sea bream with herbs
Saumon grillé	Grilled salmon
Truite meunière	Trout fried in butter
Magret de canard	Duck filets
Poulet rôti	Roast chicken
FROMAGE	CHEESE
DESSERTS	DESSERTS
Tarte aux pommes	Apple pie
Crème caramel	Cooled baked custard with caramel sauce
Sorbet: trois parfums	Sherbet: choose 3 flavours
BOISSONS	BEVERAGES
Bière	Beer
Eau minérale (gazeuse)	(Sparkling) mineral water
Une carafe d'eau	Tap water (no charge)
Vin rouge, vin blanc, rosé	Red wine, white wine, rosé
Jus de fruit	Fruit juice
MENU ENFANT	CHILDREN'S MENU
Jambon	Ham
Steak haché	Ground beef
Frites	French fried potatoes

For information on local specialities, turn to page 84.

In French restaurants and cafés, a service charge is included. Tipping is not necessary, but French people often leave the small change from their bill on their table, or about 5% for the waiter in a nice restaurant.

Basic information

Electricity

The electric current is 220 volts. Circular two-pin plugs are the rule. Adapters and converters (for hairdryers, for example) should be bought before you leave home; they are on sale in most airports. If you have a rechargeable device (video camera, portable computer, battery recharger), read the instructions carefully or contact the manufacturer or shop. Sometimes these items only require a plug adapter, in other cases you must use a voltage converter as well or risk ruining your appliance.

Metric system

France operates on the metric system. Some equivalents:

1 gram = 0.04 ounces	1 metre = 1.09 yards
1 kilogram = 2.20 pounds	1 kilometre = 0.62 miles
1 litre = 1.06 quarts	

Post and telephone

Main post offices open Monday to Friday 8am to 7pm, Saturday 8am to noon. Smaller branch post offices generally close at lunchtime between noon and 2pm and at 4pm.

Postage via air mail:
UK: letter (20g) 0.46€
North America: letter (20g) 0.67€
Australia and NZ: letter (20g) 0.79€

Stamps are also available from newsagents and *bureaux de tabac*. Stamp collectors should ask for *timbres de collection* in any post office.

Public Telephones – Most public phones in France use pre-paid phone cards *(télécartes)*, rather than coins. Some telephone booths accept credit cards (Visa, Mastercard/Eurocard). *Télécartes* (50 or 120 units) can be bought in post offices, branches of France Télécom,

bureaux de tabac (cafés that sell cigarettes) and newsagents and can be used to make calls in France and abroad. Calls can be received at phone boxes where the blue bell sign is shown; the phone will not ring, so keep your eye on the little message screen.

National calls – French telephone numbers have 10 digits. Paris and Paris region numbers begin with 01; 02 in north-west France; 03 in north-east France; 04 in south-east France and Corsica; 05 in south-west France. Numbers beginning with 08 are special rate numbers, available only when dialling within France.

International calls – To call France from abroad, dial the country code (33) + 9-digit number (omit the initial 0). When calling abroad from France dial 00, then dial the country code followed by the area code and number of your correspondent.

International dialling codes (00 + code):

Australia	☎ 61	New Zealand	☎ 64
Canada	☎ 1	United Kingdom	☎ 44
Eire	☎ 353	United States	☎ 1

To use your **personal calling card** dial:

AT&T	☎ 0-800 99 00 11	Sprint	☎ 0-800 99 00 87
MCI	☎ 0-800 99 00 19	Canada Direct	☎ 0-800 99 00 16

Emergency numbers:	
Police: 17	
SAMU (Paramedics): 15	
Fire (Pompiers): 18	

International Information,
US/Canada: 00 33 12 11

International operator:
00 33 12 + country code

Local directory assistance: 12

Minitel – France Télécom operates a system offering directory enquiries (free of charge up to 3min), travel and entertainment reservations, and other services (cost per minute varies). These small computer-like terminals can be found in some post offices, hotels and France Télécom agencies and in many French homes. 3614 PAGES E is the code for **directory assistance in English** (turn on the unit, dial 3614, hit the *connexion* button when you get the tone, type in «PAGES E», and follow the instructions on the screen).

Cellular phones in France have numbers which begin with 06. Two-watt (lighter, shorter reach) and eight-watt models are on the market, using the Orange (France Télécom) or SFR network. *Mobicartes* are pre-paid phone cards that fit into mobile units. Cell phone rentals (delivery or airport pickup provided) are available from:

Rent a Cell Express   ☏ 01 53 93 78 00, Fax 01 53 93 78 09

A.L.T. Rent A Phone   ☏ 01 48 00 06 60, E-mail altloc@jve.fr

Public holidays

Museums and other monuments may be closed or may vary their hours of admission on the following public holidays:

1 January	New Year's Day *(Jour de l'An)*
	Easter Day and Easter Monday *(Pâques)*
1 May	May Day *(Fête du travail)*
8 May	VE Day
Thur 40 days after Easter	Ascension Day *(Ascension)*
7th Sun-Mon after Easter	Whit Sunday and Monday *(Pentecôte)*
14 July	France's National Day (Bastille Day)
15 August	Assumption *(Assomption)*
1 November	All Saints' Day *(Toussaint)*
11 November	Armistice Day
25 December	Christmas Day *(Noël)*

National museums and art galleries are closed on Tuesdays; municipal museums are generally closed on Mondays. In addition to the usual school holidays at Christmas and in the spring and summer, there are long mid-term breaks (10 days to a fortnight) in February and early November.

Time

France is 1hr ahead of Greenwich Mean Time (GMT). France goes on daylight-saving time from the last Sunday in March to the last Sunday in October.

When it is **noon in France**, it is

3am	in Los Angeles
6am	in New York
11am	in Dublin
11am	in London
7pm	in Perth
9pm	in Sydney
11pm	in Auckland

R. Corbel/MICHELIN

In France «am» and «pm» are not used but the 24-hour clock is widely applied.

Conversion tables

Weights and measures

1 kilogram (kg)	2.2 pounds (lb)	2.2 pounds
1 metric ton (tn)	1.1 tons	1.1 tons

to convert kilograms to pounds, multiply by 2.2

1 litre (l)	2.1 pints (pt)	1.8 pints
1 litre	0.3 gallon (gal)	0.2 gallon

to convert litres to gallons, multiply by 0.26 (US) or 0.22 (UK)

1 hectare (ha)	2.5 acres	2.5 acres
1 square kilometre (km²)	0.4 square miles (sq mi)	0.4 square miles

to convert hectares to acres, multiply by 2.4

1 centimetre (cm)	0.4 inches (in)	0.4 inches
1 metre (m)	3.3 feet (ft) - 39.4 inches - 1.1 yards (yd)	
1 kilometre (km)	0.6 miles (mi)	0.6 miles

to convert metres to feet, multiply by 3.28, kilometres to miles, multiply by 0.6

Clothing

Women							Men
	☆	☰	✚	☆	☰	✚	
	35	4	2½	40	7½	7	
	36	5	3½	41	8½	8	
	37	6	4½	42	9½	9	
Shoes	38	7	5½	43	10½	10	Shoes
	39	8	6½	44	11½	11	
	40	9	7½	45	12½	12	
	41	10	8½	46	13½	13	
	36	4	8	46	36	36	
	38	6	10	48	38	38	
Dresses	40	8	12	50	40	40	Suits
& Suits	42	12	14	52	42	42	
	44	14	16	54	44	44	
	46	16	18	56	46	48	
	36	08	30	37	14½	14,5	
	38	10	32	38	15	15	
Blouses	40	12	14	39	15½	15½	Shirts
& sweaters	42	14	36	40	15¾	15¾	
	44	16	38	41	16	16	
	46	18	40	42	16½	16½	

Sizes often vary depending on the designer. These equivalents are given for guidance only.

Speed

kph	10	30	50	70	80	90	100	110	120	130
mph	6	19	31	43	50	56	62	68	75	81

Temperature

Celsius (°C)	0°	5°	10°	15°	20°	25°	30°	40°	60°	80°	100°
Fahrenheit (°F)	32°	41°	50°	59°	68°	77°	86°	104°	140°	176°	212°

To convert Celsius into Fahrenheit, multiply °C by 9, divide by 5, and add 32.
To convert Fahrenheit into Celsius, subtract 32 from °F, multiply by 5, and divide by 9.

Shopping

Most of the larger shops are open Mondays to Saturdays from 9am to 6.30 or 7.30pm. Smaller, individual shops may close during the lunch hour. Food shops – grocers, wine merchants and bakeries – are generally open from 7am to 6.30 or 7.30pm; some open on Sunday mornings. Many food shops close between noon and 2pm and on Mondays. Bakery and pastry shops sometimes close on Wednesdays. Hypermarkets usually stay open non-stop until 9pm or later.

People travelling to the USA cannot import plant products or fresh food, including fruit, cheeses and nuts. It is acceptable to carry tinned products or preserves.

Recovering Value Added Tax

There is a Value Added Tax in France *(TVA)* of 19.6% on almost every purchase (books and some foods are subject to a lower rate). However, non-European visitors who spend more than 183€ (amount subject to change) in any one participating store can get the VAT amount refunded. Usually, you fill out a form at the store and have to present your passport. Upon leaving the country, you submit all forms to customs for approval (they may want to see the goods, so if possible don't pack them in checked luggage). The refund is usually paid directly into your bank or credit card account, or it can be sent by mail. Big department stores that cater to tourists provide special services to help you; be sure to mention that you plan to seek a refund before you pay for goods (no refund is possible for tax on services). If you are visiting two or more countries within the European Union, you submit the forms only on departure from the last EU country. The refund is worth while for those visitors who would like to buy fashions, furniture or other fairly expensive items, but remember, the minimum amount must be spent in a single shop (though not necessarily on the same day).

Local specialities – What to bring back

Wine is the obvious choice and wine-tasting on the roadside will help you choose among the excellent wines produced in the Loire Valley.

Tempting **delicacies** from the region include Cointreau, a liqueur from St-Barthélémy d'Anjou; tasty Ste-Maure-de-Touraine or Selles-sur-Cher goat cheese; apricot-filled prunes from Tours; *muscadin*, a delicious mix of cherry, ground chestnut and black chocolate from Langeais; *cotignac*, quince jelly from Orléans sold in round wooden pots; smooth honey from the Gâtinais...

Among non-perishable goods, high-quality **handicraft**, such as wicker work from Villaines-les-Rochers and Gien earthenware, is well worth taking home.

Discovering the region

REGIONAL DRIVING TOURS

Here is a brief description of each of the tours shown on the map on page 13.

1 Haut-Anjou *170km/102mi starting from Angers*

Begin this tour in "Good King René's" city, and discover the surrounding region of Anjou Noir. Hedgerows and sunken paths cut across the landscape. The River Mayenne offers opportunities for pleasant cruises and waterside picnics. There are many lovely manor houses and impressive properties along this route.

2 Le Mans, Sarthe and Loir *240km/144mi starting from Le Mans*

Starting from the city of Le Mans, famous for the eponymous 24-hour auto race, head for the hills. The rolling landscape sparkles with good fishing streams. Meadows and woods form a patchwork. You may prefer to take your time and spend more than a day on this itinerary. Le Mans (outside of race days) is well worth a visit, and the majestic oaks of the forest seem to beckon the visitor to stop and rest a while.

3 The Loir Valley and the Vendôme region
170km/102mi starting from Châteaudun

The landscapes along the enchanting Loir Valley are a peaceful and harmonious succession of meadows, woods and vineyards. This natural beauty is further adorned with graceful Romanesque churches (some painted with remarkable frescoes), romantic ruined castles and houses built in the distinctive white stone of the region. The château at Châteaudun is considered as the northernmost of the châteaux of the Loire; from there follow the River Loir south to Vendôme, a charming, lively town. Continue on to Lavardin, one of the prettiest villages in France, dominated by the ruins of a giant medieval fortress. The route continues to Montoire-sur-le-Loir, then Troo, where dwellings have been carved out of the stone cliffs and you can visit the locally famous "talking well". Visit the Renaissance château in Poncé-sur-le-Loir or the manor of La Possonnière. This itinerary then veers north again, going through Mondoubleau, perched on a hillside. In St-Agil, the château is watched over by two magnificent lime trees, nearly 300 years old. The Knights Templar established the *commanderie* at Arvillé. Return to Châteaudun via Courtalain.

④ Orléans and Sologne *180km/108mi starting from Orléans*

Follow the River Loire as it meanders through Sologne. Much of the farmland was once an uninhabitable flood plain. Over time, fields have been recovered for farming; since the 19C, the woodlands have been a favoured hunting ground. Today, there are still wild animals roaming the pine forest, and waterfowl on the many ponds. Along the riverside, great châteaux welcomed many historic figures. From Orléans, travel to Châteauneuf-sur-Loire, where a museum presents a history of navigation on the river. Then carry on to St-Benoît, site of one of the most beautiful abbeys in France (if you are lucky, you may arrive to hear the monks singing). The château at Sully was rebuilt after the Second World War, and in Gien the brick château is now home to a hunting museum. Lamotte-Beuvron is famous for its *tarte tatin*, apple upside-down cake. Finish your tour with a relaxing stroll in the gardens of La Source.

⑤ Blois and the great châteaux of the Renaissance
120km/72mi starting from Blois

In the heart of the French region of Centre-Val de Loire, not far from Paris, and easily accessible by road or high-speed train, Blois is the gateway to the kingdom of castles. Here between the River Cher and River Loire stand some of the most elegant Renaissance buildings in the world, in such abundance that their grace and beauty are almost overwhelming. Visit the royal palaces of Chambord and Blois; the sumptuous châteaux of the nobility at Beauregard, Chaumont and Cheverny; the manor house of Villesavin. These are some of the best-known and most unforgettable monuments in the world.

⑥ Val de Touraine: drink in the beauty
150km/90mi starting from Tours

This is the land the French dream of when they reflect on all that is good in their country: the roots of history, the fruit of the vine, and unequalled *savoir vivre*. Begin in Tours and stop in Vouvray, home of the magical sparkling wine of the same name. Then on to Amboise, where François I held court, and to Clos-Lucé, where Leonardo da Vinci set up housekeeping at the king's request. In Montrichard, take the time to see the demonstration of birds of prey. Then on to the beautiful Château de Chenonceaux, gracefully arcing over the River Cher. A visit to Loches carries the imagination back to the Middle Ages. Return to Tours via the valley of the River Indre and the town of Monbazon.

⑦ The most beautiful châteaux in Touraine
130km/78mi starting from Tours

Discovering the Val de Touraine is like opening a jewellery case lined in lush green velvet, fragrant with the scent of summer roses. The jewels on the green field are royal castles. Start out from Tours and drive to the Château de Luynes, perched upon a rocky spur. Then visit Cinq-Mars-la-Pile – the name derives from a slender tower *(pile)* dating from Gallo-Roman times. Langeais presents the severe façade of a feudal fortress, but inside the decoration is evocative of life at court in ages past. In Bourgeuil, stop and visit a local vintner to taste his light-hearted wines; continue on to Chinon to compare with the slightly more robust red wines made there. Enter the Château d'Ussé quietly, so as not to disturb Sleeping Beauty. The image of Azay-le-Rideau reflected in the waters of the River Indre is a model of Renaissance elegance. Villandry is especially loved for the beauty of its carefully restored gardens: the garden of love, the water garden, the herb garden and the kitchen garden.

⑧ The Saumur region and the Layon Valley
140km/84mi starting from Saumur

This lovely region south of the River Loire is a garden of delights – or a vineyard of delights if you prefer! As you leave the town of Saumur, the sunny hillsides are covered in the vines that produce Anjou wines. Farther along the route, you will encounter a wooded landscape, and at every stage culinary pleasures await you. There are many interesting monuments and sights to visit: Brissac and its enormous eight-storey château, Doué-la-Fontine, the "city of roses", the Minières zoo, the medieval ramparts of Montreuil-Bellay, and the marvellous royal abbey of Fontevraud.

THEMATIC ITINERARIES AND VISITS

Travel itineraries on specific themes have been mapped out to help you discover the regional architectural heritage and the traditions which make up the cultural heritage of the region. You will find brochures in tourist offices, and the routes are generally well-marked and easy to follow (signs posted along the roads).

Historical routes

The Val de Loire has been on UNESCO's World Heritage list since the end of the year 2000.
To allow tourists to discover France's architectural heritage in a historical context, local authorities have set up a number of routes focusing on local architectural, cultural and traditional themes. These **routes historiques** are indicated by road signs. Each of them is detailed in a brochure available from Tourist Information Centres. Several interesting itineraries are found in the regions covered in this guide.

Route historique du roi René – This circuit takes in the most important châteaux in the Anjou area; most of which are occupied, but nonetheless open to the public.
Château de Plessis-Bourré, 49460 Écueillé, ☎ 02 41 32 06 01.

Route historique de la Vallée des Rois – The route once used by the kings of France, on the way from Gien to Saumur via Orléans, Blois and Tours.
Château des Réaux, 37140 Chouzé-sur-Loire, ☎ 02 47 95 14 40.
Thematic Michelin map 226 La Vallée des Rois.

Route historique des Dames de Touraine – Dedicated to the great ladies who showed both talent and determination in building, renovating, embellishing or simply enjoying their splendid estates, this route winds its way among the towns of Amboise, Beauregard, Montpoupon, Le Grand-Pressigny, Valençay, Chenonceau etc.
Château de Montpoupon, Céré-la-Ronde, 37460 Montrésor, ☎ 02 47 94 21 15.

Route historique François-Ier – Runs from the Blois region down to the banks of the River Cher, evoking the many visits François I and his retinue paid to the region.
14 rue St-Julien-le-Pauvre, 75005 Paris, ☎ 01 43 29 48 44.

Route historique du patrimoine culturel québécois en France – This route links places with French immigration to Quebec.
Comité Chomedey-de-Maisonneuve, Centre Culturel Maisonneuve, 10190 Neuville-sur-Vannes, ☎ 03 25 40 68 33, www.comite-maisonneuve.fr.st.

Les routes de Jeanne d'Arc – Four itineraries illustrate Joan of Arc's mission: *Les débuts* (beginnings), *La campagne de Loire* (the Loire campaign), *La campagne du sacre* (the coronation campaign) and *La capture* (taken prisoner). Locations in this guide include the towns of Beaugency, Chinon, Chécy, Gien, Loches, Orléans, Patay and Sainte-Catherine-de-Fierbois.
Association des villes johanniques, mairie, 88630 Domrémy-la-Pucelle. The association has an office in the town hall at Orléans.

Société historique des Plantagenêts – The society aims to promote a better knowledge of 12C European civilisation through the discovery of monuments and sites which testify to the wealth of the period.
Société historique des Plantagenêts, Archives Nationales, Hôtel de Soubise, 60 rue des Francs-Bourgeois, 75141 Paris Cedex 03, ☎ 01 40 27 63 50.

Parks and gardens

Route des Parcs et Jardins – The art of formal gardens which came to characterise French châteaux and parks was born in the Loire Valley in the early 16C. This tourist route leads through some of the most beautiful and ingeniously designed gardens from the Renaissance up to the present, including the Château de **Villandry**, the Château de **Chamerolles**, the Château de **Villeprévost**, the floral park at **Orléans-la-Source**, the Château de **Beauregard**, the Château de **Chaumont-sur-Loire**, the Château de **Cheverny**, the Château de **Valmer** and the priory of **St-Cosme**.

Local industry and handicraft

The following workshops or factories are open to the public, giving an insight into local crafts and industry:
Chinon nuclear power station on p 170;
Gien potteries on p 194;
Montrichard, J M Monmousseau's Champagne-method wine cellars on p 233;
Poncé-sur-le-Loir arts and crafts centre on p 308;
St-Barthélemy-d'Anjou Cointreau distillery on p 104;
St-Cyr-en-Bourg Saumur cooperative wine cellar on p 269;

St-Hilaire-St-Florent Bouvet-Ladubay sparkling Saumur wines on p 269;

Saut-aux-Loups mushroom beds on p 173;

Turquant Troglo des Pommes Tapées (dried apples) on p 174;

Vaas Rotrou corn mill on p 309;

Villaines-les-Rochers basketwork cooperative on p 113.

Mills of Anjou – The particular geographical and climatic conditions of Anjou account for the presence of many different mills in the region.

The **Association des Amis des Moulins de l'Anjou** (AMA) publishes brochures and organises visits to local mills. For information apply to 17 rue de la Madeleine, BP 725, 49007 Angers Cedex 01, ☎ 02 41 43 87 36.

Wine country

Like all wine-growers, the *vignerons* from the Loire region are extremely hospitable and eager to welcome visitors to their cellars and storehouses in order to offer tastings, talk about their profession, show their working equipment, explain winemaking techniques and... sell their wine.

The wine producers, merchants and cooperatives willing to accept visitors are too numerous for us to draw up a complete list. However, all the Tourist Information Centres and the Maisons du Vin (especially those in Amboise, Angers, Bourgueil, Chinon, Montlouis-sur-Loire, Saumur and Vouvray) will supply the necessary details:

La Maison du Vin de l'Anjou, 5 bis place Kennedy, 49100 Angers, ☎ 02 41 88 81 13.

Comité interprofessionnel des vins du Val de Loire, Hôtel des Vins La Godeline, 73 rue Plantagenêt, 49100 Angers, ☎ 02 41 87 62 57.

La Maison des vins de Nantes, Bellevue, 44690 La-Haye-Fouassière, ☎ 02 40 36 90 10.

La Maison du vin de Saumur, quai Lucien-Gautier, 49400 Saumur, ☎ 02 41 38 45 83.

Interloire, 12 rue Étienne-Pallu, BP 1921, 37019 Tours Cedex 1, ☎ 02 47 60 55 10.

The art of drinking wine – To identify and describe the qualities or defects of a particular wine, both wine buffs and wine experts use an extremely wide yet precise vocabulary. Assessing a wine involves three successive stages, each associated with a particular sense and a certain number of technical terms:

The eye – **General impression:** crystalline (good clarity), limpid (perfectly transparent, no particles in suspension), still (no bubbles), sparkling (effervescent wine) or *mousseux* (lots of fine, Champagne-type bubbles).

Colour and hues: a wine is said to have a nice robe when the colour is sharp and clean; the main terms used to describe the different hues are pale red, ruby, onionskin, garnet (red wine), salmon, amber, partridge-eye pink (rosé wine) and golden-green, golden-yellow and straw (white wine).

The nose – Pleasant smells: floral, fruity, balsamic, spicy, flinty.
Unpleasant smells: corked, woody, hydrogen sulphide, cask.

The mouth – Once it has passed the visual and olfactory tests, the wine undergoes a final test in the mouth. It can be described as agreeable (pleasant), aggressive (unpleasant, with a high acidity), full-flavoured (rich and well-balanced), structured (well-constructed, with a high alcohol content), heady (intoxicating), fleshy (producing a strong impact on taste buds), fruity (flavour evoking the freshness and natural taste of grapes), easy to drink, jolly (inducing merriness), round (supple, mellow), lively (light, fresh, with a lowish alcohol content) etc.

Quality control – French wines fall into various official categories indicating the area of production and therefore the probable quality of the wine. AOC *(appellation d'origine contrôlée)* denotes a wine produced in a strictly delimited area, stated on the label, made with the grape varieties specified for that wine in accordance with local traditional methodology. VDQS *(vin délimité de qualité supérieure)* is also produced in a legally controlled area, slightly less highly rated than AOC. *Vin de pays* denotes the highest ranking table wine after AOC and VDQS.

The table below lists the main AOC wines produced in the region described in this guide (Anjou, Orléanais, Saumur and Touraine).

Birdwatching

The French National Association for the Protection of Bird Life – **Ligue pour la Protection des Oiseaux (LPO)** – has its headquarters at La Corderie Royale, BP 263, 17305 Rochefort Cedex, ☎ 05 46 82 12 34, www.lpo-birdlife.asso.fr.

It is a non-profit-making organisation set up to protect species of wild bird as well as their environment. Its aim is to educate the general public and make people more aware of nature by organising visits, excursions and conferences on the subject of natural reserves. **LPO Touraine:** ☎ 02 47 51 81 84, **LPO Anjou:** ☎ 02 41 44 44 22, **LPO Loire-Atlantique**, ☎ 02 51 82 02 97.

The **Carrefour des Mauges** (a permanent centre whose role is to provide information about the Loire and Mauges environment, Ferme abbatiale des Coteaux, BP 44, 49410 St-Florent-le-Vieil, ☎ 02 41 71 77 30) stages a number of one-day programmes, including on-the-spot visits, during which you can identify the different bird species, study their behaviour and see them in their natural habitat *(telescopes and binoculars are supplied by the organisations)*.

Appellations	Départements	Grape varieties	R red r rosé W white
ANJOU	Maine-et-Loire	Cabernet Franc, Sauvignon	R W
ANJOU-GAMAY	Maine-et-Loire	Gamay	R
BOURGUEIL	Indre-et-Loire	Cabernet	R r
CABERNET D'ANJOU	Maine-et-Loire	Cabernet, Grolleau	r
CABERNET DE SAUMUR	Maine-et-Loire	Cabernet, Grolleau	r
CHEVERNY	Loir-et-Cher	Sauvignon, Chenin, Gamay	R r W
CHINON	Indre-et-Loire	Cabernet	R r W
COTEAUX-DU-GIENNOIS	Loiret	Sauvignon, Gamay	R r W
COTEAUX-DU-LOIR	Indre-et-Loire	Chenin, Gamay, Pineau d'Aunis	R r W
COTEAUX-DU-VENDÔMOIS	Loir-et-Cher	Chenin, Pineau d'Aunis, Pinot, Cabernet	R r W
COTEAUX-DU-LAYON	Maine-et-Loire	Cabernet Franc, Pineau	W
CRÉMANT DE LOIRE	Indre-et-Loire	Chenin, Chardonnay, Cabernet	r W
	Loir-et-Cher	Pineau d'Aunis	r W
	Indre-et-Loire	Sauvignon, Chenin, Pinot	W
MONTLOUIS	Indre-et-Loire	Chenin	W
ORLÉANAIS	Loiret	Pinot, Cabernet, Chardonnay	R r W
SAUMUR	Maine-et-Loire	Cabernet Franc, Sauvignon, Gamay	W
SAUMUR-CHAMPIGNY	Maine-et-Loire	Cabernet, Pineau d'Aunis	R
ST-NICOLAS-DE-BOURGUEIL	Indre-et-Loire	Cabernet	R r
TOURAINE	Loir-et-Cher	Pineau, Gamay, Cabernet	R r W
TOURAINE-AMBOISE	Indre-et-Loire	Chenin, Gamay, Cabernet	R r W
TOURAINE AZAY LE RIDEAU	Indre-et-Loire	Chenin, Grolleau noir	r W
TOURAINE-MESLAND	Loir-et-Cher	Chenin, Sauvignon, Gamay, Cabernet	R r W
VALENÇAY	Loir-et-Cher	Sauvignon, Chenin	R r W
VOUVRAY	Indre-et-Loire	Chenin	R

Other useful addresses:

Maison de la Nature et de l'Environnement d'Orléans, 64 route d'Olivet, 45100 Orléans, ☎ 02 38 56 69 84. This association is responsible for other sites including the Réserve naturelle de l'île de St-Pryvé-St-Mesmin and the Maison forestière d'Ouzouer-sur-Loire.

SEPN 41 (Société d'étude et de protection de la nature en Loir-et-Cher), 17 rue Roland-Garros, 41000 Blois, ☎ 02 54 42 53 71.

If you find an injured bird, please contact the LPO who will direct you to the nearest Centre de sauvegarde de la faune sauvage (Wildlife protection centre).

ANOTHER POINT OF VIEW

Tourist trains

A number of charming old steam trains are operated along parts of the Loire Valley, generally by groups of volunteers, with the result that they usually only run at weekends. It is therefore advisable to check details in advance.

Pithiviers tourist train (Loiret):
offers various short trips. Details from Pithiviers tourist office, ☎ 02 38 30 50 02.

Lac de Rillé historical railway (Indre-et-Loire):
trip round Lake Pincemaille. AECFM, ☎/Fax 02 47 24 60 19.

From Chinon to Richelieu, a Mikado 1922

Touraine steam train (Indre-et-Loire):
from Richelieu to Ligré via Champigny-sur-Veude. TVT, ☎ 02 47 58 12 97.

Loir valley tourist train (Loir-et-Cher):
from Thoré-la-Rochette to Troo. ☎ 02 54 72 80 82.

Compagnie du Blanc Argent (Loir-et-Cher):
the metric-gauge railway serves 15 stations and stops between Salbris and Luçay-le-Mâle (Indre). For details about times and rates, apply to La Compagnie du Blanc-Argent, Gare de Romorantin-Lanthenay, ☎ 02 54 76 06 51 or Romorantin tourist office.

Sarthe steam train:
from Conneré-Beillé to Bonnétable. TRANVAP, ☎ 02 43 89 00 37.

Semur-en-Vallon tourist train (Sarthe):
narrow gauge railway operating on a distance of 1.5km/1mi (25 seats).
☎ 02 43 71 30 36.

From above

Weather permitting, there are various ways of getting a bird's-eye view of the Loire Valley, from microlights (ULM, standing for *ultra-légers motorisés*), gliders, helicopters or light aircraft. Trips leave from the airport at Tours-St-Symphorien, flying over Chinon, Chambord, Chenonceau and Azay-le-Rideau, and from Blois-le-Breuil or Orléans aerodrome to fly over Amboise, Cheverny and Beaugency.
It is also possible to take a trip in a hot-air balloon (allow about half a day for 1hr-1hr 30min in the air, price from 145€ to 250€ per person).

Microlights

Aérodrome d'Amboise-Dierre, ☎ 02 47 57 93 91.

Aérodrome de Tours-Sorigny, ☎ 02 47 26 27 50.

Fédération Française de Planeur Ultra-Léger Motorisé, 96 bis rue Marc-Sangnier, BP 341, 94709 Maison-Alfort Cedex, ☎ 01 49 81 74 43, www.ffplum.com.

Gliders

Almost every airfield throughout the region has its own flying school which offers first flights and flying lessons (aboard two-seaters, gliders etc).
Fédération Française de Vol-à-Voile, 29 rue de Sèvres, 75006 Paris, ☎ 01 45 44 04 78, www.ffvv.org.

Helicopters

A helicopter ride is the ideal way to get a good overall view of the châteaux and their sumptuous architecture, as well as to take striking photographs. A number of rental companies offer helicopter rides lasting between 10min and 2hr, with prices varying accordingly (from 55€ per person).

Indre-et-Loire
Jet Systems Hélicoptères Val de Loire, Amboise-Dierre aerodrome, 37150 Dierre, ☎ 02 47 30 20 21, www.jet-systems.fr.
Air-Touraine-Hélicoptère, BP 14, 37370 Neuvy-le-Roi, ☎ 02 47 24 81 44.

Loir-et-Cher
Blois-Hélistation, pont Charles-de-Gaulle, on D 951 at the Blois-Vienne exit, ☎ 02 54 90 41 41 (booking essential).

Loire-Atlantique
Nantes Aérosystèmes Héliocéan, 44340 Bouguenais, ☎ 02 40 05 22 11.

Sarthe
Jet Systems Hélicoptères, Le Mans/Arnage aerodrome, ☎ 02 43 72 07 70.

Light aircraft

Aéro-Club Les Ailes Tourangelles, Amboise-Dierre aerodrome, 37150 Dierre, ☎ 02 47 57 93 91.
Loire Valley Aviation, Blois-Vendôme-Le Breuil aerodrome, ☎ 02 54 56 16 12.

Hot-air balloons

Travelling by hot-air balloon adds an old-world charm to the discovery of the Loire Valley from above. Balloons take off from almost anywhere (except towns of course), usually in the early morning or late evening; landing, on the other hand, greatly depends on the strength and direction of the wind and the landing spot is sometimes unpredictable. Flights last between 1hr and 1hr 30min but it is wise to allow three times that amount of time for the flight preparation and the drive back to the starting point in the vehicle which follows the balloon. The cost of the flight ranges from 145€ to 250€ per person.

Loiret: Comité départemental de tourisme, 8 rue d'Escures, 45000 Orléans, ☎ 02 38 78 04 04.

France Montgolfières, La Riboulière, 41400 Montou-sur-Cher, ☎ 02 54 71 75 40, www.franceballoons.com; meeting place: Chenonceaux, Amboise, Chaumont-sur-Loire.

Aérocom, 27 route de Saint-Sulpice, 41330 Fossé, ☎ 02 54 33 55 00. Flights from the main Loire châteaux.

Sablé-sur-Sarthe tourist office (1hr 30min trips along the Sarthe Valley), ☎ 02 43 95 00 60.

Activities children will love

The region abounds in parks, museums and various attractive features as well as leisure activities which will appeal to children; in the Sights section, the reader's attention is drawn to them by the symbol 🖾.

Towns designated by the Ministry of Culture as **"Villes d'Art et d'Histoire"** organise discovery tours and cultural-heritage workshops for children. Fun books and specially designed tools are provided and the activities on offer are supervised by various professionals such as architects, stone masons, story-tellers and actors. This scheme, called **"l'été des 6-12 ans"** (summer activities for 6-12-year-olds) operates during school holidays. The towns concerned are: Angers, Blois, Chinon, Loches, Le Mans, Tours and Vendôme.

Hot-air balloons taking off in the early morning

River cruising

For information apply to the **Comité départemental de tourisme**, Tourisme fluvial Pays de la Loire, 1 place du Président-Kennedy, 49000 Angers, ☎ 02 41 23 51 30.

Small private barges *(bateaux habitables)* can be taken on the following stretches of river:
Loire: 84km/52mi between Angers and Nantes;
Maine: 8km/5mi (at the confluence of the Mayenne and the Sarthe);
Mayenne: 131km/81.4mi between the town of Mayenne and the Maine;
Oudon: 18km/11mi between Segré and Le Lion d'Angers;
Sarthe: 136km/85mi between Le Mans and the Maine;
as well as along the canalised stretch of the **Cher** (from Montrichard when the river is suitable for cruising) and the **Canal de Berry** (from Noyers-sur-Cher, year-round, ☎ 02 54 75 08 51).

The following table provides some information on houseboats which can be hired *(no permit necessary)* for one or several nights in order to explore the Anjou region via its waterways. Day cruises on piloted boats are also available.

Departure points	Rivers	Boat companies
Entrammes	Sarthe Mayenne Oudon	Connoisseur, Île Sauzay, 70100 Gray, ☎ 03 84 64 95 20.
Angers Châteauneuf-s/Sarthe Chenillé-Changé Mayenne	Maine Mayenne Oudon Sarthe	Maine Anjou Rivières, Le Moulin, 49220 Chenillé-Changé, ☎ 02 41 95 10 83.
Daon	Mayenne	France Mayenne Fluviale, Le Port, 53200 Daon, ☎ 02 43 70 13 94.
Grez-Neuville	Maine Mayenne Oudon Sarthe	Anjou Plaisance, rue de l'Écluse, 49220 Grez-Neuville, ☎ 02 41 95 68 95.
Sablé-sur-Sarthe	Mayenne Oudon Sarthe	Anjou Navigation, quai National, 72300 Sablé-sur-Sarthe, ☎ 02 43 95 14 42. Les Croisières Saboliennes, quai National, 73200 Sablé-sur-Sarthe, ☎ 02 43 95 93 13.

River cruising is possible all year round. However, before choosing an itinerary and the dates at which you will need to book the boat, it is essential to enquire about scouring periods or *écourues (see below)* and locks, which may close at certain times of the day or on public holidays. Remember that the cruising speed is 6-8kmph/3.7-5mph and that sailing is not permitted at night.
During the **scouring periods** when the water level is lowered for maintenance work, the river sections and canals concerned are closed to navigation. Work is usually carried out in autumn from 15 September to 30 October. In the Maine basin, work alternates from river to river, affecting the Sarthe one year and the Mayenne the next. Depending on the year, cruise companies move their pleasure boats to a different river during the scouring period.

River passenger boats

There exist two types of river passenger boat: the *bateau-mouche* and the *coche d'eau*. They usually leave at set hours (often at 3pm and 5pm) between mid-April and mid-October. Some trips include the passing of locks or a fascinating and instructive commentary on local birds species or water transport in the Loire region.
Discovering the tracks of small animals like beavers and bird spotting add to the pleasure of these charming, peaceful cruises.

Starting from **Briare**, along the canal with the company Les Bateaux Touristiques;
from **Chisseaux**, 1hr 30min cruise along the Cher, gliding beneath the arches of the Château de Chenonçeau and beyond;

Chenillé-Changé – River boat centre

from **Fay-aux-Loges**, along the Orléans canal, Syndicat du canal d'Orléans, ☎ 02 38 46 82 90;
from **Montrichard**, 1hr 30min cruise along the Cher aboard the *Léonard-de-Vinci*;
from **Olivet**, 1hr 30min cruise along the Loiret aboard the *Sologne*, ☎ 02 38 51 12 12;
from **Saint-Aignan**, 1hr 30min cruise along the Cher aboard the *Val-du-Cher*.

Along the rivers of **Anjou** and **Maine**:
Batellerie Promenade, 2 rue de Beauvais, 49125 Cheffes, ☎ 02 41 42 12 12;
Sarth'Eau, Halte Nautique, rue du Port, 72210 La Suze-sur-Sarthe, ☎ 02 43 77 47 64;
Féérives, Le Moulin, 49220 Chenillé-Changé, ☎ 02 41 95 10 83;
Le Duc des Chauvières, Parc St-Fiacre, 53200 Château-Gontier, ☎ 02 43 70 37 83.

Sports and outdoor activities

Information and brochures outlining the sports and outdoor facilities available in the region can be obtained from the French Government Tourist Office or from the organisations listed below.

ALONG THE RIVER

Canoeing and kayaking

This method of exploring local waterways need not be exclusively reserved for seasoned canoeing experts. Sometimes this sport can be a pleasant way to discover secluded spots inaccessible by any other means. The main difference between a canoe and a kayak is that the former is propelled by a single-bladed paddle and the latter by a double-bladed paddle.
Canoeing trips of half a day, a whole day or more can be organised for individuals or a group (allowing for brief training and certain safety measures). The most suitable rivers are the Cisse, Conie, Cosson, Huisne, Indre, Loir, Sauldre, Thouet, Vienne and, of course, the Loire. For detailed information, contact the **Loisir Accueil** section in each *département*, or the **Fédération Française de Canoë-Kayak (FFCK)**, 87 quai de la Marne, BP 58, 94340 Joinville-le-Pont, ☎ 01 45 11 08 50.
Comité Régional de Canoë-Kayak du Centre, Maison des Sports, 1240 rue de la Bergeresse, 45160 Olivet, ☎ 02 38 49 88 80.
Ligue Canoë-Kayak des Pays de Loire, route d'Angers, 49080 Bouchemaine, ☎ 02 41 73 86 10.

Fishing

Recent French surveys reveal that freshwater fishing is the second most popular national leisure pastime after football! Swift-flowing or not, the waters of the Loire offer anglers numerous attractive possibilities.

Fish
of the Loire

Catfish
(Ictalurus melas)

Eel

Rainbow trout

Pike-perch

Perch

Catfish *(Silurus glanis)*

Pike

M. Dewynter/MICHELIN

All authorised types of fishing are open to the angler, whether fishing for gudgeon, roach and dace, or trying for pike or the striped mullet which come upstream as far as Amboise in summer, or going after the catfish, tench and carp which lurk in dips in the river bed of the Loire, the Indre and the Loir and in the pools of the Sologne which are also teaming with perch.

Trout are to be found in the Creuse, the Sauldre, the streams of Anjou or the tributaries of the Loir, whereas the Berry, Briare, or Orléans canals are home to eels and sometimes freshwater crayfish which can be caught with a net.

For salmon and shad fishing it is necessary to have a flat-bottomed boat; professionals possess specialist equipment such as nets stretched across the river, held in place by poles fixed in the river bed.

Regulations and open seasons – These differ according to whether the water is classified as first category (contains trout and salmon) or second category (coarse fish). Stricter rules apply to fish needing special protection, so salmon fishing in particular may be forbidden outright during some years, or permitted for a restricted period only between March and June. Likewise, pike may only be tackled between July and January. Generally speaking, in the case of first category rivers, the fishing season starts on the second Saturday in March and ends on the third Sunday in September. As for rivers belonging in the second category, fishing is authorised throughout the year.

Regional and national regulations should be observed. Anglers will need either to buy a special holiday fishing permit, valid for two weeks between June and September, or take out annual membership of an officially approved angling association. These officially stamped permits cover fishing with up to four lines on second category waterways administered by an angling association or one line on all public waterways. Only one line is allowed on first category waters and a supplementary tax is payable.

On private property, where the fishing rights belong to the owner of the bank, the owner's permission must be obtained. In the case of certain private lakes, which are excluded from the angling legislation, the owner's permission (annual, monthly or daily permit) is the only formality required and can be granted at any time of year.

Minimum size of catch – National regulations state that anglers must return to the water any fish they catch below the minimum permitted length (50cm/20in for pike, 40cm/16in for pike-perch, 23cm/9in for trout, 50cm/20in for salmon, 9cm/4in for crayfish).

Useful brochures and folding maps *Fishing in France (Pêche en France)* are published and distributed by the **Conseil Supérieur de la Pêche**, 134 avenue Malakoff, 75116 Paris, ☎ 01 45 02 20 20; also available from local angling organisations.

Délégation régionale du Conseil Supérieur de la Pêche, 112 faubourg de la Cueille, 86000 Poitiers, ☎ 05 49 41 29 88.

For information about regulations contact the Tourist Information Centres or the offices of the **Eaux et Forêts** (Water and Forest Authority).

Federations for fishing and the protection of rivers:

Indre-et-Loire – 25 rue Charles-Gilles, 37000 Tours, ☎ 02 47 05 33 77.

Loir-et-Cher – 11 rue Robert-Nau, Vallée Maillard, 41000 Blois, ☎ 02 54 90 25 60.

Loiret – 49 route d'Olivet, BP 8157, 45081 Orléans Cedex 2, ☎ 02 38 56 62 69.

Maine-et-Loire – 14 allée du Haras, 49100 Angers, ☎ 02 41 87 57 09.

Mayenne – 78 rue Émile-Brault, 53000 Laval, ☎ 02 43 69 12 13.

Sarthe – 40 rue Bary, BP 17, 72001 Le Mans Cedex, ☎ 02 43 85 66 01, www.unpf.fr/72.

Aquariums and angling centres

- Aquarium de Touraine at **Lussault-sur-Loire** (Indre-et-Loire)
- Aquarium Tropical at **Tours** (Indre-et-Loire)
- Aquarium de Sologne, Aliotis, at **Villeherviers** (Loir-et-Cher)
- Carrefour des Mauges at **St-Florent-le-Vieil** (Maine-et-Loire)
- Centre Piscicole at **Brissac-Quincé** (Maine-et-Loire)
- Observatoire de la Loire at **Rochecorbon** (Indre-et-Loire)
- Observatoire Fédéral at **Champigny-sur-Veude** (Indre-et-Loire)

ON DRY LAND

Cycling

The **Fédération Française de Cyclotourisme** (12 rue Louis-Bertrand, 94200 Ivry-sur-Seine, ☎ 01 56 20 88 88) and its local committees recommend a number of cycling tours of various lengths.

The Loire countryside is fairly flat, so presents few difficulties to the average cyclist. The Indre Valley, the Sologne, the numerous forest tracks and the banks of the Loire, away from the main roads, are particularly pretty. The ever-changing scenery and the rich heritage of the Loire Valley add greatly to the pleasure of a cycling tour.

Contact the Fédération Française de Cyclotourisme *(see above)* for suggested itineraries covering most of France, with information on mileage, difficult routes and sights to see. There is an IGN map (1:50 000) of cycle routes around Orléans *(1 000km à Vélo autour d'Orléans)*.

Lists of bicycle rental firms are available from the Tourist Information Centres.

For information on mountain biking (VTT, standing for *vélo tout terrain*) in the Layon region, apply to the Anjou tourist office in Angers.

Golf

The popularity of golf, which took off in the early 1980s, is steadily increasing. In 1998, more than 260 000 golf players were officially registered in France, indulging in their favourite sport on around 500 golf links.

The map *Golfs, les Parcours Français*, published by Éditions Plein Sud and based on **Michelin map no 989**, provides useful information on the location, address and type of golf course open to players throughout the country. The *Peugeot Golf Guide* published by D and G Motte in Switzerland, offers a selection of 750 courses in 12 European countries. A whole page is devoted to each site; the guide lists all the necessary information (location on Michelin map, rates, club house, nearby hotels, level of skills required) and gives its opinion on each establishment.

Fédération Française de Golf, 68 rue Anatole-France, 92309 Levallois-Perret, ☎ 01 41 49 77 00, www.ffgolf.org.

Ligue du Centre, Golf de Touraine, 37510 Ballan-Miré, ☎ 02 47 67 42 28.

Ligue de Golf des Pays de la Loire, 9 rue du Couëdic, 44000 Nantes, ☎ 02 40 08 05 06.

Hunting

The varied terrain of the Loire countryside makes it very popular with hunters for stalking, beating, coursing or shooting. The plains of the Beauce and the meadows of Touraine and Anjou provide plenty of food for partridges, quails, thrushes and larks. Hares find cover in the copses and the fields of maize and sugar beet. Wild rabbits and partridges breed in the sterile marshland whereas pheasants favour lakes and rivers. Red deer and roe deer are to be found in the thick woods around Baugé, in the forests of Château-la-Vallière and Loches and around Valençay. Wild boar favour the deep forests of Orléans and Amboise and the neighbourhood of Chambord. The islands and banks of the Loire provide nests for teal and mallard.

The Sologne is a favourite haunt for game: duck, teal and woodcock on the lakes and rivers, pheasants by the roadside, wild boar in the marshy brakes and deer in the woods. Address all enquiries to **Union nationale des fédérations départementales des chasseurs**, 48 rue d'Alésia, 75014 Paris, ☎ 01 43 27 85 76.

During the rutting season, which lasts from mid-September to mid-October, the stags are known to behave in a curious way and it is interesting to observe them in action. It is possible to do so in Chambord Forest – contact the Office National des Forêts for details, ☎ 02 54 78 55 50.

Riding and pony trekking

Not surprisingly, in view of the number of highly reputed local stud farms and the National Riding School at St-Hilaire-St-Florent near Saumur, the Loire region has numerous riding centres open to visitors. Some also serve as an overnight stop for those on pony-trekking holidays.

Guides indicating suitable routes and overnight stops are available from regional and national riding associations. Details of local equestrian centres can be obtained from the Tourist Information Centres.

Contact the **Comité nationale de tourisme équestre**, 9 boulevard Macdonald, 75019 Paris, ☎ 01 53 26 15 50, which publishes an annual brochure on exploring France on horseback. Other useful contacts include:

Association régionale de tourisme équestre des Pays de la Loire; 3 rue Bossuet, 44000 Nantes, ☎ 02 40 48 12 27 (*départements* of Maine-et-Loire, Mayenne and Sarthe);

Association régionale de tourisme équestre Centre-Val de Loire; Maison des Sports, 32 rue Alain-Gerbault, BP 719, 41007 Blois Cedex, ☎ 02 54 42 95 60 ext 411 (*départements* of Cher, Indre, Indre-et-Loire, Loir-et-Cher and Loiret).

Rambling

Short, medium and long distance footpath *Topo-Guides* are published by the **Fédération Française de la Randonnée Pédestre (FFRP)**. These give detailed maps of the paths and offer valuable information to the rambler; they are on sale at the information centre: 14 rue Riquet, 75019 Paris, ☎ 01 44 89 93 90. For further information apply to the **Comité de Touraine pour la Randonnée Pédestre**, Office de Tourisme de Tours, 78 rue Bernard-Palissy, 37042 Tours Cedex, ☎ 02 47 70 37 35.

The **Comité Départemental du Tourisme de l'Anjou** has published five IGN maps (Institut Géographique National, 1:50 000) showing routes for ramblers. There is a network of long-distance footpaths *(sentiers de grande randonnée – GR)* covering the area described in the guide:

the **GR 3** along the Loire Valley through the forests of Orléans, Russy and Chinon;

the **GR 3c** running westwards across the Sologne from Gien to Mont-près-Chambord;

the **GR 3d** through the Layon vineyards;
the **GR 31** linking Mont-près-Chambord, on the south-east edge of Boulogne Forest, to Souesmes, south through Sologne Forest;
the **GR 32** north-south through Orléans Forest;
the **GR 335**, from the Loir to the Loire, north-south between Lavardin and Vouvray;
the **GR 35** along the Loir Valley;
the **GR 36**, the footpath from the English Channel to the Pyrenees route, crossing the region described in this guide between Le Mans and Montreuil-Bellay;
the **GR 46** along the Indre Valley.

SPECTATOR SPORT

Boule de fort

This boule game is typical of the Angers area (and, to a lesser extent, of the Indre-et-Loire, the Loire-Atlantique, the Mayenne and the Sarthe). Among the many legends that explain its origins, the most common one concerns the boatmen working on the Loire: when there was little or no wind, the ships would be moored along the banks of the river and the sailors would play with large weighted balls inside. The boule in its present shape and size was created in the early 19C.

Each boule is half flattened, with an iron band circling its diameter: it has a weak side and a strong side (*fort* in French – hence the name). Originally fashioned from wood, boules are now made with synthetic materials. As in all traditional boule games, the object is to roll the boule as close as possible to a smaller ball called the *maître*. The game opposes two teams made up of two or three players.

In the old days, these boule competitions were held on playing areas covered with soil taken from the municipality of Guédeniau – a mild soapy type of clay which soaked up water without becoming sticky. Nowadays, however, the tracks, characterised by curved edges, are made with resin or flint. Playing areas are 21.5-24m/70-79ft long and about 6m/20ft wide; each boule weighs between 1.2-1.5kg/2.5-3.5lb.

Suggested reading

REGIONAL HERITAGE

A Wine and Food Guide to the Loire, Jacqueline Friedrich, Henry Holt (1998). This is an award-winning guide to the Loire, its wines and cuisine. It covers the 60 or so appellations in the five wine regions of the Loire, describing the history, soil, and vintners of each, and rates more than 600 wineries; sections on local cheeses, sausages, and fish dishes. This book is very complete and entertaining too. It will really add pleasure to your trip!

Chateaux of the Loire, Thorston Droste, Axel M Mosler (Contributor). St Martins Press (1997). This over-sized book is a collection of lavish photographs of the architecture, interiors, and gardens of the Loire chateaux, including previously unpublished photos illustrating life in the chateaux during the 19C and early 20C. Each chateau is accompanied by a text that describes architectural, historical, and travel details.

Chateaux of the Loire Valley, Jean-Marie Perouse De Montclos, Robert Polidori (Photographer). Konemann (1999). This is a beautiful book, filled with high quality photographs, portraying natural beauty of the region as well as highlighting the architecture of the famous châteaux.

Loire, Hubrecht Duijker. The Wine Lover's Touring Guides Series (March 1995). The author of this book was appointed *Officier de l'Ordre du Mérite Agricole* by the French Government for sharing his wealth of information on local treasures, from little-known villages to Gérard Depardieu's castle. Plenty of practical touring advice for an enjoyable trip, especially if you are interested in wine!

Chateau Chaumont-sur-Loire: Scale Architectural Paper Model, Jean-Marie Lemaire. Paper Models International (1992). Every detail on this 3-dimensional paper model (scale 1:250, base 8 x 13.5 inches, height 8 inches) is in precise conformity with the original. An illustrated text gives historical information and step by step instructions for assembly (in English). A good gift for a youngster before a visit – or bring one home as a souvenir (look for this and other buildings in the series in gift shops when you travel).

UNDERSTANDING THE FRENCH

Henry James: Collected Travel Writings: The Continent: A Little Tour in France/Italian Hours/Other Travels, Henry James. Library of America (1993). This 19C travelogue by the great novelist is witty, urbane and observant and includes radiant impressions of French countryside. The new hardcover edition has illustrations reproduced from the original books.

Balzac: A Biography, Graham Robb, W.W. Norton & Company (1996). This is the first major biography of the prolific French novelist *(some selected titles below)* in over 50 years. There are many references to contemporary history and culture. However, the modern sensitivity is well balanced by extensive quotes from Balzac himself. Many details convey the reality of the novelist's day and age as well as the wild disarray of his life even unto death.

France on the Brink, Jonathan Fenby, Arcade Publishing (1999). The author has culled 30 years of experience living in or writing about France into this book, which has met with both high praise and keen criticism. From Brigitte Bardot to the baguette, from the integration or exclusion of foreign cultures to hot political scandals, this portrait of contemporary France is personal, perceptive and instructive.

101 French Proverbs: Understanding French Language and Culture Through Common Sayings, Jean-Marie Cassagne, Passport Books (1998). Each proverb has the French at the top, then the translation, followed by an English equivalent. There are funny illustrations and short conversations to help with context.

Savoir-Flair: 211 Tips for Enjoying France and the French, Polly Platt, Ande Grchich (Illustrator), Distribooks Intl (2000). Useful communication and travel tips if your French is rusty or outdated. Handy phrases and explanations of cultural particularities that are easily misinterpreted by foreign visitors.

Normandy is Normandy, Burgundy is Burgundy, Provence is Provence; but Touraine is essentially France. It is the land of Rabelais, of Descartes, of Balzac, of good books and good company, as well as good dinners and good houses. ... Touraine is a land of old châteaux – a gallery of architectural specimens and of large hereditary properties. ... This is, moreover, the heart of the old French monarchy; and as that monarchy was splendid and picturesque, a reflection of that splendour still glitters in the current of the Loire. Some of the most striking events in French history have occurred on the banks of that river, and the soil it waters bloomed for a while with the flowering of the Renaissance.

Henry James – *A Little Tour in France*

NEW FICTION

Five Quarters of the Orange, Joanne Harris. William Morrow & Co (2001). The narrator of this novel is writing from the restored Loire farmhouse where she grew up and lives under an assumed identity. 65-year-old Framboise recounts her life and the terrible memories of the Second World War. The heroine is devoted to deciphering and preserving her mother's notebook of recipes and jottings. The texture, shape and aroma of bread and cakes, fruit and wine, thyme and olive become characters in this compelling and complex story.

Rabelais – Musée des Beaux-Arts, Orléans

CLASSIC FICTION

The following novels are set in the Loire region. They are readily available in paperback editions or from your local library:

Honoré de Balzac: *Eugénie Grandet, Le Curé de Tours, La Femme de Trente Ans, L'Illustre Gaudissart, Le Lys dans la Vallée;*

François Rabelais: *Gargantua and Pantagruel* comprising *Pantagruel, Gargantua, Tiers Livre, Quart Livre;*

Émile Zola: *La Terre.*

Calendar of events

In the *bouchons* (taverns) along the banks of the Loire, frequented by fishermen, old men can still be seen playing *alouette* or *bigaille*, a sailor's card game which requires a pack of 48. **Boule de Fort**, a version of boules particular to the Angers region is played regularly by around 400 clubs belonging to the Fédération de l'Ouest, along the River Loire between Tours and St-Nazaire.

Naturally, the harvesting of crops, and of grapes in particular, is an occasion to celebrate in the Loire region, frequently calling for gargantuan banquets, washed down by liberal quantities of local wine.

March to December

Fontevraud .... Itinérances Music Festival (☎ 02 41 51 73 52).

Maulévrier .... Greyhound racing at La Tuilerie racetrack (☎ 02 41 55 53 50).

Holy Saturday

St-Benoît-sur-Loire .... Great Easter Vigil (at 10pm).

Star performers of the Cadre Noir

April to September

Saumur .... Public performance by the Cadre Noir in the dressage arena of the École Nationale de l'Équitation (☎ 02 41 53 50 50).

April

Le Mans .... 24-hour motorcycle race (☎ 02 43 40 24 24).

Late April

Cholet .... Evening carnival parade (☎ 02 41 62 28 09).

First week in May

Orléans .... Joan of Arc Festival (☎ 02 38 24 05 05).

2nd week in May

Le Mans .... Festival at the abbey (☎ 02 43 81 72 72).

(Abbaye de l'Épau) .... Rencontres Imaginaires (theatre).

Mid-May

Château-Gontier .... Horse Show at Château de la Maroutière.

Le Mans .... Les Nocturnales: street theatre in Old Le Mans (2nd and 3rd weeks).

Whitsun

Châteauneuf-sur-Loire .... Whitsun Rhododendron Festival (☎ 02 38 58 41 18).

Late May

Saumur............................ International Horsemanship Competition
(☎ 02 41 51 34 15).

June

Le Mans .... 24-hour motor race on the Circuit des 24 Heures
(☎ 02 43 40 24 24).

Amboise........................... Wine Festival in the Mini-Châteaux Park.

Chambord .... Game Fair: National Hunting and Fishing Festival
(☎ 02 32 49 10 00).

Sully-sur-Loire.................. International Festival of Classical Music
(☎ 02 38 36 29 46 or 08 00 45 28 18).

Late June

Tours and around .... Touraine Music Festival (Grange de Meslay),
in which international artists take part
(☎ 02 47 21 65 08 or 02 47 11 65 15).

Chorégraphique: Contemporary Dance Festival
(☎ 02 47 64 05 06).
Tours Florilège Vocal: Choral Festival
(☎ 02 47 21 65 26).

Mid-June to mid-October

Chaumont-sur-Loire........... International Garden Show (☎ 02 54 20 99 22).

Late June to early July

Orléans .... Jazz Festival (☎ 02 38 24 05 05).

July to August

Le Mans .... Les Nocturnales: street theatre in Old Le Mans
(Wednesdays and Saturdays, ☎ 02 43 28 17 22).

July

Anjou................................ Anjou Festival in the historical sites of the Maine-et-Loire
département (☎ 02 41 24 88 77).

Mid-July

Doué-la-Fontaine .... Rose Show in the amphitheatre (☎ 02 41 59 20 49).

Blois................................ Les Montgolfiades (Hot-air balloon Festival
☎ 02 54 33 55 00).

15 July to 31 July

Loches .... Festival of Musical Drama (☎ 02 47 91 88 82).

Fourth weekend in July

La Ménitré........................ *(half-way between Angers and Samur)*

Headdress and old-fashioned costume parade with examples from the region's various
folklores (☎ 02 41 45 63 63).

Traditional Anjou costumes at La Ménitré

Last weekend in July
Saumur........................... Military tattoo with mounted, motorised and armoured divisions (☎ 02 41 40 20 66).

15 August
Molineuf
(Michelin map 64 fold 7) ..... Bric-a-brac fair; with antique dealers, antiques enthusiasts and buyers (☎ 02 54 70 05 23).

Wednesday to Saturday in the last week in August
Sablé-sur-Sarthe............... Festival of Baroque Music (☎ 02 43 95 49 96).

Early September
Amboise........................... Melon Festival (1st Wednesday of the month).
Château-Gontier .... Horse Show at Château de la Maroutière.

Penultimate weekend in October
Le Lion-d'Angers............... International Horse Show focusing on three events (dressage, cross-country, jumping). Demonstrations by the best riders in the world representing 20 nations (☎ 02 41 95 82 46).

24 December
Anjou............................... Messes des Naulets (held in a different country church every year). Groups in traditional Anjou costume sing Christmas carols in the local dialect (☎ 02 41 23 51 11).
St-Benoît-sur-Loire .... Christmas Eve vigil and Mass (at 10pm).

Main winemaking events

All year round, a great many wine fairs and wine festivals are staged at set dates in order to promote the different types of local *appellations*.

Month	Event	Venue	☎
March	Wine fair	Bourgueil	02 47 97 91 39
April	Onzain Wine Fair	Onzain	02 54 20 78 52
May	Wine Fair	Saumur	02 41 83 43 12
	Annual Saumur Wine Competition	Saumur	02 41 51 16 40
June	Champigny Biennial	Montsoreau	02 41 51 16 40
July	Wine Harvest Festival	St-Lambert-du-Lattay	02 41 78 30 58
	Saumur-Champigny Festival	Varrains	02 41 87 62 57
	Vintage Wine Festival	St-Aubin-de-Luigné	02 41 78 33 28
November	Arrival of the most recent crop of Touraine wines *(primeurs)*	Montrichard	02 54 32 05 10
	Champigny Biennial	Montsoreau	02 41 51 16 40

Son et lumière

These polished evening spectacles, which developed from an original idea of the magician Jean-Eugène Robert-Houdin *(see p 129)*, were inaugurated as a feature of the Loire Valley tourist season at Chambord in 1952.

By combining characters dressed in period costume with firework displays, illuminated fountains and image projection on huge screens, the *son et lumière* shed quite a different light on some of the Loire Valley's most famous châteaux. Nocturnal illuminations enhance the architecture of the buildings, offering a different scene from that seen during the day. Special effects using film and staging techniques, laser beam projections and an accompanying soundtrack lend ancient walls a surprisingly different aura. From time to time the theme of the *son et lumière* is changed.

You will find information about these events in the blue-bordered sections of the following chapters: Amboise, Azay-le-Rideau, Blois, Chenonceau, Loches and Valençay; it is advisable to check each programme with the local tourist office.

Useful French words and phrases

SIGHTS

abbaye . . . . abbey	**marché** . . . . market
beffroi . . . . belfry	**monastère** . . . . . . monastery
chapelle . . . . chapel	**moulin** . . . . windmill
château . . . . castle	**musée** . . . . museum
cimetière . . . . cemetery	**parc** . . . . park
cloître . . . . cloisters	**place** . . . . square
cour . . . . courtyard	**pont** . . . . bridge
couvent . . . . convent	**port** . . . . port/harbour
écluse . . . . lock (canal)	**porte** . . . . gateway
église . . . . church	**quai** . . . . quay
fontaine . . . . fountain	**remparts** . . . . ramparts
halle . . . . covered market	**rue** . . . . street
jardin . . . . garden	**statue** . . . . statue
mairie . . . . town hall	**tour** . . . . tower
maison . . . . house	

NATURAL SITES

abîme . . . . chasm	**grotte** . . . . cave
aven . . . . swallow-hole	**lac** . . . . lake
barrage . . . . dam	**plage** . . . . beach
belvédère . . . . . . viewpoint	**rivière** . . . . river
cascade . . . . waterfall	**ruisseau** . . . . stream
col . . . . pass	**signal** . . . . beacon
corniche . . . . ledge	**source** . . . . spring
côte . . . . coast, hillside	**vallée** . . . . valley
forêt . . . . forest	

ON THE ROAD

car park . . . . parking	**petrol/gas station** . station essence
driving licence . . . permis de conduire	**right** . . . . droite
east . . . . Est	**south** . . . . Sud
garage (for repairs) garage	**toll** . . . . péage
left . . . . gauche	**traffic lights** . . . . feu tricolore
motorway/highway autoroute	**tyre** . . . . pneu
north . . . . Nord	**west** . . . . Ouest
parking meter . . . horodateur	**wheel clamp** . . . . sabot
petrol/gas . . . . . . essence	**zebra crossing** . . . passage clouté

TIME

today . . . . aujourd'hui	**Monday** . . . . lundi
tomorrow . . . . . . demain	**Tuesday** . . . . mardi
yesterday . . . . . . hier	**Wednesday** . . . . . mercredi
winter . . . . hiver	**Thursday** . . . . . . jeudi
spring . . . . printemps	**Friday** . . . . vendredi
summer . . . . été	**Saturday** . . . . samedi
autumn/fall . . . . . automne	**Sunday** . . . . dimanche
week . . . . semaine	

NUMBERS

0 . . . . . zéro	**10** . . . . dix	**20** . . . . vingt
1 . . . . . un	**11** . . . . onze	**30** . . . . trente
2 . . . . . deux	**12** . . . . douze	**40** . . . . quarante
3 . . . . . trois	**13** . . . . treize	**50** . . . . cinquante
4 . . . . . quatre	**14** . . . . quatorze	**60** . . . . soixante
5 . . . . . cinq	**15** . . . . quinze	**70** . . . . soixante-dix
6 . . . . . six	**16** . . . . seize	**80** . . . . quatre-vingt
7 . . . . . sept	**17** . . . . dix-sept	**90** . . . . quatre-vingt-dix
8 . . . . . huit	**18** . . . . dix-huit	**100** . . . cent
9 . . . . . neuf	**19** . . . . dix-neuf	**1000** . . mille

SHOPPING

bank	banque	fishmonger's	poissonnerie
baker's	boulangerie	grocer's	épicerie
big	grand	newsagent,	
butcher's	boucherie	bookshop	librairie
chemist's	pharmacie	open	ouvert
closed	fermé	post office	poste
cough mixture	sirop pour la toux	push	pousser
cough sweets	cachets pour la gorge	pull	tirer
		shop	magasin
entrance	entrée	small	petit
exit	sortie	stamps	timbres

FOOD AND DRINK

beef	bœuf	lunch	déjeuner
beer	bière	lettuce salad	salade
butter	beurre	meat	viande
bread	pain	mineral water	eau minérale
breakfast	petit-déjeuner	mixed salad	salade composée
cheese	fromage	orange juice	jus d'orange
chicken	poulet	plate	assiette
dessert	dessert	pork	porc
dinner	dîner	restaurant	restaurant
fish	poisson	red wine	vin rouge
fork	fourchette	salt	sel
fruit	fruits	spoon	cuillère
glass	verre	sugar	sucre
ice cream	glace	vegetables	légumes
ice cubes	glaçons	water	de l'eau
ham	jambon	white wine	vin blanc
knife	couteau	yoghurt	yaourt
lamb	agneau		

PERSONAL DOCUMENTS AND TRAVEL

airport	aéroport	shuttle	navette
credit card	carte de crédit	suitcase	valise
customs	douane	train/plane ticket	billet de train/ d'avion
passport	passeport		
platform	voie	wallet	portefeuille
railway station	gare		

CLOTHING

coat	manteau	socks	chaussettes
jumper	pull	stockings	bas
raincoat	imperméable	suit	costume
shirt	chemise	tights	collants
shoes	chaussures	trousers	pantalon

USEFUL PHRASES

goodbye	au revoir	yes/no	oui/non
hello/good morning	bonjour	I am sorry	pardon
how	comment	why	pourquoi
excuse me	excusez-moi	when	quand
thank you	merci	please	s'il vous plaît

Do you speak English?	Parlez-vous anglais?
I don't understand	Je ne comprends pas
Talk slowly	Parlez lentement
Where's...?	Où est...?
When does the ... leave?	A quelle heure part...?
When does the ... arrive?	A quelle heure arrive...?
When does the museum open?	A quelle heure ouvre le musée?
When is the show?	A quelle heure est la représentation?
When is breakfast served?	A quelle heure sert-on le petit-déjeuner?
What does it cost?	Combien cela coûte?
Where can I buy a newspaper in English?	Où puis-je acheter un journal en anglais?
Where is the nearest petrol/gas station?	Où se trouve la station essence la plus proche?
Where can I change traveller's cheques?	Où puis-je échanger des traveller's cheques?
Where are the toilets?	Où sont les toilettes?
Do you accept credit cards?	Acceptez-vous les cartes de crédit?

Château de Chaumont-sur-Loire

Introduction

The Loire Valley

Geological formation

The Loire region is enclosed by the ancient crystalline masses of the Morvan, Armorican Massif and Massif Central and forms part of the Paris Basin.

In the Secondary Era the area invaded by the sea was covered by a soft, chalky deposit known as **tufa**, which is now exposed along the valley sides of the Loir, Cher, Indre and Vienne. A later deposit is the limestone of the sterile marshlands **(gâtines)** interspersed with tracts of sands and clays supporting forests and heathlands. Once the sea had retreated, great freshwater lakes deposited more limestone, the surface of which is often broken down into loess or silt. These areas are known as **champagnes** or *champeignes*.

During the Tertiary Era the folding of the Alpine mountain zone created the Massif Central, and rivers running down from this new watershed were often laden with sandy clays which, when they were deposited, gave rise to areas such as the Sologne and Orléans Forest. Later subsidence in the west permitted the ingress of the **Faluns Sea** as far as Blois, Thouars and Preuilly-sur-Claise, creating a series of shell marl beds *(falunières)* on the borders of Ste-Maure plateau and the hills to the north of the Loire. Rivers originally flowing northwards were attracted in a westerly direction by the sea, thus explaining the great change in the direction of the Loire at Orléans. The sea finally retreated for good, leaving an undulating countryside with the river network the most important geographical feature. The alluvial silts **(varennes)** deposited by the Loire and its tributaries were to add an extremely fertile light soil composed of coarse sand.

The limestone terraces which provided shelter and the naturally fertile soil attracted early human habitation, of which there are traces from the prehistoric era through the Gallo-Roman period (site of Cherré) to the Middle Ages (Brain-sur-Allonnes). This substratum is immediately reflected in the landscape: troglodyte dwellings in the limestone layers, vineyards on the slopes, cereals on the silt plateaux, vegetables in the alluvial silt. The marshy tracts of the Sologne were for many centuries untilled since they were unhealthy and unsuitable for any sort of culture.

The River Loire

The longest French river (1 020km/634mi) springs up beneath the Mont Gerbier de Jonc, in the Vivarais region, on the southern edge of the Massif Central mountain range. The flow of the Loire is somewhat erratic: in summer it is reduced to a few meagre streams meandering along the wide sandy river bed, but in autumn, during the rainy season, or in spring, when the thaw comes, the river is in spate, sometimes causing memorable floods (the worst recorded floods took place in 1846, 1856, 1866 and 1910).

Until the end of the 19C, the Loire was a busy waterway in spite of its unpredictable behaviour: flat-bottomed boats rigged with square sails used to sail up and down the river and its tributaries, in particular the Cher, carrying cargo and passengers between Orléans and Nantes... Horse-drawn carriages were even placed on rafts!

In 1832, the first steam-powered regular service between Orléans and Nantes was inaugurated, but the development of railways soon struck a decisive blow to boat transport.

Landscapes

The garden of France – From whatever direction one approaches the Loire region – across the immense plains of the Beauce, through the mysterious Berry countryside or the green wooded farmland *(bocage)* of the Gâtine Mancelle – one is always welcomed by the sight of vineyards, white houses and flowers. For many foreigners this peaceful,

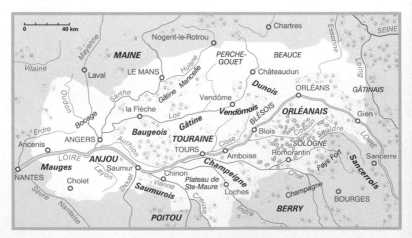

Touraine Landscape

fertile countryside is a typically French landscape. But make no mistake, the Garden of France is not simply a sort of Eden laden with fruit and flowers. The historian Michelet once described it as a "homespun cloak with golden fringes", meaning that the valleys – the golden fringes – in all their wonderful fertility bordered plateaux whose harshness was tempered only by occasional fine forests.

Northern Berry – This region lying between the Massif Central and the Loire country includes the **Pays Fort**, an area of clay soil sloping down towards the Sologne. The melancholy atmosphere of the landscape is described by Alain-Fournier in his novel *Le Grand Meaulnes (The Lost Domain)*. Between the Cher and the Indre is the **Champeigne**, an area of limestone silt pock-marked with holes *(mardelles)*.

Orléanais and Blésois – Below Gien the valley opens out, the hills are lower and a refreshing breeze makes the leaves tremble on the long lines of poplars and willows. This is the gateway to the Orléanais which covers the Beauce, the Loir Valley (ie the Dunois and Vendômois), the Sologne and Blésois (Blois region). In the vicinity of St-Benoît, the valley, commonly known as the **Val**, is a series of meadows; beyond, horticulture predominates with the growing of seedlings and rosebushes on the alluvial deposits known locally as *layes*. There is a proliferation of greenhouses, some with artificial heating. Orchards and vineyards flourish on the south-facing slopes.

From Orléans to Chaumont along its northern bank, the Loire eats into the Beauce limestone and then into the flinty chalkland and tufa. On the south the river laps the alluvial sands brought along by its own waters. This area, where asparagus and early vegetables are grown, features large expanses of dense brushwood peopled with game where the kings of France once used to hunt. The great châteaux then begin: Blois, Chambord, Cheverny, Chaumont...

The **Beauce**, the granary of France, a treeless plain covered with a thin layer (2m/6ft maximum) of fertile silt or loess, extends into the area between the Loire and Loir known as the Petite Beauce where silt gives way to clay in Marchenoir Forest. In the **Sologne** and the **Forest of Orléans** meagre crops alternate with lakes and woodland.

Touraine – The comfortable opulence of the **Loire Valley** will delight the visitor already charmed by the dazzling quality of the light. The blue waters of the Loire, which flow slowly between golden sandbanks, have worn a course through the soft tufa chalk. Channels abandoned by the main river are divided into backwaters *(boires)* or occupied by tributary streams such as the Cher, Indre, Vienne and Cisse.

From Amboise to Tours the flinty chalk soil of the valley slopes is clad with vineyards producing the well-known Vouvray and Montlouis wines. **Troglodyte** houses have been carved out of the white tufa. The **Véron**, lying between the Loire and the Vienne, is a patchwork of small fields and gardens bordered by rows of poplars.

The **Gâtine** of Touraine, between the Loir and Loire, was once a great forest; the area is now under cultivation, although large tracts of heath and woodland have survived (Chandelais and Bercé forests). The main features of the Touraine **Champeigne**, where the fields are studded with walnut trees, are the forests of Brouard and Loches and the Montrésor Gâtine. The plateaux of Montrichard and Ste-Maure are similar in many ways to the Champeigne.

Anjou – The north bank of the Loire consists of a fertile alluvial plain **(varenne de Bourgueil)** where spring vegetables thrive, surrounded by the famous vineyards planted on warm, dry gravels lying at the foot of the pine-covered hills. Between the Loire and the Authion, lined with willows, green pastures alternate with rich market gardens growing vegetables, flowers and fruit trees. The land below Angers is covered with vineyards, especially the famous Coulée de Serrant vineyard.

The pleasant **Saumurois**, which lies south of the Loire and extends from Fontevraud and Montsoreau to Doué-la-Fontaine and the Layon Valley, has three differing aspects: woods, plains and hillsides – the slopes of which are often clad with vineyards, producing excellent wine including the white wine to which the town of Saumur has given its name. The many caves in the steep, tufa valley sides of the Loire around Chêne-hutte-les-Tuffeaux are now used for mushroom growing. North of the river lies the sandy **Baugeois**, an area of woods (oak, pine and chestnut) and arable land.

Angers marks the border between the schist countryside of Black Anjou and the sharply contrasting limestone of White Anjou. The countryside is greener, heralding an area of wooded farmland – the Bocage Segréen and **Les Mauges** – which is characterised by a patchwork of small fields surrounded by hedge-topped banks crisscrossed by deep lanes leading to small farmsteads. Around Angers, nursery and market gardens specialise in flowers and seedlings.

Maine – Only the southern part of this region is included in the guide.
The Lower Maine **(Bas-Maine)** otherwise known as Black Maine, is a region of sandstones, granites and schists and wooded farmland. Geographically this area is part of the Breton Armorican Massif. The Upper Maine **(Haut-Maine)**, covering the Sarthe and Huisne basins, is known as the White Maine because of its limestone soils.

H. Dewynter/MICHELIN

Fruit of the earth

A well-disposed lie of the land, fertile soil and temperate climate make the Loire Valley ideal for the cultivation of trees and market gardens. Fruit and vegetables make a significant contribution to the economy of the Centre-Val de Loire and Pays de la Loire regions, accounting for around 20% of domestic production. The cultivation of many of the varieties to be found in the Loire Valley dates from as early as Roman rule, whereas others introduced to the region during the Renaissance continue to thrive.

Fruit – Ripening well in the local climate, the succulent fruits of the region are renowned throughout France. The most common are apples, pears and more recently blackcurrants. Many have a noble pedigree: *reine-claude* greengages are named after Claude de France, the wife of François I, *bon-chrétien* pears originated from a cutting planted by St Francis of Paola in Louis XI's orchard at Plessis-lès-Tours. They were introduced into Anjou by Jean Bourré, Louis XI's Finance Minister. Rivalling the latter are the following varieties: *de Monsieur*, *Williams*, a speciality of Anjou, *passe-crassane* and autumn varieties such as *conférence*, *doyenné du comice* and *beurré Hardy*.

Melons were introduced to the region by Charles VIII's Neapolitan gardener. Already in the 16C the variety and quality of the local fruit and vegetables were much praised, namely by Ronsard. The walnut and chestnut trees of the plateaux yield oil and much-prized wood (in the former case) and edible chestnuts (in the latter), often roasted during evening gatherings.

Alongside traditional varieties like the *reinette* apple from Le Mans are more prolific varieties better adapted to market demands such as the Granny Smith and Golden Delicious.

Early vegetables – A wide variety of vegetables is grown in the Loire Valley. There are two main areas of production: the stretch of valley between Angers and Saumur and the Orléans region. Vegetables cultivated under glass or plastic include tomatoes, cucumbers and lettuces, especially around Orléans. Early vegetables are a speciality in the Loire Valley since, in general, they are ready two weeks before those of the Paris region. Asparagus from Vineuil and Contres, potatoes from Saumur, French beans from Touraine, onions and shallots from Anjou and Loiret and artichokes from Angers are dispatched to Rungis, the main Paris market.

One of the region's more unusual crops is mushrooms; over 60% of French button mushrooms come from the Loire Valley. They are grown in the former tufa quarries near Montrichard, Montoire, Montsoreau, Tours and particularly in the Saumur area.

Flowers and nursery gardens – Pots of geraniums or begonias, borders of nasturtiums and climbing wisteria with its pale mauve clusters adorn the houses. The region of Orléans-la-Source, Olivet and Doué-la-Fontaine is famous for its cultivated flowers – roses, hydrangeas, geraniums and chrysanthemums – which are grown under glass. Tulips, gladioli and lilies are grown (for bulbs) near Soings.

Nursery gardens proliferate on the alluvial soils of the Loire. The lighter soils of Véron, Bourgueil and the Angers district are suitable for the growing of artichokes, onions and garlic for seed stock. The medicinal plants that were cultivated in the Chemillé region during the phylloxera crisis are attracting renewed interest.

Mushroom beds in Le Saut-aux-Loups

Livestock – Dairy stock are generally reared outdoors in the fields, except in winter, when they are kept inside and given corn silage. However, in the case of beef cattle, the animals spend most of the year feeding on pastures in the Maine, Anjou and Touraine valleys. The main dairy cattle breeds are Prim'Holstein, Normandy and Pie-Noire, whereas the best-known beef breeds are Normandy, Maine-Anjou and especially Charolais. Dairy production is concentrated in Maine, Anjou, the Mayenne Valley, Les Mauges and in the west of the Sarthe Valley. Sheep rearing is confined to the limestone plateaux of the Upper Maine where the black-faced Bleu du Maine and Rouge de l'Ouest prosper.

Pigs can be found everywhere but particularly in Touraine, Maine and Anjou; the production of potted pork specialities – *rillettes* and *rillons* – is centred in Vouvray, Angers, Tours and Le Mans. Recently, in the Sarthe *département* a *label rouge* (red label), guaranteeing the highest quality, was awarded to free-range pigs raised on farms.

The ever-growing demand for the well-known goats' cheeses, in particular the *appellation d'origine contrôlée* (AOC) brands, Selles-sur-Cher and, more recently, Sainte-Maure, have led to an increase in goat keeping. Market days in the west country are colourful occasions: the liveliest are the calf sales in Château-Gontier and the cattle and goat sales in Cholet and Chemillé.

Poultry – Poultry rearing, firmly established in the Loire region, has developed quite considerably; its expansion is linked to the food industry and local co-operatives. This sector has two main characteristics: the high quality of its produce, thanks to many labels, in particular the most prestigious ones recommending the free-range poultry of Loué, and variety – chickens, capons, ducks, guinea fowl, turkeys, geese, poulards, quails, pigeons and, generally speaking, all game birds.

Mills of Anjou

Very early on, the extensive network of waterways encouraged the construction of a great many **watermills** of all kinds (barge-mills, bank-mills, mills with hanging wheels). But the region is furthermore exposed for most of the year to strong winds blowing from the south-west to the north-west – a fact which led to the proliferation of various types of windmill as early as the 13C. Some of these have been restored or converted and are still standing today.

Turquant – Moulin de la Herpinière

The region still features many structures sometimes open to the public during the summer season or on request. They fall into three categories:

Corn mills – Characteristic of the Anjou landscape, the corn mill consists of a conical stone base called the cellar, surmounted by a wooden cabin bearing the shaft and sails. The cellar was used for storing grain, flour and spare parts; in some cases, it also housed stables and a shed.

Post-mills – The post-mill was a huge wooden structure supporting the sails, the mill-stone as well as the whole mechanism. Unfortunately, because it was made entirely of wood, its age of glory was short-lived, either through lack of maintenance or because the shaft suffered damage.

Tower mills – By far the most common type of mill, the tower mill – built in stone – has remained comparatively intact over the centuries. The conical roof, with its rotating cap, carries the sails.

A birds' paradise

The Loire is frequently referred to as the "last untamed river in Europe". During the summer months, along some of its banks, the local climate can tend to resemble more that of African climes. This phenomenon, known as a topoclimate, favours the growth of many tropical plants. The Loire is also inclined to overflow, flooding the surrounding meadows and filling the ditches with water. When it eventually withdraws, leaving the gravel pits and sandbanks to dry out, it creates many natural niches and shelters, the perfect environment for myriad animal and plant species. Consequently, the banks of the Loire are home to many forms of bird life attracted by the relative peace and calm of the river's waters, which are well stocked with food (water insects, larvae, tiny shellfish and amphibians etc).

Les Rosiers – Moulin des Basses-Terres

E. Baret

More than 220 officially listed species of bird live in, nest in or migrate to the Loire Valley every year. To get the most out of bird-watching, without disturbing the birds while respecting their nesting places, visitors need to identify the particular habitat associated with each species. Along the banks of the Loire, suitable habitats include islets, gravel banks, tributary channels or *boires*, alluvial plains and marshes.

Islets and gravel banks – The islets, long sandbanks and high grasses found in midstream, provide safe refuges for the **common heron**, the **kingfisher**, the **great crested grebe** and the **cormorant**, who can rest peacefully, protected from intruders by a stretch of water. The irregular flow of the Loire appears to suit their reproductive pattern as it offers many open shores suitable for building nests. Downstream from Montsoreau, the **Île de Parnay** (a protected site closed to the public from 1 April to 15 August) alone is home to more than 750 pairs of birds between March and late June, including **black-headed gulls**, **common gulls**, **Iceland gulls**, **common terns** and **little ringed plovers**. The **Île de Sandillon**, 15km/10mi upstream of Orléans, is home to 2 500 such pairs.

Boires – This is the name given to the networks of channels filled with stagnant water which line either side of the Loire, and which flow into the river when it is in spate. These channels, teeming with roach, tench and perch, provide shelter to the **bittern**, the **moorhen**, the **coot**, the **garganey**, and small perchers like the **great reed warbler**, which builds its nest 50cm/20in above the water, solidly attached to three or four reeds.

Alluvial plains – Meadows and pastures which can sometimes be flooded after heavy rains offer hospitality either to migratory birds like the **whinchat** and the gregarious **black-tailed godwit**, or to more sedentary species such as the **corncrake** (March to October).

Marshes and pools – Among the many migratory birds, the **bald buzzard**, which feeds on fish, had practically disappeared from French skies in the 1940s; fortunately, its population is now on the increase. It is indeed an impressive sight to see it hovering over the water while it looks for its prey, then darts forward, claws open, to pounce on a 30-40cm/12-15in long fish. The **water rail** is another breed which finds comfort in the long reeds and bulrushes surrounding the marshes.

Water-rail

J.-L. Lemoine/JACANA

Little ringed plover

W. Winfried/JACANA

Black-tailed godwit

A. Shah/JACANA

Lapwing

J. Brun/JACANA

Reed-bunting

H. Chaumeton/JACANA

Golden plover

Ph. Prigent/JACANA

Pochard

J.-C. Maes/JACANA

Historical table and notes

Gallo-Roman Era and the Early Middle Ages

52 BC	Carnutes revolt. Caesar conquers Gaul.
AD 1C-4C	Roman occupation of Gaul.
313	Constantine grants freedom of worship to Christians (Edict of Milan).
372	St Martin, Bishop of Tours (dies at Candes in 397).
573-594	Episcopacy of Gregory of Tours, author of *the History of the Franks*.
7C	Founding of the Benedictine abbey of Fleury, later to be named St-Benoît.
late 8C	Alcuin of York's school for copyists *(see TOURS)*. Theodulf, Bishop of Orleans.
768-814	Charlemagne.
840-877	Charles the Bald.
9C	Vikings invade Angers, St-Benoît and Tours. Rise of Robertian dynasty.

The Capets (987-1328)

987-1040	Fulk Nerra, Count of Anjou.
996-1031	Robert II, the Pious.
1010	Foundation of the Benedictine abbey at Solesmes.
1060-1108	Philippe I.
1101	Foundation of Fontevraud Abbey.
1104	First Council of Beaugency.
1137-1180	Louis VII.
1152	Second Council of Beaugency. Eleanor of Aquitaine marries Henry Plantagenet.
1154	Henry Plantagenet becomes King of England as Henry II.
1180-1223	Philippe Auguste.
1189	Death of Henry II Plantagenet at Chinon. Struggle between Capets and Plantagenets.
1199	Richard the Lionheart dies at Châlus and is buried at Fontevraud.
1202	John Lackland loses Anjou. The last of the Angevin kings, he dies in 1216.
1215	Magna Carta.
1226-1270	Louis IX (St Louis).
1285-1314	Philippe IV, the Fair.
1307	Philippe the Fair suppresses the Order of the Knights Templars.

The Valois (1328-1589)

1337-1453	Hundred Years War: 1346 Crécy; 1356 Poitiers; 1415 Agincourt.
1380-1422	Charles VI.
1392	The King goes mad *(see Le MANS)*.
1409	Birth of King René at Angers.
1418	The Massacre at Azay-le-Rideau.
1422-1461	Charles VII.
1427	The Dauphin Charles establishes his court at Chinon.
1429	Joan of Arc delivers Orléans but she is tried and burnt at the stake two years later *(see CHINON and ORLÉANS)*.
1453	Battle of Castillon: final defeat of the English on French soil.
1455-1485	Wars of the Roses: Margaret of Anjou leader of Lancastrian cause.
1461-1483	Louis XI.
1476	Unrest among the powerful feudal lords.
1477	The region's first printing press is set up in Angers.
1483	Death of Louis XI at Plessis-lès-Tours.
1483-1498	Charles VIII.
1491	Marriage of Charles VIII and Anne of Brittany at Langeais.
1494-1559	The Campaigns in Italy.
1496	Early manifestations of Italian influence on French art *(see AMBOISE)*.

1498	Death of Charles VIII at Amboise.
1498-1515	Louis XII. He divorces and marries Charles VIII's widow.
1515-1547	François I.
1519	French Renaissance: work on Chambord starts. Da Vinci dies at Le Clos-Lucé.
1539	Struggle against Emperor Charles V. He visits Amboise and Chambord.
1547-1559	Henri II.
1552	The sees of Metz, Toul and Verdun join France. Treaty signed at Chambord.
1559-1560	François II.
1560	Amboise Conspiracy. François II dies at Orléans.
1560-1574	Charles IX.
1562-1598	Wars of Religion.
1562	St-Benoît Abbey is pillaged by the Protestants. Battles at Ponts-de-Cé and Beaugency.
1572	The St Bartholomew's Day Massacre in Paris.
1574-1589	Henri III.
1576	Founding of the Catholic League by Henri, Duke of Guise to combat Calvinism. Meeting of the States-General in Blois.
1588	The assassination of Henri, Duke of Guise and his brother, the Cardinal of Lorraine *(see BLOIS)*.

The Bourbons (1589-1702)

1589-1610	Henri IV.
1589	Vendôme recaptured by Henry IV.
1598	Edict of Nantes. Betrothal of César de Vendôme *(see ANGERS)*.
1600	Henri IV weds Marie de Medici.
1602	Maximilien de Béthune buys Sully.
1610-1643	Louis XIII.
1619	Marie de Medici flees from Blois.
1620	Building of the Jesuits college at La Flèche.
1626	Gaston d'Orléans, brother of Louis XIII, is granted the County of Blois.
1643-1715	Louis XIV.
1648-1653	Civil war against Mazarin. The Fronde.
1651	Anne of Austria, Mazarin and young Louis XIV take refuge in Gien.
1669	Première of Molière's play *Monsieur de Pourceaugnac* at Chambord.
1685	Revocation of the Edict of Nantes by Louis XIV at Fontainebleau.
1715-1771	Louis XV.
1719	Voltaire exiled at Sully.
1756	Foundation of the Royal College of Surgeons at Tours.
1770	The Duke of Choiseul in exile at Chanteloup.

The Revolution and First Empire (1789-1815)

1789	Storming of the Bastille.
1792	Proclamation of the Republic.
1793	Execution of Louis XVI. Vendée War.
	Fighting between the Republican Blues and Royalist Whites *(see CHOLET and Les MAUGES)*.
1803	Talleyrand purchases Valençay.
1804-1815	First Empire under Napoleon Bonaparte.
1808	Internment of Ferdinand VII, King of Spain, at Valençay.

Constitutional Monarchy and the Second Republic (1815-1852)

1814-1824	Louis XVIII.
1824-1830	Charles X.
1830-1848	July Monarchy: Louis-Philippe.
1832	The first steamboat on the Loire.
1832-1848	Conquest of Algeria.
1848	Internment of Abd El-Kader at Amboise.
1848-1852	Second Republic. Louis Napoleon-Bonaparte, Prince-Président.

The Second Empire (1852-1870)

1852-1870	Napoleon III as Emperor.
1870-1871	Franco-Prussian War.
1870	Proclamation of the Third Republic on 4 September in Paris.
	Frederick-Charles of Prussia at Azay-le-Rideau. Defence of Châteaudun.
	Tours made headquarters of Provisional Government.
1871	Battle of Loigny.

The Third Republic (1870-1940)

1873	Amédée Bollée completes his first car, *L'Obéissante (see Le MANS)*.
1908	Wilbur Wright's early trials with his aeroplane.
1914-1918	First World War.
1919	Treaty of Versailles.
1923	The first 24-hour race at Le Mans.
1939-1945	Second World War.
1940	Defence of Saumur. Historic meeting at Montoire.
1945	Reims Armistice.

Contemporary times

1946	Fourth Republic.
1952	First *son et lumière* performances at Chambord.
1958	Fifth Republic.
1963	France's first nuclear power station at Avoine near Chinon.
1972	Founding of the *Centre* (later called *Centre-Val-de-Loire)* and *Pays de la Loire* regions.
1989	Inauguration of the TGV (high-speed train) Atlantique.
1993	Opening of the International Vinci Congress Centre in Tours.
1994	The Centre region is renamed Centre-Val de Loire.
1996	Pope John Paul II visits the city of Tours.
2000	The Val de Loire (between Sully-sur-Loire and Chalonnes-sur-Loire) is placed on the UNESCO World Heritage List.

A long and eventful history

Antiquity and the Early Middle Ages

During the Iron Age the prosperous and powerful people known as the **Cenomanni** occupied a vast territory extending from Brittany to the Beauce and from Normandy to Aquitaine. They minted gold coins and put up a long resistance to both barbarian and Roman invaders.

The Cenomanni reacted strongly to the invasion of Gaul by the Romans and in 52 BC the **Carnutes**, who inhabited the country between Chartres and Orléans, gave the signal, at the instigation of the Druids, to raise a revolt against Caesar. It was savagely repressed but the following year Caesar had to put down another uprising by the Andes, under their leader Dumnacos.

Peace was established under Augustus and a period of stability and prosperity began. Existing towns such as Angers, Le Mans, Tours and Orléans adjusted to the Roman model with a forum, theatre, baths and public buildings. Many agricultural estates *(villae)* were created or extended as the commercial outlets developed. They reached their peak in the 2C. By the end of the 3C instability and danger were so rife that cities had been enclosed behind walls.

At the same time Christianity was introduced by St Gatien, the first bishop of Tours; by the end of the 4C it had overcome most opposition under **St Martin**, the greatest bishop of the Gauls, whose tomb later became a very important place of pilgrimage (St Martin's Day: 11 November).

In the 5C the Loire country suffered several waves of invasion; in 451 Bishop Aignan held back the Huns outside Orléans while waiting for help. Franks and Visigoths fought for domination until the Frankish king Clovis was finally victorious in 507.

His successors' endless quarrels, which were recorded by Gregory of Tours, dominated the history of the region in the 6C and 7C while St Martin's Abbey was establishing its reputation. In 732 the Saracens, who were pushing north from Spain, reached the Loire before they were repulsed by Charles Martel. The order achieved by the Carolingians, which was marked by the activities of **Alcuin** and **Theodulf**, did not last. In the middle of the 9C the Vikings came up the river and ravaged the country on either side, particularly the monasteries (St-Benoît, St-Martin). **Robert**, Count of Blois and Tours, defeated them but they continued their depredations until 911 when the Treaty of St-Clair-sur-Epte created the Duchy of Normandy.

During this period of insecurity the Robertian dynasty (the forerunner of the Capet dynasty) gained in power to the detriment of the last Carolingian kings. A new social order emerged which gave rise to feudalism.

Princely power

The weakness of the last Carolingian kings encouraged the independence of turbulent and ambitious feudal lords. Although Orléans was one of the favourite royal residences and the Orléans region was always Capet territory, Touraine, the county of Blois, Anjou and Maine became independent and rival principalities. This was the age of powerful barons, who raised armies and minted money. From Orléans to Angers every high point was crowned by an imposing castle, the stronghold of the local lord who was continually at war with his neighbours.

The counts of Blois faced a formidable enemy in the counts of Anjou, of whom the most famous was **Fulk Nerra**. He was a first-

Alcuin and Rabanus Maurus (National Library, Vienna)

Archives Snark/ÉDIMÉDIA

class tactician; little by little he encircled Eudes II, Count of Blois, and seized part of his territory. His son, Geoffrey Martel, continued the same policy; from his stronghold in Vendôme he wrested from the house of Blois the whole county of Tours. In the 12C the county of Blois was dependent on Champagne which was then at its peak.

At the same period the counts of Anjou reached the height of their power under the **Plantagenets**; when Henri, Count of Anjou, became King Henry II of England in 1154 his kingdom stretched from the north of England to the Pyrenees. This formidable new power confronted the modest forces of the kings of France but they did not quail under the threat of their powerful neighbours and skilfully took advantage of the quarrels which divided the Plantagenets.

In 1202 King John of England, known as **John Lackland**, lost all his continental possessions to **Philippe Auguste** – the Loire country returned to the French sphere of interest. In accordance with the wishes of his father Louis VIII, when Louis IX came to the throne he granted Maine and Anjou as an apanage to his brother Charles, who abandoned his French provinces, including Provence, and tried to establish an Angevin kingdom in Naples, Sicily and the Near East, as did his successors. Nonetheless, Good **King René**, the last Duke of Anjou, earned himself a lasting place in popular tradition.

The cradle of feudalism

Feudalism flourished in France in the 11C and 12C in the region between the Seine and the Loire under the **Capet** monarchy. The system was based on two elements: the **fief** and the lord. The fief was a *beneficium* (benefice), usually a grant of land made by a lord to a knight or other man who became his vassal.

The numerous conflicts of interest which arose from the system in practice produced a detailed code of behaviour embodying the rights of the parties. During the 12C the services due were defined, such as the maximum number of days to be spent each year in military service or castle watch. Gradually the fiefs became hereditary and the lord retained only overall ownership. In the case of multiple vassalage, liege homage was paid to one lord and this was more binding than homage to any other.

An almost perfect hierarchical pyramid was created descending from the king to the mass of simple knights. The more important vassals had the right of appeal to the king in the event of a serious dispute with their suzerain; it was by this means that King John (John Lackland) was deprived of his French fiefs by Philippe Auguste early in the 13C.

All the inhabitants of an estate were involved in the economic exploitation of the land; the estate had evolved from the Carolingian method of administration and was divided into two parts: the domain, which was kept by the lord for himself, and the holdings, which were let to the tenants in return for rent. The authority exercised by the lord over the people who lived on his estate derived from the royal prerogative of the monarch to command his subjects which passed into the hands of powerful lords who owned castles. This unlimited power enabled them to impose military service, various duties (road mending, transport etc) and taxes on their tenants.

16C: Royal munificence and religious tumult

The 16C saw in the Renaissance an explosion of new ideas in the fields of art and architecture, resulting in one of the liveliest periods in the history of the Loire region.

The Renaissance – The University of Orléans with its long-established reputation attracted a number of **humanists**: Nicolas Béraud, Étienne Dolet, Pierre de l'Estoille, Anne du Bourg. The world of ideas was greatly extended by the invention of printing – the first printing press in the Loire Valley was set up in Angers in 1477 – which made learning and culture more accessible. By the middle of the century the **Pléiade** was formed in the Loire Valley and attracted the best local talent.

By choosing Touraine as their favourite place of residence the kings made a significant contribution to the artistic revival of the region. The chief instigators of the great French Renaissance were **Charles VIII** and even more so **Louis XII** and **François I**, who had all travelled in Italy. These monarchs transformed the Loire Valley into a vast building site

François I (16C painting)

where the new aesthetic ideals flourished at Amboise, Blois and especially Chambord. The great lords and financiers followed suit and commissioned the building of elegant houses (Azay-le-Rideau, Chenonceau) while graceful mansions were erected in the towns.

The Renaissance was the expression of a new way of thinking which redefined man's place in the world and presented a radically different view from that which had been held in the past; this gave rise to the desire for harmony and the cult of beauty in all fields: poetry, music, architecture as an expression of nature shaped by man.

LAUROS/GIRAUDON

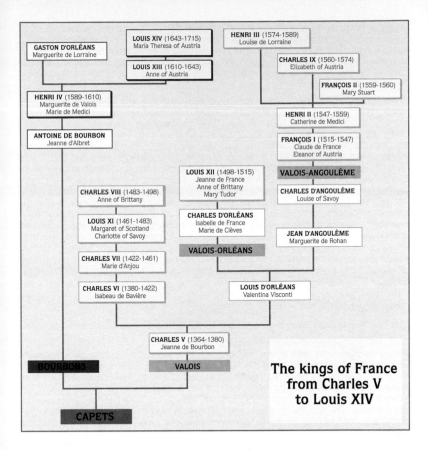

GASTON D'ORLÉANS
Marguerite de Lorraine

LOUIS XIV (1643-1715)
Maria Theresa of Austria

HENRI III (1574-1589)
Louise de Lorraine

LOUIS XIII (1610-1643)
Anne of Austria

CHARLES IX (1560-1574)
Elizabeth of Austria

FRANÇOIS II (1559-1560)
Mary Stuart

HENRI IV (1589-1610)
Marguerite de Valois
Marie de Medici

HENRI II (1547-1559)
Catherine de Medici

ANTOINE DE BOURBON
Jeanne d'Albret

FRANÇOIS I (1515-1547)
Claude de France
Eleanor of Austria

LOUIS XII (1498-1515)
Jeanne de France
Anne of Brittany
Mary Tudor

VALOIS-ANGOULÊME

CHARLES VIII (1483-1498)
Anne of Brittany

CHARLES D'ANGOULÊME
Louise of Savoy

LOUIS XI (1461-1483)
Margaret of Scotland
Charlotte of Savoy

CHARLES D'ORLÉANS
Isabelle de France
Marie de Clèves

JEAN D'ANGOULÊME
Marguerite de Rohan

CHARLES VII (1422-1461)
Marie d'Anjou

VALOIS-ORLÉANS

CHARLES VI (1380-1422)
Isabeau de Bavière

LOUIS D'ORLÉANS
Valentina Visconti

CHARLES V (1364-1380)
Jeanne de Bourbon

BOURBONS

VALOIS

The kings of France from Charles V to Louis XIV

CAPETS

Religious tumult – The Renaissance excited not only intellectual activity but also the need for a moral and religious revival. Despite several local experiments (eg Le Mans), the Roman Church did not succeed in satisfying these aspirations. Naturally the ideas of **Luther** and **Calvin** (who stayed in Orléans between 1528 and 1533) were well received in cultivated circles. In 1540 the Church responded with repression; several reformers died at the stake but the Reform movement continued to grow; nor was support confined to the elite but extended to the mass of the people, craftsmen and tradesmen. The dispute between Protestants and Roman Catholics inevitably led to armed conflict. In 1560 the **Amboise Conspiracy** failed disastrously and ended in bloodshed. Catherine de' Medici tried to promote conciliation by issuing edicts of tolerance but in April 1562 the Huguenots rose up, committing numerous acts of vandalism: damaging places of worship and destroying statues, tombs and relics.

The Roman Catholics under Montpensier and Guise regained the upper hand and exacted a terrible vengeance, particularly in Angers. From 1563 to 1567 there was relative peace, but in 1568 the armed struggle broke out anew; the Catholic and Protestant armies, the latter under Condé and Coligny, indulged in regular waves of violence. The inhabitants of Orléans suffered their own **massacre of St Bartholomew** with nearly 1 000 deaths. During the last quarter of the century the Reformed Churches had become much weaker and **Henri III's** struggle with the Catholic League came to the fore. In 1576 Touraine, Anjou and Berry were granted to François d'Alençon, the king's brother and head of the League, as a conciliatory gesture but the Guises would not compromise and conspired against the king who, seeing no other solution, had them assassinated at Blois in December 1588. The population divided into Royalists and Leaguers, who were powerful in the Loire region. Henri III, who had been forced to withdraw to Tours, allied himself with Henri of Navarre and was marching on Paris when he himself was assassinated on 2 August 1589.

It took Henri IV nearly 10 years to restore peace to the region. The brilliant period in the history of the Loire Valley, which coincided with the last years of the Valois dynasty, ended in tragedy.

17C and 18C: Peace is restored

The Loire country ceased to be at the centre of political and religious ferment. There were admittedly a few alarms during the minority of Louis XIII and the Fronde uprising, in which the indefatigable conspirator, Gaston d'Orléans, played a significant role. Order was restored under Louis XIV with centralisation under the crown stifling the slightest sign of autonomy: the districts of Orléans and Tours were administered by energetic treasury officials while the towns lost the right to self-government.

As far as religious life was concerned, the Roman Catholic Church re-established itself: a growth in number of convents and seminaries, the reform of the old monastic foundations and the suppression of sorcery went hand in hand with the improvement in the intellectual level of the clergy. Protestantism had a struggle to survive, except in Saumur thanks to the Academy, and was dealt a devastating blow by the **Revocation of the Edict of Nantes** in 1685.

A developing economy – Human enterprise benefited from the general stability. Agriculture developed slowly: cereals in the Beauce, raw materials for textiles (wool, linen, hemp), market gardening together with fruit growing and winemaking in the Loire Valley were a considerable source of wealth whereas cattle raising remained weak. Rural crafts played an important role together with urban manufacturing: hemp cloth round Cholet, cheesecloth in the district of Le Mans, sheeting in Touraine and Anjou, bonnets in Orléanais. The silk weavers of Tours earned themselves a good reputation. Nevertheless in the 18C, except for sheets from Laval and Cholet, the textile industry fell into decline. Orléans, the warehouse of the Loire, specialised in sugar refining and the finished product was distributed throughout the kingdom. The Loire, under the control of the community of merchants *(see Vallée de la LOIRE: Boats and Boatmen)*, was the main axis for trade: wine from Touraine and Anjou, wool from the Berry, iron from the Massif Central, coal from the Forez, wheat from the Beauce, cloth from the Touraine and cargoes from exotic countries – everything travelled by water. On the eve of the Revolution these activities were waning but the region featured two million inhabitants and several real towns: Orléans (pop 40 000), Angers (pop 30 000), Tours (pop 20 000) and Le Mans (pop 17 000).

The Revolution

The Touraine and Orléanais regions accepted the Revolution but Maine and Anjou rose in revolt.

Social conflict – At first it was social conflict in which the country peasants were opposed to the townspeople and the weavers from the villages. Townspeople, who had been won over by the new ideas, were enthusiastic about the new political order while peasants became increasingly disillusioned. Religious reform upset parish life and the administrative reforms aroused criticism and discontent because they favoured the townspeople. The national guards in their blue uniform were increasingly disliked: they were sent out from the towns to impose revolutionary decisions on the populace, if necessary by force. The decree imposing mass conscription in March 1793 was seen as an unacceptable provocation in rural areas and the peasants rose in a body. Les Mauges in particular was immediately in the forefront of the battle.

The Vendée War – The Angevin rebels appointed leaders from among their own class: countrymen like Stofflet and Cathelineau, as well as noblemen like Bonchamps. For four months their armies won several important engagements in support of the Church and the king; they captured Cholet, Saumur and then Angers. The Convention, the Republican government of France between September 1792 and November 1795, replied by sending in several army units. The royalist Whites were severely defeated at Cholet on 17 October by General Kléber and General Marceau and compelled to retreat. As they fled, they were pitilessly massacred and the remnants of the great Catholic and Royal Army were exterminated in the Savenay Marshes beyond Nantes. By way of reprisal against the local population the Convention appointed General Turreau in January 1794 to clean up the country. From February to May his **infernal columns** converged on the centre, killing women and children and setting fire to villages.

The Chouans – The war was followed by sporadic outbursts of guerrilla activity: daring exploits, ambushes and even assassinations. **Jean Cottereau**, also known as Jean Chouan, was the leading figure who gave his name to the movement. The country people maintained a relentless resistance. At the end of August a faint peacemaking gesture was made under the authority of **General Hoche**. Charette and Stofflet, who continued the struggle, were arrested and shot in February and March 1796. The insurrection in the Vendée came to an end under the Consulate, a triumvirate including a certain General Bonaparte set up in 1799 to provide stronger government than the existing Republican regime with its divided factions. The war left in its wake widespread ruin and an entrenched bitterness which was revealed later in the very rigid political attitudes of the people of Maine and Anjou.

From war to war

October 1870-January 1871 – After the fall of the Empire, France recovered its balance under the stimulus of Gambetta who arrived in Tours by balloon on 9 October, having escaped the Paris siege. The Bavarians, who were victorious at Artenay, had already captured Orléans (11 October) and indicated that they would link up with the Prussian army at Versailles via the Beauce. Châteaudun put up a heroic resistance for 10hr on 18 and 19 October and was bombarded and set on fire in reprisal.

The army of the Loire was formed under the command of **General d'Aurelle de Paladines**; two corps, the 15th and 16th (Chanzy), formed in the Salbris camp, set out from Blois for Orléans. The engagement took place at Marchenoir and then at Coulmiers on

9 November: the French were victorious and General Von der Thann was forced to evacuate Orléans. Meanwhile the 18th and 20th Corps tried to check the advance of the Duke of Mecklenburg on Le Mans and Tours but they were beaten on 28 November at Beaune-la-Rolande by Prince Frederick-Charles who had hastened south from Metz. On 2 December the 16th and 17th Corps were defeated at Patay and Loigny where the Zouaves under Lt Col de Charette, the great-nephew of the famous Vendéen Royalist, fought with distinction. Although cut in two the first army of the Loire survived. Orléans had to be abandoned while the government retreated to Bordeaux (8 December).

A second Loire army was formed under **General Chanzy**; it resisted every enemy attack and then retrenched on the Loir. On 19 December the Prussians captured Château-Renault and two days later arrived in front of Tours but did not besiege the town. The decisive battle was fought between 10 and 12 January on the Auvours plateau east of Le Mans. Chanzy was forced to retreat towards Laval; Tours was occupied and Prince Frederick-Charles took up residence at Azay-le-Rideau. The armistice was signed on 28 January 1871.

1917-1918 – The Americans set up their headquarters in Tours while the first Sammies disembarked at St-Nazaire and were billeted along the Loire.

1940-1944 – On **10 June 1940** the French Government moved to Tours, and Cangé Château, on the south-east edge of the town, became the temporary residence of the President of the Republic. On 13 June the Franco-British Supreme Council met in Tours; at Cangé the Council of Ministers decided to transfer the government to Bordeaux. During that week of tragedy the bridges over the Loire were machine-gunned and bombarded; floods of refugees choked the roads. The towns were badly damaged. Two thousand cadets from the Cavalry School at Saumur excelled themselves by holding up the German advance for two days along a 25km/15mi front *(see SAUMUR)*. On 24 October 1940 Marshal Pétain met Hitler at **Montoire** *(see p 228)*, and agreed to his demands; collaboration was born. The Gestapo in Angers unleashed a reign of terror in the region.

The Resistance was born in 1941; the information and sabotage networks, the underground forces and the escape agents (the demarcation line followed the River Cher and ran between Tours and Loches) hampered the movements of the occupying forces who responded with torture, deportation and summary execution. In August and September 1944 the American army and the forces of the Resistance achieved control of the area with heavy losses.

Châteaux and castle life

Development of the châteaux

The first châteaux (5C-10C) – In the Merovingian period the country was protected by isolated strongholds: some had evolved from Gallo-Roman villas (country estates) which had been fortified; others were built on high ground (Loches, Chinon). Generally they covered a fairly large area and served several purposes: residence of important people, place of worship, a place for minting money, an agricultural centre and a place of refuge for the population. This type of stronghold continued under the Carolingians but the growing insecurity in the second half of the 9C introduced a wave of fortification in an attempt to counter the Viking threat. The early castles, which were built in haste, rested on a mound of earth surrounded by a wooden palisade; sometimes a central tower was erected as an observation post. The structure contained very little masonry. Until the 10C castle building was a prerogative of the king but thereafter the right was usurped by powerful lords; small strongholds proliferated under the designation of towers – the keep had been invented.

The motte castle (11C) – The motte was a man-made mound of earth on which erected a square wooden tower, the **keep**. An earth bank protected by a ditch supported the perimeter fence, which consisted of a wooden palisade and enclosed an area large enough to contain people from the neighbourhood. The keep was built either as the last place of refuge or at the weakest point in the perimeter fence; some castles had more than one motte. In several of the Angevin castles built by Fulk Nerra the keep protected a residential building erected at the end of a promontory, as at Langeais, Blois and Loches, which are typical of the Carolingian tradition.

The stone castle (12C-13C) – By the 11C some castles had defensive works built of stone. The keep was still the strongest point and took the form of a massive quadrangular structure. The keeps at Loches, Langeais, Montbazon, Chinon (Coudray) and Beaugency are remarkable examples of 11C architecture.

The 12C keep overlooked a courtyard which was enclosed by a stone **curtain wall**, gradually reinforced by turrets and towers. Within its precincts each castle comprised private apartments, a great hall, one or more chapels, soldiers' barracks, lodgings for the household staff and other buildings such as barns, stables, storerooms, kitchens etc.

The tendency grew to rearrange the buildings more compactly within a smaller precinct. The keep comprised a storeroom on the ground floor, a great hall on the first and living rooms on the upper floors. The compact shape and the height of the walls made it difficult to besiege and only a few men were needed to defend it.

In the 13C, under the influence of the crusades and improvements in the art of attack, important innovations began to make their presence felt. Castles were designed by experts to be even more compact with multiple defensive features so that no point was unprotected. The curtain wall bristled with huge towers and the keep was neatly incorporated into the overall design.

A circular plan was adopted for the towers and keep; the walls were splayed at the base; the depth and width of the moat were greatly increased. Sometimes a lower outer rampart was built to reinforce the main rampart; the intervening strip of level ground was called the lists. Improvements were made to the arrangements for launching missiles: new types of loophole (in a cross or stirrup shape), stone machicolations, platforms, brattices etc. The 13C castle, which was more functional and had a pronounced military character, could be built anywhere, even in open country. At the same time a desire for indoor comfort began to express itself in tapestries and draperies and furniture (chests and beds), which made the rooms more pleasant to live in than they had been in the past.

The late medieval castle – In 14C and 15C castle-building the accent moved from defence to comfort and decoration. The living quarters were more extensive; large windows to let in the light and new rooms (state bedrooms, dressing rooms and lavatories) appeared; decoration became an important feature.

In the military sphere there were no innovations, only minor improvements. The keep merged with the living quarters and was surmounted by a watchtower; sometimes the keep was suppressed altogether and the living quarters took the form of a rectangular block defended by huge corner towers. The entrance was flanked by two semicircular towers and protected by a barbican (a gateway flanked by towers) or by a separate fort. The top of the curtain wall was raised to the height of the towers which were crowned by a double row of crenellations. In the 15C the towers were capped by pointed, pepper-pot roofs.

Other fortified buildings – Churches and monasteries, which were places of sanctuary and therefore targets of war, were not excluded from the fortification movement, especially during the Hundred Years War. The towns and some of the villages also turned their attention to defence and built ramparts round the residential districts. In 1398, 1399 and 1401 Charles VI issued letters and ordinances enjoining the owners of fortresses and citizens to see that their fortifications were in good order.

From the end of the 13C fortified houses were built in the country districts by the lords of the manor; they had no military significance but are similar in appearance to the smaller châteaux.

Siege warfare – The attackers' first task was to besiege the enemy stronghold. The defences they constructed (moat, stockade, towers, forts or blockhouses) were intended both to prevent a possible sortie by the besieged and to counter an attack from a relief army. In the great sieges a fortified town grew up in its own right to encircle the site under attack. In order to make a breach in the defences of the besieged place the attackers used mines, slings, battering rams, siege towers... For this they had specialist troops who were experts in siege operations.

R. Corbel/MICHELIN

The advent of the cannon altered siege technique. Both attackers and defenders used artillery: the firing rate was not very high and the aim was even less accurate. Military architecture was completely transformed; towers were replaced by low thick bastions and curtain walls were built lower but much thicker. This new system of defence was perfected by Vauban.

Château de Cheverny – The Armoury

The Renaissance château – In the 16C military elements were abandoned in the search for comfort and aesthetic taste: moats, keeps and turrets appeared only as decorative features, like at Chambord, Azay-le-Rideau and Chenonceau. The spacious attics were lit by great dormer windows in the steep pitched roofs. The windows were very large. The spiral turret stairs were replaced with stairs that rose in straight flights in line with the centre of the main façade beneath coffered ceilings. The gallery – a new feature imported from Italy at the end of the 15C – lent a touch of elegance to the main courtyard.

Whereas the old fortified castle had been built on a hill, the new château was sited in a valley or beside a river where it was reflected in the water. The idea was that the building should blend in with its natural surroundings, although these were shaped and transfigured by human intervention; the gardens, laid out like a jewel casket, were an integral part of the design. Only the chapel continued to be built in the traditional style with ogive vaulting and Flamboyant decoration.

From castle to château, daily life

The medieval household – In the 10C and 11C life in a castle was thought to be somewhat primitive. The whole family lived, ate and slept in the same room on the first floor of the keep. Furniture was sparse and tableware rudimentary.

The owner of a castle had to be self-sufficient and lived in an atmosphere of great insecurity. When the lord was out hunting or fighting his neighbours or off on a crusade, his lady would take over the administration of his affairs.

The Great Hall – In the 13C living quarters began to improve. In the Near East the crusaders experienced a comfortable lifestyle and soon acquired a taste for it. From this period on public and private life were conducted in separate rooms. The finest room in the castle was the Great Hall, where the lord held audience and dispensed justice, and where feasts and banquets were organised. The earlier loopholes were replaced by windows, fitted with panes and shutters. The walls were hung with paintings and tapestries, the floor tiles were covered with rush mats or carpets on which one could sit or lie; flowers and greenery were strewn on the floor and, in summer, in the fireplaces.

The bedchamber – The bedchamber opened off the Great Hall. Except in royal or princely households, a married couple slept in the same room. Over the centuries the furnishings grew richer; the bed was set on a dais and surrounded with sumptuous curtains; there were Venetian mirrors, tapestries, costly drapes, benches with backs, a princely chair, a prie-dieu, library steps and cushions, a dresser, a table, chests and a cupboard. To entertain the ladies there was an aviary, often with a parrot.

Near the bedchamber was a study which was also used for private audiences, a council chamber and an oratory or chapel. A special room was set aside for the guards. In the larger houses there was also a stateroom where the ceremonial clothes were on display.

Food – Food at court was good and the meals gargantuan. When eaten in private, meals were served in the bedchamber or in the Great Hall. Before and after eating, basins and ewers of scented water were provided for the diners to rinse their hands since fingers often took the place of forks. The plates were made of silver. At banquets the diners sat along one side of a great table since the central area was used by the jugglers, acrobats and musicians who provided entertainment in the intervals.

Bathing and hygiene – Near the bedchamber or in a separate building was the bathhouse. Until the 14C bathing was the fashion in France. The common people used to go to the public baths once a week; the upper classes often took a daily bath. The bathhouse contained a sort of pool which was filled with warm water and a chamber for the steam bath and massage. A barber or a chambermaid was in attendance, for it was the fashion to be clean shaven.

In the absence of a bathhouse, baths were taken in a tub made of wood or bronze or silver. Often people took supper together while bathing. Before a meal guests would be offered a bath. Men and women bathed together without being thought immoral. These habits of cleanliness disappeared from the Renaissance until the Revolution. The preachers inveighed against the communal baths which they asserted had become places of debauchery. In the 13C there were 26 public baths in Paris; by the time of Louis XIV's reign there were only two. In other respects medieval castles were well enough provided with conveniences.

Troubadours – Peterborough Psalter (1390)

Entertainment – Castle life had always had plenty of idle hours and a variety of distractions had developed to fill them. Indoors there was chess, spillikins, dice, draughts and, from the 14C, cards. Outdoors there was tennis, bowls and football, wrestling and archery. Hunting with hounds or hawks and tournaments and jousts were the great sports of the nobles. The women and children had dwarfs to entertain them; at court the jester was free to make fun of people, even the king.

There were frequent festivities. Performances of the Mystery Plays, which sometimes lasted for 25 days, were always a great success.

The Court in the Loire Valley

A bourgeois court – The court resided regularly in the Loire Valley under **Charles VII** whose preference was for Chinon and Loches. These visits ended with the last of the Valois, Henri III. Owing to the straitened circumstances, to which the King of France was reduced, Charles VII's court was not particularly glittering; but the arrival of Joan of Arc in 1429 won the castle of Chinon a place in the history books. **Louis XI** disliked pomp and circumstance. He installed his wife Charlotte of Savoy at Amboise but he himself rarely went there. He preferred his manor at Plessis-lès-Tours where he lived in fear of an attempt on his life. According to Commines, his only interests were hunting and dogs. The queen's court consisted of 15 ladies-in-waiting, 12 women of the bedchamber and 100 officers in charge of various functions including the saddler, the librarian, the doctor, the chaplain, the musicians, the official tasters and a great many butlers and manservants. Charlotte was a deep-thinking woman and a great reader; her library contained over 100 volumes, a vast total for that time. They were works on religious thought, ethics, history, botany and domestic science. A few lighter works, such as the *Tales of Boccaccio*, relieved its solemnity. In fact, compared with that of Charles the Bold, the royal lifestyle seemed homely rather than princely.

A luxurious court – In the late 15C, **Charles VIII** acquired a considerable amount of furniture and numerous other decorative objects in order to embellish the interior of the Château d'Amboise. He installed hundreds of Persian carpets, Turkish woollen pile carpets, Syrian carpets, along with dozens of beds, chests, oak tables and dressers. The rooms and sometimes the courtyards (in the case of prestigious events) were hung with sumptuous tapestries from Flanders and Paris. He also endowed the château with an extensive collection of beautifully crafted silverware, and a great many works of art, mainly from Italy. The Armoury (note the inventory dating back to 1499) contains several sets of armour and outstanding weapons having once belonged to Clovis, Dagobert, St Louis, Philip the Fair, Du Guesclin and Louis XI.

A gallant court – **Louis XII**, who was frugal, was the «Bourgeois King» of Blois. But under **François I** (1515-47) the French court became a model of elegance, taste and culture. The Cavalier King invited men of science, poets and artists to his court. Women, who until then had been relegated to the Queen's service, were eased by the king into a more prominent role in public life as focal points of a new kind of society. He expected them to dress perfectly and look beautiful at all times – and gave

Porcupine (Louis XII) – Cominus et Eminus
(Hand to hand and out of hand's reach)

them the means to do so. The King also ensured that these ladies were treated with courtesy and respect. A code of courtesy was established and the court set an example of good manners.

François I shared his time between Amboise and Blois. The festivities he organised were of unprecedented brilliance. Weddings, baptisms and the visits of princes were lavishly celebrated. Sometimes these celebrations took place in the country, as on the occasion when the reconstruction of a siege was organised; a temporary town was built to be defended by the Duke of Alençon while the King led the assault and capture. To increase the sense of realism, the mortars fired huge balls. Hunting, however, took pride of place; 125 people were employed in keeping the hounds while 50 looked after the hawks.

Upon his return from Italy, he had Chambord built and spent the rest of his life there.

The last Valois – Under **Henri II** and his sons, Blois remained the habitual seat of the court when it was not at the Louvre palace in Paris. It was **Henri III** who drew up the first code of etiquette and introduced the title His Majesty, taken from the Roman Emperors. The Queen Mother and the Queen had about 100 ladies-in-waiting. Catherine de' Medici also had her famous **Flying Squad** of pretty girls, who kept her informed and assisted her in her intrigues. About 100 pages acted as messengers. In addition there were 76 gentlemen servants, 51 clerks, 23 doctors and 50 chambermaids.

Salamander (François I) – Nitrusco et Extinguo
(I Nourish the Good and Destroy the Bad)

The King's suite included 200 gentlemen-in-waiting and over 1 000 archers and Swiss guards. There was a multitude of servants. Princes of the blood and great lords also had their households. Thus, from the time of François I, the royal entourage numbered about 15 000 people. When the court was on the move, 12 000 horses were needed. By way of comparison, in the 16C only 25 towns in the whole of France had more than 10 000 inhabitants!

Queens and great ladies

Whether they were queen or the current royal mistress, women at court played an increasingly important political role, while the lively festivities with which they surrounded themselves made a major contribution to the sphere of cultural and artistic influence of the royal court.

Agnès Sorel graced the court of Charles VII at Chinon and at Loches. She gave the King good advice and reminded him of the urgent problems facing the country after the Hundred Years War, while the Queen, Marie d'Anjou, moped in her castle.

Louise of Savoy, mother of François I, was a devout worshipper of St Francis of Paola. This religious devotion, mingled with the superstitions of her astrologer Cornelius Agrippa, was barely enough to keep her insatiable ambition in check. She lived only for the accession of her son to the throne and to this end she upset the plans of **Anne of Brittany** by making him marry Claude, daughter of Louis XII.

Ermine (Anne of Brittany) – Potius Mori quam Foedari *(Better to Die than Betray)*

The love life of François I featured many women, including Françoise de Châteaubriant and the **Duchess of Étampes**, who ruled his court until his death.

Diane de Poitiers, the famous favourite of Henri II, was a remarkably tough woman. She retained her energy, both physical and mental, well into old age, to the amazement of her contemporaries. She made important decisions of policy, negotiated with the Protestants, traded in Spanish prisoners, distributed honours and magistracies and, to the great humiliation of the Queen, saw to the education of the royal children. Such was her personality that almost every artist of the period painted her portrait.

The foreign beauty of **Mary Stuart**, the hapless wife of young King François II, who died at the age of 17 after a few months' reign, lent an all too brief lustre to the court in the middle of the 16C. She is recalled in a drawing by Clouet and some verses by Ronsard.

A different type altogether was **Marguerite de Valois**, the famous Queen Margot, sister of François II, Charles IX and of Henri III. Her bold eyes, her exuberance and her amorous escapades caused a great deal of concern to her mother, Catherine de' Medici. Her marriage to the future King Henri IV did little to calm her down and was in any case later annulled.

Catherine de' Medici married the Dauphin Henri in 1533 and was a prominent figure at court for 55 years under five different kings. Although eclipsed for a while by the beautiful Diane de Poitiers, she had her revenge on the death of Henri II by taking Chenonceau from her and building the two-storey gallery across the River Cher.

With the accession of Charles IX she became regent and tried to uphold the authority of the monarchy during the Wars of Religion by manoeuvring skilfully between the Guises and the Bourbons, making use of diplomacy, marriage alliances and family intrigue. Under Henri III her influence waned steadily against that of younger women.

The finest French in France

"Le beau parler"– Since the Loire Valley was the cradle of France, it is here that old France is recalled in the sayings which have shaped the French language. It is said that the best French is spoken in the Touraine region. This does not mean that one hears nothing but the most sophisticated, high-brow language. However, the French language, with its balance and clarity, has certainly found some of its finest expression in the Loire Valley, where the peace and beauty of the countryside have fostered many leading French writers.

Middle Ages – In the 6C, under the influence of St Martin, Tours became a great seat of learning. Bishop **Gregory of Tours** wrote the first history of the Gauls in his *Historia Francorum* and **Alcuin of York** founded a famous school of calligraphy at the behest of Charlemagne, while art in the 11C came under the influence of courtly life in the Latin poems of **Baudri de Bourgueil**. At the beginning of the 13C Orléans witnessed the impact of the popular and lyrical language of the *Romance of the Rose*, a didactic poem by two successive authors – the mannered **Guillaume de Lorris**, who wrote the first 4 000 lines, and the realist **Jean de Meung**, who added the final 18 000. The poem was widely translated and exerted tremendous influence throughout Europe. **Charles d'Orléans** (1391-1465) discovered his poetic gifts in an English prison. He was a patron of the arts and author of several short but elegant poems; at his court in Blois he organised poetic jousts – **François Villon** won a competition in 1457.

Hitherto a princely pastime, poetry in the hands of Good King René of Anjou became an aristocratic and even mannered work of art. In Angers, **Jean Michel**, who was a doctor and a man of letters, produced his monumental *Mystery of the Passion;* its 65 000 lines took four days to perform.

Renaissance and Humanism – When the vicissitudes of the Hundred Years War obliged the French court to move from Paris to Touraine, new universities were founded in Orléans (1305) and Angers (1364). They very soon attracted a vast body of students and became important centres in the study of European humanism.

Among those who came to study and to teach were Erasmus and William Bude, Melchior Wolmar, a Hellenist from Swabia, and the reformers Calvin and Theodore Beza; **Étienne Dolet**, a native of Orléans, preached his atheist doctrines for which he was hanged and burned in Paris.

François Rabelais (1494-1553), who was born near Chinon, must be about the best-known product of the Touraine. After studying in Angers, he became a learned Benedictine monk and then a famous doctor. In the adventures of Gargantua and Pantagruel he expressed his ideas on education, religion and philosophy. He was very attached to his native country and made it the setting for the Picrocholine war in his books. His comic and realistic style, his extraordinarily rich vocabulary and his universal curiosity made him the foremost prose writer of his period.

The Pléiade – A group of seven poets from the Loire founded a new school, named after a cluster of stars in the Taurus constellation, which was to dominate 16C French poetry; they aimed to develop their language by imitating Horace and the Ancients. Their undoubted leader was **Pierre de Ronsard**, the Prince of Poets from near Vendôme, but it was **Joachim du Bellay** from Anjou who wrote the manifesto of the group, *The Defence and Illustration of the French Language*, which was published in 1549. The other members of the group were **Jean-Antoine de Baïf** from La Flèche, Jean Dorat, Étienne Jodelle, Marot and Pontus de Tyard who all held the position of Court Poet; their subjects were nature, women, their native country and its special quality, *la douceur angevine*.

Classicism and the Age of Enlightenment – At the end of the Wars of Religion, when the king and the court returned north to the Paris region (Île-de-France), literature became more serious and philosophical. The **Marquis of Racan** composed verses on the banks of the Loir and the Protestant Academy in Saumur supported the first works of **René Descartes**. In the following century, **Néricault-Destouches**, from Touraine, followed in Molière's footsteps with his comedies of character; Voltaire stayed at Sully; Rousseau and his companion Thérèse Levasseur lived at Chenonceau; Beaumarchais, who wrote *The Barber of Seville*, settled at Vouvray and visited the Duke of Choiseul in exile at Chanteloup.

Romanticism – The pamphleteer **Paul-Louis Courier** (1772-1825) and the songwriter **Pierre-Jean de Béranger** (1780-1857), both active during the second Bourbon restoration, were sceptical, witty and liberal in politics. **Alfred de Vigny** (1797-1863), a native of Loches who became a soldier and a poet, painted an idyllic picture of Touraine in his novel, *Cinq-Mars*.

The greatest literary genius of Touraine was however **Honoré de Balzac** (1799-1850). He was born in Tours and brought up in Vendôme; he loved the Loire Valley and used it as a setting for several of the numerous portraits in his vast work, *The Human Comedy*.

Contemporary writers – The poet **Charles Péguy** born in Orléans, wrote about Joan of Arc and his beloved Beauce. **Marcel Proust** also returned to the Beauce in his novel *Remembrance of Things Past*. Another poet, **Max Jacob** (1876-1944), spent many years in work and meditation at the abbey of St-Benoît-sur-Loire.

The Sologne calls to mind the young novelist, **Alain-Fournier**, and his famous work, *Le Grand Meaulnes (The Lost Domain)*. The character of Raboliot the poacher is a picturesque evocation of his native country by the author **Maurice Genevoix** (1890-1980), a member of the Academy. The humorist **Georges Courteline** (1858-1929) was born in Touraine which was also the retreat of several writers of international reputation: Maeterlinck (Nobel Prize in 1911) at Coudray-Montpensier; Anatole France (Nobel Prize in 1921) at La Béchellerie; Bergson (Nobel Prize in 1927) at La Gaudinière. **René Benjamin** (1885-1948) settled in Touraine where he wrote *The Prodigious Life of Balzac* and other novels. Angers was the home of **René Bazin** (1853-1932), who was greatly attached to the traditional virtues and his home ground, and of his great-nephew, **Hervé Bazin** (1911-96), whose violent attacks on conventional values were directly inspired by his native town.

J. Benazet/PIX

Balzac (Musée des Beaux-Arts, Tours)

Art

ABC OF ARCHITECTURE

Ecclesiastical architecture

LE MANS – Ground plan of St-Julien Cathedral (12C-15C)

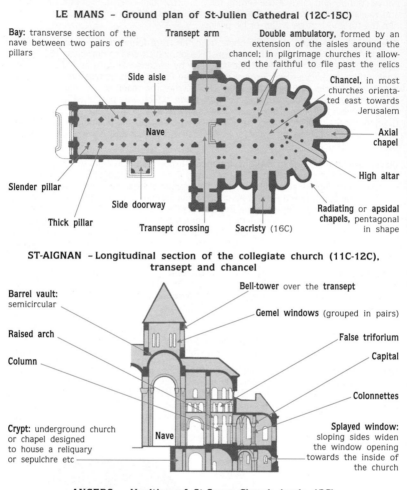

Bay: transverse section of the nave between two pairs of pillars

Transept arm

Double ambulatory, formed by an extension of the aisles around the chancel; in pilgrimage churches it allowed the faithful to file past the relics

Side aisle

Chancel, in most churches orientated east towards Jerusalem

Nave

Axial chapel

High altar

Slender pillar

Side doorway

Thick pillar

Transept crossing

Sacristy (16C)

Radiating or **apsidal chapels,** pentagonal in shape

ST-AIGNAN – Longitudinal section of the collegiate church (11C-12C), transept and chancel

Barrel vault: semicircular

Bell-tower over the **transept**

Gemel windows (grouped in pairs)

Raised arch

False triforium

Column

Capital

Colonnettes

Crypt: underground church or chapel designed to house a reliquary or sepulchre etc

Nave

Splayed window: sloping sides widen the window opening towards the inside of the church

ANGERS – Vaulting of St-Serge Church (early 13C)

This type of domical vaulting is known in France as **Angevin** or **Plantagenet vaulting**. It is curved so that the central keystone is higher than the supporting arches, unlike ordinary Gothic vaulting where they are at the same level. Towards the end of the 12C, Angevin vaulting became lighter, with slimmer, more numerous ribs springing from slender round columns. Early in the 13C, church interiors became higher, beneath soaring lierne vaulting decorated with elegant sculptures.

Quarter or **cell,** in brick

Keystone

Rib

Lierne: auxiliary rib

Capital

Rib vault

Pillar or **column**

R. Corbel/MICHELIN

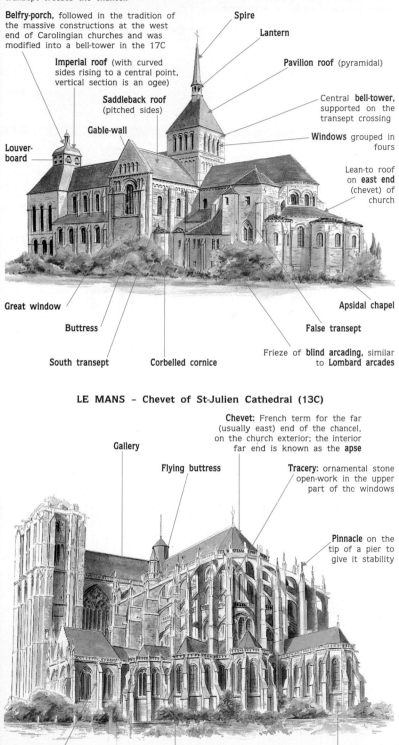

ST-BENOÎT-SUR-LOIRE – Basilique Ste-Marie (11C-12C)

Romanesque church. Ground plan with double transept is rare in France; the small, or false, transept crosses the chancel.

Belfry-porch, followed in the tradition of the massive constructions at the west end of Carolingian churches and was modified into a bell-tower in the 17C

Spire

Lantern

Imperial roof (with curved sides rising to a central point, vertical section is an ogee)

Pavilion roof (pyramidal)

Saddleback roof (pitched sides)

Central **bell-tower,** supported on the transept crossing

Gable-wall

Windows grouped in fours

Louver-board

Lean-to roof on **east end** (chevet) of church

Great window

Apsidal chapel

Buttress

False transept

South transept

Corbelled cornice

Frieze of **blind arcading,** similar to **Lombard arcades**

LE MANS – Chevet of St-Julien Cathedral (13C)

Gallery

Chevet: French term for the far (usually east) end of the chancel, on the church exterior; the interior far end is known as the **apse**

Flying buttress

Tracery: ornamental stone open-work in the upper part of the windows

Pinnacle on the tip of a pier to give it stability

Buttress: external support for a wall, built against it or projecting from it

Pier: solid masonry support structure absorbing the thrust of the arches

Apsidal chapel. In churches not dedicated to Our Lady, this chapel in the main axis of the building is often consecrated to her (Lady Chapel)

R. Corbel/MICHELIN

TOURS – Façade of St-Gatien Cathedral (13C-16C)

St-Gatien is a fine example of a harmonious combination of styles: Romanesque at the base of the towers, Flamboyant Gothic on the façade, and Renaissance at the top of the bell-towers which are crowned with **lantern-domes**.

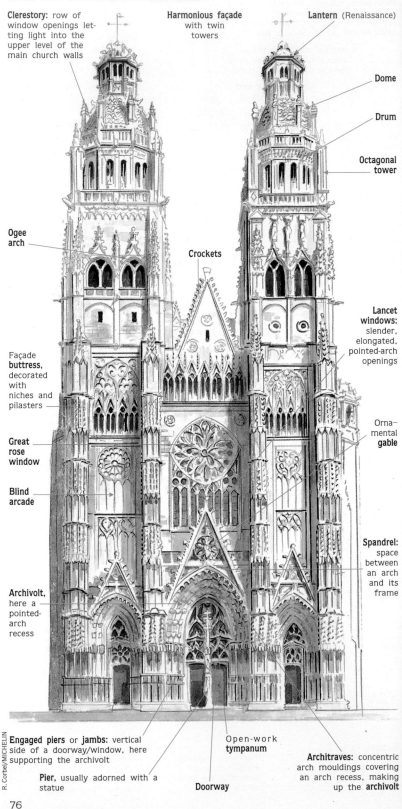

Clerestory: row of window openings letting light into the upper level of the main church walls

Harmonious façade with twin towers

Lantern (Renaissance)

Dome

Drum

Octagonal tower

Ogee arch

Crockets

Lancet windows: slender, elongated, pointed-arch openings

Façade buttress, decorated with niches and pilasters

Ornamental gable

Great rose window

Blind arcade

Spandrel: space between an arch and its frame

Archivolt, here a pointed-arch recess

Engaged piers or **jambs:** vertical side of a doorway/window, here supporting the archivolt

Pier, usually adorned with a statue

Open-work **tympanum**

Doorway

Architraves: concentric arch mouldings covering an arch recess, making up the **archivolt**

LORRIS — Organ case (15C) in Notre-Dame Church

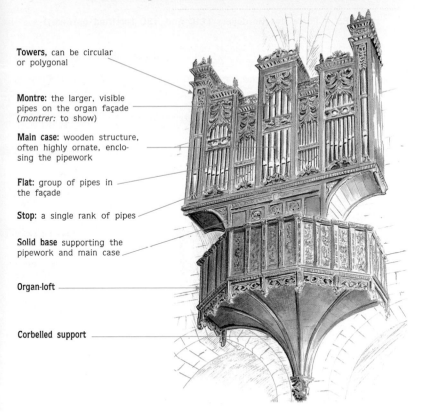

Towers, can be circular or polygonal

Montre: the larger, visible pipes on the organ façade (*montrer:* to show)

Main case: wooden structure, often highly ornate, enclosing the pipework

Flat: group of pipes in the façade

Stop: a single rank of pipes

Solid base supporting the pipework and main case

Organ-loft

Corbelled support

ANGERS — Monumental 19C pulpit in St-Maurice Cathedral

This work by Abbé René Choyer is a pastiche (1855) of 13C Gothic art. As a whole, the pulpit embodies an in-depth knowledge of medieval architecture and sculpture.

Finial: detached formal ornament in the shape of a stylised flower adorning the top of a pinnacle

Canopy: richly ornate baldaquin above a statue or an altar etc

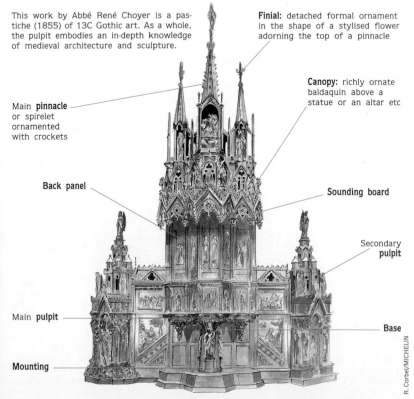

Main **pinnacle** or spirelet ornamented with crockets

Back panel

Sounding board

Secondary pulpit

Main **pulpit**

Base

Mounting

LOCHES – Porte des Cordeliers (11C and 13C fortified gateway)

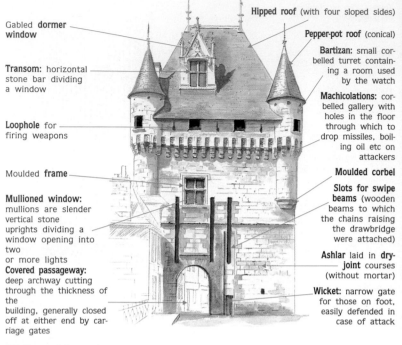

Gabled **dormer window**

Transom: horizontal stone bar dividing a window

Loophole for firing weapons

Moulded **frame**

Mullioned window: mullions are slender vertical stone uprights dividing a window opening into two or more lights

Covered passageway: deep archway cutting through the thickness of the building, generally closed off at either end by carriage gates

Hipped roof (with four sloped sides)

Pepper-pot roof (conical)

Bartizan: small corbelled turret containing a room used by the watch

Machicolations: corbelled gallery with holes in the floor through which to drop missiles, boiling oil etc on attackers

Moulded corbel

Slots for swipe beams (wooden beams to which the chains raising the drawbridge were attached)

Ashlar laid in **dry-joint** courses (without mortar)

Wicket: narrow gate for those on foot, easily defended in case of attack

Civil architecture

BLOIS – Château, François-1er staircase (16C)

The spiral stairway is built inside an octagonal staircase half set into the façade. It opens onto the main courtyard in a series of balconies which form loggias. The king and his court would view all sorts of entertainment from here: the arrival of dignitaries, jousting, hunting or military displays.

Candelabrum: an ornamental torch-shaped spike on top of a tower, chimney etc

Ornate **gable** over dormer window

Cornice of shell motifs, very common ornamentation under François I

Sculpted stone **corbels**

Stone **canopy: baldaquin** decorated with tiny arches and pinnacles, designed to protect statues

Field: plain background to decorative motif

Plain surface left bare of ornamentation

Medallion: sculpted portrait or other subject in a circular frame

Chimney stack

Gargoyle: drain in the shape of an imaginary and often grotesque animal, through whose mouth rainwater would be projected away from the castle walls

Balustrade

Sculpted **parapet** (filled-in protective wall)

Rampant arch: arch with ends springing from different levels

Sculpted **bracket** (projecting support, smaller than a corbel)

Crowned salamander: decorative motif of François I, sculpted in low relief

SERRANT – Château (16C-17C)

Brown schist, white tufa and grey-blue slate lend great character to this luxurious residence in which Renaissance and Classical styles are harmoniously combined.

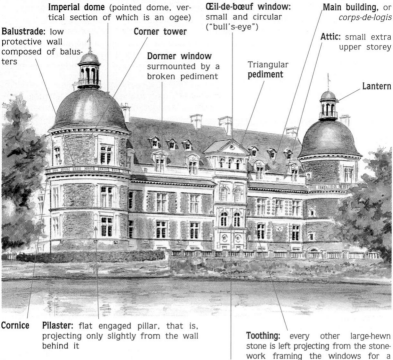

Imperial dome (pointed dome, vertical section of which is an ogee)

Œil-de-bœuf window: small and circular ("bull's-eye")

Main building, or *corps-de-logis*

Balustrade: low protective wall composed of balusters

Corner tower

Attic: small extra upper storey

Dormer window surmounted by a broken pediment

Triangular **pediment**

Lantern

Cornice

Pilaster: flat engaged pillar, that is, projecting only slightly from the wall behind it

Toothing: every other large-hewn stone is left projecting from the stonework framing the windows for a more solid – and more decorative – bond with the adjoining schist walls

Avant-corps: part of a building projecting from the rest of the façade for the entire height of the building, roof included

VILLANDRY — Layout of the Jardins d'Amour (Renaissance style)

The four gardens on the theme of love consist of box borders punctuated by clipped yews and filled with flowers. Each box parterre is laid out in the form of symbolic images: tragic love is represented by sword blades and daggers; unfaithful love by cuckolds' horns, ladies' fans and love letters etc

Monumental fountain in a niche against the wall

Arbour: trellised row of clipped hornbeams

Viewing terrace: commanding a view of the gardens

Mall: tree-lined avenue originally used for games of pall-mall, a precursor of croquet

Espalier wall

Hedge formed by clipped shrubs

Canal

Path covered in *mignonnette* (sand from the Loire which resembles coarse-ground pepper, hence its name)

Box-edged **bed**

Basin

Box edging: low box border (basic element of topiary art)

Topiary: free-standing clipped shrub. Topiary art involves clipping and trimming trees and shrubs to create figurative or geometric shapes verging on sculpture.

SECULAR ARCHITECTURE

Gothic period

In addition to the castles built for the dukes of Anjou, such as Saumur, manor houses and mansions were constructed in the 14C for merchants who had grown rich through trade. The 15C saw a proliferation in the lively ornate Gothic style of châteaux built of brick with white stone facings, such as the château at Lassay, of manor houses such as Le Clos-Lucé near Amboise, of town mansions with projecting stair turrets and high dormers, and of half-timbered houses. The finest examples of Gothic houses are to be found in Le Mans, Chinon and Tours.

Gardens – Monastic gardens, such as those belonging to the abbeys in Bourgueil, Marmoutier and Cormery, consisted of an orchard, a vegetable patch with a fish pond and a medicinal herb garden.

In the 15C they were succeeded by square flower beds created by King René at his manor houses in Anjou and by Louis XI at Plessis-lès-Tours. A fresh note was introduced with shady arbours and fountains where the paths intersected; entertainment was provided by animals at liberty or kept in menageries or aviaries.

Renaissance period

The Renaissance did not spring into existence at the wave of a magic wand at the end of the Italian campaigns. Before the wars in Italy, Italian artists had been welcomed to the French court and the court of Anjou; Louis XI and King René had employed sculptors and medallion makers such as Francesco Laurana, Niccolo Spinelli and Jean Candida. New blood, however, was imported into local art by the arrival of artists from Naples in 1495 at the behest of Charles VIII.

At Amboise and Chaumont and even at Chenonceau, Azay or Chambord, the châteaux still looked like fortresses but the machicolations assumed a decorative role. Large windows flanked by pilasters appeared in the façades which were decorated with medallions; the steep roofs were decorated with lofty dormers and carved chimneys. Italian influence is most apparent in the low-relief ornamentation. At Chambord and Le Lude the decor was refined by local masters such as Pierre Trinqueau.

The Italian style is most obvious in the exterior of the François I wing at Blois where Il Boccadoro copied Bramante's invention of the rhythmic façade which featured alternating windows and niches separated by pilasters. Later, as in Beaugency town hall, came semicircular arches and superimposed orders, then the domes and pavilions which mark the birth of Classical architecture.

The Italians created new types of staircases: two spirals intertwined as at Chambord, or straight flights of steps beneath coffered ceilings as at Chenonceau, Azay-le-Rideau and Poncé.

The Renaissance also inspired a number of towns halls – Orléans, Beaugency, Loches – and several private houses – Hôtel Toutin in Orléans, Hôtel Gouin in Tours and Hôtel Pincé in Angers.

Gardens – In his enthusiasm for Neapolitan gardens, Charles VIII brought with him from his kingdom in Sicily a gardener called **Dom Pacello de Mercogliano**, a Neapolitan monk, who laid out the gardens at Amboise and Blois; Louis XII entrusted him with the royal vegetable plot at Château-Gaillard near Amboise.

Pacello popularised the use of ornate flower beds bordered with yew and fountains with sculpted basins. The gardens of Chenonceau and Villandry give a good idea of his style.

The extraordinary vegetable garden at Villandry, whose decorative motifs were highly popular during the Renaissance, has retained a number of traditional and monastic features dating from the Middle Ages; the rose trees planted in a symmetrical pattern symbolise the monks, each digging in his own plot.

Classical period (17C-18C)

Following the removal of the court to the Paris region (Île-de-France), architecture in the Loire Valley fell into decline. Handsome buildings were still constructed but the designers came from Paris. In the more austere climate of the 17C the pompous style of the Sun King displaced the graceful fantasy of the Renaissance and the picturesque asymmetry of medieval buildings. The trend was towards pediments, domes (Cheverny) and the Greek orders (Gaston-d'Orléans wing at Blois). Tower structures were abandoned in favour of rectangular pavilions containing huge rooms with monumental fireplaces decorated with caryatids and painted ceilings with exposed beams; they were covered with steep roofs in the French style.

There was a new wave of château building – Ménars, Montgeoffroy – but the main legacy of the 18C is in the towns. Great terraces were built in Orléans, Tours and Saumur with long perspectives aligned on the axis of magnificent bridges which had level roadways.

RELIGIOUS ARCHITECTURE

Romanesque art (11C-12C)

Orléanais – The church in Germigny-des-Prés, which dates from the Carolingian period, and the Benedictine basilica of St-Benoît are particularly fine examples of Romanesque art in the Orléans area. There are two pretty churches in the Cher Valley at St-Aignan and Selles.

Touraine – Various influences from Poitou are evident: apses with column buttresses, domed transepts, doorways without pediments. The bell-towers are unusual: square or octagonal with spires surrounded at the base by turrets.

Anjou – Angevin buildings are clustered round Baugé and Saumur. The church in Cunault shows the influence of Poitou in the ogive-vaulted nave buttressed by high aisles with groined vaulting. The domes roofing the nave of the abbey church at Fontevraud and the absence of aisles are features of the Aquitaine School.

From Romanesque to Gothic

The **Plantagenet style**, which is also known as **Angevin** takes its name from Henry Plantagenet. It is a transitional style which reached the height of its popularity in the early 13C and died out by the end of the century.

Angevin vaulting – Unlike standard Gothic vaulting in which all the keystones are placed at the same level, Angevin vaulting is domical so that the central keystones are higher than the supporting arches. The best example is the cathedral of St-Maurice in Angers. This type of vaulting evolved to feature an ever finer network of increasingly fragile-looking ribs, which were eventually adorned with sculptures.
The Plantagenet style spread from the Loire Valley into the Vendée, Poitou, Saintonge and the Garonne Valley. At the end of the 13C it was introduced into southern Italy by Charles of Anjou.

Gothic art (12C-15C)

Gothic art is characterised by the use of intersecting vaults and the pointed arch. The triforium, which originally was blind, is pierced by apertures which eventually give way to high windows. The tall, slender columns, which were crowned by capitals supporting the vaulting, were originally cylindrical but later flanked by engaged columns. In the final development the capitals were abandoned and the roof ribs descended directly into the columns.
The **Flamboyant style** follows this pattern; the diagonal ribs are supplemented by other, purely decorative, ribs called liernes and tiercerons.
The Flamboyant style (15C) of architecture is to be found in the façade of La Trinité in Vendôme and of St-Gatien in Tours, in Notre-Dame-de-Cléry and in the Sainte-Chapelle at Châteaudun.

Renaissance and Classical styles (16C-17C-18C)

Italian influence is strongly evident in the decoration of **Renaissance** churches: basket-handle or round-headed arches, numerous recesses for statues. Interesting examples can be seen at Montrésor, Ussé, Champigny-sur-Veude and La Bourgonnière.
In the **Classical** period (17C-18C) religious architecture was designed to create a majestic effect, with superimposed Greek orders, pediments over doorways, domes and flanking vaulting. The church of Notre-Dame-des-Ardilliers in Saumur has a huge dome whereas the church of St-Vincent in Blois is dominated by a scrolled pediment.

STAINED GLASS

A **stained-glass window** is made of pieces of coloured glass fixed with lead to an iron frame. The perpendicular divisions of a window are called **lights**. Metal oxides were added to the constituent materials of white glass to give a wide range of colours. Details were often drawn in with dark paint and fixed by

14C stained-glass window in the Abbaye de la Trinité, Vendôme "Le Repas chez Simon"

firing. Varied and surprising effects were obtained by altering the length of firing and by the impurities in the oxides and defects in the glass. The earliest stained-glass windows to have survived date from the 12C (The Ascension in Le Mans Cathedral).

12C-13C – The colours were vivid with rich blues and reds predominating; the glass and leading were thick and smoothed down with a plane; the subject matter was naïve and confined to superimposed medallions.
The Cistercians favoured *grisaille* windows which were composed of clear-to-greenish glass with foliage designs on a cross-hatched background which gives a greyish effect.

14C-15C – The master-glaziers discovered how to make a golden yellow; lighter colours were developed, the leading became less heavy as it was produced using new tools and techniques, the glass was thinner and the windows larger. Gothic canopies appeared over the human figures.

16C – Windows became delicately coloured pictures in thick lead frames, often copied from Renaissance canvases with strict attention to detail and perspective; there are fine examples at Champigny-sur-Veude, Montrésor and Sully-sur-Loire.

17C-19C – Traditional stained glass was often replaced by vitrified enamel or painted glass without lead surrounds. In the cathedral of Orléans there are 17C windows with white diamond panes and gold bands, along with 19C windows portraying Joan of Arc.

20C – The need to restore or replace old stained glass stimulated a revival of the art. Representational or abstract compositions of great variety emerged from the workshops of the painter-glaziers: **Max Ingrand, Alfred Manessier, Jean Le Moal, M Rollo**.

MURAL PAINTING AND FRESCOES

In the Middle Ages the interiors of ecclesiastical buildings were decorated with paintings, motifs or morally and spiritually uplifting scenes. A school of mural painting akin to that in Poitou developed in the Loire region. The surviving works of this school are well preserved owing to the mild climate and low humidity. The paintings are recognisable by their weak matt colours against light backgrounds. The style is livelier and less formalised than in Burgundy or the Massif Central whereas the composition is more sober than in Poitou. Two techniques were used: **fresco work**, which was done with watercolours on fresh plaster thus making it impossible to touch it up later; and **mural painting**, where tempera colours were applied to a dry surface, producing a less durable work of art.

Romanesque period – The art of fresco work with its Byzantine origins was adopted by the Benedictines of Monte Cassino in Italy, who in turn transmitted the art to the monks of Cluny in Burgundy. The latter used this art form in their abbeys and priories, from where it spread throughout the country.

The technique – The fresco technique was the one most commonly used, although beards and eyes were often added once the plaster was dry with the result that they have since disappeared. The figures, drawn in red ochre, were sometimes highlighted with touches of black, green and the sky-blue so characteristic of the region.

The subject matter – The subjects were often inspired by smaller-scale works. The most common theme for the oven vaulting was Christ the King Enthroned, majestic and severe; the reverse of the façade (at the opposite end of the church from the apse) often carried the Last Judgement; the walls depicted scenes from the New Testament whereas the Saints and Apostles adorned the pillars. Other subjects portrayed frequently are the Conflict of the Virtues and Vices, and the Labours of the Months.

The most interesting examples – Good examples of fresco painting are to be found throughout the Loir Valley in Areines, Souday, St-Jacques-des-Guérets, Lavardin and best of all in the chapel of St-Gilles at Montoire. There is also a fine work in St-Aignan in the Cher Valley. The crypt of the church in Tavant in the Vienne Valley is decorated with lively paintings of high quality.
In Anjou a man called Fulk seems to have supervised the decoration of the cloisters in the abbey of St-Aubin in Angers. His realistic style, although slightly stilted in the drawing, seems to spring from the Poitou School. More characteristic of the Loire Valley are the Virgin and Christ the King from Ponginé in the Baugé region.

Gothic period – It was not until the 15C and the end of the Hundred Years War that new compositions were produced on themes which were to remain in fashion until the mid-16C. These were really more mural paintings than frescoes and new subjects were added to the traditional repertoire; a gigantic St Christopher often appeared at the entrance to a church *(see AMBOISE)*, whereas the legend of the Three Living and Three Dead, represented by three proud huntsmen meeting three skeletons, symbolized the brevity and vanity of human life. In the Loire Valley such paintings are to be found in Alluyes, Lassay and Villiers. Two compositions with strange iconography adorn the neighbouring churches in Asnières-sur-Vège and Auvers-le-Hamon.

Renaissance – In the 16C paintings in churches became rarer. There are however two surviving examples from this period: the Entombment in the church in Jarzé and the paintings in the chapter-house of Fontevraud Abbey.

SECULAR PAINTING

During the 15C and 16C, the French School asserted itself, first through the work of Jean Fouquet (c 1420-80), a portrait painter and miniaturist native of Tours who travelled to Italy, and later through the paintings of the Master of Moulins (late 15C), sometimes identified with Jean Perréal (c 1455-1530).

The Flemish artist Jean Clouet, commissioned by Louis XII and François I, and his son François Clouet (1520-72), who was born in Tours, became famous for their portraits of the Valois.

Last but not least, Leonardo da Vinci (1452-1519) spent the last three years of his life at the court of François I.

TAPESTRIES FROM THE LOIRE WORKSHOPS

Hanging tapestries, which had been in existence since the 8C to exclude draughts or divide up huge rooms, became very popular in the 14C. The weavers worked from cartoons or preparatory sketches using wool woven with silk, gold or silver threads on horizontal (low warp – *basse lisse*) or vertical (high warp – *haute lisse*) looms.

Religious tapestries – Their value made tapestries ideal for use as investments or diplomatic gifts; as well as those commissioned for châteaux or even specific rooms, some were hung in churches or even in the streets. The most famous is the 14C Apocalypse tapestry *(see ANGERS)*.

Mille-fleurs – The *mille-fleurs* (thousand flowers) tapestries evoked late medieval scenes – showing an idealized life of enticing gardens, tournaments and hunting scenes – against a green, blue or pink background strewn with a variety of flowers, plants and small animals. These are attributed to the Loire Valley workshops (c 1500). Good examples can be seen in Saumur, Langeais and Angers.

From the Renaissance to the 20C – The use of cartoons (full-scale designs, usually in reverse) instead of paintings, and more sophisticated weaving techniques and materials rendered greater detail possible. The number of colours increased and panels were surrounded by wide borders. In the 18C the art of portraiture was introduced into tapestry work.

In the 20C **Jean Lurçat**, originally a tapestry renovator, advocated the use of natural dyes. Contemporary weavers started to experiment with new techniques in order to create relief and three dimensional effects.

Le Chant du Monde by Jean Lurçat, 1958
(Musée Jean-Lurçat, Angers)

Musée Lurçat, Angers/(c) Adagp, Paris 2002

GEMMAIL

Gemmail is a modern art medium consisting of assembling particles of coloured glass over a light source. The inventor of this art form was **Jean Crotti** (1878-1958). The Malherbe-Navarre brothers, an interior decorator and a physicist, provided the technical expertise; they discovered a bonding agent which did not affect the constituent elements.

Food and wine

The Loire Valley is a region renowned for its simple healthy cooking, enjoyable wines and relaxed way of making the most of life.

The following menu lists a few local specialities and the wines best suited to accompany them.

Hors-d'œuvre: various types of potted pork; sausage stuffed with chicken meat *(boudin blanc)*.

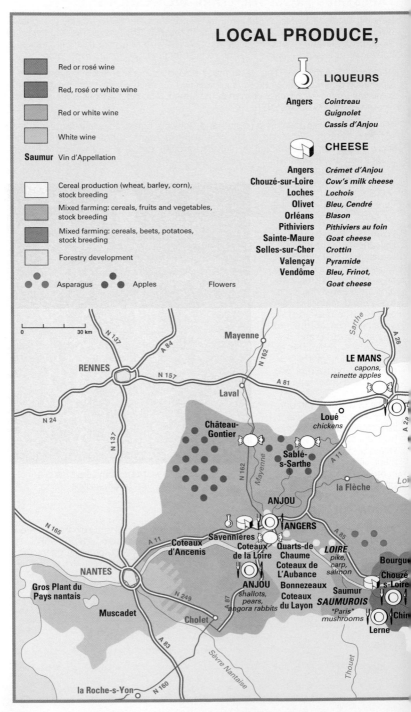

LOCAL PRODUCE,

Red or rosé wine

Red, rosé or white wine

Red or white wine

White wine

Saumur Vin d'Appellation

Cereal production (wheat, barley, corn), stock breeding

Mixed farming: cereals, fruits and vegetables, stock breeding

Mixed farming: cereals, beets, potatoes, stock breeding

Forestry development

Asparagus   Apples   Flowers

LIQUEURS

Angers	*Cointreau*
	Guignolet
	Cassis d'Anjou

CHEESE

Angers	*Crémet d'Anjou*
Chouzé-sur-Loire	*Cow's milk cheese*
Loches	*Lochois*
Olivet	*Bleu, Cendré*
Orléans	*Blason*
Pithiviers	*Pithiviers au foin*
Sainte-Maure	*Goat cheese*
Selles-sur-Cher	*Crottin*
Valençay	*Pyramide*
Vendôme	*Bleu, Frinot,*
	Goat cheese

0   30 km

Mayenne

LE MANS
capons, reinette apples

RENNES

Laval

Loué
chickens

Château-Gontier

Sablé-s-Sarthe

la Flèche

ANJOU

Coteaux d'Ancenis

Savennières

ANGERS

Coteaux de la Loire

Quarts-de-Chaume

Coteaux de L'Aubance

LOIRE
pike, carp, salmon

Bourgu

Chouzé-s-Loire

NANTES

Gros Plant du Pays nantais

Muscadet

ANJOU
shallots, pears, angora rabbits

Cholet

Bonnezeaux

Coteaux du Layon

Saumur

SAUMUROIS
"Paris" mushrooms

Chin

Lerne

la Roche-s-Yon

Fish: pike, salmon, carp or shad with the famous *beurre blanc* (white butter) sauce; small fried fish from the Loire, rather like whitebait *(friture)*; stuffed bream and casserole of eels simmered in wine with mushrooms, onions and prunes (in Anjou).

Main course: game from Sologne; pork with prunes; veal in a cream sauce made with white wine and brandy; casserole of chicken in a red wine sauce or in a white wine and cream sauce with onions and mushrooms; spit-roasted capon or pullet.

Rillauds, rillons and rillettes: all three words derive from the French 16C term *rille*, meaning small dice of pork. *Rillons*, sometimes referred to as *grillons*, are made with pork meat, both lean and fat, which is cut into small morsels. These are then sautéed in fat until they are golden brown and served cold. To make *rillettes*, take some *rillons*, slice them

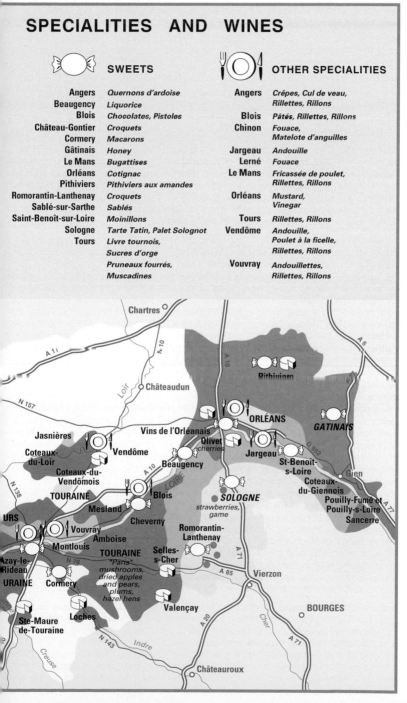

SPECIALITIES AND WINES

SWEETS

Angers	Quernons d'ardoise
Beaugency	Liquorice
Blois	Chocolates, Pistoles
Château-Gontier	Croquets
Cormery	Macarons
Gâtinais	Honey
Le Mans	Bugattises
Orléans	Cotignac
Pithiviers	Pithiviers aux amandes
Romorantin-Lanthenay	Croquets
Sablé-sur-Sarthe	Sablés
Saint-Benoît-sur-Loire	Moinillons
Sologne	Tarte Tatin, Palet Solognot
Tours	Livre tournois, Sucres d'orge, Pruneaux fourrés, Muscadines

OTHER SPECIALITIES

Angers	Crêpes, Cul de veau, Rillettes, Rillons
Blois	Pâtés, Rillettes, Rillons
Chinon	Fouace, Matelote d'anguilles
Jargeau	Andouille
Lerné	Fouace
Le Mans	Fricassée de poulet, Rillettes, Rillons
Orléans	Mustard, Vinegar
Tours	Rillettes, Rillons
Vendôme	Andouille, Poulet à la ficelle, Rillettes, Rillons
Vouvray	Andouillettes, Rillettes, Rillons

finely and put them back to cook on a low fire. They are kept in a pot where the fat rises to the surface, ensuring perfect conservation. *Rillettes* can also be made with goose meat. Anjou *rillauds* are chunks of belly of pork cooked in a vegetable stock enhanced with aromatic herbs for several hours. When the sauce has been reduced, some lard can be added for the final stages of cooking. The dish is best served with a glass of Vouvray.

Vegetables: green cabbage with butter; Vineuil asparagus; mushrooms – stuffed or in a cream sauce; lettuce salad with walnut oil dressing.

Cheese: St-Benoît, Vendôme and St-Paulin are made from cows' milk. Chavignol, Valençay, Selles-sur-Cher, Ste-Maure and Crémets d'Anjou are made from goats' milk (the latter are small fresh cream cheeses); Olivet is factory-made with a coating of charcoal.

Fruit: plums, prunes and melons from Tours; strawberries from Saumur; apricots and pears from Angers; Reinette apples from Le Mans.

Dessert: macaroons from Cormery; apple pastries; quince and apple jelly *(cotignac)*; preserves from Orléans and pastries from Tours; caramelised upside-down apple tart *(tarte tatin see the recipe below)*.

Liqueurs: there are excellent *marcs* and fruit liqueurs, including the famous Cointreau.

Marcs: pure white spirit obtained from pressed grape skins and pips.

Wine

Local wines – The vestiges of an early stone winepress were discovered at Cheille, near Azay-le-Rideau, testifying to the existence of winemaking in the Loire Valley under Roman rule, towards AD 100. It is believed that the great St Martin himself ordered vines to be planted on the slopes of Vouvray in the 4C. From then onwards, this activity became firmly established in the area. Over the centuries, Anjou, Touraine and the Orléanais have adopted a number of grape varieties coming from different natural regions, which accounts for the great diversity of the *cépages.*

The best-known white wines are Vouvray, a dry, mellow wine tasting of ripe grapes, and Montlouis, known for its delicate, fruity flavour. Both are made from the Chenin Blanc grape, referred to locally as **Pineau de la Loire**.
The best-known red wine, known as Breton, is made from the Cabernet Franc grape which originally came from Bordeaux and produces the fine, light wines of Bourgueil and those from Chinon which have a stronger bouquet; the same grape is used to make a dry rosé which has charm and nobility. Among the wines of Anjou are the Rouge de Cabernet and the Saumur-Champigny which have a fine ruby glow and the subtle taste of raspberries. The Cabernet de Saumur is an elegant dry rosé with a good flavour. Another red wine comes from the Breton vines grown on the Loudun slopes. The wines of Sancerre, on the eastern fringe of the châteaux country, are made from the Sauvignon grape and are known for their gun-flint flavour. Less famous wines are the *gris meuniers* from the Orléanais and the *gascon,* which are pale and have a low alcohol content.
The slopes of the Loir produce a dry white and an acid-tasting red which improve with ageing. A light and pleasant white wine is made from the Romorantin grape which is grown only in the Sologne. The slopes of the Loire produce 15% of the entire *Muscadet* crop. The Ancenis-Gamay wine, made from Burgundy Gamay vines, is less well known than the Gros Plant from Nantes as it is produced in smaller quantities. This light, dry, fruity wine, a perfect accompaniment to pork and other cold cuts, is produced in a 350ha/865-acre area around Ancenis.
The character of the region is most apparent in the wine cellars which are often old quarries hollowed out of the limestones slopes at road level. They are therefore easily accessible so that the owner can drive his vehicles straight in. The galleries often extend for several hundred metres. Some open out into chambers where local societies hold their meetings and festivities.
The wine cellars also host meetings of the *confréries vineuses* which preserve the tradition of good wine in the Loire Valley and joyously initiate new members *(chevaliers)* to their brotherhoods: *Les Sacavins* in Angers, *Les Bons Entonneurs Rabelaisiens* in Chinon, *La Chantepleure* in Vouvray and *La Côterie des Closiers* in Montlouis.

In the temple of Bacchus – Picture the scene... The prospective wine-buyer contemplates the latest vintage in the barrel. The owner of the vineyard fills the glasses and the ruby-red nectar is held up to the light. The tumblers have no stem or foot so they cannot be set down until they are drained.
The wine should be savoured first for its bouquet and then, after a knowing glance at one's neighbour, tasted in small sips. On emptying the glass, a simple click of the tongue is enough to signal appreciation. The owner, his eyes shining, will say *"ça se laisse boire...".*

Once inside the cellar, all round, projecting from recesses in the rock, are coloured bottle tops – red, yellow, blue and white: full-bodied Sancerre; Vouvray which is said to "rejoice the heart" (you will notice the motto etched on the glasses there); heady Montlouis; Chinon with its aftertaste of violets; Bourgueil with its hint of raspberries or wild strawberries; and their Angevin brothers, sparkling Saumur, lively and spirited, white Saumur, dry and sprightly, wines from La Coulée de Serrant and the Layon.

For a guide to the best years, and advice on the best combinations of foods and wines see the list printed in The Red Guide France.

S. Sauvignier/MICHELIN

Château de Chambord

Ph. Gajic/MICHELIN

Sights

AMBOISE★★
Population 11 457
Michelin map 317: O-4, 238 fold 14 or 4037 F3
Local map see BLOIS

The town of Amboise, which lies on the south bank of the Loire below the proud remains of its castle, appears at its most picturesque when it is seen from the bridge or the north bank of the river.

The rock spur dominating the town, on which the château ruins stand, has been fortified since the Gallo-Roman period. From the terrace overlooking the river, there is a fine overall view of the Loire Valley and of the blue-slate roofs of the town.

Charles VIII's taste for luxury – The golden age of Amboise was the 15C, when the château was enlarged and embellished by Louis XI and Charles VIII, who spent his childhood in the old castle. Since 1489 the king had dreamed of enlarging and redecorating it to satisfy his desire for luxury.

Work began in 1492 and for the five following years two ranges of buildings were added to the older structure. Hundreds of workmen laboured continuously, if necessary by candlelight, to meet the king's demands. In the meantime, the king visited Italy, where he was dazzled by the high artistic standards and extravagant lifestyle. He returned to France laden with furniture, works of art, fabrics etc. He also recruited to his service a team of scholars, architects, sculptors, decorators, gardeners and tailors... even a poultry breeder who had invented the incubator. 1496 therefore marked the beginning of Italian influence over French art, although there is little to attest to these changes at Amboise, since the new building was by then well advanced. The Italian style was to gain in popularity under Louis XII and flourish under François I.

Charles VIII was particularly impressed by Italian gardens: "They lack only Adam and Eve to make an earthly paradise". On his return he instructed Pacello to design an ornamental garden on the terrace at Amboise. Among the architects whom he employed were Fra Giocondo and Il Boccadoro; the latter, a leading figure in the introduction of Renaissance ideas into France, had worked at Blois and Chambord and on the Hôtel de Ville in Paris.

The Amboise Conspiracy (1560)

This conspiracy was one of the bloodier episodes in the château's history. During the turbulent years leading up to the Wars of Religion, a Protestant aristocrat known as **La Renaudie**, gathered a body of reformists around him in Brittany. These were dispatched to Blois in small groups to request of the young king, François II, the freedom to practise their religion. While they were there, the intention was that they should also try to lay hands on the Guises, the deadly enemies of the Huguenots.

The plot was uncovered and the court promptly withdrew from Blois, which was indefensible, to Amboise where the king signed an edict of pacification in an attempt to calm things down. The conspirators persisted, however, and on 17 March they were arrested and killed as fast as they arrived. La Renaudie also perished. The conspiracy was harshly suppressed; some of the conspirators were hanged from the balcony of the château, some from the battlements, others were thrown into the Loire in sacks, whereas the noblemen were beheaded and quartered. In 1563 there was a truce followed by an Act of Toleration, signed at Amboise, which brought an end to the first War of Religion. The country settled down to four years of peace.

The destruction of the château – Together with Blois, Amboise passed into the hands of Gaston d'Orléans, Louis XIII's brother and a great conspirator *(see BLOIS)*. During one of his many rebellions, the château was captured by royalist troops and the outer fortifications were razed in 1631. It reverted to the crown and was used as a prison where Fouquet, his financial adviser, and the Duke of Lauzun, a notorious womanizer, were imprisoned by Louis XIV.

Later Napoleon granted the château to Roger Ducos, a former member of the Directory. As there were no subsidies for its upkeep, he had a large part of it demolished.

★★CHÂTEAU ⓥ 45min

Terrace – The château is entered by a ramp which opens on to the terrace overlooking the river. From here there is a magnificent **view**★★ of the Loire meandering through the lush valley, and of the town's pointed roofs and walls. The silhouette of the **Tour de l'Horloge** (15C belfry) can be seen rising above the rooftops not far from the old ramparts, and to the west that of the imposing **church of St-Denis** with its squat bell-tower, whereas Le Clos-Lucé can be glimpsed to the south-east.

In the time of Charles VIII the terrace was entirely surrounded by buildings. Festivals were held in this enclosed courtyard: tapestries adorned the walls, and a sky-blue awning decorated with sun, moon and stars gave protection from the weather.

The Château d'Amboise seen from across the River Loire

Chapelle St-Hubert – Curiously set astride the fortified town walls, this jewel of Flamboyant Gothic architecture dating from 1491 is all that remains of the buildings which once lined the ramparts.

The transept houses the tomb thought to contain the body of the great artist Leonardo da Vinci, who died at Amboise.

Outside, admire the Gothic door panels and the finely carved lintel: on the left the legend of **St Christopher** and on the right the legend of **St Hubert**, the patron saint of hunting.

Logis royal – The Royal Apartments are the only part of the château which escaped demolition between 1806 and 1810. The Gothic wing, which overlooks the ramparts above the Loire, was built by Charles VIII (1483-98), as was the adjoining Tour des Minimes. However, the Renaissance wing set at right angles to it was constructed by Louis XII and had another storey added to it under François I.

The tour starts from the lower storey of the Gothic wing, where the guards kept watch. The **Salle des Gardes nobles**, or guard-room *(recently opened to the public)*, is roofed with vaulting supported on a single column, forming a Gothic palm-tree of ribs. A spiral staircase leads up to the **Salle des Tambourineurs** (named after the drummers who accompanied the king on royal visits), where Charles VIII withdrew from the public gaze. The room features some interesting pieces of furniture (Cardinal Georges d'Amboise's pulpit) and a beautiful Brussels tapestry (16C) on the wall, **Homage to Alexander the Great**. Leading on from the Salle des Tambourineurs is the **Salle du Conseil**, also known as the Salle des États (Hall of State). This features a double stone vault supported by a line of columns down the centre of the room, liberally adorned with motifs of the Kingdom of France and the Duchy of Brittany, the fleur-de-lis and ermine. It was here that the king presided over the State Council which decided on policies of the realm.

Continue the visit in the second wing, built at the beginning of the 16C and furnished in early French Renaissance style: winewaiter's sideboard, a Gothic piece with a distinctive linen-fold motif, carved extendable tables and chests in walnut. In **Henri II's bedchamber** *trompe-l'œil* decoration is echoed in the furniture and wall hangings.

La Salle du Conseil

Eating out

BUDGET

La Bonne Étape – *962 quai des Violettes – 2km/1mi NE of Amboise on D 751 – ☎ 02 47 57 08 09 – closed 20 Feb-9 Mar, 18 Dec-8 Jan, Sun evening and Mon – 11.89/39.94€*. Follow the road beside the Loire to get here. This recently built restaurant has two dining rooms with classic decor. The traditional menus tend slightly towards regional flavours. Functional, well-soundproofed rooms.

L'Épicerie – *46 pl. Michel-Debré – ☎ 02 47 57 08 94 – closed 5 Nov-20 Dec, Mon evening and Tue, except Jul-Sep – reservation required in high season – 10.37€ lunch, 17.53/34.3€*. This well-placed restaurant near the castle has a good reputation. The warmly tinted decor and large mirror which enhances the dining room lend an attractive light. Traditional cooking and pleasant staff.

MODERATE

La Cave aux Fouées – *76 quai des Violettes – ☎ 02 47 30 56 80 – closed Sun evening, Tue lunchtime and Mon – 9.15€ lunch, 18.27/27.40€*. An original place, situated in a huge troglodytic cave. You can sample *rillettes* and other regional specialities, accompanied by *fouées*, which are little flat bread rolls cooked in a wood-fired oven while you wait. Disco next door.

Where to stay

BUDGET

Chambre d'hôte Le Petit Clos – *7 r. Balzac – ☎ 02 47 57 43 52 – closed 15 Oct-15 Mar except by reservation – ⊘ – 3 rooms 45/54€*. On the northern bank of the Loire, this bed and breakfast provides three rooms with a separate entrance. After a good night's sleep, what could be nicer than an excellent breakfast in the garden? The bread is home-made, and your hostess is willing to let you help her make it.

On the first floor, three adjoining rooms, the suite of apartments fitted out for Louis-Philippe, display a collection of furniture and portraits of the d'Orléans family, including a grand piano (1842), armchairs bearing the manufacturer's stamp of Jacob, a portrait (1789) of Adelaïde de Bourbon Penthièvre by Vigée-Lebrun and paintings from the workshop of German master painter Winterhalter.

Tour des Minimes or Tour Cavalière – This round tower adjoining the Logis Royal is famous for its wide ramp which horsemen could ride up, ensuring easy access for the provisioning of supplies from the outbuildings in the gardens. The ramp spirals round an empty core which provides air and light. From the top (40m/130ft above the Loire) there is a sweeping **view★★** of the Loire Valley, the Gothic wing of the château and, to the left, the balcony from which several of the conspirators of 1560 were hanged.

> The Wars of Religion have left here the ineffaceable stain which they left wherever they passed. An imaginative visitor at Amboise today may fancy that the traces of blood are mixed with the red rust on the crossed iron bars of the grim-looking balcony, to which the heads of the Huguenots executed on the discovery of the conspiracy of La Renaudie are rumoured to have been suspended. There was room on the stout balustrade – an admirable piece of work – for a ghastly array.
>
> **Henry James** – *A Little Tour in France*

Gardens – These pleasant gardens, redesigned in the 19C under Louis-Philippe, lie within the rampart walls where parts of the château once stood. Most of the park is laid out in the informal English style and a border of lime trees has replaced the 16C Italian Renaissance garden. A bust of Leonardo da Vinci stands on the site of the collegiate church, where the master of the Renaissance was originally buried.

Tour Heurtault – This tower set in the château's south wall features a spiral ramp like the Tour des Minimes, to which it forms a counterpart. The detail on the sculpted corbels supporting the rib vaulting is particularly interesting. The tower leads directly to the town of Amboise.

In summer, visitors may try their hand at traditional games played during the Renaissance, such as croquet, skittles or boules.

MODERATE

Hôtel Le Blason – *11 pl. Richelieu –* ☎ *02 47 23 22 41 – closed 15 Jan-1 Feb, Wed lunchtime, Sat lunchtime and Tue –* 28 rooms 41.16/45.73€ – ☞ *5.34€ – restaurant 11/37€.* A 15C building near the town centre which has retained its original walls. The hotel offers rooms with exposed beams, some of which are attic rooms (shower only). Terrace in an inner courtyard.

A bird's-eye view

A **helicopter ride** is an exceptional way to get an admirable view of the Loire Valley châteaux, and makes for memorable photographs. Tours may last from 15min to 2hr, and prices vary accordingly. Contact Jet Systems Hélicoptères Val-de-Loire, Aérodrome Amboise-Dierre, 37150 Dierre, ☎ 02 47 30 20 21. www.jet-systems.fr.

Son et lumière

At the Court of King François (À la cour du Roy François)
This *son et lumière*, entirely written, staged and acted out by local volunteers, features around 400 jugglers, horsemen, fire-eaters and extras assisted by some highly sophisticated technology (fireworks, fountains, huge images projected onto the surroundings). The show evokes the building of the château, the arrival of Louise of Savoy, the childhood and adolescence of François I, the Italian campaign, as well as daily life and festivities at Amboise to honour the King and his court.
Performances Wednesdays and Saturdays (except on 14 July) from late June to 31 August *(1hr 30min)*. The show starts at 10.30pm in June and July and 10pm in August. 3.81€ to 15.24€. Contact Animation Renaissance Amboise, ☎ 02 47 57 14 47 or the tourist office, ☎ 02 47 57 09 28.

✦LE CLOS-LUCÉ ⊘ – LEONARDO DA VINCI'S HOUSE *1hr*

The manor house of Le Clos-Lucé, in red brick highlighted with white stone, was acquired by Charles VIII in 1490. François I, Margaret of Navarre and their mother, the regent Louise of Savoy, also resided here. In 1516, François I invited **Leonardo da Vinci** to Amboise and lodged him at Le Clos-Lucé where the great artist and scholar organised the court festivities and lived until his death on 2 May 1519 at the age of 67.
The wooden gallery in the courtyard, all that remains of a medieval construction, gives a good view of the manor's main façade. On the first floor is the bedroom, restored and furnished, where Da Vinci died, as well as his studio. This is where he is believed to have worked on his project for the draining of the Sologne and his design for a palace at **Romorantin** for Louise of Savoy.
The ground floor includes the oratory built by Charles VIII for Anne of Brittany, the salons with 18C wainscots where Da Vinci probably had his workshops, the Renaissance reception room and the kitchen with its monumental chimney-piece.

The basement houses the museum of Leonardo's **fabulous machines**, a collection of models made by IBM based on the designs of this polymath who was painter, sculptor, musician, poet, architect, engineer and scholar all in one, and whose ideas were four centuries ahead of his time. Note the entrance to the secret passageway which the King used on his visits to Da Vinci.
The grounds include gardens laid out in the Renaissance style; the terrace affords a view of the château and the river.

Le Clos-Lucé –
One of Leonardo da Vinci's fabulous machines

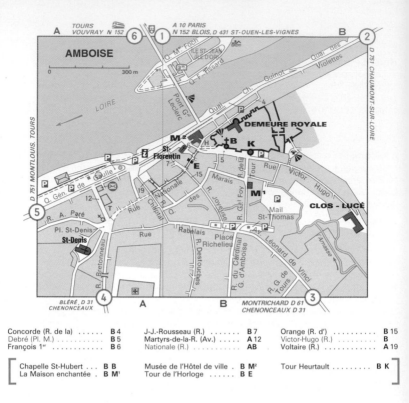

Concorde (R. de la)	**B 4**	J.-J.-Rousseau (R.)	**B 7**	Orange (R. d')	**B 15**
Debré (Pl. M.)	**B 5**	Martyrs-de-la-R. (Av.)	**A 12**	Victor-Hugo (R.)	**B**
François 1er	**B 6**	Nationale (R.)	**AB**	Voltaire (R.)	**A 19**

Chapelle St-Hubert	**B B**	Musée de l'Hôtel de ville	**B M²**	Tour Heurtault	**B K**
La Maison enchantée	**B M¹**	Tour de l'Horloge	**B E**		

ADDITIONAL SIGHTS

Musée de l'Hôtel de ville ⊙ – *Entrance on rue François-1er.* The former town hall, which was built early in the 16C for Pierre Morin, treasurer to the King of France, now houses a museum containing examples of the royal signature, a 14C carving of the Virgin Mary, Aubusson tapestries, portraits of the Duke of Choiseul and six rare 18C gouaches of the Château de Chanteloup, depicting it at the height of its splendour. Nearby on the old town ramparts stands a church, the **Église St-Florentin**, built on the orders of Louis XI.

Tour de l'Horloge – The clock tower, also known as the Amboise belfry was built in the 15C at the expense of the inhabitants on the site of a town gateway called L'Amasse. It spans a busy pedestrian street.

La Maison enchantée ⊙ – ⊚ The magic atmosphere of this enchanted house may be ascribed to the exuberant yet studied sense of disorder that reigns in the rooms, bringing to mind the carefree memories of childhood. The various exhibits – dolls, puppets, large mannequins and automata – are arranged with humour (the dentist's surgery and its waiting room, the saloon, the funfair and its roundabout), sensitivity (sitting on the bench, the toys in the attic) and refinement (the fashion parade, the animals' ball).

Église St-Denis – This compact little church dates mostly from the 12C. Most remarkable are the Angevin vaulting and the fine Romanesque capitals. The south aisle has a 16C Entombment, the recumbent figure known as the Drowned Woman *(Femme noyée)* and an interesting 17C painting, *Charles VIII Welcoming St Francis of Paola to Amboise.*

Parc des Mini-Châteaux ⊙ – *South of town, along the Chenonceaux road (D 81).* ⊚ This 2ha/5-acre park is home to 60 or so models (scale 1:25) of great châteaux and smaller manor houses of the Loire Valley, displayed in a setting commensurate with their size (bonsai trees, miniature TGV railway and boats on the river etc). By night, fibre-optical illuminations lend a fairy-tale atmosphere to the scene.

Le Fou de l'âne ⊙ – *South of town, along the Chenonceaux road (D 81).* ⊚ Donkey lovers will be interested in this park which is home to about 50 donkeys of various types, in reconstructions of their natural habitat. Besides admiring the donkeys themselves, visitors can look at the collection of saddles, harnesses and other equipment, as well as assorted literature on the subject of donkeys, and enjoy cart rides.

EXCURSIONS

★**Pagode de Chanteloup** ⊙ – *3km/2mi S on D 31.* The **pagoda** standing on the edge of Amboise Forest is all that remains of the splendid château built by the **Duke of Choiseul**, one of Louis XV's ministers, in imitation of Versailles. It was later abandoned and demolished in 1823 by estate agents.

When Choiseul was exiled to his estates to please Madame du Barry, he turned Chanteloup into an intellectual and artistic centre.

He commissioned the pagoda (1775-78) from the architect Le Camus as a memorial to his friends' loyalty. This unusual building looks somewhat out of place on the banks of the Loire but it shows how popular anything with a Chinese flavour was in the 18C.

The **setting★** of the pagoda evokes the sumptuous surroundings of Choiseul's exile; there is a plan of the whole structure inside the building. The large fan-shaped pool, now overgrown, and the traces of the alleys in the park, which can be made out from the balconies of the pagoda, help to resurrect the original design. The pagoda is 44m/144ft high and consists of seven storeys, each smaller than the one below. From the top (149 steps) there is a fine **panorama** of the Loire Valley as far as Tours and Amboise Forest.

Have fun in the park where you'll find outdoor games of bygone days.

Chanteloup Pagoda

B. Kaufmann/MICHELIN

★Aquarium de Touraine – *8km/5mi W along D 751. On leaving Lussault-sur-Loire, take D 283 and follow the signposted route.*

Devoted chiefly to European freshwater fish, this aquarium has the particularity of presenting the 70 species forming its stock in open-air basins. The advantage of this new technique is that it allows the fish to live according to the seasons, just as they would do in their natural environment.

Each of the 38 aquariums has been designed to present a specific natural setting. One evokes a mountain torrent, another shows rivers and streams of the Upper Loire. Note the pike-perch and crucian carp swimming along a carefully reconstituted bank of the River Loire. The most impressive aquarium is no 20, a 400 000l/88 000gal basin accommodating giant sturgeon, also known as *acipenser baeri* or *transmontanus*.

The Green Guide makes a point of describing the most interesting and remarkable sights of a particular region. However, some monuments may occasionally have been omitted at the request of the owner.

Leonardo da Vinci on CD-ROM

On his death at Le Clos-Lucé in 1519, Leonardo da Vinci left several thousand pages of manuscript, executed in his unique mirror-writing to preserve his ideas from the prying eyes of potential competitors. His writings, illustrated with diagrams, cover a wide range of subjects – engineering, music, sculpture, painting, science – in keeping with the universal scope of his genius. This valuable legacy became the property of Francesco Melzi, one of Leonardo's students. When Melzi died in 1570, the collection was divided by his heirs. The manuscripts were bound into volumes, or codices, the largest of which is the *Codex Altanticus* comprising 1 119 leaves, now kept at the Biblioteca Ambrosiana in Milan. The *Codex Leicester*, formerly the *Codex Hammer*, is the smallest of these volumes, with 36 folios (2 pages) setting out some of Leonardo's thoughts on hydrology, palaeontology and cosmology. It is the only manuscript of Leonardo's to be owned privately – by none other than Bill Gates, since November 1994. It cost the founder and president of Microsoft over 30 million dollars at Christie's in New York, breaking all previous records for the price fetched at auction by a manuscript. Gates became the latest in a long line of owners of the manuscript, but he is the only one not to have given it his name, preferring it to retain the name of the British family who owned it from the early 18C to 1980. Following his purchase, Gates organised exhibitions of the *Codex Leicester* in Rome, New York and Paris. The fragile state of the manuscripts make it difficult to display them for any but the most superficial of viewings, so a CD-ROM version has been brought out by Gates and his computer graphics company Corbis for those seeking to read the manuscripts in detail. The *Codex Leicester* is now on show back in Seattle, prior to being transferred for safe-keeping to a specially designed cabinet in the library of Gates' magnificent new home there.

ANGERS★★★

Conurbation 226 843
Michelin maps 317: F-4 or 232 fold 31

The former capital of Anjou stands on the banks of the Maine, formed by the confluence of the Mayenne and the Sarthe, 8km/5mi before it flows into the Loire. Modern Angers is a lively university town with a quality of life renowned for its excellence; it is also one of the prettiest French cities, with numerous parks and gardens ablaze with flowers in season. The attraction of the distinctive local architecture lies not least in its striking combination of pale tufa and dark slate.

Angers boasts a flourishing trade based on Anjou wines, liqueurs (Cointreau), early fruit and vegetables, seeds, flowers, medicinal plants and other horticultural products. Home to the famous medieval **Apocalypse tapestry** and its modern replica, **Le Chant du Monde**, as well as to the **Jean-Lurçat Museum of Contemporary Tapestry**, Angers has become an international centre for the art of tapestry making.

The **Anjou Festival** *(see p 48)*, with its many and varied entertainments (drama, music, dancing, poetry, art etc), takes place in July throughout the Maine-et-Loire *département* and draws large appreciative audiences thanks to the high quality of its performances. Angers also offers a programme of cultural events and entertainment during the summer months.

HISTORICAL NOTES

From Romans to Vikings – In the Late Empire the city fell into decline and the population level dropped under the combined effect of the threat of invasion by Germanic tribes and general impoverishment. Christianity, on the other hand, continued to gain influence and in AD 453 a church council met in Angers. Bishop Thalaise was one of the important ecclesiastical figures of the period, a scholar who protected and defended his city.

The abbeys of St-Aubin and St-Serge were founded in the 6C and 7C and soon attracted new settlements. Under the Carolingians the town recovered but was soon destabilised by the revolts of the nobility and Viking invasions. In December 854 the Vikings pillaged Angers but subsequently withdrew. In 872 they returned and held the town for over a year. Charles the Bald, assisted by the Duke of Brittany, laid siege to the invaders and succeeded in dislodging them; a more or less legendary tradition says that Charles dug a canal intending to divert the waters of the Maine and when the Vikings realised that their ships would be grounded they fled in panic.

First House of Anjou (10C-13C) – Under the early counts, who were called Fulk, Angers flourished.

The founders – The weakness of the throne in the late 9C encouraged the emergence of independent principalities. The first Angevin dynasty was established in 898 by **Fulk the Red**, Viscount and then Count of Angers, a title which he handed down to his descendants. Fulk II the Good extended his territory into Maine showing scant regard for the King of France, delicate Louis IV of Outre-Mer, whom he openly despised.

Fulk Nerra and his successors – The rise of the Angevin dynasty to the height of its power in the 11C and 12C was due to its members' exceptional political skill, uninhibited by any scruples, remarkable ability in warfare and keen eye for alliances through marriage.

Fulk III Nerra's son Geoffrey II (1040-60) continued his father's work consolidating the conquest of Maine and Touraine. The succession was divided between his two nephews who lost no time in quarrelling. **Fulk IV the Morose**, finally gained the upper hand over Geoffrey III, at the cost of the Saintonge, Maine and Gâtinais, which he was too lazy to try to recover. In 1092 his second wife, the young and beautiful Bertrade de Monfort, was seduced, abducted and married by King Philip I. For this scandalous behaviour the King was excommunicated *(see BEAUGENCY)*. The family's fortunes were salvaged by Geoffrey IV Martel, killed in 1106, and most of all by **Fulk V the Younger** (1109-31), who took advantage of Anglo-French rivalry and made judicious marriage alliances. He recovered Maine through his own marriage in 1109; later on, with the family's approval, he married his two daughters to the kings of France and

---

Fulk the Terrible

Fulk III Nerra (987-1040) was the most formidable of this line of feudal giants. Hot-blooded and aggressive, he was always waging war to extend his territory; he obtained Saintonge, annexed Les Mauges, extended his boundaries to Blois and Châteaudun, captured Langeais and Tours (he was expelled from the latter by Robert the Pious), intervened in the Vendômois, took Saumur etc. Ambitious, predatory, covetous, brutal and criminally violent, Fulk Nerra (the Black – owing to his very dark complexion) was typical of the great feudal lord in the year 1000. Every so often he would have sudden fits of Christian humility and penitence when he would shower gifts on churches and abbeys or take up the pilgrim's staff and depart for Jerusalem. He also built many fortresses throughout the Loire Valley.

England. His greatest success was the marriage in 1128 of his son Geoffrey to Mathilda of England, daughter and heir to Henry I and widow of the German Emperor Henry V. His ultimate achievement concerned himself: in 1129, by then a widower, he married Melisand, daughter of Baldwin II and heir to the kingdom of Jerusalem. He founded a new Angevin dynasty in the Holy Land and consolidated the position of the Frankish kingdoms.

Geoffrey V (1131-51), known as Plantagenet because he wore a sprig of broom *(genêt)* in his hair, ruled with a rod of iron over Greater Anjou (Anjou, Touraine and Maine) and tried to exercise his wife's rights over Normandy, which he annexed in 1144, and England, where Stephen of Blois had been king since 1135.

Plantagenets and Capets – In 1152 **Henry Plantagenet**, son of Geoffrey and Mathilda, married Eleanor of Aquitaine whom Louis VII had recently divorced. He already held Anjou, Maine, Touraine and Normandy; by his marriage he acquired Poitou, Périgord, the Limoges and Angoulême regions, Saintonge, Gascony and suzerainty of the Auvergne and the County of Toulouse. In 1153 he forced Stephen of Blois to recognise him as his heir and the following year he succeeded him on the throne of England. He was then more powerful than his Capet rival. Henry II of England spent most of his time in France, usually at Angers.

England's Lion

"Henry II was a redhead, of medium height, with a square, leonine face and prominent eyes, which were candid and gentle when he was in a good humour but flashed fire when he was irritated. From morning to night he was involved in matters of State. He was always on the go and never sat down except to eat or ride a horse. When he was not handling a bow or a sword, he was closeted in Council or reading. None was more clever or eloquent than he; when he was free from his responsibilities he liked to engage in discussion with scholars." (M Pacaut)

Successive Anjou dynasties (13C-15C) – During the regency of Blanche of Castille, Anjou was again lost as a result of the barons' revolt when Pierre de Dreux surrendered the province to Henry III. Taking advantage of a truce in 1231 Blanche and her son Louis began to build the impressive fortress of Angers.
Anjou returned to the Capet sphere of influence and in 1346 St Louis gave it, together with Maine, to his younger brother Charles as an apanage. In 1258 it was confirmed as a French possession by the Treaty of Paris. In 1360 Anjou was raised to a duchy by John the Good for his son Louis. From the 13C to the 15C Anjou was governed by the direct line of Capet princes and then by the Valois. The beginning and end of this period were marked by two outstanding personalities, Charles I and King René.

Charles of Anjou – Charles was an unusual character – deeply religious and at the same time wildly ambitious. At the request of the Pope, he conquered Sicily and the Kingdom of Naples and established his influence over the rest of the Italian peninsula. Intoxicated with his success, he dreamt of adding the Holy Land, Egypt and Constantinople to his conquests but the Sicilian Vespers awoke him rudely to reality: on Easter Monday 1282 the Sicilians revolted and massacred 6 000 Frenchmen, half of whom were Angevins.

Good King René – The last of the dukes was Good King René – titular monarch of Sicily. He had one of the most cultivated minds of his day. Having mastered Latin, Greek, Italian, Hebrew and Catalan, he also painted and wrote poetry, played and composed music and was knowledgeable about mathematics, geology and law. He was an easygoing, informal ruler who liked to talk to his subjects; he organised popular festivities and revived the old games of the age of chivalry. He loved flower gardens and introduced the carnation and the Provins rose. At the age of 12 he married Isabelle de Lorraine and was devoted to her for 33 years until her death, shortly after which, at the age of 47, he married Jeanne de Laval who was only 21. Despite the odds, this was also a happy marriage. Towards the end of his life René accepted the annexation of Anjou by Louis XI philosophically. As he was also Count of Provence he left Angers, which he had greatly enriched, and ended his days in Aix-en-Provence at the age of 72 (1480).
During the period of the duchy a university was founded in Angers which flourished with 4 000 to 5 000 students from 10 nations.

Henri IV to the present – The Wars of Religion took on a bitter twist at Angers where there was a strongly entrenched Calvinist church; a dispute on 14 October 1560 brought death to numerous townspeople. Thereafter confrontations grew more frequent and in 1572 the town experienced its own St Barthlomew's Day massacre.

Eating out

BUDGET

La Ferme – *2 pl. Freppel –* ☎ *02 41 87 09 90 – closed 20 Jul-12 Aug, Sun evening and Wed – reservation required – 10.37€ lunch, 14.03/26.98€.* A well-known restaurant near the cathedral, where you can enjoy traditional local cooking in a simple setting. The terrace is one of the nicest in town.

Provence Caffé – *9 pl. du Ralliement –* ☎ *02 41 87 44 15 – closed 31 Jul-20 Aug, 25 Dec-7 Jan, Sun and Mon – reservation required – 14.94/22.71€.* This popular restaurant next to the Hôtel St-Julien is often full both at lunch-time and in the evenings. The patron is from the south of France and the menu reflects this, with its Mediterranean flavours. The dining room has a Provençal atmosphere too. Carefully prepared cuisine at moderate prices.

Le Relais – *9 r. de la Gare –* ☎ *02 41 88 42 51 – closed 13 Aug-4 Sep, 23 Dec-8 Jan, Sun and Mon – 15.09/25.15€.* The woodwork and the murals in this charming tavern recall the vineyard and the harvest. The traditional cooking is satisfying and simple, at affordable prices.

MODERATE

Le Lucullus – *5 r. Hoche –* ☎ *02 41 87 00 44 – closed during Feb school holidays, 1-22 Aug, Sun and Mon except public holidays – 18.29/42.69€.* A pleasant restaurant not far from the castle, with two dining rooms in the vaulted cellars. The 15C local stone walls provide a cool setting for your meal. Simple cooking with fresh produce.

Where to stay

BUDGET

Hôtel Mail – *8 r. des Ursules –* ☎ *02 41 25 05 25 –* 🅿 *– 26 rooms 37.35/57.17€ –* ☕ *5.95€.* The thick walls of this former Ursuline convent in a peaceful street prevent the noise from the nearby town centre from penetrating. The fairly spacious rooms have a personal touch and are under the sloping roof on the top floor.

Chambre d'hôte Le Grand Talon – *3 rte des Chapelles – 49800 Andard – 11km/6.8mi E of Angers on N 147 (towards Saumur) then D 113 –* ☎ *02 41 80 42 85 –* ✉ *– 3 rooms 38/57€.* This elegant 18C house just outside Angers, decked out with leafy vines of Virginia creeper, is a haven of peace. You can picnic in the park, or relax in the lovely square courtyard. The rooms are pretty and the owners extend a very warm welcome.

MODERATE

Le Progrès – *26 r. D.-Papin –* ☎ *02 41 88 10 14 – 41 rooms 42.69/50.31€ –* ☕ *6.71€.* Conveniently located near the train station, this is a friendly place with modern, well-lit and practical rooms. Before setting out to tour the château, enjoy your coffee in the breakfast room, with its decor inspired by the bright colours of Provence.

Hôtel Cavier – *La Croix-Cadeau – 49240 Avrillé – 8km/5mi NW of Angers on N 162 –* ☎ *02 41 42 30 45 –* 🅿 *– 43 rooms 40.40/59.46€ –* ☕ *5.95€ – restaurant 15/28€.* The sails of this 18C windmill still turn! Inside its old stone walls is the dining room, near the original machinery. Modern bedrooms in a recent wing. Terrace next to the outdoor pool.

On the town

L'Écubier – *20 r. Château-Gontier –* ☎ *02 41 88 15 26 – Mon-Sat 6pm-2am.* In this small wine bar, the wood panelling is reminiscent of a ship's hold, the atmosphere is friendly and the conversation absorbing. Those who enjoy Loire wines can come and sample Muscadet, red Anjou, St-Nicolas-de-Bourgueil, or a glass of mead. Theatre and gallery (painting and sculpture).

La Movida – *22 r. Beaurepaire –* ☎ *02 41 87 36 68 – Mon-Sat 6pm-2am.* A pleasant little bar offering Spanish specialities: tapas, Spanish drinks (sangria, muscatel, fino sherry) and Latino music. Discreet clientele of students and regulars.

Pub Saint-Aubin – *71 r. St-Aubin –* ☎ *02 41 87 42 30 – daily 9am-1am.* This brasserie seems to be transforming itself into a high-class restaurant. Anjou wines hold pride of place, for the owner is the son of a wine-grower. The pub is popular with local business people.

Showtime

Nouveau Théâtre d'Angers – *12 pl. Imbach* – ☎ *02 41 88 99 22* – *nouveau.theatre@wanadoo.fr* – *box office Mon-Sat 11am-7pm*. This national drama centre manages several venues for the performing arts: the Beaurepaire Theatre (theatre, music and dance) and the Atelier Jean Dasté (theatre).

Sit back and relax!

La Coursive – *7 bis bd Foch* – ☎ *02 41 25 13 87* – *Mon-Sat 6pm-2am – closed for a fortnight in Aug*. This café is set up in a long, narrow building, and organises concerts once or twice a week, mostly of acoustic music. The entrance is shaped like a sailing ship and the decor is nautical, with a compass on a barrel and gangway lights. Breton atmosphere. House specialities: beer, barley beer, mead, cider.

Les Délices de la Tour – Chocolats Benoît – *1 r. des Lices* – ☎ *02 41 88 94 52* – *benoit-chocolats@worldonline.fr* – *Mon-Sat 9.15am-12.30pm, 2-7.30pm*. Since 1975, this shop has been a haven for those who love fine chocolate. Anne-Françoise Benoît, an extraordinary chocophile, has created a bright and fragrant environment for selling more than 70 flavours of chocolate, sweet and bitter, classic and inventive. Her concoctions include some surprising ingredients such as fennel, tea and ginger.

Maison du vin de l'Anjou – *5 bis pl. Kennedy* – ☎ *02 41 88 81 13* – *Apr-Sep: daily except Mon 9am-1pm, 3-6.30pm; Mar and Oct-Dec: daily except Sun-Mon*. In the centre of town, near the château, this wine shop offers a good selection of Anjou and Saumur wines, which you can taste.

Matt Murphy's – *25 bd Foch* – ☎ *02 41 87 00 61* – *daily 11.30am-2am*. This Irish pub is in one of the liveliest streets of Angers, busy with comings-and-goings both day and night. Once a month, there are concerts with Celtic music. The atmosphere is relaxed and usually quiet enough to allow for good conversation with friends.

Outdoor leisure activities

Parc de loisirs du Lac de Maine – This 200ha/494-acre park offers various facilities such as swimming, tennis, windsurfing, canoeing, kite-flying etc.

Maison de la Nature et de l'Environnement – This nature information centre organises various activities including environment-awareness courses.

Public gardens and parks – They are usually open from 8am to 8pm in summer and from 8am to 5pm in winter: Jardin des Plantes, Jardin du Mail (bandstand), Jardin Médiéval (at the foot of the castle), French-style gardens in the moat and Parcs de l'étang St-Nicolas on the outskirts of town.

It was at the Château d'Angers in 1598 that Henri IV finally brought the fomenting discontent of the Catholic League to an end by promising his son **César** *(see VENDÔME)* to Françoise de Lorraine, daughter of the Duc de Mercœur, the leader of the Catholic party. The promise of marriage was signed on 5 April, when the future bride and groom were six and three years old. A week later the Edict of Nantes came into force; the Protestants had obtained freedom of worship. In 1652, although held by the forces of the Fronde, Angers had to submit to Mazarin; in 1657 the town lost its right to elect local magistrates. After his arrest in Nantes, Louis XIV's Finance Minister, **Fouquet**, spent three weeks in the château in the governor's apartments, guarded by d'Artagnan. By then the town numbered 25 000 inhabitants and was only slightly industrialised.

At the outbreak of the Revolution in 1789, Angers declared enthusiastically for the reformers. The cathedral was sacked and turned into a Temple of Reason. In 1793 the defection of the Girondin administration allowed the Royalist Vendée party to capture the town between 20 June and 4 July. The Republicans lost no time in retaking it and the Terror claimed many victims.

In the early 19C Angers dozed until awakened by the arrival of the railway line from Paris to Nantes: the station was opened in 1849 by Louis Napoleon. Modern development had begun and, apart from a brief lull early in the 20C, it has continued to expand over recent decades.

★OLD TOWN *allow half a day*

Walking through the streets of the old town is like visiting an open-air museum. If the weather is nice, you can enjoy a pleasant break for a picnic lunch in the Jardin des Plantes.

Start from the château entrance and take the narrow rue St-Aignan.

Hôtel du Croissant – This 15C mansion, with mullion windows and ogee arches, housed the registrar of the Order of the Crescent (Ordre du Croissant), a military and religious chivalrous order founded by King René. The blazon on the façade bears the coat of arms of St Maurice, patron of the order, a 4C Christian legionary put to death because he refused to kill his fellow Christians. Opposite stand some interesting half-timbered houses.

Continue to Montée St-Maurice, a long flight of steps which leads to the cathedral square (fine view of the cathedral).

★★ **Cathédrale St-Maurice** ⊘ – The cathedral is a fine 12C and 13C building. The Calvary standing to the left of the façade is the work of David d'Angers.

Façade – This is surmounted by three towers, the central tower having been added in the 16C. The **doorway** was damaged by the Protestants and the Revolutionaries, and in the 18C by the canons, who removed the central pier and the lintel to make way for processions. Notice the fine statues on the door splays.

The tympanum portrays Christ the King surrounded by the four symbols depicting the Four Evangelists; the gracefully executed folds of the garments show skilful carving. Above at the third-storey level are eight niches containing roughly carved, bearded figures in 16C military uniforms: St Maurice and his companions.

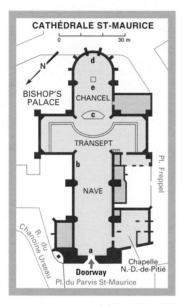

CATHÉDRALE ST-MAURICE

0   30 m

BISHOP'S PALACE

CHANCEL

TRANSEPT

NAVE

Pl. Freppel

R. du Chanoine Urseau

Doorway

Chapelle N.-D.-de-Pitié

Pl. du Parvis St-Maurice

Interior – The single nave is roofed with one of the earliest examples of Gothic vaulting which originated in Anjou in the mid-12C. This transitional style known as Angevin or Plantagenet vaulting has the characteristic feature that the keystones of the diagonal (ogive) arches are at least 3m/10ft above the keys of the transverse and stringer arches giving a more rounded or domical form. In Gothic vaulting all the keys are at roughly the same level. The vaulting of St-Maurice covers the widest nave built at that time measuring 16.38m/54ft across, whereas the usual width was 9-12m/30-40ft; the capitals in the nave and the brackets supporting the gallery with its wrought-iron balustrade feature remarkable carved decoration.

The Angevin vaulting in the transept is of a later period than that in the nave, with more numerous and more graceful ribs. The chancel, finished in the late 12C, has the same Angevin vaulting as the transept. Its **13C stained glass**★★ has particularly vivid blues and reds.

The church is majestically furnished: 18C great organ (**a**) supported by colossal telamones, monumental 19C pulpit (**b**) *(see illustration p 77)*, high altar (**c**) surmounted by marble columns supporting a canopy of gilded wood (18C), 18C carved stalls (**d**) in front of which is a marble statue of St Cecilia (**e**) by David d'Angers. The walls are hung with tapestries, mostly from Aubusson.

Walk past the Bishop's Palace (Évêché) to reach rue de l'Oisellerie.

At nos 5 and 7, there are two lovely half-timbered houses dating from the 16C.

Take the first road on the right.

★ **Maison d'Adam** – This 16C half-timbered house has posts decorated with numerous carved figures. It owes its name to the apple tree which appears to hold up the corner turret and which was flanked by statues of Adam and Eve until the Revolution. Ironically, in the 18C, this house was inhabited by a magistrate called Michel Adam.

Continue along rue Toussaint.

No 37 has a Classical doorway, once the entrance to the **abbey of Toussaint** (All Saints'). It leads to an elegant little courtyard flanked by a turret on a squinch to the right.

Walk back and follow rue du Musée. For a description of the Galerie David-d'Angers (a former church turned into a museum) and of the Musée des Beaux-Arts see ADDITIONAL SIGHTS.

Logis Barrault (Musée des Beaux-Arts) – This beautiful late-15C residence housing a **Fine Arts Museum** was built by Olivier Barrault, the King's Secretary, Treasurer to the Brittany States and Mayor of Angers. In the 17C it was taken over by the seminary, whose pupils included **Talleyrand** *(see VALENÇAY)*, the future Bishop of Autun.

Tour St-Aubin – This is the belfry (12C) of the former monastery of St-Aubin, a wealthy Benedictine abbey founded in the 6C. The tower takes its name from St Aubin, Bishop of Angers (538-50), who was buried here.

★ **Monastery buildings** ◷ – *Rue de la Préfecture*. The abbey buildings, extensively restored in the 17C and 18C, presently house local government offices. On the left side of the courtyard is a glazed-in **Romanesque arcade★★**, part of the cloisters, with sculptures of remarkably refined craftsmanship. The door with sculpted arch mouldings led to the chapter-house; the arcades support a gallery from which those monks who had no voice in the chapter could listen to the proceedings; decorating the twin bay on the right of the door is a Virgin in Majesty with two censing angels whereas on the archivolt a multitude of angels bustle about; beneath this is painted the scene of the Three Wise Men: on the left Herod is depicted sending his men to massacre the Innocents, whereas on the right the star is guiding the Wise Men.

The last arch on the right has the best-preserved scene of all: in the centre the unequal combat between David armed with his sling and the giant Goliath in his coat of chain mail is about to start; on the right the victorious David is cutting off the head of the vanquished giant and on the left he is offering his trophy to King Saul.

Take rue St-Martin to reach place du Ralliement.

Place du Ralliement – This lively square marks the centre of town. Its shops are dominated by the monumental façade of the theatre, embellished with columns and statues.

Walk along rue Lenepveu then take the first turning on the left, rue de l'Espine, past Hôtel Pincé (see ADDITIONAL SIGHTS).

St-Laud district – The small rue St-Laud is the axis of a pleasant pedestrian and shopping district, where a number of very old façades can be admired: particularly fine examples include no 21 rue St-Laud (15C) and no 9 rue des Poëliers (16C).

Take rue St-Étienne and rue du Commerce, then cross boulevard Carnot to reach the church of St-Serge.

★ **Église St-Serge** – Until 1802 this was the church of the Benedictine abbey of the same name founded in the 7C. The 13C **chancel★★** *(see illustration p 74)* is remarkably wide, elegant and well lit, a perfect example of the Angevin style, with its lierne vaulting descending in feathered clusters onto slender columns. In contrast, the 15C nave seems narrower because of its massive pillars. The high windows at the end are filled with graceful 15C stained glass with monochrome backgrounds depicting the Prophets *(north side)* and the Apostles *(south side)*. On the rear wall of the chancel is a Flamboyant sacrarium where relics were kept.

Jardin des Plantes – Located behind the Centre des Congrès and opposite the old conventual buildings (18C) of St-Serge abbey church, this botanical garden is home to some beautiful, rare species of tree (such as the *Davidia*, or handkerchief tree). There is a pool in the lower part of the garden. Parrots can be heard squawking in the aviary. The small Romanesque church of St-Samson, restored in the 16C and 17C, was once the parish church of the old town of St-Serge.

Château d'Angers

★★★ CHÂTEAU ⏱ 2hr

The **fortress**, which incorporates the former Plantagenet fief, was built by St Louis between 1228 and 1238 and is a fine specimen of feudal architecture in dark schist alternating with courses of white stone. The castle moats are now laid out as splendid gardens.

The towers were originally one or two storeys taller and crowned with pepper-pot roofs and machicolations. They were reduced to the level of the curtain walls under Henri III during the Wars of Religion. The original order had been to demolish the fortress entirely, but the governor simply removed the tops of the towers and laid down terraces.

From the top of the highest tower, **Tour du Moulin** (Mill Tower), on the north corner, there are interesting **views★** over the town, the cathedral towers and St-Aubin, the banks of the Maine and the gardens laid out at the foot of the castle, and, in the castle precincts, the series of towers on the curtain wall, the sophisticated design of the gardens, the chapel and the **Logis royal** (Royal Apartments), residence of the dukes of Anjou in the 15C.

Follow the **rampart walk** along the east side where a charming medieval garden is laid out with lavender, marguerites and hollyhocks growing in profusion near a vine like those which King René loved to plant.

★★★ **Apocalypse tapestry** – Housed in a gallery especially designed to ensure maximum preservation conditions, this legendary tapestry is the oldest, apart from the Bayeux Tapestry, to survive until the present. It was commissioned by Nicolas Bataille for Duke Louis I of Anjou and probably made in Paris at the workshops of Robert Poinçon between 1373 and 1383, after cartoons by Hennequin of Bruges, based on an illuminated manuscript belonging to King Charles V. It was subsequently hung in the courtyard of the bishop's palace in Arles to celebrate the marriage of Louis II of Anjou to Yolande of Aragon in 1400. Donated to Angers Cathedral by Good King René (d 1480), it was often displayed during religious festivities up to the late 18C, when it fell into oblivion. However, Joubert, one of the cathedral canons, had it restored between 1843 and 1870.

Originally 133m/436ft long and 6m/20ft high, it consisted of six sections of equal size, each featuring a main character seated under a canopy, eyes turned towards two rows of seven pictures, whose alternating red and blue backgrounds form a chequered design. Two long borders represent Heaven, peopled with angel-musicians, and the Earth, strewn with flowers *(missing in the first part)*.

Angers – Passion tapestry:
Angel carrying Pilate's Ewer

The 76 scenes which have survived form a superb piece of work. The tapestry closely follows the text of the Apocalypse as recounted in the Revelation of John, the last book of the New Testament, in which a divine revelation foretells the coming of a new Jerusalem, or Christ's kingdom on earth. To rekindle the hope of Christians shattered by violence and persecution all around them, the artist depicts the ultimate victory of Christ in the form of prophetic visions and, after many ordeals, the triumph of his Church.

Chapelle and Logis royal – These 15C buildings, which house the chapel and Royal Apartments, stand inside the rampart wall. In the vast and well-lit chapel, note the finely sculpted Gothic leaves of the door, the small separate ducal chapel with its fireplace and, on a keystone, a representation of the Anjou cross *(see BAUGÉ)*. The adjoining staircase, the work of King René, leads to the upper floor of the apartments.

★★ **Passion and Mille-fleurs tapestries** – The Royal Apartments house a beautiful collection of 15C and 16C tapestries including the four hangings of the late-15C **Passion tapestry**, which are wonderfully rich in colour, and several *mille-fleurs* tapestries. Among these is the tapestry entitled **Angels Carrying the Instruments of the Passion**, which is unusual in that it has a religious theme, the admirable 16C **Lady at the Organ** and a fragment showing **Penthesilea**, the Queen of the Amazons, from a hanging of the Nine Heroines, women with chivalrous virtues.

ADDITIONAL SIGHTS

★ **Galerie David-d'Angers** ⊘ – *33 bis rue Toussaint.* The gallery in this restored 13C abbey church houses the vast majority of plaster casts donated by the sculptor **David d'Angers** (1788-1856) to his native town. The Angevin vaulting has been replaced by a vast iron-framed glass roof, so that weather conditions play a major part in the lighting of the exhibition.

The well-displayed collection comprises monumental statues (King René, Gutenberg, Jean Bart, Larrey), funerary monuments (eg of General Bonchamps whose tomb is in the church of **St-Florent-le-Vieil**), busts of famous authors (Chateaubriand, Victor Hugo, Balzac) and medallions in bronze depicting contemporary figures.

In a windowed recess stands the *Young Shepherd*, set off to perfection against the greenery of the gardens of the modern public library.

To the south of the church stand the 18C cloisters with two remaining galleries *(restored)*.

★ **Hôtel Pincé** ⊘ – This Renaissance mansion, built for a mayor of Angers and bequeathed to the town in 1861, houses the **Musée Turpin-de-Crissé**, originally based on the fine personal collection of this local painter (1772-1859) who was chamberlain to Empress Josephine and a member of the Institut de France.

There are Greek and Etruscan vases on the ground floor and an Egyptian collection on the first floor. But the main attraction is displayed on the second floor – a beautiful collection of Japanese ceramics, masks and engravings, as well as a Chinese collection (ceramics, bronzes, fabrics).

Musée des Beaux-Arts (Logis Barrault) ⊘ – On the first floor are collections belonging to the Archaeological Museum, evoking the history of Anjou from the 12C to the 14C (enamels, carved wooden works, statuary etc). Note the 12C reliquary cross, the fine 13C mask on the recumbent statue and the 16C terracotta **Virgin of Tremblay**. A display case is devoted to precious arts exhibits, splendid ivories and painted enamels. The second floor is devoted to paintings: lovely Primitive works, two remarkable small portraits of Charles IX as a young man and Catherine de' Medici after Clouet; 17C paintings (Philippe de Champaigne, Mignard) and above all works of the 18C and 19C French School. There are also canvases by the local painters Lenepveu and Bodinier, and pastels (separate room) by Alexis Axilette, who was born in Durtal.

★ **Musée régional de l'Air** ⊘ – *Aéroport d'Angers-Marcé, 18km/11mi via the Paris motorway.* This aircraft museum illustrates the early days of flying with a display of old aeroplanes such as René Garnier's biplane (1908), the 1930 autogiro, the Cri-cri (smallest twin-engine plane in the world, 1970), the *starck* (the ancestor of microlights).

Short **flights** ⊘ aboard light aircraft are organised by the Aéroclub d'Angers-Marcé.

NORTH BANK OF THE RIVER MAINE

★★ **Musée Jean-Lurçat et de la Tapisserie contemporaine** ⊘ – This Museum of Contemporary Tapestry is housed in the **Ancien hôpital St-Jean★**, a hospital founded in 1174 by Étienne de Marçay, Seneschal to the Plantagenet King Henry I, which provided treatment and care for the sick until 1854.

The vast hospital ward features Angevin vaulting resting on slender columns; to the right of the entrance is the 17C **dispensary★** with glazed earthenware jars and trivets on wooden shelves. In the central recess stands a splendid pewter vessel (1720) which once contained treacle, an antidote to snake bites.

The room is hung with Lurçat's famous series of tapestries called the **Chant du Monde★★** (Song of the World). **Jean Lurçat** (1892-1966), who was largely responsible for reviving the art of tapestry, had discovered the **Apocalypse tapestry** *(see above)* in 1938 and had been profoundly impressed by it, declaring it to be one of the masterpieces of Western art. Nineteen years later he began work on the tapestry series displayed here, which constitutes his masterpiece. It consists of 10 compositions with a combined length of 80m/260ft, the fruit of years of research carried out by the artist himself. It is coarsely woven and characterised by an almost total lack of perspective and deliberate restriction of the range of colours. Evoking the joys and agonies of humanity in the face of life and death, it is an extraordinary synthesis of forms, colours and rhythms.

The doorway in the west wall leads to the Romanesque cloisters and a little garden containing a collection of stonework. Further west still is the former **granary** with its twin bays.

A short distance away, at no 3 boulevard Daviers, the **Centre régional d'Art textile**, which consists of a group of workshops for about 20 warp-weavers, organises guided tours and introductory training courses in the art of tapestry. The weavers here produce remarkable creations, displayed at national and international exhibitions, which can be subsequently bought or hired.

An annexe contains the Simone Lurçat bequest of paintings, ceramics and other tapestries made by her husband. One of the rooms is devoted to tapestries constituting the Thomas Gleb donation. The ground floor is used for temporary exhibitions.

ANGERS

Académie (Pl. de l') .... AZ
Alsace (R. d') .... CYZ
Anjou (R. d') .... BZ
Arago (Bd) .... ABY
Aragon (Av. Yolande d') . AY 2
Arnaud (Bd H.) .... AY
Ayrault (Bd) .... BCY
Baudrière (R.) .... BY 5
Baumette (Rd-Pt de la) . AZ
Bazin (Q. R.) .... BY
Beaurepaire (R.) ...... AY
Berges (Voie des) ..... BY
Besnardière (Av.) ..... CY
Bessoneau (Bd) ...... CY
Bichat (R.) .... AY 8
Blancheraie (Av. de la) . AZ
Bon-Pasteur (Bd du) ... AY 9
Boreau (R.) .... CY
Bosnet (R.) .... BCY
Botanique (Sq.) ...... CY
Bout-du-Monde
   (Prom. du) .... AY 12
Bressigny (R.) .... CZ
Carmes (Q. des) ..... AY
Carnot (Bd) .... CY
Célestin Port (R.) ..... CZ
Chaperonnière (R.) .... BYZ 15
Château-Gontier (R.) .. CZ
Clemenceau (Bd) ..... AY
Commerce (R. du) .... CY 19
Constitution (Av. de la) . CY
David-d'Angers (R.) .... CY 21
Daviers (Bd) .... ABY
Denis-Papin (R.) ..... BZ 22
Descazeaux (Bd) ..... AY
Dr-Bichon (Pl. du) .... AY
Desjardins (R.) ...... CZ
Droits-de-l'Homme (Av.) CY 25
Dumesnil (Bd G.) ..... AY
Espine (R. de l') ..... BY 27
Estoile (Sq. J. de l') ... AY 28
Faidherbe (R.) .... AZ
Félix-Faure (Q.) ...... BCY
Fèvre (Q. R.) .... AY
Foch (Bd du Mar.) .... BCZ
Foulques-Nerra (Bd) ... AY
Freppel (Pl.) .... BY 31
Gambetta (Quai) ..... BY
Gare (R. de la) ...... BZ 32
Gaulle (Bd du Gén.- de) AZ
Guitton (R. J.) .... CY
Hanneloup (R.) ...... CZ
Haras (R. du) .... BZ
Hoche (R.) .... AZ
Imbach (Pl. Louis) .... CY
La Rochefoucauld
   Liancourt (Pl.) ..... ABY 38
Laiterie (Pl. de la) .... AY
Leclerc (Pl. du Mar.) .. CY
Lenepveu (R.) .... CY 40
Leroy (Pl. A.) .... CZ
Lices (R. des) .... BZ
Ligny (Quai) .... AY
Lionnaise (R.) .... AY
Lise (R. P.) .... CY 43
Lycée (Pl. du) .... CZ
Mail (R. du) .... BCYZ
Maillé (R.) .... BCY
Maine (R. du) .... CY
Marceau (R.) .... AZ 45
Marengo (Pl.) .... BZ
Meignanne (R. de la) .. AY
Mendès-France (Pl. P.) . CY
Mirault (Bd) .... BY 49
Mitterrand (Allée F.) ... CY
Mitterrand (Pl. F.) .... BCY
Molière (R.) .... BY
Mondain-Chanlouineau
   (Sq.) .... BY 51
Monge (Quai) .... ABY
Oisellerie (R.) .... BY 53
Paix (Pl. de la) ...... AY
Parcheminerie (R.) .... BY 54
Pasteur (Av.) .... CY 55
Paul Bert (R.) .... BCZ

Pilori (Pl. du) .... CY 56
Plantagenêt (R.) ..... BY 57
Pocquet-de-Livonnières
   (R.) .... CY 58
Poëliers (R. des) ..... CY 59
Pompidou (Allées) ... CY 60
Port-Ligny (Espl. du) .. AY 62
Prés.-Kennedy (Pl. du) AZ
Quiconce (R. du) .... CZ
Ralliement (Pl. du) ... BY 66
Rennes (R. de) ..... CY
Résistance-et-de-la-
   Déport. (Bd) ..... CY 68
Robert (Bd) .... BY 69

Roë (R. de la) .... BY 70
Roi René (Bd du) .... BZ
Ronceray (Bd du) .... AY 71
St-Aignan (R.) .... AY 72
St Aubin (R.) .... BZ 73
St-Étienne (R.) ...... CY 75
St Julien (R.) .... BCZ
St-Laud (R.) .... BY 77
St-Lazare (R.) .... AY 79
St-Martin (R.) .... BZ 80
St-Maurice (Mtée) ... BY 82
St-Maurille (R.) ..... CY 83
St-Michel (Bd) ...... CY 84
St-Nicolas (R.) ...... AY

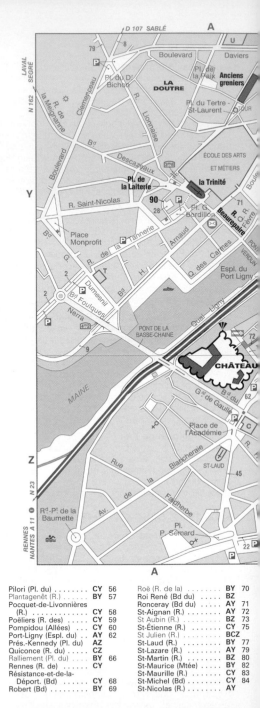

★ **La Doutre district** – The district the other side of the Maine *(d'outre Maine)* has kept its old timber-framed houses in good repair: on the pretty **place de la Laiterie**, in rue Beaurepaire running from the square to the bridge (note in particular no 67, the house of the apothecary Simon Poisson, ornamented with statues and dating from 1582) and along rue des Tonneliers.
The church of **La Trinité** is a 12C building crowned by a 16C belfry.

EXCURSIONS

St-Barthélemy-d'Anjou – *Take the Le Mans road, E on the town plan; then turn right onto boulevard de la Romanerie.*

Musée Cointreau ⓥ – The distillery was founded in 1849 by the Cointreau brothers who invented the famous clear, orange-flavoured liqueur. Various attempts to fake it are on display in the museum, as is the firm's own publicity material. The visit

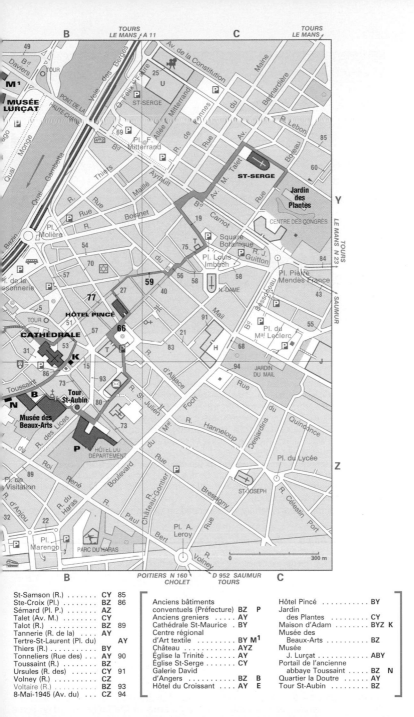

St-Samson (R.)	**CY**	85	Anciens bâtiments			Hôtel Pincé	**BY**
Ste-Croix (Pl.)	**BZ**	86	conventuels (Préfecture)	**BZ**	**P**	Jardin	
Sémard (Pl. P.)	**AZ**		Anciens greniers	**AY**		des Plantes	**CY**
Talet (Av. M.)	**CY**		Cathédrale St-Maurice	**BY**		Maison d'Adam	**BYZ K**
Talot (R.)	**BZ**	89	Centre régional			Musée des	
Tannerie (R. de la)	**AY**		d'Art textile	**BY M¹**		Beaux-Arts	**BZ**
Tertre-St-Laurent (Pl. du)	**AY**		Château	**AYZ**		Musée	
Thiers (R.)	**BY**		Église la Trinité	**AY**		J. Lurçat	**ABY**
Tonneliers (Rue des)	**AY**	90	Église St-Serge	**CY**		Portail de l'ancienne	
Toussaint (R.)	**BZ**		Galerie David			abbaye Toussaint	**BZ N**
Ursules (R. des)	**CY**	91	d'Angers	**BZ**	**B**	Quartier la Doutre	**AY**
Volney (R.)	**CZ**		Hôtel du Croissant	**AY**	**E**	Tour St-Aubin	**BZ**
Voltaire (R.)	**BZ**	93					
8-Mai-1945 (Av. du)	**CZ**	94					

covers four areas: the "product" area, where the production processes are explained and stills are on display; the "business" area, illustrating 150 years of traditions and innovations; the "communication" area, which covers the bottling process and, finally, the "tasting" area, undoubtedly the most convivial, where aromas reign supreme!

★ **Château de Pignerolle** ⊘ – *8km/5mi E on D 61, just past St-Barthélemy-d'Anjou.* This château, which stands in a large public park of over 70ha/170 acres, is a replica of the Petit Trianon in Versailles. It was built in the 18C by an Angevin architect, Bardoul de la Bigottière, for Marcel Avril, the king's equerry and master of the Riding Academy of Angers. During the Second World War the castle served successively as the seat of the Polish government in exile, the headquarters of the German admiral Doenitz, who made it his radio communications centre with the submarine fleet, and, after the Liberation of France, the quarters for American units under General Patton.

Musée européen de la communication. Angers

Musée européen de la Communication
Wireless transmitter set up on the Eiffel Tower

The château now houses the **Musée européen de la Communication** ⊙★★ (European Museum of Communication). The rich collection of scientific apparatus displayed in an instructive and lively manner traces the fascinating history of communication, the major steps in its development and the various modes of expression employed from the tom-tom to the satellite. The ground floor, dedicated to Leonardo da Vinci, illustrates the origins of communication. On the first floor is an extensive retrospective from wireless to radio – which made instantaneous communication possible – (an entire room is devoted to radio sets from 1898 to 1960) and television (there is a reconstruction of a 1950 recording studio). The second floor displays reconstructions of the salon in Jules Verne's *Nautilus* and Armstrong's landing on the moon.

The well-designed and carefully tended château grounds are a pleasant place for a stroll.

St-Sylvain-d'Anjou – *9km/5.6mi NE on the Le Mans road.* Archaeologists and master carpenters have worked closely together to reconstruct as faithfully as possible a medieval **motte-and-bailey** ⊙, like those which made an appearance at the beginning of the Middle Ages. Shows with period settings and costumes help to recreate daily life c 1033.

At the end of the 10C and during the 11C and 12C, these wooden strongholds built on a steep man-made earthen mound *(motte)* with a lower courtyard (the bailey or ward), were a common defensive feature. The feudal lord and his family, together with the chaplain and some guardsmen, would take up residence in the keep. The rest of the soldiers, craftsmen and servants would live in buildings down in the bailey, enclosed by a ditch and a bank of earth surmounted by a palisade. Other buildings to be found in the bailey included stables, byres, barns, ovens and occasionally an oratory.

Les Ponts-de-Cé – *7km/4mi S on N 160.* This is a straggling town about 3km/2mi long; its main street spans a canal and several arms of the Loire, affording some fine views from its four bridges. The history of this small town includes many bloody episodes in French history. Under Charles IX 800 camp-followers were thrown into the Loire; when the château was taken from the Huguenots in 1562, any surviving defenders were treated to a similar fate. In 1793 numerous Royalists were shot on the island that surrounds the château.

On the edge of the road, overlooking the Loire, stand the remains of a château, an ancient 15C fortress crowned with machicolations.

The Gothic church of **St-Aubin** has recently been restored after being gutted by fire in 1973. Some interesting furnishings survived the fire: altarpieces and statues (note the Christ in Captivity).

The **Angers golf course** ⊙, laid out in the park of the Château de St-Jean-des-Maurets, on the banks of the River Maine, will appeal to visitors wishing to combine the practice of a sport with a relaxing stroll in a romantic setting.

Trélazé – *7km/4mi E on the road to Saumur.* Trélazé is famous for its **slate** which has been quarried since the 12C. When the Loire was still a commercial highway, the blue-grey slates were transported upstream by boat to provide roofs for all the châteaux, manor houses and more modest residences which lined the banks of the river.

A slate museum, the **Musée de l'Ardoise** ⊙, has been set up on a 3ha/7-acre site near a disused quarry and presents the geological formation of slate, traditional methods used in quarrying, the life of the men who worked in the quarries and the latest quarrying techniques. A demonstration of old-style slate splitting is provided by former slate men.

★LA LOIRE MAUGEOISE

Downstream to Champtoceaux *83km/50mi about 4hr*

Leave Angers by boulevard du Bon-Pasteur and turn left on D 111, travelling towards Bouchemaine.

Beyond the riverside settlement of La Pointe the road leaves the Loire to wind through the vineyards to Épiré, before dropping into the valley of a stream which joins the Loire at Savennières.

Savennières The attractive village **church** has a Romanesque south door, and chevet ornamented with modillions and carved friezes. The walls of the nave are built of schist decorated with a herringbone pattern in brick (10C). Two well-known, dry, white Savennières wines are the Coulée de Serrant and the Roche aux Moines.

★ **Béhuard** – Béhuard Island has accumulated round a rock on which the little church stands. A short path, beside the Calvary where religious ceremonies take place, leads down to the Loire and a broad sandy beach.

In the pagan era there was a shrine on the island dedicated to a marine goddess, which was replaced in the 5C by a small oratory where prayers were said for sailors in peril on the Loire. In the 15C Louis XI, who believed he had been saved from a shipwreck by the intercession of the Virgin Mary, built the present church which became an even more popular place of pilgrimage than in the past and was dedicated to the Virgin Mary, the protector of travellers, since she herself had experienced the dangers of travel during the Flight into Egypt.

Église Notre-Dame – The church, which is dedicated to the Virgin Mary, faces the souvenir shop which stands on the site of the old **King's Apartment** (Logis du Roi) built in the 15C, so it is said, for the visits of Louis XI; a small stairway leads to the church.

Part of the nave is composed of the island rock. Votive chains, presented by a lucky man who escaped from the barbarian galleys, hang in the chancel; the 16C stalls have misericords carved with delightfully mischievous images. The statue of Our Lady of Béhuard stands in a niche in the chancel. The late-15C window of the Crucifixion in one of the aisles shows the donor, Louis XI *(left)*.

On your way out, stroll through the picturesque old **village**★ with its 15C and 16C houses.

Rochefort-sur-Loire – Rochefort lies in a rural setting on the Louet, an arm of the Loire. The neighbouring slopes produce the famous **Quarts de Chaume**, a distinctive and heady white wine. Several old houses, with turrets or bartizans stand on the square beneath D 751.

★ **Corniche Angevine** – From Rochefort to Chalonnes the road (D 751) along the south bank of the Loire twists and turns through many tight bends cut into the cliff face, making a scenic stretch known as the Corniche Angevine. Beyond La Haie-Longue there are superb views of the riverside villages lying in the broad valley.

La Haie-Longue – In a bend in the road at the entrance to La Haie-Longue stands a chapel dedicated to **Our Lady of Loretto**, the patron saint of aviators. Legend has it that her house was carried by the breeze from Nazareth to the Dalmatian coast and thence to Loretto on the Italian coast where it is venerated as the Santa Casa (Holy House). Opposite stands a monument in honour of René Gasnier, a pioneer in aviation; behind the monument there is an orientation table. The **view**★ is lovely: the river shimmers silver and the countryside unfolds to reveal turreted manor houses and hillside vineyards. The grapes grown here are used to make Coteaux de Layon wine.

Chalonnes-sur-Loire – Chalonnes, which was the birthplace of St Maurille, Bishop of Angers in the 5C, is pleasantly situated. From the quayside on the Loire there is a pretty view of the river. The old port now harbours more pleasure craft than fishing boats.

West of Chalonnes the road (D 571) skirts the edge of the plateau from which small streams flow north to join the Loire.

Montjean-sur-Loire – The narrow streets of Montjean (pronounced Montejan) are confined on a rocky promontory overlooking the Loire.

The buildings of the old forge house an interesting **museum** ⊙ devoted to traditional local activities like the hemp industry, shipping on the Loire, lime-kilns and coal mining. From the terrace near the church there is a broad **view** of the Loire valley, of the suspension bridge over the river and of numerous villages with their grey-slate roofs.

From Montjean to St-Florent take D 210.

The **road**★ along the river embankment provides views over the Loire *(right)* and of the slopes rising to the south of the Thau, once a tributary of the Loire *(left)*. There is a beautiful **view** on reaching Ingrandes.

Ingrandes – In the 17C and 18C Ingrandes was a major port on the River Loire. From the south bank of the river the low walls which protect the town when the river is in spate can be seen. Its position just south of the Breton border made Ingrandes an important centre for smuggling salt. Anjou was subject to the salt tax *(gabelle)* which was particularly unpopular since salt was the only means of preserving food; Brittany, however, was exempt.

The modern church (1956) is built of granite with a slate bell-tower; the huge glass bays were made by the Ateliers Loire after cartoons by Bertrand.

Champtocé-sur-Loire – *6km/4mi E of Ingrandes on N 23*. On the north-east side of the town stand the ruins of the castle of **Gilles de Rais** (1404-40), a disturbing character who may have inspired Charles Perrault to write his story about Bluebeard. He was a powerful lord, a Maréchal de France by the age of 25 and the faithful companion of Joan of Arc whom he attempted to rescue from prison in Rouen. He left the king's service in 1435 and retired to Tiffauges, in Vendée, where for many years he terrorised the surrounding population, as he attempted to redress the massive debts he had run up with his profligate lifestyle, by dabbling in alchemy and reputedly sacrificing large numbers of children. When he was finally taken to court in Nantes and charged with alchemy, raising the devil and the massacre of children, records suggest that – on pain of torture – he confessed his crimes in astoundingly great detail, hesitating only about the number of his victims: 100, 200 or maybe more... On 26 October 1440 Gilles de Rais was hanged between two of his accomplices and his body then burned before an enthusiastic crowd.

Tomb of Bonchamps by David d'Angers

Pratt-Pries/PHOTONONSTOP

St-Florent-le-Vieil – The hill on which St-Florent is built can be seen from a distance. From the bridge over the Loire there is a good **view** of the town and its hilltop church.

Church – The church, once attached to the old Benedictine monastery, stands at the top of Glonne hill. It boasts towers and a west front in a forthright Classical style (early 18C). In one of the north chapels is the white-marble **tomb of Bonchamps**★ (1825) with David d'Angers' representation of the White leader as a hero of Antiquity. Like the chancel, the crypt was restored in the late 19C; it has a 15C painted sculpture of the Virgin Mary.

The Mercy of Bonchamps

The revolt in the Vendée began in St-Florent on 12 March 1793. The Whites were defeated at Cholet and retreated to St-Florent on 18 October with their prisoners and their wounded, including **Charles de Bonchamps** who was close to death. Incensed by the atrocities committed by Westermann and the Mayence Army, the Whites prepared to avenge their leader by massacring the Republicans imprisoned in the church. Hearing by chance of their impending fate, Bonchamps begged his cousin Autichamps to obtain a reprieve for the prisoners. Autichamps ran to the church shouting that Bonchamps wanted the prisoners to be spared and they were spared. Among their number was the father of David d'Angers, the sculptor, who in gratitude produced the moving monument in the church.

The tree-lined **esplanade** near the church ends in a column which was erected in honour of the Duchess of Angoulême, daughter of Louis XVI. From the terrace there is an extensive **view**★ of the Loire Valley.

Musée d'Histoire locale et des Guerres de Vendée ⊘ – This museum housed in the 17C Sacré-Cœur Chapel contains documents, costumes (old-fashioned types of traditional headgear), uniforms and weapons mostly relating to the Vendée War and its leaders.

Ferme abbatiale des Coteaux ⊘ – The once-fortified buildings of this abbey farm now house the **Carrefour des Mauges** (Environmental Centre) with thematic displays on the natural and man-made heritage of the Mauges region and aquariums containing varieties of freshwater fish found in the River Loire.

West of St-Florent-le-Vieil the road (D 751) winds through gently rolling hills.

★**Chapelle de la Bourgonnière** ⊘ – South of D 751, between Bouzillé and Le Marillais, is the modest entrance to the former chapel of a castle destroyed during the Revolution. Towers, turrets and buttresses adorn the edifice which is decorated with shells, the initials LC and tau crosses (T-shaped) – all symbols of the Antonians, properly known as the Hospital Brothers of St Anthony. The order was protected by Charles du Plessis and Louise de Montfaucon who had the sanctuary built between 1508 and 1523. The Antonians nursed people afflicted with ergotism, a violent fever, also known as St Anthony's Fire since St Anthony was invoked to relieve the suffering.

The beautiful doorway is surmounted by a sculpted lintel and the door panels are marked with tau crosses. The star vaulting above the nave is ornamented with coats of arms and pendants. The oratory *(right)* contains a rare feudal bench decorated with 16C Italianate grotesques. Above the high altar is a remarkable statue of the Virgin, attributed to Michel Colombe, between St Sebastian and St Anthony the Hermit.

The **altarpiece**★ *(left)*, decorated with foliated scrolls and cherubs, as well as the central altarpiece, is probably the work of an Italian artist. There is a remarkable Christ in Majesty, clothed in a long tunic, crowned and nailed to a cross, against a painted background depicting the Angels bearing the Instruments of the Passion, as well as Charlemagne and St Louis, the patrons of the donors.

Joachim du Bellay (1522-60)

Du Bellay, like his friends the poets of the **Pléiade**, was brought up on Greek and Latin poetry, and he sought to provide the French language with literary works of the same stature as those he admired in the Ancient Classical languages. He was the author of the group's manifesto, *The Defence and Illustration of the French Language*, which appeared in Paris in 1549. He signed it IDBA which stands for Ioachim du Bellay Angevin and shows his affection for his native province. In 1553 he went to Rome with his cousin, the cardinal, and wrote his finest work *The Regrets*.

> ...Plus que le marbre dur me plaît l'ardoise fine,
> Plus mon Loire gaulois que le Tibre latin,
> Plus mon petit Liré que le mont Palatin,
> Et plus que l'air marin la douceur angevine.
> *(I love thin slate more than hard marble,*
> *my Gallic Loire more than the Latin Tiber,*
> *my little Liré more than the Palatine Hill,*
> *and more than the sea air the sweetness of Anjou.)*

Joachim du Bellay *Les Regrets*

Liré – The village of Liré in the Loire Valley owes its fame to **Joachim du Bellay**, the poet, who was born not far from here.

The **Musée Joachim-du-Bellay** ⊘ occupies a 16C house *(restored)* in the middle of the town. Mementoes of the poet are displayed on the first floor; the ground floor is devoted to local traditions and customs.

Ancenis – The houses of Ancenis, built of schist and roofed with slate, stand in tiers up the north bank of the Loire overlooking the suspension bridge, which is 500m/1 640ft long. The town fortifications and the castle ramparts, now in ruins, once commanded the valley so that Ancenis was known as the key to Brittany. The town used to be a busy port in the shipment of wine, in particular *muscadet*, and was active in the sailcloth industry.

Ancenis is still an important agricultural market and has one of the largest cooperatives in France, the CANA (Cooperative Agricole La Noëlle d'Ancenis), which is involved in many activities. The Vignerons de La Noëlle group of producers cultivates 350ha/865 acres of vineyards for the wines of Nantes and Anjou.

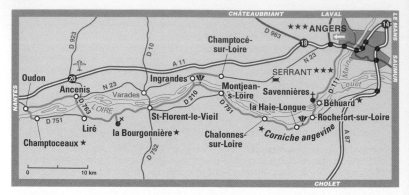

Oudon – The dominant feature of this town is the medieval keep, built between 1392 and 1415. From the top of the **tower** ⊙ there is a beautiful view of the valley.

★ **Champtoceaux** – Champtoceaux is built on an impressive **site**★ on the top of a ridge overlooking the Loire Valley.

The terrace behind the church, **Promenade de Champalud**★★, is like a balcony above the Loire which divides into several channels round the islands in midstream *(viewing table)*.

Beyond the terrace are the ruins of the fortress which was demolished in 1420 and an old toll bridge over the river. The local white wines are delicious.

> **LUXURY**
>
> **Château de la Colaissière** – *49270 St-Sauveur-de-Landemont* – *7km/4.3mi S of Champtoceaux on D 153* – ☎ *02 40 98 75 04* – *closed Jan* – **P** – *16 rooms 105.95/212.33€* – ⌷ *11.43€* – *restaurant 21/50€.* From the Middle Ages to the Renaissance, the centuries have left their mark on this majestic castle, set in a park. A refined atmosphere, with genuine antique furniture and tapestry hung stone walls. Some rooms have four-poster beds.

AZAY-LE-RIDEAU

Population 3 100
Michelin map 317: L-5, 232 fold 35 or 4037 D4

A luxuriant setting on the banks of the Indre provides the backdrop to the Château d'Azay-le-Rideau, one of the gems of the Renaissance. Similar to Chenonceau, but less grandiose, its lines and dimensions suit the site so perfectly that it conveys an unforgettable impression of elegance. It is named after one of its lords, Ridel or Rideau d'Azay, who was knighted by Philippe Auguste and built a strong castle.

The most tragic incident in its history was a massacre which occurred in 1418. When Charles VII was Dauphin he was insulted by the Burgundian guard as he passed through Azay. Instant reprisals followed. The town was seized and burnt and the captain and his 350 soldiers were executed. Azay was called Azay-le-Brûlé (Azay the Burnt) until the 18C.

★★★CHÂTEAU

A financier's creation (16C) – When it rose from its ruins Azay became the property of **Gilles Berthelot**, one of the great financiers of the time. He had the present delightful mansion built between 1518 and 1527. His wife, **Philippa Lesbahy**, directed the work, as Catherine Briçonnet had directed that of Chenonceau.

François I confiscated Azay and gave it to one of his companions in arms from the Italian campaigns, **Antoine Raffin**.

In 1870, when Prince Frederick-Charles of Prussia was staying in the château, one of the chandeliers crashed down on to the table. The Prince thought that his life was being threatened and Azay barely escaped further retribution. In 1905 the château was bought by the French State for 200 000 francs.

TOUR ⊙ *45min*

Though Gothic in outline, Azay is forward-looking in its bright appearance and the handsome design of its façades.

The medieval defences are purely symbolic and testify only to the high rank of the owners. The massive towers of earlier periods have given way to harmless turrets with graceful outlines. Dormer windows spring from the corbelled sentry walk, the machicolations lend themselves to ornamentation and the moats are mere reflecting pools. Partly built over the Indre, Azay-le-Rideau consists of two main wings set at right angles. The reflections in the water add to the chimerical quality of the site and, together with the rows of houses and gardens along the River Indre, make excellent subjects for photographs.

The château's most striking feature is the **grand staircase** with its three storeys of twin bays forming loggias opening onto the courtyard and its elaborately decorated pediment. At Blois the staircase is still spiral and projects from the façade; at Azay it is internal and features a straight ramp.

The interior is lavishly decorated and furnished with some pieces of truly outstanding beauty: late-15C oak canopy throne, fine brocade bed dating from the late 17C, credence tables, cabinets etc. A splendid collection of 16C and 17C **tapestries★** are exhibited on the walls: *verdures* (landscapes dominated by flower and plant motifs) from Antwerp and Tournai; lovely compositions woven in Oudenaarde (scenes from the Old Testament) and Brussels (*Story of Psyche* series); the fine *Tenture de Renaud et Armide*, executed in the Parisian workshops of the Faubourg St-Marcel after cartoons by Simon Vouet; and superb 17C hunting scenes which have retained their beautiful colours.

⌐ **Summer treat**: An actor leads children aged 6-13 on a tour of the castle to find the key to an enigma.

Eating out

BUDGET

Les Grottes – *23 ter r. Pineau – 37190 Azay-le-Rideau – ☎ 02 47 45 21 04 – closed 2 Jan-7 Feb and Thu – 15.24/30.64€*. The slight coolness of this restaurant is natural, as this old house is hewn out of solid rock. The good, contemporary style cooking will warm you up. You can eat on the terrace in fine weather.

La Cave St-Antoine – *37130 Lignières-de-Touraine – 6km/3.75mi NW of Azay-le-Rideau on D 57 – ☎ 02 47 96 39 87 – www.la-cave-saint-antoine.fr – closed during Christmas holidays, Sun evening, Mon and Tue, except public holidays – 16/26€*. This restaurant in a former mushroom-growing cave hewn out of the limestone rock is an unexpected find. The decor is simple, the main feature being the natural stone which is enhanced by careful lighting. Traditional cooking.

MODERATE

Auberge du XIIe Siècle – *37190 Saché – 6.5km/4mi E of Azay-le Rideau on D 17 – ☎ 02 47 26 88 77 – closed 9-29 Jan, 5-12 Jun, 27 Aug-5 Sep, Sun evening and Mon – reservation required on Sun – 25.92/48.78€*. This old half-timbered inn in the village centre is famous for its cuisine. The exposed beams and stone walls, together with the fireplace, give a warm atmosphere to the two dining rooms. Terrace for eating outside.

Where to stay

BUDGET

Chambre d'hôte La Petite Loge – *15 rte de Tours – 37190 Azay-le-Rideau – ☎ 02 47 45 26 05 – lapetiteloge@free.fr – closed Dec-Feb – ⌐ – 5 rooms 39/43€*. Despite being near the road, this local-style house just outside Azay is a quiet place to stay. The simple rooms have a separate entrance, and a fully equipped kitchen is available for the guests to use. In summer you can enjoy the garden and barbecue.

MODERATE

Chambre d'hôte Le Clos Philippa – *10 r. de Pineau – 37190 Azay-le-Rideau – ☎ 02 47 45 26 49 – 5 rooms 42.69/68.60€*. An 18C house close by the castle gardens. The rooms are spacious and well decorated, and the main sitting room is a pleasant place to mingle with other guests. In fine weather, the generous breakfast is served in the garden. Regional wine tasting.

Son et lumière

Visitor-spectators are free to walk round this *son et lumière* display in the park and château at their own pace. The illuminated façades, the music seeming to drift out of the surrounding woodland and the play of lights upon the water combine to create a fairy-tale atmosphere of this royal estate and summon up the spirit of that powerful surge of creativity seen here during the Renaissance. *Allow 1hr for the walk.*

Gates open daily at 10.30pm in May, June and July, at 10pm in August and 9.30pm in September. Closes at 12.30am (midnight in September), last tickets sold at 11.45pm. 9.15€ (free for children under 12). ☎ 02 47 45 42 04 or 02 47 45 44 40.

Château d'Azay-le-Rideau

B. Kaufmann/MICHELIN

ADDITIONAL SIGHT

Église St-Symphorien – This curious 11C church, altered in the 12C and 16C, has a double gabled **façade★**. Embedded to the right are remains of the original 5C and 6C building: two rows of statuettes and diapered brickwork. To the left above the basket-handle arched porch, there is a Flamboyant window *(restored)* which dates from the 16C.

Musée Dufresne – Laffly pavement cleaner and sweeper

Musée Maurice-Dufresne, Azay-le-Rideau

Jouets d'autrefois, rêves d'aujourd'hui ⊘ – *31 rue Nationale*.
⬚ Interesting collection of model trains (JEP), lead soldiers and Meccano (for amateur engineers!).

EXCURSIONS

Marnay – *6km/4mi NW on D 57, then D 120*.

★Musée Maurice-Dufresne ⊘ ⬚ Set up in a former paper mill, this museum is largely devoted to locomotion. It displays all kinds of machines over an area of 7 000m²/8 400sq yd. The exhibits were painstakingly gathered over 30 years, restored and painted in their original bold colours. Presented with informative cards explaining how and where they were discovered, they take the visitor on an unexpected and unusual tour through the ages: American, German and French military vehicles from the First and Second World Wars, converted into farming machinery, gypsy caravans from the turn of the 20C, the first French machine used for making draught beer, a Blériot monoplane, identical to the one that crossed the Channel in July 1909... Each presentation enlightens us on the history of mankind: a small Bauche tractor found in an attic, entirely dismantled to avoid being requisitioned; a Hanomag mine extractor-excavator which helped to erect the Wall of the Atlantic; or one of the several hundred Fordson tanks that landed in Arromanches on 6 June 1944.

VALLÉE DE L'INDRE

26km/16mi round tour E of Azay-le-Rideau – about 2hr

Leave Azay going south by the bridge over the Indre which gives an attractive view of the château through the trees of the park.

Bear left immediately onto D 17 and then right onto D 57.

Villaines-les-Rochers – Wickerwork has always been the mainstay of the village. In the 19C Balzac wrote from the neighbouring Château de Saché: "We went to Villaines where the local baskets are made and bought some very attractive ones". The black and yellow water-willow and green rushes are cut in winter and steeped in water until May when they are stripped and woven. This craft was traditionally handed down from father to son who worked in troglodyte workshops (several such dwellings can be seen).
The **Société coopérative agricole de vannerie** ⊙ of Villaines, which was founded in 1849 by the parish priest, numbers about 80 families; several basketwork workshops have been set up where young craftsmen are trained. The workshops can be visited and the craftsmen's work is on sale.

Rejoin D 17 via D 217 which runs beside the River Villaine.

Saché – Saché won a degree of renown through its association with the novelist **Honoré de Balzac** who stayed there on several occasions. A more recent famous resident was the American sculptor, **Alexander Calder** (1898-1976), who created mobiles and stabiles in abstract forms; one of his mobiles is displayed in the main square of Saché which bears his name.

Château de Saché ⊙ – The 16C and 18C château is set in a pleasant park. In the last century it belonged to M de Margonne, a friend of **Balzac**. The writer loved to escape to Saché from the bustle of Paris and the dunning of his creditors (he came here every year from 1828 to 1838); in the peaceful surroundings of the château he wrote easily and the action of one of his novels, *Le Lys dans la vallée*, is set in the Indre Valley between Saché and Pont-de-Ruan. He found plenty of material locally for characters and places which appeared in his *Scènes de la vie de province*. The room where Balzac worked remains as it was in his lifetime. Other rooms in the château contain portraits, manuscripts, corrected proofs, first editions and various other mementoes of the great writer.

Pont-de-Ruan – A beautiful scene is revealed as the road crosses the Indre; two windmills, each on an island, set among trees. The site is described at length by Balzac in *Le Lys dans la vallée*.

Return to Azay on D 84.

The background information contained in the Art and architecture section of the Introduction will make your visits to local sights and monuments far more interesting and instructive.

Mobiles and stabiles

Having studied mechanical engineering, **Alexander Calder** turned to art, enrolling on a course in New York. He was a skilled draughtsman, able to capture a subject in a few swift strokes. Before long he had moved into making wire sculptures, initially of figurative, and later abstract subjects. From the early 1930s he began producing abstract constructions which moved, either by means of a motor or when touched. In 1932 Marcel Duchamp, a fellow member of the Abstraction-Création group in Paris in which Calder became involved at this time, coined the name "mobiles" for these, whereupon Arp came up with "stabiles" for Calder's non-moving sculptures. Calder is best-known for the mobiles he made of tin shapes which were usually suspended or balanced in such a way as to move in response to draughts of air or even their own weight. Calder referred to them as his four-dimensional drawings and made no secret of the fact that his abstract geometrical creations were influenced in part by Mondrian.
Calder's reputation rests to no small degree on the fact that he was one of the first artists to include movement in sculptural art. Although he might be regarded as a precursor of Kinetic art, Calder was far more concerned with exploring free movement, rather than the more controlled motion produced by Kinetic artists. Most of Calder's works are on show in the United States (such as the enormous motorised mobile *Red, Black and Blue* hanging at Dallas airport), but others are displayed at the Tate Modern Art Galley in London and the Pompidou Centre in Paris.

BAUGÉ

Population 3 663
Michelin map 317: I-3, 232 fold 21 or 4049 I3

Baugé, a peaceful town with noble dwellings, is the capital and market town of the surrounding region, a countryside of heaths, forests and vast clearings. There is a good view of the town with its ruined walls from rue Foulques-Nerra to the west.

Under the sign of the Cross of Anjou – Baugé, which was founded in 1000 by **Fulk Nerra**, became one of the favourite residences of Yolanda of Aragon, Queen of Sicily, and her son, King René, in the 15C. Yolanda, who was a faithful supporter of Charles VII and Joan of Arc, repulsed the English from Anjou at the battle of Le Vieil-Baugé (1421) in which Sir Guérin de Fontaines distinguished himself at the head of the Angevins and Scottish mercenaries.

René painted, wrote verses and hunted wild boar in its lair *(bauge)* in the nearby forests; he also prayed before the relic of the True Cross which was venerated at the abbey of La Boissière.

Once Louis XI had gained possession of Anjou, Baugé went into decline: the saying *"Je vous baille ma rente de Baugé"* (I'll give you my rent from Baugé) means "I can give you nothing".

BAUGÉ

Angers (Av. d')	Y	2
Beausse (R. M. de la)	Y	3
Clemenceau (R. G.)	Y	
Cygne (R. du)	Y	4
Dr-Thuau (R. du)	Z	5
Dr-Zamenhof (R. du)	Y	6
Église (R. de l')	Z	7
Gaulle (Av. du Gén.-de)	Z	8
Girouardière (R. de la)	Z	9
Le-Gouz-de-la-B. (Av.)	Z	10
Lofficial (R.)	Y	12
Melun (R. A. de)	Y	14
St-Nicolas	Z	16
Victor-Hugo (R.)	Z	17

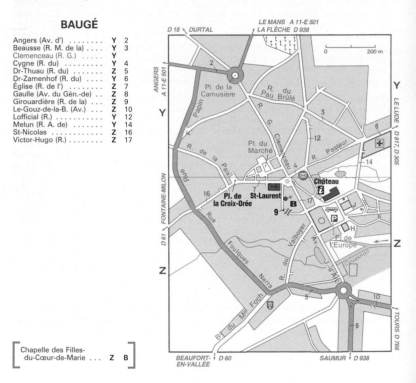

Chapelle des Filles-du-Cœur-de-Marie	Z	B

SIGHTS

Château ⊘ – This 15C building now serves as a tourist office and museum (collections of weapons, porcelain and old coins).

In 1455 King René himself supervised the building of the turrets, dormer windows and the oratory as well as the bartizan on the rear façade, where the master masons are portrayed.

An ogee-arched doorway gives access to the **spiral staircase** which terminates with a magnificent palm tree vault, decorated with the Anjou-Sicily coat of arms and other emblems: angels, tau crosses (T-shaped), symbols of the cross of Christ and stars which, in the Apocalypse, represent the souls of the blessed in eternity.

Chapelle des Filles-du-Cœur-de-Marie ⊘ – Formerly part of an 18C hospice, the chapel now houses a particularly valuable piece of treasure.

★★ **Cross of Anjou** – The cross with two transoms (the upper one carried the inscription), which was also known as the Cross of Jerusalem, was venerated as a piece of the Cross of Christ by the dukes of Anjou and in particular by King René. At the end of the 15C after the Battle of Nancy in which René II, Duke of Lorraine, a descendant of the dukes of Anjou, defeated Charles the Bold, the Lorraine troops adopted the Cross of Anjou as their own symbol in order to recognize one another in battle and the cross became known henceforward as the Cross of Lorraine. It is supposed to be made from a piece of the True Cross, brought back from the Holy Land after the crusade in 1241; it is a marvel of the goldsmith's craft, set with precious stones and fine pearls and was created at the end of the 14C for Louis, first Duke of Anjou, by his brother Charles V's Parisian goldsmith. It is unusual in that it has a figure of Christ on both sides *(see p 211)*.

Hôtels – The quiet streets of old Baugé are lined with noble mansions *(hôtels)* with high doorways: rue de l'Église, rue de la Girouardière and place de la Croix-Orée.

Église St-Laurent – Late-16C to early-17C church; the organ, dating from 1644, was restored in 1975.

The Cross of Anjou

THE BAUGEOIS REGION

82km/51mi – about 3hr

Leave Baugé on D 141 E along the Couasnon Valley.

Dolmen de la Pierre couverte – *Leave the car at the side of the road 3.5km/2mi from Baugé.* Some steps on the left lead to the dolmen standing in a forest clearing.

Return to the car and take D 141 towards Pontigné. There are fine views to the right of the Couasnon Valley and the forested massif of Chandelais.

Pontigné – The **church** dedicated to St Denis, whose effigy rises above the Romanesque portal, is crowned by an unusual twisting spiral bell-tower. Inside, Angevin vaulting covers the nave whereas the capitals of the transept present monstrous heads and water-lily leaf motifs and the charming central apse is supported by a complex network of radiating tori.

In the apsidal chapels 13C-14C **mural paintings★** depict Christ in Majesty and the Resurrection of Lazarus on one side and the Virgin Enthroned, surrounded by two angels bearing incense and scenes of Christ's childhood.

Follow the road behind the church and turn right onto D 766.

The road affords a fine view of the orchards in the valley.

Bear left and then turn right in the direction of Bocé.

★**Forêt de Chandelais** – This is a magnificent state-owned forest, covering 800ha/2 000 acres. The splendid fully grown oak and beech trees are replanted every 210 years.

Follow the forest road to the central crossroads before turning right in the direction of Bocé. Turn left on reaching D 58.

Mouliherne – Mouliherne stands on a rock on the north bank of the Riverolle, at the heart of the Baugé region. The quiet, peaceful atmosphere of the area makes it ideal for bicycle rides.

The **church** is all that remains of a fortress belonging to the counts of Anjou; built on a mound, it has a beautiful square 13C bell-tower with splayed windows and a twisting spire typical of the Baugé region.

The vaulting of the interior, which ends in oven-vaulted apses, demonstrates the evolution of the Angevin style. The chancel is covered with broken-barrel vaulting, whereas the south transept features an early example of quadripartite vaulting. A more refined version of this is found again above the north transept and the transept crossing, supported on beautiful Romanesque capitals decorated with water-lily leaves and fantastic animals. The wide Gothic vaulting above the nave, dating from the 12C-13C, is more refined still. The vaulting nearest the transept was redone in the late 15C. Behind the high altar in the chancel are 9C-10C Carolingian sarcophagi executed in conchitic stone with no ornamentation.

Twisted spires of the Baugé region

Their origin is a highly controversial subject: according to water diviners, the spires follow the path of underground water running beneath the churches... according to poets, they are like windmills facing the wind... sailors think they were built by inexperienced shipwrights... whereas joiners believe that the timber used for building them was still green and became warped with time.

Linières-Bouton – *5km/3mi E on D 62.* This is a quiet village just off the main road. The **church** has a beautiful **chancel** built in the Plantagenet style; there is a painting of the Annunciation (1677), a huge Baroque cross in gilded wood and a sculpture of the Holy Family, probably 17C.
Turn left onto D 767 then follow a road to the right which leads to Breil.

Breil – ◪ The path to Breil through Baugeois Woods makes a pleasant walk.
The semicircular apse and the tall stone spire of the **church** are characteristically Romanesque exterior features; note the fine Plantagenet vaulting in the chancel.

Parc et château de Lathan ☉ – Opposite the church stands a double formal park dating from the 17C. It features charming arbours, a long sweep of green lawn adorned with clipped yews and a double avenue of lime trees. There is a delightful view along the ornamental canal with an elegant 18C gazebo at the end of it. Note the Islet of Love (Île d'Amour) and the underground labyrinth.
Follow D 62 until you reach D 938 then turn right.

Cuon – Behind the church with the curious conical spire is a charming 15C manor house. Opposite the church an old inn still bears the inscription *"Au Soleil d'Or"* (The Golden Sun) where travellers on foot or on horseback could find lodging.
From Cuon take the road to Chartrené.
The wooded park on the left marks the site of the Château de la Grafinière.

Beyond Chartrené turn left onto D 60. After 4.5km/3mi follow D 211 to the right, crossing heaths and woodlands, to reach Fontaine-Guérin.

Fontaine-Guérin – The belfry of the heavily restored Romanesque **church** is crowned by a twisting spire. Inside, the 15C roof is decorated with 126 painted panels (15C-16C) with secular themes.
◉ The road D 211 towards St-Georges-du-Bois leads to an artificial lake with facilities for swimming, sailboarding and picnicking.
From St-Georges-du-Bois, follow D 59 to Jarzé.

Jarzé – The countryside around Jarzé-en-Baugeois is equally divided between pasture, crops and woodland. The castle was built in 1500, burnt down in 1794 and restored in the 19C.

Church – This was originally a collegiate church built in the Flamboyant Gothic style on the foundations of an 11C building. The seigneurial chapel *(right)* is covered with lierne and tierceron vaulting. The 16C stalls in the chancel are decorated with amusing carvings.
A niche in a pillar on the right of the chancel contains a late-15C statuette of St Cyr, clad in robe and bonnet, holding a pear in his hand; St Cyr, the son of St Juliette of Tarsus, was martyred at the tender age of three. The young child depicted here is more likely to be the son of Jean Bourré, reminding us that his father introduced the *bon-chrétien* pear variety into Anjou.
At the back of the apse are traces of a beautiful early-16C **mural** of the Entombment.

Chapelle Notre-Dame-de-Montplacé ☉ – *2.5km/1.2mi on D 82 towards La Flèche; take the first turning on the right.* The chapel, standing in splendid isolation on its bluff, can be seen from some way off. The neighbouring farm buildings add a touch of simplicity to its elegant appearance. There is a fine 17C west doorway dedicated to the Virgin Mary.

Around 1610 the previous chapel on this site was being used as a sheepfold although it still contained an ancient statue of the Virgin. One day when the shepherdess brought in her sheep the statue was glowing. Next day the whole neighbourhood came to see; it was not long before miraculous healings were being reported on this site and it became the object of ever-increasing religious fervour. Eventually, the generosity of pilgrims was such that the present chapel was built towards the end of the 17C. A tradition was established of making a pilgrimage to the Protector of the Baugeois region, and there is still a great annual Marian Festival held on 15 August.

Enter through the side door.

The three large altars are in the purest Baroque style. In the niche in the left-hand altar is the ancient statue venerated by the pilgrims. It is a *Pietà* carved in walnut showing traces of its original colouring. The walls are hung with numerous votive offerings.

Follow D 766 to Échemiré then turn right towards D 61.

Le Vieil-Baugé – The old village crowns a hilltop overlooking the Couasnon Valley.

Église St-Symphorien – Notice the slender twisted spire which leans as a result of the distortion of the internal wooden framework. The nave is partially 11C and the handsome **chancel**★ is 13C with Angevin vaulting.

The façade and the south transept are by the Angevin architect Jean de Lespine, and date back to the Renaissance days.

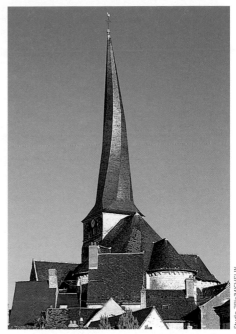

Studio 3Bis/MICHELIN

Le Vieil-Baugé – Twisted spire

BEAUGENCY★

Population 7 106
Michelin map 318: G-5, 238 fold 4 or 4045 A5

Beaugency recalls the Middle Ages. It is best to enter the town from the south, crossing the River Loire by the age-old multi-arched bridge *(attractive view)*. The oldest parts of the bridge date from the 14C but an earlier bridge used as a toll was already in existence in the 12C.

The two councils of Beaugency (12C) – Both councils were called to deal with the marital problems of Philippe I and Louis VII. While visiting **Fulk IV** in Tours, Philippe seduced his host's wife, the Countess Bertrade, and shortly afterwards repudiated Queen Bertha. The King thought that he would easily obtain the annulment of his marriage by raising a vague claim of consanguinity but Pope Urban II refused to comply with his request. The King persisted and was excommunicated so he was unable to join the First Crusade (1099). Eventually the excommunication was lifted by the Council of Beaugency in **1104** and four years later the King died at peace with the church. He was buried according to his wishes at St-Benoît-sur-Loire.
Far more important was the Council of **1152** which annulled the marriage of Louis VII and **Eleanor of Aquitaine**. The beautiful and seductive Eleanor, who was the daughter and heir of the Duke of Aquitaine, had married Louis in 1137. For 10 years the royal couple lived in perfect harmony, Eleanor exercising great influence over her husband. In 1147 they set out together on the Second Crusade but once in Palestine their relationship took a turn for the worse.
Louis grew jealous of Eleanor's partiality for Raymond of Poitiers. They had a quarrel and returned to France separately. Divorce became inevitable and on 20 March 1152 the Council of Beaugency officially dissolved the union of Louis and Eleanor for prohibited kinship: both descended from Robert the Pious.
Eleanor was not without suitors; almost immediately she married **Henry Plantagenet**, the future King of England, so that her dowry, a large part of south-west France, passed on to the English crown.
This event, one of the most important in the Middle Ages, was to lead to many centuries of Anglo-French rivalry.

Eating out

BUDGET

Le Relais du Château – *8 r. du Pont –* ☎ *02 38 44 55 10 – closed during Feb and Oct school holidays, Tue evening from Sep to Jun and Wed – 12.20/26.68€.* A good central place to stop for lunch while visiting this pretty medieval town. Tasty cooking and a good choice of reasonably priced menus.

La Chanterelle – *21 av. de la Loire – 41500 Muides-sur-Loire – 16km/10mi SW of Beaugency on N 152 towards Chambord –* ☎ *02 54 87 50 19 – closed 8-22 Jan, Sun evening, Tue lunchtime and Mon – 12.96/19.82€.* Just after the bridge across the Loire, this little restaurant has a terrace shaded with lime trees in front of it. The dining room is brightly coloured, and the menu changes with the seasons. Good local reputation.

Where to stay

BUDGET

Hôtel Sologne – *Pl. St-Firmin –* ☎ *02 38 44 50 27 – closed 25 Dec-8 Jan – 16 rooms 38.11/51.83€ –* ⊐ *6.10€.* You can't miss this local-style building with its pretty double flower-decked entrance steps, between St-Firmin Tower and the castle. The rooms are simply decorated. Reading room on the veranda.

Chambre d'hôte Le Clos de Pontpierre – *115 r. des Eaux-Bleues – 45190 Tavers – 2km/1mi SW of Beaugency towards Blois –* ☎ *02 38 44 56 85 – le.clos.de.pontpierre@wanadoo.fr –* ⊠ *– 4 rooms 40/50€ – evening meal 16€.* Don't worry about being near the road, as behind this old farmhouse is a lovely swimming pool set in a huge garden. The simple rooms overlook the country-side for maximum peace and quiet. In fine weather dinner is served in the shade of a 100-year-old horse chestnut tree.

A disputed town – Beaugency commanded one of the few bridges that spanned the Loire between Blois and Orléans before modern times. For this reason the town was often attacked. During the Hundred Years War (1337-1453) it fell into English hands four times: in 1356, 1412, 1421 and 1428. It was delivered by Joan of Arc in 1429. The town was then caught up in the turmoil of the Wars of Religion (1562-98). Catholic Leaguers and Protestants held it by turns.

BEAUGENCY

Abbaye (R. de l')	2
Bretonnerie (R. de la)	3
Change (R. de)	4
Châteaudun (R. de)	5
Cordonnerie (R. de la)	6
Dr-Hyvernaud (Pl.)	8
Dunois (Pl.)	9
Maille-d'or (R. de la)	10
Martroi (Pl. du)	
Pellieux (Passage)	12
Pont (R. du)	
Puits-de-l'Ange (R. du)	14
Sirène (R. de la)	15
Traîneau (R. du)	17
Trois-Marchands (R. des)	18

Maison des Templiers	...	F
Hôtel de ville	....	H

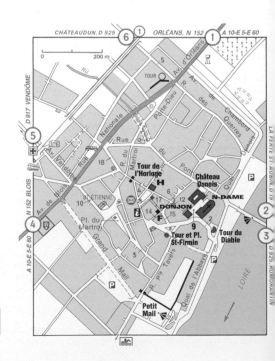

Hôtel de Ville, Beaugency – Detail of the façade

TOWN WALK

Tour de l'Horloge – This was originally the Exchange Tower. In the 12C it became one of the main gateways in the town wall.

Hôtel de ville ⊘ – The Council Chamber on the first floor is hung with eight beautiful pieces of **embroidery★**, executed with remarkable skill. Four of them, depicting the four continents known at that time, are 17C; the others (gathering mistletoe and pagan sacrifices) are 18C.

Follow rue du Pouët-de-Chaumont and rue du Pont. Walk beneath St George's archway.

Château Dunois – The medieval fortress was converted into a typical 15C residence by Dunois, Lord of Beaugency, one of Joan of Arc's followers. At the back, the painstakingly recreated medieval garden is a fitting backdrop to the restored façade.

★ **Musée Daniel Vannier** ⊘ – The rooms of Château Dunois now house a fine collection of furniture and costumes from the Orléans district. Traditional arts and crafts are on display as well as souvenirs of local celebrities: **Jacques Charles**, the physicist (1746-1823), **Eugène Sue**, the writer (1804-57). From the loft one can see the 15C timberwork of the roof.

★ **Église Notre-Dame** – The 12C Romanesque abbey church has been restored. In the chancel a series of twinned arches alternates with the windows and larger arches; the huge round columns in the nave with their massive carved capitals represent the calm strength of the purest Romanesque art, despite the false wooden vaulting in the nave which was put up after the fire in 1567.

Near the church are 18C buildings belonging to the old abbey.

Place Dunois, the square in front of the abbey church and the keep, and **place St-Firmin** form a picturesque combination. Lit by old lanterns, the two squares are equally attractive after dark.

★ **Donjon** – This keep is a fine example of 11C military architecture. At this period, keeps were rectangular and buttressed; later they became circular. The five-storey interior is in ruins.

Tour du Diable – At the bottom of the narrow rue de l'Abbaye stands the Devil's Tower which was part of the fortifications defending the bridgehead; in the Middle Ages the Loire flowed at its foot.

Tour St-Firmin – A street used to run under this tower, which is the sole remaining feature of a 15C church destroyed during the Revolution. You can hear the chimes of the Angelus bell at noon and 7pm.

Maison des Templiers – This Templars' house has fine Romanesque windows.

Petit Mail – This little tree-lined avenue, stretching beyond the Porte Travers, overlooks the River Loire. Fine view of the valley.

Château de BEAUREGARD★

Michelin map 318: F-6 or 238 fold 15

The château stands in a vast park overlooking the Beuvron Valley. The building has kept its Renaissance appearance despite 17C additions and the 20C roof extension.

TOUR ⊘ 45min

After going through the antechamber and the former kitchens on the ground floor, take the flight of steps up to the South Gallery (fine 16C and 17C furniture) which leads to the Cabinet des Grelots.

★ **Cabinet des Grelots** – This charming little room, the work of Scibec de Carpi who was also active at Fontainebleau and Anet, was fitted out towards the middle of the 16C for Jean du Thier, Secretary of State to Henri II and then Lord of Beauregard. His coat of arms, azure with three spherical gold bells *(grelots)*, decorates the coffered ceiling; the bells reappear as a decorative motif on the oak panelling which lines the room and conceals the cupboards where the château archives are kept.

★★ **Galerie des Illustres** – Above the ground floor arcade is a portrait gallery which was decorated for Paul Ardier, Lord of Beauregard at the beginning of the 17C and Treasurer of the Exchequer under Louis XIII. The long room has retained its splendid old

Portrait Gallery

Delft tiling depicting an army on the march: cavalry, artillery, infantry, musketry... The panelling and the ceiling were painted by Pierre Mosnier. The ceiling was covered in 1624 with a rich blue paint made from ground lapis lazuli, an extremely expensive mineral.

The most interesting feature of the gallery is the collection of over 327 historical portraits. They are arranged in bays, each devoted to a different reign making a complete succession of monarchs from the first Valois, Philippe VI, to Louis XIII. Round the portrait of each king are grouped the queen, the chief courtiers and important foreign contemporaries; thus, next to Louis XII are Isabella of Castille, her daughter Joan the Mad and Amerigo Vespucci, the Florentine explorer who gave his name to America. Each reign is complete with its dates and the king's emblem.

The works are gradually being restored to their original splendour.

Jardin des Portraits – Conceived by the landscape gardener Gilles Clément, this new garden laid out in the middle of a 70ha/173-acre park echoes the design of the portrait gallery: 12 alternating squares of plants and flowers separated by arbours, forming a small maze that reproduces the same colours as the paintings on display.

Forêt de BERCÉ

Michelin map 310: L-8, 232 folds 22 and 23 or 4072 G6

Bercé Forest is all that remains of the great Le Mans Forest which used to extend from the River Sarthe to the River Loir; its foliage covers a fine plateau (5 391ha/13 322 acres) cut across by small valleys and natural springs.

The magnificent trees – immensely tall sessile oaks (sometimes over 45m/148ft high) mixed with chestnuts and slim beeches – provide cover for a herd of deer.

In the 16C Bercé Forest was crown property; it is now carefully exploited for high quality oak. The trees, which are felled on a rotation of between 200 and 240 years, yield a pale yellow wood with a fine grain much in demand in cabinet-making (veneers) and for export throughout Europe.

Pines (maritime, Scots) and larches predominate on the poorer soil to the west of the forest.

TOUR ⊘

Several waymarked mountain-bike itineraries of varying lengths (6-41km/3.7-25mi) crisscross the forest; the overall difference in height never exceeds 100m/328ft, which makes these itineraries ideal for beginners. Free maps are available on request. ☎ *02 43 39 95 00.*

The trees which are destined to be felled are marked on the trunk; those with a number (oaks and beeches) are to be retained.

Fontaine de la Coudre
– The spring, which is the source of the River Dinan, a tributary of the Loir, flows slowly under the tall oaks known as the Futaie des Forges.

🔲 A path is marked with instructive notices for children explaining the uses of the forest.

★ **Sources de l'Hermitière** – A deep valley thick with towering oaks and beeches hides the pure waters of these springs.

★ **Futaie des Clos** – This is the finest stand of oaks in the forest. Two violent storms in 1967 caused great gaps among the trees. While some of the giant oaks (300 to 350 years old) are very decrepit, others are splendid specimens.

Park under the trees in the car park.

🚶 A path leads to the Boppe oak, or rather to its stump, protected by a roof, since the ancient tree was struck by lightning in 1934 at the venerable age of 262; its circumference was 4.77m/15ft 9in at 1.3m/4ft from the ground. Its neighbour, Roulleau de la Roussière, is still flourishing after more than 350 years; it has grown to a height of over 43m/141ft.

BLOIS★★

Conurbation 65 989
Michelin map 318: E-6 or 238 fold 3

Blois is situated on the north bank of the Loire, half way between Orléans and Tours. The town is built on the hillside overlooking the river; many of the medieval streets still remain, steep and twisting and occasionally linked by flights of steps. The terracing of the houses produces the characteristic tricoloured harmony of Blois, the white façades of its buildings contrasting with their blue-slate roofs and red-brick chimneys.

The magnificent royal castle where many an intrigue was plotted and a famous crime perpetrated, illustrates a Flamboyant Gothic style influenced by the fantasy and inventiveness of the Italian Renaissance (the splendid main staircase) and later by the more rigorous order of the Classical style.

A ROYAL CITY

From the counts of Blois to the dukes of Orléans – In the Middle Ages the counts of Blois were powerful lords with two estates: Champagne and the region of Blois and Chartres.

One of the counts of Blois married the daughter of William the Conqueror and their son, Stephen, became King of England in 1135. At this period the House of Blois reached its peak under Thibaud IV. After his death in 1152, attention was concentrated on Champagne, and the Loire area was somewhat abandoned together with England, where the Plantagenets took over in 1154.

In 1392 the last count, Guy de Châtillon, sold the county to Louis, Duke of Orléans and brother of Charles VI. Thereafter the court of Orléans was held at Blois. Fifteen years later Louis d'Orléans was assassinated in Paris on the orders of the Duke of Burgundy, John the Fearless. His widow, Valentina Visconti, retired to Blois where she expressed her disillusion by carving on the walls: *"Rien ne m'est plus, plus ne m'est rien"* ("Nothing means anything to me any more"); she died inconsolable the following year.

Seated on the north bank of the Loire, it presents a bright, clean face to the sun, and has that aspect of cheerful leisure which belongs to all white towns that reflect themselves in shining waters. It is the waterfront only of Blois, however, that exhibits this fresh complexion; the interior is of a proper brownness, as befits a signally historic city.

Henry James – *A Little Tour in France*

An aristocratic poet: Charles d'Orléans (1391-1465) — Charles, the eldest son of Louis d'Orléans, inherited the castle and spent some of his youth there. At the age of 15 he married the daughter of Charles VI, but she died in childbirth. At 20 he married again but soon departed to fight the English. He proved a poor general at the Battle of Agincourt where he was wounded and taken prisoner but his poetic gift helped him to survive 25 years of captivity in England. He returned to France in 1440 and being once more a widower he married, at the age of 50, Marie de Clèves, who was then 14. The Château de Blois was his favourite residence. He demolished part of the grim fortress and built a far more comfortable mansion. Charles formed a little court of artists and men of letters. Great joy was granted to him in old age; at 71 he had a son and heir, the future Louis XII. He died at Amboise in 1465.

The golden age of the Renaissance — Louis XII was born at Blois in 1462 and succeeded Charles VIII in 1498. Blois became the royal residence rather than Amboise. The King and his wife, **Anne of Brittany**, liked Blois and embarked on considerable improvements: the construction of a new wing and the laying out of huge terraced gardens, designed by the Italian gardener Pacello, who also worked at Amboise. These gardens covered the modern place Victor-Hugo and extended towards the current railway station.

François I spent his time between Amboise and Blois. He commissioned the architect Jacques Sourdeau, to build a new wing at Blois; it is the most beautiful part of the château and bears the King's name.

The assassination of the Duke of Guise (1588) — The historical interest of the château reached its peak under **Henri III**. The States-General twice met at Blois. The first time was in 1576, when there was a request to suppress the Protestant Church. In 1588 **Henri de Guise**, the Lieutenant-General of the kingdom and all-powerful head of the League in Paris, supported by the King of Spain, forced Henri III to call a second meeting of the States-General, which was then the equivalent of Parliament. Five hundred deputies, nearly all supporters of Guise, attended. Guise expected them to depose the King. The latter, feeling himself to be on the brink of the abyss, could think of no other means than murder to get rid of his rival.

The date is 23 December 1588, around 8 o'clock in the morning. Of the 45 impoverished noblemen who are Henri III's men of action, 20 have been chosen to deal with the Duke. Eight are waiting in the Chambre du Roi (King's Chamber), with daggers hidden under their cloaks, sitting on chests and seeming innocently to be swapping yarns. The 12 others, armed with swords, are in the Cabinet Vieux (Old Cabinet). Two priests are in the oratory of the Cabinet Neuf (New Cabinet), where the king is making them pray for the success of his enterprise.

The Duke of Guise is in the Salle du Conseil (Council Chamber) with various dignitaries. He has been up since 6 o'clock, after spending the night with one of the girls from Catherine de' Medici's Flying Squad, and is cold and hungry. First he warms himself at the fire and eats a couple of the prunes in his comfit box. Then the Council begins. Henri III's secretary tells Guise that the King would like to see him in the Old Cabinet.

To reach this room Guise has to go through the king's chamber as, only two days previously, the door between the council chamber and the old cabinet had been walled up. The Duke enters the king's chamber and is greeted by the men there as if nothing were amiss. He turns left towards the old cabinet but, as he opens the door leading into the corridor outside it, he sees men waiting for him with swords drawn in the narrow passage. He tries to retreat but is stopped by eight men, who are now clearly assassins, in the king's chamber. They fall upon their victim, seizing him firmly by his arms and legs and trapping his sword in his cloak.

The Duke, who is an exceptionally strong man, manages to strike down four of his assailants and wound a fifth with his comfit box. He gives his murderers a run for their money for the entire length of the king's chamber, but with the odds so heavily stacked against him his valiant efforts are in vain and he finally collapses, riddled with stab wounds, by the king's bed, gasping, *"Miserere mei Deus"*. Henri III emerges from behind the wall hanging where he has been hiding and ventures up to the corpse of his rival. According to some accounts, he slapped his face, marvelling at the dead man's size and commenting that he seemed almost bigger now than he did when alive. The dead man's pockets are found to contain a letter with the observation, "It costs 700 000 *livres* every month to sustain a civil war in France".

Afterwards, Henri III is reported to have gone down to his mother, Catherine de' Medici, and told her joyfully, "My comrade is no more, the King of Paris is dead!". His conscience apparently clear, Henri goes to hear Mass in the chapel of St-Calais as an act of thanksgiving.

The next day, the Duke of Guise's brother, the Cardinal de Lorraine, imprisoned immediately after the murder, was also assassinated. His body was put with Guise's somewhere in the château — speculation surrounds the precise location of the room where the bodies were kept. Finally, the bodies were burned and the ashes thrown into the Loire. The Queen Mother failed to survive these dramatic events and she passed away about 12 days later. Eight months later Henri III himself succumbed to the dagger of Jacques Clément.

Eating out

BUDGET

Le Bistrot du Cuisinier – *20 quai Villebois-Mareuil – ☎ 02 54 78 06 70 – bistrot.du.cuisinier@wanadoo.fr – closed 22 Dec-4 Jan – 16.01/22.11€.* You'll find a real bistro atmosphere here. The decor is simple, and from the front dining room there is a splendid view of Blois and the Loire. The cordial and inventive owner has established monthly themes for his culinary creations, and encourages you to try different wines by the glass. The children's menu will tempt the fussiest eaters to try something new and special.

MODERATE

Au Bouchon Lyonnais – *25 r. des Violettes – ☎ 02 54 74 12 87 – closed Jan, Sun and Mon except public holidays – reservation recommended – 17.99€ lunch, 25.92€.* Located just at the bottom of the hill crowned by the château, this restaurant is a favourite with residents of Blois, who enjoy the rustic decor with exposed beams and stone walls. The menu features regional fare.

Au Rendez-vous des Pêcheurs – *27 r. Foix – ☎ 02 54 74 67 48 – closed 2-14 Jan, 29 Jul-20 Aug, Mon lunchtime and Sun – reservation recommended – 22.87€.* A provincial-style bistro in the old part of Blois. Stained-glass windows filter the light in the quiet dining room. Fish features prominently among the fresh market produce on the menu.

Where to stay

MODERATE

Hôtel Anne de Bretagne – *31 av. J.-Laigret – ☎ 02 54 78 05 38 – closed 9 Jan-6 Feb – 28 rooms 44.97/57.93€ – ☕ 5.79€.* This small family hotel is near the castle and the terraced Jardin du Roi. The rooms are decorated in attractive colours and well soundproofed; those on the third floor are under the sloping roof.

Chambre d'hôte La Villa Médicis – *1 r. St-Denis, Macé – 41000 St-Denis-sur-Loire – 4km/2.5mi NE of Blois on N 152 towards Orléans – ☎ 02 54 74 46 38 – reservation required in winter – 6 rooms 53.36/94.52€ – evening meal 30.49€.* Marie de Medici came to take the waters at the springs in the park in which this 19C villa was built, as a hotel for spa patrons at the time. Enjoy a peaceful stay in one of the rooms or the suite. Breakfast is served in the park in summer.

Chambre d'hôte Domaine des Bidaudières – *R. du Peu-Morier – 37210 Vouvray – 3km/1.8mi W of Vouvray towards Château-Renault – ☎ 02 47 52 66 85 – www.bandb-loire-valley.com – ⊄ – 6 rooms 60.98/103.67€.* The rooms in this 18C castle have plenty of character, with four-poster beds, carefully chosen fabrics, and views of the park, lake or vineyards surrounding the property. The breakfast nook is carved into the cliff side, or you may choose to sit under the veranda.

Chambre d'hôte Château de Nazelles – *16 r. Tue-la-Soif (behind the post office) – 37530 Nazelles-Négron – 3km/1.8mi N of Négron on D 5 – ☎ 02 47 30 53 79 – 3 rooms 71.65/88.42€ – evening meal 23€.* It would be hard to remain indifferent to the charms of this 16C property, built on a hillside and designed by Thomas Boyer, architect of the Château de Chenonceau. The rooms display a successful mix of ancient and modern styles. There is a swimming pool hewn out of natural rock and a terraced garden.

LUXURY

Chambre d'hôte Château de Montgouverne – *37210 Rochecorbon – ☎ 02 47 52 84 59 – 6 rooms 106.71/167.43€.* Set among the vineyards of Vouvray, this 18C castle with its pretty pepper-pot towers is an incentive to prolong your stay. Each room and suite has its own individual style. French-style garden for pleasant strolls.

On the town

Le Boulot – *9 r. Henri-Drussy – ☎ 02 54 74 20 20 – Mon-Sat noon-2pm and from 6pm.* The moustachioed owner opened his first pizzeria in the small town of Blois over 20 years ago. He is eager to share his knowledge about wine, and offers a different choice of wines by the glass every week, to be enjoyed with the dish of the day or a snack.

Rond-point de la Résistance – There are three cafés near this roundabout by the river. It is more pleasant to go late in the evening, to avoid the car exhaust fumes: L'Époque, Le Maryland and Le Colonial Café. Nearby is a tobacconists and newsagents which stays open late.

Rue Foulerie – In this narrow street on the edge of the old part of town you will find a disco, a piano bar and a couple of pubs.

Shopping

Rue du Commerce – Rue du Commerce and the adjacent streets in this pleasant pedestrian-only district (rue du Rebrousse-Pénil, rue St-Martin) offer all kinds of shopping opportunities.

Sit back and relax

La Salsa – *4 ruelle Ronceraie* – ☎ *02 54 78 28 67 – sekou-kassogué@wanadoo.fr – Tue-Sun 8pm-2am.* A cross between an old-fashioned youth club and Savoyard chalet-restaurant in appearance, this bar is rather out of the ordinary, perhaps because it started out as a cooperative and the present owner, who took over when the coop failed, still has a certain contempt for commerce. The atmosphere is very easy-going, to the beat of salsa and African music.

Le Bistrot – *12 r. Henry-Drussy* – ☎ *02 54 78 47 74 – daily 8am-2pm except Sun noon-2am.* The attractive, slightly old-fashioned decor of this bistro provides a contrast to the crowd of smart young regulars, who are quite happy to listen to accordion music or the Sex Pistols, as the mood strikes. "Everyone knows each other, but I don't know everyone" admits the owner, whose long terrace set among the acacias in place Ave-Maria is much in demand on fine days.

Son et lumière

Alain Decaux of the Académie Française wrote the texts that retrace the history of Blois – "a thousand years' history spanning 10 centuries of splendour" – and they are read by famous French actors including Michael Lonsdale, Fabrice Luchini, Robert Hossein, Pierre Arditi and Henri Virlojeux. Enormous projectors, combining photographs with special lighting effects, and the very latest in sound transmission systems make for a lively, entertaining and visually stimulating show, despite there being no live actors participating in the show. *Performances (45min) every evening between 9.30pm and 10.30pm (sunset) from late April to mid-September; Ascension-Whitsun: weekend only. 9.15€ (children: 4.57€).* ☎ *02 54 78 72 76.*

A conspirator: Gaston d'Orléans (17C) – In 1617 **Marie de Medici** was banished to Blois by her son, Louis XIII. A little court in exile grew up in the château; the leading figure was **Richelieu**, the Queen Mother's confidant and cardinal-to-be, but he became involved in intrigues and decided to flee to Luçon hoping for a more favourable occasion to pursue his ambition.

On 22 February 1619 the Queen Mother escaped; despite her embonpoint, she succeeded in climbing down a rope ladder into the moat at night. After such a feat she and her son were reconciled... through the mediation of Richelieu!

In 1626 Louis XIII gave the country of Blois and the duchies of Orléans and Chartres to his brother, **Gaston d'Orléans**, who was scheming against Cardinal de Richelieu. However, Gaston soon grew bored with his new estates and turned to conspiracy again, but his inconstancy prevented him from carrying any project to its conclusion: one day he would talk of killing Richelieu, the next day he would be reconciled with him. He went into exile, returned to France, started a new conspiracy and then left again. He was reconciled with the King in 1634 and was at last able to devote himself to his residence in Blois for which he had grandiose schemes. He sent for Mansart and commissioned a vast new building which would have entailed the destruction of the old château. Between 1635 and 1638 a new range of buildings was erected but then work had to stop owing to lack of funds. The birth of the Dauphin released Richelieu from the need to humour the King's brother so the latter returned to his old ways. In 1642 he was a party to the plot hatched by the Duc de Bouillon and the Marquis de Cinq-Mars. He escaped conviction but was deprived of his claim to the throne. From 1650 to 1653 he played an active part in the Fronde against Mazarin and was banished to his estates; after this further failure he finally settled down. He lived in the François-I wing, embellishing the gardens, until his death in 1660.

★★★CHÂTEAU ⊙ *2hr*

Place du Château – This vast esplanade was once the farmyard of the château. Slightly below, the terraced gardens offer a wide view of the bridge spanning the Loire beyond the rooftops and place Louis XII at the foot of the retaining wall; to the right are the spires of the church of St-Nicolas and to the left the cathedral with its Renaissance tower.

Successive building stages –
– Medieval period: Salle des États-Généraux (13C); Tour du Foix (13C)
– Transition period (Gothic-Renaissance): Galerie Charles d'Orléans (late 15C, early 16C); Chapelle St-Calais (1498-1508); Louis-XII wing (1498-1501)
– Renaissance period: François-I wing, façade (1515-24)
– Classical period: Gaston-d'Orléans wing

The **façade** of the château – "one of the most beautiful and elaborate of all the old royal residences in this part of France" (Henry James) – on the esplanade has two main parts: the pointed gable of the Salle des États-Généraux

(Chamber of the States-General), relic of the former feudal castle (13C), on the right and then the pretty building of brick and stone erected by Louis XII. In keeping with the endearing whimsicality which characterizes buildings from the Middle Ages, this has a random, asymmetrical arrangement of window openings. Two windows on the first floor have balconies. That on the left opened from Louis XII's bedroom. His Minister, the Cardinal d'Amboise, lived in a neighbouring mansion, which was destroyed in June 1940 and has since been rebuilt with only moderate success. When the King and the Cardinal took the air on their balconies they were able to exchange pleasantries.

The great Flamboyant **gateway** is surmounted by an alcove containing an equestrian statue of Louis XII, a modern copy (made in 1857 by Seurre) of the original. The window consoles are adorned with spirited carvings. The coarse humour of the period is sometimes displayed with great candour (first and fourth windows to the left of the gateway).

The inner courtyard – Cross the courtyard to reach the delightful terrace (good **view** of the church of St-Nicolas and the Loire) on which stands the 13C **Tour du Foix**, a tower which formed part of the medieval fortified wall.

Chapelle St-Calais – Of the King's private chapel, which was rebuilt by Louis XII, only the Gothic chancel remains. Mansart demolished the nave when he built the Gaston-d'Orléans wing. The modern stained-glass windows depicting the life of St Calais are by Max Ingrand.

Galerie Charles-d'Orléans – Although it is named after Charles d'Orléans, this gallery probably dates from the Louis XII period. Until alterations were made in the 19C the gallery was twice its present length and connected the two wings at either end of the courtyard. Note the unusual basket-handle arches.

Aile Louis-XII – The corridor or gallery serving the various rooms in the wing marks a step forward in the quest for greater comfort and convenience. Originally rooms opened into one another. At each end of the wing a spiral staircase gave access to the different floors. The decoration is richer and Italianate panels of arabesques adorn the pillars.

Aile François-I – The building extends between the 17C Gaston-d'Orléans wing and the 13C Salle des États-Généraux (Chamber of the States-General). Only 14 years passed between work finishing on the Louis-XII wing and beginning on the François-I wing, but in this time an important milestone had been passed, heralding the triumphant arrival of the Italian decorative style.

French originality, however, persisted in the general composition. The windows were made to echo the internal arrangement of the rooms, without regard for symmetry; they could be close together in some places and far apart in others; their mullions might be double or single; and pilasters might flank the window openings or occupy the middle of the opening. A magnificent **staircase** *(see illustration p 78)* was added to the façade. Since Mansart demolished part of the wing to make room for the Gaston d'Orléans buildings, this staircase is no longer in the centre of the façade. It climbs spirally in an octagonal well, three faces of which are recessed into the building. This masterpiece of architecture and sculpture was evidently designed for lavish receptions. The well is open between the buttresses and forms a series of balconies from which members of the court could observe the arrival of prominent guests.

Aile Gaston-d'Orléans – This wing designed by François Mansart between 1635 and 1638 in the Classical style is in sharp contrast to the rest of the building.

Château de Blois – François-I staircase

Royal apartments (Aile François-I) and museums – Inside the Gaston-d'Orléans wing, a projecting gallery runs round the base of the cupola crowning the grand staircase, sumptuously decorated on all but the lower level with trophies, garlands and masks. Many plans displayed on the ground floor illustrate the various alterations of the château.

Musée archéologique ⊙ – *Ground floor of the François-I wing to the left of the grand staircase.* The Archaeological Museum presents artefacts resulting from digs carried out in the Loir-et-Cher *département*, laid out in the rooms which served as kitchen quarters under François I. A great many exhibits were uncovered on the medieval site of the castle, a small hillock. Note the outstanding artefacts dating back to Carolingian times.

Apartments in the François-I wing – The François-I staircase leads up to the Royal Apartments on the first floor where a succession of rooms containing splendid fireplaces, tapestries, busts, portraits and furniture can be seen. The interior decoration was restored by Duban in the 19C. The smoke from the open fireplaces, candles and torches used during the years the château served as a royal residence would have blackened the decor in no time.

The most interesting room on the **first floor** is that of Catherine de' Medici. It still has its 237 carved wood panels concealing secret cupboards which may have been used to hide poisons, jewels or State papers, or may simply have been made to cater for the then prevalent taste for having wall cupboards in Italian-style rooms. They were opened by pressing a pedal concealed in the skirting board.

The **second floor** was the scene of the **murder of the Duke of Guise**. The rooms have been altered and the old cabinet demolished to make way for the Gaston-d'Orléans wing. It is therefore rather difficult to follow the phases of the assassination.

Take the grand staircase down to the first floor and cross the guard-room.

Salle des États-Généraux – This is the oldest (13C) part of the château, the feudal hall of the old castle of the counts of Blois. From 1576 to 1588 the States-General, the French Parliament, used to convene in this hall. The twin barrel vaults are supported by a central row of columns.

★ **Musée des Beaux-Arts** ⊙ – *First floor in the Louis-XII wing.* The main interest of this Fine Arts Museum lies in the 16C and 17C paintings and portraits. The **portrait gallery** contains paintings from the Château de St-Germain-Beaupré (Creuse *département*) and Château de Beauregard. In the gallery of 17C and 18C works, there is an outstanding collection of 50 terracotta **medallions** by Jean-Baptiste Nini. The Guise Gallery houses several works on the theme of the events of 1588, such as *Meeting of the Duke of Guise and Henri III* by Pierre-Charles Comte. Finally, the wrought-iron and locksmithing gallery contains the Frank collection in which one of the star exhibits is the remarkable fire-pan destined for the Count of Chambord, executed by local ironsmith Louis Delcros.

★ OLD BLOIS *2hr*

Every street corner of this fascinating town has something to offer the dedicated visitor prepared to stroll through the old districts.

★ **Pavillon Anne-de-Bretagne** – This graceful little building of stone and brick, crowned by a high slate roof, once the belvedere of the Royal Gardens, is now the tourist centre. Note the cable mouldings which emphasize the corners, and the open-work sculptured stone balustrade with the initials of Louis XII and Anne of Brittany, his wife. On the right along avenue Jean-Laigret, the pavilion extends into a long half-timbered wing, also built under Louis XII, which was later used as an *orangery (now a restaurant)*. Walk along place Victor-Hugo, which is lined on the north by the façade of the 17C church of **St-Vincent** built in the style known as Jesuit, and on the south by the beautiful **Façade des Loges** of the château.

Jardin des simples et des fleurs royales – This small terraced garden, is all that remains of the vast château gardens. Standing near the balustrade one has an excellent **view**★ to the left over the Pavillon Anne-de-Bretagne, the church of St-Vincent and place Victor-Hugo; on the right rises the Façade des Loges (François-I wing of the château) and the end pavilion of the Gaston-d'Orléans wing. Down below, a modern garden (1992) designed by Gilles Clément is a delightful tribute to Renaissance gardens.

Façade des Loges – The interior part of François I's initial construction backed on to the medieval rampart wall and had no outside view. This troubled the King and so he decided to add a second building with as many openings as possible against the outside of the ramparts. Since from here it is a sheer drop into the gully, the new building had to be shored up on a stone substructure.

Following the king's wish to copy the most recent Roman buildings, the architect drew his inspiration from the Vatican palace; however, the loggias do not communicate and the addition of bartizans adds a somewhat medieval note to the overall effect. The top storey is underlined by fine gargoyles.

Returning to place des Lices, one can take in at a glance the majestic **Gaston-d'Orléans façade** which overlooks the moat.

Façade des Loges

★Église St-Nicolas – A beautiful building from the 12C and 13C, of great unity, the church was once part of the Benedictine abbey of St-Laumer whose sober monastic buildings, in Classical style, extend as far as the Loire. The layout is characteristically Benedictine, with a large chancel surrounded by an ambulatory and radiating chapels. Note the lovely historiated capitals in the chancel and the unusual 15C altarpiece dedicated to St Mary of Egypt to the left.

Couvent des Jacobins – *Rue Anne-de-Bretagne.* As early back as the 15C-16C, these convent buildings already housed the **Musée d'Art religieux** ☉ devoted to religious art collections on the first floor and, on the second floor, beneath a fine timber roof shaped as an inverted hull, the **Muséum d'Histoire naturelle** ☉, where stuffed and mounted animals vividly portray the wildlife of the region.
There is a fine view of the Jacques-Gabriel bridge from the banks of the Loire.

Walk to square Augustin-Thierry via rue St-Lubin (note the Fontaine Louis XII, a copy of the Flamboyant-Gothic fountain erected by King Louis XII and now kept in the castle) and rue de la Voûte-du-Château.

Hôtel de la Chancellerie – This late-16C mansion is one of the largest in Blois. Behind the 17C carriage entrance note the superb staircase with straight banisters at the back of the courtyard.

Hôtel d'Alluye ☉ – *At no 8 rue St-Honoré.* This fine private mansion was built in 1508 for **Florimond Robertet**, treasurer successively to Charles VIII, Louis XII and François I. When accompanying Charles VIII on his expedition to Naples, the financier took a liking to Italian art. Behind the façade of the mansion with its delicate Gothic Renaissance sculptures, a large **courtyard** opens up with pure Renaissance Italianate **galleries★**. The building now houses the head office of a group of insurance companies founded in 1820.

Tour Beauvoir ☉ – This square keep (11C) belonged to a separate fief from the château and was later incorporated into the town's fortifications. The cells which can be visited today were used until 1945.
From the terrace there is a fine **view★** of Blois and the surrounding area.
Old half-timbered façades line rue Beauvoir (nos 3, 15 and 21), surrounding a 15C stone house (no 19).

Escaliers Denis-Papin – At the top of this flight of steps a sweeping panorama suddenly opens up towards the south. Dominating the view is the statue of **Denis Papin**, recognized as the father of the steam machine.

Denis Papin, the unfortunate inventor

Born in Chitenay *(12km/8mi S of Blois)* in 1647, Papin was forced into exile by the Revocation of the Edict of Nantes and published his memorandum on "How to soften bones and cook meat quickly and cheaply" in England; his «digester» known as Papin's cooking pot, thus became the forerunner of today's pressure cooker. In Germany, under the patronage of the Landgrave of Hesse, Papin discovered a new way of raising water by the use of fire; in 1706 in Kassel he carried out public tests demonstrating the motive power of steam. After the death of his patron, he died in poverty in 1714.

BLOIS

Abbé-Grégoire
  (Quai H. de l') . . . . Z 2
Anne-de-Bretagne (R.) . . . Z 3
Beauvoir (R.) . . . . Y 6
Bourg-St-Jean (R. du) . . . . Y 10
Chemonton (R.) . . . . Y 16
Clouseau (Mail) . . . . Y 17
Commerce (R. du) . . . . Z
Cordeliers (R. des) . . . . . . Y 18
Fontaine des Élus (R.) . . . . Z 22
Fossés-du-Château (R. des) Z 23
Jeanne-d'Arc (R.) . . . . Z 30
Laigret (Av. J.) . . . . Z 32
Lices (Pl. des) . . . . Z 34
Lion-Ferré (R. du) . . . . Z 35
Louis-XII (Pl.) . . . . Z 38

Maunoury (Av. du Mar.) . . Y 39
Monsabre (R. du Père) . . . Z 41
Orfèvres (R. des) . . . . Z 43
Papegaults (R. des) . . . . . Y 44
Papin (Escaliers Denis) . . Y 45
Papin (R. Denis) . . . . Z
Pierre-de-Blois (R.) . . . . . Z 46
Poids-du-Roi (R. du) . . . . . Z 47
Porte-Côté (R.) . . . . Z 48
Président Wilson (Av.) . . . . Z 51
Puits-Châtel (R. des) . . . . . Y 52
Remparts (R. des) . . . . Z 53
Résistance (Rd-Pt de la) . . Z 55
St-Honoré (R.) . . . . YZ 59
St-Jean (Q.) . . . . Y 60
St-Louis (Pl.) . . . . Y 62
St-Martin (R.) . . . . Z 63
Trois-Marchands (R. des) . Z 67

Trouessard (R.) . . . . Y 69
Vauvert (R.) . . . . Z 70
Villebois-Mareuil (Q.) . . . . Z 75

Fontaine Louis-XII . . . . Z B
Hôtel d'Alluye . . . . YZ E
Hôtel
  de la Chancellerie . . . Z K
Hôtel de ville . . . . Y H
Jardin des simples
  et des fleurs royales . . Z L
Maison Denis-Papin . . . Y N
Maison des Acrobates . . Y R
Musée de l'Objet . . . . . Y M¹
Pavillon
  Anne de Bretagne . . . . Z S

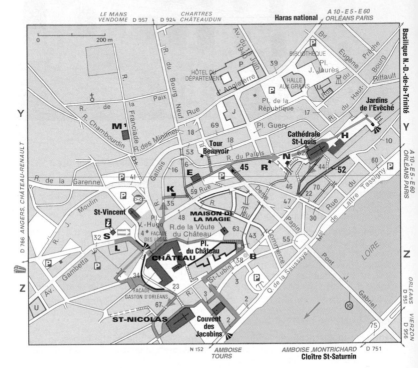

Maison des Acrobates – *At no 3 place St-Louis.* This is a typical medieval house, with its half-timbered façade, its two corbelled storeys, its posts carved with acrobats, jugglers... and its foliage ornamentation.

Cathédrale St-Louis – Rebuilt in the 16C and flanked by a high Renaissance tower with a lantern, the cathedral was almost entirely destroyed in 1678 by a hurricane. Thanks to the intervention of Colbert, whose wife was a native of Blois, it was rapidly rebuilt in the Gothic style. The simplicity of the contemporary stained-glass windows in the nave and side aisles offers a striking contrast to the rich decoration of those in the chancel dating from 1860. The base of the tower (12C) is part of the original collegiate church built by St Solenne, Bishop of Chartres in the 5C, who taught Clovis his catechism and assisted at his baptism by St Rémy. The **Crypte St-Solenne** *(entrance to the right of the chancel)* dates from the 10C and was enlarged in the 11C to accommodate the crowds of pilgrims; it was the largest of its day and contained the tomb of St Comblée.

Hôtel de ville and Jardins de l'Évêché – *Access through the gate to the left of the cathedral.* Situated behind the cathedral, the town hall lies in the former bishop's palace, built at the beginning of the 18C by Jacques-Jules Gabriel, father of the architect of place de la Concorde in Paris.
Further towards the east, the gardens of the bishop's palace form a terrace overlooking the Loire, with a lovely **view★** *(stand near the statue of Joan of Arc)* over the river, its wooded slopes and the roofs of the town; to the south is the pinnacle of the church of St-Saturnin and to the right on the north bank, the pure spires of the church of St-Nicolas. Lovely view also of the cathedral chevet.

Maison Denis-Papin – Also called Hôtel de Villebresme, this lovely Gothic house at the top of rue Pierre-de-Blois spans the road with a timber-framed footbridge. At the bottom of rue Pierre-de-Blois on the left a fine Renaissance door stands out bearing the Latin inscription *Usu Vetera Nova* which can be translated "through use, the new becomes old" or vice versa "the old becomes new again".

The King of Magicians: Robert-Houdin (1805-71)

The son of a local watchmaker, Jean-Eugène Robert-Houdin was not only a gifted illusionist and an exceptional magician, he was also a remarkable inventor with a sound scientific background. Along with his conjuring tricks and automata, he invented the filament bulb 15 years before Edison, as well as the electricity meter and many other curious devices (including several related to ophthalmology).

In his house Le Prieuré, which he would jokingly call the Abbey of Tricks, he was known to entertain friends and neighbours with a host of ingenious inventions. The magician would give free rein to his imagination to improve home automation long before the term was coined: doors would swing open before visitors, bells would start chiming as people walked past, a gardener-robot would rake up dead leaves in the garden, a mechanical, electrically operated hermit would read passages of the Bible, a system of remote control levers would automatically feed oats to horses in the stables... a series of technical achievements which in those days seemed to verge on the extraordinary.

Rue des Papegaults – The street, which owes its name to the wooden parrots used as targets by the town's archers, is lined by fine Renaissance houses (nos 15, 13, 10, 8 and 4).

Rue du Puits-Châtel – Many interior courtyards are worth a glance through half-open entrance doors.

At no 3 there is an outside staircase with a half-timbered balcony (16C); at no 5 the staircase turret is in stone and there are vaulted galleries and sculpted balconies on the landings (early 16C); next door at no 7 the Hôtel Sardini has a courtyard with Renaissance arcades, and above the door of the staircase turret is Louis XII's porcupine.

ADDITIONAL SIGHTS

★ **Maison de la Magie Robert-Houdin** ⊘ – Set up in a 19C *hôtel particulier* facing the château, the Maison de la Magie enlightens visitors on the history of magic and serves as a national centre for the art of illusionism *(open to professional conjurers and researchers only)*. The museum is dedicated to the great Robert-Houdin.

A six-headed dragon, operated by a highly sophisticated computer system, welcomes visitors to this attractive mansion made with tufa and painted bricks. The tour starts with a guided visit through the history of conjuring, illustrating the chronological developments in this fascinating world. Visitors then become part of the exhibition, walking through a giant kaleidoscope and stepping into a picture gallery before they reach the foyer devoted to magicians of international renown such as Georges Méliès, who was to pave the way for special effects in the film industry.

On the first floor, set against an elegant and theatrical backdrop, the **Cabinet fantastique Robert-Houdin** displays exhibits relating to the world of magic. Posters, engravings, manuscripts and miscellaneous accessories evoke Houdin's performances, which would attract large crowds of Parisian socialites to the Palais-Royal Theatre.

The **Théâtre des Magiciens★** (400 seats set up under the château esplanade) has been especially designed for high-class conjuring acts and offers a 20min show of dazzling expertise, performed by some of the world's leading illusionists.

Musée de l'Objet ⊘ – *Rue Franciade*. The collections presented in the former Couvent des Minimes are unusual in that they were made with extremely simple, mundane objects designed for everyday use. They are the work of contemporary artists who have deliberately chosen these materials in order to turn them into something different: this novel approach based on manipulating matter has given birth to a new art form. A ready-made composition by Marcel Duchamp (1887-1968) welcomes visitors, who may then explore a series of curious or striking exhibits laid out on three levels, executed by leading names such as César, Christo or Isou.

Mur des Mots – On the corner of rue Franciade and rue de la Paix, one of the walls of the Conservatoire is covered with graffiti stating axioms and proverbs.

Haras national ⊘ – *East of town, 62 avenue du Maréchal-Maunoury*. This stud farm, which has occupied an old Carmelite convent since 1810, is home to about 30 blood stallions, in particular French saddle horses, and 20 or so draught stallions, most of which are Percherons. From March to July these horses are divided between the 11 riding centres in the Cher, Eure-et-Loir, Indre, Indre-et-Loire, Loir-et-Cher and Loiret *départements*. While visiting the handsome 19C buildings, there will be opportunities to meet technicians and national agents.

Cloître St-Saturnin ⓥ – *Entrance indicated on quai Villebois-Mareuil.* This former cemetery with timber-roofed galleries, was built under François I. The cloisters serve as a Lapidary Museum, containing fragments of sculptures from the houses of Blois destroyed in 1940.

Basilique Notre-Dame-de-la-Trinité – *North-east of the plan. Take rue du Prêche.* This basilica designed by the architect Paul Rouvière, built between 1937 and 1949, has some fine stained glass and a Stations of the Cross sculpted out of cement by Lambert-Rucki. The 60m/200ft-high campanile affords an extensive view of the surrounding countryside *(240 steps)*. The **carillon** consists of 48 bells, the largest weighing over 5t. It is one of the best in Europe.

EXCURSIONS

Boat trips – Sailing along the Loire in a traditional boat will offer you the opportunity of observing at leisure the local fauna and flora. *For information apply to the tourist office.*

Orchaise – *9km/6mi W on D 766.* Situated near the church, the **Priory Botanical Gardens** ⓥ, covering an area of 3ha/7 acres, boast a superb collection of rhododendrons, azaleas, camellias and peonies, as well as numerous evergreen plants.

Maves – *19km/12mi N.* Note the 15C post **windmill** ⓥ.

Mulsans – *14km/9mi NE along D 50.* Mulsans is a small farming village on the edge of the Beauce, heralded by the village's traditional walled-in farmyards which are characteristic of this region. The charming **church** ⓥ has Flamboyant windows and a fine Romanesque bell-tower decorated with blind arcades and twin round-arched window openings. There is a Renaissance gallery supported by carved wooden columns extending the full width of the nave and incorporating the porch; this is a regional feature known as a *caquetoire* where people would pause to talk after Mass.

Ménars – *6km/3.7mi NE along N 152.* This village's claim to fame is the château where the famous Marquise de Pompadour once took up residence.

★**Suèvres** – *11km/6.8mi NE along N 152.* The ancient Gallo-Roman city of Sodobrium hides its picturesque façades below the noisy main road on the north bank of the Loire. The **church of St-Christophe** beside the road is entered through a huge porch *(caquetoire)* where the parishioners could pause to engage in conversation. The stonework is decorated with various fishbone and chevron patterns characteristic of the Merovingian period.
The houses at no 9 and no 14 bis in rue Pierre-Pouteau date from the 15C. Turn right into a picturesque cul-de-sac, rue des Moulins, running beside the stream which is spanned by several footbridges. Tamarisks and weeping willows are reflected in its waters.
Go back to the turning and cross the stone bridge.

The washing place is at the corner of rue St-Simon; on either side of the street are traces of an old fortified gate. Further on through the trees *(left)* emerges the two-storey Romanesque tower of the **Église St-Lubin** ⓥ with its attractive south door (15C).

LA LOIRE TOURANGELLE

Downstream to Tours *89km/55mi – allow 4hr*

Leave Blois along N 152 towards Tours.

This stretch of road offers numerous views of the Loire which is broken up in a number of places with sandbanks covered in greenery in summer. The Chaumont metal bridge leads to the Château de Chaumont on the south bank.

"The most striking and the most noble feature of the Loire is the huge limestone barrier which follows the steep north bank, combining sandstone, burrstone and clay, and which changes magically before your eyes, running from Blois to Tours, with incomparable variety and spirit, switching from wild rock to landscape garden, planted with trees and flowers, crowned with thriving mushrooms and smoking chimneys, weathered like a sponge, swarming like an ant hill."

Victor Hugo – *En Voyage*

★★**Château de Chaumont-sur-Loire** – *See Château de CHAUMONT-SUR-LOIRE.*
Return to the north bank.

Shortly after Le Haut-Chantier, the Château d'Amboise is visible from the road.

★★**Amboise** – *See AMBOISE.*
Leave Amboise on D 81 then at Civray-de-Touraine bear left to Chenonceau.

★★★**Château de Chenonceau** – *See Château de CHENONCEAU.*
Return towards Amboise along D 40; at La Croix de Touraine bear right onto D 31.

★ Pagode de Chanteloup – *See AMBOISE: Excursions.*

In Amboise cross the river and turn left onto N 152 which runs along the river bank towards Tours.

Négron – Standing below N 152 this village has a charming square overlooked by the church and a Gothic house with a Renaissance front.
Turn right onto D 79 and drive on to the Château de Valmer.

Château de Valmer ⓥ – The park and gardens of Valmer Castle occupy a remarkable position on a hillside overlooking the River Brenne. The castle has disappeared, destroyed by fire in 1948. But the beautiful Italian-style terraced gardens, the vast kitchen garden and the park enclosed by a wall have remained as they were in the 17C. An unusual chapel hewn into the cliff-side has retained two 16C stained-glass windows.
The estate produces fine Vouvray wine.
Follow D 46 on the left then turn right beyond Chançay onto D 62 towards the Château de Jallanges.

Château de Jallanges ⓥ – This brick-and-stone edifice comes into sight on a small ridge rising out of a sea of vineyards. It is Renaissance with a 17C chapel and a superb park.
Rejoin D 46 after it passes beneath the TGV Atlantique line.

Vernou-sur-Brenne – Vernou's attractive old houses are surrounded by Vouvray vineyards against a hillside riddled with caves.

Vouvray – At the heart of the famous vineyard is the village of Vouvray which is set on the south-facing slopes of the hills that overlook the north bank of the Loire upstream from Tours. There are one or two old cliff-side dwellings in the village. Vouvray boasts a statue of Gaudissart, the famous travelling salesman whom Balzac described in one of his novels. **Honoré de Balzac** was born in Tours and often came to visit friends in Vouvray. The atmosphere and characters of 1830 have gone but the charm of the landscape described in his novels still remains.
Still or sparkling white **Vouvray wines** are some of the most famous of Touraine. Many wine producers and merchants have cellars *(caves)* open to the public.
On approaching **Rochecorbon**, a small town at the foot of a bluff riddled with dwellings hewn in the rock, note

Au Virage Gastronomique – *25 av. Brûlé – 37210 Vouvray – ☎ 02 47 52 70 02 – closed 10-20 Sep and Tue – 13.72/41.16€.* Enter via the small veranda and choose between the country-style dining room and the shady terrace, weather permitting. The owner does the traditional cooking himself, and charges reasonable prices.

the **lantern**, a watchtower on the top of the hill. Further on, at the end of a long wall *(right)* stands an imposing 13C doorway, part of the **Abbaye de Marmoutier**, which was founded by St Martin in 372 and fortified in the 13C and 14C.
Drive to Tours along N 152 from the E.

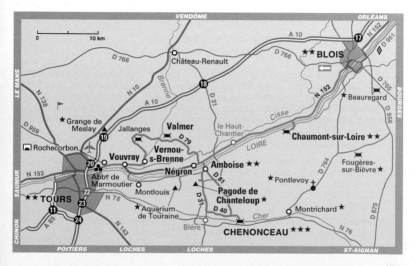

BONNEVAL

Population 4 285
Michelin map 311: E-6 or 237 fold 38

Bonneval developed in the Middle Ages round the 9C Benedictine monastery of St-Florentin on the River Loir. The old town walls are reflected in the waters of the surrounding moat.

An angler's paradise, the Bonneval region offers visitors its attractive small churches, often decorated with frescoes, and fine walks along the shaded banks of the river.

Ancienne abbaye – A specialist hospital centre now occupies the former abbey buildings. The beautiful 13C **fortified gateway★** with its pointed archway was integrated into the abbot's lodging, which was built by René d'Illiers, Bishop of Chartres in the late 15C. The lodge is an attractive building of chequered stonework, flanked by two machicolated towers and capped with pinnacled gables over the dormer windows. In front of the abbey stretches the **Grève**, a large shaded promenade beside the moat. For an attractive view of the old towers and the church spire, go to the end of rue des Fossés-St-Jacques to the west of the town.

Église Notre-Dame – The early-13C church was built in the pure Gothic style: a fine rose window above the flat chevet, an elegant triforium in the nave, fine woodwork behind the font and a 17C figure of Christ.

From the nearby bridge there is a picturesque view of the fortifications and of the moat lined with wash-houses.

Porte St-Roch and Tour du Roi – Several pointed arches mark the old houses which line rue St-Roch, the street which leads to St-Roch Gate with its two round towers. Beside it stands the King's Tower, the old keep, pierced by loopholes and capped with a pepper-pot roof.

Porte Boisville and Pont du Moulin – To the west of the town, between the railway and the by-pass, stands the Boisville Gate (13C); the only remaining part of the first town wall, it was reduced in size in the 15C.

EXCURSIONS

Alluyes – *7km/5mi NW*. All that is left of the old **castle** is the great round tower of the keep and a fortified gate spanning the moat.

On the east bank of the river stands the **church** ⊘ (15C-16C). On the left wall of the nave are two Gothic murals depicting *St Christopher* and the *Legend of the Three Living and the Three Dead*. On the left of the nave is a 16C Virgin Mary bearing a representation of the Trinity on her breast and the arms of Florimond Robertet at her feet.

Dangeau – *9km/5.6mi W*. The village square is bordered by old houses of brick and timber construction (15C). The **Église St-Pierre**, which was built in the early 12C by monks from Marmoutier, is a vast, well-balanced structure in pure Romanesque style. The buttresses and facings are in ironstone. The door in the south porch is embellished with scrolls and strange symbols carved on the lintel: the Cross appears between the Sun and the Moon which have been given human faces. Avarice is shown as a demon holding a purse, whereas Lust is portrayed as a female figure. The wooden ceiling in the nave is supported on archaic pillars. There are several statues in the aisles: the two figures on horseback are typical of popular 15C-17C sacred art. The baptistery contains a marble triptych of the Passion and the Resurrection, dated 1536.

★UPPER REACHES OF THE LOIR

77km/47mi – allow one day

The Loir wends its way in a leisurely fashion through a peaceful landscape defined by rolling hills, green meadows, smart towns and charming villages, which have earned the region the name La Douce France (Gentle France). Originally the river was navigable up to Château-du-Loir but now the only boats are occupied by fishermen who appreciate the variety and abundance of the fish and the beauty of the quivering poplars and silvery willows at the water's edge.

Leave Bonneval to the S.

There are uninterrupted views of the surrounding countryside as the road cuts through the plateau. Before **Conie** the road crosses the river of the same name and follows it (D 110) downstream to **Moléans** with its 17C castle. In the pretty village of **St-Christophe** the road rejoins the slow waters of the Loir which it follows (D 361) to Marboué.

Marboué – Once a Gallo-Roman settlement, the village is known for its tall 15C bell-tower and crocketed spire and for its bathing beach on the river.

★★Châteaudun – *See CHÂTEAUDUN*.

★ **Montigny-le-Gannelon** – This fortress on the north bank of the Loir can be seen from afar on N 10. The name Montigny comes from Mons-Igny meaning Signal Hill; Gannelon evokes either the traitor who betrayed Roland to his enemies, or more likely the priest of St-Avit in Châteaudun who inherited the fortress in the 11C.

Church ⊙ – This church, dedicated to St Giles and St Saviour, contains the shrine of St Felicity.

★ **Château** ⊙ – A second fortified wall with five gates used to enclose the château, which is now approached through the park, in full view of the highly composite west façade. The combination of brick and stonework is striking. Two towers – Tour des Dames and Tour de l'Horloge – are the only remains of the Renaissance château which was rebuilt from 1475 to 1495 by Jacques de Renty. The château contains interesting information on the illustrious **Lévis-**

Montigny-le-Gannelon

S. Sauvignier/MICHELIN

Mirepoix family. To the right of a large Renaissance staircase adorned with portraits of Marshals of Lévis in medallions are the Gothic cloisters with a fine collection of 16C Italian faience plates. The richly furnished rooms that follow contain numerous portraits and mementoes of the Montmorency and Lévis-Mirepoix families. They are the Salon des Colonnes, Salon des Dames, Grand Salon (Portrait of Gilles de Montmorency-Laval, Sire of Rais, said to have inspired Charles Perrault for his character Bluebeard, *see p 108*) and the Salle à Manger Montmorency (portraits of Louis XVIII and Charles X by the Baron Gérard)

In the grounds, a colourful collection of ostriches, emus, nandus (a South American ostrich), waterfowl and pheasants roams through a cluster of trees over 150 years old. Hidden behind a screen of greenery is the former riding school and stables for coach teams, a vast shed on a frame of steel girders which was built at the same time as the Eiffel Tower. Today it contains old farm implements, carriages and stuffed animals.

Cloyes-sur-le-Loir – Cloyes, once a fortified town and staging post on the pilgrim road to Santiago de Compostela, straddles a bend in the Loir on the southern edge of the Beauce region. It is a welcoming town with several picturesque old houses and a church with a 15C belfry. In 1883 **Émile Zola** stayed in Cloyes to study the local customs for his novel *The Earth* which is set in Cloyes and **Romilly-sur-Aigre**.

The Children's Crusade – In 1212 a young shepherd from Cloyes called Estienne gathered a following of about 20 000 children on a pilgrimage to the Holy Land. Neither their parents nor their friends could deter them. The expedition was doomed to failure: some children died on the road, others perished at sea and some were even sold to the Saracens.

Leave Cloyes on D 81 E to Bouche-d'Aigre.

Chapelle d'Yron – *1km/0.5mi S on D 35 (towards Vendôme), then turn right onto D 8¹; entrance in the garden of the old people's home.*
This Romanesque chapel is decorated with well-preserved **mural paintings** in red and ochre tones. Those in the nave are 12C and depict the Flagellation and the Offering of the Magi *(left)*, the Kiss of Judas and an abbot (St Bernard) *(right)* and the Apostles *(apse)* below a gentle-featured Christ in Majesty (14C) on the oven vault of the apse.

A picturesque road *(D 145⁷)* follows the east bank of the Loir south through **St-Claude** with its pointed church on the hill.

St-Jean-Froidmentel – On the west bank is the village of St-Jean-Froidmentel. Its church has an attractive Gothic Renaissance doorway.
Return to the east bank.

Only a row of poplars separates the road from the river. Between Morée and Fréteval there are fishing huts on the bank and one or two pretty riverside houses with flat-bottomed boats moored nearby.

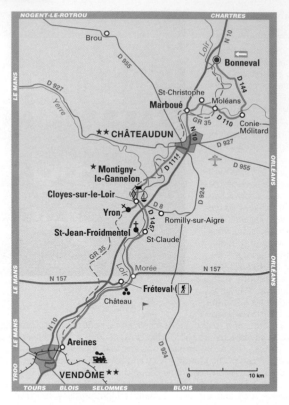

Fréteval – The ruins of a **medieval castle** *(15min on foot there and back)* look down from their bluff on the east bank to Fréteval on the far bank which is a favourite meeting place for fishermen. Soon after this the signposted tourist road leaves the river bank.

Areines – This village lying in the Loir plain, was an important town in the Roman era.

Church – The plain façade is adorned by a 14C Madonna; the church itself is 12C. The interior is decorated with a group of interesting **frescoes**, executed with graceful draughtsmanship and a fresh palette. On the oven vault of the apse lies a majestic figure of Christ surrounded by symbols of the Evangelists; note the lion of St Mark, in stylised Byzantine manner; below are the Apostles with sky-blue haloes, typical of Loire Valley art *(see p 54)*; in the central bay are warrior saints, also with haloes.

The chancel vault shows the Lamb adored by Angels; on the sides are the Annunciation and the Visitation, elegantly depicted, and a somewhat damaged Nativity scene. The frescoes on the walls of the chancel seem to be of a later period; the Marriage of the Virgin is on the right.

BOURGUEIL

Population 4 109
Michelin map 317: J-5, 232 fold 34 or 4037 A4
Local map see CHINON: Excursions

Bourgueil enjoys a fortunate location in a fertile region between the Loire and the Authion at the eastern end of the Anjou Valley where the hillsides are carpeted with vines and woods. French poet **Pierre de Ronsard** (1524-85) was a frequent visitor and it was there that he met the Marie mentioned in his romantic ballads. Nowadays the little town's renown derives from the full-bodied red wines yielded by the ancient Breton vines found only in that area. Rabelais makes reference to them in his works. The great French actor **Jean Carmet** (1921-94) was a native of this region, and he was particularly fond of these wines.

Church ⊘ – Illuminated by lancet windows, the large Gothic chancel of this parish church is roofed with ribbed vaulting. Its width contrasts with the narrow and simple 11C Romanesque nave.

Market – Opposite the church backing on to the old town hall is the elegant covered market place *(halles)* with stone arcades.

Abbey ⊘ – *E of town on the road to Restigné.* The abbey was founded at the end of the 10C by the Benedictines and was one of the richest in Anjou. Its vineyards stretched over the entire hillside and its woods reached down to the Loire. In the 13C and 14C it was fortified and surrounded by a moat. The elegant building by the roadside containing the **cellar** and **granary** dates from the same period.

The tour includes the building constructed in 1730: dining room with 18C panelling, monumental staircase with wrought-iron banisters and huge vaulted hall. On the first floor the monks' cells have been converted into a museum with displays of costumes, bonnets and tools from the early years of this century.

Musée Van-Oeveren ⓥ – This small museum on the art of fencing, duelling and hand-to-hand fighting occupies the Château des Sablons (19C). The splendid armoury is where the château owner gives fencing lessons.

Moulin bleu ⓥ – *2km/1.3mi N.* The Blue Windmill is of a similar type to the one at La Herpinière near Turquant; a wooden cabin is perched on top of a cone made of ashlar-work supported by a vaulted substructure, so that the top can pivot to bring the sails into the wind. The tannin obtained from grinding the bark of the chestnut tree was used in the tanneries in Bourgueil.
From the terrace, there is a fine **view** down on to the vineyards of Bourgueil and south to the Loire Valley.

Cave touristique de la Dive Bouteille ⓥ – The cool chamber (12°C/54°F), hollowed out of the rock, contains a collection of old presses – one of which dates from the 16C – and of photographs of the vineyard. Wine tasting sessions are available.

Eating out

BUDGET

Auberge de Touvois – *Rte de Gizeux – 37140 Touvois – 4km/2.5mi N of Bourgueil on D 749, towards Gizeux – ☎ 02 47 97 88 81 – closed 19-26 Feb, 25 Jun-2 Jul, Tue and Mon lunchtime from 1 May to 30 Jun – reservation required for weekends – 12.96/31.20€.* This friendly inn is hidden in the countryside on the wine route. The cuisine is mainly traditional, combining different herbs and spices in interesting ways. Enjoy the shaded terrace in summer.

Where to stay

MODERATE

Chambre d'hôte Le Château des Réaux – *37140 Chouzé-sur-Loire – 4km/2.5mi S of Bourgueil on D 749, towards Port Boulet – ☎ 02 47 95 14 40 – www.chateaux.france.com/-reaux – closed 15 Nov-1 Mar – 17 rooms 53.36/215€ – ☕ 11€ – evening meal 46€.* If you've always dreamt of staying in a castle, now's your chance, in this historic 15C château flanked by two machicolated towers, decorated with a checked pattern of brick and stone. Reserve one of the sumptuous rooms and enjoy your daydreams while you stroll around the park.

EXCURSIONS

Restigné – *5km/3mi E.* The wine-growing village lies just off the main road clustered round the **church**. The façade is decorated with a diaper pattern and the lintel of the south doorway is carved with fantastic beasts and Daniel in the lion's den. The Romanesque nave is roofed with early-16C timberwork; the beams are decorated with the heads of monsters.

Les Réaux – *4km/2.5mi S.* This charming **château** ⓥ, dating from the late 15C, later belonged to Tallemant des Réaux, who wrote a chronicle, *Historiettes*, of early 17C French society. The château is surrounded by a moat and the entrance pavilion is flanked by two machicolated towers; the defensive features have however been subordinated to the decorative ones: chequerwork in brick and stone; gracefully carved ornamentation in the shell-shaped dormer windows; the salamander above the entrance; and soldiers for weather vanes.

Chouzé-sur-Loire – *7km/4mi SW.* The attractive village on the north bank of the Loire was once a busy port; the deserted dockside where the mooring rings are rusting and the **Musée des Mariniers** ⓥ (Nautical Museum) recall the past. The charming 15C **manor house** in rue de l'Église is where Marie d'Harcourt, wife of Dunois, the famous Bastard of Orléans *(see CHÂTEAUDUN)*, passed away on 1 September 1464.

Varennes-sur-Loire – *15km/9mi SW.* From the old river port on the Loire there is a very attractive **view** of **Montsoreau Château**. The towpath makes a pleasant place for a walk.

Brain-sur-Allonnes – *10km/6mi W.* Excavations in a 14C house have uncovered the medieval site of the **Cave peinte** ⓥ (Painted Cellar). Some beautiful faience tiles are displayed in the adjoining **museum** ⓥ.

Château de BRÉZÉ★★

Michelin map 317: I-5, 232 fold 33 or 4049 I5

The castle's imposing outline towers above one of the oldest vineyards of the Loire Valley. Apart from that, nothing seems to distinguish this elegant edifice from its prestigious neighbours. However, a closer examination of the deep dry moat (18m/59ft deep and 13m/43ft wide) reveals intriguing openings, the only outward signs of more than 1km/0.6mi of underground galleries and of the most extensive underground fortress discovered to date!

The lords of Brézé built the original fortress in the 11C. Their descendants, the Maillé-Brézé, erected the Renaissance living quarters. The Grand Condé, a leader of the uprising known as the "Fronde", which took place at the beginning of Louis XIV's reign, found refuge inside the castle with his whole army. In 1682, he exchanged the property against the Galissonnière estate belonging to the Dreux, who subsequently took the name of Dreux-Brézé. Their descendants still live in the château.

TOUR ⊘

★ **Château** – Beyond the moat stands the elegant Renaissance edifice remodelled in 1824 by Hodé. Surrounding the courtyard are the main building, the gallery and the gatehouse flanked by two large round towers; a terrace makes up the fourth side. From the rooftop, the panoramic view reveals the different stages of construction of the castle.

The visit of the apartments with its fine furniture and 19C decor illustrates the lifestyle of that period.

★★ **Ensemble troglodytique** – ⊙ A discreet door opening onto the main courtyard gives access to a gallery dug out in the 15C, which penetrates deep into the rock and leads to a vast underground network steeped in mystery. Its complexity is due to the various uses to which it was put through the centuries: stone quarry for the construction of the castle, cellars for storing the wine production etc.

★ **Roche de Brézé** – Located beneath the castle, these underground living quarters were mentioned in the 9C; hewn out of the rock, the rooms surround a light shaft. The area was originally accessed through a well-guarded narrow corridor with a bend in it. The large storing silos nearby testify to the wealth and power of the owner.

A corridor leads from this area to the underground watch-path with loopholes opening into the moat. It was dug c 1448 by Gilles de Maillé-Brézé who wished to make his castle impregnable. The path ends in the moat via a drawbridge spanning a pit.

On the other side of the moat, there is another underground network which comprises the five huge halls used by the Grand Condé's soldiers. They have been turned into cellars, including a winepress cellar.

★ **Underground bakery** – Reached by a narrow staircase hewn out of the rock, the superb bakery has an imposing fireplace and an impressive baking oven. Opposite, the quarters allotted to the baker's boy amount to a recess resembling a mezzanine dug in the rockface. The heat from the ovens made the bread dough stored in the room above rise more quickly and enabled silk-worm breeding to take place in the adjacent room.

Winepress and cellars – The vast winepress cellar was used in the making of the famous Brézé white wines. The harvest fell directly into the winepress from a well dug into the rock, which opened in the middle of the vineyards. The grape juice then flowed directly into the vats, along channels running at ground level. This method was used until 1976. Casks were stored in the cold cellars.

★ **Cathédrales d'images** – An audio-visual show about the underground world takes place in the last three cellars. Murals, architecture and old photographs displayed on the walls illustrate this unusual, fascinating environment through the centuries.

BRIARE

Population 5994
Michelin map 318: N-6, 238 fold 8 or 4045 H6

This quiet town on the banks of the Loire is the meeting point of two canals which connect the basins of the River Seine and River Loire. The **Briare Canal** was completed in 1642, 38 years after its conception. Along its 57km/36mi path, six locks move the waters from the Loire Lateral Canal (which runs alongside that river) to the Loing Canal. It was the first canal in Europe designed to link up two different canal networks in this way. At Rogny-les-Sept-Écluses, about 15km/9mi north on the towpath, the seven original locks, no mean feat of engineering at the time, are no longer in use; they form a sort of giant's stairway, in an admirable natural setting.

Today, commercial navigation has given way to leisure, and the town marina has been newly equipped to accommodate recreational boating.

SIGHTS

★★ **Pont-Canal** – The canal bridge (662m/2 172ft long by 11m/37ft wide), completed in 1890 and inaugurated in 1896, may no longer fulfil an important economic role in the transportation of merchandise, but it does transport the visitor who takes the time to stroll along the towpaths. The waters of the Loire ripple below while ducks glide on the calm surface of the brimming canal, suspended high above and resting on 15 masonry piers. The ironwork, which can be seen from stairs down to the river, was created by the Société Eiffel. To commemorate the inaugural

centennial, the elaborate waterworks plant *(usine élévatoire)*, where machinery pumps water up to the bridge, has been renovated and now houses temporary exhibits.

Musée de la Mosaïque et des Émaux ⊘ – This museum devoted to the local enamel crafts is located in the manufactory, which is still in operation. One main theme is the history of Jean-Félix Bapterosses, a skilled mechanic and technician and inventor of the first machine able to produce buttons in industrial quantity, a step ahead of the British, who were still stamping them out one at a time. The collection on display is impressive in its variety. The museum also presents late-19C mosaic work typical to the town, and in particular the work of Art Nouveau precursor Eugène Grasset. The mosaic technique has been used to decorate the floor of the town's church, where a winding pattern, recalling the waters of the Loire, swirls around images representing the ages of man and the five senses.

Château de BRISSAC★★

Michelin map 317: G-4, 232 fold 32 or 4049 G4

The château is set in a fine park shaded by magnificent **cedar trees★**. The building is unusual both because it is exceptionally tall (48m/157ft), and because it comprises two juxtaposed buildings one of which was intended to replace the other, rather than stand next to it. Built c 1455 by Pierre de Brézé, Minister to Charles VII and then to Louis XI, the château was bought by René de Cossé in 1502 and has remained in the family ever since. It was severely damaged during the Wars of Religion. René's grandson, **Charles de Cossé**, Count of Brissac, was one of the leaders of the League, the Catholic party

Château de Brissac

which supported the Guises *(see BLOIS)* in the 16C. In 1594, as Governor of Paris, he handed the keys of the city to Henri IV who had arrived newly converted to Roman Catholicism at the city gates. In gratitude the King raised him to the status of duke. The new duke began to rebuild his house but work was brought to a halt by his death in 1621 and the château has been left unaltered ever since.

TOUR ⏱ *1hr*

The main façade is flanked by two round towers with conical roofs, ringed by elegantly sculpted machicolations, traces of the medieval château.

Inside, the French **ceilings**, often embellished with sculptures, are still adorned with their original 17C paintings; the walls are hung with superb **tapestries** and the rooms are enhanced by fine furniture.

The dining room has a large painting of the old Bercy Château and park in Paris and in the Grand Salon there are superb 18C furnishings, Venetian crystal chandeliers and a pastel portrait of the 8th Duke of Brissac by Élisabeth Vigée-Lebrun.

The Louis XIII staircase leads to the imposing guard-room on the first floor, as well as to the bedchamber where Louis XIII and his mother, Marie de Medici, were at least temporarily reconciled after the Battle of Les Ponts-de-Cé in 1620, and to the Hunting Chamber (Chambre des Chasses) hung with magnificent 16C Flemish tapestries.

Beyond the Picture Gallery, with its portrait of the famous Widow Clicquot, is

> **THE HILLTOP**
>
> **Le Haut Tertre** – *1 pl. du Tertre – 49320 Brissac-Quincé –* ☎ *02 41 91 79 95 – closed Sun evening, Mon evening and Thu evening – 8.84€ lunch, 11.28/24.24€.* You will be made to feel welcome in this little restaurant, an elegant oasis of calm. The friendly atmosphere and its setting near the château makes it an ideal place to stop and eat without spending a fortune. The cooking features fresh produce.

the chapel; here there is a moving low-relief sculpture by David d'Angers as well as finely worked choir stalls in the Italian Renaissance style.

The second floor presents a delightful 17C-style theatre *(restored)*, built in 1883 by the Vicomtesse de Trédern, who had a beautiful pure soprano voice.

The tour ends with the cellars of the château.

The vineyards on the estate yield 1 500 bottles of Anjou-Village wine every year.

EXCURSION

Centre de découverte du milieu aquatique et de la pêche ⏱ – *Take D 748 S of Brissac-Quincé and follow the signposted route.* This fish-breeding centre, located on a lovely site on the banks of the **Étang de Montayer**, enlightens visitors on the river and local efforts to protect its ecosystem. Besides viewing fish typical of the Loire Basin, visitors can watch the various stages involved in the breeding of pike, from the hatching of eggs to the growing of young fry in basins.

🚶 A botanical trail reveals the flora characteristic of shores and wetlands. A pretty footpath around the lakeshore is an agreeable way to round off the visit.

BROU

Population 3 713
Michelin map 311: C-6 or 237 folds 37 and 38

Although Brou was once a barony in Le Perche-Gouet, it is more characteristic of the rich and fertile agricultural region of the Beauce; it is a market town centred on its market place where poultry and eggs are the main commerce.

There are many old street names which have remained unchanged since the Middle Ages.

Place des Halles – On the corner of rue de la Tête-Noire stands an old house with projecting upper storeys, which dates from the early 16C; the timberwork is decorated with carved motifs.

In rue des Changes near the market place there is another 16C house with a curved façade; the corner post bears the figures of St James and a pilgrim, since Brou lies on the old pilgrimage route from Chartres to Santiago de Compostela in Spain.

> **ONLY IN FRANCE**
>
> **L'Ascalier** – *9 pl. Dauphin –* ☎ *02 37 96 05 52 – closed during autumn school holidays and Mar – reservation required – 14.94/38.11€.* There are several good reasons to eat at this restaurant near the market hall: good, yet simple cooking, reasonable prices, a flower-decked terrace and a lovely 16C staircase which leads to the first-floor dining room. Definitely worth a visit.

EXCURSIONS

Église de Yèvres – *1.5km/1mi E.* The **church** dates mainly from the 15C and 16C. The elegant Renaissance doorway is framed by carved pilasters (Instruments of the Passion) and surmounted by a double pediment.

The interior contains some remarkable classical **woodwork★**: the pulpit which is decorated with effigies of the Virtues; the retable on the high altar; the altars in the side chapels; and an eagle lectern. The door into the baptismal chapel (fine carved wood ceiling) is beautifully carved with scenes of the Martyrdom of St Barbara and the Baptism of Christ.

The sacristy contains Louis XIII woodwork and collections of 18C and 19C sacred vessels.

★LE PERCHE-GOUET

There are guided tours of this region labelled "Pays d'Art et d'Histoire"; information is available from tourist offices.

97km/60mi round tour – allow one day

Take D 15 NW.

Le Perche-Gouet, which is sometimes known as Lower Perche, was named in the 11C after **William Gouet** who owned five baronies within the jurisdiction of the Bishop of Chartres: Alluyes la Belle, Brou la Noble, La Bazoche la Gaillarde, Authon la Gueuse and Montmirail la Superbe.

Le Perche-Gouet covers a sort of crescent between the Loir and the Huisne; the soil is composed of chalk marl and banks of sand or clay. Much of the immense forest which once covered the land has been replaced by fields and orchards. The eastern part of Le Perche-Gouet is very similar to the Beauce but is distinguished from it by its scattered farms and the abundance of hedges and trees. Most of the streams flow east into the Loir; only the Rhône drains north-west into the Huisne at Nogent-le-Rotrou.

The farms hidden in the deep lanes were originally built of wattle and daub or within a brick framework. Their owners raise cattle, particularly dairy herds, which have replaced the breeding (in slight progress) of the Percheron draught horses, their coats dappled grey, roan or black.

Frazé – Frazé is a little village in the valley beside the River Foussarde. Its origins are Gallo-Roman; later it was fortified and surrounded by water. The village square, place de la Mairie, provides a charming view of both the church and the château. The **château** ⊙ was first built to a square ground plan in 1493 and protected by a moat and a pool; it was completed in the 16C and 17C with the outbuildings which form an entrance porch. The surviving buildings include: a watchtower; two towers of which one stands alone and is decorated with machicolations and a moulding; a fort flanked by towers and ornamented with

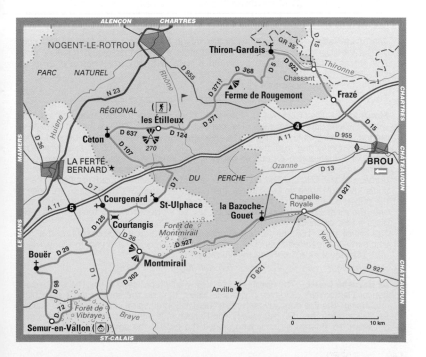

sculpted corbels; and an interesting chapel with historiated ornaments. An old well, gardens, canals and terraces enhance the courtyard and the park.
The **church** has an attractive Renaissance doorway supported by three atlantes.

Once in Chassant, take D 922. The road runs through the southern part of the Parc naturel régional du Perche (1998) which extends as far as Montmirail Forest.

Thiron-Gardais – The village has developed on the south bank of the Thironne, which flows out of the Étang des Moines (Monks' Pool) near the abbey founded by St Bernard in 1114 and dedicated to the Holy Trinity. Tiron Abbey (written without the "h" in those days) was especially prosperous in the 12C and 13C. Among the abbots in the 16C were Charles de Ronsard, the poet's brother, and Philippe Desportes, himself a poet. In 1629 the Benedictines of St-Maur moved in. The **abbey church** is still a huge building even though the chancel collapsed in 1817. Near the entrance *(left)* is the tombstone of John II of Chartres, Abbot of Tiron in the 13C; the monks' stalls in the nave are 14C; the woodwork and stalls in the present chancel date from 1740. A few buildings from the 17C college still exist.

Continue S by D 5 and then D 371³.

Ferme de Rougemont – From the road (D 371³) passing this farm there is an extensive **view** of the Ozanne Valley.

Les Étilleux – ◪ South of the village near a small farm on D 13 take the path *(signposted)* which climbs to the top of a mound (270m/886ft; at the foot of the television aerial) from where there are beautiful **views** of the Ozanne Valley, the hills of Le Perche and the Huisne Valley.

Follow D 637 to Ceton.

Ceton – The **church of St-Pierre** *(recently restored)* derives its importance from the Cluniac priory to which it belonged from 1090. The tower is Romanesque, the Gothic nave and chancel were built in the 13C-16C. Each bay in the side aisles has its own roof at right angles to the nave in the Percheron manner. A touchingly naïve 16C Entombment stands out in the interior among the fine statues.

St-Ulphace – Half way up the slope stands the **church** ⊙ (15C-16C), with a powerful façade flanked by a tower and a Renaissance doorway.

Courgenard – In this small village with its pretty gardens, the door of the **church** ⊙ is carved with low-relief statues in the Renaissance style. The right wall of the nave is decorated with 16C murals depicting Hell and the Legend of the Three Living and the Three Dead; there is also an interesting Baroque altarpiece.

Château de Courtangis – Among the tall trees in an idyllically isolated valley are the turrets, dormers and steeply pitched mansard roofs of a graceful early-16C manor house.

Turn right onto D 125 towards Lamnay and St-Maixent.

Bouër – Bouër is a tiny little village hidden in the hills overlooking the Huisne Valley. The slate spire of the **church** is joined to the bell-tower by scrolls. There are two attractive wooden altars in front of the chancel. From the terrace there is a fine view of the Huisne Valley.

Semur-en-Vallon – This is an attractive village by a man-made lake. In the valley on the western edge of Vibraye Forest stands a 15C moated and turreted **castle**. The entrance façade, flanked by round towers with lanterns, was altered in the 17C. Note the pretty, steeply pitched French roofs.
◙ The Decauville **tourist train** ⊙ runs on a 1.5km/1mi long circuit.

Pretty D 72, then D 302 cut across a section of Vibraye Forest.

Montmirail – The little town of Montmirail, once strongly fortified, was built on a site with excellent natural defences. The **castle** ⊙, built in the 15C on top of a medieval mound, was altered in the 18C by the Princesse de Conti. It still has the original underground works dating from the 11C and 14C. On 9 January 1169, the castle was the scene of a memorable encounter between the kings of England and France in the course of which the exiled Archbishop of Canterbury, **Thomas Becket**, reaffirmed the primacy of the Church. The apartments of the Princesse de Conti (the daughter of Louis XIV and Louise de La Vallière), including the Louis XV Grand Salon, are open to the public, as are the dungeons and armouries. The Classical west façade, contrasting with the medieval south and east fronts, can be viewed from the terrace, which also gives a vast **panorama★** over the countryside of Le Perche-Gouet.
The **church** (12C-16C) has a 16C stained-glass window in the chancel and a realistic early-17C painted sepulchre in the left aisle. Opposite is a carved stone which, until the Revolution, contained a reliquary.

A picturesque road (D 927) runs through Montmirail Forest.

La Bazoche-Gouet – The **church**, 12C or 13C, was altered early in the 16C by the addition of Flamboyant windows in the side aisles; that on the south side is particularly interesting. The fine doorway features niches resting on spiral columns. Inside, a square tower supports the 16C bell-tower. The Renaissance windows in the chancel were a gift from the Bourbons-Conti, who owned the estate; the detail and realistic expressions are remarkable the subject is the Passion copied from German engravings.

Château de CHAMBORD★★★

Michelin map 318: G-6 or 238 fold 3
Local map see ORLÉANS: Excursions

"Chambord is truly royal – royal in its great scale, its grand air, its indifference to common considerations" (Henry James). This château, the largest by far of the Loire châteaux, is built on a scale foreshadowing that of the château at Versailles. It looms into sight suddenly, at the end of a long avenue, and as the view of its white mass gradually expands on approaching, its detail becoming ever clearer, it makes a striking impression on the viewer, even more so at sunset. This magnificent building also owes its impact to its fine architectural unity, sumptuous Renaissance decoration, dating from the period when this style was at its most splendid, and finally two particularly outstanding features: the great staircase and the roof terrace. *See photo p 88.*

All year round, from sunset to midnight, a sophisticated system of floodlighting allows visitors to feast their eyes on the château's outstanding architecture, set off by a dazzling kaleidoscope of red, white, yellow and blue.

FANTASY AND GRANDEUR

Grandiose creation of François I (16C) – The counts of Blois had built a small castle in this isolated corner of the forest of Boulogne, which was excellent hunting country. As a young man François I liked to hunt in the forest and in 1518 he ordered the old castle to be razed to make room for a sumptuous palace.

Several designs were put forward and no doubt Leonardo da Vinci, the King's guest at Le Clos-Lucé, drew up a plan which was made into a model by Le Boccador. As work progressed, the original plans were altered and large sums of money were swallowed up but the King refused to cut corners. Even when the Treasury was empty and there was no money to pay the ransom for his two sons in Spain, when he was reduced to raiding the treasuries of the churches or to melting down his subjects' silver, work went on. It suffered only one interruption, from 1524 to 1525, during the Italian campaign which resulted in the defeat of Pavia. In his enthusiasm the King even proposed in 1527 to divert the course of the Loire so that it should flow before the château but in view of the enormity of this task a smaller river, the Cosson, was chosen instead.

By 1537 the major construction work was completed. Only the interior decoration remained to be done. In 1538 the King commissioned a pavilion linked to the keep by a two-storey building, and a second symmetrical wing to be added to the west side. The whole complex measured 117m/380ft by 156m/510ft. In 1539 the King was able to receive Charles V at Chambord. The visitor, charmed by the warm reception he was granted and amazed by the château itself, said to his host "Chambord is a compendium of human industry". In 1545 the royal pavilion was finished but François I, who until then had lived in the north-east tower, leaving him little time to enjoy it as he died two years later. Henri II continued his father's work by building the west wing and the chapel tower while the curtain wall was completed. At his death in 1559 the château was still unfinished.

The Château de Chambord is a jewel of the Renaissance, the result of "a real mathematicization of architecture" (Jean Jacquart); it comprises 440 rooms, 365 fireplaces, 13 main flights of stairs and 70 backstairs.

Louis XIV and Molière – François II and Charles IX came frequently to hunt in the forest. Henri III and Henri IV hardly put in an appearance at Chambord, but Louis XIII reforged the royal link. Louis XIV stayed at Chambord nine times between 1660 and 1685 and had considerable restoration work done.

Molière wrote *Monsieur de Pourceaugnac* at Chambord in a matter of a few days. During the première the King did not seem at all amused. Lully, who had written the music and was playing the role of an apothecary, had an inspiration; he jumped feet first from the stage on the harpsichord and fell through it. The King burst out laughing and the play was saved.

Le Bourgeois gentilhomme caused Molière renewed anguish. The King was icy at the first performance. The courtiers who were made fun of in the play were ready to be sarcastic. But after the second performance the King expressed his pleasure and the whole court changed their criticism into praise.

From the Revolution to the Restoration – In 1809 Napoleon gave Chambord as an entailed estate to Berthier, Prince of Wagram. Berthier sold the timber and left the estate unoccupied. After his death the Princess was authorized to sell it.

It was bought by public subscription in 1821 for the Duke of Bordeaux, heir to the throne.

The affair of the white flag (1871-73) – In 1871, Henri, Count of Chambord and, since the fall of Charles X in 1830, legitimate heir to the French throne, was close to achieving his goal. This was the year when, following the disruption of the Franco-Prussian War, the French elected a monarchist assembly in favour of restoring the monarchy. However, the monarchists were divided into two groups: the legitimists who supported the traditional conception of absolute monarchy and the Orléanists, more modern in their outlook, who upheld the principles of 1789. Eventually both parties agreed on the name of the heir; **Henri V**, the last of the Bourbon line. As he had lived in exile for 40 years, Henri was not well-informed of the realities of French politics when he returned to his native soil. He went to live at Chambord where on 5 July 1871 he proclaimed his convictions in a manifesto which ended with these words "Henri V will not give up the white flag of Henri IV".

Where to stay

MODERATE

Hôtel Grand St-Michel – *Pl. St-Michel – 41250 Chambord – ☎ 02 54 20 31 31 – closed 12 Nov-20 Dec –* 🅿 *– 38 rooms 44.21/68.60€ –* ☐ *6.40€ – restaurant 16/34€.* This regional-style building opposite the castle benefits from the peace of its magnificent park. The only sound that might disturb your sleep is the mating call of the stags. A few rooms offer a splendid view of the castle. Large dining room with glass roof and huge fireplace.

Chambre d'hôte Manoir de Clénord – *998 rte de Clénord – 41250 Mont-près-Chambord – 15km/9mi SW of Chambord on D 112, then D 923 from Bracieux –* ☎ *02 54 70 41 62 –* www.clenord.com *– closed 15 Nov-15 Mar – 6 rooms 45.66/152.67€.* Set in a park which reaches all the way to Chambord Forest, this luxurious 18C manor is distinguished by unaffected elegance. The rooms are quiet and each is distinctive, with parquet floors and fine old furnishings. Pool, tennis court.

Hôtel Bonnheure – *41250 Bracieux – 8km/5mi S of Chambord on D 112 –* ☎ *02 54 46 41 57 – closed beginning Dec to mid-Feb –* 🅿 *– 13 rooms 49.55/57.93€ –* ☐ *6.86€.* This Sologne-style house and its pretty garden are hidden behind a *porte cochère.* Peaceful rooms opening onto the terrace or balconies. Two apartments and a studio flat with kitchenette for family holidays.

LUXURY

Chambre d'hôte Le Château de Colliers – *41500 Muides-sur-Loire – 8km/5mi NE of Chambord on D 112, D103 and D 951 towards Tours –* ☎ *02 54 87 50 75 – 5 rooms 91.47/129.38€.* A long, tree-lined drive leads to this little 18C folly, built to satisfy the whim of one of Louis XV's knights. Stately bedrooms where open fires can warm you at the first hint of wintry weather; nearly all have views of the Loire. Elegant reception rooms.

The effect of this declaration on public opinion was a disaster: the royalists lost the elections. The Count of Chambord stubbornly refused to reconsider the matter and returned to Austria. Two years later in October 1873 a final attempt to compromise – a tricolour flag dotted with fleur-de-lis – failed. The National Assembly accepted the situation and voted for the Republic. Henri did not succeed to the throne and died in 1883. The Château de Chambord, which had witnessed the final hours of the monarchy, was handed down to his nephew, the Duke of Parma. In 1932 his descendants sold it to the State for about 11 million francs.

TOUR ⏱ *1hr 30min*

Visitors enter through the Porte Royale. Leaflets with a detailed ground plan of the château are available from the reception.

Although the ground plan of Chambord is feudal – a central **keep** with four towers, which qualifies as a château in its own right, set in an enclosed precinct – the architecture is Renaissance and makes no reference to war. The château is a royal palace built for pleasure. During the construction two wings were added, one containing the royal apartments and the other the chapel; the façades are particularly impressive, their appeal deriving from the Italian influence in the sculptures and wide bays.
Chambord is the personal creation of François I. The name of the architect has not been recorded but the architecture seems to have been inspired by the spirit of Leonardo da Vinci who had been staying at the French court and died in the spring of 1519 just as work on the château began. François I never saw the finished château; it was Henri II who added the second storey of the chapel and Louis XIV who completed the building.

Main courtyard – From the entrance there is a fine view of the keep linked to the corner towers by two arcades surmounted by galleries. A gallery was added to the façade towards the end of the reign of François I at the same time as the two spiral staircases in the north corners of the courtyard.

Double staircase – The famous double staircase, undoubtedly conceived by Leonardo da Vinci, stands at the intersection of the cross formed by the four guard-rooms. The two flights of steps spiral round each other from the ground floor to the roof terrace. The stonework at the centre and round the outside is pierced by many openings so that one can see from one flight across to the other.

State apartments – The State Rooms on the ground floor and on the first floor contain a superb collection of French and Flemish tapestries. The Salle des Soleils, named after the sunbursts decorating the shutters, contains a number of interesting paintings, including *The Recognition of the Duke of Anjou as King of Spain* by Baron François Gérard, and a Brussels tapestry, *The Call of Abraham.*

François I's rooms were in the north tower on the **first floor**. In the King's Bed-chamber the bedspread and hangings are made of gold embroidered velvet (16C Italian); it was on one of the window panes that the King is supposed to have engraved a melancholy couplet: *"Souvent femme varie, bien fol est qui s'y fie"* (Woman often changes, he who trusts her is a fool). In François I's dressing room the salamander, the King's emblem, and the letter F alternate in the coffers of the barrel-vaulted ceiling; the room was used as an oratory by Queen Catherine Opalinska, wife of Stanislas Leszczynski. The Queen's Bedchamber in the Tour François-Ier is hung with Paris tapestries relating the History of Constantine, after cartoons by Rubens.

The King's Suite which follows is decorated with tapestries and historic portraits; the rooms in the centre of the north-west façade of the keep were furnished by Louis XIV. The Royal or State Bedchamber, which was used successively by Louis XIV, Stanislas Leszczynski and the Maréchal de Saxe, has the original Regency style panelling fitted in 1748 for the Maréchal; the room next door at the exact centre of the building gives a remarkable view of the park. Maurice de Saxe left his mark in the King's Guard-Room in the form of a huge porcelain stove.

The Dauphin's Suite in the East Tower, contains many mementoes of the Count of Chambord: paintings, the State bed presented by his admirers, statues of Henri IV and the Duke of Bordeaux, the first and last counts of Chambord, as children, and a collection of miniature artillery given to the young Prince for his amusement and instruction the cannon fired shot which could pierce a wall.

Maréchal de Saxe (18C)

Louis XV presented the estate, with a revenue of 40 000 *livres*, to the Maréchal de Saxe as a reward for his victory over the Dutch and English at the Battle of Fontenoy in 1745. The extravagant, proud and violent Maréchal entertained a lively, exciting lifestyle. To satisfy his taste for arms, he made room to accom-modate two regiments of cavalry composed of Tartars, Wallachians and natives of Martinique. These unconventional troops rode high-spirited horses from the Ukraine which were trained to assemble at the sound of a trumpet. The Maréchal imposed iron discipline on his entourage. If the slightest offense was committed, the culprits would be hanged from the branches of an old elm. More by terror than by courtship, Maurice de Saxe won the favours of a well-known actress, Mme Favart, and compelled her to remain at Chambord. He re-erected Molière's stage for her amusement. Monsieur Favart played the triple role of director, author and consenting husband.

The Maréchal died at 54, some said, in a duel with the Prince de Conti whose wife he had seduced. Others ascribed his death to a neglected chill. Vainglorious even in death, Maurice de Saxe had given orders that the six cannon he had placed in the main courtyard of the château should be fired every quarter of an hour for 16 days as a sign of mourning.

The rooms on the **second floor** are devoted to a **Hunting and Wildlife Art Museum**, laid out around four different themes, each located in a separate part of the keep. The first exhibition focuses on the public's perception of hunting seen through mythology. The second display outlines the similarities between hunting and the arts. The last two galleries present hunting practices and traditions from the 16C to the 18C. All these collections feature an impressive number of trophies, weapons, paintings, tapestries and engravings. The most remarkable exhibits include *The Story of Diana* (resulting from the joint collaboration of Rubens and Jean Brueghel) and several canvases by Desportes, Oudry and Dürer.

Roof terrace – The terrace, a direct inspiration from castles such as Méhun-sur-Yèvre and Saumur, is unique: a maze of lanterns, chimneys, stairs and dormer windows, all intricately carved and curiously decorated with a sort of mosaic of inset slates cut in various shapes – lozenges, circles and squares – in imitation of Italian marble. The stair continues above the terrace in a single spiral enclosed in a magnificent lantern 32m/105ft high.

It was here that the court spent most of its time watching the start and return of the hunts, military reviews and exercises, tournaments and festivals. The thousands of nooks and crannies of the terrace invited the confidences, intrigues and assig-nations which played a great part in the life of that glittering society.

The decoration reflects this: François I's initials, crowned salamander, candelabras, fleurs-de-lis and recesses designed for statues as well as slates cut in the shape of diamonds, circles or squares to form a kind of mosaic lining the chimneys.

Sport of kings – The château estate was richly stocked with game and also lent itself to hawking. At one time there were more than 300 falcons. The royal hunt packs received unremitting care and attention, and for breeding purposes the best dogs were brought from the four corners of Europe to improve the strain.

Hunting was the favourite medieval sport and princes were brought up to it from their earliest days. Louis XII took 5m/16ft ditches on horseback without flinching. Despite his delicate constitution, Charles IX would hunt for as long as 10hr at a stretch, exhausting five horses in the process and often coughing up blood such were his exertions. It was he who accomplished the feat of hunting down a stag without the help of hounds.

Park ⊙ – Since 1948 the park has been a national hunt reserve covering 5 500ha/13 591 acres of which 4 500ha/11 120 acres are taken up by forest; it is enclosed by a wall, the longest in France, 32km/20mi long and pierced by five gates at the end of six beautiful drives.

🗓 Walkers are admitted to a restricted area on the west side offering paths and tracks suitable for rambling. Four observation hides have been built so that people can watch the herds of deer and wild boar browsing for food.

🎠 Fun for kids

Écuries du Maréchal de Saxe – A **display of horsemanship** ⊙ *(45min)* is held in the ruins of the former stables belonging to the Maréchal de Saxe. It retraces the history of the château from the Renaissance period to the days of the Comte de Chambord. For tired tots, why not suggest a ride in a **horse-drawn carriage** ⊙ as a way of enjoying the scenery and relieving tired feet. Or you may prefer a **boat trip** ⊙ on the River Cosson, around the moat and down the grand canal, which will reveal the extraordinary perspective of the castle and park as Louis XIV imagined them.

Contemporaries of Chambord (1519-47)

ENGLAND	LOIRE VALLEY		PARIS REGION
Bridewell Palace 1	Azay-le-Rideau	Gué-Péan	Chantilly
Compton Wynyates	Beauregard	Talcy	(Petit Château)
Hampton Court	Blois	Valençay	Ecouen
Palace of Nonsuch 2	Champigny-sur-	Villandry	Fontainebleau
St James	Veude 3	Villesavin	Louvre
	Chaumont (decor)		(Vieux Louvre)
	Chenonceau		St-Germain-en- Laye
			(Château Vieux)

EXCURSION

★ **Château de Villesavin** ⊙ – Villesavin derives from Villa Savini, the name of a Roman villa which stood beside the Roman road built by Hadrian which passed through Ponts-d'Arian (Hadrian's Bridges) on the south side of the River Beuvron. The **château** was built between 1527 and 1537 by Jean Le Breton, Lord of Villandry and superintendent of works at Chambord. It is a charming Renaissance building with certain Classical tendencies and consists of a central block flanked by symmetrical pavilions.

The handsome dormer windows in the attics and the inscription on the rear façade add to the beauty of the château's harmonious proportions. The 16C white-marble Italian **basin** in the courtyard is a very fine example of Renaissance decorative sculpture.

A **collection**★ of wedding accessories (1835-1950) is on display in some of the furnished rooms.

There are some vintage cars in the outbuildings.

To the left of the château stands a large 16C **dovecot** with 1 500 pigeon-holes; it is in a good state of preservation, with its revolving ladder still intact.

The park is peopled with various breeds of carthorses and mules from France.

Pigeons as a status symbol

The right to keep pigeons – held essentially by large landowners – was one of the privileges that disappeared with the Revolution. The size of the dovecot depended on the size of the estate: there was one pigeon-hole containing a couple of birds for each acre of land. In the Middle Ages, dovecots were built to attract pigeons and doves for two reasons: not only did the birds provide meat, but their droppings were also highly prized as a fertilizer – though it was so rich in nitrates that it could be used only in the rainy season, when it would be naturally diluted. It is thought that the practice of keeping pigeons was brought back by the Crusaders from the Middle East where the land has always been fertilized with pigeon manure.

CHÂTEAUDUN★★

Population 14 543
Michelin map 311: D-7 or 237 fold 38
Local map see BONNEVAL: Excursions

Châteaudun and its castle stand on a bluff, indented by narrow valleys called *cavées*, on the south bank of the Loir at the point where the Perche region joins the Beauce.

Birth of the Alexandrine metre – It was at Châteaudun in the 12C that the poet **Lambert le Tort** was born. He was one of the authors of the *Story of Alexander*, a heroic poem inspired by the legend of Alexander the Great which was very popular in the Middle Ages. Its 22 000 lines were written in the heroic metre, with 12 feet or syllables to the line, which subsequently came to be known as the Alexandrine metre.

Dunois, the Bastard of Orléans (1402-56) – Handsome Dunois, the faithful companion of Joan of Arc, was the bastard son of Louis I of Orléans and Mariette d'Enghien. He was brought up by **Valentina Visconti**, Louis' wife, who loved him as much as her own children. From the age of 15 Dunois fought the English for several decades. In 1429 he rallied the army to the defence of Orléans and delivered Montargis. He took part in all the great events of Joan of Arc's career. Towards the end of his life, having won all the honours it is possible for one man to win, he retired to Châteaudun in 1457, where he founded the Sainte-Chapelle and received the poet François Villon. Dunois was buried in the church of Notre-Dame at Cléry. He was well educated and well read and Jean Cartier, the chronicler, described him as "one of the best speakers of the French language".

A heroic defence – On 18 October 1870 the Prussians attacked Châteaudun with 24 cannons and 12 000 men. Confronting them were only 300 local members of the national guard and 600 free fighters, who managed to hold out all day behind their barricades, despite heavy bombing which lasted from noon to 6.30pm. Finally, they had to admit they were outnumbered and consented to retreat. The Prussians promptly set fire to the town and 263 houses were razed. In recognition of services rendered to France, Châteaudun received the Legion of Honour and adopted the motto *Extincta revivisco* ("I rise again from the ashes").

A wise financier

A local man called **Dodun** gradually worked his way up from nothing to become Financial Controller under the Régence (of Philippe d'Orléans, 1715-23). In 1724 his portrait was painted by Rigaud; in 1727 Bullet built him a magnificent mansion in rue de Richelieu in Paris; the château and the marquisate of Herbault also came into his possession.
Dodun showed loyalty to his region by finding the money to rebuild Châteaudun after the town had burnt down in 1723. Reconstruction work was directed by Jules Hardouin, nephew of Jules Hardouin-Mansart; he was responsible for the part of the town which is laid out on the grid system.

★VIEILLE VILLE

Rue du Château, which is lined by overhanging houses, opens onto a charming little square with two old houses: the one with pilasters, beams and carved medallions is 16C; the other, heavily restored, is a corner house with a carved corner post showing the Virgin and St Anne *(badly damaged)*.
It is prolonged by rue de la Cuirasserie (fine 16C house with a corner turret), which opens onto a square named after **Cap-de-la-Madeleine**, a town in the province of Quebec in Canada founded in the 17C by a priest from Châteaudun. On the right is the Hôtel-Dieu founded in 1092 and modernised in 1762; on the left is the Palais de Justice (Law Court) housed in a former Augustinian abbey, built in the Classical style. The **Église de la Madeleine** ⊙★, is built into the ramparts; its north façade is topped by pointed gables, a common local feature. The

> **Hôtel St-Michel** – *5 r. Péan –* ☏ *02 37 45 15 70 – closed 20 Dec-6 Jan –* 19 rooms *25.92/47.26€ –* ⊑ *5.79€*. Just off the main square, place du 18-Octobre, 500m/550yd from the castle, this hotel has two entrances, linked by an old passageway between two streets, now a flower-decked patio under a glass canopy. Comfortable rooms.

interior is vast; the church was built in the 12C to an ambitious plan and never completed owing to insufficient funds. The south door, overlooking a steep drop, is Romanesque with human figures and fantastic animals carved over the arch.
Continue down rue des Huileries to rue de la Porte-d'Abas; on the left, near the ruins of a Roman gate, stands the 16C Loge aux Portiers (Porters' Lodge) decorated with a carefully restored statue of the Virgin Mary.
Walk up rue St-Lubin, lined with impressive houses (nos 2 and 12), to return to the front of the château.

Go through the arch at the beginning of rue de Luynes and onto impasse du Cloître-St-Roch, then turn right onto a narrow, winding street, venelle des Ribaudes, which opens onto a small square on the edge of the bluff; from here there is a pleasant **view** of the River Loir and its valley. On the right of the square stands a 15C house with a Flamboyant door and mullion windows.

Take rue Dodun back to the château.

Promenade du Mail – The mall walk, which runs along the edge of the bluff above the river valley, has been widened and turned into a public garden. The **view★** stretches westward across the two branches of the Loir, the suburb of St-Jean and beyond to the hillsides of the Perche region.

★★CHÂTEAU ⊘ *1hr*

Châteaudun is the first of the Loire châteaux to come into sight on the road from Paris. It stands on a bluff rising steeply above the River Loir (there is an excellent view from the north bank at the level of an old mill near the bridge).

Crude and fortress-like from the outside, the buildings resemble a stately mansion when seen from the courtyard. The keep, which is 31m/102ft high without the roof, dates from the 12C; it is one of the earliest circular keeps, as well as one of the most impressive and best preserved.

H. Dewynter/MICHELIN

Châteaudun – The Keep

The **basement rooms** extend into the Dunois wing *(entrance at the bottom of the Gothic staircase)*. Two of these rooms, beautifully decorated with intersecting ribbed vaulting, housed the kitchens, each with a double fireplace running the whole width of the room. The small rooms on the north side were occupied by the guards in charge of the cramped prison cells, some of which feature ogee vaulting.

Sainte-Chapelle – Dunois was responsible for this elegant 15C building; it is flanked by a square belfry and two oratories and the chancel ends in a three-sided apse. The upper chapel, which was provided for the servants, has a panelled wooden ceiling; the lower chapel has ogee vaulting.

The south oratory is decorated with a well-preserved 15C mural of the Last Judgement. The charming collection of 15 **statues★★** is an excellent example of the work produced in the workshops in the Loire Valley in the late 15C. Note in particular St Mary the Egyptian, clothed only with her own hair, St Radegund with her sceptre, St Apollonia with forceps gripping a tooth, St Barbara with her tower, St Catherine holding the wheel and the sword that killed her and St Martha with a dragon at her feet.

Aile de Dunois – This wing was begun towards 1460 and is built in the true Gothic tradition, although the interior furnishings suggest the desire for comfort which followed the Hundred Years War.

The huge living rooms have massive overhead beams and are hung with tapestries, including, on the first floor, a superb series from Brussels depicting the Life of Moses. Visitors then come to the Salle de Justice (Court Room), where the Lord of the Manor passed judgement and which was panelled in the 17C and painted with the arms of Louis XIV for an occasion when the King visited Châteaudun. This room served as a Revolutionary tribunal in 1793.

Aile de Longueville – In completing his father's work, François I de Longueville had a staircase built in the Gothic style. The design echoes the transition between the medieval turreted staircase of the Dunois wing and the Renaissance at the east end of the Longueville wing.

The Longueville wing was built between 1510 and 1520 by François II de Longueville and then by his brother the Cardinal on foundations which date from the preceding century, but it was never completed. At roof level an Italian cornice supports a Flamboyant balustrade. The staircase at the east end is richly decorated with Renaissance motifs set in a Gothic setting. The ground floor rooms, including the Renaissance gallery, are hung with 17C Paris and

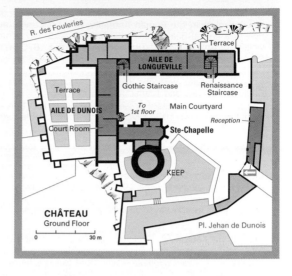

Amiens tapestries. In the Grand Salon on the first floor there are carved 16C chests and, facing each other, two monumental chimney-pieces, one in the Gothic and one in the Renaissance style.

ADDITIONAL SIGHTS

Musée des Beaux-Arts et d'Histoire naturelle ⊙ – This Fine Art and Natural History Museum is worth visiting for its remarkable **collection of stuffed birds★** (2 500) from countries all over the world. The room on the ground floor devoted to Egyptian archaeology contains funerary objects from the early Dynastic Period

CHÂTEAUDUN

Cap-de-la-Madeleine (Pl.)		**A** 3
Château (R. du)		**A** 4
Cuirasserie (R. de la)		**A** 5
Dunois (Pl. J. de)		**A** 6
Gambetta (R.)		**AB**
Guichet (R. du)		**A** 7
Huileries (R. des)		**A** 8
Luynes (R. de)		**A** 10
Lyautey (R. Mar.)		**A** 12
Porte d'Abas (R. de la)		**A** 14
République (R.)		**AB**
St-Lubin (R.)		**A** 18
St-Médard (R.)		**A** 19
18 Octobre (Pl. du)		**A** 21

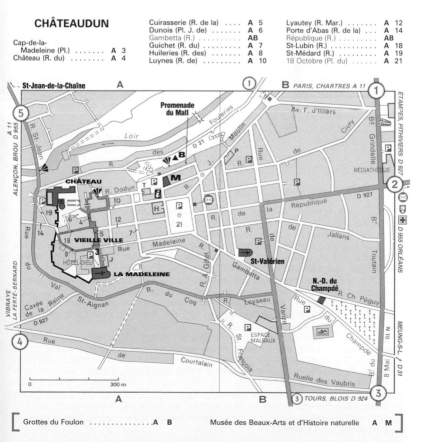

| Grottes du Foulon | A B |
| Musée des Beaux-Arts et d'Histoire naturelle | A M |

(3100-2700 BC) discovered at Abydos. The same room also displays **mummies** and sarcophagi from the Roman Antiquity. Local history is evoked by the reconstitution of a typical Beauce domestic interior, a display of artefacts excavated in the vicinity of Châteaudun and by souvenirs of the 1870 War.

On the first floor, the section on Asian and Oceanian art presents French East India Company porcelain, together with a great many pieces belonging to the Wahl-Offroy collection: weapons from the Middle and Far East, Chinese jewellery, Buddhist statuary and Islamic miniatures.

The new Painting Gallery presents a series of 19C Eure-et-Loir landscapes along with fragments of 16C polychrome wooden retables attributed to the Antwerp workshops.

Église St-Valérien – This 12C church features a tall square tower and crocketed spire (15C); on the south side there is a fine Romanesque multifoil doorway.

Chapelle Notre-Dame-du-Champdé – All that remains of this funerary chapel, destroyed at the end of the 19C, is a Flamboyant façade with finely worked ornamentation; a delicate balustrade is supported by sculpted consoles at the base of the gable which holds an effigy of the Virgin Mary, to whom the chapel is dedicated.

Grottes du Foulon ⊙ – *35 rue des Fouleries*. Lining the roadside like the many other caves in the area, and clearly visible, these caves owe their name to the activity of the fullers *(fouleurs)* who used to work here. Hollowed out in Senonian limestone by the waters of the Loir, the cave roofs have flinty concretions which in places have been transformed into geodes of chalcedony or quartz by the effects of crystallisation.

Église St-Jean-de-la-Chaîne – *Exit ⑤ on the town plan*. In the suburb of St-Jean on the north bank of the Loir stands an early-16C ogee-arched gate at the entrance to the churchyard. The **church of St-Jean** was built mainly in the 15C but the apses date from the 11C and 12C.

From this side of the river there is a fine view of the north façade of the château.

EXCURSIONS

Lutz-en-Dunois – *7km/4mi E along D 955*. Lutz has a charming Romanesque **church** with a low bell-tower crowned by a saddleback roof. The interior is decorated with 13C **murals** in red and yellow ochre: those on the oven-vault above the apse depict the Apostles and Bishop Saints; on the walls of the nave are Christ's Entry into Jerusalem, the Entombment, the Resurrection and the Descent into Limbo.

Abbaye du Bois de Nottonville ⊙ – *18km/11mi E; take D 927 to Varize and then follow the signs*. The 11C priory (restored in the 15C) belonged to Benedictine monks from Marmoutier. Note, in particular, the fortified doorway, the barn with a roof shaped like an inverted ship's hull, and the dovecot.

CHÂTEAU-GONTIER

Population 11 131
Michelin map 310: E-8 or 232 fold 19

On the border between Brittany and Maine, Château-Gontier is a striking old town, the capital of the Mayenne country. It was founded in the 11C by **Fulk Nerra**, Count of Anjou, who constructed a castle on the rocky spur overlooking the river and put it in the charge of one Gontier, an officer in his army. The area around belonged to the Benedictines of the abbey of St-Aubin at Angers, and it was they who built the 11C priory of St-Jean-Baptiste by the side of the castle.

The town was one of the centres of Royalist resistance *(chouannerie)* to the French Revolution. The Royalist leader and friend of Cadoudal (leader of the Royalist rebels known as the Chouans), **Pierre-Mathurin Mercier**, was born the son of an innkeeper in rue Trouvée. Cadoudal and Mercier passed through the town in October 1793 with the forces of the Vendée.

Château-Gontier is divided into two distinct areas: the upper town bisected by Grande-Rue on the west bank of the river, and the suburb around St-Julien Hospital on the east bank. The town has always been a great centre for fairs and markets, and every Thursday Parc St-Fiacre hosts a market for sheep and calves, one of the most important of its kind in Europe.

The quaysides are a reminder of the days when Château-Gontier was a port on the canalised Mayenne *(for details of boat trips on the Mayenne, see p 40)*.

Several itineraries for walking, cycling or riding through the surrounding area are available from the tourist office.

UPPER TOWN *1hr 30min*

Start from place St-Jean.

Jardin du Bout du Monde – These pretty gardens laid out in the grounds of the old priory are a pleasant place for a stroll and afford glimpses of the river and the far bank.

Viewpoint – From under the elm trees on the terrace built on the old ramparts, downhill from the church, there is a fine view of the far bank of the river.

Église St-Jean-Baptiste – The church is built in flint and red sandstone. The **interior★** reflects a remarkably forceful yet pure Romanesque style. The nave has modern stained glass and irregularly spaced columns supporting impressive arcades, whereas the crossing is roofed by an unusual dome resting on pendentives ending in colonnettes. Although there are remains of 13C and 14C frescoes in the nave, those in the transepts date from the 12C: in the north transept they illustrate God's creation of the birds, domestic animals and Adam and Eve (the figures of the Three Wise Men can be discerned in the chapel of St-Benoît); in the south transept are representations of Noah and the Ark.
The beautiful crypt is crowned by groined vaulting resting on two rows of columns.

The walk down to place St-Just gives a glimpse of the steep rise known as montée du Vieux-Collège. Walk along montée St-Just to Grande-Rue.

At the corner of Grande-Rue and rue de la Harelle there is a fine 15C timber-framed house and, opposite, the old salt store built in tufa and with a turret dating from the 16C.

Go up Grande-Rue and turn left onto rue de Thionville, then right onto rue d'Enfer.

This cobbled street is bordered on the left by the foundation structure of the church of St-Jean-l'Évangéliste.

To the right, rue de Lierru leads to rue Jean-Bourré, a reminder of the fame that this son of the town acquired as Financial Secretary and Treasurer of France during the reign of Louis XI *(see p 248)*.

CHÂTEAU-GONTIER

Alsace-Lorraine (R. et R. d')	R ?	Lierru (R. de)	B 25
Bourg-Roussel (R.)	A 5	Olivet (R. d')	A 29
Coubertin (Q. P. de)	B 7	Pasteur (Q.)	B 31
Foch (Av. Mar.)	B 9	Pilori (Pl. du)	A 33
Fouassier (R.)	A 10	République (Pl.)	A 30
Français-Libres (Pl. des)	A 12	St-Jean (Pl.)	A 39
Gambetta (R.)	A 14	St-Just (Pl.)	B 40
Gaulle (Quai Ch. de)	B 15	Thionville (R. de)	B 45
Horno (R. René)	A 18		
Joffre (Av. Mar.)	A 20		
Leclerc (R. de la Division)	A 22		
Lemonnier (R. Gén.)	B 24		

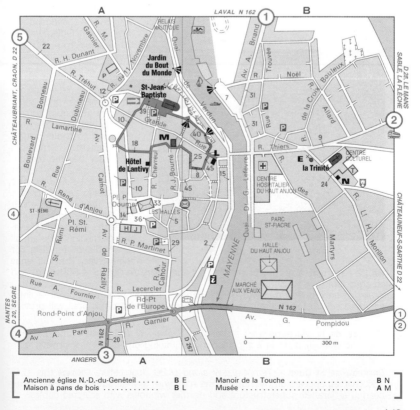

Ancienne église N.-D.-du-Genêteil	B E	Manoir de la Touche	B N
Maison à pans de bois	B L	Musée	A M

Musée d'Art et d'Archéologie ⓥ – Housed in the lovely 17C Hôtel Fouquet, the archaeological museum has a number of good paintings and sculptures as well as Ancient Greek and Roman remains: an unfinished painting by Le Brun of the *Battle of Constantine and Maxentius*; 17C Dutch pictures; a fine wooden statue of St Martha (15C French) and a 14C marble Virgin Mary. Local artists are represented by engravings by Tancrède Abraham and watercolours by Louis Rénier (19C).

Go up rue du Musée (note the building on the corner with rue Bruchemotte which has an elegant turret) and onto rue Chevreul.

Hôtel de Lantivy – This town house (no 26) has a particularly interesting 16C façade.

Take rue René-Homo to the left, then on the right rue Fouassier and rue de l'Allemandier to place St-Jean.

EAST BANK SUBURB *30min*

There are fine views of the upper town from the Pierre-de-Coubertin quayside.

Église de la Trinité ⓥ – The former Ursuline convent was built in the 17C by Pierre Corbineau and his son Gilles, architects from Laval. A statue of St Ursula adorns the pilastered façade of the church. Inside there is a monumental 18C altarpiece and the convent parlour grille.

To the right of the church is the elegant 15C manor house known as the **Manoir de la Touche**.

THE GOLDEN CALF

Le Veau d'Or – *Parc St-Fiacre* – ☎ *02 43 07 28 65* – *closed 11-18 Feb, 15-20 Jul, Sun evening and Mon* – *reservation recommended for weekends* – *14.49€ lunch, 16/36.60€*. This restaurant gets its name from the most important calf market in Europe, which is held every Thursday in the park. The house speciality is *tête de veau sauce gribiche*, a speciality made of calf's head, and other veal dishes.

Ancienne église Notre-Dame-du-Genêteil ⓥ – This austere little Romanesque church built of schist used to be a college chapel and is now used to house temporary art exhibitions.

EXCURSIONS

Refuge de l'Arche ⓥ – *On the outskirts of town along D 267.*

⬛ Half way between a zoo and a veterinary clinic, this 10ha/25-acre sanctuary is committed to the shelter, care and protection of sick, wounded or abandoned animals (not including domestic pets such as cats or dogs). It has around 800 house guests, fed and cared for mainly by volunteer workers. When the animals have recovered, and if they are fit enough to survive on their own, they are returned to their natural environment. The animals who have become too dependent on man are kept at the refuge. Among the long-term residents are *Tsavo*, the bear with a collar, *Djina* the tigress, *Sambaur* the leopard and *Namanga* the lion, who are all incapable of fending for themselves. The visit ends with a terrarium, a grotto for reptiles, a huge aviary (4 000m²/4 800sq yd) and an aquarium.

Ph. Gajic/MICHELIN

⬛ A playing ground fitted with slides, cable-cars and other recreational facilities has been set up for children. In bad weather, a covered picnic area will provide shelter for visitors.

Château de la Maroutière ⓥ – *3km/2mi S along N 162.* Built in the 13C and 14C, the château is set in a superb park containing one of the last private racecourses.

Château de St-Ouen – *7km/4mi SW along D 20.* Just before **Chemazé** this 15C-16C château appears on the right of the road with a great square staircase tower bearing a tiara-like superstructure and dormer windows with sculpted gables.

★VALLÉE DE LA MAYENNE

71km/44mi – allow one day

The quiet Mayenne follows a picturesque and winding course between steep wooded banks as it flows south to join the Loire. The river was made navigable in the 19C when 39 locks were built between Laval and Angers and it is now ideal for pleasure craft.

The valley is too steep for any houses to be built beside the river so it has been preserved in its natural state. The route described below passes through the villages of low red-stone houses with slate roofs which crown the top of the slopes. There are good views of the river, some from a bridge and some from the by-roads which lead down to a picturesque site on the river bank to a mill or an isolated château.

Daon – The village and its 16C manor house are superbly sited on a slope above the Mayenne. Daon was the birthplace of Abbé Bernier who negotiated the peace between the Chouans and the Republicans.

In Daon take D 213 E, turn left then left again.

A long avenue of lime and plane trees leads straight to the attractive 16C moated **Manoir de l'Escoublère**.

Beyond Daon, turn right off D 22 onto D 190 to Marigné.

Chenillé-Changé – This is one of the most attractive villages in the Segréen region with its **fortified watermill** ☉, dating from the turn of the 19C and still in use, as the white streaks of flour on the schist walls

> For information on hiring a houseboat to travel through the countryside at a leisurely pace, contact **Tourisme fluvial** *(Maine-Anjou Rivières – Le Moulin – 49220 Chenillé-Changé – ☏ 02 41 95 10 83).*

show. The old houses, 11C church and a **river boat centre** *(see Practical information)* with small barges moored along the shady banks of the Mayenne, all add to the peace and beauty of the scene.

Take the road across the river to Chambellay and turn right onto D 187.

La Jaille-Yvon – The village is perched on the cliff above the river. From the east end of the church there is an extensive view of the fields and meadows in the valley.

Take D 189 W and turn left onto N 162 going S.

Shortly after the turning to Chambellay the imposing 15C-17C buildings of the **Château du Bois-Montbourcher** come into sight *(left)*, surrounded by lawns and woods on the edge of a vast lake.

Le Lion-d'Angers – The town occupies a picturesque site on the west bank of the River Oudon just north of the confluence with the Mayenne. It is a horse breeding centre, particularly of half-breeds; the horse racing and competitions held here are famous throughout Anjou.

Église St-Martin ⊙ – The tracery decoration above the church door is pre-Romanesque, whereas the nave with its wooden vaulting is Romanesque. On the left wall of the nave above the entrance door are some 16C murals showing the Devil vomiting the Seven Deadly Sins, a Crucifix and St Christopher. In a recess there is a diptych of an Ecce Homo.

★ **Haras national de l'Isle-Briand** ⊙ – *1km/0.5mi E of Le Lion-d'Angers.*
⌖ In 1974, the premises of the national stud farm, which were too cramped in Angers city centre, was transferred to the Isle-Briand estate, where they now house an ultra-modern establishment. About 55 selected horses are stabled here. The tour of the stud farm includes the barns, the harness room, the forge (with oak flooring, more comfortable for the horses' hooves) and the riding school. The loose boxes are grouped according to the different types of horses: Normandy cob, Breton or Percheron draught horses, Anglo-Arabs, pure-bred Arabs, saddle horses, trotters and ponies. Horses which have won numerous prestigious races are brought here to pass on their genes, in the hope of producing another generation of winners.

Every year, the Mondial du Lion international race meeting is held on the third weekend in October; the elite of the racing fraternity from around 20 countries takes part in the event *(see Calendar of events on p 49).*

A. Laurioux/Haras national du Lion d'Angers

Out for a trot

Grez-Neuville – This picturesque village in the heart of the Maine basin slopes gently down to the banks of the Mayenne, its slate-roofed bell-tower reflected in the water. Grez-Neuville is the departure point for **river cruises** *(see p 40)* along the Mayenne and Oudon. In season, a Percheron horse can be seen on the towpath pulling a boat for about 1km/0.5mi.

The road down the east bank *(D 191)* sometimes overhangs the river; it passes *(left)* **Château du Sautret**, an impressive building with a dry moat.

In Feneu take D 768 S across the river to Montreuil-Juigné then follow N 162 to Angers.

CHÂTEAU-LA-VALLIÈRE

Population 1 535
Michelin map 317: K-3, 232 fold 22 or 4037 B2

This calm, small town ideal for tourists seeking a quiet haven is situated in a wooded region interspersed with many stretches of water.

Louise de La Vallière

Louise de La Baume le Blanc (1644-1710), better known as the Duchess of La Vallière, spent her childhood at La Vallière Manor, near the village of Reugny to the north-east of Tours.
Lady-in-waiting to Charles I of England's widow, Henrietta Maria, the gentle, gracious Louise captured the heart of the Sun King, Louis XIV, at Fontainebleau in 1662. She remained the royal mistress for five years before being ousted by the haughty Mme de Montespan. Following her fall from favour, she retired to the Carmelite convent in rue St-Jacques in Paris and eventually took the black veil from the hands of Queen Maria-Theresa; the preacher was Bossuet. For the 36 years of her convent life her piety, modesty and tolerance never failed her.

Étang du Val Joyeux – ⊚ This vast stretch of water *(bathing and sailing facilities)*, formed by the River Fare, lies in an attractive wooded setting. The nearby hill is crowned by a church.

Forêt de Château-la-Vallière – Except on the north side, the town is surrounded by a vast forest of pines and oaks, dotted with stretches of heath, which spreads over 3 000ha/7 410 acres and is ideal for hunting.

EXCURSION

Château de Vaujours – *3.5km/2mi SE.* Standing in front of the romantic ruins of this château *(closed to the public)* are a fortified barbican and a rampart wall interrupted at intervals by round towers, one of which has survived almost in its entirety, complete with battlements. The courtyard is bordered by the remains of the chapel and main building dating from the 15C. Louis XI came to the château several times to stay with his half-sister, Jeanne, the daughter of Charles VII and Agnès Sorel. Louise de La Vallière also held the title of the Duchess of Vaujours but visited the château only once in 1669.

CHÂTEAUNEUF-SUR-LOIRE

Population 7 032
Michelin map 64 fold 10, 237 fold 41, 238 fold 6 or 4045 E4

On the site of the old fortified castle to which the town owes its name, where Charles IV, the Fair, died in 1328, Louis Phelypeaux de la Vrillière, Secretary of State to Louis XIV, built a small-scale imitation of the château of Versailles. After the Revolution the château was sold to an architect from Orléans who had it demolished; only the 17C rotunda and gallery, the outbuildings and the pavilions in the forecourt, some of which are used as the town hall, remain.

Château grounds – The park is bordered by a moat; the western section is filled with water and spanned by an elegant stone footbridge. It is at its best at the end of May or in early June when the exotic plants and giant **rhododendrons** are in bloom.

Musée de la Marine de Loire ⊙ – The Nautical Museum, housed in the former stables of the château, contains collections made up for the most part of donations from descendants of Loire boatmen, which testify to the importance of the great river through the ages. Among the displays are carpentry tools as well as objects, garments, jewellery and a beautiful collection of Nevers faience. Visitors will learn about nautical techniques, river planning and maintenance, the ferrying of men and goods and the natural phenomena of river floods and pack ice.

Chambre d'hôte Cervina – *28 route de Châteauneuf – 45110 Germigny-des-Prés – 3km/1.9mi SE of Châteauneuf via D 60* – ☏ *02 38 58 21 15 – 5 rooms 33/43€ – meal 13€.* This house extends a friendly welcome to its guests but don't expect any luxury in the small bedrooms: two of them are attic rooms, the other three give directly onto the garden where it is possible, in summer, to have a barbecue and eat in the shade of the arbour. Meals are served from October to March.

Faience adorned with a boat sailing down the Loire

Along the quayside you will see the reconstruction of various boats which once sailed on the river.

Église St-Martial – The church was built late in the 16C in the Gothic style but lost its nave in a fire in 1940; all that remains is a double arch through which the old market hall of St-Pierre can be seen. Inside stands the marble **mausoleum**★ of Louis Phelypeaux de la Vrillière who died in 1681. This imposing Baroque monument, framed by two skeletons acting as caryatids, was carved in Italy by a pupil of Bernini.

Halle St-Pierre – Next to the church stands this picturesque building supported on wooden columns; originally built as a boathouse, it became the corn market in 1854.

CANAL D'ORLÉANS: LOIRE REACH

The Seine Reach is described on p 210.

The Orléans Canal, which links the Loire to the Loing just north of Montargis, was built between 1677 and 1692. The 79km/49mi-long canal was the scene of intense activity, mainly the transport of timber and coal to Paris, for 250 years. The canal was closed in 1954 with the decline of river traffic on the Loire and the competition from the railways. Repairs are being carried out on the canal to make it navigable again for pleasure boats. The stretch between Fay-aux-Loges and Combreux is now open to boats and barges.

Chécy – *15km/9mi W along N 960.* This village was originally founded by the Carnutes, a Celtic tribe. The church of St-Pierre-St-Germain, with its 12C belfry-porch, offered hospitality to Joan of Arc on 28 April 1429, on the eve of the Orléans siege. Behind the church the small **Musée de la Tonnellerie** ⊙ (Cooperage Museum) and a restored farmhouse remind visitors that in days gone by most of the local people were wine-growers.

Fay-aux-Loges – *9km/5.6mi NW along D 11.* This village on the banks of the Orléans Canal has a handsome low-roofed **church** (11C-13C). The fortified house behind the church is the vicarage.

Combreux – *13km/8mi NE along D 10 and D 9.* The town clusters on the picturesque south bank of the Orléans Canal. On the north side of the town and the canal, along D 9, stands an eye-catching **château** (16C-17C), built of brick with stone dressings and surrounded by a moat.

★ **Étang de la Vallée** – *2km/1mi W of Combreux.* ⊚ The reservoir which feeds the Orléans Canal is on the eastern fringe of Orléans Forest in a wild setting of dense trees and tall reeds where ducks and moorhens can be heard quacking, clucking and cackling. There are facilities for swimming, fishing, windsurfing, sailing and picnics.

CHÂTEAU-RENAULT

Population 5 538
Michelin map 317: O-3, 238 fold 1 or 4037 F2

Château-Renault was founded in 1066 by Renault, son of Geoffroi de Château-Gontier, on a tongue of land between the River Brenne and the River Gault at the point where they meet. The main street runs in a large curve down to the river bank. The shaded terraces laid out beneath the castle keep offer fine views of the two rivers and their valleys.

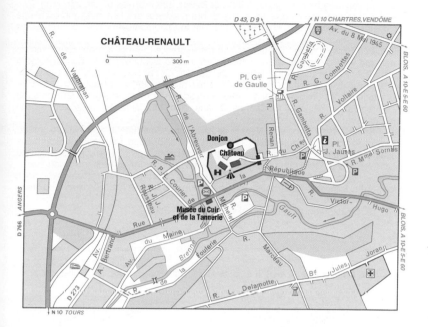

Musée du Cuir et de la Tannerie ⊙ – Housed in an old tannery, this Leather and Tanning Museum displays the various stages of traditional manufacture with, among other things, a collection of old currying machinery.

Château – A 14C gate, surmounted by a hoarding (to enable the defenders to protect the entrance) leads onto the terraces shaded by lime trees, from where there is an attractive **view**★ over the town.

The top of the 12C **keep** *(donjon)* has been demolished. The town hall occupies the 17C château. This belonged to the owners of the château in Châteaudun and then to two illustrious sailors: the Marquis de Château-Renault under Louis XIV and, under Louis XVI, the Count of Estaing who died under the guillotine in 1793.

EXCURSION

St-Laurent-en-Gâtines – *9km/5.6mi W.* At the roadside stands a massive brick and stone edifice. Known for many years as **La Grand' Maison** (Great House), it was once the residence of the abbots of Marmoutier, who owned the land of St-Laurent-en-Gâtines. The building was constructed in the 15C and converted into a church in the 19C; a spire was added to the polygonal tower which housed the stairs and two large Flamboyant windows were inserted on one side.

Château de CHAUMONT-SUR-LOIRE★★

Michelin map 318: E-7 or 238 fold 14

The Château de Chaumont is as well sited as Amboise on the south bank of the Loire, overlooking the town and the river. The feudal austerity of the edifice is softened by its Renaissance influence, its elegant stair tower and its sumptuous Council Room.

The original fortress of Chaumont was demolished twice; it was rebuilt between 1445 and 1510 by Pierre d'Amboise, Charles I d'Amboise, the eldest of Pierre's 17 children, and Charles II, his grandson.

In 1560 Catherine de' Medici, the widow of Henri II, acquired the castle purely as a means of exacting revenge against **Diane de Poitiers**, the mistress of the late King. The Queen forced her rival to give up her favourite residence at Chenonceau in exchange for Chaumont. Diane de Poitiers never set foot in Chaumont, however, but retired to Anet where she died in 1566.

Catherine de' Medici's stay at Chaumont and the existence there of a room connected by a staircase with the top of a tower have given rise to plenty of speculation. The room has been said to be the study of **Cosimo Ruggieri**, the Queen's astrologer, and the tower the observatory from which Catherine and her master plotter consulted the stars. It was apparently at Chaumont that Catherine read in the future the grim fate awaiting her three sons, François II, Charles IX and Henri III, and the accession of the Bourbons with Henri IV of Navarre.

Exiled from Paris by Napoleon, **Madame de Staël** spent some time in 1810 at Chaumont. She worked there, surrounded by her court which included Benjamin Constant and Madame Récamier. When her guests praised the landscape of the Loire, she replied sadly "Yes, it's an admirable scene, but I so much prefer my gutter in rue du Bac".

In 1875 the castle was bought by **Mlle Say**, heiress to an industrial fortune, who soon became the Princesse de Broglie; for Chaumont this was an era of luxury and magnificent festivities.

Since 1938 Chaumont has belonged to the French State.

TOUR *45min*

Park ⊙ – A 10min walk uphill will bring you to the castle. This pleasant stroll is an opportunity to admire the fine landscaped gardens designed by Henri Duchêne at the end of the 19C. The paths wind their way through cedars, lime trees and redwoods. The **view★** from the terrace is remarkable.

The building – The outer west façade, which is the oldest, has an austere and military appearance. Most of the windows that can be seen now did not exist originally. The two other façades, despite their feudal aspect, reflect the influence of the Renaissance.

Chaumont-sur-Loire – Ruggieri's Bedchamber

At ground-floor level there is a frieze bearing the interlaced Cs of Charles de Chaumont-Amboise, alternating with the rebus of the castle a volcano or *chaud mont* (Chaumont). The emblem of Diane de Poitiers is carved in front of each machicolation on the fortress and the east wing; it consists of intertwined Ds or of the hunting horn, bow and quiver of Diana the Huntress.

The entrance gate is adorned with the arms of France and the initials of Louis XII and Anne of Brittany on a field of fleur-de-lis and ermine in homage to the then reigning monarchs.

Apartments ⊙ – Note the room of the two rivals, Catherine de' Medici and Diane de Poitiers, and also Ruggieri's study and the Council Room, which is paved with 17C Spanish majolica tiles bought in Palermo, Sicily, by the Prince of Broglie. These apartments contain fine 16C and 17C tapestries, good furniture and a collection of the terracotta medallions made by Nini, an 18C Italian artist who set up his workshop in the stables.

Stables ⊙ – *About 50m/55yd from the château.* The size and luxurious fittings of these stables give an idea of the part played by horses in the lives of princely families.

Built in 1877 by the Prince de Broglie and fitted with electric lighting in 1906, the stables include stalls for the horses and ponies, boxes for the thoroughbreds, a kitchen, a remarkable harness room, horse-drawn carriages and a second courtyard known as the guests' courtyard, in which there is a small riding centre. Note in a corner of the stables the unusual double-roofed tower, the former dovecot, converted into an oven for Nini, which later became the riding school for children staying at the château.

The stables organise **rides in horse-drawn carriages**.

Conservatoire international des Parcs et Jardins du Paysage ⊙ – The château farmhouse houses a permanent information and training centre offering thematic workshops aimed at enlightening visitors on the fascinating world of botany and horticulture. It also runs university level courses in gardening and landscaping. An important **International Garden Festival** is held here every summer from mid-June to mid-October.

Chaumont hosts the International Garden Festival

After walking over an unusual gangway, the visitor enters a curious and fascinating plant kingdom. It is neither a landscape garden nor a botanical park, rather a unique, changing site that pays tribute to the beauty of nature, where the creative genius of gardeners and horticulturists can be given free rein. This annual festival, which was held in Chaumont for the first time in 1992, aims to familiarize the general public with contemporary creations, new possibilities for garden layout and unusual, daring combinations of plants and flowers. Every summer, the work of the previous year is removed and a new theme is suggested to 30 landscape gardeners, some of international renown. These experts are required to draw on their powers of imagination and originality to design the most attractive garden on the 250m²/300sq yd plot allotted to each of them.

The beautiful Château de Chenonceau *(the town of Chenonceaux is written with an "x" but not the château)* stretches across the River Cher in a harmonious natural setting of water, greenery, gardens and trees. To this perfection is added the elegance of the château's architecture, interior decor and magnificent furniture.

A magnificent avenue of plane trees leads to the château. Tourists with a fanciful imagination can try to imagine the entry of Charles IX, among mermaids, nymphs and satyrs.

A CHATEAU SHAPED BY WOMEN

The first château was built between 1513 and 1521 by **Thomas Bohier**, Treasury Superintendent under François I. Bohier's acquisition of Chenonceau and the château's frequent change of ownership thereafter make up an eventful tale. For 400 years the main protagonists in this, both happy and sad, were women, be they royal wives, mistresses or queens.

Catherine Briçonnet, the soul of an architect – In 1512, Chenonceau was put up for sale, whereupon Bohier bought it for 12 400 *livres*. He immediately demolished all the old buildings except for the keep. As he was kept busy by his duties and often had to be with the army near Milan, he could not supervise the building of his new residence. It was his wife Catherine, from a family of great financiers in Touraine, who took charge and was the creative spirit behind the project. It is possible to detect a certain feminine influence and eye for convenience and comfort in the site chosen for the building and the simplicity of its layout, consistent with the requirements of someone used to running a household.

The new building was completed in 1521 but Bohier and his wife had little time in which to enjoy it as they died in 1524 and 1526 respectively. A few years later, Bohier's accounts were examined and he was shown to owe a large sum of money to the Treasury. In order to pay his father's debts, Antoine Bohier gave up the château in 1535 to François I who would use it as a hunting lodge.

Diane de Poitiers, the everlasting beauty – When Henri II came to the throne in 1547 he gave Chenonceau to Diane de Poitiers. She was 20 years older than him but was still radiantly attractive. "I saw her," wrote a contemporary, "at the age of 70 (in fact she died at 67), as beautiful to look at and as kind as at 30. She had very white skin and wore no make-up on her face." Diane was the widow of Louis de Brézé, for whom she had a splendid tomb built in Rouen Cathedral, and in honour of whom she always wore black and white, the colours of mourning. Her influence over Henri II was such that, in addition to all the other favours she received, she made him wear mourn-

ing too, to the despair of the rejected and humiliated Queen.

Diane was an able manager and set out to exploit her estate and her position; she took an interest in agriculture, in the sale of wine, in her income from taxes and in anything else that brought in money. She found an excellent source of revenue in the 20 *livres* tax on bells, of which she received a good share; Rabelais said, "The king has hung all the bells of the kingdom round the neck of his mare". Diane was a woman of good taste; she created a beautiful garden and had a bridge built linking the château with the north bank of the Cher. She spent some happy times here with Henri II.

When Henri II was killed in a tournament in 1599, Diane found herself face to face with Catherine de' Medici who was now regent. While her husband was alive the queen had been patient and dissembling and had accepted the situation, but now she wanted vengeance.

Château de Chenonceau – Study of Diane de Poitiers

B. Kaufmann/MICHELIN

Knowing that Diane was very attached to Chenonceau, she forced her to give up the property in exchange for Chaumont. After a brief attempt at resistance, Diane gave in, left the banks of the Cher and retired to Anet Château where she died seven years later.

Catherine de' Medici, the lady of leisure – Catherine de' Medici satisfied her love of the arts and her thirst for magnificence on a grand scale at Chenonceau. She had a park laid out, built a graceful two-storey gallery on the bridge and added extensive outbuildings. She held one magnificent feast after another, greatly impressing her contemporaries. She put on a huge party for the arrival of François II and Mary Stuart, and an even more sumptuous one for Charles IX. No expense was spared at these festivities, which included banquets, dances, fancy dress balls, fireworks and even a naval battle on the Cher.

Louise de Lorraine, the inconsolable widow – Catherine bequeathed Chenonceau to her daughter-in-law, Louise de Lorraine, wife of Henri III. After the King's assassination by Jacques Clément, Louise retired to the château and according to royal custom put on white mourning which she continued to wear until the end of her life, earning herself the nickname White Queen or White Lady. For 11 years Louise remained faithful to the memory of her husband, passing her time by praying, embroidering or reading.
From Louise de Lorraine Chenonceau passed on to her niece, Françoise de Lorraine, wife of César de Vendôme, the son of Henri IV and Gabrielle d'Estrées who had stayed at the château in 1598.

Madame Dupin, the literary spirit – In 1733 it became the property of Dupin, the farmer-general who was the tax collector. Madame Dupin held a salon which was attended by all the famous names of the time. **Jean-Jacques Rousseau** was her son's tutor and it was for the benefit of this boy that he wrote his treatise on education, *Émile*. In his *Confessions* the philosopher writes warmly of those happy days, "We had a good time in that beautiful place, we ate well, I became as fat as a monk".
Madame Dupin grew into old age encircled by the affection of the villagers, with the result that the château survived the Revolution unscathed. At her request she was buried in the park.
The Château de Chenonceau now belongs to the Menier family.

Eating out

BUDGET

Hostellerie La Renaudière – *24 r. Bretonneau – 37150 Chenonceaux – ☎ 02 47 23 90 04 – closed 7 Jan-8 Feb, 15 Nov-21 Dec except weekends – 16 rooms 38.11/96.04€ – ☐ 5.34€ – restaurant 15/30€.* This early-19C building near the castle has retained its period charm. The trees in the park have been classified as national treasures! It is lovely to eat outside in fine weather. The veranda in the dining room overlooks the beautiful landscape, as do some of the rooms.

MODERATE

La Roseraie – *7 r. Bretonneau – 37150 Chenonceaux – ☎ 02 47 23 90 09 – closed 1 Dec-Feb – ▣ – 18 rooms 51.07/83.85€ – ☐ 7.32€ – restaurant 15/28€.* The façade of this typical regional building near the castle is covered in flowers and Virginia creeper. Spacious rooms with a countrified decor. Meals are served on the terrace, or by the big fireplace in the dining room in winter. Shady garden with heated outdoor pool.

LUXURY

Château de la Bourdaisière – *25 r. de la Bourdaisière – 37270 Montlouis-sur-Loire – 18km/11.25mi N of Chenonceaux on D 40 – ☎ 02 47 45 16 31 – ▣ – 20 rooms from 107€.* If you're tempted to stay in a castle, then this Renaissance-style property, set among vineyards, is for you. The rooms have a personal touch, often with period furniture, and they overlook a huge park planted with cedars and sequoias. While you're enjoying the grounds, be sure to have a look at the vegetable garden.

Shopping

Cave des Dômes – *37150 Chenonceaux – ☎ 02 47 23 90 07.* This is where you will find and enjoy the delicious Chenonceaux wine, bottled at the château.

Son et lumière

The Ladies of Chenonceau (Au temps des Dames de Chenonceau)
Under the influence of six women, Chenonceau evolved from a fortified mill into an elegant residence where sumptuous parties were held.
Performances daily 1 July to 31 August at 10.15pm. 7.62€. ☎ 02 47 23 90 07.

> "The Château de Chenonceau, shrouded in aristocratic dignity, exudes a strangely suave atmosphere. It lies at some distance from the village, which stands respectfully to one side. It can be glimpsed at the end of a wide avenue enhanced with greenery, surrounded by woods, framed by a vast park boasting fine lawns. Built on rippling waters, it rears its pretty turrets and square chimneys into the skies. The Cher runs beneath it, swirling at the foot of its arches, whose pointed features break up the sparkling current. The general feeling is one of gentle peace, elegance and comforting strength. Its stillness is not remotely boring and its melancholy is never conducive to remorse."
>
> Gustave Flaubert – *Par les Champs et les Grèves* (1847)

TOUR ⏱ *2hr*

Approach – As you walk towards the castle and pass between two sphinxes, the outbuildings erected after the plans of Philibert Delorme (wax museum, restaurant and tea house) can be seen on the right.

After crossing a bridge the path reaches a terrace surrounded by a moat. To the left is Diane de Poitiers' Italian garden; to the right, that of Catherine de' Medici, bounded by the great trees in the park. On the terrace stands the keep of the former 15C Château des Marques.

Château – The château consists of a rectangular mansion with turrets at the corners. It stands on two piers from the old mill, which rest on the bed of the Cher. The library and the chapel are corbelled out on the left. Catherine de' Medici's two-storeyed gallery stretches across the bridge over the river. This building has a classical simplicity contrasting with the ornate and exuberant appearance given to the older section which now looks like an annexe.

Ground floor – The four main rooms lead off the hall which features ribbed vaults with keystones aligned along a zigzag axis. The old guard-room *(left)* is paved with majolica tiles and adorned with 16C Flemish tapestries; in the chapel is a 16C marble low-relief sculpture of a Virgin and Child; the fireplace in Diane de Poitiers' bedroom was designed by Jean Goujon note the touching Virgin and Child believed to be the work of Murillo.

Pictures by Jordaens and Tintoretto and a 16C Brussels tapestry hang in Catherine de' Medici's **Green Cabinet**. The 16C ceiling is lined with fine layers of pewter decorated in green. The small adjacent room overlooking the River Cher was Catherine de' Medici's library; it has retained its splendid coffered ceiling in carved oak, dating from 1525.

The **Great Gallery★** overlooking the Cher is 60m/197ft long and has black and white chequered paving. During the First World War the gallery was converted into a military hospital and from 1940 to 1942 the demarcation line ran right through the middle.

At the end of the gallery, a drawbridge, raised every evening, leads to the wooded area on the south bank of the Cher and to Madame Dupin's grave.

Note the remarkable Renaissance fireplace in **François I's Bedchamber★★**, which contains paintings by Van Loo *(Three Graces)* and Il Primaticcio *(Diane de Poitiers as the Huntress Diana)*, and a handsome 15C Italian piece of furniture inlaid in ivory and mother-of-pearl. In a salon with a magnificent French-style ceiling are works by Rubens *(Jesus and St John)*, Mignard, Nattier *(Mme Dupin)* and a portrait of *Louis XIV* by Rigaud, in a sumptuous frame.

First floor – This is reached by a straight staircase, which at the time it was built was an innovation in France. From the vestibule, with its Oudenaarde tapestries depicting hunting scenes, walk through to Gabrielle d'Estrées' Bedchamber, then the Royal or **Five Queens' Bedchamber★**, then Catherine de' Medici's Bedchamber and finally to that of César de Vendôme.

Second floor – The bedchamber of Louise de Lorraine, who never stopped mourning her husband, Henri III, has an impressive funeral decor. The furniture is covered with black velvet, the curtains are made of black damask and the ceiling is decorated with crowns of thorns and cable motifs painted in white over a black background.

A small convent for Capuchin nuns was set up in the attics, complete with a drawbridge which was raised at night to segregate the nuns from the other occupants of the castle.

Kitchens – Set up in two hollow piers of the château, resting on the very bed of the river, the kitchen quarters consist of several rooms: the butlery, the pantry, a larder for storing meat, the actual kitchen where royal meals were prepared and the refectory for staff members.

From the bridge giving access to the kitchens, take a look at the mini-harbour through which supplies were delivered to the castle and which Diane de Poitiers is said to have used as a swimming pool.

Musée de Cires ⊙ – The Waxworks Museum is housed in the Dômes building, so called because of the shape of its roof. There are 15 scenes evoking life in the château and the personalities associated with it.

★★ **Park** – This stretches along the banks of the Cher, offering picturesque views of the château. There are picnic areas along the moat.

THE CHER VALLEY

Round trip of 60km/37mi – allow 1hr 45min

Leave Chenonceaux eastwards (towards Montrichard), cross the Cher and take N 76 W towards Tours.

Bléré – At the entrance to Bléré, on place de la République, stands an elegant monument with particularly fine Italian-style sculpted decoration; this is the **funerary chapel** (1526) of Guillaume de Saigne, Treasurer of the Royal Artillery under François I.

Beyond Bléré, continue along N 76 then follow D 45, drive through Athée then turn towards Le Grais.

Prieuré de Saint-Jean-du-Grais ⊙ – This tastefully restored priory set in pleasant surroundings offers an insight into 12C monastic life as visitors walk through the chapter-house, the dormitory and the refectory.

Drive along D 82 leading to N 76 then towards Bléré for 1km/0.6mi before turning left.

Château de Leugny ⊙ – This elegant château on the Cher was built by André Portier, a pupil of Gabriel, for his own use. It is furnished in the Louis XVI style.

Rejoin N 76 towards Tours.

Véretz – This smart little town tucked between the Cher and the hillside makes a charming picture from the north bank of the river: the houses and church lead the eye west to the tree-lined paths and terraces of the château. Among those who once strolled in the château grounds were the Abbé de Rancé (1626-1700) who reformed the Trappist Order, the Abbé d'Effiat and Madame de Sévigné, the Princesse de Conti and the Abbé de Grécourt who wrote light verse; Voltaire stayed at the Château de Véretz in his youth. In the village square stands a monument to **Paul-Louis Courier** (1772-1825), an officer under the Empire who bought the Chavonnière estate with its large house on the Véretz plateau in 1816 and settled there with his young wife. From his country retreat he began to harass the government with wittily caustic pamphlets, such as "A petty village tyrant under the Restoration". Despite his talent his quarrelsome temperament made him unpopular, and on 10 April 1825 he was assassinated in Larçay Forest under mysterious circumstances.

Take D 85 N across the River Cher to Montlouis.

Montlouis-sur-Loire – Montlouis is built in terraces up a hillside of tufa which is riddled with caves. Its vineyards on the south-facing plateau between the Loire and the Cher produce a heady, fruity white wine made from the famous Pinot de la Loire grape. Beside the church stands a Renaissance mansion (now the priest's house) with dormer windows decorated with shell motifs.

The Babou family

In the 16C Montlouis was ruled by the Babous of La Bourdaisière, a turbulent family whose main residence, the **Château de la Bourdaisière**, lay a few miles to the south on the banks of the Cher. Montlouis was built c 1520 by Philibert Babou, silversmith to François I. His wife, Marie Babou, lived in it. She was known as La Belle Babou and was the first to admit she had a roving eye; she boasted of having known François I, Charles V and many others. Gabrielle, the beautiful daughter born in 1573 to Antoine d'Estrées and Françoise Babou, also went on to enjoy royal favour; she was the mistress of Henri IV and when she died the King turned to another Babou for consolation.

Maison de la Loire ⊙ – *Quai A.-Baillet.* Exhibitions on the fauna and flora of the Loire region are displayed here.

Drive out of Montlouis towards Amboise then turn right to La Bourdaisière.

Château de la Bourdaisière ⊙ – Part of the château, the outbuildings, the gardens and the **kitchen garden**★ (specialising in tomato growing with more than 400 varieties) can be visited.

Follow D 40 to St-Martin-le-Beau.

St-Martin-le-Beau – The **church** has a finely sculpted Romanesque doorway.

Return to Chenonceaux on D 40.

Château de CHEVERNY★★★

Michelin map 318: F-7 or 238 fold 15

Standing on the edge of Sologne Forest, not far from the châteaux of Blois and Chambord, Cheverny owes its charm to the harmonious proportions of its symmetric design, and to its sumptuous interior decoration. Its Classical façade is built of attractive white stone from the Bourré quarries *(28km/17mi SW)* and is crowned by a splendid slate roof. The château is still home to the descendants of the Hurault de Cheverny family who have perpetuated the tradition of deer hunting; between autumn and Easter each year the hunt rides out in the surrounding woodland.

TOUR ○ 45min

Château – Construction work was carried out uninterruptedly by Count Hurault de Cheverny between 1604 and 1634; consequently, the château displays a rare unity of style, both in the architecture and the decoration.

The symmetric design and harmonious grandeur of the façade are characteristic features of the period of Louis XIII. On either side of the single bay containing the main entrance and staircase are steep-roofed central sections, themselves flanked by massive corner pavilions with square domes topped by open-work belfries. At first-floor level there are oval niches housing the busts of Roman emperors, whereas the Hurault coat of arms above the main doorway is surrounded by two concentric collars, one symbolising the Order of the Holy Ghost, the other, the Order of St Michael.

The interior is sumptuously appointed, with beautiful furniture, sculptures, gilt work, marble and multicoloured panelling.

Eating out

BUDGET

Le Grand Chancelier – *2 r. du Chêne-des-Dames – 41700 Cheverny – ☎ 02 54 79 22 57 – closed Jan, Feb, Tue out of season and Wed except lunchtime in season – reservation recommended in high season – 9€ lunch, 15/36€.* You can eat at a stone's throw from the castle, in the dining room with its exposed beams, or outdoors on the terrace. The chef's ideas are original, using regional or traditional cuisine. Brasserie menu in the afternoon in high season for famished tourists.

La Ferme de la Pinsadière – *41700 Contres – 12km/7.5mi S of Cheverny towards Romorantin, then D 99 and minor road – ☎ 02 54 98 77 21 – closed Dec, Jan, Tue evening and Wed – 15.24€.* This pretty Sologne farm is hidden away, but fortunately the road to it is well signposted. The restaurant is famous for its spit-roasted meat, and the terrace facing a small lake is an invitation to linger. Impeccable service.

MODERATE

La Rousselière – *41700 Cheverny – S on D 102 – ☎ 02 54 79 23 02 – www.golf-cheverny.com – closed evenings from Sep to Easter – reservation recommended – 16.77/25.92€.* This restaurant overlooking the golf course is well known to golfers, who come and eat between rounds. The dining room has exposed timbers and is decorated in soft, pretty cream and orange tones. Terrace overlooking a small lake. Traditional cooking.

Where to stay

BUDGET

Le Clos Bigot – *41120 Chitenay – 2km/1mi SE of Chitenay towards Contres then follow a lane – ☎ 02 54 44 21 28 – closed 16 Nov-28 Feb – ⊅ – 4 rooms 36.59/83.85€.* A peaceful 17C longhouse with three rooms under a sloping roof and an apartment complete with dovecot, converted into a bathroom. The sitting room is comfortably furnished with traditional pieces, inviting you to relax in front of the wood stove.

Chambre d'hôte Le Béguinage – *41700 Cour-Cheverny – ☎ 02 54 79 29 92 – le.beguinage@wanadoo.fr – ⊅ – 6 rooms 42/60€.* The wooded park and the lake are not the only treasures hidden behind the gates of the ivy-covered town house. The rooms are spacious, elegant and unpretentious, with parquet or terracotta floors and exposed beams. Reasonable prices.

Chambre d'hôte La Raboullière – *Chemin de Marçon – 41700 Contres – 10km/6.25mi S of Cheverny on D 102 and minor road – ☎ 02 54 79 05 14 – ⊅ – 5 rooms 45.73€.* This lovely Sologne longhouse is in fact a complete reconstruction! It owes its authentic appearance to the fact that it has been built with old materials recuperated from neighbouring farms. Richly furnished rooms. Breakfast is served in front of the fire in winter or in the garden in summer.

Château de Cheverny

A. de Valroger/MICHELIN

Dining room – To the right of the hall is the dining room hung with a fine 17C Flemish tapestry. The room has retained its French-style painted ceiling and small murals depicting the story of Don Quixote; both are by Jean Mosnier (1600-56), a native of Blois. The walls are covered with Cordoba leather embossed with the Hurault coat of arms.

Private apartments in the west wing – Access to the west wing is via the splendid main staircase with its straight flights of steps and rich sculptural decoration. The private apartments consist of eight rooms, all magnificently furnished.

★ **Armoury** – The armoury is the largest room in the château. The ceiling, the wainscots and the shutters were painted by Mosnier, who also executed the painting on the gilt wood chimney-piece, depicting the death of Adonis. A collection of arms and armour from the 15C to the 17C is displayed on the walls along with a tapestry from the Gobelins factory (1610) showing the *Abduction of Helen*.

★★ **King's Bedchamber** – The King's Bedchamber is the most splendid room in the château. The ceiling is coffered in the Italian style, gilded and painted by Mosnier, as is the rich Renaissance chimney-piece, embellished with telamones, cherubs and plant motifs. The walls are hung with tapestries from the Paris workshops (1640) after Simon Vouet; beneath them are wainscots decorated with small pictures. The canopied bed is covered with Persian silk embroidered with flowers (1550). A remarkable red-and-blue tapestry (*Fishermen returning*, after Teniers) hangs in the ante-room.

Grand Salon – *Back to the ground floor*. In the antechamber, note the superb red-and-blue tapestry depicting *The Fishermen's Return* after Teniers (the other part is in the Tapestry Room). The Grand Salon is decorated with 17C and 18C furniture and paintings. The ceiling is entirely covered, as is the wall panelling, with painted decoration enhanced with gilding. The paintings on either side of the mirror include a portrait of *Cosimo de' Medici* by Titian, another of *Jeanne d'Aragon* from the School of Raphaël and, on the chimney-piece, a portrait by Mignard of *Marie-Johanne de Saumery*, Countess of Cheverny.

Gallery, Petit Salon, Library – The **Gallery** is furnished with magnificent Régence chairs and contains several paintings, including three splendid **portraits by François Clouet★★**, a portrait of *Jeanne d'Albret* by Miguel Oñate and a *Self-Portrait* by Rigaud. The **Petit Salon** is hung with 16C, 17C and 18C pictures. The **Library** features some fine woodwork and a beautiful parquet floor; it also contains some very fine bindings.

Tapestry Room – The smaller salon is hung with five 17C Flemish tapestries after cartoons by Teniers. Both rooms contain Louis XIV and Louis XV period furnishings, including a Louis XV Chinese lacquered commode and a magnificent Louis XV **clock★★** decorated with bronzes by Caffieri.

Park – The château is surrounded by a lovely 100ha/247-acre park.

⊙ Visitors of all ages will enjoy a tour of the grounds aboard an electric car and a boat trip. Fans of Tintin and Captain Haddock will delight in the permanent exhibition displayed in the château's former smithy.

Outbuildings – There is **kennelling★** for a pack of 90 hounds, cross-breeds from English foxhounds and the French Poitou race, and the **Trophy Room** displays 2 000 deer antlers.

L'Orangerie – Some 200m/220yd from the northern steps, on the way out of the château grounds, stands a magnificent early-18C orangery, now entirely restored. Receptions are held here all the year round and, in summer, exhibitions.

EXCURSION

Château de Troussay ⊘ – *3.5km/2mi W skirting the Cheverny park as far as D 52; turn left and take the first fork on the right.* This small Renaissance château was refurbished in the late 19C by the historian Louis de la Saussaye with features from other historic buildings of the region then in a state of neglect. Note particularly the stone carving of a **porcupine**, the emblem of Louis XII, on the rear façade taken from the Hurault de Cheverny mansion in Blois and the beautiful **chapel door**★ carved with delicate scrollwork. The tiles on the ground floor date from the reign of Louis XII, the Renaissance windows came from the Guise mansion in Blois and the *grisaille* on the ceiling in the little salon are attributed to **Jean Mosnier**. The château, which is lived in, is furnished with fine pieces dating from the 16C to the 18C. The outbuildings round the courtyard house a small **museum** evoking past domestic and agricultural life in the Sologne.

The background information contained in the Art and architecture section of the Introduction will make your visits to local sights and monuments far more interesting and instructive.

CHINON★★

Population 8 716
Michelin map 317: J-5, 232 fold 34 or 4037 B5

Chinon lies at the heart of a well-known wine region, surrounded by the fertile **Véron countryside** and beautiful **Chinon Forest**. The well-preserved old houses of this medieval town are strung along the banks of the Vienne beneath the crumbling walls of its gigantic ruined fortress. A **medieval market** held here every year plunges visitors back into the lively atmosphere of the Late Middle Ages.

> *Chinon, Chinon, Chinon,*
> *Small town, great renown,*
> *Resting on its weary stones,*
> *Above, the thick forests,*
> *Below, the River Vienne.*

Rabelais

The road approaching Chinon from the south gives the best **view**★★ of the spectacular setting of town and castle brooding over the River Vienne.

*Park along quai Danton to take in the sweeping panorama and get out your camera for a few photographs! A small **tourist train** ⊘ offers guided tours of the town in summer.*

From the quayside, the different parts of the castle can be clearly distinguished: on the left, Fort du Coudray; in the centre, the massive Château du Milieu stretching as far as the slender clock tower with its roof and machicolations; on the right, the site where Fort St-Georges, now demolished, once stood.

River Vienne at Chinon

Joan of Arc at Chinon

Escorted by six men-at-arms, Joan travelled from Lorraine to Chinon, arriving on 6 March, without encountering any of the armed bands which were ravaging the country. The people took this as a clear sign of divine protection. Waiting to be received by Charles VII, Joan spent two days at an inn in the lower town, fasting and praying.

When the 18-year-old peasant girl was finally admitted to the palace, an attempt was made to put her out of countenance. The great hall was lit by 50 torches and 300 courtiers in rich apparel were assembled there. The King was hiding among the crowd while a courtier wore his robes. Joan ventured forward, immediately recognized the real King and went straight up to him. "Gentle Dauphin," she said – for Charles, not having been crowned, was only the Dauphin to her – "my name is Jehanne la Pucelle (Joan the Maid). The King of Heaven sends word by me that you will be anointed and crowned in the city of Reims, and you will be the Lieutenant of the King of Heaven, who is the King of France." Charles was consumed with doubts about his birthright as a result of the scandalous behaviour of his mother, Isabella of Bavaria. When Joan said to him, "I tell you in the name of Our Lord Christ that you are the heir of France and the true son of the King", he was reassured and almost believed in the courageous girl's mission.

His advisers were more stubborn, however. Joan was made to appear before the court at Poitiers. A tribunal of doctors and midwives was set up to decide whether she was inspired by God or the devil. For three weeks she was cross-examined. The simplicity and swiftness of her responses, her piety and her confidence in her heavenly mission convinced even the most sceptical and she was declared to be truly a "Messenger of God". She returned to Chinon, where she was given the necessary armed men and equipment. She left on 20 April 1429 to fulfil her miraculous and tragic destiny.

Rabelais's childhood home – **François Rabelais** (1494-1553) was born near Chinon at La Devinière and grew up in Chinon where his parents had a house in rue de la Lamproie. He was the author of the spirited adventures of Pantagruel and his father Gargantua, two giants whose earthy realism invariably delights the reader. Written in the manner of a burlesque farce, his books were intended for the budding bourgeoisie: they denounced priggishness and ignorance and praised a moral society based on free, honest citizenship.

From the Plantagenets to the Valois – Chinon was originally a Gallo-Roman camp and then a fortress belonging to the counts of Blois. In the 11C it passed to their enemies, the counts of Anjou, one of whom, **Henry Plantagenet**, built the major part of the present castle. In 1154 he became King of England but Chinon, at the heart of his continental possessions, was one of his favourite residences; he died there on 6 July 1189. However, it was during the Angevin period from 1154 to 1204 that Chinon truly flourished.

Studio 3Bis/MICHELIN

John Lackland, the youngest son of Henry II, inherited the Plantagenet kingdom on the death of his elder brother Richard the Lionheart, who was killed at Châlus in 1199. His deceitful character and his underhand plotting earned him many enemies. First he quarrelled with his nephew Arthur of Brittany who sought refuge at the French court. Then he abducted Isabelle d'Angoulême, the fiancée of the Count of La Marche, and married her at Chinon on 30 August 1200. Discontented with the behaviour of their overlord, the knights of Poitou appealed to the royal court in Paris. John refused to attend the hearing, at which he was condemned to forfeit his French fiefs.

John was reduced to being King of England and, one by one, Philippe Auguste recaptured all the former English strongholds in France; in 1205 Chinon passed to the French crown. John tried to fight back but in vain; after the truce of 26 October 1206 he was forced to give up. He sought, nonetheless, to exact revenge and in 1213 he took part in the Anglo-German coalition against Philippe Auguste.

He was defeated the following year by the future Louis VIII at the Battle of La Roche-aux-Moines near Angers. The French victory was confirmed by the Treaty of Chinon on 18 September 1214. John, who had alienated all the knights in his kingdom and richly deserved his nickname of Lackland, died two years later.

The Court of the King of Bourges (early 15C) – With the accession of **Charles VII** Chinon moved into the limelight. France was in a terrible predicament. Henry VI, King of England, was also King of Paris; Charles VII was only King of Bourges when he set up his little court at Chinon in 1427. The following year he called a meeting of the States-General of the central and southern provinces which had remained faithful to him. They voted 400 000 *livres* for organizing the defence of Orléans besieged by the English *(see ORLÉANS)*. Then, in 1429, Joan of Arc appeared on the scene...

★★OLD CHINON *45min*

Formerly surrounded by high walls which earned it the name Ville-Fort (Fortified Town), the old city (Le Vieux Chinon) with its pointed roofs and winding streets lies tucked between the banks of the River Vienne and the castle bluff. There are numerous medieval houses with picturesque details: half-timbered houses with carved corbels, stone gables with corner turrets, mullioned windows and sculpted doorways.

Eating out

BUDGET

La Crémaillère – *22 r. du Commerce* – ☏ *02 47 98 47 15* – *closed Wed* – *13.42/16.77€*. This long, narrow little restaurant is original, to say the least: the wooden dining room is divided into compartments, with little friezes of pine trees and walls painted with floral motifs, giving the impression of a Savoyard chalet. Pleasant little terrace in summer. Family-style cooking.

La Maison Rouge – *38 r. Voltaire* – ☏ *02 47 98 43 65* – *closed beginning Nov-end Mar except during school holidays, and Mon except Jul-Aug* – *12€ lunch, 14/31€*. This half-timbered restaurant in the medieval quarter of town is the place to indulge in generous helpings of regional specialities worthy of Rabelais, without breaking the bank. Enjoy a glass of Chinon with your meal to make the experience complete.

MODERATE

Les Années 30 – *78 r. Voltaire* – ☏ *02 47 93 37 18* – *closed first fortnight in Mar, 1 week in Jun, last fortnight in Oct, Tue lunchtime, Thu lunchtime and Wed* – *reservation required* – *21.34/28.20€*. This restaurant is located in a 14C building between the Musée du Vieux Chinon and the Musée du Vin et de la Tonnellerie. The atmosphere is friendly and the prices reasonable.

Where to stay

BUDGET

Chambre d'hôte La Pilleterie – *37420 Huismes* – *6km/3.75mi N of Chinon on D 16* – ☏ *02 47 95 58 07* – ✍ – *4 rooms 44.21/53.36€*. This property in the heart of the country is a delight for those seeking absolute peace and quiet. Pleasant, rustic-style rooms. The owners keep sheep, geese and other farm animals, sure to entertain any youngsters in your party!

MODERATE

Hôtel Agnès Sorel – *4 quai Pasteur* – ☏ *02 47 93 04 37* – *10 rooms 43/92€* – ⌑ *6.50€*. Not far from the town centre, this hotel on the banks of the Vienne is almost like home. Each room is decorated in a different colour – ask for the green room, it has a private terrace! Bikes for hire and picnics provided for walkers.

Visiting Chinon

There are several fairs and other events organised in Chinon, don't miss them if you're in town! In April visit the Salon des Vins (wine fair); in late June and on 15 August, there are horse races. In July the town is the venue of a Festival of Musical Comedy. An old-fashioned market is held on the 3rd Saturday in August. It isn't easy to get around town by car in the summer months, so we suggest you leave your car in the riverside parking area and use the little tourist train which leaves from the Hôtel de Ville.

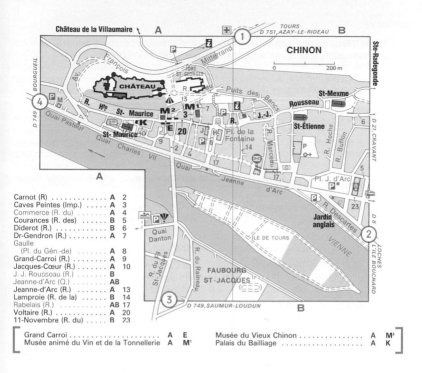

Château de la Villaumaire · **A**

TOURS
D 751, AZAY-LE-RIDEAU · **B**

CHINON

Ste-Radegonde →

BOURGUEIL

D 749

Av. François Mitterrand

FORT
ST-GEORGES

Puits des Bancs

St-Mexme

CHÂTEAU

R. Hte St- Maurice

M² M¹
3

R. J.-J.

Rousseau

St-Étienne

St-Maurice

Quai Pasteur

Quai Charles VII

20

Pl. de la
Fontaine

14

P

D 21, CRAVANT

R. Hoche

R. Buffon

6

5

Quai Jeanne d'Arc

Pl. J. d'Arc

P

D 8

LOCHES L'ILE BOUCHARD

Quai Danton

R. Descartes

Jardin
anglais

23

ILE DE TOURS

VIENNE

R. du Rineau

R. du Fg St-Jacques

FAUBOURG
ST-JACQUES

D 749, SAUMUR-LOUDUN · **B**

0   200 m

A

Carnot (R) . . . . **A** 2
Caves Peintes (Imp.) . . . . . **A** 3
Commerce (R. du) . . . . **A** 4
Courances (R. des) . . . . . **B** 5
Diderot (R.) . . . . **B** 6
Dr-Gendron (R.) . . . . **A** 7
Gaulle
   (Pl. du Gén.-de) . . . . . . **A** 8
Grand-Carroi (R.) . . . . **A** 9
Jacques-Cœur (R.) . . . . . . **A** 10
J. J. Rousseau (R.) . . . . . . **B**
Jeanne-d'Arc (Q.) . . . . . . **AB**
Jeanne-d'Arc (R.) . . . . **A** 13
Lamproie (R. de la) . . . . . **B** 14
Rabelais (R.) . . . . **AB** 17
Voltaire (R.) . . . . **A** 20
11-Novembre (R. du) . . . . . **B** 23

Grand Carroi . . . . **A**   **E**   Musée du Vieux Chinon . . . . **A**   **M²**
Musée animé du Vin et de la Tonnellerie **A**   **M¹**   Palais du Bailliage . . . . **A**   **K**

One of the many pleasant activities Chinon has to offer is a walk along the banks of the Vienne, particularly to be recommended in the English-style landscape garden, the **Jardin anglais**, where flourishing palm trees are a testimony to the mild climate of the Loire Valley.

Start from rue Haute-St-Maurice, which is the main axis of the old town.

Église St-Maurice (12C-16C) – The high pointed vaulting in the nave and the chancel is in the pure Angevin style.

Palais du Bailliage – *No 73 rue Haute-St-Maurice*. Walk round onto rue Jacques-Cœur to admire the southern façade of this building which houses the Bailiff's Court and the Hôtellerie Gargantua with its pretty corbelled turret and crocketed gable.

★★**Grand Carroi** – (*carroi* meaning crossroads). Despite its small size, which hardly merited such a grand name, this was the centre of town in the Middle Ages, where rue Haute-St-Maurice intersected rue du Grand-Carroi.
The prettiest courtyards are not far from one another: the broad stone doorway of no 48, the 17C **Hôtel du Gouvernement** (Government House), opens into an at-

Chinon – La Maison Rouge

H. Dewynter/MICHELIN

tractive courtyard lined with elegant arcades; another half-timbered house, no 45, is decorated with statues serving as columns; no 44, the **Hôtel des États-Généraux** (States-General House), is a handsome 15C-16C brick building, which houses the Museum of Old Chinon; no 38, called the **Maison rouge** (Red House – 14C), is half-timbered with brick and an overhanging upper storey.

Hôtel Torterue de Langardière (18C) – The Classical façade of this 18C mansion is enhanced by handsome wrought-iron balconies.

Further on, rue Jeanne-d'Arc starts its steep climb up to the castle; a plaque marks the **well** where, according to tradition, Joan of Arc is said to have placed her foot on dismounting from her horse when she arrived in Chinon.

Note the 14C half-timbered house at no 19 rue Voltaire.

Impasse des Caves-Painctes – This narrow alley leading up the hillside will take you to the **Caves Painctes** (Painted Cellars), where Pantagruel drained many a glass of cool wine according to his creator Rabelais, who was known to patronise the establishment on frequent occasions. The paintings have since disappeared but these old quarries have always been dedicated to the Sacred Bottle; it is on these premises that the annual ceremony of the **Bons Entonneurs Rabelaisiens** ⊘ (Wine-Growers' Brotherhood) is held.

Rue Jean-Jacques-Rousseau – Several striking medieval houses can be seen, especially nos 71 and 73 at the crossroads with rue du Puy-des-Bancs.

Église St-Étienne – This church was built c 1480 by the governor of Chinon, Philippe de Commines, and features a beautifully sculpted Flamboyant Gothic doorway carved with his coat of arms.

Collégiale St-Mexme – Two imposing towers overlooking place St-Mexme and the nave and the narthex are all that is left of this 10C-11C church.

Chapelle Ste-Radegonde ⊘ – *Access on foot up the steep path which begins northeast of the church of St-Mexme.* The steep rise is bordered by troglodyte houses. In the 6C a pious hermit had his cell built in the cave. **Radegund**, the wife of King Clotair I, came to consult the hermit about her intention to leave the court and found the convent of the Holy Cross (Ste-Croix) in Poitiers – the cell was later enlarged into a chapel where the hermit was buried. A Romanesque portal leads into the chapel. On the left is a 13C Romanesque fresco depicting a Royal Hunt; on the right 17C paintings recount St Radegund's life. Also of interest to visitors are the **cave dwelling**, adjoining the chapel, and the **Musée des Arts et Traditions populaires** (Folk Museum).

★★ CHÂTEAU ⊘ *1hr*

It is best to approach the château by route de Tours (D 751) which skirts the massive walls on the north side. Note the reconstructions of ancient fighting machines including a ballista (catapult for launching stones) and a trebuchet, used in siege warfare until the 14C.

Built on a spur overlooking the Vienne, this vast fortress (400x70m/1 312x230ft) dates mostly from the reign of Henry II (12C). Abandoned by the court after the 15C and bought in the 17C by Cardinal de Richelieu, the castle was dismantled little by little until Prosper Mérimée undertook to preserve it. These majestic ruins evoke eight centuries of history.

The fortress consisted of three buildings separated by deep dry moats.

Fort St-Georges – The eastern fort, which is now demolished, protected the vulnerable side of the castle which was accessible from the plateau.

Château du Milieu – The entrance to the Middle Castle is across the moat and through the 14C **Tour de l'Horloge** (Clock Tower) which is unusually shallow (only 5m/16ft deep). A bell, the Marie Javelle, which is dated 1399, sounds the hour from the lantern at the top of the tower. Inside, several rooms house displays evoking the great moments in the life of Joan of Arc. Visitors are free to stroll in the gardens and explore the ruined towers, in particular the **Tour des Chiens** (Dogs' Tower). The south curtain wall commands a very picturesque **view★★** of the slate roofs of Old Chinon, the Vienne and the river valley.

Fort du Coudray – West of the gardens another bridge crosses the moat to the Fort du Coudray on the point of the rock spur. The keep *(right)* was built by Philippe Auguste early in the 13C; the Templars *(see p 227)* were imprisoned here by Philip the Fair in 1308 and it was they who carved the famous graffiti on the north wall of the present entrance.

Logis royaux – Joan of Arc was received in the great hall on the first floor, of which only the fireplace remains. The guard-room on the ground floor, hung with a 16C Flemish tapestry *(Bear Hunt in a Park)*, displays a large model of the castle as it was in the 15C. In the kitchens you can admire two 17C tapestries from Flanders belonging to the same series – *The Wedding of Thetis and Peleus* and *The Judgement of Paris* – flanked by four busts from Cardinal de Richelieu's collection of antiques. The Royal Apartments also house an interesting 17C Aubusson tapestry, *The Recognition of the Dauphin by Joan of Arc.*

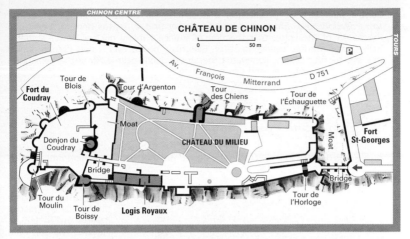

ADDITIONAL SIGHTS

Musée animé du Vin et de la Tonnellerie ⊘ – 🖾 Housed in a wine cellar, the Wine and Cooperage Museum presents the work carried out in a vineyard, various winemaking techniques and the cooper's art, with the help of life-size automata.

Chinon, a great wine at the heart of the Val de Loire

The actual plot of land entitled to carry the Chinon *appellation* is spread out over 2 000ha/5 000sq yd covering 19 winemaking localities. Red Chinon is usually made with a single grape variety, which is Cabernet-Franc. Graced with a subtle bouquet of violets and wild strawberries, Chinon is definitely a wine for laying down, sometimes for many years. However, depending on the *terroir*, some bottles may also be drunk young, as early as Easter. Generally speaking, Chinon provides a perfect accompaniment to red meat, poultry and game and can round off a meal nicely when served with a mild cheese.

The serving temperature should be between 14°C/57.2°F and 16°C/60.8°F for reds and between 8°C/46.4°F and 12°C/53.6°F for rosés and whites, of which there are far fewer varieties.

For details, apply to the Syndicat des Vins de Chinon, impasse des Caves-Painctes, ☎ 02 47 93 30 44.

Musée du Vieux Chinon ⊘ – The museum is housed in the Hôtel des États-Généraux, where Richard the Lionheart is said to have died in 1199 after being wounded at the siege of Châlus in the Limousin, and where the States-General – the French Parliament – met in 1428 at the request of Charles VII to provide him with the money to continue waging war against the English.

The museum is devoted to the history of the town, as well as to river transport. The ground-floor exhibits are mainly concerned with folk art and archaeological finds. The main hall on the first floor has a full-length portrait of Rabelais by Delacroix. The second floor, where the roof is in the form of a ship's hull, contains the collections of a local historical society.

Maison de la Rivière ⊘ – *12 quai Pasteur.*
🖾 This riverside museum illustrates inland water transport in the Loire Valley; note the reconstruction of a shipwright. There are various exhibits connected with the traffic on the Vienne and the Loire and models of the different kinds of vessels: flat-bottomed barges, lighters and expendable pinewood boats. There is also a section on fishing.

EXCURSIONS

Huismes – *8km/5mi N along D 16.*
Château de la Villaumaire ⊘ The castle is much older than you might assume from its vast 19C neo-Gothic façade. in fact, it has retained its **medieval kitchens** where you are invited to enjoy delicious flat bread baked in the original oven. The underground cellars and galleries can also be visited. The pleasant park covers 32ha/79 acres.

Centre nucléaire de production d'électricité de Chinon ⊙ – *12km/8mi NW towards Bourgueil. Entrance near Port-Boulet bridge.* It was here at Avoine, on the banks of the Loire, that the first of France's many nuclear power stations, EDF 1, was put into service in 1963. Electricity production is now carried out on this site by four 900-million-watt generators which meet 40% of the demand in the Loire Valley, Brittany and central France.

★RABELAIS COUNTRY

☐ 25km/15mi round tour

Leave on ③ on the town plan. The road runs through a tunnel of tall plane trees to St-Lazare; turn right onto D 751ᴱ, an old Roman road; after 3km/2mi turn left onto D 759; then right onto D 24 and continue along D 117.

La Devinière

La Devinière ⊙ – This farmhouse was the birthplace of **François Rabelais** (1494-1553). He was the son of a Chinon lawyer and after a studious childhood, he became a monk, fell in love with Ancient Greek and studied the humanists. He transferred to the secular clergy, studied medicine at Montpellier and became a famous doctor, under the patronage of such great names as cardinal Jean du Bellay and his brother the Governor of Piedmont; in 1551 the Cardinal arranged for his appointment to the parish of Meudon.

With the publication of *Pantagruel* in 1532 Rabelais, the distinguished Hellenist, revealed the humorous side of his character by choosing burlesque farce and every kind of comedy to express his philosophy.

At La Devinière visitors can see Rabelais' room and a small museum illustrating his life and work; there is an interesting study on the origins of his hero Gargantua.

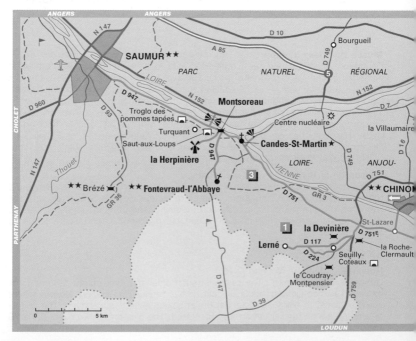

Rejoin D 117 and turn right.

On the opposite side of the valley stands the beautiful **Château du Coudray-Montpensier** (15C) with its numerous roofs, restored in the 1930s. Next comes **Seuilly-Côteaux**, a long straggling street of troglodyte houses.

It was in the abbey at Seuilly that Rabelais was educated; he used it as the setting for one of his characters in *Gargantua*.

Lerné – Yellow stone buildings make the village picturesque. In Rabelais' book this was the village from which the bakers *(fouaciers)* of a special sort of bread set out to sell their goods *(fouaces)* in Chinon market; it was a dispute between them and the shepherds from Seuilly that sparked off the comic Picrocholean War between Picrochole, King of Lerné, an aggressive fighter, and Grandgousier, the wise Prince of Seuilly, who was Gargantua's father.

Return to Chinon along D 224 through Seuilly-Bourg.

At the bottom of the slope; near the junction with D 749 *(right)* stands **Château de la Roche-Clermault** which was taken by assault by Picrochole and his men in Rabelais' tale.

★VALLÉE DE LA VIENNE

☑ **60km/38mi round tour** *about 3hr*

Leave Chinon to the E on rue Diderot and D 21.

The road follows the chalky hillside through the well-known vineyards of Cravant-les-Coteaux.

Vieux Bourg de Cravant – *1km/0.5mi N of Cravant-les-Coteaux*. The **church** ⊙ *(disused)* in this old town is particularly interesting because of its age. The nave is a rare example of the Carolingian style (early 10C), built of characteristically small stones. The 11C south portal is adorned with cable moulding; just at the entrance to the chancel two rectangular pillars have been adorned with Merovingian interlacing. These pillars used to support the roof of the south portal.

In the south chapel, added in the 15C, there are the remains of a fresco (on the west wall) depicting the chapel's donors, who were probably Georges de la Trémoille, Minister to Charles VII, Catherine de l'Île-Bouchard, his wife, and their children. Small Lapidary Museum.

Follow D 21 to Panzoult and then take D 221 to Crouzilles.

Crouzilles – Built in the 12C and covered with Angevin vaulting in the 13C, the **church** is particularly interesting because of the way in which the statues have been incorporated into its structure. The buttresses on either side of the Romanesque door have been carved with a niche to hold a statue; in the apse, statues have been placed at the springing line of the vault: St Peter, the Virgin Mary, St John, St Paul and in the south-east corner of the south transept a figure known as the Beau Dieu de Crouzilles.

Take D 760 W to L'Île-Bouchard.

L'Île-Bouchard – *See L'ÎLE-BOUCHARD.*

The road passes in front of the church of St-Gilles, then crosses the Vienne to the other half of the town.

Take D 18 E to Parçay-sur-Vienne.

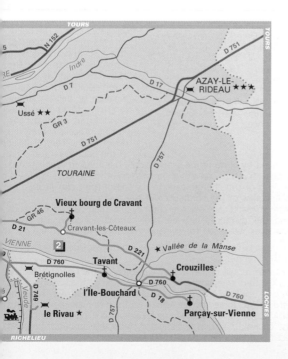

Parçay-sur-Vienne – This 12C **church** ⊙ has a fine Romanesque doorway flanked by blind arcades. It is decorated with carved archivolts representing bearded faces (33 in total), foliated scrolls and palmettes, and the ensemble is surmounted by a motif resembling fish scales. The capitals in the chancel are ornamented with imaginary animals of astounding ugliness inspired by the Apocalypse of St John the Divine.

Return to L'Île-Bouchard and take D 760 westwards along the south bank of the Vienne.

Tavant – The Romanesque **church** ⊙ here is of special interest because of the 12C **frescoes★** which adorn the vaulting, apse and crypt. More markedly in the crypt than in the church, the figures embody a force of expression and a degree of realism extremely rare during the Romanesque period. Note the capitals in the chancel.

About 3km/2mi further on, beyond Sazilly, the road (D 760) passes the **Château de Brétignolles** *(left)*, a Louis XII-style building with turrets.

Turn left onto D 749.

★ **Château du Rivau** ⊙ – Erected in the 13C and fortified in the 15C by Pierre de Beauvau, Chamberlain to Charles VII, the Château du Rivau is a fine building of great distinction. Joan of Arc found horses for her soldiers here on her way to the siege of Orléans. The château is circled by a dry moat and defended by a drawbridge. Its harmonious proportions reflected the influence of the Renaissance period, when the vaulted stables and outbuildings (including the dovecot) were completed. Rivau is also reminiscent of Rabelais' work since Gargantua gave the castle to one of his knights after the Picrocholean War.

The **gardens**, recreated on the basis of 15C documents, evoke both the Late Middle Ages and the beginning of humanism through a series of ornate compositions (secret garden, carpet of flowers etc). Rabelais drew inspiration from these horticultural arrangements when he imagined the grounds surrounding the Abbaye de Thélème.

Return to Chinon along D 749.

★★★LA LOIRE SAUMUROISE

③ From Chinon to Saumur *38km/24mi – allow 3hr*

Leave Chinon on ③ on the town plan then turn right onto D 751 to Saumur.

Just before entering Candes turn right onto D 7, which crosses the Vienne, to enjoy a good view of the pretty **setting★** of this village at the Loire-Vienne confluence.

Return to the south bank of the Vienne.

★ **Candes-St-Martin** – The village of Candes stands on the south bank of the Vienne at its confluence with the Loire; the church was built on the spot where St Martin died in 397 and it was from here that the saint's body was taken on its miraculous journey up the Loire to Tours *(see TOURS)*.

Auberge de la Route d'Or – *2 pl. de l'Église – 37500 Candes-St-Martin –* ☎ *02 47 95 81 10 – closed 13 Nov-7 Feb, Tue evening except Jul-Aug, and Wed – 19.82/28.97€.* A small inn near the church, which has retained its original 17C exterior. A good place to stop and eat in the dining room with its fireplace, or on the terrace in fine weather. Classic cuisine at reasonable prices.

★ **Collegiate church** – The building was erected in the 12C and 13C and fitted with defensive features in the 15C. The roadside façade is remarkable for its combination of military architecture and lavish ornamentation, such as the ribbing gracefully reaching down to the central pillar of the doorway.

Inside, the nave is buttressed by aisles of the same height. The Angevin vaulting rests on soaring piers; the whole structure conveys an impression of tremendous lightness. A narrow path on the right of the church leads to the top of the slope *(15min on foot there and back)*; fine **view** of the confluence of the rivers.

Another walk along rue St-Martin, below the church, and then rue du Bas ends near a plaque showing the distances between the various ports on the Loire, recalling how much the river was used for transporting goods in days gone by.

Montsoreau – Montsoreau is famed for its château which overlooks the confluence of the Loire and the Vienne.

Château ⊙ – The château was rebuilt in the 15C by a member of the Chambes family, famed for its bold warriors and enterprising women. An event in the history of the family and the château was used by Alexandre Dumas in one of his novels, *La Dame de Montsoreau*. The heroine was forced by her jealous husband to make a rendezvous with her lover, Bussy d'Amboise, at the Château de la Coutancière (on the north bank of the Loire) where the cuckold had him assassinated. After this outburst, husband and wife lived in perfect harmony until they died 40 years later.

The river front, which was once at the water's edge, is an impressive example of military architecture.

The façade giving onto the courtyard features far more gentle contours and presents two staircase turrets; one of these, built around 1530, is embellished in the early French Renaissance style.

Diane de Méridor – *12 quai Philippe-de-Commines – 49730 Montsoreau –* ☎ *02 41 51 71 76 – closed 2 Jan-8 Feb, Tue and Wed except Jul-Aug – 15.09/32.78€.* This old building on the banks of the Loire is a nice place to stop and eat, with a view of the castle. The restaurant is neat and tidy, and cozy too, with a fireplace and exposed beams. Traditional cooking using fresh local products.

A permanent audio-visual presentation, **Les Imaginaires de Loire★**, takes you on an enchanting journey through the landscapes and history of the Angevine part of the Loire Valley and brings to life the legend of the château of Montsoreau.

Birds of the Loire

The Loire, the last wild river in Europe, with its islands, backwaters, long sand banks and grassy shores, is one of the natural regions in France where the flora and fauna are particularly abundant and diverse. Among the birds that build their nests along its banks are the common and little tern, the little ringed plover and the common sandpiper.

From March to the end of June, Parney Island below Montsoreau is home to over 750 pairs of gulls – black-headed, Mediterranean, common and Iceland – and common and little terns. Lastly, in August and September, among the many migratory species on the river is the osprey which makes spectacular dives into the slow waters.

The **Moulin de la Herpinière**, a corn mill dating back to 1514 and still operational, stands out against the skyline between Montsoreau and **Turquant**.

★★ **Fontevraud-l'Abbaye** – *See FONTEVRAUD-L'ABBAYE.*

Return to Montsoreau.

From the bridge over the Loire west of Montsoreau there is a fine view upstream of Montsoreau and Candes and downstream of Saumur Château which is just visible. The road (D 947) is bordered by troglodyte dwellings and white Renaissance houses.

Small wine villages nestle between the road and the limestone cliffs, which are riddled with caves and old quarries, some of which are now used for growing mushrooms. At **Saut-aux-Loups** ⊙ just beyond Montsoreau on the Maumenière hillside, galleries display the different stages of mushroom cultivation and exhibit some of the rarer varieties, like the *pied-bleu* which smells slightly of aniseed or the *pleurotus* (oyster mushroom), which can be yellow or pink (the latter, also known as *salmoneo straminens*, has recently been cultivated on an experimental basis; its shape and colour make it look like a flower). In season, it is also possible to taste the famous somer-

Montsoreau

> **Dried apples**
>
> The apples are peeled, placed in flat wicker baskets and dried for five days in tufa ovens. When flattened for preservation may be kept for several months. They are eaten in a preparation made with local red wine flavoured with cinnamon.
>
> This technique for preserving fruit, which was in use at the time of the Revolution and continued until the beginning of 1914, reached its height in about 1880 when wine-growers, forced to abandon their vines in the wake of the phylloxera plague, turned to the drying of apples. With the advent of machines for peeling and drying, the activity developed from a craft into an industry and tons of dried apples were exported to Belgium, Great Britain and Sweden.
>
> Historical archives on the Loire Valley show that a similar method for preserving fruit was used at Rivarennes near Ussé *(see p 299*, where the making of dried pears became a thriving industry.

sault mushrooms known as *galipettes.* These large button-mushrooms, picked when fully mature and cooked in bread ovens hollowed out of the tufa, probably owe their name to the fact that in the olden days they were grown in stacks and when they reached a certain stage of maturity fell to the ground, somersaulting as they went.

The sloping vineyards produce a dry or medium dry white wine, a Cabernet rosé called **Cabernet de Saumur**, and a red wine called **Champigny**.

Troglo des pommes tapées ⊘ – *At Val-Hulin in the Turquant district.* Yet another example of local agricultural heritage. The art of drying apples *(pommes tapées)* has been revived in an enormous cave decorated with ancient farming implements *(see inset)*.

Aux mille et un casse-tête du monde entier ⊘ – *Place St-Aubin, Turquant.* This museum, the first of its kind, contains no fewer than 1 001 brain-teasers!

Continue along D 947 to Saumur past the elegant church of Notre-Dame-des-Ardilliers (see p 268).

PARC NATUREL RÉGIONAL LOIRE-ANJOU-TOURAINE

Maison du Parc, 7 rue Jehanne-d'Arc, 49730 Montsoreau, ☎ 02 41 53 66 00, www.parc-loire-anjou-touraine.fr.

French *Parcs naturels régionaux* are zones set aside for both protection and development. Unlike nature reserves or other national parks, these zones are inhabited, and measures are taken to stimulate environmentally friendly economic activities

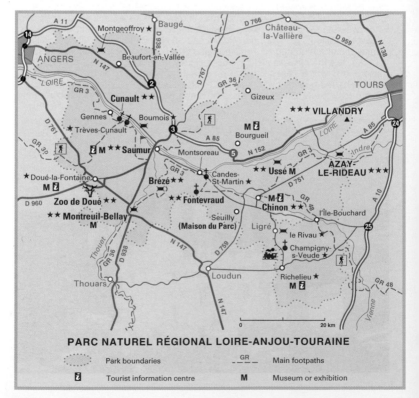

PARC NATUREL RÉGIONAL LOIRE-ANJOU-TOURAINE

Park boundaries	Main footpaths
Tourist information centre	Museum or exhibition

which respect the traditions and customs of the region. Thus craftsmanship and quality agricultural are promoted, along with the creation or preservation of local museums and architecture, and access to natural sites is improved.

The parks are managed by local authorities acting with representatives of associations and inhabitants. Each park has a charter signed by all interested parties, defining the goals and objectives as well as the boundaries of the park.

Created in 1996; the **Parc naturel régional Loire-Anjou-Touraine** includes 136 *communes* from the *départements* of Indre-et-Loire (*région* Centre) and Maine-et-Loire (*région* Pays de la Loire), and covers 235 000 ha/580 685 acres. The River Loire flows through it, as well as its tributaries, the rivers Indre, Vienne and Thouet. The environment is typical of landscapes criss-crossed by rivers in this way: valleys and wooded groves, meadows and farms criss-crossed by hedgerows.

CHOLET

Conurbation 54 204
Michelin map 317: D-6, 232 fold 30 or 4049 D6

Cholet is a thriving industrial town, with a long-standing tradition as a textile centre. Surrounded by the pastures of **Les Mauges** *(see below)*, it is also an important cattle market.

There is scarcely a building in Cholet which dates from before the Revolution since the town suffered sorely in the Vendée War (Royalists versus Republicans).

SIGHTS

★ **Musée d'Art et d'Histoire** ⊙ – *27 avenue de l'Abreuvoir*. Housed in a building opposite the Hôtel de Ville, the Art and History Museum consists of two separate galleries.

Galerie d'Histoire – The History Gallery evokes Cholet in 1793, as well as the Vendée wars (1793-96, 1815, 1832) and the chronological sequence of events which was to ravage the city and plunge it into mourning during the period of revolutionary unrest (maps, arms, table coverings, everyday objects). Note *The Machecoul Massacre* by François Flameng, *The Rout of Cholet* by Girardet, *General Moulin's Suicide* by Benoît-Lévy and above all the series of famous full-length portraits of some of the leaders of the Vendée resistance, in particular those of *Henri de La Rochejaquelein* by Pierre Guérin and *Cathelineau*, commissioned by Louis XVIII for the guard-room of the old Château de St-Cloud just west of Paris.

Galerie d'Art – The Art Gallery has a strong 18C collection with works by the local artist Pierre-Charles Trémolières (1703-39), Carle Van Loo, Hallé, Nattier, De Troy, Coypel and De Loutherbourg. Sculptures by Hippolyte Maindron and paintings by Troyon, Diaz de la Peña and Maufra represent the 19C. As far as the 20C is concerned, the main movement represented is Geometrical Abstraction with works by Vasarely, Gorin, Nemours, Herbin, Claisse, Valmier, Honegger, Magnelli and especially Morellet.

Musée du Textile ⊙ – This Textile Museum has been set up in an old bleaching house by the River Sauvageau, a remarkable piece of 19C industrial heritage. The museum visit begins in an unusual modern building, modelled on Crystal Palace in London *(see The Green Guide London)*. This demonstration room, which shares some similarities with weaving factories (plenty of light, metal structure etc), houses four looms still in working order, the oldest of which dates from 1910. Next comes the steam-engine room in which the furnace and enormous machinery, no longer extant, generated the necessary energy for the entire factory. Other rooms contain a display on the history of textiles. Finally, a textiles garden has also been laid out to show visitors some of the plants used in the manufacture and dyeing of cloth.

A working loom in the Textile Museum

Hôtel de Ville de Cholet

Eating out

BUDGET

Au Passé Simple – *181 r. Nationale –* ☏ *02 41 75 90 06 – closed 5-20 Aug, Sun evening and Mon – 12.20/27.44€*. A small, unpretentious restaurant with a friendly atmosphere in its country-style dining room. The menus feature fresh produce and change according to the season. A selection of regional wines to sample.

Thermidor – *40 r. St-Bonaventure –* ☏ *02 41 58 55 18 – closed 1-6 Jan, Tue evening and Wed – 14.48/30.49€*. This restaurant in the heart of Cholet has two country-style dining rooms, one of which was formerly a weaving workshop. The stone walls provide a fitting decor for the good, old-fashioned fare.

Where to stay

BUDGET

Hôtel du Parc – *4 av. A.-Manceau –* ☏ *02 41 62 65 45 – 46 rooms 33.54/50.31€ –* ☕ *6.10€*. This hotel, built in the 1970s, lies slightly out of the town centre and is a useful place to stay for those passing through. The decor in the rooms is not very recent, but the prices are affordable and the level of comfort leaves nothing to be desired. The rooms at the back are the best.

On the town

Cyberpub du Cadran – *105 r. Nationale –* ☏ *02 41 62 00 78 – www.cadran.net – Mon-Sat 11am-2am*. One of the most popular venues in town, especially among the young of Cholet, this lively bar has the advantage of being situated in a passageway, with a terrace that is sheltered from cars and neighbours. In the basement are computers to surf the Web, a DJ and a dance floor; the cyberpub sponsors concerts and theme evenings. On the ground floor is a bar with a good choice of beers, Tex-Mex and Cuban drinks. Restaurant upstairs.

Showtime

Théâtre municipal de Cholet – *Pl. Travot –* ☏ *02 41 49 26 00 – box office Tue-Sat 3.30-6.30pm, Wed 10.30am-12.30pm*. A venue for touring theatre, dance, classical music, jazz, rock and variety concerts, operettas, recitals and stand-up comics.

Sport

C.I.S.P.A. – *Port de Ribou –* ☏ *02 41 62 12 77 – open all year, daily except Sun*. Situated on the outskirts of town, the Centre d'Initiation aux Sports de Plein-Air (outdoor sports centre) occupies a vast site in a green valley next to a huge artificial lake. All the necessary equipment can be hired on the spot for water sports such as sailing, wind-surfing, canoeing and kayaking, or for other activities such as tennis, archery, golf, climbing and mountain biking. Accommodation available.

Art

Le Jardin de Verre – *13 bd Gustave-Richard –* ☏ *02 41 65 13 58 – open Mon-Fri 9am-noon, Sat 2-6pm*. Formerly a police station – although you wouldn't guess it – this cultural centre can be adapted for all kinds of creative performance, from cabaret, theatre and concerts to clowns, jazz and world music. The bar is a favourite place for holding those long philosophic discussions the French so love; there is an exhibition space and Cholet fashion school students regularly put on events to display their creative designs.

Sit back and relax

Le Grand Café – *1 pl. Travot –* ☏ *02 41 65 82 41 – daily 11am-2am*. Situated in Cholet's former town hall, recognisable by its monumental staircase which leads to the restaurant and reception rooms, this café is the ideal place to relax, either indoors (newspapers available, old jazz and French songs as background music) or on the terrace, which is the biggest in town.

Cholet handkerchiefs

Weaving is a long-established industry in Cholet, where hemp and flax have been cultivated and spun since the 11C. In the 16C the handkerchief was introduced into France from Italy. In the 17C, as the practice of bleaching cloth became ever more widespread, local manufacturers came up with a whiteness for which Cholet was to become famous, by spreading their cloth out to bleach in the sun on green meadows where the damp clay soil prevented it drying out too much. In the 18C Cholet cloth was part of the cargo of manufactured goods which the shipowners of Nantes and La Rochelle traded on the coasts of Africa in exchange for slaves who were then sold in the West Indies, from where the rum bought with the profits was imported into France, in the notorious trade triangle.

Despite the devastation wrought on the town during the revolutionary wars, Cholet was not destroyed; it re-established its crafts and tenaciously fostered its textile industry throughout the 19C. Cholet table and bed linen is now renowned for its high quality and as well known as the traditional red Cholet handkerchief, which is holding its own against stiff competition from abroad and from the disposable handkerchief industry. Many French department stores traditionally hold cut-price sales of table and bed linen in January – *le mois du blanc*: the «white sale» is an idea which originated in Cholet!

Old houses – A pedestrian precinct has been created in the town centre, where place Rougé, rue du Devau and its continuation rue du Commerce have a number of old houses with rare 18C wrought-iron balconies. On the south side of the street the **Jardin du Mail** makes a pleasant garden setting for the law courts.

The **Parc de Moine**, a 13ha/32-acre public garden in the very centre of town, is one of the favourite haunts of Cholet's inhabitants.

LES MAUGES

The southern part of Anjou on the borders of the Vendée and Poitou, which is known as Les Mauges, is a peaceful, somewhat secluded region delimited by the Loire to the north, by the Layon Valley to the east and the *départements* of the Vendée and Deux-Sèvres to the south and west. Les Mauges is a mixture of woodland and pasture used for cattle raising, where the Durham-Mancelle breed is fattened before being sold in its thousands at the markets in Chemillé and Cholet.

The straight main roads, which were laid down during the Revolution and under the Empire for political reasons, are superimposed on a network of deep lanes well-suited to the ambushes which played a prominent part in the Vendée War. The windmills still crowning the hillsides were often used by the Royalist Whites to send signals.

Drive NW out of Cholet along D 752.

The Vendée War (1793-96)

At the beginning of the peasant insurrection the town was captured by the Royalist Whites (15 March 1793) who then regrouped before marching victoriously on Saumur and Angers. On 17 October Cholet was captured by Kléber after a bloody battle in which 40 000 Whites faced 25 000 Blues; the victor described it as a "battle between lions and tigers"; the dead numbered 10 000. Some 60 000-80 000 Whites – panic-stricken men, women and children – crossed the Loire. In an episode that became a byword for brutality in French annals, the survivors were massacred in their thousands, shot down or drowned in the Loire. General Westermann wrote a chilling account of events to the Convention; "There is no more Vendée; it has died under our sword of liberty... I have had the children crushed under horses' feet and the women massacred. I have not a single prisoner with which to reproach myself".

On 10 March 1794 after vicious hand-to-hand fighting in the streets Stofflet won Cholet back for the Whites, but a few days later the «infernal columns» under General Turreau put Cholet to fire and the sword. On 18 March Stofflet returned once more but was soon driven out by General Cordellier, leaving the town of Cholet in ruins.

Memorials of the Vendée War

Throughout the region there are monuments to the events of 1793-1796. At **Maulévrier** there is a pyramid commemorating Stofflet and a martyrs' cemetery. At the crossroads on N 149 and D 753 near **Torfou** stands a column celebrating the victory of the Whites over the Mayence army (19 September 1793). Bonchamps was buried at **St-Florent-le-Vieil**. A cross was put up by the road to Nuaillé near **Cholet** where La Rochejaquelein fell on 29 January 1794.

Beaupréau – Beaupréau is a small town built on a steep slope on the north bank of the River Èvre. In 1793 it was the headquarters of the Whites; their leader, D'Elbée, owned a manor at St-Martin, on the east side of the town, which now houses the public library. The 15C **château** overlooking the River Evre (good view from the south bank) is now a clinic. Although it was set on fire in 1793, the entrance has retained its character: two large towers flanking a 17C pavilion which has a pyramidal roof flanked by two small slate cupolas.

Continue along D 752 then turn left onto D 17.

Le Fuilet – Le Fuilet and the neighbouring hamlets – Les Challonges, Bellevue, Les Recoins etc – stand on an excellent clay soil which has given rise to numerous brickworks and potteries producing a variety of articles (ornamental, horticultural or artistic).

The potteries are open to the public during working hours preparation and shaping of the clay by hand or by machine according to the work.

Retrace your steps and drive along D 17 to St-Laurent-de-la-Plaine.

St-Laurent-de-la-Plaine – ⌖ A museum of traditional crafts, the **Cité des métiers de tradition** ⊘, is housed in a complex of several buildings, among them the 18C vicarage, one of the only two houses in the village which survived the ravages of the Republicans in 1794. About 70 trades are illustrated with implements collected from all over France (weaving equipment from St-Étienne, a saw from the Vosges, a paddle-wheel...). In addition to the traditional exhibition rooms (lace), a number of **workshops** – clog-maker, oil dealer, blacksmith, wax chandler, laundry – have been reconstructed inside a magnificent timber-built barn.

Leave Saint-Laurent E along D 17 then turn right onto D 961.

Chemillé – This town, which spreads along the valley of the Hyrôme, is an important centre for stock-raising and for the production of medicinal plants (demonstration garden with some 300 species of plants in the grounds of the town hall). In July 1793 Chemillé was the scene of a fierce struggle between the Blues and the Whites, in the course of which 400 Blues who had been taken prisoner were saved from death only by the intervention of General d'Elbée. In place du Château there is a 13C doorway with honeycomb decoration, a vestige of the old citadel. The disused church of Notre-Dame has an interesting Romanesque **bell-tower** with blind arcading and two levels of richly decorated window openings.

Stained-glass windows

Many churches in Les Mauges and the Saumur region have stained-glass windows that illustrate forcefully and realistically the Vendée War and relate the great deeds of its heroes. The windows, particularly in Vihiers, La Salle-de-Vihiers, Montilliers, Chemillé, Chanzeaux, St-Laurent-de-la-Plaine, Le Pin-en-Mauges and further north at La Chapelle-St-Florent, were mostly the work of local glassmakers including Clamens, Bordereau, Megen, and more recently, Rollo, who by both restoring and creating stained glass, has continued the tradition of this craft in Anjou.

The 12C **church of St-Pierre**, which was thoroughly restored at the beginning of the 20C, has a fine stained-glass window (1917) by Jean Clamens. It illustrates the **Vendée Pater** incident when D'Elbée, one of the great leaders of the Vendée War, made his soldiers, who were pressing to kill their prisoners, recite the Our Father. They were thus encouraged to forgive them their trespasses and the men were spared.

Drive SE along D 756.

Château du Coudray-Montbault – The moated 16C château with its two massive round towers of brick and stone and green lozenge decoration was built on the ruins of a 13C castle. A ruined chapel in the park contains a recumbent figure and an Entombment.

Turn right onto D 960 then, as you leave Coron, take D 196 left.

Forêt de Maulévrier – The **Cimetière des Martyrs** in the Maine-et-Loire, which is situated between Chanteloup-les-Bois and Yzernay beside the road (D 196), is surrounded by a forest of tall oak trees. During the Vendée War, **Stofflet** used the inaccessibility of this cemetery to conceal his headquarters where the wounded were brought for treatment. On 25 March 1794, however, the Blues penetrated the forest and massacred 1 200 of the Whites; two days later the latter took their revenge with a second massacre. The commemorative chapel standing alone in the forest is now a peaceful place.

Continue along D 196 to Maulévrier.

Maulévrier – The name Maulévrier is believed to date from the Merovingian period and means bad greyhound *(mauvais lévrier)*. Fulk Nerra built the first castle here in 1036 and set up a barony which, under Louis XIV, was passed on to Colbert's brother, whose descendants owned it until 1895. **Stofflet**, the famous Vendée leader, was gamekeeper to one of them in 1774. He is commemorated by a stele in the park.

The castle, which was partly destroyed during the Revolution, was rebuilt to its original plan in the 19C. At the end of the century, a manufacturer from Cholet called upon the architect **Alexandre Marcel** to restore it and lay out an oriental-style park in the grounds.

Nowadays Maulévrier is well known for its greyhound races.

Alexandre Marcel (1860-1928)

The Parisian architect Alexandre Marcel restored many old buildings before gaining recognition for his thermal baths *(Grands Thermes)* in Châtelguyon, private mansions in Paris and Cholet, and a magnificent palace for the Maharajah of Kapurthala.

His love for the Orient resulted in La Pagode *(now a cinema)* in rue Babylone in Paris and acclaimed buildings for several international exhibitions. He designed the Round the World Panorama *(Panorama du Tour du Monde)* hall for the French shipping company Messageries Maritimes, and the Cambodian Pavilion, in which he reproduced parts of the Temple of Angkor Wat, for the Universal Exhibition in 1900.

Thanks to these constructions he was brought to the notice of King Leopold II of Belgium who asked him to rebuild, in Laeken Park (Brussels), the Japanese Tower and Chinese Pavilion which would otherwise have been demolished *(see The Green Guides Brussels and Belgium/Luxembourg).*

Parc oriental de Maulévrier ⊘ – The terraces of Colbert Castle overlook the oriental park of 28ha/70 acres that was laid out by Alexandre Marcel between 1899 and 1910. Designed to resemble a Japanese garden, it was laid out around a peaceful lake to represent the changing seasons and the progression of living things, with symbols of the life process from birth to death (rising and setting sun).

🏃 A path with Japanese lanterns leads around the lake through exotic species of shrubs and trees (Japanese maples, magnolia stellata, cryptomerias, flowering cherries and aucubas) to a pagoda and garden with a spring, the symbol of birth and light. There is also a Khmer temple *(used by Buddhists)* approached by steps adorned with lions, a red bridge leading to the Crane and Tortoise islands (symbols of paradise), a hill of meditation, a rise of azaleas, and so on.

Beyond the shadowy lanes of conifers are a bonsai exhibition and a Raku earthenware workshop.

The best time of year to visit the park is from mid-April to mid-May and from mid-October to mid-November.

Drive W out of Maulévrier along D 20 towards the Verdon and Ribou lakes.

Lac du Verdon – This lake lies immediately downstream from the Lac de Ribou and covers an area of 280ha/692 acres. One end of the lake stretches into the hills. The lake has become a nature reserve for migratory birds which flock here in thousands.

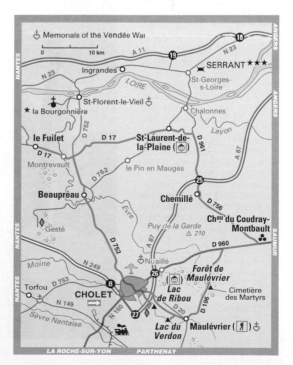

Lac de Ribou – 🖭 This vast reservoir encircled by hills provides facilities for a variety of water sports including windsurfing, rowing, sailing etc as well as fishing *(CISPA, Port de Ribou)*. The gently sloping, grassy shores are suitable for other sports such as archery, golf and riding. There is also a camp site.

The **Ferme de la Goubaudière** ⊘ is a farmhouse which has been converted into a museum devoted to rural life, the **Musée de la Paysannerie**, showing a typical late-19C domestic interior from the Cholet region, with furniture, everyday articles and a display of tools and farming machinery in use from 1900 to 1950.

Basilique de CLÉRY-ST-ANDRÉ★

Population 2 718
Michelin map 318: H-5, 238 fold 4 or 4045 B5

In 1280, some labourers set up a statue of the Virgin Mary they had found in a thicket in a humble chapel which was to become the present **church**. Worship of this statue spread throughout the district, and the chapel, too small to accommodate the pilgrims, was transformed into a church served by a college of canons. This was destroyed in 1428 by the English commander Salisbury during his march on Orléans. Charles VII and Dunois supplied the first funds for rebuilding, but the great benefactor of Cléry was **Louis XI**. During the siege of Dieppe, while still only the Dauphin, he vowed to give his weight in silver to Notre-Dame de Cléry if he were victorious. His prayer was answered and he kept his vow. When he became King, Louis XI dedicated himself to the Virgin Mary and in doing so strengthened his attachment to Cléry. He was buried there at his request and the building was completed by his son, Charles VIII. The house (now a school) in which Louis XI stayed during his visits to Cléry is on the south side of the church opposite the transept entrance.

Every year a popular **pilgrimage** is held on 8 September and the following Sunday.

★**TOUR** *30min*

Notre-Dame de Cléry Basilica is a 15C building with the exception of the 14C square tower abutting the north side of the church, the only part of the original structure to have escaped destruction by the English. *Enter through the transept.*
Although slightly austere, the interior of the church is suffused with light and conveys great elegance; it should be imagined with tapestries adorning the walls.

Tomb of Louis XI – The tomb stands on the north side of the nave and is aligned with the altar dedicated to Our Lady, so that it lies at an oblique angle to the axis of the church. It was commissioned during the King's lifetime.

The marble statue of the King is the work of an Orléans sculptor, Bourdin (1622). It took the place of the original bronze statue, which was melted down by the Huguenots.

Funerary vault of Louis XI – Louis XI's bones and those of his wife, Charlotte de Savoie, are still in the vault which opens onto the nave near the tomb. The two skulls, sawn open for embalming, are in a glass case. Note the decorative mourning band *(litre)* which runs round the vaulting.

Tanguy de Châtel, who was killed during a siege while saving the life of Louis XI, is buried under a flagstone alongside the royal vault. Further to the right another stone covers the urn containing the heart of Charles VIII. The inscription on this urn is repeated on the nearest pillar.

★ **Chapelle St-Jacques** – *South aisle*. The church dean, Gilles de Pontbriand, and his brother built this chapel, dedicated to St James, to

St James

serve as their tomb. The chapel's Gothic decoration is extremely ornate. The vaulting is decorated with girdles and pilgrims' purses, for Cléry is on the pilgrimage route to St James' shrine in Santiago de Compostela, Spain. The walls are studded with ermines' tails and bridges (the arms of the Pontbriands). There are three fine statues: two in wood, of St James in a pilgrim's cloak (16C) and St Sebastian (17C); and one in stone of the Virgin Mary with very delicate features (16C). The Breton-style wooden grille in front of the chapel was donated by Louis XIII in 1622.

Chapelle de Dunois – *From the Chapelle St-Jacques, the second door on the left.* Dunois and his family are buried here *(see CHÂTEAUDUN)*. The church at Cléry was already finished when this chapel was added (1464) hence the construction of the vaulting was complicated by the presence of a buttress.

Stalls – These were presented by Henri II. Their seats are carved with a variety of human masks and the initials of the donor and his mistress, Diane de Poitiers *(see cheekpieces of the second row of stalls on the right)*.

Chancel – On the 19C high altar is a statue in wood of Notre-Dame de Cléry. In the central window a fine piece of 16C stained glass – the only one from this period in the church – represents Henri III founding the Order of the Holy Spirit.

Sacristy and oratory of Louis XI – In the second ambulatory bay on the right is the beautiful door to the sacristy, in pure Flamboyant style. Above it, a small window opens into an oratory *(spiral staircase in the sacristy)* from which Louis XI could follow Mass.

CRAON

Population 4 659
Michelin map 310: D-7 or 232 fold 18

Craon (pronounced Cran) is a quiet Angevin town on the River Oudon surrounded by woodland and pastures, devoted to arable farming and cattle raising. It is famous for its horse racing (August and September).

The riverside château, one of the finest examples of Louis XVI architecture, is surrounded by an English-style park. A few fine old timber-framed houses line the narrow streets of the old town, in particular the Grande-Rue.

Craon was the birthplace of **Volney** (1757-1820), a philosopher who enjoyed great fame in his lifetime.

★ **Château** ⊙ – Built c 1770 in the local white tufa, this elegant château has a curvilinear pediment and windows embellished with festoons characteristic of the Louis XVI period. The courtyard façade is in a severe neo-Classical style. Several 18C rooms with fine woodwork and Louis XVI furnishings are on show. Note the splendid wrought-iron ramp adorning the hall.

The pretty formal French **gardens** around the château and the fine landscape **park** (42ha/104 acres) in the English style running down to the river have recently been restored. Many of the trees can be identified with the aid of descriptive labels. There is a kitchen garden with its 19C greenhouses, a laundry building where clothes were steamed over wood-ash and an underground ice house, built in the 19C. In winter it was filled with ice and packed snow to serve as a cold chamber for the preservation of food in summer.

EXCURSIONS

Cossé-le-Vivien – *12km/8mi N via N 171.* In 1962, the painter and ceramicist **Robert Tatin** (1902-83), gave free rein to his architectural fantasies around the old farmhouse called La Frénouse. The result has now become the **Musée Robert-Tatin** ⊙★.

The museum is approached along an avenue lined with strange statues leading to the Giants' Gate and the figure of a dragon with jaws agape. Then come three major coloured structures made of reinforced concrete, representing Our Lady of the Whole World, the Moon Gate and the Sun Gate, which stand reflected in a pool shaped like a cross and lined by representations of the 12 months of the year. The architecture, painting and ceramics seem to have been drawn from experience of a symbolic, initiatory nature.

The museum itself, which is reminiscent of Art Brut, takes the visitor into the fantastic world of this self-taught artist, whose naïve and visionary creations draw on Oriental, Pre-Colombian and even Celtic sources, merging them into an art of universal significance – a bridge between East and West.

Renazé – *10km/6mi SW.* Having reached their heyday in the early years of the 20C, the quarries at Renazé continued to produce their finely grained slate up until 1975. The Longchamp site has now been turned into the **Musée de l'Ardoise** ⊙, with displays of slate-working tools and machinery, demonstrations of the slate-worker's skills and a slide show *(15min)* evoking the dark world of the underground slate mines which have gradually replaced conventional quarrying.

Château de Mortiercrolles ⊙ – *11km/7mi SE on D 25 and a track to the left beyond St-Quentin-des-Anges.* This beautiful château was built in the late 15C by Pierre de Rohan, Marshal of Gié. A broad moat surrounds the long curtain wall with its four corner towers, which is guarded by a remarkable **gatehouse★** with alternating courses of brick and stone and fine machicolations in tufa. In the courtyard the building housing the main apartments *(right)* is decorated with superb dormer gables. At the rear of the courtyard an elegant chapel of brick with stone courses was re-roofed in 1969: note the pretty Renaissance side door and the piscina ornamented with shells.

DESCARTES

Population 4 019
Michelin map 317: N-7, 232 fold 48 or 4037 E6

It was in Descartes, which used to be called La Haye, that **René Descartes** (1590-1650), the famous French philosopher, physicist and mathematician was baptised, although the family home was in the neighbouring town of Châtellerault. At the age of eight he was sent to the Jesuit College of Henri IV in La Flèche where he received a semi-military education, before joining the army under the Prince of Nassau. While pursuing his military career, he travelled widely throughout Europe, devoting most of his time to study, and the pursuit of his life's mission as it was revealed to him on 10 November 1619. In 1629 he returned to Holland where he stayed for 20 years, studying at various universities and writing and publishing some of his most famous works. In 1649 he accepted an invitation to the Swedish royal court, where he died on 11 February 1650.

Cartesian thought – Written in French rather than in the Latin of all philosophical or scientific works published hitherto, Descartes' *Discourse on Method* (1637) was intended to be accessible to everyone. Published four years after Galileo's condemnation by the Inquisition, this seminal work met with a quite different reception and was destined to confound the sceptics; it marked the beginning of modern thought and scientific rationalism. In it, Descartes broke with scholasticism and founded a way of thinking based entirely on reasoned methodology and the systematic application of doubt, to the extent of questioning one's own existence, which he however resolved in the following way. "I who doubt, I who am deceived, at least while I doubt, I must exist, and as doubting is thinking, it is indubitable that while I think, I am". Descartes' work gave birth to an intellectual revolution, one of whose first fruits was analytical geometry.

Musée Descartes ⊙ – *29 rue Descartes.* This museum is Descartes' childhood home. Documents illustrating his life and works are on display.

EXCURSIONS

Château du Châtelier – *10km/6.2mi E along D 100.* Standing on a rocky outcrop, commanding the Brignon Valley, this austere castle (rebuilt in the 15C and 17C) has preserved some of its medieval fortifications: moats, drawbridges and, to the east of its rampart, an imposing round keep with large window openings, some of which are mullioned.

Ferrière-Larçon – *16km/10mi E along D 100.* The picturesque tile roofs of this village climb haphazardly up the valley slopes. The **church** presents an interesting combination of styles with a narrow Romanesque nave (12C) and a vast, luminous Gothic chancel (13C). The elegant Romanesque bell-tower has an octagonal stone spire with rounded mouldings on the ridges and a pinnacle at each corner.

DOUÉ-LA-FONTAINE★

Population 7 450
Michelin map 317: H-5, 232 fold 32 or 4049 H5
Local map see Vallée du LAYON

Doué and its outskirts are built on a chalk plateau which is riddled with caves; some are old quarries, others were excavated to provide housing or storage, as a wine cellar or a stable. The caves cannot be seen from the street since they were not hollowed out of the hillside as in the valley of the Loire and its tributaries, but were below ground level and opened laterally into a broad ditch forming a courtyard. Some are still in use but have long since been abandoned.

The town's main activities are nursery gardening and rose growing; examples of these arts are on display at the famous flower show, **Journées de la rose**, which takes place each year in mid-July in the arena, and at a large park, where some late-18C stables belonging to Baron Foullon have been converted into an open-air museum of old-fashioned shops *(see below)*.

SIGHTS

Maisons anciennes – In addition to its cliff-face dwellings (rue des Perrières and rue d'Anjou), Doué still has a number of old houses with turrets and external stairs. On the way out of town along the Saumur road, a fine-looking **windmill** is the lone survivor of the many that used to cover the region.

Arènes ⊙ – In the 15C an old quarry in the **Douces** district was converted into an arena when terraces of seats were hewn out of the solid rock. It is now used for theatrical and musical performances and the flower show *(see above)*. Beneath the terraces are vast caves which were for a long time inhabited, and kitchens and other rooms are still visible. Royalists were imprisoned here during the revolutionary wars.

Musée des Commerces anciens ⊙ – Rue de Soulanger, towards St-Georges-Du Layon. ⊚ The stables of Baron Foullon, the only remaining part of the château, provide a splendid setting for this museum of 20 or so old-style shops along two reconstructed streets. Covering about a century (1850-1950) of local retail trade, the museum includes stores formerly belonging to an apothecary, a hatter, a corn chandler, an ironmonger, a barber, a grocer etc. Each shop has been reconstructed with great attention to detail and equipped with the relevant accessories (display counters, shop windows, tills etc) for the period.

★★**Zoo de Doué** ⊙ – The zoo is situated on the western edge of Doué on the road to Cholet (D 960), in a remarkable troglodyte **setting**★. ⊚ The old conchitic stone quarries, with their vast underground caverns and lime kilns, make an unusual habitat for the 500 or more animals which have their home here, more or less at liberty. The setting has been enhanced with features such as waterfalls, rocky outcrops, acacias and bamboo to make it as natural an environment as possible for the various species, several of which are endangered. Breeding them in captivity in zoos such as this is an important contribution towards ensuring their survival.

Fearless visitors may like to go into one of the quarries which has been turned into a huge aviary containing about 20 vultures. Then there is the Leopard Canyon, specially adapted to be home to three families of beautiful big cats: snow leopards, Sumatra tigers and jaguars. A colony of 35 penguins has been incorporated into the zoo and a large transparent tank affords close-up views of dwarf hippopotamuses indulging in underwater antics. The design of the zoo and the many species of leafy trees enable visitors to observe and photograph the animals in a natural setting at close range.

There are several displays, including those in the **naturoscope** on wildlife conservation and environmental protection, housed in an old farm. The Faluna Gallery contains animal fossils from the park itself.

> **WELCOME INN**
>
> **Auberge Bienvenue** – *Rte de Cholet (opposite zoo)* – ☎ *02 41 59 22 44 – closed during Feb school holidays, Wed evening from Oct-Mar, Sun evening and Mon – 17.53/45.73€.* A flower-decked inn, a little way from the town centre, opposite the zoo. Two spacious and airy dining rooms have arcades opening onto a shaded terrace. Good choice of menus at reasonable prices.

Zoo de Doué-la-Fontaine

Dwarf hippopotamuses

La Cave aux sarcophages ⊘ – *1 rue de la Croix-Mordret, S of the road leading to Montreuil-Bellay.* Numerous excavations have revealed fine Merovingian sarcophagi. These monoliths were produced in great quantities in the Doué region (more than 30 000 dating from the 5C and 6C) and the finds offer an opportunity to discover the secrets of this flourishing production on an almost industrial scale.

Maison carolingienne – *Boulevard du Docteur-Lionnet, on the southern outskirts of the town near the road to Argenton-Château (D 69).* This 9C fortified Carolingian house was later transformed into a keep.

Les Chemins de la rose ⊘ – *Route de Cholet.* A recent park covering 5ha/12 acres has been chosen as the setting for thousands of roses representing more than 800 varieties from all over the world, from the Damascus rose brought back by crusaders in the 13C to the York-Lancaster rose from England.

EXCURSIONS

Louresse – *6km/4mi N on D 69 and D 177.*

Village troglodytique Rochemenier ⊘ – 🖼 The underground village of Rochemenier, an example of a typical settlement adapted to the conditions of the plain, was dug out of the marly deposit known as faluna. Although it extends over a wide area, it is now hidden by the dwellings at ground level where the majority of the local people live. Two of the old farmsteads, abandoned around 1930, are open to the public.

Maisons troglodytes de Forges ⊘ – *5.5km/3mi N on D 214.*

🖼 Excavations in 1979 revealed this fine example of a type of rural architecture which was formerly unappreciated; the hamlet used to house three families until it was abandoned in the 1940s. Like the *bories* of Provence it shows how the peasants adapted to living underground. The various chambers were hollowed out below ground around a sunken courtyard, similar to dwellings found in Tunisia; only the chimneys protruded above ground level. Ovens and chimneys were dug straight into the earth, as were the rooms for storing grain and vegetables.

Caverne sculptée de Dénezé-sous-Doué ⊘ – *5.5km/3mi N on D 69.*

🖼 This cave (14ºC/57ºF only!) is most unusual; its walls are carved with hundreds of strange figures. From the attitudes, dress and musical instruments archaeologists have dated the carvings to the 16C; they are probably the work of a secret society of stonemasons and depict their initiation rites. Guides are at hand to give a detailed explanation of the different scenes.

La FERTÉ-BERNARD★

Population 9 239
Michelin map 310: M-5, 232 folds 11 and 12 or 4072 H2
Local map see BROU

The Renaissance houses of La Ferté-Bernard cluster round the church of Notre-Dame-des-Marais. The lush pastures of the Huisne Valley are watered by this river, its tributary the Même, and the Sarthe. The old fortified town, which grew up round the castle *(ferté)* was erected on stilts in the middle of the marshes. It was distinguished by the name of the first feudal lord, Bernard, whose descendants held the domain until the 14C. Under Louis XI it was made the property of the Guise family; in the 16C it enjoyed a period of economic prosperity giving rise to some remarkable buildings which contribute to the charm of the town. After siding with the

A FOREST INN OUTSIDE OF TOWN

Auberge de la Forêt – *38 r. Gabriel-Goussault – 72320 Vibraye – 16km/10mi S of La Ferté-Bernard towards St-Calais, then D 211 – ☎ 02 43 93 60 07 – closed 27 Jan-19 Feb, Sun evening and Mon – 16.77/41.92€.* You'll feel happy and well satisfied after a copious meal of local produce at this inn. The dining room displays paintings which are for sale, if the fancy takes you.

Catholic League and being defeated by the troops of Henri IV, La Ferté was sold to Cardinal de Richelieu in 1642 and was held by his heirs until the Revolution.

La Ferté-Bernard was the birthplace of the poet **Robert Garnier** (1544-90), whose best-known tragedy, *The Jews,* echoes Corneille and foreshadows Racine.

Every year, the city of La Ferté-Bernard organizes ARTEC, the International Festival of Art and Technology during which the French Cup and the European Cup of Robotics (E=M6), are held.

TOWN WALK

Porte St-Julien – This gate, which is protected by two round towers and machicolations, was built in the 15C under Louis XI; the moat was fed by the River Huisne. There was a postern and a double gate for vehicles guarded by a portcullis and a drawbridge.

Porte St-Julien

Old houses – East of the Porte St-Julien in rue de l'Huisne are a few Renaissance houses (no 15 features a telamone).

There are several old houses in rue Carnot including a pilgrim inn (15C) on the road to Santiago de Compostela and a house (butcher's shop) decorated with painted telamones representing a pilgrim (ground floor) being stared at by a madman and a grimacing Moor and two people (first floor) stoning St Stephen.

Halles – The market hall *(restored)* on place de la Lice and in rue Carnot was built in 1535. The façade overlooking the square is decorated with Guise lions on each gable and an extensive tile roof pierced by dormers and supported by a splendid timber frame.

Fountain – *Place Carnot.* The granite fountain (15C-16C) is fed by a spring in the Guillottières district which is channelled beneath the Huisne.

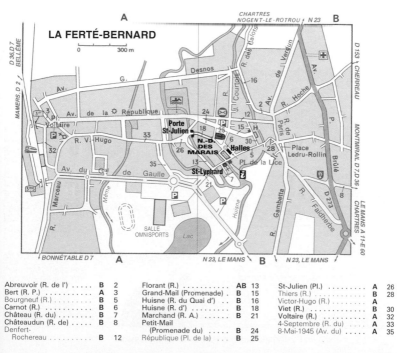

Abreuvoir (R. de l')	**B**	2	Florant (R.)	**AB**	13	St-Julien (Pl.)	**A**	26
Bert (R. P.)	**A**	3	Grand-Mail (Promenade)	**B**	15	Thiers (R.)	**B**	28
Bourgneuf (R.)	**B**	5	Huisne (R. du Quai d')	**B**	16	Victor-Hugo (R.)	**A**	
Carnot (R.)	**B**	6	Huisne (R. d')	**B**	18	Viet (R.)	**B**	30
Château (R. du)	**B**	7	Marchand (R. A.)	**B**	21	Voltaire (R.)	**A**	32
Châteaudun (R. de)	**B**	8	Petit-Mail			4-Septembre (R. du)	**A**	33
Denfert-			(Promenade du)	**B**	24	8-Mai-1945 (Av. du)	**A**	35
Rochereau	**B**	12	République (Pl. de la)	**B**	25			

Chapelle St-Lyphard ⊘ – Thorough restoration work has revealed the chapel of an 11C feudal castle. The outbuildings *(private property)* also remain. The chapel, which was originally built against the main body of the castle and given a small side oratory in which a Virgin in Majesty may be seen, is decorated with modern stained-glass windows portraying Louis, Duke of Orléans, and his wife Valentina Visconti, lord and lady of La Ferté-Bernard to whom the castle was endowed in 1392.

ADDITIONAL SIGHT

★★ **Église Notre-Dame-des-Marais** ⊘ – This magnificent church is a fine example of the Flamboyant Gothic style with early touches of the Renaissance. The nave, the transept and the square tower were built between 1450 and 1500; from 1535 to 1544 Mathurin Delaborde worked on the church and between 1550 and 1590 the Viet brothers were in charge of the construction of the spacious chancel (completed in 1596).

Exterior – There are Renaissance motifs in the carved decoration of the chancel the south side is ornamented with scrollwork and busts of Roman emperors in the spandrels there are niches in the buttresses. The low gallery is supported on a carved cornice of shells and busts in relief between the corbels. On the balustrade stand some unusual little statues of the king of France and his 12 peers; in the spaces are the words Regina Cæli. The upper gallery spells out the letters of Ave Regina Cælorum. *Enter via the Flamboyant south door.*

Interior – At the west end are the original Renaissance holy water stoups; the nave contains the organ pipes supported on a Flamboyant corbel.
The skilfully constructed, elegant chancel consists of soaring arches, each one surmounted by a small statue on a dais, a light and simple Renaissance triforium and tall windows filled with light 16C and 17C glass.
The three **apsidal chapels**★ are particularly interesting. The right chapel has an astonishing ceiling of ogive vaulting meeting in a crown-shaped pendant; the windows, the delicate carved cartouches and the stoup are all 16C. In the central chapel the spaces between the ribs are decorated with stalactites and honeycombs; the Renaissance window *(left)* shows the meal at Bethany with Mary Magdalene at Jesus' feet. The left chapel has an unusual ceiling. The altarpiece in the side chapel on the left of the chancel shows the instruments of the Passion.

La FERTÉ-ST-AUBIN

Population 6 783
Michelin map 318: I-5, 238 fold 5 or 4045 C5

The town extends north-south between the main road (N 20) and the railway line. The old district has a few typical local houses: low, timber-framed constructions with brick infill and huge roofs of flat tiles. A splendid Classical château stands among greenery, on the banks of the River Cosson.

The château on the banks of the Cosson

★**Château** ⊙ – Built in brick relieved with courses of stone, this is an impressive edifice, albeit an asymmetrical one; to the left is the Little Château still with its 16C diamond-patterned brickwork and, to the right, the Big Château, built in the mid-17C with a Classical façade topped by sculpted dormers. The centrepiece is formed by a pedimented portal flanked by domed pavilions.

Inside *(access via the ramp)*, the Dining Hall and the Grand Salon have kept their 18C furnishings as well as a number of portraits including one of the *Marquis de la Carte* attributed to Largillière and another of *Louis XV* at the age of 54. The Marshals' Room is devoted to the memory of **Maréchal de la Ferté**, who distinguished himself at the Battle of Rocroi, and of Ulrich de Lowendal, a contemporary of Maréchal de Saxe, his neighbour at Chambord.

On the first floor of the right wing *(access on the right)*, are 17C, 18C and 19C state apartments and the guard-room with its fine French-style ceiling. On the second floor are a number of rooms with displays on traditional trades from the Sologne.

The basement houses the spacious 17C kitchens where a permanent display enlightens visitors on the culinary subtleties of baking small, honey flavoured, sponge cakes *(madeleines au miel)*, which they can then taste as they come piping hot out of the traditional oven.

The main courtyard is defined by two identical buildings; that on the left houses the **stables** and the **saddlery**, and that on the right the orangery.

▣ **The park** – To round off the tour, you can visit the **menagerie** and its little model farm or else take a walk through the English-style parkland with its charming network of islets. The **Île enchantée** (Enchanted Island) presents small-scale houses especially designed for children, where they can play games featuring their favourite heroes, pretending to be Alice or Lancelot.

Église St-Aubin – 12C-16C church. The tall tower over the entrance overlooks the Cosson Valley.

La FLÈCHE★

Population 15 241
Michelin map 310: I-8, 232 fold 21 or 4072 D5
Local map see VENDÔME

This charming Angevin town, pleasantly situated on the banks of the Loir, is renowned for its Prytanée, a military school which has trained generations of officers.
Students tend to group around the Henri IV fountain (on the square of the same name); a stroll along boulevard Latouche and Carmes gardens is also pleasant.
The surrounding area boasts a number of châteaux, the fine Chambiers Forest and the pretty villages of Bazouges and Durtal in their green riverside setting.
In July, the Festival des Affranchis is brought to life by a group of travelling actors who give street performances using the city's old fountains or wells as their setting.

Henri IV – La Flèche was given as part of a dowry to Charles de Bourbon-Vendôme, grandfather to Henri IV of Navarre, of "Paris is well worth a Mass" fame.
It was here that the young Prince Henri happily spent his childhood and where in 1604 he founded a Jesuit college, which was to become the Prytanée.

A breeding-ground for officers – The Jesuit college grew rapidly and by 1625 there were 1 500 pupils. Carried away by their success, the good fathers started a dispute with the Governor of the town who wanted to prevent them fishing in their moat; the dispute became known as the War of the Frogs. Following the expulsion of the Jesuits from France in 1762, the college became a military school and then a military academy *(prytanée)* in 1808. Over the years it has produced a great many celebrities who have distinguished themselves in the service of their country: Charles Borda, René Descartes, Marshalls Bertrand, Clarke, Pelissier, Gallieni, and more recently astronauts Patrick Baudry and Jean-François Clervoy and the actor Jean-Claude Brialy. Not to mention more than 2 000 generals and a number of government ministers.

Ph. Gajic/MICHELIN

The Muslim Warrior

Missionaries in Canada – Jérôme le Royer de la Dauversière, a native of La Flèche, was one of the founders of Montreal. The paganism of the Canadian Indians moved him to create the Society of Our Lady for the Conversion of the Savages which started a little colony in 1642, now the capital of Quebec. Another old pupil of the college in La Flèche, **François de Montmorency-Laval**, became the first bishop of Nouvelle-France in 1674.

Unhappy exile – Under the monarchy La Flèche was a peaceful town with nothing to offer by way of entertainment but a hairdresser's, two billiard halls and a café. The witty poet **Jean-Baptiste Gresset** (1709-77) composed the heroic-comic masterpiece on the adventures of the parrot Ver-Vert, for which he is famous *(see The Green Guide Burgundy-Jura)*, while in exile in La Flèche for the indiscreet use of his tongue and his pen.

SIGHTS

★ **Prytanée national militaire** ⊙ – Located on the same site as the prestigious 17C Jesuit college, this military academy currently educates a total of 900 students, housed in two pavilions, named respectively after Henri IV and Gallieni. This State establishment offering an all-round education is open to any young French boy wishing to prepare for entrance to the national service academies *(grandes écoles militaires)* such as the École Polytechnique, the École Spéciale Militaire in Coëtquidan, the École Navale in Brest, the École de l'Air at Salon-de-Provence and academies specialised in engineering. A monumental Baroque doorway, surmounted by a bust of Henri IV, marks the entrance to the former Jesuit college. It opens into the main courtyard, also known as the Austerlitz courtyard; at the far end stands a Louis XVI-style house (1784) which houses the staff. The school boasts an excellent library containing around 45 000 volumes, some of which date back to the 15C.

★ **Église St-Louis** ⊙ – 1607-37. The chapel is laid out in the typical Jesuit manner: nave bordered by side chapels, large galleries, plentiful light. The Baroque decor is impressive, from the great retable on the high altar to the magnificent organ (1640) in its graceful **organ loft**★. Set in an upper niche in the left transept is a heart-shaped, lead gilt urn which contains the ashes of the hearts of Henri IV and Marie de Medici.

Chapelle Notre-Dame-des-Vertus – This is a charming Romanesque chapel with a semicircular-arched doorway and oven-vaulted apses. The wooden vaulting in the nave is completely decorated with 17C paintings (scrolls and medallions). Note the superb Renaissance **woodwork**★ and the Muslim warrior on the back of the main door.

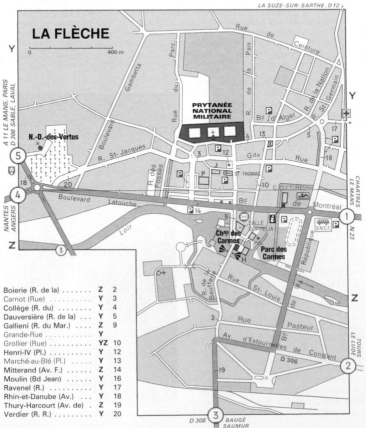

LA FLÈCHE

Boierie (R. de la)	Z	2
Carnot (Rue)	Y	3
Collège (R. du)	Y	4
Dauversière (R. de la)	Y	5
Gallieni (R. du Mar.)	Z	9
Grande-Rue	Y	
Grollier (Rue)	YZ	10
Henri-IV (Pl.)	Y	12
Marché-au-Blé (Pl.)	Y	13
Mitterand (Av. F.)	Z	14
Moulin (Bd Jean)	Y	16
Ravenel (R.)	Y	17
Rhin-et-Danube (Av.)	Y	18
Thury-Harcourt (Av. de)	Z	19
Verdier (R. R.)	Y	20

Eating out

BUDGET

Le Moulin des Quatre Saisons – *R. Gallieni* – ☎ *02 43 45 12 12* – *closed 2-25 Jan, Wed evening, Sun evening and Mon* – *16.01/23.17€*. Your first impression on arriving at this 17C watermill in summer will be the scent of wisteria that overhangs the front path. The restaurant overlooks the Loir and features cooking from the south of France, whereas the decor is Alsatian.

Where to stay

MODERATE

Relais Cicero – *18 bd d'Alger* – ☎ *02 43 94 14 14* – *closed 20 Dec-4 Jan and Sun* – *21 rooms 66.32/103.51€* – ☕ *7.62€*. A 17C property which has retained a sense of history within its ivy-covered stone walls. Luxurious rooms with antique furniture where you can relax by the hearth. You will sleep peacefully in the personalised and well-decorated rooms.

Château des Carmes – The 17C buildings erected on the ruins of a 15C fortress now house the town hall. The façade facing the Loir consists of a steep gable flanked by two machicolated turrets. The **Parc des Carmes**, which is open to the public, stretches down to the river; from the bridge there is a fine view of the calm water reflecting the garden and the château.

EXCURSIONS

★**Parc zoologique du Tertre rouge** ⊘ – *5km/3mi E. Leave La Flèche on* ② *on the plan and turn onto D 104; the zoo is 1km/0.5mi after the third level crossing.*
⌖ The zoo covers 7ha/17 acres in a forest setting. There are mammals (big game, monkeys, deer, elephants etc), many birds and numerous reptiles housed in two vivariums (pythons, boas, crocodiles, tortoises etc). Sea-lions appear at scheduled performances. The **Musée de Sciences naturelles** (Natural Science Museum) displays a diorama on regional fauna. The 600 stuffed animals in the collection of the naturalist Jacques Bouillault are on show in reconstructions of their natural habitats.

Bazouges-sur-le-Loir – *7km/4.3mi. Drive W out of La Flèche and follow N 23.* From the bridge there is a charming **view**★ of the river with its wash-houses and river gate, of the castle and the mill, of the church and its tower in the square and of the gardens climbing towards the roofs of Bazouges.

Château ⊘ – The Château de Bazouges, together with its watermill, was built on an attractive site on the banks of the Loir in the 15C and 16C by the Champagne family, one of whom, Baudoin (Baldwin), was chamberlain to Louis XII and François I.
The entrance is flanked by two massive towers, with machicolations and pepper-pot turrets; one of them contains the 15C chapel decorated with Angevin vaulting and two old statues portraying St Barbara and St John.
The guard-room over the gateway leads to the sentry walk. Another more imposing guard-room with a stone chimney-piece is on view as well as the 18C State Rooms and the formal French park which is planted with cypresses and yew trees and circled by water.

Church ⊘ – The building dates from the 12C. A solid tower rises above the crossing. The nave vaulting, which is made of oak shingles, is painted with 24 figures (12 Apostles and 12 angels) separated by trees each bearing an article from the Creed (early 16C).

Durtal – *12km/7.5mi W along N 23*. Durtal occupies a charming site in the shelter of its château on the Loir.
▣ **Chambiers Forest** on the southern edge of the town provides 1 300ha/5sq mi of walks among the oak and pine trees; broad rides radiate from the Table au Roy (King's Table). The racecourse is a popular meeting place for the sporting fraternity.

Château ⊘ – This grand stronghold on the Loir belonged to François de Scépeaux, Marshal of Vieilleville, who was host to Henri II, Charles IX and Catherine de' Medici. It came through the Revolution relatively unscathed.
The 15C wing is flanked by round towers with machicolations and pepper-pot roofs. The highest one (5 storeys) affords a good view of the **Loir Valley**. The Renaissance Gallery, lavishly decorated with paintings, overlooks the river. The Schömberg Pavilion, characterised by string courses, cordons and cornerstones with vermiculated bossage, prefigures the Classical period.
A tour of the interior will take you through the guard-room, the kitchen quarters, the dungeons, the Renaissance Gallery and the Great Tower (Grande Tour).

Porte Verron – This 15C gate flanked by two turrets is part of the original curtain wall of the castle.

Vieux Pont – This old bridge commands a nice **view** of the River Loir, the watermills, the pointed roofs of the town and a medieval round tower upstream.

Fontevraud Abbey stands on the borders of Anjou, Touraine and Poitou. Despite the ravages of history, it remains the largest group of monastic buildings in France, having retained some interesting features typical of Anjou architecture, in particular the lofty vaulting of the abbey church and the impressive kitchen. There is a good view of the abbey from the Loudon road on the south side of the village.

An aristocratic Order – The success of the new Order was immediate and it quickly took on an aristocratic character; the abbesses, who were members of noble families, procured rich gifts and powerful protection for the abbey. The **Plantagenets** showered it with wealth and a dozen or so of their number elected to be buried in the abbey church. Henri II, his wife Eleanor of Aquitaine and their son Richard the Lionheart are buried in the crypt. Later transfers to the crypt include the hearts of John Lackland and of his son Henry III, who rebuilt Westminster Abbey.

The abbey became a refuge for repudiated queens and daughters of royal or highly placed families who, voluntarily or under compulsion, retired from the secular world. There were 36 abbesses, half of whom were of royal blood including five from the House of Bourbon, between 1115 and 1789. Louis XV entrusted the education of his four younger daughters to the Abbess **Gabrielle de Rochechouart de Mortemart** (the sister of Madame de Montespan).

Over the centuries, several energetic reforming abbesses made the abbey a spiritual and cultural centre of great renown.

Foundation of the abbey (1101)

The monastic order at Fontevraud was founded by **Robert d'Arbrissel** (c 1045-1117) who had been a hermit in Mayenne Forest before being appointed by Urban II to preach in the west of France. He soon gained a large group of disciples of both sexes and chose this place to found a double community.

From the beginning the abbey was unique among religious houses in that it had five separate buildings accommodating priests and lay brothers (St-Jean-de-l'Habit), contemplative nuns (Ste-Marie), lepers (St-Lazare), invalids (St-Benoît) and lay sisters (Ste-Marie-Madeleine). Each body led its own life, with its own church and cloister, chapter-house, refectory, kitchen and dormitory. Robert d'Arbrissel had ordained that the whole community be directed by an abbess chosen from among widows; she was later designated as Head and General of the Order and this female supremacy was to be maintained right up to the French Revolution.

Violation of the abbey – The Huguenots desecrated the abbey in 1561; in 1792 the Order was suppressed by the Revolutionaries who completely destroyed the monks' priory in the following year.

In 1804 Napoleon converted the remaining buildings into a State prison which was closed only in 1963.

Cultural vocation – In 1975 the abbey embarked on a new vocation as a venue for cultural events. The **Centre culturel de l'Ouest** ⊘ (Cultural Centre of the West) administers the buildings and organises concerts, exhibitions, seminars and lectures.

Accommodation for visitors is provided in the old priory of St-Lazare, a short distance away from Fontevraud's other buildings.

VILLAGE

★**Église St-Michel** – Although the church was enlarged and remodelled in the 13C and 15C, an inner arcade with small columns and typical Angevin vaulting remains from the original Romanesque building.

The church contains numerous **works of art**★. The high altar of carved and gilded wood was made at the behest of Abbess Louise de Bourbon, in 1621 for the abbey church. In a north side chapel is a 15C wooden Crucifix which somehow exudes an impression of both torment and peace, and an impressive 16C *Crowning with Thorns*. In a Crucifixion painted on wood in an archaic style by Étienne Dumonstier, the artist sought to portray the shameful waste of the struggles between Catholics and Protestants by depicting the protagonists at the foot of the Cross. Viewers can make out Catherine de' Medici as Mary Magdalene, Henri II as the soldier piercing the heart of Christ, and their three sons, François II, Charles IX and Henri III. Mary Stuart is the Holy Woman with a crown; the Virgin Mary has the features of Elizabeth of Austria. The modest nun in the foreground is Abbess Louise de Bourbon who was host to Mary Stuart in 1548, Charles IX in 1564 and Catherine de' Medici in 1567.

Chapelle Ste-Catherine – This 13C chapel stands in what was originally the churchyard; it is crowned by a lantern of the dead.

A QUIET RETREAT

Hôtellerie Prieuré St-Lazare – *R. St-Jean-de-l'Habit – ☎ 02 41 51 73 16 – closed 2 Nov-31 Mar – 25.92/53.36€.* A haven of peace in the heart of the Fontevraud Abbey gardens, the old priory of St-Lazare encourages spiritual repose; guests stay in the old monastic cells. The smaller cloister is used as a restaurant today, whereas the chapel has been converted into a reception hall. The menu features contemporary dishes.

ROYAL ABBEY FARM

Chambre d'hôte Domaine de Mestré – *1km/0.5mi N of Fontevraud on D 947, towards Montsoreau – ☎ 02 41 51 72 32 – www.dauge-fontevraud.com – closed 24 Dec-1 Mar (open weekends in Mar) – ⊠ – 12 rooms 38.85/52.60€ – ⊑ 6.85€ – evening meal 22.85€.* Like the pilgrims on their journey to Santiago de Compostela, spend a night or two at the old royal abbey farm on your way through the Loire Valley. A good night's sleep guaranteed, home-grown produce to enjoy and refined decor. Lovely park planted with centuries-old cedar and lime trees.

★★ ABBEY ⊙ *2hr*

Among the buildings around the entrance court, most of which date from the 19C are, on the left, the vast 18C stables *(fannerie)* and, on the right, the 17C and 18C abbess' house adorned with garlands and low-relief sculptures. The entrance is situated in the former barracks which, during the 19C, housed the military in charge of the prison (a standing exhibition presenting Fontevraud's history can be seen on the first floor).

Every evening in August, the abbey organises **Les Rencontres Imaginaires**, *an open-air* **son et lumière** *performance involving artists as well as professional and amateur actors.*

★★ **Abbey church** – This imposing 12C abbey church, divided into storeys at the time when it served as a prison, has been restored to its original purity.
The vast nave (15x60m/49x197ft) with its delicately carved capitals is roofed by a series of domes, a characteristic of churches found in the south-west of France (Cahors, Périgueux, Angoulême etc). Fontevraud is the northernmost example of these curious domed churches and this can be explained by the important links between Anjou and Aquitaine during the Plantagenet reign.

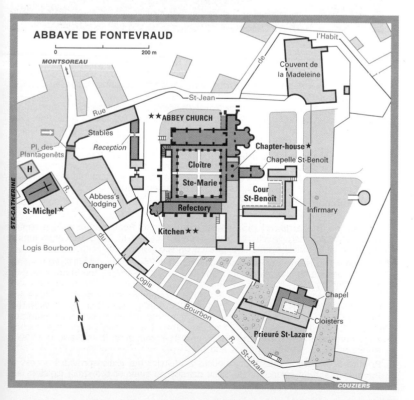

ABBAYE DE FONTEVRAUD

Fontevraud abbey kitchen

Built several decades earlier than the nave, the transept and chancel are reminiscent of the Benedictine plan: an ambulatory and radiating chapels where the luminosity and repetition of vertical lines – slender columns, arcades, pillars – signify the aspiration to reach up to heaven.

The building houses 13C **polychrome recumbent figures of the Plantagenets★**, representing Henry II, Count of Anjou and King of England, his wife Eleanor of Aquitaine, who died at Fontevraud in 1204, their son Richard the Lionheart and lastly Isabella of Angoulême, second wife of their son, King John of England.

Cloître Ste-Marie – The cloisters in the nuns' convent have Renaissance vaulting except on the south side, which is Gothic inspired. A richly carved doorway in the east gallery, paved with the Bourbon coat of arms, opens into the **chapter-house★** which has 16C murals representing some of the abbesses.

Cour St-Benoît – This 17C-18C courtyard leads to the infirmary. The north wing includes the 12C **Chapelle St-Benoît**.

Refectory – This large hall (45m/148ft long) with its Romanesque walls is roofed with Gothic vaulting which replaced a timber ceiling in 1515. A chronological sequence of historical events is projected on the walls.

★★ **Kitchen** – This is the only Romanesque kitchen in France to have survived the centuries – despite its alterations. In many respects it resembles the abbot's kitchen at Glastonbury.

This most intriguing building is roofed with overlapping lozenge-shaped stones and topped by numerous chimneys, added in 1904 during restoration by the architect Magne. Originally, the building was free-standing, built on an octagonal plan and capped by an octagonal hood (27m/88ft high). The kitchen's large size is commensurate with the size of the abbey and its community; it was also used as a smoke room for preserving meat and fish.

Prieuré St-Lazare – This priory houses a hostelry but it also provides access to the chapel and its splendid 18C **spiral staircase**; in summer the small cloisters are used as a restaurant.

Château de FOUGÈRES-SUR-BIÈVRE★

Michelin map 318: F-7 or 238 fold 15 – 8km/5mi NW of Contres

In the charming village of Fougères, surrounded by nursery gardens and fields of asparagus, stands the austere yet noble north façade of the feudal-looking château of Pierre de Refuge, Chancellor to Louis XI. It is not too difficult to imagine the original moats, drawbridge and arrow slits – replaced in the 16C by windows – and the keep's battlements which disappeared when the roof was added.

TOUR ⏱ *30min*

The present building was begun in 1450 with the construction of the two wings giving onto the courtyard, dedicated to Jeanne de Faverois, the wife of Jean de Refuge.

In 1470, Pierre de Refuge was granted royal permission to fortify his castle and, shortly afterwards, he erected the north wing, whose defensive features were aimed to impress, playing a purely symbolic role in times of peace.

However, when completed by his grandson, Jean de Villebresmes, the château acquired a certain grace: the east wing in the main court has a gallery of arcades with lovely dormer windows; the attractive turreted staircase in the north-west corner has windows flanked by pilasters with Renaissance motifs; the large windows added in the 18C to the south wing made it ideal as a spinning mill in the 19C.

The size of the rooms seen from within is impressive; so are the wooden roof-frame of the main building which is shaped like a ship's hull, and the conical roof-frame of the towers.

GIEN★

Population 15 332
Michelin map 318: M-5, 238 fold 7 or 4045 G5

Built on a hillside overlooking the north bank of the Loire, Gien, a small town with many a pretty garden, is well known for its glazed blue-and-yellow earthenware or faience and for its splendid hunting museum housed in the castle, said to have been built by Charlemagne. It was here, in 1410, that the Armagnac faction was set up in support of Charles d'Orléans against the Burgundians in the civil war which led up to the last episode in the Hundred Years War. The castle was later rebuilt by **Anne de Beaujeu** (1460-1522), the Countess of Gien, who was Louis XI's eldest daughter. Aged 23 when her father died, she was appointed regent during the minority of her brother Charles VIII (1483-91).

In 1652 during the **Fronde**, the armed revolt mounted by the great princes against the King forced Anne of Austria, Mazarin and the young Louis XIV to flee from Paris. They took refuge in Gien while Turenne, at the head of the royal troops, defeated the Fronde insurgents at Bléneau *(E of Gien)*.

Eating out

BUDGET

Le Régency – *6 quai Lenoir* – ☎ *02 38 67 04 96* – *closed during Feb school holidays, 1-15 Jul, Sun evening and Wed* – *14.50/26€.* Opposite the old stone bridge across the Loire, this small, town-centre restaurant provides a friendly welcome. Simple, tasty cooking.

Where to stay

BUDGET

Chambre d'hôte Le Domaine de Ste-Barbe – *45500 Nevoy* – *4km/2.5mi NW of Gien towards Lorris, take 2nd left after the level crossing and follow the signs* – ☎ *02 38 67 59 53* – *www.france-bonjour.com/sainte-barbe* – *closed 20 Dec-6 Jan* – ⌨ – *4 rooms 34/58€.* A pleasant house with an old-fashioned atmosphere. Terracotta floor tiles, floral fabrics, knick-knacks, old furniture and four-poster beds decorate the pretty rooms overlooking the garden. Small Sologne-style house available as a holiday cottage.

MODERATE

Hôtel Anne de Beaujeu – *10 rte de Bourges on D 941* – ☎ *02 38 29 39 39* – *closed 24 Dec-2 Jan* – 🅿 – *30 rooms 42.69/64.03€* – ⌨ *7.47€.* Near the old bridge across the Loire, this hotel is slightly out of the town centre. Functional rooms with contemporary furniture. Those at the back are quieter.

SIGHTS

From the 18C bridge there is a lovely **view**★ of the château, the houses lining the quay and the River Loire.

★★ **Musée international de la Chasse** ⊙ – Gien **château**★ stands on the eastern fringe of Orléans Forest and the Sologne, a region abounding in game, making it an ideal setting for a Hunting Museum.

The château, which dominates the town, was rebuilt shortly before 1500 with red brick and a slate roof. The decoration is restrained: a pattern of contrasting dark bricks and bands of white stone and a few stair turrets.

The French Hunting Horn

There exist two types of hunting horn used in France, which are both held on the player's arm. The **trompe de chasse** is made up of several conical brass tubes welded together with a flared end measuring 38cm/15.2in in diameter. The total length of the instrument is invariably 4.545m/14.9ft, usually forming three and a half coils, although this number may vary depending on the model (Dampierre, Maricourt, Dauphine or d'Orléans). The sound, always a D note, is produced towards the back of the horn. On the other hand, the **cor de chasse** is straighter and produces an E flat, which it projects forwards.

In France there are around 120 hunts staged on horseback every year. However the official number of horn players is estimated at 10 000, many of whom do not hunt big game. Players traditionally wear cotton gloves so that the moisture from their hands does not affect the metal and therefore the pure quality of the sound.

The Musée de la Chasse et de la Nature set up in the Hôtel Guénégaud in Paris, the Musée du Veneur in Montpoupon Château and the Musée International de la Chasse in Gien display fine collections of instruments whose musical variations have inspired many great composers: Lully, Mozart, Vivaldi, Rameau, Bach etc.

The rooms of the château with their beamed ceilings and fine chimney-pieces form an attractive backdrop to the exhibition of fine art inspired by hunting – tapestries, porcelain, cut glass, paintings etc – as well as weapons and accessories used in hunting since the prehistoric era: powder flasks, porcelain plates and jugs, decorated pipes, hunting knives, fashion plates, chimney plaques, crossbows, harquebuses, pistols and guns with detailed ornamentation.

Hunting Hound by François Desportes

CP/Musée International de la Chasse/ACPA

Beneath its superb roof the Great Hall is devoted to the work of **François Desportes** (1661-1743) and **Jean-Baptiste Oudry** (1686-1755), great animal painters attached to Louis XIV. Particularly noteworthy is the collection of some 4 000 blazer buttons decorated with hunting motifs. There is also a collection of hunting horns as well as 500 antlers, given to the museum by the great hunter, Claude Hettier de Boislambert, and various sculptures of animals by Brigaud and Fath.

The château terrace affords an extensive **view**★ of the River Loire and the slate roofs of the town, reconstructed in traditional style with pointed gables and diaper patterning in the brickwork.

Église Ste-Jeanne-d'Arc – The church standing on the north side of the château was entirely rebuilt in brick in 1954 apart from the 15C bell-tower which is all that remains of the collegiate church founded by Anne de Beaujeu. The slender round pillars of the interior create an atmosphere conducive to meditation, much like that found in Romanesque churches.

Faïencerie ⊙ – *West of the town. Access by quai Lenoir or rue Paul-Bert.* An old paste store has been converted into a **Faience Museum**; some of the very large pieces were made for the Universal Exhibition in 1900. There is also a display of the current production and a shop where factory pieces can be purchased at reduced prices.

Gien earthenware

When the faience (glazed earthenware) factory was founded in 1821 Gien was chosen because it was near the deposits of clay and sand needed for the paste, as well as having plentiful supplies of wood to fire the kilns, and because the Loire provided a means of transporting the finished product. Gien was well known for its dinner services and objets d'art; at the end of the 19C it developed a new technique called Gien blue *(bleu de Gien)* which produced a deep blue glaze enhanced with golden yellow decoration. As well as continuing the early handmade pieces, the factory also produces modern services.

EXCURSIONS

St-Brisson-sur-Loire – *6km/4mi SE along D 951*. Here in the borderlands between Berry and the Orléans region stand the remains of a 12C hilltop **fortress** ⊙ deprived of its original keep and crenellated south wall. The east wing and the staircase tower were restored in the 19C. The cellars of the old castle are open to the public, as is a suite of rooms with mementoes from the D'Estrades and Séguier families. In the library is a letter written by Jean-Jacques Rousseau. Replicas of medieval weaponry (mangonel, swivel gun) have been set up in the moat. Archery demonstrations are regularly staged on Sunday afternoons from mid-June to mid-September.

Dampierre-en-Burly – *13km/8mi NW along D 952*. The flat-tiled roofs of Dampierre present an attractive spectacle to anyone approaching from the west on D 952 from Ouzouer-sur-Loire; as the road crosses the tree-lined lake by a causeway, the ruins of a château loom into sight. Beyond what remains of the towers and curtain wall of the castle rises the church tower.

In the square by the church stands one of the château gatehouses, an elegant early-17C building, in brick and stone, decorated with bossed pilasters beneath a pyramidal roof.

Centre nucléaire de production d'électricité CNPE ⊙ – *3km/2mi S of Dampierre*. The four gigantic cooling towers (165m/541ft high and 135m/443ft diameter at the base) rising out of the flat Loire Valley belong to the nuclear power station which, like those at Chinon and St-Laurent-des-Eaux, uses the river to supply water to the cooling system. The Dampierre complex, which was commissioned in 1980 and 1981, consists of four pressurized water reactors each generating an output of 900 million watts.

The way in which the reactors work is described in the **information centre**, named after **Henri Becquerel** (1852-1908), a physicist whose family lived at Châtillon-Coligny, 30km/21mi away.

La Bussière – *10km/6.2mi NE along D 622*. The village is known for its **Château des Pêcheurs★**, an old fortress rebuilt in the 17C, which now houses a Museum of Freshwater Fishing *(see The Green Guide Burgundy-Jura)*.

GIZEUX

Population 510
Michelin map 317: K-4, 232 fold 34 or 4037 B3

East of the village, along a tree-lined avenue, stands an imposing château of the Angers area, which was the fief of the Du Bellay, princes of Yvetot, from 1330 to 1661 and which has been occupied by the same family since 1786.

Château ⊙ – The central building, flanked by two perpendicular wings, was erected on the site of the old fortress in 1560. All that remains of the former building is the machicolated tower in the front of the Court of Honour. The interior boasts a fine set of Louis XV furniture. **Salle François-Ier** is decorated with paintings on wood executed by Italian artists. The **Galerie des Châteaux★** features 17C frescoes depicting royal châteaux (Chambord, Vincennes, Fontainebleau, Versailles).

The château is extended to the north by a series of interesting outbuildings, including stables, dating from the mid-18C.

EXQUISITE AND ROMANTIC

Chambre d'hôte La Butte de l'Épine – *37340 Continvoir – 2km/1mi E of Gizeux on D 15 – ☎ 02 47 96 62 25 – closed 24 Dec-5 Jan – ⌦ – 3 rooms 48.78/53.36€*. This 16C-17C property has been charmingly restored. The main room has old furniture and a huge fireplace, the bedrooms are really exquisite and romantic, and the park is full of flowers. Sweet dreams!

Église – Not far away stands the church, which contains 17C tombs of the Du Bellay family. On the right are two kneeling figures in white marble: René du Bellay (d 1611) in armour, and his wife Marie in an open-necked dress and bonnet. On the left is Martin du Bellay, their son, and his wife, both wearing ruffs.

EXCURSIONS

Parçay-les-Pins – *6km/3.7mi N along D 15 and D 86*. The **Musée Jules-Desbois** ⊘ houses sculpture by Rodin's friend, a group of sensual works *(Leda and the Swan)* displayed to full advantage in this former farmhouse.

Vernoil – *10km/6.2mi W along D 215 and D 206*. The **church** has a massive bell-tower. Enter the priory yard *(right)* to see the solid octagonal turret and mullioned windows of the old prior's lodging.

Vernantes – *2km/1.2mi W of Vernoil*. A 12C tower marks the site of the **church**, of which only the chancel is still standing. The nave, destroyed by lightning in the 19C, has been replaced by a simple porch. A new church has been built on the other side of the square.

Blou – *21km/12.4mi W along D 206*. The Romanesque **church** ⊘ with its massive buttresses has curious 11C diapering on its north transept. A 13C bell-tower rises above the transept crossing.

Le GRAND-PRESSIGNY

Population 1 119
Michelin map 317: N-7, 232 fold 48 or 4037 E6

Le Grand-Pressigny stands in an attractive location facing the confluence of the River Claise and River Aigronne. It was once protected by its hilltop castle.
The site is well-known in the field of prehistory on account of its many flint work-shops where large numbers of blades were made at the end of the Neolithic Era. These have been found far afield; some even in Switzerland.

A steep narrow street lined with old houses leads straight to the castle. The ter-races offer superb views of the valley below.

★ **Château** ⊘ – The castle which provides a setting for the Prehistory Museum has retained characteristics of the medieval fortress of Guillaume de Pressigny: ram-parts flanked by towers, fortified gateway, keep and late-12C underground gallery. Amid the carefully tended gardens stands the 16C seigneurial home, which we owe to the renovation work carried out by Honorat de Savoie; the elegant Renaissance gallery opens through a pretty portico onto the Court of Honour, laid out as French gardens. At the top of the Vironne tower, the parapet walk affords an extremely pleasant **view** of the village and the Claise Valley.
The **Musée départemental de Préhistoire**, opened in 1912, traces the different stages of prehistoric evolution through displays of discoveries made in major sites in the Touraine. There are special facilities for the blind.
Six galleries illustrate the main periods of prehistory and the evolution of flint cutting through the ages.
The 16C coach house, containing a section on palaeontology, displays fossils from the Touraine, in particular those found in deposits from the Faluns Sea to the north and south of the Loire.

EXCURSION

La Celle-Guenand – *8.5km/5mi NE along D 13*. La Celle-Guenand has a harmo-niously proportioned church with a sober Romanesque façade. The covings in the façade's central doorway have been finely carved with masks and imaginary figures. To the right of the entrance, an enormous monolith decorated with masks serves as a stoup (12C).

L'ÎLE-BOUCHARD

Population 1 764
Michelin map 317: L-6, 232 folds 34 and 35 or 4037 C4

The ancient settlement of L'Île-Bouchard, once one of the ports on the River Vienne, derives its name from the midstream island where in the 9C the first known lord, Bouchard I, is said to have built a fortress which was destroyed in the 17C. The estate was purchased by Cardinal de Richelieu and it belonged to his descendants until 1789. The surrounding area, crisscrossed by small winding roads and dotted with windmills, is ideal touring country.

Prieuré St-Léonard ⊙ – *S of the town, signposted.* The priory church stood on the lower slopes of the valley. There are few vestiges of the original edifice: the 11C Romanesque apse in white tufa, an ambulatory and radiating chapels. The arcades were reinforced by additional arches one century later.

The church contains some remarkable **capitals★** sculpted with narrative scenes depicting *(left to right)*:

1st pillar – Annunciation and Visitation, Nativity, Adoration of the Shepherds, Adoration of the Magi;

2nd pillar – Presentation, Massacre of the Innocents, Flight into Egypt, Baptism of Christ;

3rd pillar – Last Supper, Kiss of Judas, Crucifixion;

4th pillar – Jesus' Entry into Jerusalem, Descent into Hell, Beheading of St John the Baptist.

Église St-Maurice ⊙ – The octagonal tower dating from 1480 is capped by an open-work stone spire. The main church building is in the transitional Flamboyant-Renaissance style and supported on pilasters decorated with Renaissance medallions. The very beautiful early-16C **cathedra★** (bishop's throne) in the chancel is adorned with most graceful Renaissance carvings portraying the Annunciation, the Nativity and the Flight into Egypt; the sculptors are shown on the cheekpieces.

St Léonard priory church

Beside the church stands a charming early-17C manor house with pedimented dormers.

Église St-Gilles – This 11C-12C church on the north bank of the Vienne was enlarged (Gothic chancel) in the 15C. The two attractive Romanesque doorways have no tympanum but are decorated with plants and geometric figures. The dome on squinches over the transept crossing supports a Romanesque tower.

Eating out

BUDGET

Ferme-auberge Le Moulin de Saussaye – ☎ *02 47 58 50 44* – 🍽 – *reservation required* – *15/23€*. There's something for everyone here: an inn on a working farm where you can feast on home-made produce. The watermill still works and river fishing is available. If you're tempted by the idea of a peaceful night, book one of the three rooms.

Where to stay

MODERATE

Chambre d'hôte Domaine de Beauséjour – *37220 Panzoult – 5km/3mi NW of Bouchard on D 757 and D 21 towards Chinon* – ☎ *02 47 58 64 64* – *3 rooms 60.98/76.22€*. A chance to appreciate the vineyards of the Chinon region, much praised by Rabelais. Attractive rooms in a house built with local materials. Under your window, the grapes slowly ripen to become excellent wines. Outdoor pool. Peace and quiet.

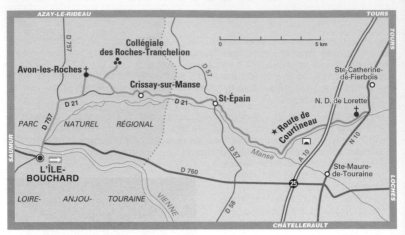

★VALLÉE DE LA MANSE

Upstream from L'Île-Bouchard *27km/17mi – about 2hr*

The River Manse flows west through quiet picturesque countryside away from the main roads to join the Vienne at L'Île-Bouchard.

Leave L'Île-Bouchard to the N along D 757.

Avon-les-Roches – The 12C-13C **church** ⊘ has a stone spire over the right transept. The arches of the porch and the door are decorated with archivolts and delicately carved capitals; an inscription in the porch *(left)* tells of the death of Charles the Bold.

Take the road E towards Crissay; after 1km/0.5mi turn left.

Collégiale des Roches-Tranchelion – The ruins of this Gothic collegiate church (1527) can be seen from some way off. *Car drivers can take the steep earth track which leads up to the church.* These ruins perched on a hill overlooking the surrounding countryside bear witness to past greatness. Little remains of the church vaulting but the elegant façade is still standing, decorated with delicate carving; note the seated figure above the great window under the triumphal arch, and the Renaissance decoration of pilasters and medallions representing the local feudal lords.

Crissay-sur-Manse – The ruins of the partly troglodytic 15C castle *(left)*, the stone spire of the village church *(right)* and the several 15C houses with square turrets make up a charming scene.

St-Épain – The village **church** (12C, 13C and 15C) is capped by a 13C square tower. Adjoining it is a **fortified gate**, all that remains of the 15C curtain wall. Above the arch, the **Hôtel de la Prévôté** can be seen with its mullioned window and overhanging upper storey. Go through the doorway to admire the mansion's other façade, which is flanked by a round tower.

On the other side of the main street stands a house with a watch turret where the road bends south-east to Ste-Maure.

This road leads up the pretty Manse Valley and its luxuriant vegetation.

After passing under the railway, bear left.

★ **Route de Courtineau** – This small scenic road winds between the stream hidden amid the trees and the cliff dotted with dwellings hewn out of the rock. The **Chapelle Notre-Dame-de-Lorette**, a small 15C oratory, has been carved into the cliff face beside a small dwelling of the same period.

ILLIERS-COMBRAY

Population 3 329
Michelin map 311: D-6 or 237 S of fold 26

Illiers, on the upper reaches of the River Loire, is a market town serving both the Beauce and the Perche regions.

Combray – It was under this name that **Marcel Proust** (1871-1922) portrayed Illiers in his novel *Remembrance of Things Past* in which he analysed his feelings and those of the people he had known.

Marcel Proust spent his holidays in Illiers where his father Dr Proust was born; the impressions young Marcel experienced here, like the taste of a madeleine sponge cake dipped in tea, were later to become "that great edifice of memories".

The town is divided into the bourgeois district – *le côté de chez Swann* – facing the rich wheat fields of the Beauce, and the aristocratic district – *le côté de Guermantes* – overlooking the Perche region and its horses. In the novel the Loir becomes the Vivonne.

SIGHTS

Maison de tante Léonie ⊙ – *4 rue du Docteur-Proust*. Some of the rooms (kitchen, dining room) in this house belonging to Proust's uncle, Jules Amiot, are still as they were in the novel. The bedrooms have been arranged to match Proust's descriptions of them. The **museum** evokes the writer's life, work and relationships, and has portraits and mementoes as well as a number of early photographs taken by Paul Nadar.

Pré Catelan – *South of the town on D 149*. Designed by Jules Amiot, the gardens, which include a serpentine, a dovecot, a pavilion and some fine trees, make a pleasant place for a walk beside the Loir. The garden is evoked by Proust in *Jean Santeuil*, and its hawthorn hedge in *Swann's Way*.

Château de LANGEAIS★★

Population 3 865
Michelin map 317: L-5, 232 folds 34 and 35 or 4037 C4

The town's white houses nestle beneath the high walls of the château. Facing the château there is a lovely Renaissance house decorated with pilasters; the church's tower is also Renaissance.

Louis XI's château – At the end of the 10C Fulk Nerra, Count of Anjou, built a **donjon**, the ruins of which still stand in the gardens, which is thought to be the oldest surviving castle keep in France.

The château itself was built by Louis XI from 1465 to 1469 as a stronghold on the road from Nantes, the route most likely to be taken by an invading Breton army. This threat vanished after the marriage of Charles VIII and Anne of Brittany was celebrated at Langeais itself in 1491.

★★CHÂTEAU ⊙ *1hr*

The château was built in one go – a rare event – and has not been altered since – all the more rare. It is one of the most interesting in the Loire Valley owing to the patient efforts of Jacques Siegfried, the last owner, who refurnished it in the style of the 15C and who bequeathed it to the Institut de France.

Where to stay

MODERATE

Chambre d'hôte Domaine de Châteaufort – *800m/0.5mi from the centre of Langeais* – ☎ *02 47 96 85 75* – *closed Nov-Mar* – ⊠ – *6 rooms 70-100€* – *evening meal 26€*. This property near the castle provides spacious, plainly decorated rooms. You will be won over by the peace of the wooded park and the friendly welcome. The rooms on the second floor are the nicest. Reasonably priced.

LUXURY

Le Vieux Château – *Rte de Gizeux – 37340 Hommes* – ☎ *02 47 24 95 13* – *5 rooms from 77.75€* – *meal 27€*. This charming little 15C château is in a lovely setting deep in the countryside. The rooms, in the former tithe barn, are beautifully furnished. In the dining room, a superb suit of armour seems to be watching over the lucky guests.

On the town side, it resembles a feudal fortress: high walls, round towers, a crenellated and machicolated sentry walk and a drawbridge spanning the moat. The façade facing the courtyard is less severe, suggesting a manor house with mullioned windows and pointed dormers decorated like the doors of the stair turrets. The buildings consist of two wings set at a right angle; on the west side of the courtyard a terraced garden climbs to the keep.

★★★ **Apartments** – These apartments with their beautiful period furnishings exude an atmosphere which is much more alive than in most other old castles. They also convey an accurate picture of what aristocratic life was like in the 15C and early Renaissance. There are many fine tapestries, most of which are Flemish, including a series portraying the Nine Heroes and some *mille-fleurs*. Note the interlaced initials K and A for Charles VIII and Anne of Brittany.

The guard-room, converted into a dining room by J Siegfried, has a monumental chimney-piece, the hood of which represents a castle with battlements manned by small figures.

One of the first-floor, in the Crucifixion room, note an early four-poster bed, a 17C panel from Brussels depicting Christ on the Cross between St John and the Virgin Mary, a credence table and a Gothic chest. The next bedchamber has a fine 15C Gothic chest and three 16C tapestries decorated with motifs of climbers with yellow flowers. The Wedding room contains seven early-16C tapestries and Anne de Bretagne's wedding chest.

On the second floor, do not miss, in the *mille-fleurs* tapestry room, one of the first Renaissance wardrobes; and, in Charles VIII's bedchamber, a curious 17C clock with only one hand as well as two 16C tapestries. The upper great hall has a chestnut timber roof in the form of a ship's hull; 15 wax figures recreate the scene of Charles VIII and Anne of Brittany.

The sentry walk, a covered gallery running the length of the façade, offers views of the Loire and the city rooftops.

Three weddings and a funeral

In 1490, Anne de Bretagne, who was barely 14, was married by proxy to Maximilian of Austria. However, the marriage was annulled a year later so that Anne could marry the king of France, Charles VIII. Brittany was thus united with France and the wedding contract stipulated that if the king died, she should marry his successor... which is exactly what she did six years later when Louis XII succeeded Charles VIII.

EXCURSIONS

Cinq-Mars-la-Pile – *5km/3mi E on N 152*. The place name is derived from a curious brick-built monument in the shape of a slender tower *(pile)* which dominates the ridge east of the village. The structure is 5m/16ft square and 30m/98ft high and is topped by four small pyramids, one at each corner. It could be a funerary monument or a navigation light but it is most likely a Gallo-Roman mausoleum built in the 2C AD.

Château ⊘ – Two 13C round towers on the hillside mark the site of the medieval castle where Henri d'Effiat, Marquis of Cinq-Mars, was born. He was the favourite of Louis XIII but was convicted of conspiring against Richelieu and beheaded in Lyon in 1642 at the age of 22. His castle was dismantled.

Each tower contains three superimposed rooms, roofed with eight-ribbed ogive vaulting. From the top there is an extensive view of the Loire Valley. The surrounding **park**★ is particularly beautiful: here a romantic garden, there a complicated maze, elsewhere dense woodland. The bushes are clipped and the paths neatly edged but with a light touch that does not detract from the natural charm.

St-Étienne-de-Chigny – *7.5km/4.7mi NE on N 152; fork left onto D 76 and left again onto D 126 towards Vieux Bourg*. Set back from the village which lies on the Loire embankment is the **Vieux Bourg** nestling in the Bresme Valley, featuring several old houses with steep gables.

The **church** ⊘★ was built in 1542 on the orders of Jean Binet, major-domo to François I and Mayor of Tours, whose arms appear both inside and on the outer façade in the shape of a mourning band. The nave is covered by a remarkable **hammerbeam roof**; the tie beams are carved with enormous grotesque masks and, in the chancel, Jonah in the belly of the whale. The 16C **stained-glass window** in the chevet shows the Crucifixion flanked by the figures of the donors, Jean Binet and his wife, Jeanne de la Lande. In the north transept hangs a 16C painting, *Virgin and Child*, by the French School; there is also a mural portraying St Clement, Pope and patron saint of boatmen. The font dates from the 16C.

Cadillac-sur-Loire

The most prestigious American car manufacturer, which saw the light of day in Detroit at the turn of the last century, was named after the French founder of the town, Antoine de la Mothe Cadillac. Served by the exceptional talent of the designer Harley Earl, Cadillac became the pride and joy of General Motors during the roaring twenties. After the war it came to symbolise the era of glamour with its 62-series coupés, its Eldorado cabriolet models with extravagant rocket-shaped fins, its daring Dagmars (bumper terminals shaped like bombs), its greedy radiator grills and its curved windscreens resembling a plane's cockpit.

★**Château de Champchevrier** ⊙ – *12km/8mi N on D 15 then D 34; turn right when leaving Cléré-les-Pins.* The château stands on the site of an old stronghold, which played a defensive role in the area for many centuries. The present building, dating originally from the 16C, was modified in the 17C and 18C. It has been occupied by the same family since 1728, testifying to the strong social and geographical attachment of these people to their land.

The château is completely surrounded by a late-17C moat. The interior is enhanced by superb **Regency furniture**; the original upholstery, with fine colours which have remained intact, was woven in the Beauvais workshops. The series of **tapestries**★ called *Loves of the Gods*, which can be admired in several rooms, was executed by the Manufacture Royale d'Amiens after cartoons by Simon Vouet; note the variety of different shades, which are still surprisingly vivid. The wood panelling of the wide staircase and its polychrome coffers were taken from the **Château de Richelieu** *(see RICHELIEU)*, demolished in 1805. The staff quarters (laundry room, kitchen) provide an interesting insight into the daily routine of a large family mansion.

Located at the heart of a wooded area in which wolves roamed for many years, Champchevrier is the seat of the most long-standing equipage in France (1804). It perpetuates hunting traditions through its many trophies and collections; it also houses a series of kennels where visitors can befriend 70 large dogs belonging to an Anglo-French pack, specialised in deer hunting.

LAVARDIN★

Population 262
Michelin map 318: C-5 or 238 fold 1
Local map see VENDÔME

The crumbling ruins of Lavardin Fortress are perched on a rocky pinnacle towering above the village and the River Loir, which is spanned by a Gothic bridge, forming a picturesque scene. The castle was the principal stronghold of the counts of Vendôme in the Middle Ages and its strategic importance greatly increased in the 12C owing to its location half way between the kingdom of France under the Capets and the possessions of the Angevin kings. In 1188 Henry II of England and his son Richard the Lionheart besieged the castle, but in vain.

In 1589 the troops of the Catholic League captured the castle but the following year it was besieged by Henri IV's soldiers under the Prince de Conti and surrendered. The King ordered the castle to be demolished.

Old houses – One is 15C and half-timbered whereas the other is Renaissance with an overhanging oratory, pilastered, mullioned dormer windows and a loggia overlooking the courtyard.

The **mairie** ⊙ (town hall) contains two beautiful 11C rooms with handsome 15C vaulted ceilings; that on the ground floor is used for exhibitions.

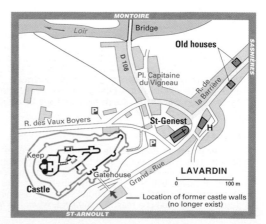

A bridge over tranquil waters

The 13C **bridge** offers an attractive view of the lush green banks of the river.
🚶 A narrow lane behind the church climbs half way up the hill and leads to a group of interesting cave dwellings.

Castle ⊙ – The path and flight of steps skirting the south side of the castle ruins offer a good view of the gatehouse and the keep.

Although well worn by the weather and the passage of time, the ruins are still impressive and give a good idea of the three lines of fortified walls, the gatehouse (12C-15C) and the rectangular 11C keep (26m/85ft high) which was reinforced in the following century with towers of the same height. The innermost defensive wall is the best preserved.

Église St-Genest – The priory was built in an archaic Romanesque style with a square belfry porch. Low-relief sculptures have been reused in the structure; those in the apse represent the signs of the zodiac.

Interior – The church is divided into three parts by square piers capped by delicately carved early-12C imposts. The chancel, which is entered through a triumphal arch, ends in an oven-vaulted apse, where curious Romanesque pillars, probably part of an earlier building, support roughly hewn capitals. The windows in the north aisle are framed by delightful twisted Romanesque colonnettes.

The **mural paintings** date from the 12C to 16C. The oldest, most stylized and majestic ones are on the pillar at the entrance to the left apsidal chapel, depicting the Baptism of Christ and a Tree of Jesse. The well-conserved group in the chancel and apse shows scenes from the Passion *(right)* and the Washing of the Feet *(left)* on either side of a Christ in Majesty surrounded by the symbols of the Evangelists. In the right apsidal chapel note a St Christopher and Last Judgement (15C) where Paradise *(above)* and Hell are colourfully portrayed. On the pillars in the nave and aisles are 16C figures of saints venerated locally. Note the Martyrdom of St Margaret on the wall of the south aisle and the Crucifixion of St Peter on a pillar on the north side of the nave.

EXCURSION

Parc et jardin du domaine de Sasnières ⊙ – *6km/3.7mi SE by D 108*.
🚶 This attractive 3.5ha/8.5-acre English-style garden enhanced by clumps of trees and shrubs surrounds a pretty lake laid out at the foot of a hill. It presents a wide range of plants belonging to many different species and is particularly appealing in spring and summer on account of its blossoming roses and magnolias. The autumn season too is a feast for the eyes, when the foliage takes on superb shades of russet.

Vallée du LAYON

Michelin map 317: E-4 to H-6, 232 folds 31 and 32 or 4049 E4 to H6

The Layon, which was canalised under Louis XVI, flows into the Loire downstream of Angers.

The region is a pretty one with vineyards, fields of crops interspersed here and there with fruit trees (walnut, peach, plum etc), hillsides crowned with windmills and wine-growing villages with graveyards in which dark green cypresses grow.

The Coteaux-du-layon – The delicious mellow white wines of the Layon vineyards are produced by the *chenin*, a variety of grape often known as *pineau*. They are harvested in late September when the grapes begin to be covered with a mould known as noble rot *(pourriture noble)*. **Bonnezeaux** and **Quarts de Chaume** are two well-known wines from this area.

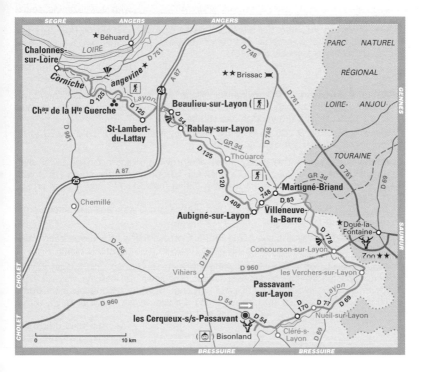

VINEYARDS AND WINES IN THE LAYON VALLEY

72km/45mi – about 3hr 30min

Les Cerqueux-sous-Passavant – The grounds of a 19C Landes château are home to **Bisonland** ⊙, a stock-breeding farm of buffaloes and fallow deer. Typical dwellings of various American Indian tribes (tepee, lodge, wigwam) and a Tatanka camp have been recreated, offering an unusual approach to learning about these remote societies. Traditional craftwork on show.

Follow the road towards Cléré-sur-Layon (D 54). At the entrance to the village turn left to Passavant.

Passavant-sur-Layon – This pretty village on the edge of a lake formed by the Layon, is enhanced by the eye-catching ruins of its castle. The church has a Romanesque chancel.

Take D 170 to Nueil-sur-Layon, turn right after the church onto D 77; after the bridge over the Layon bear left onto D 69 towards Doué-la-Fontaine.

The landscape at this point is still typical of the Poitou with its hedgerows, sunken roads and farmsteads roofed with Mediterranean-style tiles. The **vineyards** are grouped on the exposed slopes and at Nueil the slate roofs, more typical of northern France, make an appearance.

Beyond Les Verchers bear left onto D 178 towards Concourson.

The road runs parallel with the Layon through fertile countryside; beyond Concourson it offers an extensive view of the river valley.

In St-Georges-sur-Layon take the road N towards Brigné, turning left onto D 83 to Martigné-Briand.

Martigné-Briand – This wine-growing village lies clustered round a château which suffered extensive damage during the Vendée War. It was built in the early 16C, and the north façade has glazed windows with Flamboyant motifs.

Take D 748 SW towards Aubigné, turning right to Villeneuve-la-Barre.

ALFRESCO

Le Relais de Martigné – *Rte de Vihiers – 49540 Martigné-Briand – ☎ 02 41 59 42 14 – closed during Feb school holidays, Tue evening (except Jul-Aug), Wed evening and Sun evening – 11.89/24.69€.* This modest restaurant is a good place to stop for a meal while exploring the valley and discovering its wine production. The decor is not very inspiring, but the simple cooking makes up for it, especially as the prices are extremely reasonable. Terrace.

Villeneuve-la-Barre – The road leads through this attractive village with its numerous gardens to the **monastère des bénédictines**, in a pretty setting with a welcoming courtyard. Visitors can ask to see the rather austere chapel, which occupies an old barn and has plain, leaded glass windows with abstract motifs.

Aubigné-sur-Layon – This delightful village still has several elegant old town houses. Near the 11C church stands an old fortified gateway where the remains of the portcullis and drawbridge can still be seen.

Leave Aubigné on D 408 to Faveraye-Mâchelles and turn right onto D 120. After crossing D 24 bear left onto D 125.

Rablay-sur-Layon – This pretty little wine-growing village occupies a well-sheltered site. In Grande-Rue there is a brick and half-timbered tithe house (15C) with an overhanging upper storey. A building dating from the 17C now houses artists' studios.

The road *(D 54)* crosses the Layon, then skirts a cirque with vine-clad slopes; from the plateau there is a broad view of the valley.

🚶 A disused railway line converted into a footpath follows the Layon over a distance of 25km/15.5mi, offering pleasant strolls in pastoral surroundings.

Beaulieu-sur-Layon – This wine-growing village *(viewing table)* amid the Layon vineyards has attractive mansard-roofed houses. The town hall building was once the residence of the steward of the Abbess of Ronceray. There are 13C frescoes in the **church**. To the west of Beaulieu *(to right of D 55)* is a wine cellar, **Caveau du vin** ⊙, with a collection of old Angevin wine bottles and glasses.

AFTER DARK ...

Le Métro – *Les Grandes Noues – 49750 Beaulieu-sur-Layon – ☎ 02 41 78 30 97 – Thu-Sat from 11pm.* The biggest disco in the region, capable of entertaining 2 000 people. There's always a crowd, a good atmosphere, and all types of music. To get there, follow the lasers which light up the sky for a radius of 10km/6mi around.

The main road drops into the valley, past the steep sides riddled with caves and quarries. At Pont-Barré there is an attractive view of the narrow course of the Layon and a ruined medieval bridge, scene of a bloody struggle between Royalists and Revolutionaries on 19 September 1793 *(see CHOLET).*

Drive to N 60 and follow it S.

St-Lambert-du-Lattay – **Musée de la Vigne et du Vin d'Anjou** ⊙ is housed in the Coudraye wine cellars. Wine-growing and cooperage tools, illustrations, a collection of presses and commentaries embody the living memory of a people who have always been engaged in the cultivation of the grape. The room entitled *L'Imaginaire du Vin* appeals to visitors' senses of sight, smell and taste in a display on wine which emphasizes variety of bouquet and flavour.

The road to St-Aubin-de-Luigné winds its way up and down the slopes which produce Quarts-de-Chaume wine.

Before entering St-Aubin turn left onto D 106 and soon after turn right.

Château de la Haute-Guerche ⊙ – This castle was built in the reign of Charles VII and burned down in the Vendée Wars; all that can now be seen from the valley are its ruined towers. There is an extensive view of the surrounding countryside from the site.

Return to St-Aubin then drive onto Chaudefonds and continue to Ardenay to reach the Corniche Angevine (see ANGERS: La Loire Maugeoise).

Population 6 328
Michelin map 317: O-6, 238 S of folds 13 and 14 or 4037 G5

Loches is a small town on the south bank of the Indre; the old town, huddled on the slopes of a bluff above the river, still resembles a medieval fortified town, with two of its original three defensive walls remarkably well preserved. From the entrance to the public gardens, there is a pretty **view★** of the church of St-Ours, the imposing castle, famous for its associations with the beautiful Agnès Sorel, and in the foreground the houses lining the banks of the River Indre.

Loches was the birthplace of the Romantic poet, **Alfred de Vigny** (1797-1863), whose mother's family had been closely involved with the town's history since the Renaissance. The poet left the town when he was only an infant.

LOCHES

Anciens A.F.N. (Pl. des)	.	Z
Auguste (Bd Ph.)	......	Z
Balzac (R.)	....	ZY
Bas-Clos (Av. des)	.....	Y 2
Blé (Pl. au)	....	Y 3
Château (R. du)	......	YZ 5
Descartes (R.)	....	Y 7
Donjon (Mail du)	....	Z
Droulin (Mail)	....	Z
Filature (Q. de la)	.....	Y 8
Foulques-Nerra (R.)	....	Z 9
Gaulle (Av. Gén.-de)	....	Y 10
Grand Mail (Pl. du)	.....	Y 12
Grande-Rue	....	Y 13
Lansyer (R.)	....	Z 14
Marne (Pl. de la)	....	Y
Mazerolles (Pl.)	....	Y 15
Moulins (R. des)	....	Y 16
Pactius (R. R.)	....	Z 17
Picois (R.)	....	Y
Poterie (Mail de la)	.....	Z
Ponts (R. des)	....	Y 18
Porte-Poitevine		
(R. de la)	....	Z 19
Quintefol (R.)	....	YZ
République (R. de la)	....	Y
Ruisseaux (R. des)	.....	Z 20
St-Antoine (R.)	....	Y 21
St-Ours (R.)	....	Z 22
Tours (R. de)	....	Y
Verdun (Pl. de)	....	Y
Victor-Hugo (R.)	......	Y
Vigny (R. A.-de)	......	Y
Wermelskirchen (Pl. de)	.	Y 29

Chancellerie	....	Y B
Hôtel de ville	....	Y H
Maison Lansyer	.....	Z M
Porte Picois	....	Y C
Tour Agnès-Sorel	...	Z K
Tour St-Antoine	.....	Y N

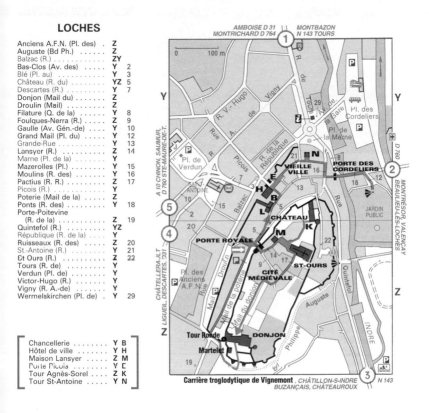

★★MEDIEVAL TOWN *3hr – park the car in the Mail Droulin*

Loches is somewhat similar to Chinon: once you have reached the centre you will not see any modern buildings. The whole district seems to have remained as it was in the 15C and at the time of the Renaissance, except for the shops and the numerous stalls which liven up the lower part of the town on market days.
The 12C wall surrounding the medieval city is more than 1km/0.6mi long with only two gates.

★**Porte Royale** – The Royal Gate (11C) had powerful defences; it was flanked by two towers in the 13C; the machicolations and the slots for the drawbridge chains are still visible.

Go through the gateway; turn left onto rue Lansyer to reach the museum.

Maison Lansyer ⊙ – *No1.* The family home of the artist **Emmanuel Lansyer** (1835-93) seems to cling to the ramparts; a pupil of Gustave Courbet and a friend of the poet José-Maria de Heredia, Lansyer was influenced by the landscape painters of the Barbizon School. In addition to Lansyer's own works, the museum contains the artist's collections of prints (Canaletto, Millet, Corot...) and of Japanese art.

★**Église St-Ours** – In 1802 the old collegiate church of Notre-Dame became the parish church dedicated to St Ours, a local apostle in the 5C. Its most characteristic features are the two octagonal pyramids (built by Prior T Pactius in the 12C), between its towers of the type commonly used for belfries, kitchens *(see p 192)* or lavabos in monasteries which form the vaulting of the nave and, with the eight-

Porte des Cordeliers and Château de Loches by Emmanuel Lansyer

Musée Lanoyer

sided dome surmounting the transept crossing, evoke the silhouette of Aquitaine cupolas. The Angevin porch shelters a **Romanesque doorway**, richly decorated with unusual carved animals; the upper part (badly damaged) represents the Adoration of the Three Wise Men. A holy-water stoup has been hollowed out in a Gallo-Roman column.

As you come out of the church, the castle is on your right.

★★ **Château** ⊘ **(Castle)** – The tour starts from the **Tour Agnès Sorel**, a tower dating from the 13C traditionally referred to as the Beautiful Agnès Tower.

Logis Royaux (Royal Apartments) – From the terrace, which commands a fine view of Loches and the Indre Valley, it is clear that the château was built at two different periods. The Vieux Logis (14C), the older, taller building, is heavily fortified with four turrets linked by a sentry walk at the base of the roof. It was enlarged under Charles VIII and Louis XII by the addition of the more recent Nouveau Logis, in the Flamboyant Gothic style.

Enter the **Vieux Logis** through the room known as Charles VII's antechamber, leading to the great hall with the large fireplace where on 3 and 5 June 1429 Joan of Arc came to urge Charles VII to go to Reims.

A thousand-year-old fortress

Loches is built on a natural strong point which has been occupied since at least the 6C when Gregory of Tours made reference to a fortress commanding a monastery and a small town. From the 10C to the 13C Loches was under the sway of the counts of Anjou who altered the fortress by building a residential palace and a moated keep at the tip of the promontory. Henry II of England reinforced the defences. On his death in 1189 his son Richard the Lionheart took possession of the land before leaving on crusade with Philippe Auguste. In the Holy Land Philippe Auguste, an artful schemer, abandoned Richard and hurried back to France (1191) where he plotted with John Lackland, Richard's brother, who agreed to give up the fortress (1193). When Richard was finally ransomed – he had been held captive in Austria – he hastened to Loches and seized the castle in less than three hours (1194), an exploit which was celebrated in all the chronicles of the day. When Richard died, Philippe Auguste recaptured the castle by way of revenge but much less impressively: the siege lasted a whole year (1205). Loches was given to Dreu V de Mello, son of the victorious besiegers' leader, and repurchased by Louis IX in 1249.

Loches took on the role of royal residence for a succession of monarchs. In 1429, after her victory at Orléans, Joan of Arc rejoined Charles VII at Loches and insisted that he should set out for Reims.

The alabaster **recumbent figure of Agnès Sorel★** is of special interest. During the Revolution, soldiers took the favourite of Charles VII for a saint, chopped up her statue, desecrated her grave and scattered her remains. The monument was restored in Paris under the Empire. Agnès is shown recumbent, with two angels supporting her lovely head and two lambs – the symbol of gentleness and her name – lying at her feet. In the same room is displayed the portrait by Fouquet of the Virgin Mary, whose face is that of the beautiful Agnès, amid red and blue angels *(the original is displayed in Antwerp)*; the hairstyle, for which women had to have half their skull shaved to reveal a bare forehead, first became fashionable in Venice.

Recumbent figure of Agnès Sorel

B. Kaufmann/MICHELIN

Another room contains an interesting **triptych★** from the 15C School of Jean Fouquet, which originally came from the church of St-Antoine, with panels evoking the Crucifixion, the Carrying of the Cross and the Deposition.

La Dame de Beauté

Agnès Sorel was the owner of Beauté Castle (at Nogent-sur-Marne) near Paris and also a great beauty, so that her title, **La Dame de Beauté**, was doubly apt. She was born at Fromenteau Castle in Touraine in 1422. She became Charles VII's favourite, but left the court at Chinon, where the Dauphin, the future Louis XI, was making life impossible for her, to come and live at Loches. Her influence on the King was often beneficial – she cured him of his depression and encouraged him in his effort to save his kingdom – but her taste for luxury coupled with great generosity was a heavy burden on the slender royal purse. She died on 9 February 1450 at Jumièges where she had gone to be with Charles VII. Her body was brought back to Loches and buried in the collegiate church. Some years later the canons, who had benefited from her largesse, asked Louis XI to transfer her tomb to the castle. He agreed on condition that the gifts went too, whereupon the canons let the matter drop!

The tour ends with Anne of Brittany's **oratory**, a tiny room decorated with finely worked motifs of the ermine of Brittany and the girdle of St Francis. Executed in the pure Gothic style, this oratory was originally polychrome: a bright blue background with gilded cable moulding and silver-coated ermines.

Make for the keep through the streets of the medieval town.

★★ **Donjon** ⊘ – This keep was built in the 11C by Fulk Nerra to defend the fortified town from the south. It is a solid square construction which, together with the Ronde and Martelet towers, forms an imposing defensive system.

Inside the dungeon, the floors of the three storeys have vanished but three sets of fireplaces and windows can still be seen on the walls. A staircase of 160 steps leads up to the top of the 37m/121ft-high keep from which there is a fine view of the town, the Indre Valley and Loches Forest.

Tour ronde – Like the Martelet it was built in the 15C to complete the fortifications. To the left, in the entrance pavilion, Philippe de Commines' cell presents an iron collar weighing 16kg/35lb and the reconstitution of one of Louis XI's famous cages.

A flight of 102 steps leads up to a terrace from which there is a view of the moat and, beyond, a vast panorama of Loches.

Louis XI's Cages (late 15C)

A tour of the castle will include the dungeons and barred cells, but not the cages in which Louis XI liked to confine his prisoners; these monuments of tyranny were destroyed by the inhabitants of Loches in 1790. The cages were made of a wooden framework covered with iron. The more comfortable measured 2x2m/6ft 7inx6ft 7in on all sides but there was a shallower model in which the prisoner could only lie or sit. Legend has it that prisoners never came out alive; in fact, the cages were used only at night or to transport prisoners. Cardinal **Jean Balue**, who is said to be the inventor of these cages, knew them well. He was greatly in favour under Louis XI who bestowed honour after honour on him, but he plotted secretly with the Duke of Burgundy; in 1469 he was discovered and imprisoned in Loches until 1480; he died 11 years later.

Martelet – The most impressive dungeons, occupying several floors below ground, are to be found in this building. The first was that of **Ludovico Sforza**, Duke of Milan, nicknamed the Moor, who was taken prisoner by Louis XII.

For four years, he paid for his tricks and treachery. On the day of his release the sunlight was so bright and the excitement of freedom so great that he fell down dead. Ludovico, who was Leonardo da Vinci's patron, covered the walls of his prison with paintings and inscriptions. Next to the stars, cannon and helmets may be seen a phrase, hardly surprising in the circumstances: *Celui Qui n'est Pas Contan* (He Who is Not Content).

Below, lit by a solitary ray of light, is the dungeon where the bishops of Autun and Le Puy, both implicated in the change of allegiance to the Emperor Charles V by the Constable of France, Charles, Duke of Bourbon, found leisure to hollow out of the wall a small altar and a symbolic Stations of the Cross.

At the foot of the Martelet tower, galleries branch off to quarries, which in the 16C provided stone for the small fortified covered passageways *(caponnières)* flanking the ramparts.

As you come out of the Martelet, walk back to the Porte Royale and turn right onto rue du Château for a stroll through the old town which developed at the foot of the fortress.

★OLD TOWN

Located inside the second perimeter wall, the old town is crisscrossed with narrow streets lined with old houses built of tufa. A leisurely walk will take you past the **chancellerie**, dating from the Henry II period (mid-16C), embellished with fluted columns, pilasters and wrought-iron balconies; nearby is the **Maison du Centaure**, which owes its name to the low-relief sculpture on the façade, which depicts the centaur Nessus abducting Deianira; proceed to the 15C **Porte Picois**, also with machicolations. This tower stands next to the **hôtel de ville★**, an elegant Renaissance building with flower-decked balconies. From there, head for the 16C **Tour St-Antoine**, one of the rare belfries to be found in central France and continue to the late-15C **Porte des Cordeliers★**; this and the Porte Picois are the only two remaining gates of the town's original four. It was the main gate of the city on the road to Spain. Go through the gate to see its riverside façade lined with machicolations and flanked by bartizans.

Walk across the bridge to the public garden which offers a fine view of the medieval town.

Eating out

BUDGET

L'Estaminet – *14 r. de l'Abbaye – 37600 Beaulieu-lès-Loches – ☎ 02 47 59 35 47 – closed 25 Aug-3 Sep, Sun and Mon – 11/15€.* In a pretty, shady square near the 11C abbey, this little country café is reminiscent of the north of France. While the locals play cards in the bar, you can sample the family-style cooking in the small dining room or on the terrace.

Where to stay

MODERATE

Chambre d'hôte Le Clos du Petit Marray – *37310 Chambourg-sur-Indre – 5km/3mi N of Loches on N 143 towards Tours – ☎ 02 47 92 50 67 – ⌂ – 4 rooms 47/62€ – evening meal 21€.* An imposing country property set in a large garden, with a small lake. The rooms are spacious and attractively decorated.

Son et lumière

Féerie nocturne (magic in the night): performance Fridays and Saturdays from the second Friday in July until the end of August. 10.30pm in July, 10pm in August. 10.67€ (children: 6.10€). ☎ 02 47 59 01 76.

EXCURSIONS

* **Carrière troglodytique de Vignemont** ⊙ – *55ter rue des Roches, S towards Châteauroux (warm clothing recommended)*. The 600m/656yd tour of the quarry explains all there is to know about the extraction and use of the famous white limestone which brightens up castles and villages of the Loire Valley; it is an excellent introduction to a visit of the area.

Beaulieu-lès-Loches – *1km/0.6mi E along the east bank of the River Indre*. This old village contains the ruins of a famous abbey founded in 1004 by Fulk Nerra, who was buried there at his request. The **abbey church** is dominated by a majestic square Romanesque tower, surmounted by an octagonal spire. The arms of the transept also date from the Romanesque period but the nave and chancel were rebuilt in the 15C after being destroyed by the English in 1412; beyond the chancel are a few traces of the original Romanesque apse.
The interior is adorned with a 15C *Pietà*, some 18C terracotta statues in the chancel and some 17C portraits and a low-relief carving of the Last Supper in the sacristy. A curious outdoor pulpit adjoins the old abbot's lodgings on the site of the old cloisters to the right of the church.
The 13C **Église St-Laurent** has retained its Romanesque tower and its three fine aisles roofed with Angevin vaulting.

Bridoré – *14km/9mi SE via N 143 and D 241*. The late-15C **church** here, dedicated to St Roch, houses a monumental 15C statue of the Saint (nave to the right). The legend of St Hubert is evoked on a 16C low-relief sculpture. The **castle** ⊙, which belonged to Marshal Boucicaut in the 14C, was altered in the 15C by Imbert de Bastarnay, Secretary to Louis XI. It is an imposing, well-preserved complex, bordered by towers, *caponnières* and a deep dry moat on three sides. Note the gateway flanked by a machicolated round tower and the Louis XII porch-keep with its side bartizans topped by pepper-pot roofs; the **logis seigneurial** (main living quarters) is adjacent to the keep.

*VALLÉE DE L'INDRE

27km/16mi NW via N 143 and D 17 – about 1hr

From Chambourg-sur-Indre to Esvres the road (D 17) follows a pretty route beside the Indre which meanders lazily past a windmill here or a boat there moored in the reeds.

Azay-sur-Indre – Azay stands in a pleasant setting at the confluence of the Indre and the Indrois. Adjoining it is the park of the château that once belonged to La Fayette.

Reignac-sur-Indre – Visible from the bridge spanning the Indre (on the road to Cigogné) is Reignac windmill, standing on a small lake set in lush, verdant surroundings.

Take D 58 towards N 143 until you reach the locality named Le Café Brûlé.

Cormery – Cormery, which is famous for its macaroons, sits prettily beside the Indre with inns on either bank. Near the bridge, half-hidden under the weeping willows is an **old mill**; downstream the river feeds the old washing place.

Abbey ⊙ – The Benedictine abbey, which was founded in 791, was suppressed 1 000 years later during the Revolution; the buildings were confiscated and sold by the French Republic and most of them were subsequently demolished. The few remains conjure up a picture of the complete abbey; the model shows it as it was in the 14C and 15C.
Rue de l'Abbaye, which begins beside the town hall *(on N 143)*, passes under a tall ruined tower, the **Tour St-Paul**, the huge 11C bell-tower above the entrance to the church; note the Romanesque low-relief ornamentation and the scale and lozenze motifs below the upper windows. The 15C **Logis du Prieur** (Prior's Residence) at the foot of the tower features an elegant staircase turret. In the street on the left are the arches of the **old refectory** (13C). Of the church itself, which would have been on the far side of the tower, nothing remains; the street follows the line of the nave. The elegant Gothic chapel (left), reserved for the abbot, was originally next to the apsidal chapel of the church and linked to the **Logis abbatial** (Abbot's Residence) which has a turret and a half-timbered penthouse.

Église Notre-Dame-du-Fougeray – The church of Our Lady of Fougeray, which dominates the valley, is a 12C Romanesque building with elements typical of the Poitou region: a large apse with three apsidal chapels, historiated brackets, a frieze and a dome on pendentives over the transept crossing.
In the cemetery opposite the church there is an altar and a 12C lantern of the dead.

Cross the Indre and follow N 143 towards Tours for 1km/0.6mi then bear left onto D 17 to Esvres.

LORRIS★

Population 2 674
Michelin map 318: M-4, 237 fold 42, 238 fold 7 or 4045 G4

Lorris is famous for the charter of freedom which was granted to it in 1122 by Louis VI. The town was a hunting seat for the Capet kings and a place of residence for Blanche of Castille and her son Louis IX of France. In 1215 it became the birthplace of Guillaume de Lorris, who wrote the first part of the *Romance of the Rose (Roman de la Rose)*, a poem of courtly love which influenced Chaucer in his writings.

★**Église Notre-Dame** – The church is interesting not only for the purity of its architecture (12C-13C) but also for its furnishings. An elegant Romanesque door leads into a well-lit Gothic nave. High up in the nave are a **gallery** and the early-16C **organ loft★** *(see illustration in Art and architecture: Ecclesiastical architecture)*, both ornately carved. The late-15C **choir stalls★** are decorated with the Prophets and Sibyls on the cheekpieces and scenes from The Golden Legend, the New Testament and everyday life on the misericords. Above the old altar hang two 18C angels. Also worth a closer look are the polychrome statues in the ambulatory and an alabaster Virgin Mary (late 15C) near the font.

A **museum** dedicated to the organ and old musical instruments in general has been set up under the eaves.

Le Sauvage – *Pl. du Martroi* - ☎ *02 38 92 43 79 – closed Feb, 1-20 Oct, Sun evening and Fri – 19.06/45.73€.* Don't be misled by the name of this restaurant – the only "wild" thing about the dining room is the winter garden under a glass roof. A few nice rooms available for guests.

Musée départemental de la Résistance et de la Déportation ⊘ – This museum is housed in the old station which has now been restored, against a backdrop of trees and greenery. Its impressive collections relate the history of the Second World War and its consequences in this region. The course of events, from the underlying causes of the war until the liberation of France, is illustrated in detail with the aid of documents, dioramas (the exodus of refugees and a reconstruction of a camp of members of the Resistance movement in a forest), figures in costume, models and other miscellaneous exhibits.

Place du Martroi – The 16C **town hall**, built of brick with stone courses and heavily ornamented dormer windows, stands in the main street overlooking the huge town square; opposite is the **market** *(halles)* covered with an oak roof (1542).

CANAL D'ORLÉANS: SEINE REACH

For the Loire reach of the canal see p 154. 14km/9mi, following D 44 NW then turning left onto D 444.

Grignon – The hamlet is set deep in the countryside on the banks of the canal. It makes a most attractive picture with its towpaths, locks and lock-keeper's house. Continue south to **Vieilles-Maisons** where the church has a timber-framed porch.

Étang des Bois – *Due S of Vieilles-Maisons.* This is another of the reservoirs associated with the Orléans Canal. The little lake is fringed with oak, beech and chestnut trees and is a popular spot in summer (camp site, bathing, fishing, windsurfing, canoeing and picnic areas).

No longer used for commercial navigation, sections of the canal are now being renovated for recreational purposes.

Ph. Gajic/MICHELIN

Château du LUDE★★

Michelin map 310: J-9, 232 fold 22 or 4072 E6
Local map see VENDÔME

This magnificent château, lying on the south bank of the Loir and surrounded by a beautiful park, offers visitors a fascinating mixture of Gothic, Renaissance and Louis XVI styles. The 11C fortress of the counts of Anjou was replaced in the 13C-14C by a castle which withstood several assaults by the English before it fell in 1425; it was recaptured two years later by Ambroise de Loré, Beaumanoir and Gilles de Rais. In 1457 the castle was acquired by Jean de Daillon, a childhood friend of Louis XI. His son built the present château on the foundations of the earlier fortress: it kept the traditional square layout with a massive tower at each corner but the large windows and the delicate decoration make it a country house in the fashion of its age. Remodelled in the 18C, the castle has remained the property of the same family until now.

Tour of the château ⊙ – The U-shaped, early-17C courtyard was closed off in the late 18C by an arched portico.

Façades – Facing the park, to the right, is the François I wing. Its façade is a pleasing combination of the fortress style, with its round medieval towers, and Renaissance refinement: windows framed by pilasters, pedimented dormer windows, medallions and carved ornamentation.

Overlooking the river, the Louis XVI wing in white tufa stone exemplifies the Classical style; it is sober and symmetrical, its façade broken only by a central projecting section topped by a carved pediment. The north wing *(visible from rue du Pont which skirts the château)* is the earliest wing (early 16C); it was altered in the 19C when the stone balconies and equestrian statue of Jean de Daillon were added.

A kitchen fit for a king

Interior – The Louis XII wing houses a large 19C library with 2 000 books that belonged to the Duke of Bouillon and a ballroom restored in the 15C and 16C style. The 18C building contains a fine suite of rooms including a splendid oval salon in pure Louis XVI style with carved woodwork and mirrors, an 18C bedroom and a 16C oratory decorated with murals from the School of Primaticcio illustrating biblical scenes and the *Triumphs* of Petrarch; note the ceiling painted in the Italian grotesque style. In the François I wing a small library contains a 17C Gobelins tapestry; in the dining room, where the window recesses reveal the thickness of the medieval walls, there is a vast chimney-piece with a carved salamander and ermine, whereas on the walls hang three Flemish tapestries including a *verdure* showing a red parrot.

The underground passages and 13C guardroom beneath the parterre of the former fortress are now open to the public *(access from the outside)*.

Maison des Architectes *– 3 rue du Marché-au-Fil near the entrance to the château.* The house, built in the 16C by the architects who designed

the château, features ornamentation typical of the Renaissance period: mullioned windows, pilasters with Corinthian capitals decorated with roundels and lozenges and a frieze running between the lower and upper floors *(not open to the public)*.

THE QUEST FOR THE CROSS OF ANJOU

Round trip of 28km/17mi – about 1hr 30min.

Drive S out of Le Lude on D 257.

Genneteil – The Romanesque **church** has a 13C bell-tower with a stair turret and a beautiful 11C doorway; the arch stones are carved with the signs of the zodiac and human faces. The left-hand chapel is decorated with Romanesque frescoes. Depicted on the vaulting is a procession of wise and foolish virgins looking towards a Virgin and Child; the Presentation is also represented and there is a medallion featuring Christ offering his blessing.

Take D 138 E to Chigné.

Chigné – The fortified **church** (12C-15C) features an interesting façade flanked by a round tower. Above the triple-arched doorway note the line of carved brackets and the primitive carvings which have been incorporated, much altered, in the building.

Continue via Les Quatre-Chemins to La Boissière.

La Boissière ⊙ – The name of La Boissière is linked with a precious relic: the **Cross of Anjou** *(see p 114)*. The cross was brought from the Middle East in the 13C by a crusader and given to the Cistercians at La Boissière who built a chapel for it. During the Hundred Years War the cross was kept in Angers Château. It returned to La Boissière in about 1456 and remained there until 1790 when it was transferred to Baugé. In the 18C the **abbey buildings** were converted into a château; the 12C church was reduced to the chancel   note the altarpiece and Gothic recumbent figures.

Chapelle de la Vraie-Croix – The 13C Chapel of the True Cross *(restored)* on the road to Dénezé features three bays of Angevin vaulting inside.

Drive back towards Le Lude on D 767; in La Croix-Beauchêne turn right onto D 138.

Broc – The attractive **church** has a squat Romanesque tower and a row of carved brackets on the chevet. The broad nave is roofed with lierne and tierceron vaulting; the Romanesque apse is decorated with 13C frescoes: Christ in Majesty *(on half-dome)*, the Annunciation *(left)* and the Virgin in Majesty *(right)*. On the nave wall is a very beautiful sculpted wood Crucifix of the Louis XIII period.

Return to Le Lude via La Croix-Beauchêne then turn right onto D 307.

Le MANS★★

Conurbation 194 825
Michelin map 310: K-6, 232 folds 10 and 22 or 4072 F3

Le Mans *(54min from Paris by the high-speed TGV train)* stands on the banks of the Sarthe at its confluence with the Huisne. It is a thriving provincial capital renowned for its good food: potted pork *(rillettes)* and poultry accompanied by sparkling cider and the famous local Reinette apple... as well as for its 24-hour motor race.
Art lovers will find plenty to satisfy their thirst for beauty in the impressive cathedral, its fine east end, doorways, stained-glass windows and funeral monuments; visitors in general will appreciate a stroll through the old town, along its narrow streets and river embankments.

THE FORTUNES AND MISFORTUNES OF LE MANS

In the 4C the ancient town of *Vindinium* surrounded itself with ramparts to resist the barbarian invasions.

The Plantagenet dynasty – When **Geoffrey Plantagenet**, Count of Anjou, married Matilda, the grand daughter of William the Conqueror, he added Normandy and Maine to his estates. Geoffrey often resided at Le Mans and on his death in 1151 he was buried here. His son, who in 1154 became **Henry II** of England, was the founder of the Coëffort Hospital and it was to Le Mans, his birthplace, that he retired in his old age only to be expelled by one of his rebellious sons **Richard the Lionheart**, then in alliance with the French king. While on the Third Crusade Richard married **Queen Berengaria** of Navarre and it was to her in her widowhood that Philippe Auguste gave the county of Maine which he had reconquered from Richard's younger brother, John Lackland. Berengaria founded Épau Abbey *(see EXCURSIONS)* where she was buried. During the Hundred Years War Le Mans remained under English control until 1448.

The drama of 5 August 1392 – In the summer of 1392 King **Charles VI** of France launched a campaign against the Duke of Brittany, who supported the English. On 5 August the King left Le Mans with his troops and rode westwards. Suddenly, as they approached a leper house, an old man, hideously disfigured and with his clothes in tatters, blocked the King's path and cried "Don't go any further, noble king, you have been betrayed."

Charles was deeply affected by this incident but continued on his way. A little later, when they were pausing to rest under the hot sun, a soldier let his lance fall against a helmet causing a strident clang in the silence. Charles jumped. Gripped by a sudden surge of fury and believing he was being attacked, he drew his sword and shouted out that he was being delivered to his enemies. He killed four men, gave his horse free rein and galloped wildly about for some while without anyone being able to intervene. Finally he wore himself out and one of his knights was able to mount behind and bring the horse under control. They laid the King in a wagon and tied him down; then they took him back to Le Mans convinced that he was about to die.

This terrible onset of madness in the middle of the Hundred Years War had serious consequences. Deprived of its ruler and a prey to princely rivalries, the kingdom grew weak. From time to time Charles VI would regain his senses only to lapse back into madness. Henry V of England was quick to take advantage of the situation: in 1420 he imposed the famous Treaty of Troyes by which Charles VI disinherited his son and recognized Henry as his heir. Charles VI finally died in 1422, 30 years after the drama near Le Mans had occurred.

The Comic Novel – The cathedral chapter in Le Mans had several members of note: Arnould Gréban, author of a *Mystery of the Passion* (c 1450), a poem of 30 000 lines; Ronsard, who was a canon in 1560; Jacques Pelletier, a friend of Ronsard; and Paul Scarron.

Paul Scarron (1610-60), a poet, was an unordained canon of Le Mans Cathedral by his mid-20s; this worldly cleric, who had a lively social life at court where he spent most of his time, enjoyed excellent health, a prebend and a house attached to the cathedral. Unfortunately for him, since he preferred city life, he was obliged to spend some time in Le Mans every now and then, where he consoled himself with the local food and wine. In 1638 Scarron fell victim to a noxious drug dispensed to him by a charlatan physician and found himself paralysed.

His hard lot was mitigated first by Marie de Hautefort, a former mistress of Louis XIII who had been exiled to Le Mans and who offered her friendship, and then by the Muse who inspired his *Comic Novel (Le Roman Comique)*, a burlesque work relating the adventures of a troupe of actors in Le Mans and its neighbourhood.

In 1652 Scarron married **Françoise d'Aubigné**, grand daughter of the Calvinist poet Agrippa d'Aubigné, who said, "I would rather marry a cripple than the convent". When she was widowed she was elevated to the rank of **Marquise de Maintenon** before her secret marriage to Louis XIV (1683) over whom she exerted considerable influence.

The birthplace of the French motor-car industry

In the second half of the 19C, **Amédée Bollée** (1844-1917), a local bell-founder, began to take an interest in the incipient motor-car industry. His first car *(L'Obéissante)* was completed in 1873. Later he built the *Mancelle*, the first car to have the engine placed in front under a bonnet and to have a transmission shaft. The Austrian emperor, Franz-Joseph went for a ride in the *Mancelle*.

Bollée's son Amédée (1867-1926) devoted himself mainly to racing cars; they were fitted with **Michelin** tyres and reached 100kph/62mph. After the First World War he began to produce an early form of piston rings which became the main line of manufacture in his factory.

On 27 June 1906, the first prize on the Sarthe circuit was won by Szisz driving a Renault fitted with Michelin detachable rims.

In 1908 his brother, Léon Bollée, invited **Wilbur Wright** to attempt one of his first flights in an aeroplane at Les Hunaudières. When asked how the aircraft had performed Wright replied, "Like a bird". In 1936 Louis Renault set up his first decentralized factory south of Le Mans in the Arnage plain.

Radiator of a 1912 Amédée Bollée

Eating out

BUDGET

La Botte d'Asperges – *72230 Guécelard – 18km/11mi S of Le Mans on N 23 – ☎ 02 43 87 29 61 – closed 4-11 Mar, 5-28 Aug, Sun evening and Mon except public holidays – 15.09/41.92€*. A simple little restaurant, in a former staging inn. The picture-hung dining room is very pleasant. Unpretentious cooking with good menus, including one for children.

MODERATE

Chez Jean – *9 r. Dorée – ☎ 02 43 28 22 96 – closed 27 Aug-9 Sep, 26 Nov-2 Dec, 31 Dec-6 Jan, Tue lunchtime Apr-Oct, Wed evening Nov-Mar, Sun evening and Mon – 24.24/28.81€*. This half-timbered restaurant in a small pedestrian-only street is a stone's throw from the old town. Countrified dining room with big stone fireplace and Louis XIV-style chairs. Wide choice of tempting menus and small terrace in summer.

OUTSIDE TOWN

Auberge du Rallye – *13 r. des Gesleries – 72210 Fillé-sur-Sarthe – 12km/7.5mi S of Le Mans on D 147[E], D 23 towards Allones, then D 51 – ☎ 02 43 87 40 40 – closed Wed evening and Thu – reservation required for weekends – 18.29/33.54€*. It's good to get away from the noise of the city and eat in a country setting in the Sarthe, on a shaded terrace. At this restaurant the chef concocts his daily dishes from fresh market produce.

La Petite Auberge – *By the bridge – 72270 Malicorne-sur-Sarthe – ☎ 02 43 94 80 52 – closed 15 Feb-15 Mar, 20 Dec-10 Jan, Mon and evenings Sep-Jun except Sat – 19.67/22.41€*. The river with its pleasure boats flows past the terrace of this restaurant, though in cooler weather the dining room with its large fireplace is preferable. Traditional cooking with a contemporary flavour.

Where to stay

BUDGET – OUT OF TOWN

Chambre d'hôte Le Petit Pont – *3 r. du Petit-Pont – 72230 Moncé-en- Belin – 11km/6.8mi S of Le Mans on D 147 towards Arnage, then D 307 – ☎ 02 43 42 03 32 – 5 rooms 32/39.64€ – evening meal 15.24€*. A healthy, simple place with a warm welcome. The rooms are non-smoking, simply decorated and well equipped. The property is situated on a working farm.

Chambre d'hôte Mme Bordeau – *Le Monet – 72190 Coulaines – 5km/3mi N of Le Mans towards Mamers, then Ballon on D 300 – ☎ 02 43 82 25 50 – ⌿ – 4 rooms 32/42€*. A chance to stay in the countryside, but not too far from town. This typical regional house has been completely restored but has retained its original character, as can be seen in the bedrooms, with their heavy rustic furniture. You will also appreciate the carefully tended, shady garden.

MODERATE

Hôtel Émeraude – *18 r. Gastelier – ☎ 02 43 24 87 46 – closed 4-26 Aug and 24 Dec-2 Jan – 33 rooms 57.93/60.98€ – ⌺ 7.62€*. A useful, very reasonably priced little hotel near the station. The rooms are simple but well kept.

On the town

La Péniche Excelsior – *Z.A. La Raterie – ☎ 02 43 80 35 06 – opening hours according to events and concerts*. The Excelsior is a barge moored to the banks of the Sarthe which, although limited for space (99 places), offers reasonably priced contemporary music concerts, such as afro, techno, ethnic and house.

Le Saint-Flaceau – *9 r. St-Flaceau – ☎ 02 43 23 24 93 – daily 4pm-1am*. This cocktail bar is something really different: the setting is an 18C apartment in the old town, complete with parquet floors and mouldings, and furnished with old sofas and chairs. Wide choice of drinks at reasonable prices, and a wonderful terrace on the old Roman walls overlooking the town – which was the main reason for converting this bar from an apartment.

Showtime

L'Espal – *60-62 r. de l'Estérel* – ☎ *02 43 50 21 50* – *open Tue 10am-7pm, Wed-Fri 10am-1pm, 2-7pm, Sat 10am-5pm.* The Espal centre is both a community arts centre and a cultural venue. It organises workshops and courses (dance, lithography) as well as putting on shows of choreography, theatre, exhibitions and concerts.

Leisure

Les Croisières au Mans – *101 quai de l'Amiral-Lalande* – ☎ *02 43 80 56 62* – *Mon-Sat 9am-6pm, Sun 10am-12.30pm.* Make your reservation through the tourist office for a boat trip or cruise (with a meal) on the Sarthe. A different way of discovering the history, geography and even zoology of Le Mans and its surroundings.

Pony rides ⊙ – ☎ *02 43 87 66 52.* On Sundays, take a ride through the old town, starting from square du Bois, above the tunnel.

Cultural centre

MJC Jacques-Prévert – *97 Grande-Rue* – ☎ *02 43 24 73 85* – *opening hours according to events.* An arts centre in a lovely 17C building where there is always something going on. Radio Alpha (107.3) is Le Mans' latest community radio station, whose studios are open to the public. In the vaulted cellar, the Inventaire holds concerts of rock, jazz and French songs, as well as theatre performances. Two cinemas show art and experimental films, always in original version.

Sit back and relax

Café Crème – *2 r. de la Barillerie* – ☎ *02 43 14 26 29* – *Mon-Fri 11am-2am, Sat 2pm-2am.* With its upper floor, hidden corners and bench seats, this café on the corner of place de la Sirène is known as a smart place to go. The terrace with its elegant teak furniture is particularly appealing.

Hollyrock – *46 r. du Dr-Leroy* – ☎ *02 43 23 00 00* – *daily 6pm-4am.* Heavily influenced by the American 1950s style, this huge bar includes a sports hall, where transmissions of matches are shown, an exotic billiard room with fake palm trees, and a main dance floor with DJ. Theme evenings. Disco next door.

Mulligan's – *44 r. du Dr-Leroy* – ☎ *02 43 14 26 65* – *Mon-Fri 11am-2am, Sat 2pm-2am, Sun and public holidays 4pm-2am* – *concerts Thu and Fri.* In this fine Irish pub, furnished with benches and barrels instead of tables, the landlord speaks the language of James Joyce with an accent as authentic as the Guinness he serves. Theme evenings.

Reignier – *19 r. de Bolton* – ☎ *02 43 24 02 15* – *Tue-Sat 9am-7pm.* Two floors (400m²/478sq yd) of high-quality wines (60 000 bottles in stock). Reignier's own-brand top-class tea and coffee, delicatessen and regional specialities.

★★OLD TOWN *1hr*

The old town (Le Vieux Mans) is built on a hill overlooking the Sarthe. Restaurants and craft shops enliven the pretty, winding streets, intersected by stepped alleys and lined with 15C half-timbered houses, Renaissance town houses and 18C *hôtels* graced by wrought-iron balconies. Clearly visible from all along the quays of the Sarthe, the well-restored **Gallo-Roman ramparts★** in their typically pinkish hues are a truly unique landmark. The overall impression of elegance is created by the alternating layers of brickwork and black and white ashlar arranged in geometrical patterns. This 1 300m/4 270ft-long military construction, interrupted by 11 towers, is one of the longest still extant in France.

Start from place des Jacobins at the bottom of the cathedral steps.

Place and Quinconces des Jacobins – The square, place des Jacobins, which is famous for its view of the cathedral chevet, was laid out on the site of a former Dominican convent. At the entrance to the tunnel through the old town stands a monument to Wilbur Wright by Paul Landowski.

Go up the steps and follow the itinerary indicated on the town plan.

Place St-Michel – Standing in the cathedral precincts is the Renaissance house where Paul Scarron lived while he was a member of the cathedral chapter. The presbytery, at no 1 bis, still features its 15C staircase turret.

Maison des Deux-Amis – *Nos 18-20 rue de la Reine-Bérengère.* The two friends *(deux amis)* are shown supporting a coat of arms. This mansion was built in the 15C and two centuries later was home to the poet and painter Nicolas Denizot, a friend of Ronsard and Du Bellay.

Le Mans – Maison du Pilier Rouge

H. Dewynter/MICHELIN

On the opposite side of rue Wilbur-Wright, which was cut through the hillside to relieve traffic congestion, is the **Maison du Pilier rouge** (Red Pillar House), a half-timbered house containing the tourist office and featuring a corner pillar decorated with a dead man's head.

At the beginning of Grande-Rue stands *(right)* the **Maison du Pilier vert** (Green Pillar House) and further on the 16C Hôtel d'Arcy.

Return to the Maison du Pilier Rouge and turn right onto the street of the same name which leads to place du Hallai, then continue along rue du Hallai to place St-Pierre lined with half-timbered houses.

Hôtel de ville – The town hall was built in 1760, within the walls of the palace of the counts of Maine. Take the steps to rue Rostov-sur-le-Don from where there is a view of the old town's south-east ramparts; on one side of the steps is a 14C tower and on the other the old collegiate church of **St-Pierre-la-Cour** ⊙, now an exhibition and concert hall.

Hôtel de Vignolles – This 16C mansion with tall French-style mansard roofs stands at the beginning of rue de l'Écrevisse on the right.

Maison d'Adam et Ève – *No 71 Grande-Rue.* This superb Renaissance mansion was the home of Jean de l'Épine, an astrologer and physician.

At the corner of **rue St-Honoré** a column shaft is decorated with three keys, the sign of a locksmith. The street is lined with half-timbered houses. The picturesque Cour d'Assé opens opposite rue St-Honoré. From here onwards Grande-Rue runs downhill between elegant Classical mansions. Bear right onto the less patrician rue St-Pavin-de-la-Cité; on the left is the Hôtel d'Argouges which has a lovely 15C doorway in the courtyard. Carry on along the street and after a vaulted passageway turn left onto rue Bouquet. At the corner of rue de Vaux a 15C niche shelters a statue of Mary Magdalene; the Hôtel de Vaux at no 12 is a late-16C mansion. Further on to the left there is a view of the Great Postern steps, part of the Gallo-Roman ramparts.

Walk back along rue de Vaux.

Note the Hôtel de Tucé-Lavardin at no 4.

River Sarthe at Le Mans

Cross rue Wilbur-Wright and climb the steps turning left onto rue des Chanoines.

At no 26 stands the St-Jacques canon's residence built around 1560.

Maison de la Tourelle – In front of the cathedral. This Renaissance mansion, with its windows and dormers decorated with delicate scrollwork, is named after the corbelled turret it features on the corner of the Pans-de-Gorron stepped alley.

Hôtel du Grabatoire – On the other side of the steps, opposite the Romanesque doorway of the cathedral, this 16C mansion stands on the site of what was originally the infirmary for sick canons, but which is now the episcopal palace. On its right stands the Maison du Pèlerin (Pilgrim's House) decorated with cockleshells, the symbol adopted by pilgrims on their way to the shrine of St James at Santiago de Compostela *(see The Green Guide Spain)*.

OTHER DISTRICTS

Pont Yssoir – This bridge affords a nice view of the cathedral, the old town, the Gallo-Roman fortified wall with its geometric decoration and a riverside walk past traces of medieval fortifications.

Close to the bridge on the north bank is the church of Notre-Dame-du-Pré.

Église Notre-Dame-du-Pré ⊘ – In a square planted with magnolia trees stands the old abbey church of the Benedictine convent of St Julian in the Fields (St-Julien-du Pré); the column capitals and chancel are Romanesque.

Jardin d'horticulture – *Rue de l'Éventail.* This beautiful horticultural garden (covering 5ha/12 acres) with its rockery and cascading stream was designed in 1851 by Alphand, the landscape gardener responsible for the Bois de Boulogne and the parks of Montsouris and Buttes-Chaumont in Paris. From the mall on the terrace there is a fine view of the cathedral.

Église de la Visitation – This church, which stands in the main square, place de la République, at the heart of the modern town, was originally a convent chapel; it was built in about 1730. The main façade, in rue Gambetta, is lavishly decorated with a portico of Corinthian columns sheltering a Rococo door; the interior decor, of the same date, is also Baroque.

★ **Église Notre-Dame de la Couture** – This church, now in the centre of the town and next to the *préfecture* housed in the old convent buildings (18C), was originally the abbey church of the monastery of St-Pierre-de-la-Couture (a corruption of *culture* which referred to the fields of crops that used to surround the church).

Sutdio 3Bis/MICHELIN

Ancien hôtel d'Arcy	E	B
Ancienne collégiale St-Pierre-la Cour	E	E
Bois de Loudon	DY	
Cathédrale St-Julien	DV, E	
Église de la Couture	DX	
Église de la Visitation	CX	
Église N.-D. du Pré	CV	
Église Ste-Jeanne d'Arc	DY	
Enceinte Gallo-Romaine	E	
Hôtel d'Argouges	E	K¹
Hôtel de Vaux	E	K²
Hôtel de Vignolles	E	K³
Hôtel de ville	DX, E	H
Hôtel du Grabatoire	E	K⁴
Maison canoniale St-Jacques	E	N¹
Maison d'Adam et Ève	E	N²
Maison de la reine Bérengère (Musée)	DV, E	M²
Maison de la Tourelle	E	N³
Maison de Scarron	E	N⁴
Maison des Deux-Amis	E	N⁵
Maison du Pilier Rouge	E	N⁶
Maison du Pilier Vert	E	N⁷
Montfort-le-Gesnois	DY	
Musée de Tessé	DV	
Tour du 14ᵉ siècle	E	R

LE VIEUX MANS

The façade is 13C. The door is framed by the Apostles defeating the Forces of Evil; on the pediment is Christ, between the Virgin Mary and St John, presiding over the Last Judgement; on the arch stones, making up the Heavenly Host, are rows of Angels, Patriarchs, Prophets (1st row), Martyrs (2nd row) and Virgins (3rd row).

The wide single nave, built in the late 12C in the Plantagenet style, is lit by elegant twinned windows surmounted by oculi. The enchanting white-marble **Virgin★★** (1571), on the pillar directly opposite the pulpit, is by Germain Pilon. The blind arcades are hung with 16C panels painted by one of the monks.

The 10C crypt, altered in 1838, has pre-Romanesque or Gallo-Roman columns and capitals; an inverted Antique capital serves as a base for one of the pillars. The 6C-7C shroud of St Bertrand, Bishop of Le Mans and founder in 616 of the monastery, is displayed at the entrance *(automatic time switch for lighting)*.

★**Église Ste-Jeanne-d'Arc** ⊘ – This church, on the site of the old Coëffort Hospital, was founded c 1180 by Henry II of England in atonement, it is said, for the murder of his former Chancellor, Archbishop **Thomas Becket** in Canterbury Cathedral. The 12C great hall or ward for the sick is now the parish church. The plain façade, pierced by an arched doorway, crowned by twinned windows, opens into a vast room divided into three naves of equal height. The elevation is elegant with slender columns topped by finely carved capitals, supporting Plantagenet vaulting.

★★CATHÉDRALE ST-JULIEN *1hr*

This magnificent cathedral, dedicated to St Julian the first Bishop of Le Mans, makes an impressive spectacle seen from place des Jacobins, where its Gothic **chevet★★★** *(see illustration in Art and architecture: Ecclesiastical architecture)* rises in a succession of tiers supported by an amazingly intricate system of Y-shaped two-tiered flying buttresses. The present building comprises a Romanesque nave, Gothic chancel and Rayonnant or High Gothic transept flanked by a tower. The interior is illuminated to show it to best effect.

Exterior

The south porch overlooking the charming place St-Michel has a superb 12C **doorway★★** contemporary with the Royal Doorway of Chartres. At the right corner of the west front is a pink-veined sandstone menhir tradition has it that visitors should place their thumb in one of the holes to claim that they have truly visited Le Mans. On either side of the doorway stand groups of figures: Christ in Majesty, the Apostles and a series of statue columns flanking the doorway. These portray St Peter and St Paul on the jambs, whereas the figures on the splay embrasures represent Solomon and the Queen of Sheba, a Prophet, a Sibyl and the ancestors of Christ. The Apostles occupy the niches of the lintel in serried ranks with Christ the King on the tympanum, surrounded by the symbols of the Evangelists, being censed by angels in the first recessed arch moulding.

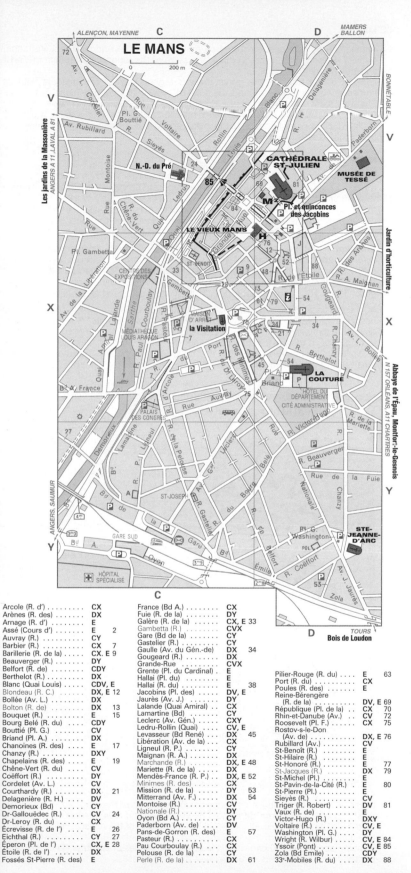

Arcole (R. d') . . . . **CX**
Arènes (R. des) . . . . . . **DX**
Arnage (R. d') . . . . **E**
Assé (Cours d') . . . . **E** 2
Auvray (R.) . . . . **CY**
Barbier (R.) . . . . **CX** 7
Barillerie (R. de la) . . . . **CX, E** 9
Beauverger (R.) . . . . . . **DY**
Belfort (R. de) . . . . **CDY**
Berthelot (R.) . . . . **DX**
Blanc (Quai Louis) . . . . **CDV, E**
Blondeau (R. C.) . . . . . . **DX, E** 12
Bollée (Av. L.) . . . . **DX**
Bolton (R. de) . . . . **DX** 13
Bouquet (R.) . . . . **E** 15
Bourg Belé (R. du) . . . **CDY**
Bouttié (Pl. G.) . . . . **CV**
Briand (Pl. A.) . . . . **DX**
Chanoines (R. des) . . . . **E** 17
Chanzy (R.) . . . . **DXY**
Chapelains (R. des) . . . **E** 19
Chêne-Vert (R. du) . . . . **CV**
Coëffort (R.) . . . . **DY**
Cordelet (Av. L.) . . . . . . **CV**
Courthardy (R.) . . . . . . **DX** 21
Delagenière (R. H.) . . . **DV**
Demorieux (Bd) . . . . . . **CY**
Dr-Gallouëdec (R.) . . . . **CV** 24
Dr-Leroy (R. du) . . . . . . **CX**
Écrevisse (R. de l') . . . . **E** 26
Eichthal (R.) . . . . **CY** 27
Éperon (Pl. de l') . . . . . **CX, E** 28
Étoile (R. de l') . . . . **DX**
Fossés St-Pierre (R. des) . **E**

France (Bd A.) . . . . **CX**
Fuie (R. de la) . . . . **DY**
Galère (R. de la) . . . . . **CX, E** 33
Gambetta (R.) . . . . **CVX**
Gare (Bd de la) . . . . . . **CY**
Gastelier (R.) . . . . **CY**
Gaulle (Av. du Gén.-de) . **DX** 34
Gougeard (R.) . . . . **DX**
Grande-Rue . . . . **CVX**
Grente (Pl. du Cardinal) . **E**
Hallai (Pl. du) . . . . **E**
Hallai (R. du) . . . . **E** 38
Jacobins (Pl. des) . . . . **DV, E**
Jaurès (Av. J.) . . . . **DY**
Lalande (Quai Amiral) . . **CX**
Lamartine (Bd) . . . . **CX**
Leclerc (Av. Gén.) . . . . **CXY**
Ledru-Rollin (Quai) . . . **CV, E**
Levasseur (Bd René) . . **DX** 45
Libération (Av. de la) . . **CX**
Ligneul (R. P.) . . . . **DX**
Maignan (R. A.) . . . . . . **DX**
Marchande (R.) . . . . . . **DX, E** 48
Mariette (R. de la) . . . . **DY**
Mendès-France (R. P.) . **DX, E** 52
Minimes (R. des) . . . . . **DX**
Mission (R. de la) . . . . **DY** 53
Mitterrand (Av. F.) . . . . **DX** 54
Montoise (R.) . . . . **CV**
Nationale (R.) . . . . **DY**
Oyon (Bd A.) . . . . **CY**
Paderborn (Av. de) . . . **DV**
Pans-de-Gorron (R. des) . **E** 57
Pasteur (R.) . . . . **CX**
Pau Courboulay (R.) . . . **CX**
Pelouse (R. de la) . . . . . **CY**
Perle (R. de la) . . . . **DX** 61

Pilier-Rouge (R. du) . . . . **E** 63
Port (R. du) . . . . **CX**
Poules (R. des) . . . . . . **E**
Reine-Bérengère
(R. de la) . . . . **DV, E** 69
République (Pl. de la) . . **CV** 70
Rhin-et-Danube (Av.) . . **CV** 72
Roosevelt (Pl. F.) . . . . . **CX** 75
Rostov-s-le-Don
(Av. de) . . . . **DX, E** 76
Rubillard (Av.) . . . . **CV**
St-Benoît (R.) . . . . **E**
St-Hilaire (R.) . . . . **E**
St-Honoré (R.) . . . . **E** 77
St-Jacques (R.) . . . . . . **DX** 79
St-Michel (Pl.) . . . . **E**
St-Pavin-de-la-Cité (R.) . **E** 80
St-Pierre (Pl.) . . . . **E**
Sieyès (R.) . . . . **CV**
Triger (R. Robert) . . . . . **DV** 81
Vaux (R. de) . . . . **E**
Victor-Hugo (R.) . . . . . . **DXY**
Voltaire (R.) . . . . **CV, E**
Washington (Pl. G.) . . . . **DY**
Wright (R. Wilbur) . . . . **CV, E** 84
Yssoir (Pont) . . . . **CV, E** 85
Zola (Bd Émile) . . . . . . **CDY**
33ᵉ-Mobiles (R. du) . . . . **DX** 88

Among the other scenes on the arch mouldings are the Annunciation, Visitation, Nativity, Presentation in the Temple, Massacre of the Innocents, Baptism of Christ and the Wedding at Cana.

Looking to the right of the porch there is a good view of the transept with its immense window openings and the 12C-14C tower (64m/210ft high).

The west front, built in an archaic Romanesque style, overlooks place du Cardinal-Grente, its sides lined with Renaissance mansions. Clearly visible is the original 11C gable which was embedded in the gable added the following century when the new vaulting was being built.

Interior

The Romanesque main building rests on great 11C round arches which were reinforced in the following century by pointed arches. The convex or Plantagenet-style vaulting springs from splendid capitals with particularly finely worked detail.

In the side aisles are eight Romanesque stained-glass windows; the most famous one represents the Ascension (**1**). The great window of the west front, heavily restored in the 19C, depicts the Legend of St Julian.

Transept – The 14C-15C transept, with its boldly soaring elevation pierced by a triforium and immense stained-glass windows, has an ethereal quality in striking contrast to the nave. The south arm is dominated by the 16C organ-loft (**2**), whereas the north arm is suffused with light transmitted through the beautiful 15C stained glass. Three 16C tapestry hangings (**3**) illustrate the Legend of St Julian.

At the entrance to the baptismal chapel (Chapelle des Fonts), which opens into the north arm of the transept, are two remarkable Renaissance **tombs**★★ opposite one another. The tomb on the left (**4**), that of Charles IV of Anjou, Count of Maine, the brother of King René, is the work of Francesco Laurana. The recumbent figure lies, in the Italian style, on an antique sarcophagus and the delicacy of the facial features recalls Laurana's talents as a portraitist. On the right, the magnificent monument (**5**) to the memory of Guillaume du Bellay, cousin to the poet, shows the figure holding a sword and a book and reclining on one elbow in the Antique manner on a sarcophagus which is adorned with an attractive frieze of aquatic divinities. A third tomb (**6**), that of Cardinal Grente, was erected in 1965.

Chancel – "The sustained height of this almost detached choir is very noble; its lightness and grace, its soaring symmetry, carry the eye up to places in the air from which it is slow to descend" *(Henry James)*. The lofty Gothic chancel (13C), encircled by a double ambulatory with a circlet of apsidal chapels, is one of the finest in France – soaring 34m/112ft high (compare Notre-Dame in Paris 35m/115ft, Westminster Abbey in London 31m/102ft).

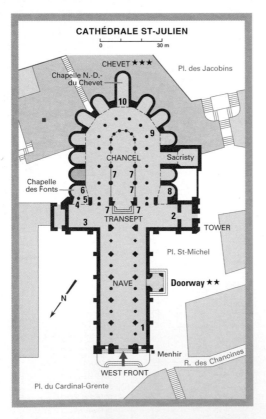

CATHÉDRALE ST-JULIEN
0 — 30 m
CHEVET ★★★
Pl. des Jacobins
Chapelle N.-D.-du Chevet
10
9
CHANCEL
Sacristy
Chapelle des Fonts
7 7
7
6
5
8
4
7 7
2
3
TRANSEPT
TOWER
Pl. St-Michel
NAVE
Doorway ★★
N
1
Menhir
R. des Chanoines
WEST FRONT
Pl. du Cardinal-Grente

The massed ranks of the tall upward-sweeping columns support lancet arches showing a definite Norman influence.

In the high windows of the chancel and first ambulatory and in the low windows of the chapels, the 13C **stained glass**★★ is a blaze of colour dominated by vivid blues and reds. Binoculars are needed to identify the rather stylized and fierce-looking figures of the Apostles, bishops, saints and donors.

Hanging above the 16C choir stalls is the famous series of **tapestries** (**7**) of the same period depicting the lives of St Gervase and St Protase.

Chancel precincts – In the first chapel on the right is a moving 17C terracotta Entombment (**8**). The sacristy door beyond used to be part of the 17C rood screen. The beautiful 16C woodwork in the sacristy originally formed the high backs of the choir stalls. The 14C Canons' Doorway features a tympanum with an effigy of St Julian (**9**).

The 13C **Lady Chapel** (Chapelle Notre-Dame-du-Chevet) is dedicated to the Holy Virgin; it is closed by a delicate 17C wrought-iron grille. A remarkable series of late-14C **mural paintings★** on the chapel vaulting was recently discovered and restored; it depicts an Angels' Concert and displays a rare degree of draughtsmanship. Forty-seven musicians and singers portrayed as angels declare their faith to Mary; they are suffused with light and compose a magnificent tableau in which colour and perspective blend harmoniously. Among the 27 musical instruments depicted in the fresco, note the *échiquier* (also spelt *eschiquier*), a rare occurrence indeed. Up to then, this instrument featuring a stringed keyboard, the ancestor of the piano, had never been represented in art although mention of it was made in the account books belonging to King John II the Good as far back as 1360. The stained-glass windows date from the 13C; they depict the Tree of Jesse (**10**) and the story of Adam and Eve.

ADDITIONAL SIGHTS

★ **Maison de la Reine-Bérengère** – *No 9 rue de la Reine-Bérengère.* This elegant house was built around 1460 for an alderman of Le Mans, over two centuries after the death of its namesake Queen Berengaria, wife of Richard the Lionheart. The decoration consists of an accolade above the door, beams supported on historiated brackets and sections of carved woodwork on the façade. The house at no 7, which dates from c 1530, is adorned with statues of St Catherine and St Barbara.

Musée de la Reine Bérengère ⊘ – The Maison de la Reine Bérengère is now a **Museum of History and Ethnography**. A Renaissance room on the ground floor contains a display of regional furniture.

On the first floor, the glazed pottery of the Sarthe region (Ligron, Malicorne, Bonnétable and Prevelles) makes a lively and imaginative display, with strikingly fresh colours – yellow, green and brown – lavished onto statuettes, altarpieces, chafing-dishes, pots, roof finials etc. On the second floor are paintings by 19C artists from the Sarthe region including Hervé-Mathé, Dugasseau and Gizard.

★ **Musée de Tessé** ⊘ – This museum, housed in the old bishop's palace built in the 19C on the site of the Tessé family mansion, contains fine collections of 19C paintings and archaeology.

Basement – This is where the **Egyptian collections** are displayed: reconstruction of the tombs of Nefertari (Ramses II's first wife) and of Sennefer (mayor of Thebes), mummy dating from 750 BC, rowing boat (1950 BC), funerary objects and jewellery.

Ground floor – A small room *(left)* contains a superb enamelled copper plaque, called the **Plantagenet enamel★**, a unique piece depicting Geoffrey Plantagenet, Count of Anjou and Maine from 1129 to 1151, Duke of Normandy in 1144 and father of Henry II of England. Originally it adorned the tomb *(no longer extant)* of this powerful knight in the cathedral.

The Italian paintings include an interesting series of 14C-15C altarpieces with gold backgrounds, a delightful female saint with narrow, slanting eyes by Pietro Lorenzetti from Siena, two panels from a marriage chest by Pesellino of Florence and a very touching portrait of the Virgin Mary suckling the Infant Jesus.

In the Renaissance Room there are two panels by the Master of Vivoin, part of an altarpiece (c 1470) from Vivoin Priory (Sarthe).

Note the Classical paintings by Philippe de Champaigne (the famous *Vanity* exhibited in the Tessé Room), Georges de la Tour *(St Francis in Ecstasy)* and Nicolas Tournier *(The Drinking Party* – in the entrance). The 18C Room displays a superb bookcase by Bernard van Risenburgh.

First floor – The Northern School of painting is represented by Van Utrecht, Kalf *(Still Life with Armour)*, several *bambocciate* (scenes of street life) and landscapes. A whole room is devoted to *The Comic Novel* by Scarron; a portrait of the author is exhibited alongside paintings by Coulom and engravings by Oudry and Pater.

Second floor – This floor is reserved for temporary exhibitions.

Musée Vert Véron de Forbonnais ⊘ – *SE, at no 204 avenue Jean-Jaurès.*
⌂ This interesting museum houses a number of collections devoted to mineralogy, palaeontology, entomology, botany and ornithology. Two rooms are reserved for children.

MOTOR RACING CIRCUITS

To the S of Le Mans between N 138 and D 139.

Circuit des 24 Heures – The 24-hour circuit (13.6km/8.5mi long) begins at the Tertre Rouge bend *(virage)* on N 138. The racetrack, which is about 10m/33ft wide, is marked in kilometres. The double bend on the private road and the Mulsanne and Arnage hairpin bends are the most exciting hazards on the 24-hour course. In 1972 the course was laid out to give the public a better view along a distance of 4km/2.5mi.

Within the confines of the circuit is Les Hunaudières racecourse for horses where Wilbur Wright made his first flight, commemorated by a stele.

Le Mans 24-hour race – In 1923 Gustave Singher and Georges Durand launched the first Le Mans endurance test which was to become a sporting event of universal interest and an ideal testing ground for car manufacturers.

The difficulties of the circuit and the duration of the race are a severe test of the quality of the machine and of the endurance of the drivers.

The track has been greatly improved since the tragic accident in 1955 when 83 spectators died and 100 were injured. Whether seen from the stands or from the fields or pine woods which surround the track, the race is an unforgettable experience:

Milestones in the Le Mans 24-hour Race

1923 – The first 24-hour race in 1923 was won by Lagache and Léonard from Chenard and Walcker; they covered 2 209.536km at an average speed of 92.064kph; the fastest circuit time was achieved by Clément in a Bentley at 107.328kph.

1971 – In 1971 when the track was 13.469km long Helmut Marko and Gijs Van Lennep covered 5 335.313km in a Porsche 917 at an average speed of 222.304kph; Siffert drove the fastest lap, also in a Porsche 917, at an average speed of 243.905kph.

1991 – The circuit was redesigned and granted new facilities, making it the first racing track of its kind in the world. Mazda came first (unprecedented victory of a Japanese firm and a rotary engine).

1993 – Peugeot's historic hat-trick: three cars on the starting line, three cars on the finishing line, and three cars winning laurels. Moreover, they succeeded in setting a new track record on the longer circuit (13.600km) covering 5 100km at an average speed of 213.358kph.

1998 – The Scot Alan McNish and the two Frenchmen Laurent Aïello and Stéphane Ortelli celebrate Porsche's 16th triumphant arrival; their GT1 performed 351 laps (4 723.78km) at an average speed of 199.32kph.

2000 – The drivers Biela, Kristensen and Pirro won the 68th race. Three Audi R8s took the first three places, the first one having gone round the track 368 times!

Pit stop during the Le Mans 24-hour race

the roaring of the engines, the whining of the vehicles hurtling up the Hunaudières section at more than 350kph/200mph, the smell of petrol mingled with the resin of the pine trees, the glare of the headlights at night, the emotion and excitement of the motor car enthusiasts.

Every year there is also a Le Mans 24-hour motorcycle race and a Le Mans 24-hour truck race. A Grand Prix de France motorcycle race is held here regularly.

From the main entrance to the track on D 139 a tunnel leads to the Bugatti circuit and the museum.

Circuit Bugatti ⊘ – Apart from being used by its school for racing drivers, the track (4.43km/2.75mi) is also a permanent testing ground for teams of racing car drivers and motorcyclists who use it for private trials.

Le Mans-Paris in 18 hours

This is exactly how long it took Amédée Bollée to cover the 230km/143mi distance separating the two cities in his car *L'Obéissante*! True, the vehicle he choose for his journey was a 12-seater driven by two engines, each one operating one back wheel. This strange contraption weighed around 1t when empty and was supposed to reach a speed of 40kph/24.9mph. However, with half an hour's stop in each *département* to obtain the right of passage and the various formalities involved in 75 tickets he was given, the average velocity was considerably reduced. Consequently, it was at 13kph/8.1mph that Amédée Bollée made his triumphant arrival in the French capital on 9 October 1875.

** **Musée de l'Automobile de la Sarthe** ⊘ – *Access is through the main entrance to the circuit (D 139 N of D 921)*. Rebuilt in 1991, the Motor Museum displays 115 vehicles in an extremely modern and instructive setting. With the help of video technology and interactive games, a series of showcases and animated maquettes illustrate the Saga of the Automobile over the past 100 years.

The section on racing cars, in particular those that won the Le Mans 24-hour race, presents a superb collection of outstanding automobiles, including a 1924 Bentley, a 1949 Ferrari, a 1974 Matra, a 1983 Rondeau, a 1988 Jaguar, a 1991 Mazda and a 1992 Peugeot.

EXCURSIONS

* **Abbaye de l'Épau** ⊘ – *4km/2.5mi E via avenue Léon-Bollée; turn right onto the ring road, cross the railway and follow the arrows*. In 1229 a Cistercian abbey was founded on the south bank of the Huisne by **Queen Berengaria**, the widow of Richard the Lionheart, who spent her last days here.

The monastic buildings were laid out around the cloisters. On the right is the **refectory** wing with the arcades of the washing place *(lavatorium)*. Opposite are the monks' quarters, including the writing room (**scriptorium** – right) and the **chapter-house** (left) with elegant ogive vaulting and the tomb of Queen Berengaria; the first floor consisted of the monks' **dormitory** covered with wooden vaulting.

On the left is the **church**, which was built in the 13C and 14C and remodelled in the 15C; this is the date of the huge, delicately carved chancel window. The church was designed to the traditional Cistercian layout: a square east end with three chapels facing east in each arm of the transept. In the south arm, the square capitals are decorated with water-lily leaf motifs.

In recent years, the abbey has hosted the **Festival de l'Épau**, a highly esteemed festival of classical music.

Arche de la Nature ⊘ – *Near the Abbaye de l'Épau*. This 450ha/1 112-acre natural site comes to life in season with activities on the theme of "rivers", "woodlands" etc. On offer are visits to the Maison de l'Eau (some afternoons), of a model farm (many animals typical of the region), rides in horse-drawn carts (April to October), hikes, sports grounds and outdoor games.

Montfort-le-Gesnois – *20km/12.5mi E of Le Mans along avenue Léon-Bollée and N 23; after 16km/10mi bear left onto D 83* . Not far from **Connerré**, a small commercial town renowned for its *rillettes* (potted meat made from pork or goose), Montfort, resulting from the merging of Pont-de-Gennes and Montfort-le-Rotrou, lies in a peaceful, attractive site which developed from the Roman bridge over the River Huisne. The narrow humpback **bridge**, built with sandstone blocks in the 15C, spans the river at a point where it widens and flows among the trees. There is a pretty view of the 13C church of St-Gilles, a mill overgrown with Virginia creeper and surrounded by weeping willows, and a little weir where the water tumbles and races.

Bois de Loudon – *18km/11mi SE along avenue Jean-Jaurès, N 223 and D 304; fork left onto D 145ᴱ and turn left again onto D 145*. Woodland tracks branch off to the right of the road (D 145) into the coniferous forest; in the autumn the sandy soil is covered with a thick carpet of heather.

Jardins du Manoir de la Massonière ⊘ – *In St-Christophe-en-Champagne, 35km/22mi W via A 11 (exit Le Mans Sud) then D 22*. Surrounding an attractive manor house, these gardens, inspired by Impressionist painting, display a splendid array of colours, perfumes and topiaries, trees and bushes trimmed in the shape of chess pieces.

MEANDERING DOWN THE SARTHE VALLEY

73km/45mi – about 3hr

The Sarthe meanders peacefully south-west through the beautiful Maine countryside. The river is navigable between Le Mans and the confluence with the Mayenne along lateral canals running parallel to it. The countryside through which it flows consists of woodland alternating with meadows and fields of cereals, potatoes and early vegetables.

Leave Le Mans on N 23 heading SW.

Spay – *10km/6mi on N 23 and D 51 via Arnage*. The 9C-12C Romanesque **church** has a beautiful altar (1773) and a very elegant 14C Virgin and Child. A valuable pyx (small spherical box made of precious metal in which the Eucharist was placed) dating from 1621 is just one of the items in the church's treasury.

Parc ornithologique ⊘ – This 6ha/15-acre landscaped park is home to some 250 species of colourful birds from five continents: humming bird, emu, marabou...

Take D 51 to Fillé.

Fillé – The village is on the north bank of the Sarthe; its **church** ⊘ contains a large painted statue of the Virgin Mary (late 16C), glazed somewhat by the fire of August 1944.

La Suze-sur-Sarthe – The bridge over the Sarthe provides a good view of the river, the remains of the castle (15C) and the church.

Leave La Suze on D 79 going W through woods towards Fercé.

Fercé-sur-Sarthe – Attractive views from the bridge and from the road up to the church.

Return across the river and turn right to St-Jean-du-Bois.

The road (D 229) passes the troubadour-style castle of La Houssaye and provides several glimpses of the Sarthe before reaching Noyen.

Noyen-sur-Sarthe – The village is built in terraces on the sloping north bank overlooking the canal which at this point runs parallel to the broad Sarthe. From the bridge there is an attractive **view** of a weir, a mill, an island of poplars, a jumble of roofs and little gardens, the beach and another island.

Pirmil – *4km/2.7mi N of Noyen along D 69*. The **church**, a Romanesque building with buttresses, dates from 1165. The capitals are beautifully carved. The springers of the ogive vaulting are decorated with figures of a saint, a bishop and a priest and a grotesque head.

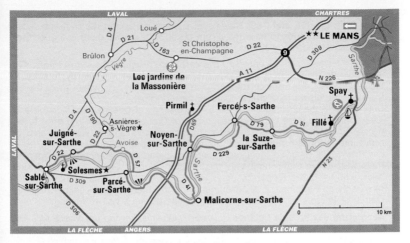

Malicorne-sur-Sarthe – Malicorne is pleasantly situated at the water's edge. From the bridge there is a pretty view of a mill and the poplars along the bank.

The 11C **church** contains a recumbent figure of one of the lords of Chaources (chapel on the right of the nave), a *Pietà* (south transept) and an attractive 16C piscina (left wall of the nave).

Downstream, set back from the south bank of the river in a beautiful park, stands the 17C **château** (altered) where Madame de Sévigné liked to stay, which belonged to the Marquise de Lavardin. The château has turrets and mansard roofs and is surrounded by a moat which is spanned by a charming humpback bridge.

Malicorne Espace faïence ⊙ – This interactive museum, devoted to the local speciality, is housed in the renovated buildings of a former factory. Workshops help to illustrate the process of making and firing earthenware, its uses and the art of potters. On the eastern side of the town, there is a working **pottery** ⊙ which produces pieces in the perforated Malicorne style, as well as reproductions of period pieces.

Take D 8 W towards Parcé, making a detour along a small country track (V 1) to the right via Dureil, which provides attractive glimpses of the River Sarthe before rejoining D 8.

Parcé-sur-Sarthe – Parcé is a charming little village grouped round a Romanesque tower with a mill on the river. The cypress-girted cemetery at the entrance to the village makes a peaceful setting for the chapel with its gable-belfry.

After crossing the river and the canal, turn left onto D 57.

On leaving Avoise note, on the left, La Perrigne de Cry *(private property)*, a 16C manor overlooking the river.

Bear left to Juigné.

Juigné-sur-Sarthe – Juigné is a pleasant village set on a promontory which juts south across the valley. There are 16C and 17C houses and the 18C château which belonged to the Marquis of Juigné. From the church square there is a view of the river below and of Solesmes Abbey downstream.

Solesmes – *See SABLÉ-SUR-SARTHE.*

Take D 22 alongside the canal and the old marble quarries to Sablé.

MEUNG-SUR-LOIRE ★

Population 6 254
Michelin map 318: H-5, 238 fold 4 or 4045 B5
Local map see ORLÉANS: La Loire Blésoise

This fortified village stretches from the Loire which laps at the roots of the tall trees lining the avenue up the slope to the main road (N 152) on the plateau. From the **old market** a narrow and twisting street, **rue Porte-d'Amont**, climbs up to an archway; little lanes skirt **Les Mauves**, a stream with many channels which runs between the houses (rue des Mauves, rue du Trianon).

The town has put up a statue in honour of its most famous son, **Jean de Meung**. In about 1280 he added 18 000 lines to the *Romance of the Rose (Roman de la Rose)* which had been written some 40 years earlier by Guillaume de Lorris and consisted of 4 000 lines. The allegorical narrative was the greatest literary achievement of a period in which readers certainly had to have stamina. Chaucer translated part of the work and was much influenced by it throughout his poetic career.

The bridge at Meung was often fought over during the Hundred Years War; it was captured by the English in 1428 and retaken by Joan of Arc on 15 June 1429.

★ Collégiale St-Liphard – This plain church building with its bell-tower and spire dates from the 11C and 13C; the chevet is semicircular and the transept unusually has rounded ends to its arms. From beyond the chevet there is a good view of the church and the château.

Castle – *Following its recent sale, the castle is currently closed to visitors.* This venerable building reflects a curious mixture of styles, having partly retained its medieval aspect, for instance the entrance façade (12C-13C), where there are still traces of the drawbridge which spanned the dry moat.

Until the 18C the château belonged to the bishops of Orléans, who administered justice in their diocese but who, being men of God, did not have the right to put people to death. Prisoners sentenced to lifelong confinement were lowered on ropes into an underground tower, the **oubliettes**, with a well at the bottom; every day they would be given the same quantity of bread and water, however many of them were down there, until they died of starvation or illness. The poet **François Villon**, who had powerful patrons, was the only one ever to come out alive; he suffered only one summer of imprisonment, for the theft of gold chalices from the church of Baccon, before Louis XI released him during a visit to Meung.

Arboretum des Prés de Culands – *Towards Orléans, beyond the Nivelle Mill.* This romantic site, famous for its display of holly, is crisscrossed by canals which form tiny islands planted with maple trees, oaks and alders.

MONDOUBLEAU

Population 1 608
Michelin map 318: C-4 or 232 fold 12

Approached from the west, Mondoubleau can be seen clustered on the east bank of the River Grenne. Perched at a precarious angle on a bluff to the south of the road to Cormenon, the ruins of a keep overlook the village where remains of the curtain wall are partly hidden among the houses and trees. Several graceful churches and properties which once belonged to the Knights Templars can be seen in the surrounding area.

Chambre d'hôte Peyron-Gaubert – *Carrefour de l'Ormeau* – ☎ *02 54 80 93 76 – closed Nov-Mar* – ⌷ – *5 rooms 35.38/46.15€* – *evening meal 20€.* All of the smooth, polished furniture in this 17C property was made by the owner, a cabinetmaker. The rooms are decorated in a soothing combination of natural wood and white. Guests may enjoy the garden.

Fortress ⊘ – At the end of the 10C, Hugues Doubleau, from whom the town has taken its name, built a red-sandstone fortress over which towered a 33m/108ft-high keep. All that remains of this imposing stronghold are half a keep, the governor's house, known as the Maison Courcillon (15C), and the baronial building (16C).

EXCURSIONS

① North of Mondoubleau

Round trip of 26km/16mi on D 921 – about 1hr

Château de St-Agil ⊘ – This is an interesting château encircled by a moat. The part of the building dating from the 13C was altered in 1720. The early-16C gatehouse is flanked by two towers decorated with a diaper pattern in red and black bricks. The machicolations guard the sentry walk and the pepper-pot roofs. The main building has a dormer window with a medallion of the lord of the manor, Antoine de la Vove. The park was landscaped by Jules Hardouin-Mansart and transformed in 1872 in the English style. The splendid lime trees were planted in 1720. Note the fine ice house from the 16C.

Commanderie d'Arville ⊘ – The road D 921 running south from Le Gault-Perche offers a good view of the Templar Commandery which later passed to the Knights of St John of Jerusalem. The ironstone building in its rural setting makes an attractive picture.

The 12C chapel housing the Commandery is crowned by a gable belfry which is linked to a flint tower, once part of the former ramparts. The town gateway (late 15C) is decorated with two brick turrets with unusual conical roofs made of chestnut slats.

The handsome tithe barn and dovecot have been restored and an information centre about military religious orders has been set up to retrace the history of the crusades and recreate the crusaders' life with the help of pictures, sounds and even smells (badian, anise...).

The Templars

The Order, which was both military and monastic, was founded in 1119 near the site of Solomon's Temple in Jerusalem. The members wore a white mantle bearing a red cross and were bound by their vows to defend the Holy City from the Muslims and protect all Christians making a pilgrimage to Jerusalem. To this end they built fortified commanderies along the main roads. A pilgrim would deposit a sum of money at his local commandery before setting out and in exchange for the receipt could draw the same sum on arrival in the Holy Land; thus the commanderies came to serve as banks in the 13C.

The Templars lent money to the popes as well as to kings and princes, and grew rich and powerful. Early in the 14C the Order of Templars numbered 15 000 knights and 9 000 commanderies. It had its own judicial system, paid no tax and took its authority directly from the Pope. Such wealth and independence earned it many enemies and brought about the Order's downfall.

In 1307 Philip the Fair persuaded the Pope that the Templars should be brought to trial; he had every single member of the Order in France arrested on the same day. The Grand Master, Jacques de Molay, and 140 knights were imprisoned in Chinon Castle; the following year they were brought to Paris. A trial was held in which they were accused of denying Christ by spitting on the Cross in their initiation ceremonies; 54 of them, including Jacques de Molay, were burned at the stake on one of the islets in the Seine.

Souday – The nave of the **church** ⊘ is extended by an interesting 16C two-storey chancel. Two flights of stairs, with wrought-iron railings which date from 1838, lead to the upper floor which is lit by Renaissance stained glass depicting the Passion and the Resurrection of Christ. The elegant ogive vaulting in the 11C crypt springs from columns without capitals. The south transept is decorated with 16C paintings of St Joseph, St Joachim and four scenes from the Life of John the Baptist; on the ceiling are the symbols of the Four Evangelists.

② South of Mondoubleau

Round trip of 24km/15mi – about 1hr

Leave Mondoubleau SE on D 151.

Le Temple – All that is left of the Templar commandery is a 13C church with a squat bell-tower and a square chevet nestling pleasantly by a pool.

Turn right onto D 156.

Sargé-sur-Braye – The **church of St-Martin** ⊘ was built in the 11C and 15C. The painted wainscots date from 1549. The murals discovered in the nave are 16C (*Pietà*, *St Martin*) and in the chancel 14C (*Christ in Majesty* and *Labours of the Months*; note the three faces of Janus symbolising January).

Baillou – The little village is attractively clustered below a great 16C-17C château.

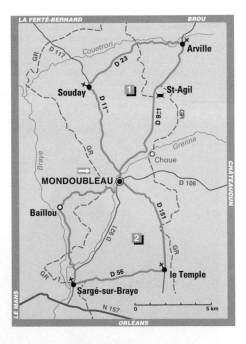

The beautiful early-16C **church** ⊘ stands alone on a mount. The Renaissance doorway is flanked by scrolled pilasters, surmounted by figures of Adam and Eve.

Inside, the south transept contains a carved altarpiece (1618) depicting the Death of the Virgin surrounded by the Apostles and the donor, a priest called Gaultier.

Take D 86 back to Mondoubleau. Fine view of the town on arrival.

MONTOIRE-SUR-LE-LOIR

Population 4 558
Michelin map 318: C-5, 232 fold 24 or 238 fold 1
Local map see VENDÔME

This charming riverside town developed round the priory of St-Gilles founded in the 7C. In the 9C Charles the Bald had a fort built to protect the country from Viking incursions. Pilgrims heading for Tours to pray at the tomb of St Martin used to stay the night in Montoire which was also on the route to Compostela in Spain. During this period leper houses were set up in Montoire and Troo.

Hitler meets Pétain

In mid-October 1940 German uniforms began appearing in ever increasing numbers, convoys of machine guns roved the streets and anti-aircraft batteries were set up on the hills. Military patrols erected barbed wire barriers across the roads and made house-to-house searches in Montoire. The electricity and telephones were cut off and German railwaymen replaced the staff of the SNCF, while people living in houses beside the railway line were ordered to close their shutters and stay indoors. A squadron of Messerschmidts frightened the cattle in the fields and two armoured trains bristling with guns patrolled the line from Vendôme to Tours, Bordeaux and Hendaye.

On 22 October Adolf Hitler and Pierre Laval met at Montoire station; in the event of an attack, Hitler's train could have withdrawn into the tunnel at St-Rimay to the east. Two days later, the famous meeting between Hitler and Maréchal Pétain took place, in which the German Chancellor tried to persuade the French Head of State to declare war against the United Kingdom.

SIGHTS

Castle ○ – A stone fortified wall encloses the 11C keep which stands on a spur of rock.

Bridge – There is a beautiful **view★** of the Loir flowing past old houses covered with wisteria where weeping willows trail their tendrils in the water among the fishing boats moored to the banks.

Renaissance houses – Two Renaissance houses stand side by side on place Clemenceau; the larger, with mullioned windows and high dormer windows, is also the older. There are two others: the 16C Antoine-Moreau Hospital in rue St-Laurent and, in rue St-Oustrille, the Maison du Jeu de Quilles, which owes its name the skittle-game house to the columns decorating the façade.

Fresco in chapelle St-Gilles

S. Sauvignier/MICHELIN

★Chapelle St-Gilles – The main gate opens on to the apse of an elegant Romanesque chapel which belonged to a Benedictine priory of which the poet Ronsard was once head. He left in October 1585 to visit his other priories, Ste-Madeleine de Croixval and St-Cosme, near Tours, where he died two months later. The chapel and the prior's lodging are set against a pleasant backdrop of lawns and yew trees.

★★Mural paintings – The paintings are to be found in the apse and transepts which are shaped like a clover leaf. Each half-dome, roof vault bears a figure of Christ painted at a different date. The oldest (first quarter of the 12C) in the apse shows a very majestic Christ surrounded by Angels; this is the **Christ of the Apocalypse.**

In the south transept is another 12C Christ, handing the keys to St Peter *(missing)*; this figure shows Byzantine influence in the tight and symmetrical folds of the garments.

The third figure in the north transept dates from the 13C and shows Christ with the Apostles at Pentecost; the more contrived attitudes and the colours – white, ochre and the blue of the haloes – are typical of the early local school. Note too the paintings on the arches of the crossing, particularly the Battle of the Virtues and Vices on the western arch.

Station ⊙ – This is where the Franco-German meeting took place on 24 October 1940.

Musikenfête ⊙ – *Espace de l'Europe, quartier Marescot*. In this show-museum of traditional music, 500 instruments come to life.

Summer street music – During the 2nd week in July, it is the turn of violins, double basses and other instruments; then from mid-August onwards, the International Folklore Festival takes over.

MONTRÉSOR★

Population 362
Michelin map 317: Q-6, 238 SE of fold 14 or 4037 G5

This interesting village with its Renaissance château and Gothic church is reflected in the River Indrois. The old market in the town is a timber-framed construction and a handsome 16C house with a watchtower in the main street is now the town hall.

Montrésor has been named one of *Les plus beaux villages de France* (the most beautiful French villages), an association which includes 140 outstanding villages selected for their beautiful setting, their fine buildings and lovely surroundings.

A visit to the Chartreuse du Liget and the church in Nouans-les-Fontaines, both situated less than 10km/6mi from Montrésor, is highly recommended.

★ **Château** ⊙ – The curtain wall with its ruined towers belongs to the fortress built by Fulk Nerra in the 11C; within it at the centre of a charming, romantic park stands the residence built in the early 16C by **Imbert de Bastarnay**, Lord of Montrésor from 1493, adviser to several kings of France and grandfather to Diane de Poitiers. This building has mullioned windows on the south front facing the river, gabled dormers and two machicolated towers. From the curtain wall above the river there is an attractive **view** of the valley and the houses of the town. In 1849 the château was restored by **Count Xavier Branicki**, a Polish émigré who accompanied Prince Napoleon to Constantinople during the Crimean War and tried to raise a Polish regiment.

The furnishings are as they were at the time of Branicki: his shooting trophies decorate the entrance hall; military souvenirs and medals and pictures by Polish and French painters are exhibited throughout. Also of interest are low-relief sculptures in wood depicting the battles of John III Sobieski of Poland (17C), a boudoir containing Italian Primitives and gold and silver plate.

Church – The church was built between 1519 and 1541 in the Gothic style – only the doorway is Renaissance and was originally a collegiate foundation set up by Imbert de Bastarnay, who built the church to house his tomb. The **Bastarnay tomb**★ in the nave consists of three recumbent figures in white marble – Imbert, his wife and his son – resting on a base decorated with statues of the 12 Apostles. Of the same date are two windows and the choir stalls, the latter in Renaissance style and richly decorated with medallions and misericords. In the chancel chapel *(left)* is a painting of the Annunciation by Philippe de Champaigne (17C).

EXCURSIONS

La Corroirie – Along the road to Loches (D 760), at the bottom of a small valley, behind a screen of trees *(left)* stands a building belonging to the charter house which was fortified in the 15C. Clearly visible are the fortified gate and the square machicolated tower with drawbridge.

Chartreuse du Liget – Slightly further on, alongside the road, on the eastern edge of Loches Forest, stands the great wall of the **charter house** ⊙. The elegant 18C **gateway**★ is flanked by numerous outbuildings which give an idea of the size and wealth of the abbey in the days preceding the Revolution.

The abbey was founded in the 12C by Henry II of England in expiation, it is said, for the murder of Thomas Becket, Archbishop of Canterbury. It was sold as State property at the end of the 18C and mostly demolished. Nonetheless the few traces which remain suggest how large and impressive the abbey complex must have been.

Walk down the central path.

In front of the house are the ruins *(left)* of the 12C church, behind which still stands one side of the great cloisters built in 1787. In the cell walls are the hatches through which the monks used to receive their meals.

Chapelle St-Jean-du-Liget ⊙ – *Return to the Loches road and 1km/0.5mi E turn left.* Standing alone in the middle of a field is an unusual round 12C building where the first monks of the charter house probably lived. The interior is decorated with some Romanesque frescoes depicting the Tree of Jesse, the Nativity, the Crucifixion and the Resurrection, as well as the Presentation and the Dormition of the Blessed Virgin. Note the soft colours and the serenity pervading the various scenes.

★VALLÉE DE L'INDROIS

From Nouans-les-Fontaines to Azay-sur-Indre

33km/20mi along D 760 and D 10 – about 2hr

The River Indrois winds its picturesque way westwards through the clay and chalk of the Montrésor marshland *(gâtine)* to join the Indre. Its course is lined by willows, alders and poplars and lush green meadows. The sunny slopes are planted with fruit trees, in orchards or espaliers, and a few vines.

Nouans-les-Fontaines – The 13C church in this village harbours a masterpiece of Primitive art (behind the high altar): the **Deposition★★**, or *Pietà of Nouans*, by Jean Fouquet. This vast painting on wood (2.36x1.47m/8x5ft) is one of the finest late-15C French masterpieces. The deliberately neutral colours, the resigned features of the characters and their majestic attitude make this a moving composition indeed.

Coulangé – At the entrance of this pleasant hamlet stands *(right)* the bell-tower of the old parish church (12C). On the opposite river bank are the remains of the fortifications of the Benedictine abbey of Villeloin.
⊚ Further on, the road *(D 10)* offers scenic views of the lake at Chemillé-sur-Indrois and the countryside east of Genillé (swimming, fishing, pedalos).

Genillé – The houses climb up from the river to the late-15C château with its corner towers and dovecot. The church presents a striking belfry with a stone spire and, inside, an elegant 16C Gothic chancel.

St-Quentin-sur-Indrois – The town occupies one of the best sites in the valley. East of the village the road *(D 10)* offers a fine view south of Loches Forest before joining the valley of the River Indre at Azay-sur-Indre.

Azay-sur-Indre – *See LOCHES: Excursions.*

MONTREUIL-BELLAY★

Population 4 112
Michelin map 317: I-6, 232 fold 33 or 4049 I6

The little town of Montreuil-Bellay, occupying a charming **site★** beside the Thouet on the border of the Poitou and Anjou regions, has retained its authentic medieval character. From the east bank of the river and bridge there are good views of the château and church.

Montreuil-Bellay

★★ CHÂTEAU ⊙

In front of the castle stretches the picturesque place des Ormeaux *(parking space)*. Imposing walls, pleasant gardens and remarkable furnishings are the main features of Montreuil Château. Beyond the **barbican**, inside the fortified gateway, stands the graceful residence built by the Harcourt family in the 15C. From the courtyard terrace there are fine views of the church, the château and the grounds which dip in great steps down to the river.

The **medieval kitchen** with its central fireplace like the one at Fontevraud *(see p 192)* was slightly altered in the 15C and is still in perfect condition, with a set of copper pans and a kitchen range (18C) with seven fire boxes fuelled by charcoal.

The 15C **canons' lodge** has four staircase turrets with conical roofs serving four separate sets of rooms, each consisting of living rooms over a storeroom (one was converted into a steam room) for the canons who served in the castle chapel.

Recalcitrant vassals

In 1025 **Fulk Nerra**, Count of Anjou, gave this stronghold to his vassal Berlay (distorted into Bellay), who made it into a powerful fortress. A century later, safe behind their stout walls, his successors plotted and intrigued against their overlord. In 1151, one of them, Giraud, held out for a whole year before he capitulated to Geoffrey Plantagenet, who then razed the keep which he had just taken with the aid of an early incendiary bomb, made by sealing a vessel full of oil, heating it to burning point and firing it at the keep with a mangonel.

When the Plantagenets acceded to the throne of England and thus became the main enemy of the King of France, the Berlays (who later became the Du Bellays) pledged allegiance to their immediate overlord; Philippe Auguste thereupon besieged their castle and demolished it.

The **château neuf** was built in the 15C. It features a beautiful staircase turret decorated with mullioned windows protected by delicately carved mock balustrades. The rooms in the château are 7m/23ft high and fully furnished. The dining room (49m²/527sq ft) has painted ceiling beams. The little **oratory** decorated with frescoes is late 15C. Visitors see the bedchamber of the **Duchess of Longueville**, Prince Condé's sister, who was one of the main instigators behind the Fronde uprising and was exiled by Louis XIV to Montreuil where she lived in luxurious style. In the Grand Salon there is a Brussels tapestry and a German marquetry cupboard; in the small music salon there is a superb bureau made by the famous cabinetmaker Boulle (1642-1732), inlaid with copper and tortoiseshell.

In the vaulted **cellar** the brotherhood of the Sacavins holds its meetings; it was founded in 1904 by the then owner of the castle, Georges de Grandmaison, to advertise Anjou wine. The winepress, into which the grapes were poured directly from the courtyard through a trapdoor, was still in use at the beginning of the last century.

Collégiale Notre-Dame – The church was built as the seigneurial chapel between 1472 and 1484 and has astonishingly sturdy walls and buttresses. Note the black mourning band in the nave and the private oratory for the owner of the castle.

TOWN WALK

As you come out of the castle, turn right onto rue du Marché, then follow rue du Tertre.

Les Nobis – Deep in the vegetation beside the Thouet are the ruins of the church of St-Pierre which was burnt down by the Huguenots in the 16C; the Romanesque apse is decorated with carved capitals. Nearby are two wings of some 17C cloisters.

Walk up the St-Pierre steps and turn right.

Maison Dovalle – *69 rue Dovalle*. The façade of this 16C house was altered in the 18C. The watchtower in the garden gives a fine view of the towers of the château, the Thouet Valley and in the far distance, Le Puy-Notre-Dame. The building is named after the Romantic poet **Charles Dovalle** (1807-29) whose collected works, *Le Sylphe*, were published posthumously with a preface by Victor Hugo.

Continue along rue Dovalle to reach *(on the left)* long stretches of the medieval wall; a path then leads to the **Porte St-Jean**, a 15C gate flanked by two large rusticated towers.

Proceed along rue Nationale, the town's high street; at the other end stands the Porte Nouvelle.

Musée de la Soie vivante ⊙ – Housed inside the Chapelle des Petits Augustins, near the 17C church and a herb garden, this museum shows the process of silkworm breeding.

Eating out

BUDGET

La Grange à Dîme – *Rue du Château* – ☎ *02 41 50 97 24* – *closed Christmas to 15 Jan, Sun evening and some days off season* – *booking essential* – *fixed menu 19.06€*. This 15C tithe barn boasting a superb timber roof in the shape of a ship's hull creates a conducive atmosphere for the enjoyment of delicious local specialities accompanied by *fouées*, bread rolls baked in wood-fired ovens.

Where to stay

BUDGET

Camping Les Nobis – *Les Nobis* – ☎ *02 41 52 33 66* – www.camping-les-nobis.com – *open Easter to Sep* – *165 places* – *16.77€*. Located at the foot of the castle walls, this 4ha/10-acre campsite lies in a pleasant verdant setting on the edge of the River Thouet. Possibility of hiring mobile homes. Numerous activities in summer.

MODERATE

Demeure des Petits Augustins – *Place des Augustins* – ☎ *02 41 52 33 88* – *closed Nov to Mar* – *3 rooms 38.11/54.55€*. Situated in the town centre, this elegant hotel is housed in a former 17C private mansion listed as a historic monument.

Les Gastines – *49260 Saint-Just-sur-Dive* – *7km/4.3mi NE of the town via D 160* – ☎ *02 41 67 39 39* – *closed Dec to Easter* – *5 rooms 45.73/58€*. Attractive, peaceful hotel with very comfortable rooms and a heated swimming pool.

EXCURSIONS

Ancienne abbaye d'Asnières ⊘ – *7.5km/5mi NW along D 761 then right to Cizay*. On the northern edge of Cizay Forest are the evocative ruins of what was once an important monastery founded in the 12C. The tall and graceful **chancel**★ with its delicately ribbed vaulting is, like the chancel of the church of St-Serge in Angers, a perfect specimen of Angevin Gothic art. The Abbot's Chapel, which was added in the 15C, has a pointed recess decorated with trefoils and festoons and a 14C Crucifix.

Le Puy-Notre-Dame – *7km/4.3mi W along D 77*. The **collegiate church**★, built in the 13C, is a remarkable example of Angevin architecture. The tower with its stone spire above the south transept is decorated with mouldings forming a recess containing a very beautiful statue of the Virgin (16C). On the north side of the church, enclosed in a cylindrical building, is the well.

In the Middle Ages people came from all over France to venerate the Virgin Mary's girdle, a relic brought back from Jerusalem in the 12C. The tall, narrow nave and aisles lend majesty to the interior; the vaulting in the chancel is ornamented with lierne and tierceron ribs. The carved stalls beyond the high altar are 16C.

Nature lovers: stay within the authorised areas in parks and gardens. Avoid collecting rare plant species and, if you cut a few flowers belonging to the more common species, take care to leave behind the roots and bulbs in the earth.

MONTRICHARD★

Population 3 624
Michelin map 318: E-7 or 238 fold 14

From the river bank and bridge over the Cher there is a good **view** of this town and its medieval houses clustered around the church below the crumbling keep.
The north bank above the town is pitted with quarries which have now been transformed into dwellings, caves for growing mushrooms and cellars for storing renowned sparkling wines.

TOWN WALK

★**Donjon** – The square keep which stands on the edge of the plateau above the River Cher is enclosed by the remains of its curtain wall and by a complex system of ramparts which protected the entrance. It was built c 1010 by Fulk Nerra, reinforced with a second wall in 1109 and then with a third in 1250. Despite having been reduced in height by 4m/13ft on the orders of Henri IV in 1589 for having fallen into the hands of the Catholic League at one stage, the keep still evokes its distant past.

Museums ⊘ retrace the archaeological history of the town and the surrounding area.

Enjoy the fine **panorama**★★ of Montrichard and the Cher Valley.

Église Ste-Croix – The church, which was originally the castle chapel, stands below the keep at the top of the flight of steps known as Grands Degrés Ste-Croix. The façade is decorated with elegant Romanesque arches; the arches of the porch are ornamented with a twisted torus. The elegant doorway is also Romanesque. **Jeanne de France**, the daughter of Louis XI, and her young cousin, the Duke of Orléans, were married in this chapel in 1476.

Old houses – There are several picturesque old façades up by the keep. **Hôtel d'Effiat** in rue Porte-au-Roi, which was built in the late 15C-early 16C, has Gothic decor with a few Renaissance elements. In the 16C it was the residence of Jacques de Beaune-Sem-blançay, Treasurer to Anne of Brittany and then to Louise of Savoy, the mother of François I. The mansion has retained the name of its last owner, the Marquis d'Effiat, who at his death (1719) presented it to the town to be converted into an old people's home.

H. Dewynter/MICHELIN

Montrichard – House with half-timbered façade

On the corner of rue du Pont stands the **Maison de l'Ave Maria** (16C) which has three gables and finely carved beams. Opposite are the Petits Degrés Ste-Croix *(steps)* which lead to some troglodyte dwellings. Further on, at the corner of rue du Prêche, stands the 11C stone façade of the **Maison du Prêche** (Sermon House).

Caves Monmousseau ⊘ – These cellars (15km/9.3mi of underground galleries) are particularly interesting as they present age-old traditional methods alongside modern, more sophisticated techniques, known as the **Dom Pérignon method**.

Église de Nanteuil – *On the road to Amboise (D 115)*. This church is a tall Gothic building with a Flamboyant doorway; the apses are Romanesque decorated with carved capitals. The high, narrow nave features Angevin vaulting.

Above the entrance porch is a chapel built by Louis XI, which can be entered up internal or external flights of steps.

There is a long-standing tradition of a pilgrimage to the Virgin Mary of Nanteuil on Whit Monday.

Jeanne de France's wedding

The 12-year-old bride, who was ugly and deformed, held no attraction for Louis d'Orléans who had been forced into the marriage by the King. Knowing that his daughter could not bear a child, Louis XI hoped in this way to bring to an end the Orléans line, a junior branch of the Valois family which chafed at royal authority.

Events, however, took a different course. In 1498 Louis XI's son, Charles VIII, died accidentally at Amboise leaving no heir since his sons had died in infancy. As the King's nearest relative Louis d'Orléans acceded to the throne as Louis XII. In his will Charles VIII had stipulated that the new King should marry his widow, Anne of Brittany.

Repudiated, Jeanne devoted herself to a life of good works; she withdrew to Bourges where she founded a religious order.

Eating out

Le Bistrot de la Tour – *34 r. de Sully* – ☎ *02 54 32 07 34 – closed Mon evening, Tue evening and Sun – 13.60/19€.* A pleasant place to stop and eat in a shady square. Plain but comfortable setting and a friendly welcome. Simple, unpretentious cooking at reasonable prices.

Where to stay

MODERATE

Chambre d'hôte Manoir de la Salle du Roc – *69 rte de Vierzon – 1.5km/1mi N of Montrichard on D 62* – ☎ *02 54 32 73 54 – 5 rooms 60/110€.* A tree-lined drive leads to this manor house, built on a rocky outcrop and set in a park with an orangery, ornamental ponds, lakes, statues and 500 different roses. The rooms are sumptuous, and book-lovers may be given access to the owner's personal library.

EXCURSIONS

Chissay-en-Touraine – *1km/0.5mi W on D 176.* The **Distillerie Fraise-Or** ⊙ presents traditional methods used for making liqueurs and fruit brandies which are typical of the region.

Bourré – *3km/2mi E.* The road carves a sinuous course between the north bank of the River Cher and the steep cliff face. The practice of digging underground galleries appears to have been widespread here since the days of Roman Antiquity and the local stone, tufa (*tuffeau*, also called *pierre de Bourré*) has often been used in the construction of châteaux. However, these quarries were gradually abandoned and subsequently used as wine cellars or mushroom beds. Among the latter, the most fascinating is undoubtedly the **Caves champignonnières des Roches** ⊙. At a depth of 50m/164ft, visitors will discover the strange and silent kingdom of mushrooms, lit by the glow of torchlights, where the *pleurotus* (oyster mushrooms), button mushroom, shiitake and *pied-bleu* varieties thrive in darkness.

La Ville souterraine ⊙ – *Champignonnières des Roches.*
⊡ This is the lively reconstruction of a village square with its church, town hall and school: a dog is pushing a door open, a housewife is looking out of her window, a pair of clogs are waiting on the window sill... the whole scene is set in stone and in time!

Thésée – *10km/6mi E along D 176.* West of the village stand the remains of the Gallo-Roman settlement of Tasciaca beside the Roman road from Bourges to Tours. During the 1C-3C it prospered from the making and selling of ceramic ware. Known as Les Maselles, the settlement extended over the area of modern Thésée and Pouillé. The buildings were made out of the soft local limestone, their stone courses laid conventionally or in herringbone pattern, reinforced with brick at their base and corners.

Musée archéologique ⊙ – Housed in the town hall (an 18C wine-grower's property in the middle of a splendid 7ha/18-acre park), the museum's archaeological collection consists of objects excavated from the sanctuary *(fanum)* and from the numerous potteries unearthed on either side of the river. Ex-votos, statuettes, coins, jewellery, buckles as well as ceramics, some of them signed, all help to evoke the life of those who once dwelt here on the banks of the Cher.

Château du Gué-Péan ⊙ – *13km/8.1mi E along D 176 then D 21.* The château is isolated in a quiet wooded valley; a picnic area has been set up in the grounds. It was built as a country house in the 16C and 17C but the plan is that of a feudal castle: three ranges of buildings round a closed courtyard with a huge round tower at each corner, surrounded by a dry moat and reached by a stone bridge. The detail is more decorative; the tallest tower (the other three were never completed) is capped with a bell-shaped roof and delicate machicolations; the other buildings, with arcades and elegant windows flanked by pilasters, are roofed in the French manner *(access to the watch-path).*
The rooms inside are furnished in the style of Louis XV and Louis XVI; Germain Pilon designed the Renaissance chimney-piece in the Grand Salon. The library houses handwritten letters and historical souvenirs. *Access to the sentry walk.*

Château de Montpoupon ⊙ – *12km/7.5mi S along D 764.* Only the towers remain of the original 13C fortress on this site. The main building, which has mullioned windows and Gothic-style gables, was built in the 15C, whereas the **fortified gatehouse** is early 16C.
Seen from the road, the whole complex conveys unmistakable elegance. A visit to the château includes the gatehouse, as well as several rooms in the main building including the fine Chambre du Maréchal (bedchamber).

A hunting museum, **Musée du Veneur**, evokes the daily life of a gentleman-hunter as well as activities linked with hunting, such as forestry, animal breeding, crafts (manufacture of hunting horns, saddlery, farriery, hunting costumes, livery buttons etc). An extensive collection of exhibits is devoted to the history of the Montpoupon Hunt which was active from 1873 to 1949.

The **outbuildings★**, which house reconstructed apartments with furniture originally in the castle, offer an excellent demonstration of the way the castle was run in the last century. The kitchen, with its oven and copper pans, was still in use in 1978; the laundry displays delicate garments, decorated with pleats and edged with lace, such as they were worn in the 19C.

The nearby **stables** still display a few carriages and the saddle and harness rooms present the harnesses used in the old days.

ORLÉANS★

Conurbation 263 292
Michelin map 318: I-4, 237 fold 40, 238 fold 5 or 4045 C4

In spite of having no castle, Orléans has a lot to offer visitors, its cathedral, its old town and Classical façades, its splendid fine arts museum, and its beautiful parks and rose gardens.

Once the capital of France, Orléans is today the capital of the Centre region (an economic division of France) and an important administrative and university town.

The **Fêtes de Jeanne d'Arc**, which are held every spring, date back to 1435 and are the occasion of great rejoicing on the part of the townspeople in celebration of their deliverance from the English.

From the Carnutes to Joan of Arc – The Gauls considered the land of the Carnutes to be the centre of their territory, Gaul; each year the Druids held their great assembly there and it was at Cenabum (Orléans) that the signal was given to revolt against Caesar in 52 BC.

A Gallo-Roman city soon rose from the Gaulish ruins. In June 451 it was besieged by Attila the Hun, but the inhabitants, inspired by their bishop, St Aignan, succeeded in driving off the invaders.

During the 10C and 11C Orléans was one of the focal points of the Capet monarchy.

THE SIEGE OF 1428-1429

This memorable siege was one of the great episodes in the history of France; it marks the rebirth of a country and a people who were sinking into despair.

The forces engaged – From the early 15C the defences of Orléans had been set up to repel any English attack. The city wall was composed of 34 towers *(tours)* and was divided into six sections, each defended by 50 men. All the townspeople took part in the defence of the city either by fighting as soldiers or by maintaining the walls and ditches. In all about 10 000 men were involved under the orders of the Governor of Orléans, **Raoul de Gaucourt**, and his captains.

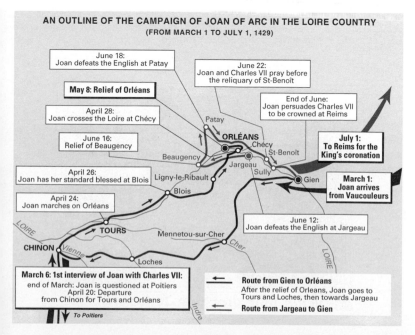

AN OUTLINE OF THE CAMPAIGN OF JOAN OF ARC IN THE LOIRE COUNTRY
(FROM MARCH 1 TO JULY 1, 1429)

June 18:
Joan defeats the English at Patay

June 22:
Joan and Charles VII pray before the reliquary of St-Benoît

May 8: Relief of Orléans

End of June:
Joan persuades Charles VII to be crowned at Reims

April 28:
Joan crosses the Loire at Chécy

June 16:
Relief of Beaugency

**July 1:
To Reims for the King's coronation**

April 26:
Joan has her standard blessed at Blois

**March 1:
Joan arrives from Vaucouleurs**

April 24:
Joan marches on Orléans

June 12:
Joan defeats the English at Jargeau

March 6: 1st interview of Joan with Charles VII:
end of March: Joan is questioned at Poitiers
April 20: Departure from Chinon for Tours and Orléans

Route from Gien to Orléans
After the relief of Orleans, Joan goes to Tours and Loches, then towards Jargeau

Route from Jargeau to Gien

Patay · ORLÉANS · Chécy · St-Benoît · Beaugency · Jargeau · Sully · Gien · Ligny-le-Ribault · Blois · TOURS · Mennetou-sur-Cher · CHINON · Loches · To Poitiers

During the summer of 1428 the commander of the English army, the **Earl of Salisbury**, had destroyed the French strongholds along the Loire and gained control of the river downstream from Orléans. His army consisted of 4 000 men-at-arms and 1 200 archers recruited in France, in all over 5 000 men.

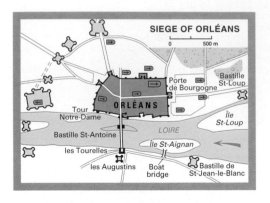

SIEGE OF ORLÉANS

The struggle began on 17 October when the English began pounding the city with bombards and heavy cannon. On the south side of the town there was a bridge spanning the Loire which was defended at its southern end by the Tourelles Fort. On 24 October, the English captured Les Tourelles but as Salisbury was inspecting the grounds, he was killed by a cannon-ball thought to have been fired from the tower of the church of Notre-Dame.

Orléans was now cut off from the rest of the French Kingdom. On 8 November the majority of the English forces withdrew to Meung-sur-Loire and the French took the opportunity to raze the other suburbs to prevent the English from re-establishing themselves there. The besiegers were not inactive, however. They surrounded the town with a series of trenches commanded by small forts.

The two sides settled down to a war of attrition punctuated by skirmishes outside the gates. From time to time feats of arms raised the morale of the besieged. The prowess and cunning of Master-Gunner Jean de Montesclerc became legendary: he killed many English soldiers and would often pretend to die so that when he reappeared the dismay and alarm of the English were redoubled. Two bombards called Rifflart and Montargis rose to fame owing to their fire power and their range which caused great damage on the south bank of the Loire.

However, food grew scarce and in February 1429 part of the garrison left. It seemed that the English were close to victory and in Orléans, Dunois was the only person to remain optimistic.

The arrival of Joan of Arc – In April 1429 Joan of Arc persuaded the future **Charles VII** to rescue Orléans. She left Blois with the royal army, crossed the river and approached Orléans along the south bank, meaning to take the English by surprise, but the river was too high and the army had to return to the bridge at Blois. Meanwhile, Joan and a few companions crossed by boat a few miles upstream of Orléans at Chécy and entered the town on 29 April through the Porte de Bourgogne. She was greeted by an enthusiastic crowd and issued her famous ultimatum to the English, that they should surrender to her, the young girl sent by God to drive them out of France, the keys of all the French towns that they had captured.

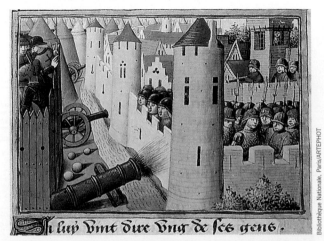

The Siege of Orléans

Eating out

BUDGET

Espace Canal – *6 r. Ducerceau* – ☎ *02 38 62 04 30* – *closed 1-20 Aug, Mon evening, Tue evening, Wed evening, Sat lunchtime and Sun* – *reservation required* – *14.48€ lunch, 20.58/26.68€*. A great place to go for fine wines, with a decor which features metal and wood. Let the cellar master advise you which wine to sample, accompanied by a carefully chosen dish to complement it.

MODERATE

Dariole – *25 r. Étienne-Dolet* – ☎ *02 38 77 26 67* – *closed 25 Feb – 5 Mar, 4-27 Aug, Wed lunchtime, Sat lunchtime and Sun all day* – ✍ – *reservation recommended* – *16.77/30.49€*. This half-timbered house is near the elegant Hôtel Cabu (1550), now home to the Museum of History and Archaeology. The old-fashioned dining room is quite attractive, and in the summer months there is alfresco dining in the back garden. Traditional French fare.

L'Épicurien – *54 r. des Turcies* – ☎ *02 38 68 01 10* – *closed 1-21 Aug, Sun and Mon* – ✍ – *19.82/42.69€*. This restaurant lives up to its name as a place for pleasure-lovers. Fine, carefully prepared cuisine served in a dining room with exposed beams.

Where to stay

BUDGET

Chambre d'hôte Les Courtils – *R. de l'Ave* – *45430 Chécy* – *10km/6.2mi E of Orléans on N 460* – ☎ *02 38 91 32 02* – ✍ – *4 rooms 38/49€*. This lovely village house overlooks the Loire. The rooms are named after climbing plants and are furnished with floral fabrics, shades of beige and white, a blend of old and modern furniture and Sologne floor tiles. Small garden with terrace.

Chambre d'hôte Les Usses – *145 r. du Courtasaule* – *45760 Marigny-les-Usages* – *12km/7.5mi NE of Orléans towards Pithiviers on N 152* – ☎ *02 38 75 14 77* – *kris.marin@wanadoo.fr* – ▣ – ✍ – *3 rooms 45/50€*. In the heart of the countryside. A peaceful former peasant's house dating from 1850, surrounded by a lovely garden. Nice rooms with wooden furniture. Breakfast is served in the old stables, attractively restored using stone and wood. Two holiday cottages are available for longer stays.

MODERATE

Jackotel – *18 cloître St-Aignan* – ☎ *02 38 54 48 48* – *closed Sun and public holidays at lunchtime* – ▣ – *61 rooms 42.70/54.90€* – ☕ *5.80€*. Near the river in the old town, this hotel is set in the lovely peaceful St-Aignan Cloister, shaded by horse chestnut trees. The simply furnished rooms are comfortable and functional.

Shopping

Martin Pouret – *236 fg Bannier* – *45400 Fleury-les-Aubrais* – *3km/1.8mi N of Orléans on D 97* – ☎ *02 38 88 78 49* – *Mon-Fri 8am-noon, 1-5.30pm*. Founded in 1797, this is the only establishment in town which still makes wine vinegar according to the authentic Orléans method.

Leisure

Base de loisirs de l'Île Charlemagne – *45650 St-Jean-le-Blanc* – *2km/1.6mi E of town via the south bank and rue de la Levée* – ☎ *02 38 51 92 04* – *open all year*. The outdoor recreation area offers swimming (May-Aug), windsurfing boards, catamarans, sailing dinghies and kayaks for hire. Beach-ball, pony club and mountain bike trails.

Sit back and relax

La Chancellerie – *27 pl. du Martroi* – ☎ *02 38 53 57 54* – *Mon-Sat 7-1am*. A high-class café-restaurant run by the Erta family since 1957 and specialising in fine wines. One of the two brothers was the top wine steward in France (1973-74). Terrace in place du Martroi. A popular place to meet in town.

Mc Ewan's Café – *250 r. de Bourgogne* – ☎ *02 38 54 65 70* – *Mon-Sat 6pm-1am (summer: 3pm-1am)*. A lively Irish pub, run by a native of Marseille, where the most popular drinks are beer and Ricard. Rock and Breton music concerts three times a month. Friendly atmosphere.

Shannon Irish Pub – *Centre commercial Halles Châtelet* – ☎ *02 38 54 53 50* – *daily 5pm-3am*. A pub with typical Irish decor and a good choice of whiskeys and beers. Irish music.

L'Absinthe – *133 r. Marcel-Belot – 45160 Olivet –* ☎ *02 38 63 76 36 – Tue-Thu 7pm-1am, Fri-Sat 7pm-3am – reservation recommended at weekends*. A very fashionable place to go for a beer in Orléans. Choice of over 200 brews, of which 90% are Belgian. Friendly atmosphere and pleasant decor. Crêpes.

Jazz festival – If you are visiting Orléans around the end of June-early July, check the posters for the yearly jazz festival, and take in a concert!

The people of Orléans rallied and prepared for battle while Joan found herself up against the hostility of the captains and the Governor. On 4 May the royal army, which Dunois had rejoined, attacked the Bastille St-Loup without warning Joan. When she learned of it she made a sortie, raising her banner, and the French were victorious. On the morning of 6 May, Joan herself led the attack against the Augustins Fort. For a second time her spirited intervention threw the English into confusion as they were engaged in pursuing the retreating French troops. This second victory increased her popularity. Joan went on the offensive again on 7 May against the advice of the Governor who tried to bar her way. While fighting in the front line outside Les Tourelles she was wounded in the shoulder by a crossbow bolt. The English thought she was done for and Dunois suggested postponing the attack until the following day but, having had the wound dressed and prayed to the saints, Joan returned to the attack with her standard raised high. With renewed vigour the French hurled themselves into the fray against the English defence. The English garrison in the fort were caught in crossfire; they were forced to abandon the fort and surrender. On Sunday 8 May the English withdrew from the last forts and raised the siege. Joan was carried back into Orléans in triumph after her victory.

The defeat threw the English plans for invasion into disarray, and gave new confidence to the Dauphin and his army. On 18 June the French forces won the Battle of Patay.

TOWN WALK

The town centre owes its stately character to the vast expanse of place du Martroi, to the elegant arcades along rue Royale, to the 18C and 19C façades of the buildings and private mansions. However, the old town nearby offers a striking contrast with its medieval and Renaissance houses lining the lively pedestrianised streets right to the edge of the River Loire.

Hôtel Groslot – Built in 1550 by the bailiff of Orléans, Jacques Groslot, this large Renaissance mansion in red brick with diaper-work in black was subject to extensive remodelling in the 19C. Admire the delicate scrollwork on the staircase pillars and the two main entrances flanked by caryatids. This was the King's residence in Orléans: François II, who died here after opening the States-General in 1560, Charles IX, Henri III and Henri IV all stayed here.

On the other side of the building is the **garden** where the façade of the old chapel of St-Jacques (15C) has been re-erected. On the other side of the road stand the **Pavillons d'Escures**, town houses in brick with stone courses dating from the early 17C.

Place Ste-Croix, a vast symmetrical esplanade, bordered by neo-Classical façades and arcades, was laid out c 1840 when rue Jeanne-d'Arc was opened up. On the south side of the square there is a bronze statue of the Loire holding the fruits of the river valley in the folds of her dress. The 15C **Hôtel des Créneaux** was the town hall from the 16C to 1790.

Place du Martroi – This square marks the symbolic centre of the town and is adorned with a statue of Joan of Arc by Foyatier (1855). The name of the square is derived from the Latin word *martyretum* which was used to refer to the 6C Christian cemetery. On the west corner of rue Royale stands the old **Pavillon de la Chancellerie** which was built in 1759 by the Duke of Orléans to house his archives. A pedestrian alleyway leads to an underground car park, where vestiges of the Porte Bannier still stand.

Rue Royale – This broad street, lined with arcades, was opened up c 1755 when the Royal Bridge **(Pont George-V)** was built to replace the old medieval bridge which had stood 100m/110yd upstream in line with rue St-Catherine, the main street of the old medieval city.

Beyond the house and the two adjoining Renaissance façades on the right there is an arch leading into square Jacques-Boucher. Standing alone in the garden is the **Pavillon Colas des Francs**, an elegant little Renaissance building, where Boucher's grandson conducted his business; a room on the ground floor houses the archives, whereas another room upstairs was where the silver was kept.

Quai Fort-des-Tourelles – Opposite a statue of Joan of Arc standing in a small square are a commemorative cross and an inscription on the low wall beside the Loire which mark the site of the southern end of the medieval bridge and of the 15C Tourelles Fort, the capture of which by Joan of Arc led to the defeat of the English and the lifting of the siege. Fine **view**★ of the whole town.

Quai du Châtelet provides a quiet shaded walk beside the river. In Sully's time, early in the 17C, this was one of the busiest parts of town; it was from here that goods bound for Paris from the Loire Valley and the Massif Central were transferred from river to road, and from here that the six-day voyage downstream to Nantes was begun.

Rue de Bourgogne – This was the main east-west axis of the old Gallo-Roman city. Now largely pedestrianised, it is ideal for window shopping. There are several old façades: no 261 is a 15C stone house with a half-timbered gable.

Along the street is the **préfecture**, housed in a 17C Benedictine convent. Opposite in rue Pothier is the façade of the old **Salle des Thèses** (Thesis Hall), a 15C library, which is the only remnant of the University of Orléans where **Jean Calvin**, the religious reformer, studied law in 1528.

Église St-Aignan – The nave of this huge Gothic church, which was consecrated in 1509, was burnt down during the Wars of Religion leaving only the choir and the transepts. Note the 11C **crypt** ⊙.

SIGHTS

★**Cathédrale Ste-Croix** – This cathedral dedicated to the Holy Cross was begun in the 13C and construction continued until the 16C, although the building was partly destroyed by the Protestants in 1568. Henri IV, the first Bourbon king, being grateful to the town for having supported him, undertook to rebuild the cathedral in a composite Gothic style. The work went on throughout the 18C and 19C.

The **west front** has three large doorways with rose windows above them crowned by a gallery with open-work design. The skill of the masons can be seen in the unusually fine quality of the stonework. At the base of the two towers admire the delicacy of the spiral staircases, also with open-work design, at each of the four corners. The huge **doorway** has four gigantic statues of the Evangelists.

Interior – In the central chapel of the apse is a fine marble Virgin Mary by Michel Bourdin (early 17C), a sculptor born in Orléans.

Splendid early-18C **woodwork**★★ adorns the chancel and the stalls. It was made after designs of Jacques V Gabriel by Jules Degoullons, one of the decorators of Versailles and designer of the stalls in Notre-Dame, Paris.

In the **crypt** ⊙ are traces of the three buildings which predated the present cathedral, and two sarcophagi; one belonged to Bishop Robert de Courtenay (13C) who collected the most precious items in the **treasury**. Among these are two gold medallions (11C) decorated with cloisonné enamel in the Byzantine manner, which used to adorn the gloves worn by the Bishop of Orléans for ceremonies and processions; 13C gold and silverware; and 17C paintings by Vignon and Jouvenet.

North transept and east end – In the north transept is a rose window with the emblem of Louis XIV at the centre. Excavations at the base have revealed the old Gallo-Roman walls and part of a tower.

The east end with its flying buttresses and pinnacles is clearly visible from the gardens of the former episcopal palace, an 18C building which now houses the municipal library.

Campo Santo – To the left of the modern Fine Arts School (École Régionale des Beaux-Arts) is a graceful Renaissance portal and on the north side of this same building is a garden edged with an arcaded gallery. The garden was a cemetery outside the city walls in the 12C, whereas the galleries were added in the 16C *(exhibitions)*.

★★**Musée des Beaux-Arts** ⊙ – The variety and high standard of the collections displayed in this Fine Arts Museum, the oldest of which date back to the days of the French Revolution, make it one of France's most outstanding cultural venues. The paintings, sculptures and objets d'art provide a fascinating insight into European art from the 16C to the 20C.

The **second floor** is devoted to the Italian, Flemish and Dutch Schools, represented by works by Correggio *(Holy Family)*, Tintoretto *(Portrait of a Venetian)*, Annibale Carracci *(Adoration of the Shepherds)*, Van Dyck, Teniers and Ruysdael.

On the **first floor**, there are works from the 17C-18C French School: large religious paintings inspired by the Counter-Reformation, *St Charles Borromeo* by Philippe de Champaigne, *Triumph of St Ignatius* by Claude Vignon. The chiaroscuro technique is illustrated in *St Sebastian* from Georges de La Tour's studio. Among the 17C canvases are *Bacchus and Ariadne*, a rare mythological work by Le Nain, and *Astronomy* by La Hire. Masterpieces from Richelieu's château include Deruet's graceful, imaginative *Four Elements*. The collection of 18C portraits includes: *Mme de Pompadour* by Drouais; *The Engraver Moyreau* by Nonotte; the *Marquis of Lucker* by Louis Tocqué. Paintings by Hubert Robert *(Landscape with Ruined Tower, The Wash House)*, Boucher *(The Dovecot)* and Watteau (the unusual *Monkey Sculptor*) are also of interest.

ORLÉANS

Albert 1ᵉʳ (Pl.)	EY	
Abert 1ᵉʳ (R.)	EY	
Alexandre Martin (Bd)	EFY	
Alsace-Lorraine (R. d')	EY	
Antigna (R.)	DY	4
Arc (Pl. d')	EY	
Augustins (Quai des)	EZ	
Bannier (R.)	DY	
Bannier (R. du Fg)	DY	
Barentin (Quai)	DZ	
Bellebat (R. de)	FY	
Bothereau (R. R.)	FY	14
Bourdon Blanc (R.)	FYZ	
Bourgogne (R. de)	EFZ	
Brésil (R. du)	FY	16
Bretonnerie (R. de la)	DEY	17
Briand (Bd A.)	FY	19
Caban (R.)	DY	
Carmes (R. des)	DY	
Champ Rond (R. du)	FY	
Champ-de-Mars (Av.)	DZ	25
Champ St-Marc (Pl. du)	FY	
Charpenterie (R. de la)	EZ	34
Charretiers (R. des)	EZ	
Châteaudun (Bd de)	DY	
Château-Gaillard (R. du)	FY	
Châtelet (Pl. du)	EZ	
Châtelet (Quai du)	EZ	
Châtelet (Square du)	EZ	32
Chollet (R. Théophile)	EY	36
Claye (R. de la)	FY	38
Coligny (R.)	FZ	39
Cordiers (R. des)	FY	
Coulmiers (R. de)	DY	
Croix de Bois (R.)	DZ	
Croix-de-la-Pucelle (R.)	EZ	43
Croix Morin (Pl.)	DY	
Cypierre (Quai)	DZ	
Dauphine (Av.)	EZ	47
Desfriches (R.)	FYZ	
Dotel (R. Étienne)	EZ	49
Ducerceau (R.)	EZ	51
Dumois (Pl.)	DY	52
Dupanloup (R.)	EFY	53
Émile Zola (R.)	EY	
Escures (R. d')	EY	55
Étape (Pl. de l')	EY	56
Ételon (R. de l')	FY	57
Foch (R. du Mal.)	DY	
Folie (R. de la)	FZ	58
Fort Alleaume (Quai du)	FZ	
Fort-des-Tourelles (Q.)	EZ	60
Gambetta (Pl.)	DY	
Gaulle (Pl. du Gén.-de)	DZ	65
George V (Pont)	EZ	
Grands-Champs (R. des)	DY	
Gratteminot (R.)	DY	
Hallebarde (R. de la)	DY	70
Illiers (R. d')	DY	
Jaurès (Bd J.)	DZ	
Java (R. de)	FY	
Jean Zay (Av.)	FY	
Jeanne d'Arc (R.)	FY	
Joffre (Pont du Mar.)	DZ	
Jugan (R. J.)	FY	
Julien (R. S.)	DZ	
Lavedan (R. H.)	FY	
Lemaître (R. J.)	EFY	
Lionne (R. de la)	DY	
Madeleine (R. Fg)	DZ	88
Manufacture (R. de la)	FY	89
Martroi (Pl. du)	EY	
Motte-Sanguin (Bd de la)	FZ	95
Murlins (R. des)	DY	
N.-D.-de-Recouvrance (R.)	DZ	97
Oriflamme (R. de l')	FZ	98
Paris (Av. de)	EY	
Parisie (R.)	EZ	100
Patay (R. de)	DY	
Péguy (Sq. Ch.)	FZ	
Poirier (R. du)	EZ	106
Pte-Madeleine (R.)	DY	108
Pte-St-Jean (R.)	DY	109
Pothier (R.)	EZ	112
Prague (Quai)	DZ	113
Pressoir neuf (R. du)	FY	115
Proust (R. M.)	EY	
Rabier (R. F.)	EY	117
République (Pl.)	EZ	121
République (R. de la)	EY	
Rocheplatte (Bd)	DY	
Roi (Quai du)	FZ	
Royale (R.)	EZ	125
St-Aignan (Cloître)	FZ	
St-Charles (Pl.)	FZ	
St-Euverte (Bd)	FYZ	126
St-Euverte (R.)	FY	127
St-Jean (R. du Fg)	DY	
St-Laurent (Quai)	DZ	
St-Marc (R.)	FY	
St-Vincent (R. du Fg)	FY	
Ste-Catherine (R.)	EZ	135
Ste-Croix (Pl.)	EYZ	139
Secrétain (Av. R.)	DZ	140
Segellé (Bd de)	FY	141
Tabour (R. du)	EZ	145
Thinat (Pont René)	FZ	
Tour Neuve (R. de la)	FZ	147
Trévise (Av. de)	DZ	
Tudelle (R.)	DZ	
Vauquois (R. de)	DY	
Verdun (Bd de)	DY	152
Vieux-Marché (Pl.)	DZ	159
Vignat (R. E.)	EY	
Weiss (R. L.)	FY	160
Xaintrailles (R.)	DY	
6-juin 1944 (Pl. du)	FY	162

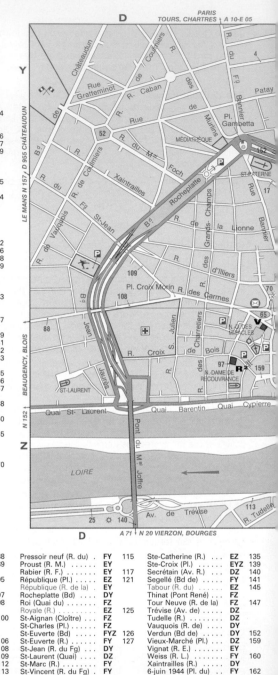

In the **Pastel Gallery** there are 18C portraits including works by Perronneau, Quentin La Tour, Chardin *(Self-Portrait with Spectacles)* and Nattier.

The rooms devoted to the **19C** offer a wealth of interesting collections covering neo-Classicism (Guérin, Gérard), Romanticism (Delacroix, Cogniet, Dauzats, Huet), Realism (Antigna) and pre-Impressionism (Daubigny, Boudin) up to the works of Gauguin. These collections are enhanced by a large display of sculptures.

The **modern art section**, housed in the basement, concentrates above all on sculpture: Rodin, Maillol, Bourdelle, Malfray and Gaudier-Brzeska. Early-20C art is present with paintings by Gromaire, Asseli, Soutine, Kisling and Kupka, whereas contemporary creation is reflected by artists such as Hélion, Le Gac, Garouste, Monory, Debré, Jan Voss etc.

Lastly, one gallery is entirely devoted to Max Jacob and his friends Picasso, Marie Laurencin and Roger Toulouse.

Ancien évêché	**FY B**	Collégiale		Musée
Ancienne Salle		St-Pierre-le-Puellier	**EFZ**	des Beaux-Arts .... **EY M¹**
des Thèses	**EZ E**	Église St-Aignan	**FZ**	Musée historique
Campo Santo	**EY**	Hôtel des Créneaux	**EZ R¹**	et archéologique ...... **EZ M²**
Cathédrale		Hôtel Groslot		Muséum .... **EY M³**
Ste-Croix	**EY**	(hôtel de ville)	**EY H**	Pavillon
Centre Charles Péguy	**EZ K**	Hôtel Toulin	**DZ R²**	de la Chancellerie ..... **EY X**
Centre		Maison de		Pavillons d'Escures ..... **EY**
Jeanne-d'Arc	**EY N**	Jeanne-d'Arc	**DZ V**	Préfecture .... **EZ P**

★ **Musée historique et archéologique** ⊙ – The Museum of History and Archaeology is housed in an elegant little mansion, **Hôtel Cabu** (1550), next to another Renaissance façade.

On the ground floor is the astonishing **Gallo-Roman treasure**★ from Neuvy-en-Sullias *(31km/19mi E of Orléans)* which consists of a series of expressive statues, a horse and a wild boar in bronze as well as a number of statuettes of great artistic value. The first floor is devoted to the Middle Ages and to the Classical period; there are sculptures from Germigny-des-Prés and St-Benoît-sur-Loire, souvenirs of Joan of Arc (15C German tapestry, 17C banner from the Joan of Arc Festival), as well as typical local ceramic ware. The second floor is occupied by local folklore, pewter ware, gold and silverware and clocks. A new exhibition room presents the history of the port of Orléans, describing the various industries associated with river traffic in the 18C-19C.

Charles Péguy (1873-1914)

Born in Orléans, Charles Péguy was the founder of the *Cahiers de la Quinzaine* (1900). He was known to be a committed poet and campaigner and his writings duly reflected the causes which he adopted and which he staunchly defended: the Dreyfus case, socialism, patriotism and Catholicism. He wrote several works devoted to the life of Joan of Arc, including a long play in 1897, followed up by *Le Mystère de la charité de Jeanne d'Arc* (1910) and *La Tapisserie de sainte Geneviève et de Jeanne d'Arc* (1912). With *La Tapisserie de Notre-Dame* (1913), Péguy signed "one of the most outstanding achievements in the history of French Christian poetry". He also produced a number of remarkable literary reviews, such as *Victor-Marie, comte Hugo*.

He was killed in Villeroy on 5 September 1914, at the beginning of the Battle of the Marne.

Centre Charles-Péguy ⊘ – This centre is housed in the old **Hôtel Euverte-Hatte**, which was built later during the reign of Louis XII. The rectangular windows are framed with Gothic friezes; the Renaissance arcade in the courtyard was added during the reign of François I. There is a library devoted to Péguy, his work and his literary, political and social environment. The Péguy Museum displays manuscripts and memorabilia.

★ **Maison de Jeanne d'Arc** ⊘ – The tall timber-framed façade contrasts with the modernity of the square, place du Général-de-Gaulle, which was heavily bombed in 1940. The building is a reconstruction of the house of Jacques Boucher, Treasurer to the Duke of Orléans, where Joan stayed in 1429. An audio-visual show on the first floor recounts the raising of the siege of Orléans by Joan of Arc on 8 May 1429; there are reproductions of period costumes and weapons of war.

Centre Jeanne-d'Arc ⊘ – The centre's resources include a book library, a film library and microfilm and photographic archives *(open to the public)*.

★ **Museum** ⊘ – The old museum, which has been completely restored and to which an extension has been added, now houses local and regional displays of a scientific and cultural nature.

Temporary exhibitions are held regularly on the ground floor. The four upper floors of the museum are devoted to the marine world, aquatic ecosystems (aquarium), reptiles and amphibians (vivarium), higher vertebrates (diorama on the Sologne region), mineralogy, geology, palaeontology and botany (greenhouses of temperate and tropical plants on the top floor). There are simultaneous displays in scientific workshops and a geology laboratory explaining various techniques including the art of keeping aquaria, stuffing animals and pressing plants. Complementary information may be obtained from a library and audio-visual and computer aids.

Hôtel Toutin ⊘ – The house was built in 1540 for Toutin, manservant to François I's son. In the small courtyard is a double Renaissance arcade covered in Virginia creeper and a statue of François I.

Collégiale St-Pierre-le-Puellier ⊘ – This 12C Romanesque collegiate church, now used to host **permanent exhibitions**, is at the heart of an old district of pedestrian streets.

EXCURSIONS

Gidy – *12km/8mi N. Take motorway A 10 and leave at the rest areas Aire d'Orléans-Saran direction Paris-Orléans or Aire d'Orléans-Gidy direction Orléans-Paris.*
Designed and created by the Geological and Mining Research Bureau (BRGM), the **géodrome** ⊘ is a garden of rocks representing an enormous relief map of the most remarkable geological features to be found in France. Eight hundred tons of rock have been laid out on but 1ha/2.5 acres of land along with the vegetation typical of each French region. A huge painted frieze 70m/230ft long illustrates a cross-section of French soil from the Alps to the Armorican Massif (Brittany).

Artenay – *20km/12.5mi N on N 20.* The entrance to this large town in the Beauce region is marked by a windmill-tower with a revolving roof (19C).
🎭 A Beauce farmhouse is the setting for the **Musée du Théâtre forain** ⊘, a museum devoted to the life of travelling theatre, which toured French towns and villages from the 19C to the 1970s. Scenery, puppets, posters and costumes combine to evoke the social, professional and family life of these wandering performers. A small theatre (200 seats) welcomes troupes who perform in the tradition of travelling theatre.
In the sheepfold there are two rooms on local archaeology and palaeontology.

★★ LA LOIRE BLÉSOISE

From Orléans to Blois

84km/52mi – about 6hr

Leave Orléans on avenue Dauphine (S of the town plan).

Nursery gardens and rose gardens line both sides of the road. Cross the Loiret which flows between wooded banks.

Olivet – Like the southern suburbs of Orléans between the Loiret and the Loire, the greater part of Olivet is given over to growing flowers, roses and ornamental plants. It is also a pleasant summer resort on the south bank of the Loiret, composed of elegant houses and old watermills, where people come for the fishing and canoeing.

Promenade des moulins – *Round trip of 5km/3mi from the bridge by the side road along the north bank of the Loiret going W and returning on D 14 going E.*
At the far end of the loop, two old mills straddle the river over their mill-races between the wooded banks of the Loiret, while ducks and swans glide up and down on the quiet river.

In Olivet take D 14 E to the Source Floral Park.

★★ Parc floral de la Source ⊘ – This park was laid out in the wooded grounds of a 17C château to host the 1967 Floralies Internationales horticultural exhibition. It covers 35ha/86 acres and is home to a wide variety of garden layouts, including symmetri-cally arranged flower beds, rockeries, wooded parkland and evergreen and flowering shrubs. As the seasons change, so does the display: in spring, the flower beds are in bloom with tulips, daffodils, then **irises★** (more than 900 varieties), rhododendrons and azaleas; mid-June to mid-July is when the rose bushes are at their best; in July and August the gardens are ablaze with summer flowers; in September the late-flowering rose bushes come into bloom with the dahlias; and finally it is the turn of the chrysan-themums, which are displayed in the exhibition hall.

This park, a real showcase for local horticulture, is a delight for everyone, from people walking through it feasting their eyes on the display to amateur gardeners, for whom it is very instructive. From the **mirror★**, a semicircular ornamental lake, there is a good view of the château and the dainty Louis XIII embroidery pattern adorning the lawns. The **Loiret spring ★**, a short tributary of the south bank of the Loire, can be seen bubbling up from the ground. The spring is in fact the resurgence of the part of the river which disappears underground near St-Benoît-sur-Loire, some 58km/36mi upstream. Throughout the year, flocks of cranes and emus and herds of deer roam the park, while flamingoes stalk by the banks of the Loiret.

The **Butterfly House** is a charming tropical garden with many colourful exotic species.

Every year, in mid-September, the Parc Floral de la Source serves as a presti-gious backdrop to an international exhibition devoted to fuchsia and other exotic plant species, organised by national and regional horticultural societies (Orléans, Le Loiret).

Take D 14 heading W.

Neat little houses with pretty gardens line the road to Cléry.

Parc Floral de la Source

S. Sauvignier/MICHELIN

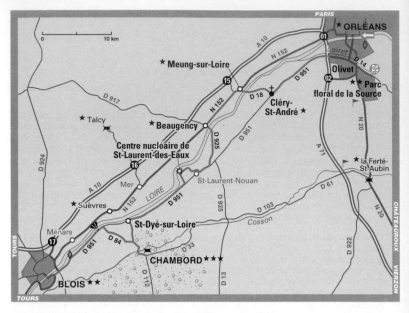

★ Basilique de Cléry-St-André – *See Basilique de CLÉRY-ST-ANDRÉ.*

★ Meung-sur-Loire – *See MEUNG-SUR-LOIRE.*

Take N 152 to Beaugency; soon the large towers of the St-Laurent nuclear power station are visible on the horizon.

★ Beaugency – *See BEAUGENCY.*

Leave Beaugency S along D 925 and turn right onto D 951. Just before St-Laurent-Nouan, follow the road leading to the power station.

Centre nucléaire de production d'électricité de St-Laurent-des-Eaux ⊙ – The nuclear power station, involving four plants, is sited on a peninsula jutting out into the Loire. Its annual output of 4 billion kWh accounts for 2.7% of the country's needs and 90% of the annual energy consumption of the six *départements* forming the Centre *région*. The power station's waste water is used to heat an extensive area of greenhouses nearby.

St-Dyé-sur-Loire – Legend has it that this little place was founded in the 6C by St Deodatus (also known as St Dié or St Dyé). There are many reminders of the days when St-Dyé's riverside was busy with the activity associated with the construction of the great Château de Chambord; 13C fortified walls looming above the quayside, little craftsmen's houses in rue de Chambord and a number of grander buildings from the 15C, 16C and 17C where their masters resided. The 16C **church** ⊙, with its impressive belfry-porch, contains the tombs of St Deodatus and his companion, St Baudemir, and has a Revolutionary inscription in the chancel. The **Maison de la Loire** ⊙ in the 17C Hôtel Fonteneau houses the tourist office as well as exhibits relating to the Loire and its valley.

The road enters the walled Chambord estate (speed restrictions).

The stately façade of the Château de Chambord comes into sight suddenly at the end of an avenue making a striking impression.

★★★ Château de Chambord – *See Château de CHAMBORD.*

Take D 84 NW to Montlivault on the banks of the Loire.

The road which follows the embankment offers beautiful **views★** of this green and leafy setting: poplars, fields of asparagus, tulips and gladioli. On the north bank stand the silhouettes of the Château de Ménars, then Blois with its basilica, cathedral and castle.

★★ Blois – *See BLOIS.*

PITHIVIERS

Population 9 242
Michelin map 318: K-2, 237 fold 41 or 4045 E2

Pithiviers is situated on the border between the Beauce and the Gâtinais regions. Its main economic activities are related to local products – cereals and sugar beet (sugar refinery at Pithiviers-le-Vieil) – but other industries are currently being introduced.

The rectangle containing the old town is enclosed on four sides by a shaded tree-lined avenue. It is pleasant to wander along the quiet old streets which radiate from place du Martroi, an irregular triangle of open space in the shadow of the great tower of the church of St-Salomon.

The city of Pithiviers has given its name to a delicious cake found in most French *boulangeries*, consisting of oblong squares of light puff pastry with an almond paste filling. St George's Fair in April is the rendezvous of gourmets.

Musée des Transports ⊙ – The Railway Museum was founded by volunteer workers in the old terminus of the Tramways à Vapeur du Loiret line. The 0.60m/2ft wide tracks designed by Decauville, who promoted this particular width for French railways, would carry passengers and sugar beet from Pithiviers to Toury *(32km/20mi W)* until 1951. Subsequently, the passenger service was dropped and the trains transported only sugar beet between 1951 and 1964.

The museum contains several steam locomotives (seven of which belong to France's national heritage), two electrical tramways and a rail car running on both electricity and oil (1923). The oldest locomotive, a Schneider model dating from 1870, is still in perfect working order.

Visitors can end their tour of the museum by taking a short trip (4km/2.5mi) in a train.

Musée municipal ⊙ – Predominantly local memorabilia are attractively displayed on the first floor of this municipal museum. The first room, on the South Sea Islands, adds a touch of the exotic. Another room is devoted to famous local people, to the more or less legendary origins of the culinary specialities of Pithiviers and to saffron, the strongly coloured aromatic derived from the crocus, which the west Gâtinais was one of the first places in Europe to cultivate. It takes 1hr to gather 1 000 flowers and 150 000 flowers are needed to produce 1kg/2.2lb of saffron.

EXCURSIONS

Malesherbes – *18km/ 11.2mi NE along N 152.* Situated along the Essonne Valley, this small town is entirely surrounded by woods. The **Duthiers** leisure park lies close to the river, in a forest setting dotted with sandstone boulders.

Château ⊙ – The 14C round towers are all that remains of the feudal castle rebuilt in the 15C. The courtyard leads to the former outbuildings: 14C tithe barns where wheat was stored four floors high; Tour des Redevances; and a pavilion known as Chateaubriand's House in memory of the famous poet who stayed in it. The 14C dovecot could accommodate 8 000 pigeons. The chapel dates from the 15C.

Inside, the ground-floor reception rooms have been refurbished as they were

> **Malesherbes**
>
> This tolerant man, who became one of Louis XVI's ministers, encouraged the introduction and circulation throughout France of Diderot's *Encyclopédie*. Having retired from public service on the eve of the Revolution, he requested the honour of defending the king before the Convention. He was later guillotined together with his daughter, his son-in-law, as well as one of his granddaughters and her husband the Marquess of Chateaubriand, the eldest brother of the writer.

before the Revolution and the visit ends with the bedroom and vaulted oratory of **Henriette d'Entragues**, who succeeded Gabrielle d'Estrées as Henri IV's official mistress. However, the king soon tired of Henriette's bad temper and she was forced to retire to Malesherbes where she spent her time plotting. The chapel contains the recumbent figure of Guillaume d'Entragues (Henriette's grandfather) by Pierre Bontemps.

PITHIVERAIS COUNTRY

95km/59mi – allow half a day
Leave Pithiviers E along D 123.

Yèvre-le-Châtel – Perched on its promontory, Yèvre overlooks the Rimarde, a tributary of the River Essonne. The ramparts date from the 13C. A fortified gate under the elm trees in the main square opens into the outer bailey of the castle.

Château fort ⊙ – The stronghold, recently restored, is diamond-shaped with a round tower at each corner containing hexagonal rooms with ogive vaulting.

The sentry walk linking the towers is now accessible.

The north-west and south towers provide a **view** of the Beauce and the Gâtinais regions. To the south the treetops of Orléans Forest darken the horizon.

Église St-Lubin – On the south side of the village among the tombstones stands the unfinished stone shell of a huge Gothic church. Its vast size seems to have been dictated by the need for a place of refuge rather than a place of worship. The church's great elegance and the speed of its construction (the first quarter of the 13C) suggest that the project had royal backing.

Drive to Estouy and turn right onto D 26 which follows the River Essonne.

Puiseaux – This busy cereal centre of the Gâtinais region developed round a priory belonging to the Parisian abbey of St-Victor, a famous theological centre in medieval times. The twisted 65m/213ft-high spire of the 13C church can be seen from afar. Inside, the nave is surmounted by pointed vaulting and the elegant transept is decorated with a fine rose window. On the keystone over the crossing, note the two different sets of the abbey's coat of arms. A chapel along the south aisle contains a beautiful 16C **Holy Sepulchre★**.

Drive S out of Puiseaux along D 948 then turn right onto D 28.

Boësse – This once fortified village stretches its winding streets on the hillside; the church is preceded by an impressive porch reminiscent of part of a cloister.

Take D 123 on the right to Givraines then turn left onto D 25 to Boynes.

Boynes – Seeing it today, it is difficult to imagine that Boynes remained the world capital of saffron during 300 years (16C-19C). Drastic changes in the agricultural world brought with them the decline of saffron and of wine-growing, but the town recalls its prosperous past at the **Maison du Safran** ⊙.

Source of saffron

Beaune-la-Rolande – Lying on the banks of the River Rolande, Beaune is a market town where sugar beet and cereals have replaced saffron and vines.

Church – The building is 15C-16C and features an elegant north side in the Renaissance style: there are pilasters bearing medallions, recesses and doorways with pediments decorated with busts.

To the left is the gate to the former cemetery with a thought for the day on the lintel. The aisles are almost as wide and high as the nave, so that the building resembles the hall-churches of the German, Late Gothic period. At the back of the left aisle there is a painting of the *Mystic Marriage of St Catherine* by Frédéric Bazille, who fell in the Battle of Beaune-la-Rolande in 1870.

The last side chapel on the left contains a 17C giltwood altar with panels depicting biblical scenes and a statue of St Vincent de Paul, earlier than the stereotyped 19C representations.

Boiscommun – *5.5km/3.4mi SW on D 9.* Of the castle only two towers and other ruins remain and these can be seen from the path which now follows the line of the former moat.

The interesting 13C **church** with its Romanesque doorway has a Gothic nave with a majestic elevation. It is relatively easy to discern the different periods of construction by looking at the changes in the capitals, the form of the high windows and openings of the triforium.

At the end of the aisle, above the sacristy door, is a late-12C stained-glass window showing the Virgin and Child. On leaving, glance at the organ loft ornamented with eight painted figures (16C) of knights; Roland, the hero of a 12C epic poem, is identified by the inscription.

Courtier and patron of the arts

Louis-Antoine de Pardaillan, **Duc d'Antin**, was the son of Madame de Montespan and Surveyor to the King. He was a model courtier: Voltaire wrote that he had a talent for flattery, not only in words but in actions.

During a visit to Petit-Bourg Château, near Paris, Louis XIV complained about a row of chestnut trees which, although very fine from the garden, obscured the view from the royal apartments. D'Antin had the trees felled during the night and all trace of the work cleared away; on waking, the King was astonished to find the view unobstructed.

D'Antin collected works of art and acted as a patron to artists. His mother was a frequent visitor to Bellegarde where he erected a series of brick buildings (1717-27).

Bellegarde – The town's colour-washed houses are grouped round a huge square and surrounded by rose nurseries, market gardens and wheat fields.

★ **Château** – Grouped round the old keep, this unusual and picturesque ensemble, built in the 14C by Nicolas Braque, Finance Minister to Charles V, stands on a platform surrounded by a moat.

The brick **pavilions** with stone dressings which frame the courtyard were built by D'Antin to house the château staff and his guests; from left to right they comprise the Steward's pavilion surmounted by a pinnacle turret, the Captain's massive round brick tower, the Salamander pavilion, the kitchen pavilion, which houses the town hall – **hôtel de ville** ⊙ – and contains the **Regency Salon** with wood panelling, and, on the other side of the gate, the D'Antin Pavilion with a mansard roof. A **rose garden** has been laid out round the moat.

A drive skirting the rose garden leads to the stables *(private property)*; the pediment is decorated with three horses' heads sculpted by Coysevox.

Church – The façade of this Romanesque building is a remarkable combination of balanced proportion and harmonious decoration. Note the ornamentation of the central doorway: wreathed and ringed engaged piers support carved capitals depicting imaginary foliage and animals.

The nave contains an interesting collection of 17C **paintings**: *St Sebastian* by Annibale Carracci and *The Infant Louis XIV as St John the Baptist* by Mignard (right wall) and *The Deposition* by Lebrun (right chapel); Louise de la Vallière may have been the model for the two female characters in these pictures.

Drive SW through Bois de la Madeleine then turn right onto D 114.

Chambon-la-Forêt – This lovely flower-decked village lies on the edge of Orléans Forest.

Drive out along D 109.

★ **Château de Chamerolles** ⊙ – On the boundaries of the Beauce and the Gâtinais region, on the edge of Orléans Forest, stands this sumptuous Renaissance building and its formal gardens restored to their former glory. The Dulac family moved here in the 15C, when Lancelot I (named after the hero immortalised in the story of the Knights of the Round Table) commissioned the construction of the present château. Lancelot, who was acquainted with Louis XII and François I, designed a medieval stronghold with very few apertures, but with an elegant, comfortable interior. Through their connections with Louise de Coligny, the Dulac family became unconditional supporters of the Protestant cause. Around the same period (1585), the **chapel** was converted into a Protestant church.

★ **Promenade des parfums** – The Chamerolles estate is given over to perfume and other olfactory delights. The south wing of the château contains a chronological exhibition of different scents from the 16C up to the present day, taking the visitor through a series of rooms decorated with objects related to perfume. The tour ends with a «perfume organ» and a fine collection of remarkable flasks designed by Daum, Lalique and Baccarat for such prestigious perfume manufacturers as Guerlain, Lancôme, Roger et Gallet, Chanel etc.

A small bridge spanning the moat allows visitors to continue their aromatic exploration by visiting the **garden★**. The six flower beds have been painstakingly restored to the layout they would have had during the Renaissance, reflecting the threefold purpose of gardens in those days: ornamentation, leisure and utility. One has been conceived as an outdoor parlour where people engaged in conversation on grass banks. The others include an elaborate "embroidered flower bed" with boxwood edging, an "exotic patch" planted with many rare aromatic species used for making perfume, a maze and two vegetable gardens containing herbs, spices, fruit trees and vegetables common in the 16C and 17C. Beyond the dazzling sheet of water, a stroll through the park takes you to the bandstand, which commands a lovely view of the château.

Return to Pithiviers along N 152.

Château du PLESSIS-BOURRÉ★★

Michelin map 317: F-3, 232 fold 19 or 4049 F3

Le Plessis-Bourré stands at the far end of a vista of meadowland dotted with copses. This white building beneath blue-grey slate roofs gives a very strong idea of what seigneurial life in the 15C would have been like.

Born in Château-Gontier, **Jean Bourré** (1424-1506) first entered royal service under Dauphin Louis, the son of Charles VII, whom he served faithfully. When Louis XI assumed the crown in 1461, Bourré was given the important post of Financial Secretary and Treasurer of France. In addition to building several châteaux – Jarzé and Vaux among others – he bought the estate of Plessis-le-Vent and in 1468 ordered work to begin on the new château. The design was inspired by the château at Langeais which he had supervised during its construction, and as Le Plessis was built in a single go it boasts magnificent unity of style.

Among the many illustrious guests that Bourré welcomed to his new residence were Pierre de Rohan, Louis XI and Charles VIII.

Château du Plessis-Bourré

TOUR ⓥ

On the outside, Le Plessis, enclosed by a wide moat spanned by a long (43m/141ft) bridge enhanced by many arches, is plainly a fortress protected by a gatehouse with a double drawbridge and four flanking towers. The largest of these is battlemented and served as a keep. A 3m/10ft-wide platform at the base of the wall provided for artillery crossfire. To the left of the gatehouse the chapel's slender spire rises above the roof.

On the inside of the entrance archway, Le Plessis has been converted into a country mansion with a spacious courtyard, low wings, an arcaded gallery, turret staircases and the high dormer windows of the seigneurial wing.

On the ground floor visitors will see the splendid, richly furnished and decorated **State Apartments,** from which there is a charming view of the gentle surrounding countryside. The wing built at right angles houses the Parliament Hall, a vast dining hall with a superb monumental fireplace.

A spiral staircase leads to the splendid guard-room, which has a coffered wooden **ceiling★★★** painted at the end of the 15C with such allegorical figures as Fortune, Truth, Chastity (a unicorn) and Lust, the Musician Ass etc. There are also humorous scenes with a moral message, depicting for example the unskilled barber at work on a client, the presumptuous man trying to wring the neck of an eel and a woman sewing up a chicken's crop. The crude realism of some of the scenes, which are accompanied by lines of verse, and their outstandingly fresh and graphic quality make them all the more striking and evocative.

The upper floor comprises two bedchambers (Empire-style and Renaissance furniture, including a monumental Spanish bed) and the library. St-Anne's chapel gives access to the main courtyard.

The castle grounds have recently been laid out as a park and make a pleasant place for a walk.

EXCURSION

Manoir de la Hamonnière ⓥ – *9km/6mi N via Écuillé.* The architecture of this manor house, which was built between 1420 and 1575, shows the evolution of the Renaissance style. The buildings laid out around the courtyard consist of a plain residential block *(right)* with a stair turret, a Henri III section *(left)* with a window bay framed by pilasters and capitals following the Classical progression of the orders, and at a right angle a low wing with two twisted columns supporting a dormer window. To the rear stands the keep, probably the last addition made in the 16C, with a staircase turret and round-arched windows, contrasting with the other architectural features.

Château du PLESSIS-MACÉ★

Michelin 317: E-3, 232 fold 19 or 4049 E3

This château set apart from the village and hidden amid greenery is protected by a wide moat. Begun in the 11C by a certain Macé, the **château** became the property in the mid-15C of Louis de Beaumont, the Chamberlain and favourite of Louis XI, who had it rebuilt into a residence fit to accommodate his royal master. The year 1510 saw the beginning of a 168-year-old ownership by the Du Bellay family.

TOUR ⊙ *1hr*

From the outside, Le Plessis still has the appearance of a fortress with its tower-studded wall and rectangular keep, stripped of all its fortifications except the battlements, and surrounded by a moat.

Once you enter the great courtyard, you will notice that the building is similar to a country residence: decorative elements in white-tufa stone enhance the dark grey of the schist; the imposing ruined keep towers over the west side of the enclosure.

To the right are the outbuildings housing the stables and guard-room. To the left are the chapel, an unusual staircase turret which gets larger as it goes up and the main residential wing surmounted by pointed gables. In the corner with the main wing is a charming **hanging gallery★**, a fine example of Flamboyant Gothic sculpture, from where the ladies would watch jousting tournaments and other entertainments. A second balcony opposite, in the outbuildings, was reserved for the servants.

The tour includes the dining room, the large banqueting hall, several bedrooms, one of which was the King's, and the **chapel**, which still features rare 15C Gothic **panelling★** forming two levels of galleries, the first reserved for the lord and his squires, the second for the servants.

PONTLEVOY

Population 1 460
Michelin map 318: E-7 or 238 folds 14 and 15

Pontlevoy is a small town situated in the agricultural region to the north of Montrichard and can still boast a number of charming old houses with stone dressings.

Some 30 panels, decorated with advertisements for Poulain chocolate, illustrate life in Pontlevoy at the turn of the 20C and the early days of motor cars.

★ABBEY *1hr 15min*

The main interest of the old **abbey** lies in its elegant 18C buildings (including two wings of the cloisters) and the 14C-15C Gothic chapel. The abbey was founded in 1034 when, legend has it, Gelduin de Chaumont, vassal of the Count of Blois, established a Benedictine community here as a token of gratitude to the Virgin Mary for his surviving a shipwreck. In the 17C, when the reform of monastic life became essential, the abbey was entrusted to the Benedictines of St-Maur and the Abbot Pierre de Bérule, who opened an educational establishment in 1644 which made Pontlevoy famous until the 19C. Made into an École Royale Militaire in 1776, the college added to the general education it offered the military training of scholarship students chosen by the King from among the lower nobility.

The façade of the abbey

S. Sauvignier/MICHELIN

Abbey church – The abbey church, which was rebuilt in the 14C and the 15C, consists solely of the chancel of the imposing building which was originally planned. In 1651 two large stone altarpieces with marble columns were added to the high altar and to the axial chapel where Gelduin de Chaumont and his immediate descendants are buried.

Conventual buildings – These 18C conventual buildings include the refectory, the remarkable staircase leading to the upper floor, and the majestic façade giving onto the gardens, decorated with emblazoned pediments at regular intervals.

Musée municipal ⊘ – Housed in the west wing of the conventual buildings, the municipal museum is devoted to key themes of the early 20C in which local people played an important part.

The first theme is advertising, one of the pioneers of which was **Auguste Poulain**, born in Pontlevoy in 1825 and founder of the famous chocolate factory at Blois. There are old posters (including some signed by Cappiello and Firmin Bouisset), chromolithographs and other publicity items.

Then there are about 100 photographs from the collection of 10 000 pictures taken by Louis Clergeau, a watchmaker with a passion for photography, and by his daughter Marcelle; they constitute a marvellous record of life in Pontlevoy between 1902 and 1960.

Finally, the heroic beginnings of aviation (1910-14) are evoked by models of the four training aircraft as well as by photographic documents.

Some 20 heavy goods vehicles built between 1910 and 1950 are displayed under the fine timber roof of the old riding school.

POUANCÉ

Population 3 307
Michelin map 317: B-2, 232 fold 17 or 4049 B2

Pouancé, in its protective ring of lakes, lies on the border between Anjou and Brittany. In the Middle Ages it played an important economic role owing to its iron foundries which were supplied with ore from the Segré Basin. The surrounding woods provided shelter for the Chouans during the Revolution.

Castle ⊘ – The main road *(N 171)* skirts the town, passing at the foot of the ruined castle (13C-15C). The towers and curtain wall of dark schist are impressive and reinforced by a firing caponier linked to the keep by a postern.

EXCURSIONS

Menhir de Pierre Frite – *5km/3mi S on D 878, bearing left onto D 6 in La Prévière and then a track to the right (signposted).* This menhir in woodland surroundings stands 6m/20ft high.

Château de la Motte-Glain ⊘ – *17km/11mi S.* The red-stone château with its strong lines was built late in the 15C by **Pierre de Rohan-Guéménée**, Counsellor to Louis XI and later one of the commanding officers of the armies of Charles VIII and Louis XII in Italy. A reminder of the château's location on the pilgrimage route from Mont-St-Michel to Compostela is given by the scallops and pilgrim's staff motifs decorating the

courtyard façade. The gatehouse is flanked by two round towers. Renaissance fireplaces and 15C-16C furniture embellish the interior of the château, together with hunting trophies, most of them of African origin.

In the chapel is a fresco from the early 16C representing the Crucifixion.

PREUILLY-SUR-CLAISE

Population 1 293
Michelin map 317: O-7, 238 fold 25 or 4037 F6

Preuilly, which has retained numerous interesting old houses and the former abbey church beneath the ruins of its fortress, rises in terraces on the north bank of the Claise amid woodland, green meadows and vineyards. The town was once considered to be the leading barony of the Touraine region, held by such illustrious families as those of Amboise, La Rochefoucauld, César de Vendôme, Gallifet and Breteuil. Five churches and a collegiate church were barely enough to accommodate the town's worshippers in its heyday.

Église St-Pierre – This old Benedictine abbey church (c 1000) is a Romanesque building in which traces of the architectural styles of the Poitou and Touraine regions are evident. Architect Phidias Vestier carried out some excellent repair work in 1846, but the church was subsequently subjected to shoddy restoration in 1873, the year when the tower was built.

COLOURS OF PROVENCE

Auberge St-Nicolas – *4 Grande-Rue –* ☎ *02 47 94 50 80 – closed 10 Sep-8 Oct, Sun evening and Mon except Jul-Aug –* *10.67€ lunch, 17.53/35.83€.* A modest town-centre restaurant decorated in Provençal colours, with three enormous old beams in the dining room. The rooms are simple, almost sparsely decorated, and impeccably clean.

Near the church, there are several 17C mansions, one of which has been turned into a hospice (previously Hôtel de la Rallière).

EXCURSION

Boussay – *4.5km/7mi SW.* The château here combines such diverse elements as 15C machicolated towers, a wing in the Baroque style of Mansart, the architect who designed much of the château at Versailles, and an 18C façade. It stands in fine gardens laid out in the French style.

RICHELIEU★

Population 2 165
Michelin map 317: K-6, 232 fold 46 or 4037 B5

Lying on the southern limits of Touraine, bordering on Poitou, Richelieu is a quiet town which comes to life on market days.

La Fontaine called the place "the finest village in the universe". It is a rare example of Classical town planning, the project of one man, the statesman and churchman **Cardinal de Richelieu**, who was eager to lodge his court near his château which was then under construction. The building of the town itself started in 1031 at a time when Versailles was still only an idea.

CARDINAL DE RICHELIEU

In 1621 when **Armand du Plessis** (1585-1642) bought the property of Richelieu it consisted of a village and manor on the banks of the Mable. Ten years later the estate was raised to the status of a duchy. On becoming Cardinal and First Minister of France, Richelieu commissioned Jacques Le Mercier, the architect of the Sorbonne and Cardinal's Palace, now Palais-Royal, in Paris, to prepare plans for a château and a walled town. Built under the supervision of the architect's brother, Pierre Le Mercier, the project was considered at the time to be a marvel of urban planning which Louis XIV was to visit at the age of 12.

Determined not to have his creation outstripped in grandeur, Richelieu created a small principality around his masterpiece and jealously razed in whole or in part many other châteaux in the vicinity. He already owned Bois-le-Vicomte and was to add to his estates Champigny-sur-Veude, L'Île-Bouchard, Cravant, Crissay, Mirebeau, Faye-la-Vineuse and even the royal residence of Chinon, which he was to allow to fall into disrepair. The great fortress of Loudon also suffered destruction at his hands, once its owner, Urbain Grandier, an arch enemy of the Cardinal, had perished at the stake. One may call it retribution or the hazard of fate but little has survived of the Cardinal's magnificent residence.

An enormous park was once the setting for a marvellous palace filled with great works of art. Two vast courtyards surrounded by outbuildings stood in front of the château proper, which was protected by moats, bastions and watchtowers.

The apartments, gallery and chapel were hung with works by Poussin, Claude Lorrain, Champaigne, Mantegna, Perugino, Bassano, Caravaggio, Titian, Giulio Romano, Dürer, Rubens and Van Dyck.

The powerful Cardinal Richelieu

The gardens were dotted with copies of Antique statues and artificial grottoes which concealed the then-popular water tricks (fountains or jets which would spring up unexpectedly, soaking unwary visitors). It was in these gardens that the first poplar trees from Italy were planted.

The dispersal of the riches gathered here began in 1727 and intensified after 1792, when the château was confiscated. After the Revolution the descendants of Richelieu ceded the château to a certain Boutron who demolished it for the sale of the building materials.

Some of the works of art collected by the Cardinal de Richelieu can be seen in the Louvre Museum in Paris (Michelangelo's Slaves and paintings by Perugino). A few antiquities and paintings are displayed in the museums of Tours, Azay-le-Ferron and Poitiers.

★THE TOWN

The walled town which Richelieu planned at the gates of his château was in itself a fine example of the Louis XIII style designed by Jacques Le Mercier.

The town embodies the sense of order, balance and symmetry which characterised the 17C, or Grand Siècle, in France. The rectangular ground plan (700x500m/766x547yd) was surrounded by ramparts and a moat. The impressive entrance gates are flanked by rusticated and pedimented gatehouses surmounted by high French roofs.

Grande-Rue – The main street crosses Richelieu from north to south. In addition to the gateways note the Louis XIII-style *hôtels* with the decorative elements in white tufa stone, especially no 17, Hôtel du Sénéchal, which has retained its elegant courtyard with busts of Roman emperors. There are two squares, one at each end of the main street.

Place du Marché – In the southern square, opposite the church, stands the 17C covered market, its slate roof supported by a fine chestnut timber frame.

Église Notre-Dame – The church, which is built of white stone in the Classical, so-called Jesuit style, exudes unmistakable harmony and elegance. The niches in the façade contain statues of the Evangelists; the chancel is flanked by two towers topped with obelisks, a rare arrangement. Inside, note the elegant 18C high altar.

Hôtel de ville ⊘ – This former law court houses a **museum**, which contains documents and works of art pertaining to both the Richelieu family and the château.

Parc du château ⊘ – A magnificent statue of Richelieu by Ramey stands at the southern end of the main street in front of the park (475ha/1 174 acres), which is crisscrossed by straight avenues of chestnut and plane trees.

Of the many splendid buildings once to be found here, there remains a domed pavilion (part of the outbuildings), which houses a small **museum** containing models of the château and historical documents on Richelieu. The canals also remain as do two pavilions, the orangery and wine cellar, at the far end of the formal gardens *(south-east)*. The old château entrance can still be seen from D 749 *(south-west)*.

Steam train of Touraine ⊘ – 📷 A genuine steam train dating from the turn of the 20C runs between Richelieu and Ligré via Champigny-sur-Veude. The museum at Richelieu station displays ancient machinery: early-20C locomotives, saloon-carriages (1900) belonging to the company PLM, an American diesel engine (a relic of the Marshall Plan) etc.

EXCURSIONS

★ **Champigny-sur-Veude** – *6km.3.7mi N along D 749*. Champigny lies in the green valley of the Veude. The collegiate chapel is a remarkable instance of Renaissance art at its height; it was part of a château built from 1508 to 1543 by Louis I and Louis II de Bourbon-Montpensier. The château itself was later pulled down on the orders of Cardinal de Richelieu. Only outbuildings remain but even these give some idea of the size and splendour of the château that was demolished.

★**Sainte-Chapelle** ☉ – The Sainte-Chapelle, which owed its name to the portion of the True Cross which was kept there, was saved by the intervention of Pope Urban VIII. Louis I of Bourbon, who had accompanied Charles VIII to Naples, wanted the chapel to be in the transitional Gothic Renaissance style.

The peristyle, which was built later on, is decidedly Italian in character: the detailed sculpted ornament is based on the insignia of Louis II of Bourbon and includes crowned and plain Ls, lances, pilgrims' staffs, flowers, fruit etc. The porch presents a coffered ceiling.

A fine wooden door dating from the 16C, carved with panels depicting the Cardinal Virtues, leads to the nave which has ogive vaulting with liernes and tiercerons. It is there that the visitor can admire the praying figure of Henri de Bourbon, last Duke of Montpensier, carved by Simon Guillain at the beginning of the 17C.

Installed in the middle of the 16C, the eleven **stained-glass windows★★** are the chapel's most precious jewel, forming a remarkable example of Renaissance glasswork. They comprise 34 portraits of the Bourbon-Montpensier House; above are scenes from the Passion. The vivid yet subtle combination of colours throughout the whole work deserve special mention, particularly the purplish blues with their bronze highlights which are truly outstanding.

Faye-la-Vineuse – *7km/4.3mi S along D 749 and D 757.* Faye-la-Vineuse stands on a rise once covered in vineyards overlooking the valley formed by a tributary of the Veude. During the Middle Ages it was a prosperous walled city of five parishes and 11 000 inhabitants. It was ruined during the Wars of Religion.

The Romanesque **Église St-Georges** ☉ was once a collegiate church surrounded by cloisters and conventual buildings. It has suffered from excessive restoration but still retains some interesting features: a tall transept crossing with a cupola on pendentives; two side aisles typical of churches in the Berry region; a chancel with a very high elevation and an ambulatory; and fascinating carved capitals – apart from the many plant motifs and imaginary animals there are also battle scenes. The 11C **crypt** is unusually large and its vaulting high. Note the two carved capitals of the Adoration of the Magi and jousting knights.

Abbaye de Bois-Aubry ☉ – *16km/10mi E on D 757 then D 58 and D 114.* The 12C Benedictine abbey in the middle of the countryside is heralded by its stone spire which may be seen standing on the horizon. The best-preserved feature of the ruins *(currently being restored)* is the square 15C bell-tower. Note also the 15C stone rood screen in Flamboyant Gothic style. The vaulting in the 13C nave has a keystone decorated with a carved coat of arms. There are 12 beautifully carved capitals in the early-12C chapter-house.

ROMORANTIN-LANTHENAY★

Population 18 350
Michelin map 318: H 7 or 238 fold 16

The point where the River Sauldre divides into several arms is the site of the former capital of the Sologne, with its pine forests, moorlands, numerous lakes... and gastronomic specialities including pumpkin pâté!

Royal associations – In the 15C Romorantin was the fief of the Valois-Angoulême branch of the French royal family and it was here that François d'Angoulême, later **François I**, spent his turbulent childhood and where his wife-to-be Claude de France, the daughter of Louis XII, was born in 1499. The King loved Romorantin and in 1517 he commissioned Leonardo da Vinci, then living in Amboise, to draw up plans for a palace destined for his mother Louise of Savoy.

In France, the Feast of the Epiphany *(fête des Rois)* is celebrated by eating a cake *(galette des rois)* which contains a bean. The finder of this bean is the bean king of Twelfth Night. On 6 January 1521, Epiphany, François I led a mock attack on the Hôtel St-Pol, where a bean king reigned. The occupants were defending themselves when some ill-advised person threw out a glowing log which landed on the royal skull. To dress the wound the doctors shaved his head, whereupon the King grew a beard. His courtiers promptly followed suit.

TOWN WALK

★**Old houses** – On the corner of rue de la Résistance and rue du Milieu stands the **chancellerie**, a corbelled Renaissance house, of brick and half-timber construction, where the royal seals were kept when the King resided in town. The corner post features a coat of arms and a musician playing the bagpipes. Opposite stands **Hôtel St-Pol**, built of stone and glazed bricks with window mouldings.

Standing at the junction of rue du Milieu and rue de la Pierre is the charming **Maison du Carroir doré** ☉ (Archaeological Museum) with its remarkable carved corner posts showing the Annunciation *(left)* and St George killing the Dragon *(right)*.

★ View from the bridges – From the north branch of the river there is a **view** of the **Château royal**, opposite the Sologne museum complex, which dates from the 15C and 16C and now houses the sub-Prefecture. Along the narrow southern branch of the river there is a row of attractive half-timbered houses.

Venerable piper

Square Ferdinand-Buisson – This is a pleasant public garden with tall trees and footbridges over the river; there are attractive views of the river banks and the fulling mill.

Église St-Étienne – Above the transept crossing of the church rises a Romanesque tower with finely executed sculptures. Beyond the nave with its Angevin vaulting is the darker chancel which is also roofed with Angevin vaulting springing from powerful Romanesque pillars; each rib of the apsidal vault supports the statue of an Evangelist.

Chapelle St-Roch – *Not open to the public*. This elegant chapel at the entrance to the St-Roch district is flanked by turrets with round-arched windows typical of the Renaissance.

SIGHTS

Espace automobile Matra ⊙ – Housed in disused factory premises, this Motor Racing Museum presents an exhibition of Matra cars, including the Formula 1 car which won the world championship in 1969, and a series of display cases retracing the technical developments in racing car construction. The museum also has a specialist library. Established in 1968, Matra is the company which employs the most people in town.

★ Musée de Sologne ⊙ – The museum is situated in the heart of the old quarter of Romorantin-Lanthenay, spanning the river. In this delightful setting, three buildings house the museum collections.

The **Moulin du Chapitre**, whose exterior still reveals traces of its former activity as a flour mill in the 19C, consists of exhibition areas laid out over four floors: the history, flora and fauna of the Sologne region; life in the châteaux and the rural community.

ROMORANTIN-LANTHENAY

Brault (R. Porte) 2
Capucins (R. des) 4
Clémenceau (R. Georges) 6
Four-à-chaud (R. du) 8
Gaulle (Pl. Gén.-de) 10
Ile-Marin (Quai de l') 13
Jouanettes (R. des) 14
Lattre-de-Tassigny (Av. du Mar. de) 15
Limousin (R. des) 17
Mail de l'Hôtel-Dieu 18
Milieu (R. du) 20
Orléans (Fg d') 22
Paix (Pl. de la) 23
Pierre (R. de la) 24
Prés-Wilson (R. du) 26
Résistance (R. de la) 28
St-Roch (Fg) 30
Sirène (R. de la) 33
Tour (R. de la) 34
Trois-Rois (R. des) 36
Verdun (R. de) 37

Ancien château royal
  (sous-préfecture) . . . . P
Espace Automobile Matra . . . . M¹
Maisons anciennes . . . . B
Maisons à pan de bois . . . . . . E
Moulin-foulon . . . . K
Musée de Sologne . . . . M²

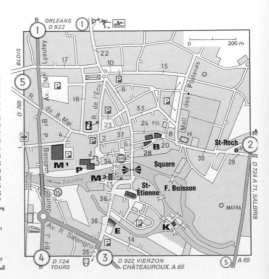

Eating out

BUDGET

Hôtel-restaurant du Brocard – *137 r. de Blois – 41230 Mur-de-Sologne – 12km/7.5mi NW of Romorantin towards Blois on D 765 – ☏ 02 54 83 90 29 – closed 20 Dec-30 Jan, Sun evening and Mon except Jun-Aug – reservation required – 11.45/38.11€.* A recently built property, but the use of terracotta floor tiles, stone, brick and wood succeeds in recreating the Sologne decor. Local produce for lovers of good food, pumpkins and gourds in season. Ground-floor rooms leading onto a small terrace. Pretty garden with lake for fishing.

MODERATE

Le Lanthenay – *Pl. de l'Église – 2.5km/1.5mi N of Romorantin on D 922 – ☏ 02 54 76 09 19 – closed 15 Jul-2 Aug, 24 Dec-15 Jan, Sun and Mon – reservation required – 17.53/48.02€.* This restaurant has earned a fine reputation among gourmets. The dining room with its exposed beams opens onto a terrace with veranda. Well-prepared dishes at reasonable prices. A few rooms, some on the ground floor.

The **Moulin de la Ville** presents the history of Romorantin, insisting on Leonardo da Vinci's plans to build a new city and royal residence.

The **Jacquemart Tower** is the oldest building in town; it is used to house temporary exhibitions.

EXCURSIONS

Lanthenay – *4km/2.5mi N.* The **Chapelle St-Aignan** here contains a painting of the Virgin Mary between St John the Baptist and St Sebastian, dating from 1523 and attributed to Timoteo Viti from Urbino who influenced Raphael in his early days. There is also a 17C canvas of the dead Christ with the Virgin Mary and St John and 16C painted wooden statues of St Francis and St Clare.

Mennetou-sur-Cher – *20km/12.4mi SE along D 922 and N 76.* This medieval town is enclosed within its original ramparts.

Ramparts – These were built in the 13C, and three out of five towers as well as the three entrance gateways are still intact. On the side of town towards Vierzon, Bonne-Nouvelle gateway is supported by a round tower which used to flank a Benedictine priory. Only the church of this has survived. En-Bas gateway, which can boast that Joan of Arc once passed through its portal, features pointed supporting arches, and its guard-room contains the original fireplace complete with hood. En-Haut gateway is adorned with a twin window.

Old houses – Grande-Rue, the steep and winding main street, leads from Bonne-Nouvelle gateway to that of En-Haut, past most of Mennetou's interesting old houses. These embody a variety of architectural styles, dating from the 13C (Gothic, with twin windows), 15C (half-timbered, with projecting upper storeys) and 16C (elegant mansions with pilastered façades).

SABLÉ-SUR-SARTHE

Population 12 716
Michelin map 310: G-7, 232 fold 20 or 4072 B5
Local map see Le MANS

Situated at a point where two tributaries, the Vaige and the Erve, flow into the Sarthe, Sablé is dominated by the austere façade of its château, which once belonged to the Colbert family and now houses the National Library's restoration and book binding workshops. The town, which is famous for its shortbread biscuits *(sablés)*, is the second largest economic centre in the Sarthe region. A favourable environment and pronounced dynamism have helped develop the foodstuff industry and diversify the local economy.

Nearby, art lovers will discover the fascinating Benedictine abbey of Solesmes and the church of Asnières-sur-Vègre, superbly decorated with Gothic murals.

TOWN WALK

In the 17C the fief belonged to Laval-Bois-Dauphin, Marquis de Sablé. In 1711 Colbert de Torcy, the nephew of the great Jean-Baptiste Colbert, Louis XIV's Minister, rebuilt the château and radically changed the appearance of the town; many houses and the hospital date from this period. Development on place Raphaël-Élizé has highlighted a fine group of 19C buildings in rue Carnot.

Hostellerie St-Martin – *3 r. Haute-St-Martin* – ☎ *02 43 95 00 03* – *closed 18-24 Feb, 27 Aug-6 Sep, Sun evening, Wed evening and Mon* – *14.48/29.73€*. A restaurant in an old building, a little way from the town centre. Old-fashioned wood-panelled dining room, or a shaded terrace for lunch outside.

The small port on the canalised part of the Sarthe used to receive sand-laden barges from the Loire. Nowadays it harbours about 20 craft for hire *(pénichettes)* as well as *Le Sablésien*, a **tourist boat** ⊙ offering leisurely rides or luncheon-cruises along the Sarthe.

EXCURSIONS

Auvers-le-Hamon – *8.5km/5mi N along D 24*. The nave of the **church** here is ornamented with 15C-16C **mural paintings** depicting a series of popular local saints and religious scenes: to the right St Mamès holding his intestines; St Martin on horseback; St Cénéré as a Cardinal; St Eutropius; St Andrew on his cross; St Luke riding a bull; the Nativity and the Flight into Egypt. To the left are a Dance of Death, St Avertin, St Apollonia whose teeth were pulled out by her torturers, St James and the Sacrifice of Isaac.

Solesmes – *3km/2mi NE along the picturesque D 22*. A few miles upstream from Sablé lies Solesmes, which has won renown through its association with the Benedictine Order. From the north bank of the Sarthe and from the bridge there is an impressive **view**★ of the north front of the abbey, a dark wall, about 50m/164ft high, which was built at the end of the 19C in the Romanesque-Gothic style. The abbey buildings are reflected in the river, next to a less imposing, but rather more inviting-looking 18C priory.

The Benedictine priory founded in 1010 by the Lord of Sablé was served by monks from St-Pierre-de-la-Couture in Le Mans *(see p 217)*. It expanded rapidly and by the early 16C had become very wealthy.

The Revolution brought ruin, but a new community was established in 1833 by a priest from Sablé, Dom Guéranger, and in 1837 the abbey became the headquarters of the Benedictine Order in France.

The name of Solesmes has been linked with the restoration of the liturgy and the revival of the Gregorian chant in France. The abbey **services**, to which the public is admitted, demonstrate the beauty of the liturgy celebrated in Benedictine monasteries.

★ **Abbaye St-Pierre** – *Only the abbey church (in the main courtyard) is open to the public*. The **church** comprises the nave and transept which date from the 11C and 15C and the domical-vaulted chancel which was added in 1865. The famous sculpture groups, which are known as the **Saints of Solesmes**★★, are in the transept.

Note in the south transept a monumental Entombment (1496) with a beautiful representation of Mary Magdalene at prayer; on the left, a terracotta *Pietà* from an earlier period, and, in the north transept, a remarkable composition depicting the scenes from the Virgin's life, which is matched, in the south transept by The Entombment of Christ dating from 1496.

★ **Asnières-sur-Vègre** – *10km/6mi NE along D 4 and D 190*. Asnières lies in an attractive setting, deep in the picturesque Vègre Valley. The road *(D 190)* from Poillé gives a pretty view over the old houses with their steeply pitched roofs, the church and a mansion called the Cour d'Asnières.

REPAST FROM THE PAST

Le Pavillon – *2 r. St-Hilaire – 72430 Asnières-sur-Vègre* – ☎ *02 43 95 30 20* – *closed Jan-1 Mar* – ✄ – *reservation required* – *13.57/24.39€*. If you like the idea of eating with your fingers, book a table at the Pavillon and order a medieval menu; other menus are also available. A warm welcome and a lot of fun in store! Enjoy the terrace in fine weather.

Bridge – This medieval humpback structure provides a charming **view**★ of the river, the old mill – still operational – against a backdrop of fine trees, and the elegant mansion with its turret and dormer windows on the right bank. Close to the mill stands a château known as the Moulin Vieux dating from the 17C and 18C.

Church ⊙ – The interior is decorated with Gothic **wall paintings**★ – 13C in the nave and 15C in the chancel. The most famous, on the inside wall of the main façade, depicts Hell. On the left Christ is preparing to release the souls trapped in Limbo by attacking the three-headed dog, Cerberus, with a lance; in the centre Leviathan is swallowing up the Damned; finally canine-headed demons are stirring a cauldron of the Damned in which the wimple of the lady of the manor and the bishop's mitre can be seen.

The scenes on the north wall of the nave portray the Adoration of the Magi, the Presentation of Jesus in the Temple and the Flight into Egypt. Note in the chancel a Baptism of Christ, a Flagellation and a Crucifixion.

Cour d'Asnières – Standing a little to the south of the church is a large, elongated Gothic building, with pretty paired windows. It was here that the canons of Le Mans, the one-time lords of Asnières, exercised their seigneurial rights, hence the name *cour* meaning court.

St-Denis-d'Anjou – *10.5km/6.5mi SW along D 309*. This village with its numerous pretty gardens has a 12C **fortified church** with keel vaulting and 12C and 15C **frescoes** which were discovered in 1947 and have been gradually restored. They depict St Christopher (west wall); the Martyrdom of St John the Baptist and the Legends of St Nicholas, St Giles and St Hubert on two levels. Opposite the church, which belonged to the Chapter of Angers, stands the 15C canons' house, which is now the town hall, and the 16C market where wine was bought and sold.

Chapelle de Varennes-Bourreau ⊙ – *10km/6mi S along D 159*. This **chapel** nestles in the lush vegetation beside the River Sarthe; it is decorated with beautiful 12C and 15C frescoes: a mandorla surrounds Christ, whose hand is raised in blessing. The village of Varennes was formerly a small port engaged in the transport of wine to Angers before the vines were destroyed by phylloxera.

Miré – *16km/10mi SW via D 309 and D 27*. In this small village, the church is roofed with wooden keel vaulting decorated with 43 late-15C painted panels depicting the Four Evangelists, Angels bearing the Instruments of the Passion and the Apostles presenting the Creed.

Château de Vaux ⊙ – *3.5km/2mi NW of Miré on D 29 towards Bierné*. The picturesque château stands well back from the road to the right. The ruined curtain wall enclosed an elegant building with a stair turret and mullioned windows. This manor house was built at the end of the 15C by **Jean Bourré**, Lord of Miré, whose main claim to fame is that he introduced a delicious fruit – *bon-chrétien* pears – to the Angevin orchards.

ST-AIGNAN★

Population 3 542
Michelin map 318: F-8 or 238 fold 15

St-Aignan stands on the south bank of the Cher at the heart of a region of woods and vineyards. Coteaux du Cher is the wine produced in Seigy and Couffy.
There is a picturesque view of the little town on its sloping site from the bridge or from the north bank on the road *(D 675)* north of Noyers-sur-Cher. Both the church and the Renaissance château are interesting and the nearby zoo boasts some rare white lions.

TOWN WALK

Château – *Not open to the public*. A great flight of steps starting from the church porch leads up to the château court-yard; pleasant view of the roofs of the town, one or two of slate among the tiles. The château consists of two buildings at right an-gles, mostly built in the 16C and backing on to the remains of the medieval fortifications on the east side of the courtyard. The elegant Renaissance dwelling has pilasters flanking the windows, carved dormer gables and a handsome stair in an octagonal turret terminating in a lantern. The terrace overlooks the turbulent Cher passing under the bridge.

Maison de la Prévôté ⊙ – *On leaving the church cross the main street, rue Constant-Ragot*. The 15C building is used for hosting temporary exhibitions.
Rue Constant-Ragot contains two Gothic houses and provides the best view of the chevet of the church. A stroll in the narrow streets and neighbouring square will reveal some 15C carved stone or half-timbered houses.

ADDITIONAL SIGHT

★ **Église St-Aignan** – The collegiate church *(see illustration in Art and architecture: Ecclesiastical architecture)* is a Romanesque building dating from the 11C and 12C with an impressive tower over the transept. A spacious tower-porch with delicately carved capitals leads into the high, radiant nave; the capitals are finely carved into

IN THE RED

Le Crêpiot – *36 r. Constant-Ragot* – ☏ *02 54 75 21 39* – *closed 19 Feb-4 Mar, Tue evening except Jul-Aug, and Mon* – *reservation required for weekends* – *10.51€ lunch, 12.05/14.94€*. Choose from grilled meats, crêpes or salads, and enjoy a simple meal in a pretty setting, with wooden beams and chairs, red and white checked tiles and matching red seats.

acanthus leaves and fantastic animals: the chancel and ambulatory have historiated capitals showing the Flight into Egypt *(north ambulatory)*, the Sacrifice of Isaac and King David *(south side)*.

** **Lower Church** – *Entrance in north transept*. Formerly known as the Church of St John or Church of the Grottoes, it was probably the early Romanesque church which was used as a stable or store during the Revolution. It is similar in plan to the chancel and decorated with **frescoes** (12C-15C): St John the Evangelist (15C) in the central chapel of the ambulatory; the Legend of St Giles in the south chapel. A great Christ in Majesty in a double mandorla (1200) fills the oven vaulting of the chancel and spreads his blessing through the mediation of St Peter and St James to the Sick who are prostrate; the vault over the transept crossing shows the figure of Christ in Judgement resting on a rainbow.

EXCURSIONS

Chapelle St-Lazare – *2km/1mi NE on the north bank of the River Cher*. The chapel of St-Lazare, standing near the road, was once part of a leper house; note the gabled belfry.

* **Zoo-parc de Beauval** ⊙ – *4km/2.5mi S along D 675*.

The road downhill to Beauval zoological park offers a fine view of the local vineyards. A haven for both animals and flowers, this 12ha/30-acre park, built on undulating woodland, has been conceived as an old-fashioned rose garden (2 000 rose bushes) and an Amazonian forest.

A visit to the zoo begins with its feathered residents. A 2 000m²/2 390sq yd **aviary under glass** is home to several hundred exotic birds (including some tiny humming birds) free to flutter about in the lush environment of an equatorial forest complete with waterfalls and streams. Outside, there are about 2 000 more birds to be seen, including 400 or so parrots, some of which are extremely rare.

The next port of call is the section of the zoo given over to mammals. The zoo is home to several species of big cat, including some rare white tigers with blue eyes, white lions, black panthers, pumas, hyenas... Numerous species of monkey and lemur are resident here as part of the European programme for the preservation of endangered species. Visitors will be fascinated by the intense, penetrating gaze and comical expression of small monkeys from the Congolese basin or the Guinean heights, whereas the acrobatics of the athletic orang-utans and various gibbons who inhabit the magnificent huge **tropical hothouse*** never fail to delight onlookers. The hothouse also contains a vivarium (with around 100 snakes) and an aquaterrarium in which turtles and crocodiles are raised. Since 1997, a new hothouse creating an equatorial environment enables visitors to closely observe gorillas and their fascinating behaviour and, for the very first time in France, a group of manatees.

Several times a day from March to mid-October, there is a 30min opportunity to watch the underwater antics of a group of sea-lions. There are also 30min flight demonstrations with 30 or so birds of prey, some of which have a wingspan of nearly 3m/10ft.

All the animals at Beauval were born in captivity.

Château de Chémery ⊙ – *12km/7mi NE on D 675 turning right after St-Romain-sur-Cher onto D 63*. The château (15C and 16C) is a mixture of medieval and Renaissance architecture. It was built on the site of a 12C fortress. In the grounds is a dovecot with spaces for 1 200 birds.

ST-BENOÎT-SUR-LOIRE**

Population 1 876
Michelin map 318: K-5, 238 fold 6 or 4045 E5

The basilica of St-Benoît-sur-Loire is one of the most famous Romanesque buildings in France. Visitors are enthralled by its harmonious proportions and its elaborate carvings steeped in golden light.

Foundation (7C) – According to Celtic tradition St-Benoît-sur-Loire was the place where the local Carnute druids assembled.

In 645 or 651 a group of Benedictine monks led by an abbot from Orléans came to this spot and founded a monastery which very soon gained the favour of the great. Around 672 the **Abbot of Fleury**, as the monastery was called, learned that the body of **St Benedict**, the father of western monasticism who died in 547, was buried beneath the ruins of the abbey of Monte Cassino in Italy. He gave orders for the precious relic, a source of miracles and cures, to be transported to the banks of the Loire where it attracted great crowds of people and brought great success to the monastery.

Theodulf, Odo, Abbo and Gauzlin – Charlemagne gave Fleury to his adviser and friend, **Theodulf**, the talented Bishop of Orléans, who founded two famous monastic schools, an external one for secular priests and an internal one for postulant monks. The scriptorium produced some beautiful work.

Theodulf, a Dignitary at Charlemagne's Court

Theodulf was a Goth, probably originally from Spain or the Ancient Roman province of Gallia Narbonensis (modern south-west France). This brilliant theologian, scholar and poet, well-versed in the culture of Classical Antiquity, came to Neustria after 782 and joined Charlemagne's erudite circle. After a long time spent journeying round the south of France as the emperor's *missus dominicus*, he was made Bishop of Orléans, then Abbot of Micy and of St-Benoît-sur-Loire. Theodulf had a villa (country estate) not far from Fleury; all that now remains is the oratory, or church of Germigny-des-Prés. The villa was sumptuously decorated, with murals depicting the Earth and the World, marble floors and superb mosaics in the oratory which date from about 806. On Charlemagne's death, Theodulf fell into disgrace, accused of plotting against Louis the Pious. He was deposed in 818, exiled and finally died in an Angers prison in 821.

The death of Theodulf and the Viking invasions upset the courses of study and the smooth running of the monastery; discipline suffered as a result.

In the 10C the situation underwent a spectacular change. In 930 **Odo**, a monk from the Touraine, became Abbot of Cluny; he imposed the Cluniac rule at Fleury and reopened the abbey school. St-Benoît regained its prosperity. Students flocked to the school, particularly from England, and the French king and princes offered gifts and extended their patronage. The Archbishop of Canterbury, Odo the Good, received the Benedictine habit from Fleury.

The late 10C was dominated by **Abbo**, a famous scholar and teacher, who enjoyed the favour of the Capets. He entered Fleury as a child, studied in Paris and Reims where he was under the celebrated Gerbert, who had himself been at Fleury, and then returned c 975 to Fleury as Head of Studies. He added to the already extensive **library** and enlarged the area of study. During his reign as abbot (from 988) the abbey was at the forefront of western intellectual life with a particularly strong influence in England and the west of France. He was also a very able organizer of the monastic life of the abbey. Abbo was very influential with Robert II and commissioned a monk called Aimoin to write a **History of the Franks**, which became the official chronicle expounding the ideology of the Capet monarchy. Abbo was assassinated in 1004 during a revolt.

The reign of Abbot **Gauzlin**, the future Archbishop of Bourges, early in the 11C is marked by the production of the so-called Gaignières **Evangelistary**, an illuminated manuscript – gold and silver lettering on purple parchment – which is the work of a Lombard painter, and by the construction of the handsome porch belfry.

The present church (crypt, chancel, transept) was built between 1067 and 1108; the nave was not completed until the end of the 12C.

From the Middle Ages to the present – In the 15C St-Benoît passed *in commendam* this meant that the revenues of the abbey were granted by the monarch to commendatory abbots, often laymen, who were simply beneficiaries and took no active part in the religious life of the community.

The monks did not always make such abbots welcome. Under François I they refused to receive Cardinal Duprat and shut themselves up in the tower of the porch. The King had to come in person, at the head of an armed force, to make them submit.

During the Wars of Religion (1562-98) one of these abbots, Odet de Châtillon-Coligny, the brother of the Protestant leader Admiral Coligny, was himself converted to Protestantism. In 1562, St-Benoît was looted by Condé's Huguenot troops.

The treasure was melted down – the gold casket containing the relics of the saint alone weighed 17.5kg/39lb – the marvellous library was sold and its precious manuscripts, about 2 000 in number, were scattered to the four corners of Europe. Some are now to be found in Berne, Rome, Leyden, Oxford and Moscow.

Le Grand St-Benoit – *7 pl. St-André –* ☎ *02 38 35 11 92 – closed 27 Aug-4 Sep, 24 Dec-23 Jan, Sat lunchtime, Sun evening and Mon – 22.11/41.92€.* A spruce, local-style house in the village centre. Exposed beams in the dining room. Contemporary, well-presented cooking at reasonable prices. Terrace on pedestrianised square.

The celebrated Congregation of St-Maur, introduced to St-Benoît in 1627 by Cardinal de Richelieu, restored its spiritual and intellectual life. The abbey was closed at the Revolution, its archives transferred to Orléans and its property dispersed. At the beginning of the First Empire the monastic buildings were destroyed and the church fell into disrepair. In 1835 it was registered as a historical monument, and it was restored on various occasions between 1836 and 1923. Monastic life was revived there in 1944.

The poet and painter **Max Jacob** (1876-1944) retired to the abbey in St-Benoît-sur-Loire, before being arrested by the Gestapo in 1944. He died in the camp at Drancy and his remains are buried in the local cemetery.

BASILICA ⊘ *45min*

This imposing basilica was built between 1067 and 1218. The towers were originally much taller.

** **Belfry-Porch** – The belfry originally stood by itself, and is one of the finest examples of Romanesque art. It is well worth taking a close look at the richly decorated Corinthian capitals with their abaci and corbels beautifully carved in handsome golden stone from the Nevers region. Stylised plants and flowing acanthus leaves alternate with fantastic animals, scenes from the Apocalypse, and events in the Life of Christ and the Virgin Mary. On the porch (second column from the left), one of the capitals is signed *Umbertus me Fecit.*

Nave – This was rebuilt in the early-Gothic style during the second half of the 12C. It is suffused with light thanks to its white stonework and high vaulting. The organ loft was added c 1700.

St-Benoît-sur-Loire – Porch of the basilica (detail)

Studio 3Bis/MICHELIN

Transept – Like the chancel, this was completed in 1108. The dome, built on superimposed squinches, carries the central bell-tower. Under the dome are the stalls dated 1413 and the remains of a choir screen in carved wood presented in 1635 by Richelieu, when he was Commendatory Abbot of St-Benoît. In the north transept is the precious 14C alabaster statue of Notre-Dame-de-Fleury. Max Jacob used to pray before this statue.

** **Chancel** – The very long Romanesque chancel was built between 1065 and 1108; note the decor of blind arcades with sculpted capitals forming a triforium. The ambulatory with radiating chapels is typical of a church built for crowds and processions; this floor plan can be found in most Benedictine churches.

The floor is paved with a Roman mosaic which was transported from Italy in 1531 by Cardinal Duprat; it is similar to the style popular in the eastern part of the Roman Empire. The recumbent figure is that of Philippe I, the fourth Capet king, who died in 1108.

* **Crypt** – This impressive masterpiece of the second half of the 11C has kept its original appearance. Large round columns form a double ambulatory with radiating chapels round the large central pillar containing the modern shrine of St Benedict, whose relics have been venerated here since the 8C.

EXCURSION

Église de Germigny-des-Prés – The little church in Germigny is a rare and precious example of Carolingian art; it is one of the oldest in France and can be compared with the Carolingian octagon in the cathedral at Aachen, Germany.

The original church, with a ground plan in the form of a Greek cross reminiscent of Echmiadzin Cathedral in Armenia, among other places, had four very similar apses. Visitors should try to imagine what it was like when the entire interior was sumptuously decorated with mosaics and stuccowork and the floor paved with inlaid marble and porphyry.

The east apse is the only original remnant. On its ceiling it has a remarkable **mosaic**** (made up of 130 000 glass cubes), depicting the Ark of the Covenant surmounted by two cherubs flanked by two archangels; at the centre of the composition appears the Hand of God. The use of gold and silver mosaic in the illustration of the archangels links this mosaic to the Byzantine art of Ravenna.

Mosaic on the ceiling of the east apse

This remarkable work of art was discovered under a thick layer of distemper in 1840 when some archaeologists saw children playing with cubes of coloured glass which they had found in the church and decided to investigate.

Other elements in the decor, such as the stucco blind arcades and the capitals, reflect a combination of several artistic influences: the Umayyads, the Mozarabs and the Lombards. In the centre, the altar is lit by a square lantern above the crossing fitted with panes of translucent alabaster (the technique for fitting glass panes was not then widespread). The present nave, which dates from the 15C, took the place of the fourth apse.

ST-CALAIS

Population 3 785
Michelin map 310: N-7, 238 fold 1 or 4072 I4

St-Calais, on the border between Maine and the Vendôme region, is a market town dominated by the ruins of a medieval château. A few old gables still look down on the narrow streets.

Five bridges span the River Anille lined with gardens.

Apple Turnover Festival – The **Fête du chausson aux pommes** has taken place every year since 1581 *(first weekend in September)* to commemorate the end of the plague.

TOWN WALK

The **quais de l'Anille** offer pleasant views of the riverside wash-houses, now overgrown with moss, and gardens of flowers against a background of picturesque roofs.

The district on the west bank developed round the Benedictine abbey which was founded in the reign of Childebert (6C) by Karilefus, an anchorite from Auvergne. The monastery was destroyed during the Revolution but the few 17C buildings which survived are now occupied by the library, the theatre and the museum.

Église Notre-Dame – Construction of the church began in 1425 with the chancel; the building is a mixture of the Flamboyant Gothic and Renaissance styles. The bell-tower is surmounted by a crocketed stone steeple.

The Italianate **façade★** was finished in 1549 and is typical of the second Renaissance. The carved panels of the twin doors portray scenes from the Life of the Virgin Mary; above in the transom are two horns of plenty framed by a semicircular arch. The whole doorway is flanked by two Ionic pilasters. The charming side doors are surmounted by curvilinear pediments and niches. A pedimented window and an oculus are set in the upper part of the gable which is surmounted by five pinnacles ornamented with statues.

The first three bays of the interior are Renaissance; the vaulting with pendentives springs from majestic columns with Ionic capitals. The 17C loft came from the abbey and the organ itself is of the same date. Restored in 1974, it is the pride and joy of the church's organists. A Baroque retable adorns the high altar and a strong cupboard to the right of the chancel contains the shroud of St-Calais which is made of Sassanid (6C Persian) material.

EXCURSION

Château de Courtanvaux ⊙ – *8km/5mi S along D 303 to Bessé-sur-Braye; from Bessé, follow the signposting.* The château, a Gothic building sheltering in the valley, was the seat of a marquisate held successively by the Louvois and Montesquiou families; one of the owners was Michel Le Tellier, **Marquis de Louvois** (1639-91) and Louis XIV's Minister for War.

In 1815, when Napoleon fell from power, the château came to life again after 150 years of neglect and became the residence of the **Countess of Montesquiou** who had been the much-loved governess to the King of Rome, Napoleon's son by Marie-Louise.

An avenue of plane trees leads to the charming Renaissance gatehouse. The buildings have typical 15C and 16C features: tall roofs, mullioned windows and pointed dormer pediments. The courtyard is overlooked by two terraces. The main block, called the Grand Château, has a suite of four rooms (47m/154ft long) on the first floor, which were redecorated in 1882.

ST-PATERNE-RACAN

Population 1 539
Michelin map 317: L-3, 232 fold 23 or 4037 C2

St-Paterne stretches out along the Escotais, which is bordered by riverside wash-houses and weeping willows.

Church – The church contains interesting works of art, some of which came from the nearby abbey of La Clarté-Dieu. The 16C terracotta group to the left of the high altar portrays the Adoration of the Magi; at the centre is a charming **Virgin and Child★**.

In the nave, 18C polychrome statues represent the four great Latin Doctors of the Church – Ambrose, Augustine, Jerome and Gregory the Great – whereas in the south chapel a large retable (Virgin of the Rosary) from the same period is accompanied by a 16C terracotta group of St Anne and the Virgin Mary.

EXCURSIONS

Château de la Roche-Racan ⊙ – *2km/1mi SE on D 28.* The Château de la Roche-Racan stands perched on a rock *(roche)* overlooking the Escotais Valley which, together with the nearby Loir, was a constant source of inspiration to the first owner and poet, **Racan**.

Born at Champmarin near Aubigné, Honorat de Bueil, Marquis de Racan (1589-1670), was a member of the well-known local family, the Bueils. Not really cut out for the life of a soldier and following a number of unlucky love affairs, Racan retired to his country seat for the last 40 years of his life, a period described in his work, *Stances à la retraite.*

There he was quite content to stroll by his fountains or hunt game or visit Denis de la Grelière, the Abbé de la Clarté-Dieu, who invited him to put the Psalms into verse. He brought up his children, pursued his lawsuits, grew beans and rebuilt his château.

In 1635 Racan commissioned a local master mason, Jacques Gabriel, a member of a long-established family of architects, to build this **château**. The main building was originally flanked by two pavilions, only one of which remains standing, pedimented and adorned with a corner turret and caryatids. Long balustered terraces, above arcades decorated with masks, overlook the park and Escotais Valley.

St-Christophe-sur-le-Nais – *2.5km/1.5mi N on D 6.* Also lying in the Escotais Valley, this village is the scene of a pilgrimage in honour of St Christopher *(penultimate Sunday in July)*. The **church** is in fact composed of two separate buildings, an old 11C-14C priory chapel and the parish church with its 16C nave and belfry. On the threshold of the nave a gigantic St Christopher welcomes the visitor. To the right in a recess is a reliquary bust of the saint. To the left of the chancel, the door leading to the prior's oratory is surmounted by a fine 14C statue of the Virgin and Child. Two Renaissance medallions adorn the church's timber roof.

Neuvy-le-Roi – *9km/6mi E on D 54.* The **church**, which dates from the 12C and 16C, has a Romanesque chancel and a nave covered with Angevin vaulting; note in the north aisle the complex pattern of vaulting with projecting keystones (16C), and to the south of the chancel the elegant seigneurial chapel, also with projecting keystones.

Bueil-en-Touraine – *8km/5mi NE along D 72 and D 5.* Set above the valley of the River Long, this village is the cradle of the Bueil family which has supplied France with an admiral, two marshals and a poet, Honorat de Bueil, Lord of Racan.

At the top of the hill stands a curious group of buildings formed by the juxtaposition of the church of St-Pierre-aux-Liens (left) and the collegiate church of St-Michel, founded at the end of the 14C.

Église St-Pierre-aux-Liens – The church is built against a large but incomplete square tower; steps lead up to the door. Inside, there is a remarkable **font** in the Renaissance style, with small statues of Christ and the Apostles on the panels. At the end of the nave are traces of early-16C frescoes and old statues. A door gives into the collegiate church.

Collégiale Saints-Innocents-St-Michel – The church was built by the Bueil family to contain their tombs. The recumbent figures of the lords of Bueil and their ladies are laid in the recesses: the first wife (right) of John V of Bueil is wearing a local headdress *(hennin)* and an emblazoned surcoat.

STE-MAURE-DE-TOURAINE

Population 3 909
Michelin map 317: M-6, 232 fold 35 or 4037 D5

This small town occupies a sunny site on a knoll commanding the Manse Valley. The settlement, which is Roman in origin, developed in the 6C round the tombs of St Britta and St Maurus, and then round the keep built by Fulk Nerra. The Rohan-Montbazon family were the overlords from 1492 to the Revolution.
The town is known for its busy poultry markets and its local goats' milk cheeses. A national Cheese Fair is held annually in June.

Church – The church dates from the 11C but its original appearance was altered when it was restored in 1866. A chapel to the right of the chancel has an attractive 16C white-marble statue of the Virgin Mary by the Italian School. In the central apse there are two painted panels, one depicting the Last Supper (16C), and the other, Christ on a gold background; the relics of St Maurus are venerated here. The crypt has a curious series of archaic Romanesque arcades and a small lapidary museum.

Covered market – The 17C covered market *(halles)* at the top of the town was built by the Rohan family.

PLATEAU DE STE-MAURE

Round trip starting from Ste-Maure *56km/35mi – about 2hr*

The plateau is dissected by the green valleys of two rivers – the Manse and the Esves – and bordered by three others – the Indre (north), the Vienne (west) and the Creuse (south). It is composed of lacustrine limestone which is easily eroded by running water; in the south there are bands of sand and shell, deposited during the Tertiary Era by the Faluns Sea and once used to improve the soil.
Leave Ste-Maure on D 59 going SE.

The line of the road running through the valleys between limestone bluffs is often marked by a row of poplars.

Bournan – The village **church** is Romanesque; it has a beautiful apse and a tower over the side chapel topped by a faceted spire.

Ligueil – Ligueil is a small town built of white stone; there are a few old houses. The decorated wooden washing place is on the edge of the town on the road to Loches (D 31).

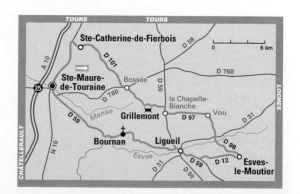

Esves-le-Moutier – The village, which lies on the south bank of the Esves, takes its name from a priory which was surrounded by a fortified wall. The **church** (10C-12C) has a massive square tower with bartizans. The interior contains a 17C wooden gilt altarpiece.

Château de Grillemont – The huge white château stands half way up a slope over-looking an attractive **valley★** of meadows round a lake; the slopes are capped by oak and pine woods. The huge round towers of the castle with their pepper-pot roofs were built in the reign of Charles VII for Lescoet, the governor of Loches Castle; in 1765 the 15C curtain wall was replaced by magnificent Classical buildings.

Drive to Bossée and follow D 101.

Ste-Catherine-de-Fierbois – The spirit of Joan of Arc hovers over this village which lies grouped round its church, east of the main road (N 10).

On 23 April 1429, following directions given by Joan of Arc, a sword marked with five crosses was found on this site. It was supposed to have been placed there by **Charles Martel** after his victory over the Saracens at Poitiers in 732. The **church** was rebuilt in 1431 and completed in the reign of Charles VIII, whose coat of arms appears on the building together with that of Anne of Brittany. The chapel, restored in 1859, is in the Flamboyant Gothic style with an interesting door beneath a pierced pediment.

Simple pleasures of the Ste-Maure region

The interior vaulting springs directly from the piers. Hanging under a glass cover on the north wall of the nave is a small but very realistic 15C Entombment. The south transept contains an unusual 15C altar; on it stands a 15C statue of St Catherine whose image is also carved on the front. Opposite is a rare confessional in the Flamboyant style, very delicately carved.

Maison du Dauphin – The door of this house (1415) to the left of the church is flanked by two sphinxes. Note the charming carving on the lip of the well in the courtyard.

N 10 leads back to Ste-Maure-de-Touraine

SAUMUR★★

Population 29 857
Michelin map 317: I-5, 232 fold 33 or 4049 I5
Local map see La Loire Angevine below

Lying on the banks of the Loire, beneath its imposing fortress, Saumur is famous for its Cavalry School, its wines – especially its sparkling wines – its medal makers and its mushrooms (local production of mushrooms represents 42% of the national figure). Every year a tattoo using horses and motor transport is given by the **Cadre Noir** on the vast place du Chardonnet *(see Calendar of events)*, drawing large numbers of spectators. Repeat performances are given in the Riding School of the National Equitation Centre in Terrefort.
From Easter to September, a **tourist train** ⊙ takes visitors on a tour of the town.

AN EVENTFUL HISTORY

Charles the Bald built a fortified monastery in the 9C to house the relics of St Florent who converted the region to Christianity in the 4C, but it was not long before it was destroyed by the Vikings. In the 11C Saumur was the subject of numerous conflicts between the Count of Blois and the Count of Anjou. In 1203 the town was captured by Philippe Auguste. The castle was destroyed on several occasions and subsequently restored or rebuilt. From the time of Louis IX (13C) Saumur shared the destiny of the **House of Anjou**.
In the late 16C and early 17C the town enjoyed its true heyday. It was one of the great centres of Protestantism. Henri III gave it as a stronghold to the King of Navarre, the future Henri IV, who appointed as Governor **Duplessis-Mornay**, a great soldier, scholar and fervent Reformer, who was known by the Roman Catholics as the Huguenot Pope. He founded a Protestant academy which won widespread renown. In 1611 a general assembly of the Protestant churches was held there to consolidate their organisation following the death of Henri IV and the departure of Sully. Louis XIII grew alarmed at the Protestant danger and ordered the town walls to be demolished in 1623. The Revocation of the Edict of Nantes in 1685 dealt Saumur a fatal blow; many of the inhabitants emigrated and the Protestant church was demolished.

École d'application de l'arme blindée et de la cavalerie (EAABC) – It is interesting to note the mementoes of officers who served in the cavalry of the African Army between 1830 and 1962: Bugeaud, Gallifet, Charles de Foucault, who was an officer before he became a recluse, Lyautey, Henry de Bournazel and Leclerc de Hauteclocque. In June 1940 the officers and cadets of the Cavalry School made it a point of honour to defend the passage of the Loire. For three days, from 18 to 20 June, although inferior in number and having only training equipment, they performed many heroic feats and succeeded in holding the Germans in check on a 25km/16mi front between Gennes and Montsoreau.

★OLD TOWN

The narrow twisting streets between the castle and the bridge still follow their original course; in some areas the old houses have been preserved whereas in others new constructions have been built in the medieval style or are resolutely modern but full of surprises (south of St Peter's Church).
Along the main shopping street, rue St-Jean, and in the square, **place St-Pierre**, half-timbered houses and 18C mansions with wrought-iron balconies stand side by side. The new market (1982) blends with the older styles.

Église St-Pierre – The church is Plantagenet Gothic except for the west front which collapsed in the 17C and was rebuilt. The beautiful Romanesque door in the south transept leads into the interior which is hung with two series of 16C **tapestries★**. Regular concerts of organ music are given here.

★ **Hôtel de ville** – Only the left-hand section of the town hall is old (16C). Originally the Loire flowed past the foundations and the building was a bridgehead and part of the town walls, hence its military appearance. The façade facing the courtyard is in the Gothic Renaissance transitional style with some fine sculpture.

★ **Église Notre-Dame-de-Nantilly** – This is a fine Romanesque church. Louis XI, who had a great devotion to the Virgin Mary, added the right aisle; his oratory was used as a baptismal chapel. A pillar on the left in the same aisle bears an epitaph composed by King René d'Anjou for his nurse Tiphaine.
The 12C painted wooden statue of Our Lady of Nantilly was placed in the apse on the right of the chancel. The organ case resting on telamones dates from 1690.
There are fine **tapestries★★** dating from the 15C and 16C except for eight in the nave which were made at Aubusson in the 17C and depict scenes from the lives of Christ and the Virgin.

Eating out

BUDGET

Les Pêcheurs – *512 rte de Montsoreau – 3km/1.8mi E of Saumur on D 947 –* ☎ *02 41 67 79 63 – closed during Feb and October school holidays – reservation recommended – 9.90/18.30€.* A visit to this unpretentious restaurant will surely make you The Fisherman's friend. The summer menu features fresh small fry *(friture)* from the Loire, and eels are a favourite with the regulars all year round.

Auberge St-Pierre – *6 pl. St-Pierre –* ☎ *02 41 51 26 25 – closed 12-26 Mar, 8-22 Oct, 24 Dec-2 Jan, Sun except lunchtime in Jul-Aug, and Mon – 12.96/22.87€.* This 15C half-timbered red-brick property near St-Pierre Church is a pleasant place to stop and eat. Friendly, family atmosphere and reasonable prices.

MODERATE

Le Relais – *31 quai Mayaud –* ☎ *02 41 67 75 20 – closed Feb, Sat lunchtime and Sun – reservation required – 20/28.97€.* A restaurant and wine bar where good traditional cooking is accompanied by the best of the local wines. The wine list will delight enthusiasts. Summer terrace in the beautiful paved courtyard.

Where to stay

BUDGET

Hôtel du Roi René – *94 av. du Gén.-de-Gaulle –* ☎ *02 41 67 45 30 – 38 rooms 44.21/48.78€ –* ☱ *6.40€ – restaurant 14/27€.* An imposing regional-style property built on an island opposite the castle, on a branch of the Loire. The rooms in this hotel are plain, functional and bright. Restaurant with a good choice of reasonably priced menus.

Chambre d'hôte Château de Beaulieu – *98 rte de Montsoreau –* ☎ *02 41 67 69 51 – 5 rooms 69/120€.* A beautiful little limestone castle. The individually named rooms are elegant and refined, with a personal touch, and you will be impressed by the peace of the surrounding park and the quality of the service. Guaranteed to please.

Village hôtelier Le Bois de Terrefort – *49400 St-Hilaire-St-Florent – 2km/1mi W of Saumur on D 751 –* ☎ *02 41 50 94 41 –* ▣ *– 13 rooms 49.54/96.04€ –* ☱ *4.88€.* A hotel-village near the national riding school, not far from Saumur, providing accommodation in simple, practical little cottages. The peaceful country setting and reasonable prices make this an ideal place to stay for those on a tight budget.

On the town

Blues Rock Magazine – *7 r. de la Petite-Bilange –* ☎ *02 41 50 41 69 – Tue-Sun 11pm-4am.* A private dance club which is the cool place to be seen in Saumur. It attracts a smart and select clientele of all ages and styles, and features authentic rock. Regular events and concerts.

L'Absynthe – *27 r. Molière –* ☎ *02 41 51 23 37 – cafe-absynthe@hotmail.com – daily 5pm-2am – closed Mon in winter.* This atmospheric bar with a Canadian influence (the owner once worked in Quebec) is probably the liveliest in the staid city of Saumur, and is popular with the younger crowd. Apart from regular concerts, the venue holds open-mike nights for amateur musicians. There are 30 kinds of beer and 40 different whiskies to please every customers.

Place St-Pierre – Several of the 18C half-timbered buildings near the Gothic church of St Pierre house cafés with shady terraces in this lovely square: Le Café du Parvis, Le Richelieu, Le Café de la Place, Le Swing...

Sit back and relax

Au Bureau – *19 pl. Bilange –* ☎ *02 41 67 39 71 – daily 10am-2am.* High-class, impeccable and very professional; these are the words that come to mind to describe the Bureau, with its terrace seating 120, its attentive waiters, its brass beer pumps, its immaculate wood panelling and carpets. Respect and tolerance for others also play a part, as the sound is kept at a reasonable level when sports events are broadcast on the TV.

Maison des vins de Saumur – *Quai Lucien-Gautier –* ☎ *02 41 38 45 83 – Tue-Sat 7am-1pm, 3-7pm, Sun 10am-1pm, Mon 3-7pm.* Located next to the tourist office, this is a good place to learn about the wines of Saumur from the selection of 42 vintage wines grown in Anjou and the Saumur area; competent and friendly specialists provide information and advice during wine tasting sessions; afterwards, it is possible to buy wine on the premises or go to the wine-growers' cellars which are open to visitors.

Distillerie Combier – *48 rue Beaurepaire –* ☎ *02 41 40 23 00.* Learn all about the art of 19C distillers and admire the shiny copper stills; after the visit, you can taste different liqueurs and buy whichever you prefer!

Château de Saumur

SIGHTS

★★ Château ⊘ – *1hr 30min.* The château is compact and solid, but the vertical lines of its pointed and ribbed towers lend it a certain grace. Despite being a fortress it is decorated in the style of a country house with sculpted machicolations and balustrades at the windows overlooking the courtyard. It stands high above the Loire Valley on a sort of pedestal created by the star-shaped 16C fortifications.

A succession of fortresses has been erected on the promontory. The present building, which succeeded Louis IX's castle, was rebuilt at the end of the 14C by Louis I, Duke of Anjou, and completed by Louis II. The interior was altered in the 15C by René d'Anjou and external fortifications were added in the late 16C by Duplessis-Mornay. Under Louis XIV and Louis XV it was the residence of the Governor of Saumur; it subsequently became a prison and then barracks and it now houses two museums. From the château terrace there is a fine **panorama★** of the town and the valleys of the Thouet *(south)* and the Loire *(east and west)*.

★★ Musée des Arts décoratifs ⊘ – The exhibits in this museum, which include the Lair Collection, form a fine display of decorative works of art from the Middle Ages and the Renaissance period: Limoges enamels, alabaster and wooden sculptures, tapestries, furniture, paintings, sacred ornaments and a collection of French faience and porcelain (17C-18C) together with furniture and tapestries from the same period. The 15C and 16C tapestries include the *Savages' Ball*, the *Return from the Hunt*, the *Coronation of Vespasian* and the *Capture of Jerusalem* (the last two make up part of a tapestry series on the *Story of Titus*).

★ Musée du Cheval ⊘ – The Equine Museum depicts the history of the saddle horse and equitation in different countries over the years: collections of saddles, bits, stirrups and spurs, fine engravings referring to the Saumur Cavalry School, horse racing and famous thoroughbreds as well as splendid harnesses from the world over (Asia, North America and Africa).

★ Musée de l'École de cavalerie ⊘ – *Entrance in avenue Foch.* In 1763 the Carabiniers Regiment, a crack corps recruited from the best horsemen in the army, was sent to Saumur. The present central building was constructed between 1767 and 1770 as their barracks.

This museum's rich display of souvenirs, created in 1936 from Barbet de Vaux collections, traces the heroic deeds of the French Cavalry and the Armoured Corps since the 18C.

★★ Musée des Blindés ⊘ – *Via boulevard Louis-Renault; follow the signposts.* This museum and information centre on tanks houses over 100 vehicles (tanks, armoured

Renault FT 17 tank

vehicles, artillery equipment), many of which are still in working order, coming from a dozen or more countries. It offers a survey of the history of the Armoured Corps and Cavalry from 1917 up to the present. The most prestigious or rare exhibits are the **St-Chamond** and the **Schneider** (the first French tanks), the Renault FT 17 (French tank used in the very last stages of the First World War), the Somua S 35, the B1bis (issued to the 2nd Armoured Division under General de Gaulle in 1940) and German tanks dating from the French Campaign until the fall of Berlin (Panzers III and IV, Panther, Tiger), the Comet A 34 (the British tank used in the Normandy landing), the Churchill A 22, the Sherman M 4 and AMX 13 and 30.

Besides examples of armoured tanks which played a part in the Allied landing of 6 June 1944 (practically all the different models are displayed) there are vehicles belonging to the UN peace-keeping forces, as well as numerous heavy and light tanks from a variety of nations (Germany, Russia, Britain, the United States, Sweden etc).

Several display windows and dioramas illustrate the way tanks are used in combat.

During the Carrousel, in July, the Tank Museum exhibits several of these vehicles, which it has carefully restored, driven by trainees from the École d'Application de l'Arme Blindée et de la Cavalerie.

SAUMUR

Anjou (R. d')	**BZ**	2
Beaurepaire (R.)	**AY**	3
Bilange (Pl. de la)	**BY**	4
Cadets (Pont des)	**BX**	5
Dr-Bouchard (R. du)	**AZ**	6

Dupetit-Thouars (Pl.)	**BZ**	7
Fardeau (R.)	**AZ**	9
Gaulle (Av. du Général-de)	**BX**	
Leclerc (R. du Mar.)	**AZ**	
Nantilly (R. de)	**BZ**	10
Orléans (R. d')	**ABY**	
Poitiers (R. de)	**AZ**	12

Portail-Louis (R. du)	**BY**	13
République (Pl. de la)	**BY**	15
Roosevelt (R. Fr.)	**BY**	16
St-Jean (R.)	**BY**	18
St-Pierre (Pl.)	**BY**	19
Tonnelle (R. de la)	**BY**	20
Vieux-Pont (R. du)	**BY**	22

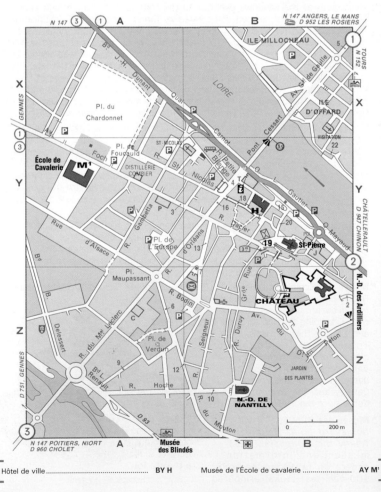

Hôtel de ville	BY	H
Musée de l'École de cavalerie	AY	M¹

Église Notre-Dame-des-Ardilliers – *On the eastern edge of the city, quai L.-Mayaud, D 947*. This beautiful 17C church building is one of the most popular places of pilgrimage in France. Devotion to Our Lady of Ardilliers began to develop in the reign of François I thanks to a miraculous statue a farm labourer was supposed to have discovered on this spot in the previous century, but it was to reach its height in the 17C when the number of pilgrims exceeded 10 000 a year.

EXCURSIONS

Bagneux – *South of Saumur. Leave town by ③ on the plan*. Bagneux, which lies at the heart of the oldest inhabited region of Anjou, is an old village on the banks of the Thouet.

The engines displayed in the **Musée du Moteur** ⊙ *(no 18 rue Alphonse-Cailleau; second street on the left after Fouchard bridge)* have been collected by mechanics enthusiasts, most of whom attended the Saumur Industrial School and wish to preserve and restore old and contemporary engines.

Return to rue du Pont-Fouchard for a short distance. Beyond the town hall, bear left onto rue du Dolmen.

Le Grand Dolmen ⊙ – The Great Dolmen, situated in the centre of the village itself, is one of the most remarkable megalithic dolmens in Europe. It measures 20m/66ft long by 7m/23ft wide and consists of 16 standing stones (weighing about 500t) forming a passage and supporting a roof 3m/10ft high which is composed of four capstones.

Château de Boumois ⊙ – *7km/4mi NW, on the north bank of the Loire*. Boumois was the birthplace in 1760 of **Aristide Dupetit-Thouars**. This highly experienced naval officer took part in the French expedition to Egypt. In the course of the Battle of the Nile, fought between the British (commanded by Nelson) and the French off Aboukir, Dupetit-Thouars preferred to die a hero's death on the quarterdeck of his ship, *The Tonnant*, rather than haul down his flag.

The apparently feudal exterior of the 16C château conceals an elegant residence in the Flamboyant and Renaissance styles. The driveway leads to the main entrance; on the left stands a 17C dovecot still with its rotating ladder and nesting places for 1 800 birds. A massive gate opens onto the main courtyard which is protected by a fortified wall, formerly reinforced by a moat.

The house itself, which is late 15C, is flanked by two huge machicolated towers. The entrance to the stair turret in the inner courtyard is closed by a door with detailed Renaissance motifs and the original and most unusual wrought-iron lock.

The Great Hall contains a marble effigy of Marguerite de Valois, a full-length portrait of Elizabeth I of England and an Indian screen from Coromandel. In the beautiful Flamboyant chapel is a Virgin and Child by Salviati and a 15C Burgundian sculpture of the Holy Family.

St-Cyr-en-Bourg – *8km/5mi S on D 93*. A visit to the **Cave des vignerons de Saumur** ⊙ is a good way of learning more about the whole winemaking process, from the grape to the finished product, in a series of underground galleries reaching 25m/82ft below ground level; a motorised vehicle circulates in the galleries. There is a commentary and wine tasting in a special chamber.

★LA LOIRE ANGEVINE

From Saumur to Angers *48km/30mi – about 3hr 30min*

Leave Saumur along D 751.

St-Hilaire-St-Florent – *2km/1mi NW*. The village consists of one long street straggling at the foot of the hill beside the River Thouet. It is in fact a suburb of Saumur, which is given over mainly to the production of a famous sparkling white wine made by the Champagne method; all along on either side of the road there is one wine cellar after another.

Caves Bouvet-Ladubay ⊙ – From its premises in galleries hollowed out of the tufa rock, this leading producer of Saumur Brut unveils the stages involved in the production of its wines, from the initial fermentation to the sophisticated design of its bottles. There is an outstanding collection of labels.

Galerie d'Art Contemporain Bouvet-Ladubay ⊙ – This contemporary art gallery consists of nine rooms exhibiting works by artists of today, following their search for new directions in their various fields (architecture, sculpture, painting). There is also a section on journalism. A delightful little theatre founded in the late 19C to entertain staff has just been reopened.

★ **École nationale d'équitation** ⊙ – The riding school was opened in 1972 on the Terrefort and Verrie plateaux. It is a modern establishment consisting of several units, each comprising a granary where foodstuffs are stored, a large dressage arena that can seat 1 200 spectators and stabling for 400 horses with harness rooms and showers. One of the vocations of the school, which comes under the auspices of the French Ministry for Youth and Sport, is to maintain the level of French horsemanship and further its renown. The **Cadre Noir** (Black Squad) has been based here since 1984. A fundamental part of the school, it is involved in all its projects and gives its traditional repeat performances of *Manège* (dressage) and *Sauteurs en liberté* (jumps) in France and all over the world.

Musée du Champignon ⊙ – Large areas of the old tufa quarries which pit the hillsides around Saumur are used for the cultivation of mushrooms which need humidity and a constant temperature (between 11°C and 14°C). Mushrooms have been grown in the quarries since the time of Napoleon I, but production has escalated to industrial scale and now takes up some 800km/497mi of galleries yielding some 200 000t.

⊚ The museum is a thriving mushroom bed which explains the various options open to growers; the oldest method of growing in mushroom beds is gradually being replaced by more modern techniques using wooden crates, plastic bags, bales of straw and the trunks of trees. Apart from button-mushrooms, new types of cultivated mushroom such as shiitake, pleurotus (oyster mushrooms) and *piedbleu* are also on show.

The visit ends with the Muséum des Champignons Sauvages, presenting several hundred different varieties of wild mushroom classified into families.

Parc miniature Pierre et Lumière ⊙ – *On the way out of St-Hilaire-St-Florent.*

⊚ This former underground tufa quarry houses remarkable sculptures by Pierre Cormant. A fascinating educational tour.

Chênehutte-les-Tuffeaux – The village **church** stands beside the road on the north side of the village. It is an attractive Romanesque building with a handsome doorway in the same style; the arch stones are carved.

Trèves-Cunault – A 15C crenellated keep is all that remains of the old castle. Tucked in beside it is the little **church**★ of Trèves, once the castle chapel. It has a beautiful interior with great arches supporting the broad Romanesque nave; the chancel arch frames the rood beam on which there is a Crucifix. The holy water stoup by the entrance is of porphyry with primitive carvings; to the right is a recumbent figure; to the left stands a tall stone tabernacle pierced with Flamboyant Gothic openwork.

★★ **Église de Cunault** – Cunault Abbey was founded in 847 by monks from Noirmoutier fleeing from the Normans; in 862 they had to move from Cunault and take refuge further away in Tournus in Burgundy where they deposited the relics of St Philibert. Cunault therefore became a rich Benedictine priory dependent on Tournus Abbey. The monastic church is a beautiful Romanesque structure dating from the 11C to the 13C.

The huge 11C bell-tower has been extended by a 15C stone spire; the broad façade is simply decorated with arches at the base and three windows above. In contrast, the tympanum over the door is richly decorated with a Virgin in Majesty in generous high relief.

On entering one is struck by the sheer size and height of the pillars. Cunault Church was built in the regular Benedictine style to provide for the liturgical ceremonies (seven per day in the Rule of St Benedict) and for the crowds which attended the pilgrimage on 8 September. The ambulatory with its radiating chapels which circumscribed the chancel and the side aisles were broad enough to take the traditional processions, and the raised chancel enabled the faithful to see the celebrant.

The church is impressive both for its pure lines and the rich decoration (11C-12C) of its 223 **capitals**. Only two, at the entrance to the chancel, are visible without binoculars: *(right)* nine monks standing and *(left)* St Philibert welcoming a sinner. The ambulatory chapels contain *(starting on the left)* a 16C *Pietà*, a 16C ash vestment wardrobe (for stiff copes) and a rare 13C carved and painted **shrine** belonging to St Maxenceul who converted Cunault in the 4C. In the 15C the church was decorated with frescoes; a few fragments and a fine St Christopher remain. The four bells in the tower come from Constantine Cathedral in Algeria. Opposite the church stands the prior's lodging, an attractive 16C house.

Cunault – Virgin in Majesty on the church tympanum

Gennes – Among the wooded hills hereabouts are numerous megaliths including the **Madeleine dolmen** south of the Doué road. Discoveries including an aqueduct, baths, an amphitheatre and the figure of a nymph point to the former existence of a Gallo-Roman shrine dedicated to a water cult.

Amphithéâtre ⊙ – Discovered as long ago as 1837 and still being excavated, this is assumed to have been the structure serving as the local amphitheatre between the 1C and 3C. It is set into a terraced slope cut into on the north-east by a podium and has an elliptical arena whose principal axis measures 44m/145ft. On the north side is the boundary wall built of sandstone, tufa and brick paralleled by a paved drainage corridor.

Église St-Eusèbe ⊙ – This church, on a hilltop overlooking the Loire, has kept only its transept, its tower from the 12C and, on the north side, a small 11C doorway. From the tower there is a vast **panorama** over Gennes and the Loire Valley from the Avoine nuclear power station to Longue and Beaufort. The churchyard has built a memorial to the cadets of the Saumur Cavalry School who fell defending the Loire crossing in June 1940.

Le Prieuré – *6.5km/4mi W of Gennes on D 751, turn left beyond Le Sale-Village.* The hamlet clusters around this charming priory whose **church** (12C and 13C) has a delightful square Romanesque tower and, inside, a fine painted wooden altar (17C).

Les Rosiers-sur-Loire – *1km/0.3mi N of Gennes.* Linked to Gennes by a suspension bridge, this village has a church whose Renaissance tower was built by the Angers architect Jean de l'Espine; the staircase turret flanking it is pierced by pretty, pilastered windows. In the church square is a statue of Jeanne de Laval, second wife of **René of Anjou**.

Cross back over the bridge; turn right immediately onto D 132 along the south bank.

Le Thoureil – This quiet, spruce little village was formerly an active river port for the handling of apples. Inside the **church**, on either side of the chancel there are two beautiful wooden reliquary shrines dating from the late 16C, which originally belonged to the abbey of St-Maur-de-Glanfeuil *(see below)*; they are adorned with statuettes of Benedictine monks (Maurus, Roman) and saints who were popular locally.

Abbaye de St-Maur-de-Glanfeuil – This ruined Benedictine abbey is believed to be named after St Maurus, a hermit who came from Angers and founded a monastery in the 6C on the site of the Roman villa of Glanfeuil on the Loire. The abbey presently houses an international ecumenical centre and is home to a religious community of Augustinians *(not open to the public).*

Cross the river via D 55. In St-Mathurin, turn right onto D 952 then left onto D 7.

Beaufort-en-Vallée – Beaufort nestles amid the rich plains of the Anjou Valley. In the 18C-19C it was one of the largest manufacturers of sailcloth in France. The town is dominated by the ruins of the **château**, which was built in the 14C by Guillaume Roger, Count of Beaufort and father of Pope Gregory XI. The Tour Jeanne de Laval was rebuilt in the 15C by King René. From the top of the bluff on which the ruins stand there is a charming **view** of the surrounding country.

Church – This was largely restored in the 19C and has a fine belfry built by Jean de Lespine and completed in 1542 over the 15C transept.

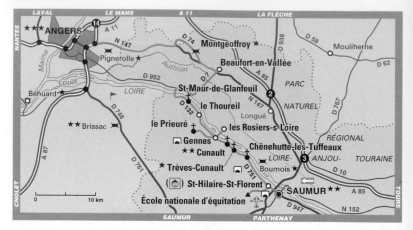

The interior contains a 17C Adoration of the Shepherds, a carved wooden altar (1617) and the earlier high altar, made of marble, which is now under the great window in the transept.

Follow N 147 then turn right onto D 74.

★**Château de Montgeoffroy** ⊙ – This elegant château, overlooking the Authion Valley, has a harmonious Louis XV façade. The two round towers attached to the wings, the curvilinear moat defining the courtyard and the chapel to the right are the only remains of the original 16C building.

The Montgeoffroy estate came into the possession of Erasme de Contades in 1676; the buildings owe their present appearance to his grandson, the famous Marshal who commanded the German army in the Seven Years War and who was Governor of Alsace for 25 years. His architect was the Parisian Nicolas Barré.

The **château** has remained in the family, and has consequently kept its original furnishings and decor, which combine to create an effect of great charm.

The **Chapelle Ste-Catherine** has Angevin vaulting and a 16C stained-glass window depicting the kneeling figure of the previous owner of Montgeoffroy, Guillaume de la Grandière.

In the **stables** is a collection of horse-drawn vehicles. The magnificent **Harness Room** fitted out in Norway spruce contains a collection of saddles, stirrups, bridles, whips and riding crops.

N 147 leads to Angers.

SEGRÉ

Population 6 410
Michelin map 317: D-2, 232 fold 18 or 4049 D2

The schist houses of Segré cascade down the slope to the river which is bordered by quays and spanned by attractive bridges.
The town is the capital of the Segréen, a region of woods and meadows devoted to mixed farming and also known for its high-grade iron ore.

Old Bridge – The humpback bridge over the River Oudon offers pretty views of the old parts of the town.

Chapelle St-Joseph – There is a good view of the old town and the Oudon Valley from this chapel.

★**Château de la Lorie** ⊙ – *On the outskirts of town, heading E along D 863.* La Lorie is an imposing 18C château approached up a long avenue of trees which meet overhead. The château stands in a setting of formal French gardens.

A dry moat surrounds a square courtyard which is bordered on three sides by ranges of buildings with white-tufa tiles; a statue of Minerva, the Bearer of Peace adorns the central range, which was built in the 17C by René Le Pelletier, Provost General of Anjou; the château's imposing dimensions are due to the addition of the two wings and the symmetrical outbuildings (late 18C).

The same nobility of line and form is echoed in the interior: the Great Gallery decorated with beautiful Chinese vases, the late-18C Marble Salon, the adjoining chapel and the 18C woodwork in the Dining Hall. The Great Salon is the most unusual as it is sumptuously decorated with Sablé marble and was designed by Italian artists in 1779; the musicians played in the overhead rotunda.

EXCURSIONS

Château de Raguin ✎ – *8.5km/5mi SW on D 923; in St-Gemmes-d'Andigné bear left onto D 183*. The old 15C castle was replaced c 1600 by Guy du Bellay, son of Pierre du Bellay (cousin of the poet), with a Renaissance-style building.

Although a marshal in the King's army, Du Bellay had a taste for luxury and he made Raguin a luxurious and elegant château. When his son Antoine married in 1648, he had the first-floor salon and another room fitted with wainscots and had the walls and ceiling entirely redecorated; in the second room, Chambre des Amours, the cherubs play with the initials of the newly-wed couple.

Vallé de l'Oudon

Round trip of 21km/13mi – allow 45min, not including the tour of Noyant-la-Gravoyère. Leave Segré on D 923 going SW towards Candé; beyond the level crossing turn right onto D 181.

Le Bourg-d'Iré – *8km/5mi W along D 181*. This town stands in the valley of the River Verzée. From the bridge there is a most attractive **view** of the river.

Take D 219 to the right. Drive through Noyant-la-Gravoyère, which once had a flourishing fine-slate industry; continue to Nyoiseau along D 775 towards Segré then take the first road on the left.

The road runs through a schist gorge, partially flooded by small lakes which make this the most picturesque section of the excursion. The land surrounding the two lakes – St-Blaise and La Corbinière – has been laid out as a **leisure park**.

Nyoiseau – The village – its name is a corruption of *Niosellum* meaning little nest – perched on the slopes of the Oudon Valley has the remains of a Benedictine abbey for women, now used as a farm as well as housing the town hall. Along the road leading to L'Hôtellerie-de-Flée stands an old Gallo-Roman bridge.

Leave Nyoiseau N.

★ **Domaine de la Petite Couère** ✎ – A pleasant setting for country walks and leisure activities, this 80ha/198-acre protected park offers a fascinating combination of rural ethnography, animal species and mechanical curiosities.

📷 Near the entrance stands a **Tractor Museum** (Musée du Tracteur), displaying around 80 vehicles from 1910 to 1950 along with many other farming vehicles. Further on, there are around 40 vintage cars, including a 1913 Brasier Phaeton. Another exhibition is the painstaking reconstitution of a small village at the turn of the 20C with its chapel, school, town hall, café-grocery and various shops. One of the attics houses a curious collection of washing machines, enlightening visitors on the history of boilers and mangles from 1880 to 1950.

🚶 Visitors can also wander from one enclosure to the next thanks to the various signposted paths (1-6km/0.5-4mi long). The park is peopled by more than 80 animal species (watussi, horses, emus, Poitou donkeys, llamas, deer) living in relative freedom, which can be approached fairly easily.

Two small trains make the 15min trip from the many picnic areas to the village *(pigeonholes have been set aside for iceboxes and picnic baskets)*.

SELLES-SUR-CHER

Population 4 775
Michelin map 318: G-8 or 238 fold 16

Selles-sur-Cher is prettily situated in a bend of the River Cher, in which the towers of its castle are reflected. The town developed round an abbey which was founded by St Eusice, a hermit who lived in that spot. Only the abbey church now remains.

The town of Selles-sur-Cher has given its name to a delicious goat's cheese sold in flat round pats dusted with charcoal. Highly popular among gourmets, it was awarded its own *appellation d'origine contrôlée* (AOC) in 1975.

SIGHTS

Église St-Eusice – The church, which dates from the 12C and 15C, was burned down by Coligny in 1562; it was partially restored in the 17C and then more thoroughly in the 19C. The façade, which is almost entirely Romanesque, has reused the columns and capitals from an earlier church which was destroyed by marauding Normans in c 903.

The **chevet**, which is well built, is ornamented with two friezes of figures; those below the windows are rough, simple and heavy but those above are better proportioned and more elegant. The lower frieze depicts scenes from the New Testament; the upper one illustrates the Life of St Eusice.

Near the north wall are low-relief carvings of the Labours of the Months; higher up and further to the right there is a beautiful Visitation, protected by the transept chapel.

In the north wall, which was built late in the 13C, there is a charming door decorated with carved capitals supporting tori separated by a chain of flowers and wild rose leaves.

The crypt contains the tomb of St Eusice (6C).

Castle – *Closed to the public*. The remains of an austere 13C fortress stand in striking contrast to a couple of light 17C buildings joined together by a long arcaded wall.

Musée du Val-de-Cher ⊙ – A variety of exhibits is displayed in the Cher Valley Museum: documents about Selles' past, tools used by wine-growers, basket-makers, coopers and watermen, and an interesting section on the preparation of gunflint, a thriving industry in the region from the middle of the 18C until the invention of the percussion cap *(see EXCURSIONS: Meusnes)*.

EXCURSIONS

Châtillon-sur-Cher – *5km/3mi W on N 76 towards St-Aignan and a turning to the left*. This little village stands on the north slope of the Cher Valley. The **Église de St-Blaise** ⊙ contains *(left wall of chancel)* a **panel★** by the School of Leonardo da Vinci depicting St Catherine between two cherubs: the treatment of the hands, a little mannered but very attractive, and the facial expression are typical of Da Vinci's style.

A statue of St Vincent, patron of wine-growers, is surrounded by the batons of their brotherhood which are carried in their processions.

Meusnes – *6.5km/4mi SW on D 956 briefly towards Valençay and then right onto D 17*. The **church** is in the pure Romanesque style. There is a triumphal arch in the transept surmounted by three charming open-work arcatures. Several beautiful 15C and 16C statues have been reinstated.

A small gunflint museum, **Musée de la Pierre à fusil** ⊙, housed in the town hall, describes this industry which flourished in the region for 300 years.

Château de SERRANT★★★

Michelin map 317: E-4, 232 fold 31 or 4049 E4
Local map see ANGERS

Although built over a period of three centuries, 16C to 18C, this sumptuous moated mansion has great unity of style and instant appeal. Its massive domed towers and the contrast between the dark schist and the white tufa give it considerable character *(see illustration in Art and architecture: Civil architecture)*.

The **Château de Serrant** ⊙ was begun in 1546 by Charles de Brie supposedly after drawings by Philibert Delorme, the architect responsible for the construction of Fontainebleau, but it was more likely designed by Jean de L'Espine, a local architect who built the central tower of Angers Cathedral. Tthe castle was bought by Hercule de Rohan, Duke of Montbazon, in 1596, and sold in 1636 to Guillaume Bautru whose granddaughter married the Marquis of Vaubrun, Lieutenant-General of the king's army. On the death of her husband, who was killed beside Turenne at the Battle of Altenheim, the Marchioness continued construction work until 1705. She commissioned Jules Hardouin-Mansart to build the beautiful chapel in memory of her husband, and Coysevox to design the white-marble mausoleum. During the 18C, the property was acquired by Antoine Walsh, a member of the Irish nobility who followed James II into exile in France and became a shipowner in Nantes. In 1830 one of his descendants married the Duc de la Trémoille and the castle is still in the hands of this illustrious family.

Tour – In addition to the superb Renaissance staircase surmounted by coffered vaulting, the whole interior is extremely attractive. The **apartments★★★** are magnificently furnished and this exceptional collection of furniture was added in November 2000 to the list of Historic Monuments. Sumptuous Flemish and Brussels tapestries hang in the reception rooms which contain rare pieces of furniture such as the unique ebony cabinet by Pierre Gole (17C) adorning the Grand Salon. Note also 17C, 18C and early-19C furniture by prestigious cabinet-makers (Saunier, JE de Saint-Georges) and Empire-style furniture by Jacob, upholstered with Beauvais tapestry, commissioned for Napoleon and Josephine's visit.

There are fine paintings representing the French and Italian schools, a bust of the Empress Marie-Louise by Canova (Empire-style bedroom on the first floor), and two terracotta nymphs by Coysevox in the sumptuous **Grand Salon★★**.

The **library★★★** also houses some treasures, including 12 000 volumes (incunabula, engravings by Piranese, first editions of La Fontaine's Fables and Diderot's Encyclopaedia). Some of the books are marked with the Trémoille seal showing four Ts symbolising the main estates owned by the family: Trémoille, Thouars, Talmont and Tarente; they are joined by the royal crown of Naples to which the Trémoilles aspired. The owners' taste for refinement is also apparent in the **kitchens**, several rooms which illustrate to perfection the art of dining in ducal households.

Opening onto the main courtyard, the chapel built by Jules Hardouin-Mansart contains the magnificent white-marble funeral monument of the Marquis de Vaubrun killed at the battle of Altenheim (1673); it was carved by Coysevox and Collignon after drawings by Lebrun.

Library

During the Second World War, Serrant was requisitioned by German officers who showed great respect for the castle. One of them painted scenes of their daily life on the walls of the basement.

EXCURSION

St-Georges-sur-Loire – *2km/1mi by N 23*. St-Georges, on the north bank of the Loire, is situated not far from the famous vineyards, the **Coulée de Serrant** and the **Roche aux Moines**, where some of Anjou's finest white wines are produced.
The **former abbey** ⊘ was founded in 1158 by the Augustinian Order. Up to 1790 it was occupied by a scholarly community, the Genovefans, who were regular canons belonging to the abbey of St-Geneviève in Paris.
The handsome building, which dates from 1684 and is occupied by the town hall, contains a grand staircase with a remarkable wrought-iron banister and the chapter-house with its original wainscoting where temporary exhibitions are held.

La SOLOGNE

Michelin map 318: H-5 to J-7 or 238 folds 3 to 7 and 16 to 19

The Sologne's wide, flat expanses of heathland stretching as far as the eye can see are a paradise for hunters, anglers and hikers. The region, which is given over to farms, forests and a great many isolated lakes, is dotted with villages which add touches of colour to the landscape with their red-brick, stone and timber buildings.
Lying between the Loire and the Cher, the Sologne is delimited to the east by the Sancerre hills and to the west by a curved line running north from Selles-sur-Cher via Chémery, Thenay and Sambin to Cheverny.
The Sologne terrain, which is composed of clay and sand, slopes very gently westwards as indicated by the direction in which the main rivers – Cosson, Beuvron, Petite Sauldre and Grande Sauldre – flow.

Development – In the past the region was a desolate wasteland ravaged by fevers caused by the stagnant water of its numerous lakes, but things changed radically for the better in the reign of Napoleon III who acquired the Lamotte-Beuvron estate and initiated a number of improvements. The Sologne Central Committee started to plant birch and Norway pines, dig canals, construct roads, clear and drain the lakes and improve the soil.
The fevers disappeared, the population soared and the Sologne took on the features of its present appearance.

Pheasant

275

Stag

The Sologne countryside – Fields of maize are widespread; it is a particularly useful crop because it provides not only fodder for the livestock but also good cover for game, thus reconciling the interests of both farmers and hunters. The dense cover provided by the forest, together with the peaceful atmosphere of the area and the presence of water, attracts a wide variety of fauna. The resident wildlife has to be regulated to protect the forest from the damage wrought by larger members of the Cervidae family as well as roe deer and rabbits in search of food. The region also features a great many biological species on account of the abundance of migratory birds.

Wherever farmers have been able to drain the land, there are fruit orchards and also farms involved in the intensive rearing of cattle, sheep and goats.

The Sologne and the Loire Valley near Blois form one of France's leading asparagus-growing areas. The cultivation of strawberries has become very specialised, leading to an increase in production. Along the Cher Valley and in the neighbourhood of Blois the production of wine has improved owing to the introduction of Sauvignon and Gamay grapes. Markets are held in certain small towns such as Gien, Sully, Romorantin-Lanthenay and Lamotte-Beuvron which is the geographical centre of the Sologne.

The recent improvement in fish farming on the lakes has increasingly rationalised traditional methods of production. Pike, sauger, eel, carp and more recently silurid are a delight to fishermen and gourmets alike.

Eating out

BUDGET

Les Copains d'Abord – *52 av. d'Orléans – 41300 Salbris –* ☎ *02 54 97 24 24 – closed 1-15 Jan, 11-22 Aug and Tue – 11.74€.* All the locals know this bistro with its happy, convivial atmosphere. You'll find good traditional cooking, and every weekend there is live jazz.

Auberge du Prieuré – *41230 Lassay-sur-Croisne –* ☎ *02 54 83 91 91 – closed Tue evening and Wed – 13.42€ lunch, 19.06€.* This restaurant in a former presbytery has a lovely setting, opposite a charming gothic church. Simple and refined decor with exposed beams and a fine carved wooden mantelpiece. The cuisine is based on fresh produce and the serving staff is attentive without being fussy.

MODERATE

Le Lion d'Or – *41300 Pierrefitte-sur-Sauldre – 15km/9.4mi SE of Lamotte-Beuvron on D 923 and D 55 –* ☎ *02 54 88 62 14 – closed 2-10 Jan, 5-13 Mar, 3-18 Sep, Mon and Tue except public holidays – 26.68/34.30€.* A smart local-style house opposite the church in the village centre, with old beams and half-timbering in the dining room. Small flower-decked garden courtyard. The menu features regional specialities.

Where to stay

BUDGET

Chambre d'hôte La Farge – *41600 Chaumont-sur-Tharonne – 4km/2.5mi NE of Chaumont towards Vouzon on minor road –* ☎ *02 54 88 52 06 – sylvie.lansier@wanadoo.fr –* ✉ *– 4 rooms 53.36/76.22€.* An elegant old Sologne-style farm in a rural setting, with a turret and brick half-timbering. The rooms are furnished in country style. An added attraction is the next-door riding centre and swimming pool. A lovely place to stay.

Domaine de Valaudran – *41300 Salbris – 1.5km/1mi SW of Salbris on D 724 –* ☎ *02 54 97 20 00 – closed 3 Jan-15 Mar – 32 rooms 68.60/99.09€ –* ☐ *12.20€ – restaurant 24/37€.* This fine brick house with its own park is a good place to relax and find peace and quiet. Follow the tree-lined drive to the house, where the rooms have views over the countryside. Eat indoors in the dining room or outside on the terrace near the heated pool.

★WOODLAND AREAS

① Between the River Cosson and River Beuvron

The Sologne is at its most attractive in the early autumn, when the russet of the falling leaves mingles with the dark evergreen of the Norway pines above a carpet of bracken and purple heather, broken by the brooding waters of an occasional lake. However, the bursts of gunfire which announce the shooting season can detract somewhat from the charm of the region.

◪ One of the best ways to appreciate the natural beauty of the Sologne is by taking a walk. Owing to the many enclosures, prohibited areas and animal traps it is definitely advisable to keep to the waymarked footpaths such as the GR 31 and the GR 3C.

La Ferté-St-Aubin – *See La FERTÉ-ST-AUBIN.*

Drive NW out of La Ferté along D 61 towards Ligny-le-Ribault.

In **Ligny-le-Ribault**, the **Maison du Cerf** ⊘ is devoted to this splendid animal acknowledged as the "king" of forests.

D 61 then becomes D 103; in Couy-sur-Cosson, turn left onto D 33.

The **Pavillon de Thoury** marks the entrance to the Chambord estate.
Hikers and visitors are welcome along footpaths. An observation area is available for keen picture hunters wishing to catch a glimpse of deer and wild boar on the move.

★★★Château de Chambord – *See Château de CHAMBORD.*

Follow D 112 S, turn left at the Chambord intersection, then right at King Stanislas' crossroads onto the forest road to Neuvy.

Neuvy – Neuvy is located on the southern edge of Boulogne Forest on the north bank of the River Beuvron.
The village **church** ⊘ stands on its own in its graveyard near a half-timbered farmhouse with brick infill on the opposite bank. It was partially rebuilt in 1525. The rood beam supports 15C statues; in the south transept there is a 17C painting of the dead Christ supported by two angels.

La Ferté-Beauharnais – The small 16C church contains some fine carved stalls. The village has retained several old houses (Maison du Carroir, Cour à l'Écu, Relais du Dauphin) worth a detour.

Drive E along D 923 then turn left onto D 123.

Chaumont-sur-Tharonne – The line of the old ramparts can be traced in the layout of the town which is picturesquely situated round its 15C-16C church on a bluff in the centre of the Sologne region.

Tarte Tatin

(Caramelised Upside-Down Apple Tart)

The Tatin sisters, who were innkeepers in Lamotte-Beuvron during the 19C, invented this delicious dessert.

Ingredients:

225g/8oz plain flour	1 egg
5 tbsp castor sugar	1 tbsp cold water
pinch of salt	6-8 large crisp apples
225g/8oz unsalted butter	(such as coxes)

Method:
Make up pastry base using the flour, 1 tbsp of sugar, 140g/5oz of butter, a pinch of salt and the egg. Add water if necessary. Cover dough ball and leave in a cool place for a couple of hours.
Preheat the oven to 200ºC (400ºF/Gas 6). Grease a 20-25cm/9-10in baking tin (fairly deep) with some of the remaining butter, and sprinkle some of the sugar over the bottom.
Peel, core and slice the apples, and arrange them in a couple of neat layers on the bottom of the tin. Dot the top with knobs of the remaining butter and cover with the rest of the sugar.
Roll out the pastry into a fairly thin (about 0.5cm/0.25in thick) circle and place over the apples, trimming it to fit just inside the rim of the tin. Cut some air holes with the tip of a sharp knife.
Bake for 30-45min in the upper half of the oven. When cooked, turn out onto a serving dish so that the layers of apple are on top and place under a red-hot grill for a few minutes to caramelise the top.
Serve warm, with lashings of *crème fraîche*.

Lamotte-Beuvron – Soon after Napoleon III acquired the château, this simple hamlet got its own railway station and promptly became the main rendezvous of hunters in the Sologne region. Public buildings and most of the private brick-built houses date from the decade of 1860-70.

Souvigny-en-Sologne – This attractive village, typical of the area, is well worth a visit. The 12C-16C church, preceded by a vast timber porch (known as a *caquetoir* or gossip place), is surrounded by timber-framed houses including the former presbytery, now a holiday cottage.

🏃 The immediate surroundings are crisscrossed by 80km/50mi of marked footpaths *(detailed map available in the local shops)*.

Ménestreau-en-Villette – *7km/4.3mi E from La Ferté-St-Aubin by D 17.* In this Sologne village, the **Domaine du Ciran** ⊙ (Conservatoire de la Faune Sauvage de Sologne) is devoted to the Sologne region, its flora and its fauna, both past and present. Visitors are offered an insight into the natural resources of the area thanks to a discovery trail featuring around 20 display cases framed with wood. The diversity of the Sologne vegetation can be glimpsed through the many paths cutting across forests and coppices and skirting lakes and rivers. Observation points have been set up all along, providing opportunities for taking unexpected photographs of deer, wild boar, foxes, martens and roe deer, especially at sunrise or sunset.

The farmhouse, devoted more specifically to raising goats and cattle, produces a delicious cheese. The objectives of this farm are to serve both the economy and the environment it aims to maintain traditional rural practices while increasing visitors' awareness of the fragile ecology of the region.

Special tours focusing on themes such as bees, mushrooms, ponds and lakes, forests and wild animals are available on request.

🏃 The Domaine du Ciran is crisscrossed by discovery trails. For a close look at the natural environment, take advantage of walking tours which last several days *(accommodation on-site)* and witness the astonishing variety of the Sologne flora and fauna. *Don't forget to bring your camera, binoculars and sturdy shoes!*

"How can I convey to you the nostalgic charm of the Sologne lakes, in the vicinity of St-Viâtre? They stretch endlessly across the landscape, set against a backdrop of birches and pine trees. The night fraught with perils oozes thick drops of blood evidenced by long carmine trails. The mother duck teaches her young charges to swim and beware of danger. Occasionally, the melancholy screech of the bittern shatters the stillness of the night. At the water's edge, nestled in the leafy treetops, the crimson heron casts a watchful eye over the nearby forests and lakes. Huge pike can be seen dozing beneath the surface. Frogs rejoice in a perpetual concert."

Maurice Constantin-Weyer – *Le Flâneur sous la tente*

Detailed information about the lakes of the Sologne region is available from the **Maison des Étangs**, ☎ 02 54 88 23 00.

★LAKES AND MOORS

② Round trip from Romorantin-Lanthenay

★**Romorantin-Lanthenay** – *See ROMORANTIN-LANTHENAY.*
Drive E out of Romorantin along D 724.

Villeherviers – The village is set among asparagus fields in the broad valley of the Sauldre. There is Plantagenet vaulting in the 13C **church** ⊙.

★**Aliotis, les poissons du monde entier** ⊙ – *E of Villeherviers on D 724; follow the signposted route as far as the Moulin des Tourneux.*
📷 This aquarium set up in the heart of nature comprises eight different sections. The first section, consisting of 10 large 10 000-115 000l/2 200-25 300gal basins, presents freshwater fish found in France, coming from rivers, both small and large, waterways, lakes in mountains and plains, ponds, estuaries etc. The second section comprises an impressive 600 000l/132 000gal basin, home to some enormous fish from France and other European countries (such as catfish); two smaller basins contain a collection of Japanese koi – a multicoloured variation of the carp. The two tanks in the third section are devoted to the sea. The fourth section showcases aquatic life from Latin America and includes two aquaterrariums which simultaneously show life above and below water level in a South American river. The fifth section is on Africa. The sixth is devoted to waterfalls. Section seven, Ocean and Mirror, displays fish from tropical seas. Finally, section eight explains the ecological balance of lagoons. A laboratory is open to visitors eager to see more (microscopes etc).

Selles-St-Denis – This village lies on the north bank of the Sauldre. The **chapel**, which dates from the 12C and 15C and has side chapels and an apse in the Flamboyant style, is decorated with 14C murals of the Life of St Genoulph to whom it is dedicated.

Salbris – Salbris, on the south bank of the Sauldre, is a busy crossroads and a good centre for excursions into the forest.

The stone and brick **church of St-Georges** was built in the 15C and 16C. The centre of the retable on the high altar is occupied by a *Pietà* (16C). The transept chapels have interesting coats of arms of the donors on the keystones of the vault and attractive pendant sculptures representing the Three Wise Men and the Virgin and Child *(south)* and the symbols of the Evangelists *(north)*.

At Salbris station, you can take the **petit train du Blanc-Argent**, a metric-gauge railway, which goes up to Luçay-le-Mâle, offering a pleasant tour of the Sologne region.

Drive N out of Salbris along N 20, turn left onto D 121 then right 10km/6.2mi further on towards St-Viâtre on D 73.

St-Viâtre – This smart little town was formerly a place of pilgrimage containing the relics of St Viâtre, a hermit who retired here in the 6C and, so the legend says, made himself a coffin from the trunk of an aspen tree.

The 15C transept gable of the **church** is built of brick with a black diaper pattern and edged with spiral rosettes. A sturdy bell-tower porch shelters the 14C door. At the chancel step stands a remarkable carved wood desk (18C) of surprising size. In the south transept are four **painted panels**★ dating from the early 16C, giving a realistic evocation of the life of Christ and of St Viâtre.

Reposoir St-Viâtre – This small brick building (15C) at the north entrance to the village is a wayside altar.

Continue W along D 63 to Vernou-en-Sologne.

South of the village stands the beautiful Château de Laborde *(not open to the public)*. Note the slate inlays underlining the openings.

Drive to Bracieux along D 60 via Bauzy.

Bracieux – Bracieux is a smart village on the border of the Sologne and the region round Blois. The houses are grouped round the 16C market on the south bank of the Beuvron which is spanned by a pretty bridge.

★ **Château de Villesavin** – 2km/1.2mi from Bracieux along D 102. See CHAMBORD: Excursion.

★★★ **Château de Cheverny** – See Château de CHEVERNY.

Drive out of Cheverny along D 765 then turn left onto D 78.

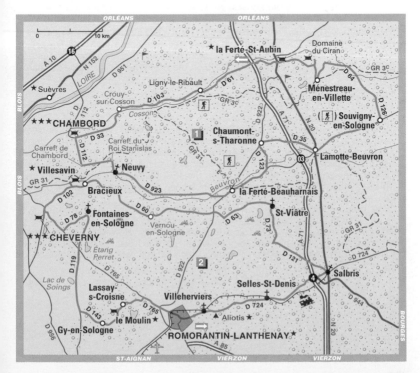

Château du Moulin

Fontaines-en-Sologne – The **church**, which dates for the most part from the 12C, shows how widespread the Angevin style was: flat chevet, nave with remarkable domed vaulting. It was fortified in the 17C. Beside the church there are some pretty, half-timbered houses with roofs of small flat tiles, commonly found in the region.

D 119 runs S along Perret Lake then along Soings-en-Sologne Lake.

The water level of the lake is liable to change abruptly without any apparent reason; in the past, this gave rise to many local legends!

In Rougeou, turn onto D 143.

Gy-en-Sologne – The typical Sologne cottage here, **Locature de la Straize** ⊘, dates from the 16C.

Lassay-sur-Croisne – Lassay is a village in the Sologne, a region of woodland and vast lakes. A cluster of old houses, crowned with long slate roofs, add a colourful touch to the urban landscape thanks to their stone and brick architecture.

Église St-Denis ⊘ – This charming little 15C church has a beautiful rose window and a slender spire. In the left transept, above the recumbent figure of Philippe du Moulin, there is an attractive early-16C **fresco** depicting St Christopher; on the right the artist has painted Lassay Church and on the left in the background the Château du Moulin.

★ **Château du Moulin** ⊘ – *1.5km/1mi W on a track beside the River Croisne.* The Château du Moulin stands in a rural setting, its red-brick walls reflected in the water of the moat.

It was built between 1480 and 1506 by **Philippe du Moulin**, a prominent nobleman devoted to the service of Charles VIII and Louis XII, who saved the life of Charles VIII at the Battle of Fornoue in 1495. The original castle was built on the square ground plan typical of fortresses, surrounded by a curtain wall reinforced with round towers. In keeping with the traditions of the 15C, the buildings are decorated with diaper pattern brickwork and bands of stone, giving an effect which is more elegant than military.

The keep or seigneurial residence features large mullioned windows and is furnished in the style contemporary with the period in which it was built: the bedrooms contain tester beds and Flemish tapestries. However, 19C comfort is represented by the chimney plaques which provided central heating. Near the entrance, left of the drawbridge, is the vaulted kitchen with its huge fireplace; the spit was turned by a dog.

SULLY-SUR-LOIRE★

Population 5 907
Michelin map 318: L-5, 238 fold 6 or 4045 F5

The Château de Sully commanded one of the Loire crossings. Its history is dominated by four great names: Maurice de Sully, Bishop of Paris who commissioned the building of Notre-Dame; Joan of Arc; Sully and Voltaire.
Today an olde worlde charm pervades the mellow stones of the fortress reflecting in the still waters of the moat and bathed in the soft light of the Loire Valley.
The international music festival which takes place in June is one of the major cultural events in the whole region.

The determination of Joan of Arc – In 1429 Sully belonged to Georges de la Trémoille, a favourite of Charles VII. The King was living in the castle when Joan of Arc defeated the English at Patay and captured their leader, the famous Talbot, Earl of Shrewsbury. Joan hastened to Sully and eventually persuaded the indolent monarch to be crowned at Reims. She returned to the castle in 1430 after her check before Paris, and there felt the jealousy and hostility of La Trémoille gaining influence over the King. She was detained and almost made prisoner but escaped to continue the struggle.

Sully's capacity for work – In 1602 **Maximilien de Béthune**, the Lord of Rosny, bought the château and the barony for 330 000 *livres*. Henri IV made him Duc de Sully, and it was under this name that the great Minister passed into history.
Sully had begun to serve his King at the age of 12. He was a great soldier, the best artilleryman of his time and a consummate administrator. He was active in all the departments of State: Finance, Agriculture, Industry and Public Works. A glutton for work, Sully began his day at 3am and kept four secretaries busy writing his memoirs; he entitled them *Wise and Royal Economies of State*. Fearing indiscretions, he had a printing press set up in one of the towers of the château and the work was printed on the spot, although it bore the address of a printer in Amsterdam. The old Duke had a mania for orderly accounts. Every tree to be planted, every table to be made, every ditch to be cleaned was the subject of a legal contract. Sully had an awkward character and he frequently brought legal actions, especially against the Bishop of Orléans. Since the Middle Ages it had been the custom for the Lord of Sully to carry

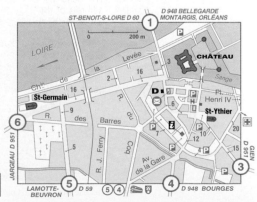

SOLOGNE CHARM

Auberge du Faisan Doré – *45600 St-Florent-le-Jeune* – *10km/6.25mi SE of Sully on D 951 and D 63* – ☎ 02 38 36 93 83 – *12.50€ lunch, 21.50/30.50€*. A fine example of a charming Sologne property with its half-timbered brick walls. Exposed beams, old terracotta floor tiles, open fireplaces, nooks and crannies and different floor levels all add to the picturesque effect. The cuisine uses fresh produce and is much appreciated by the regular clientele. A few simple but smart rooms.

the Bishop's chair on the day of his entry into Orléans. The Minister, very much the ducal peer and a Protestant to boot, refused to comply with this custom. Finally he obtained permission to be represented at the ceremony.
Sully's career came to an end with the assassination of Henri IV in 1610. The Minister retired but he assured Louis XIII of his loyalty and encouraged his co-religionists to do the same. Cardinal de Richelieu made him a Marshal of France.

TOWN WALK

Collégiale de St-Ythier – A chapel dedicated to Notre-Dame-de-Pitié was built in 1529 and enlarged in 1605, whereupon it became the collegiate church of St-Ythier. There are two 16C **stained-glass windows**: the one at the end of the south aisle shows pilgrims on their way to St James' shrine in Compostela; the second, showing the Tree of Jesse with the Virgin Mary and the Infant Jesus, is in the central apse. In the north aisle there is a 16C *Pietà* above the high altar.

SULLY SUR-LOIRE

Abreuvoir (R. de l') 2
Béthune (R. de l') 3
Champ-de-Foire (Bd du) 4
Chemin de Fer (R. du) 5
Grand-Sully (R. du) 6
Jeanne-d'Arc (Bd) 7
Marronniers (R. des) 9
Porte-Berry (R.) 10
Porte-de-Sologne (R.) 12
St-François (R. du Fg) 15
St-Germain (R. du Fg) 16
Venerie (Av. de la) 20

Maison Renaissance . . **D**

Renaissance house – Above the façade decorated with medallions and pilasters, the roof features dormer windows with twin bays surrounded by caryatids.

Église St-Germain ⊙ – The 13C church has been severely damaged several times over the centuries and is presently undergoing restoration *(not open to visitors)*. It has a remarkably slender spire rising to a height of 38m/125ft.

★CHÂTEAU ⊙ *45min*

The castle is an imposing feudal fortress dating largely from before 1360. The keep, which faces the Loire, was built at the end of the 14C by Guy de la Trémoille. It is rectangular with massive round towers at the corners. The upper part is equipped with machicolated sentry walks, loopholes and holes for crossbows illustrating the evolution of military architecture during the Hundred Years War. The wing added to house Sully's living quarters, known as Le Petit Château, dates from the early 15C.

The spirit of Voltaire (18C)

Exiled from Paris by the Regent for his scathing epigrams, Voltaire spent several seasons with the Duke of Sully, who surrounded himself with philosophers and freethinkers. At the time Voltaire was 22. His gaiety and wit made him the life and soul of the castle. In the shade of the park among the trees which he described as "carved upon by urchins and lovers", young François-Marie Arouet (he had not yet adopted his pen name) indulged in flirtations which he transferred to the stage. A theatre was built for him in the castle where he produced *Œdipus*, *Les Nuits galantes* and *Artemis*, with his friends playing the roles.

The tour of the château begins in the great lower hall in which six tapestries from the Parisian workshops, precursors of the Gobelins, are on display. They relate the stories of *Psyche*, *Venus* and *Cupid*.

The main hall, another enormous room (300m²/3 230sq ft) on the first floor, was the part of the seigneurial residence used during the Middle Ages for dispensing justice and holding feasts. It was decorated by Maximilien de Béthune in the 17C. Portraits of the descendants of the first Duke of Sully and of his brother Philippe adorn the walls, which are hung with red fabric. This is the room where Voltaire performed his plays. In the window splays, the Grand Duke of Sully's ancestors are depicted in *trompe-l'œil*. An iron door concealed in the panelling leads to the old exercise room from where the guards operated the drawbridge and the trapdoor. Nowadays called the **oratory**, this room was also the Duke's treasury in the 17C. The bed in the centre of the king's bedchamber has blue and gold curtains in honour of Dauphin Louis XIV's stay here during the Fronde uprising. Finally, on the second floor, there is the single room crowned by its famous timber roof. The visit ends with a tour of the sentry walk in view of the Loire.

S. Sauvignier/MICHELIN

Château de Sully-sur-Loire

★★ Timber roof – The upper half of the keep has one of the finest timber roofs to have survived from the Middle Ages. It was built towards the end of the 14C by the master carpenters of Orléans and is impressive in size (35m/115ft long and 15m/50ft high). Its good state of preservation is due to the infinite pains taken by its builders, both in treating the timber and in the way it was put together. Felled in winter under a waning moon, the trees were squared off, stripped of the sap wood, and sawn up following the grain. Immersion in water for a period of several months got rid of the sap. The wood was subsequently dried in the air over a period of many years, after which the precious material was smoked or cured to protect it from rot and decay. The final treatment consisted of coating it with an alum-based solution.

Petit Château – This part of the château was built some years after the keep and houses the Duke of Sully's apartments, notably his bedchamber and its coffered ceiling adorned with mottoes and motifs related to his title of Grand Master of the Artillery (cannon-balls, flashing explosions etc), reflecting the high esteem in which the Duke held his king, Henri IV. The apartments contain some interesting pieces of furniture and paintings.

Château de TALCY★

Michelin map 318: F-5 or 238 fold 3

This austere-looking **château** on the borders of the Loire Valley and Beauce region stands well off the beaten track. Once inside the courtyard, however, visitors discover a charming, Renaissance manor house which inspired two of France's greatest poets, Pierre de Ronsard and Agrippa d'Aubigné.
The 13C manorial dwelling was bought in 1571 by a rich Florentine, Bernardo Salviati, a cousin of Catherine de' Medici. The Salviati family, who became famous in literary history, retained the estate until 1667. Bernardo was the father of Cassandra, to whom **Ronsard** dedicated so many sonnets, and of Giovanni Salviati, whose daughter, Diana, similarly inspired the young Agrippa d'Aubigné. Cassandra's daughter married Guillaume de Musset and one of her direct descendants was the great poet **Alfred de Musset** (1810-57).

TOUR ⊘

The keep, part of which dates from the 15C has a double doorway (postern and carriage gate), two corner turrets and a crenellated sentry walk which looks medieval although it dates from 1520.
The first courtyard owes its charm to a graceful gallery and an attractive well. In the second courtyard is a large 16C **dovecot**, with its 1 500 pigeon-holes in a remarkably good state of preservation. The old **winepress** is still in very good working order.
Most unusually, the house itself has retained the interior decor and furniture it would have had in the 17C and 18C. Fine furniture (17C 18C) and Gothic tapestries adorn the guard-room, office, kitchen, bedrooms and salons which are roofed with French-style ceilings (with decorated exposed beams).
The gardens have been redesigned as an orchard-conservatory which will give pride of place to the apple and the pear.

TOURS★★

Conurbation 297 631
Michelin map 317: N-4, 232 folds 35 and 36, 238 fold 13 or 4037 E3
Local map see Excursions below

Tours, the capital of Touraine, is traditionally a centre for excursions into château country but it has many attractions of its own: its clear light, slate roofs, orderly street plan, squares and gardens, churches, monasteries, museums and pedestrianised shopping areas.

A EUROPEAN METROPOLIS

The Gallo-Roman capital – During the Roman period the settlement known as Turons became a prosperous free city with the name Caesarodunum (Caesar's Hill) and extended over a densely populated area of about 40ha/100 acres. Late in the 3C however, invasions obliged the inhabitants to take refuge in the present cathedral district which included the arena. A wall was built to enclose the city and traces of it can still be seen near the castle and in the nearby street, rue des Ursulines.
In 375 the town, which had reverted to its former name Turones, became the seat of government of the third Lyonnaise, a province comprising Touraine, Maine, Anjou and Armorica.

F. Joly/Bibliothèque Municipale, Tours

St Martin cutting his cloak (14C Missal, Tours)

St Martin's city (4C) – The man who became the greatest bishop of the Gauls started as a legionary in the Roman army. At the gates of Amiens the young soldier met a beggar shivering in the cold wind. He cut his cloak in two with his sword and gave half to the poor man. The following night in a dream he saw Christ wearing half his cloak, so he had himself baptised and embarked upon his mission. At Ligugé in Poitou he founded the first monastery on Gallic soil. His faith and charity spread his fame far afield. In 372 the people of Tours begged him to become their bishop. The monastery of Marmoutier was built at the gates of Tours.

St Martin died in Candes in 397. The monks of Ligugé and Marmoutier quarrelled over his body; while the men of Poitou slept, the men of Tours transferred the saint's body to a boat and rowed hard upstream for home. Along the way a miracle occurred: although it was November, as the saint's body passed by trees turned green, plants burst into flower and birds sang – a St Martin's summer. In 471 a basilica was built over his tomb; it measures 50?20m/164?66ft and has 120 columns, 32 windows in the apse and 20 in the nave.

Gregory of Tours

In 563 a young deacon in poor health, who was heir to a noble Gallo-Roman family in the Arverne (later Auvergne), visited St Martin's tomb. His name was Gregory. He was cured and settled in Tours. Owing to his piety and probity, coupled with the renown of several of his relatives (he was the great-nephew of St Nizier of Lyon) he was elected bishop in 573. Gregory of Tours produced many written works, especially the *History of the Franks* which has been the main source of information about the Merovingian period. He also wrote eight *Books of Miracles* and the *Lives of the Fathers*. Under his enlightened direction the town developed and an abbey grew up round St Martin's Basilica. Gregory died in 594.

A popular pilgrimage – In 496 or 498 **Clovis** came to St Martin's Basilica to meditate and promised to be baptised if he defeated the Alemanni. He returned in 507 during the war against the Visigoths and commanded his army not to despoil the territory of Tours out of respect for St Martin. After his victory at Vouillé, near Poitiers, he did not forget to visit the basilica on which he bestowed many presents in thanksgiving. For the occasion he wore the insignia of the consulship which the Emperor of the East had conferred on him. These visits by Clovis were the beginning of the special protection which the Merovingians granted to the prestigious sanctuary.

For many years pilgrims had been flocking to Tours for cure or counsel. The shrine of St Martin acquired a great reputation, which was assisted by skilful propaganda about the numerous miracles which had taken place round his tomb. Besides the ordinary pilgrims in search of the supernatural, kings, princes and powerful lords came seeking absolution for their many crimes and abuses. The sanctuary was also a place of asylum, an inviolable refuge for both the persecuted and the criminal. The popularity of the cult of St Martin brought the abbey great wealth; its estates, the result of many donations, extended as far as Berry and Bordelais. Royal favour was expressed in the abbey being granted the right to mint money.

From the early Capets to Louis XI – The Viking invasions reached Tours in 853: the cathedral, the abbeys and the churches were set on fire and destroyed. The relics of St Martin were removed and hidden in the Auvergne. The ancient abbey fell into decline and passed to the Robertians who were lay priests. In 903, after further attacks, the abbey was surrounded by a wall and a new town grew up to the west of the old city; it was called Châteauneuf or Martinopolis.

The Robertians in charge of St Martin's Abbey held immense temporal power and the opportunity to pursue ecclesiastical careers; abbots, bishops and archbishops were appointed from among the 200 canons attached to the abbey. The nickname **Capet** by which King Hugh was known at the end of the 10C comes from an allusion to the *cappa* (cloak) of St Martin, thus proving that the success of the new royal dynasty owed much to the famous monastery. One of Hugh Capet's vassals, Eudes I, Count of Blois and Tours, obtained from his King c 984 the neighbouring abbey of Marmoutier which was to acquire greater importance in the 11C.

Abbot Alcuin (c 735-804)

At the end of the 8C Tours added to its fame by becoming an intellectual and artistic centre under the influence of Alcuin, an Anglo-Saxon monk, originally from York in England, who had met Charlemagne in Italy and accompanied him back to France.

The French King wanted to raise the standard of learning in his kingdom and he opened a large number of schools to train a well-informed clergy capable in its turn of instructing the population. At his palace in Aix-la-Chapelle (Aachen) he organised a meeting of a group of scholars led by the great figure of Alcuin, inspirational behind the Carolingian Renaissance.

After serving energetically at court, where he set up a palace library, Alcuin decided to retire; Charlemagne offered to appoint him abbot of St-Martin of Tours (796). Although the community counted over 200 monks, it was not very active. Alcuin undertook to renew its prestige. He reformed the abbey school, creating two levels of study: one was elementary, the other consisted of the seven liberal arts (grammar, rhetoric, logic, arithmetic, geometry, music and astronomy). Students came from all over Europe. He revived the scriptorium where the copyists designed a new calligraphy for illuminated manuscripts. He also produced a revised version of the *Vulgate Bible* which became the authorised text throughout the kingdom. He remained in close touch with Charlemagne who sought his advice and visited him just before his coronation in December 800. Alcuin died on Whit Sunday in 804.

In the 50 years that followed his death, Tours continued to be a thriving cultural centre. In 813 a council met in Tours and ordained that the clergy should comment on the Bible in French rather than Latin. In the 840s the scriptorium of St Martin's Abbey produced some splendid masterpieces: the so-called Alcuin Bible, the so-called Moutier-Grandval Bible and the famous Bible of Charles the Bald. Artists from Aix-la-Chapelle and Reims renewed and enriched the illustrative technique of the abbey scriptorium.

In 997 a huge fire destroyed Châteauneuf and St Martin's Abbey which had to be completely rebuilt, including the basilica which dated from 471. The rivalry in the 11C between the houses of Blois and Anjou, whose domains met in Touraine, ended with victory for the Angevins.

When Pope Alexander III held a great council in Tours in 1163, Touraine belonged to the Plantagenets but in 1205 **Philippe Auguste** captured the town which then remained French. The 13C was a period of peace and prosperity; the **denier tournois**, the money minted in Tours and thereafter in other cities in the kingdom, was adopted as the official currency in preference to the *denier parisis*. Early in the 13C a monk from Marmoutier, John, author of the *History of the Counts of Anjou* and of the *Life of Geoffroi le Bel*, painted a very flattering portrait in his *In Praise of Touraine* of the citizens of Touraine and their wives. "They are always celebrating and their meals are of the very best; they drink from gold and silver cups and spend their time playing at dice and hunting. The women are astonishingly beautiful, they make up their faces and wear magnificent clothes. Their eyes kindle passion yet they are respected for their chastity."

In 1308 Tours played host to the États Généraux (French Parliament). Less welcome events soon followed; the arrival of the **Black Death** (1351) and the beginning of the Hundred Years War forced the citizens to build a new wall in 1356 enclosing Tours and Châteauneuf. Touraine, which had been coveted by the great royal vassals, was raised to a duchy for the future Charles VII and he solemnly entered the town of Tours in 1417. In 1429 Joan of Arc stayed in Tours while her armour was being made. Charles VII settled in Tours in 1444 and on 28 May he signed the Treaty of Tours with Henry VI of England. Under **Louis XI** Tours was very much in favour; the city acted as the capital of the kingdom and a mayor was appointed in 1462. The King liked the region and lived at the Château de Plessis-lès-Tours *(see below)*. Once again life became pleasant and the presence of the court attracted a number of artists of which the most famous was **Jean Fouquet** (born in Tours c 1420) who painted the magnificent miniatures in the *Great Chronicle of France* and *Jewish Antiquities*.

The abbey once again enjoyed royal favour and recovered some of its former prestige. Louis XI died in 1483 at Plessis, whereupon the court moved to Amboise.

Silk weaving and the Wars of Religion – Louis XI had promoted the weaving of silk and cloth of gold in Lyon but the project had not met with much enthusiasm so the weavers and their looms were moved to Touraine. The industry reached its highest output in the middle of the 17C when 11 000 looms were at work and two fairs were held each year.

In this world of craftsmen, intellectuals and artists, the **Reformation** found its first supporters and Tours, like Lyon and Nîmes, became one of the most active centres of the new religion. In 1562 the Calvinists caused great disorder, particularly in St Martin's Abbey. The Roman Catholics were merciless in their revenge; 10 years before Paris, Tours had its own St Bartholomew's Day massacre, with 200-300 Huguenots being drowned in the Loire. In May 1589 Henri III and the Parliament retreated from Paris to Tours which once again resumed its role as royal capital.

Eating out

BUDGET

Le Trébuchet – *18 r. de la Monnaie* – ☏ *02 47 64 01 57* – *closed 2 weeks in Aug and Sun* – *reservation required* – *12/23€*. This restaurant in the old part of Tours has a friendly atmosphere, and extends a warm welcome. The menu changes according to the owner's whim and local market produce. Tasty cooking at reasonable prices. Definitely worth a visit.

Le Mérimée – *66 r. Colbert* – ☏ *02 47 61 32 34* – *closed Feb school holidays, 28 Jul-4 Aug, Fri lunchtime and Sun* – *reservation required for weekends* – *14.33/19.06€*. If you are one of those people who likes to read and eat at the same time, you will enjoy deciphering and contemplating the sayings of the poet Mérimée, which are reproduced on the walls and menus. Sandwiches, salads, regional produce and more traditional cooking are also bound to satisfy.

MODERATE

Léonard de Vinci – *19 r. de la Monnaie* – ☏ *02 47 61 07 88* – *closed Mon* – *reservation required in evenings* – *11.89€ lunch, 19.97/30.95€*. A taste of Tuscany in the heart of the Touraine. This Italian restaurant's claim to fame is that it doesn't serve pizzas! A chance to discover different Italian dishes, in a decor that highlights models of Leonardo da Vinci's inventions.

La Furgeotière – *19 pl. Foire-le-Roi* – ☏ *02 47 66 94 75* – *closed 1-15 Jan, Feb school holidays, 1-7 Jul, Tue and Wed* – *16.33€ lunch, 22.44/39.23€*. This restaurant has a charming decor, with half-timbering and limestone. The owners love life, good food and their work. Original, inventive cuisine should satisfy all appetites.

LUXURY

La Roche Le Roy – *55 rte de St-Avertin* – ☏ *02 47 27 22 00* – *closed Feb school holidays, 1-27 Aug, Sun and Mon* – *38.11€ lunch, 57.93€*. The restaurant in this Touraine manor house was created under a lucky star and will be much appreciated by gourmets. Sample the cooking, which varies with the seasons, in the intimate dining room or the pretty enclosed courtyard in summer, and enjoy fine wines from the cellar hewn into the cliff face.

Where to stay

BUDGET

Hôtel Le Manoir – *2 r. Traversière* – ☏ *02 47 05 37 37* – *36.59/48.78€* – ⊠ *4.57€*. This hotel in a quiet part of town near the *préfecture* is a former gentleman's residence. The rooms are comfortable and well kept; those on the third floor are under the sloping roof with exposed beams.

Chambre d'hôte Le Moulin Hodoux – *37230 Luynes* – *14km/8.75mi W of Tours on N 152 and minor road* – ☏ *02 47 55 76 27* – *closed 17 Feb-4 Mar and 28 Dec-6 Jan* – ⊄ – *4 rooms 48/53€*. In a peaceful country setting not far from Tours, near the castle at Luynes, this 18C-19C watermill provides comfortable, well-equipped rooms. In the lovely garden there are tables, chairs and a barbecue for visitors' use, as well as a swimming pool.

MODERATE

Central Hôtel – *21 r. Berthelot* – ☏ *02 47 05 46 44* – 🅿 – *40 rooms 53.36/144.82€* – ⊠ *8.39€*. A quiet, comfortable hotel in the old part of Tours, near the busy pedestrian-only districts. The staff are reserved but pleasant. There is a small, peaceful garden to enjoy behind the hotel in summer, and you can eat breakfast on the terrace.

On the town

Aux Trois Pucelles – *19 r. Briçonnet* – ☏ *02 47 20 67 29* – *Mon-Fri 7.45am-midnight, Sat 9am-3.30pm*. The oldest bar in Tours is in a 15C building. Away from the bustle of place Plumereau, this café is popular among university students. The owner may tell you how it got its name (Three Young Virgins").

Le Corsaire – *187 av. de Grammont* – ☏ *02 47 05 20 00* – *daily except Sun 6pm-4am*. A smart bar offering a choice of over 400 cocktails. The decor is designed to look like a boat's hold, with real portholes and ship's lanterns. Discreet clientele and atmospheric music, mainly jazz.

Le Hamac – *21 r. de la Rôtisserie* – ☏ *02 47 05 25 71* – *daily 7pm-2am*. A peaceful cocktail bar which is a popular place to go in the evening in Tours. An ideal place for an ice cream (from a choice of 40) or a cocktail (180). Romantic couples will appreciate the sofas on the first floor.

Sit back and relax

Le Gambrinus – *69 bis r. Blaise-Pascal* – ☎ *02 47 05 17 00* – *daily except Tue 10am-2am – closed in Aug.* This bar specialises in Belgian beers, offering around 100, some of which are not normally available in France. Regular clientele.

Le Vieux Mûrier – *11 pl. Plumereau* – ☎ *02 47 61 04 77* – *Tue 2pm-2am, Wed-Sat 11am-2am, Sun 2pm-1am.* This is one of the oldest cafés in place Plumereau, and it has that extra hint of character that is so often missing from modern establishments, with a decor reminiscent of a museum. Lovely terrace in the square.

Pub St James – *7 r. des Orfèvres* – ☎ *06 60 77 44 97* – *daily 6pm-2am.* A truly English place with the friendly atmosphere of a pub with its regulars (not many students among them). Specialities: beers and 25-year-old whiskies.

In the latter half of the 18C, extensive town planning by royal decree opened up a wide road on a north-south axis along which Tours was to develop in the future.

In the 19C development was slow; there was some building and improvement but little industry. The railway acted as a stimulant and the station at St-Pierre-des-Corps was the focus of renewed activity.

Wars – Owing to its communications facilities Tours was chosen in 1870 as the **seat of the Government for the National Defence** but three months later, in the face of the Prussian advance, the government withdrew to Bordeaux. In June 1940 the same chain of events took place but at greater speed. The town was bombed and burned for three days. In 1944 the bombings resumed. In all, between 1940 and 1944, 1 543 buildings were destroyed and 7 960 damaged; the town centre and the districts on the banks of the Loire were the most badly hit.

★★★OLD TOURS *1hr 30min*

The vast restoration work begun about 1970 around place Plumereau and the building of the Faculté des Lettres beside the Loire have brought the old quarter to life; its narrow streets, often pedestrian precincts, have attracted shops and craftsmen, and the whole quarter near the university has become one of the liveliest parts of town.

★Place Plumereau – This picturesque and animated square, once the hat market *(carroi aux chapeaux)*, is lined with fine 15C timber-framed houses alternating with stone façades. Pavement cafés and restaurants overflow onto the square during

Place Plumereau

the fine season. On the corner of rue du Change and rue de la Monnaie there is a lovely house featuring two slate-roofed gables and posts decorated with sculptures. Continue to the corner of rue de la Rôtisserie where there is an old façade with wooden lattice-work.

To the north of the square a vaulted passageway opens on to the attractive little **place St-Pierre-le-Puellier**, with its pleasant gardens. Excavations have uncovered a 1C Gallo-Roman public building, 11C and 13C cemeteries and the foundations of the old church after which the square is named. Part of the nave is still visible on one side of the square and from rue Briçonnet. To the north, a large ogive-vaulted porch opens on to a small square.

Rue du Grand-Marché – This is one of the most interesting streets in old Tours, with a great number of half-timbered façades embellished with bricks or slates.

Rue Bretonneau – At no 33 stands a 16C *hôtel* with pretty Renaissance carved foliage; the northern wing was added towards 1875.

★ **Rue Briçonnet** – This charming street is bordered by houses showing a rich variety of local styles, from the Romanesque façade to the 18C mansion. Off the narrow rue du Poirier, no 35 has a Romanesque façade, no 31 a late-13C Gothic façade; opposite, at no 32, stands a Renaissance house with lovely wooden statuettes. Not far away, an elegant staircase tower marks the entrance to place St-Pierre-le-Puellier. Further north, on the left, no 23 has a Classical façade. No 16 is the **Maison de Tristan**, a remarkable stone and brick construction with a late-15C pierced gable: it is used as the premises of a modern languages centre, the Centre d'Études de Langues Vivantes. One of the window lintels in the courtyard bears the inscription *Prie Dieu pur*, an anagram of the name of Pierre Dupui, who built the mansion.

Rue Paul-Louis-Courier – In the inner courtyard, above the doorway of the 15C-16C Hôtel Binet (no 10) is an elegant wooden gallery served by two spiral staircases.

Place de Châteauneuf – There is a fine view of the **Tour Charlemagne**, and the remains of the **Ancienne basilique St-Martin** built in the 11C and 13C over the tomb of the great Bishop of Tours, after the Vikings had destroyed the 5C sanctuary. The new building was as famous as the old one for its size and splendour. Sacked by the Huguenots in 1562, it fell into disrepair during the Revolution and its vaulting collapsed. The nave was pulled down in 1802 to make way for the construction of rue des Halles. Since that time, Tour Charlemagne, the tower which dominated the north transept, has stood alone. It collapsed partially in 1928, but after careful restoration, it has retained its original elegance.

Opposite, the 14C ducal residence, **Logis des ducs de Touraine**, houses a centre for military servicemen, the Maison des Combattants, whereas the late-15C **church of St-Denis** has been converted into a music centre. Further along rue des Halles stands the **Tour de l'Horloge**, a clock tower marking the façade of the basilica which was crowned with a dome in the 19C.

In its crypt, the **Nouvelle basilique St-Martin**, built between 1886 and 1924 in neo-Byzantine style, houses the shrine of St Martin, which remains the object of pilgrimages.

★★CATHEDRAL DISTRICT *2hr*

This charming peaceful district has retained a few fine mansions and the Archbishop's Palace nestling round the cathedral.

★★ **Cathédrale St-Gatien** – Work on the cathedral started in the mid-13C and was completed in the 16C. It demonstrates the complete evolution of the French Gothic style: the chevet typifies the early phase, the transept and nave the development of the style and the Flamboyant west front belongs to the final phase *(see illustration in Art and architecture: Ecclesiastical architecture)*. The first traces of the Renaissance are visible in the tops of the towers.

Despite the mixture of styles the soaring **west front** is a harmonious entity. A slight asymmetry of detail ensures that the façade is not monotonous. The foundations of the towers are a Gallo-Roman wall and solid buttresses indicate that the bases are Romanesque. The rich Flamboyant decoration was added to the west front in the 15C: pierced tympana, festooned archivolts, ornamented gables over the doorways. The buttresses, which rise to the base of the belfries, were decorated at the same period with niches and crocketed pinnacles.

It is a very beautiful church of the second order of importance, with a charming mouse-coloured complexion and a pair of fantastic towers. There are many grander cathedrals, but there are probably few more pleasing; and this effect of delicacy and grace is at its best toward the close of a quiet afternoon, when the densely decorated towers, rising above the little place de l'Archevêché, lift their curious lanterns into the slanting light, and offer a multitudinous perch to troops of circling pigeons.

Henry James – *A Little Tour in France*

The upper section of the north tower, which dates from the 15C, is surmounted by an elegant lantern dome in the early Renaissance style. The south belfry, which was built in the 16C on the Romanesque tower, is also surmounted by a lantern dome, here in the early Renaissance style.

The **interior** of the cathedral has a striking purity of line. The 14C and 15C nave blends perfectly with the older **chancel**, which is one of the most beautiful works of the 13C and is reminiscent of the Sainte-Chapelle in Paris.

The **stained-glass windows**★★ are the pride of the cathedral of St-Gatien. Those in the chancel with their warm colours are 13C. The rose windows in the transept are 14C; the south window is slightly diamond-shaped and the north one is divided by a supporting rib. The windows in the third chapel in the south aisle and the great rose window in the nave are 15C.

The chapel which opens into the south transept contains the **tomb**★ of the children of Charles VIII, an elegant work by the School of Michel Colombe (16C), mounted on a base carved by Jerome de Fiesole.

★ **Place Grégoire-de-Tours** – This square gives a fine view of the east end of the cathedral and the Gothic flying buttresses; to the left is the medieval gable of the **Archbishop's Palace** (now the Musée des Beaux-Arts) – the decisions of the ecclesiastical court were read out from the Renaissance gallery. Note, in rue Manceau, a 15C canon's house with two gabled dormers and, at the beginning of rue Racine, a tufa building with a 15C pointed roof which housed the Justice des Bains – the seat of jurisdiction of the metropolitan chapter. This had been built over the ruins of a Gallo-Roman amphitheatre which, during the Renaissance, was mistakenly believed to have been baths.

Continue to place des Petites-Boucheries and take rue Auguste-Blanqui, then bear right onto rue du Petit-Cupidon.

On the corner of rue du Petit-Cupidon and rue des Ursulines is an arched passage through buildings which leads into the garden of the Archives of the Indre-et-Loire *département*.

This spot contains the best-preserved part of the Gallo-Roman walls and the ancient city of *Caesarodunum* with one of its defence towers, known as the Tour du Petit Cupidon, and, carved out of the wall, the southern postern which would have been the entrance to a Roman road.

Further along rue des Ursulines, on the left, is the 17C **Chapelle St-Michel** in which Mary of the Incarnation is remembered *(see ADDITIONAL SIGHTS)*.

★ ST-JULIEN DISTRICT *1hr*

The streets near the bridge over the Loire suffered considerable bomb damage in the Second World War, but behind the regular modern façades in rue Nationale some charming little squares have survived.

Église St-Julien – The 11C belfry porch is set back from the street in front of the 13C church. The sombre Gothic interior is lit through stained-glass windows (1960) executed by Max Ingrand and Le Chevalier. Originally it had adjoining cloisters (now a garden) and conventual buildings. The Gothic chapter-house still exists, and the **Celliers St-Julien** (12C) is a huge vaulted chamber which now houses a local Wine Museum, the **Musée des Vins de Touraine** *(see ADDITIONAL SIGHTS)*.

★ **Beaune-Semblançay Garden** – *Entrance through a porch, 28 rue Nationale.* The **Hôtel de Beaune-Semblançay** belonged to the unfortunate Minister of Finance who was hanged during the reign of François I. This Renaissance mansion has suffered badly from the ravages of history; there remain only an arcaded gallery supporting a chapel; a beautiful façade decorated with pilasters and surrounded by plants; and the charming, finely carved **Beaune fountain**.

In rue Jules-Favre stands the sober and elegant façade of the **Palais du Commerce** (Chamber of Commerce) which was built in the 18C for the merchants of Tours; the courtyard is more elaborately decorated.

Rue Colbert – Before Wilson Bridge was built, this street together with its extension, rue du Commerce, was the main axis of the city. The half-timbered house at no 41 bears the sign *À la Pucelle armée* (The Armed Maiden); Joan of Arc's armour is believed to have been made by the craftsman living here in April 1429. Rue Colbert and rue de la Scellerie, which is reached via rue du Cygne, are home to several antique dealers.

Place Foire-le-Roi – This was the site of the free fairs established by François I; it was also the stage for the mystery plays which were performed when the kings visited Tours. The north side is lined by 15C gabled houses. The beautiful Renaissance mansion (no 8) belonged to Philibert Babou de la Bourdaisière *(see p 161)*. On the west side, a side street leads into the narrow and winding passage du Cœur-Navré (Broken-Heart Passage) which leads onto rue Colbert.

TOURS

Amandiers (R. des) . . . . CY 4
Aumônes (Pl. des) . . . . CZ
Avisseau (R.) . . . . DY
Barbusse (R. H.) . . . . . AZ
Barre (R. de la) . . . . . . CY
Béranger (Bd) . . . . ADZ
Berthelot (R.) . . . . BCY 7
Blaise Pascal (R.) . . . . CZ
Blanqui (R. A.) . . . . . . DY
Bons Enfants (R. des) . BY 8
Bordeaux (R. de) . . . . CZ
Bourde (R. de la) . . . . . AZ
Boyer (R. Léon) . . . . . AZ 10
Bretonneau (R.) . . . . . AY
Briçonnet (R.) . . . . AY 13
Buffon (R. de) . . . . . . CYZ
Carmes (Pl. des) . . . . BY 16
Cathédrale (Pl. de la) . CY
Cerisiers (R.) . . . . AY
Chanoineau (R.) . . . . . BZ
Charpentier (R. J.) . . . . AZ
Châteauneuf (Pl. de) . . . BY 17

Châteauneuf (R. de) . . . . AY 18
Cité A. Mame (R. de la) . AZ
Clocheville (R. de la) . . . BZ
Clouet (R. F.) . . . . DY
Cœur-Navré (Passage du) CY 21
Colbert (R.) . . . . CY
Commerce (R. du) . . . . . BY 22
Comte (R. A.) . . . . CZ
Constantine (R. de) . . . . BY 24
Cordeliers (R. des) . . . . CY
Corneille (R.) . . . . CY 25
Courier (Rue Paul-Louis) BY 27
Courset (R. de) . . . . . . AZ
Courteline (R. G.) . . . . AY 28
Cygne (R. du) . . . . . . CY 29
Delperier (R. G.) . . . . . AYZ
Déportés (R. des) . . . . BY
Descartes (R.) . . . . . . BZ 33
Desmoulins (R. C.) . . . . DZ
Dr-Desnoyelle (R. du) . . DZ
Dr-Herpin (R. du) . . . . . DZ
Dolve (R. de la) . . . . . . BZ 35
Dublineau (Pl.) . . . . DZ
Entraigues (R.) . . . . . . BZ

Favre (R. Jules) . . . . . . BY 38
Foch (R. du Mal.) . . . . . BY
Foire-le-Roi (Pl.) . . . . . . CY
France (Pl. A.) . . . . BY
François 1er (Jardin) . . . BY
Frumeaud (Pl. N.) . . . . AZ
Fusillés (R. des) . . . . . BY 41
Gambetta (R.) . . . . DZ 43
Georget (R.) . . . . AZ
Gille (R. Ch.) . . . . CZ
Giraudeau (R.) . . . . . . AZ 46
Grammont (Av. de) . . . . CZ
Grand Marché (Pl. du) . . AY 49
Grand Marché (R. du) . . ABY
Grand Passage . . . . . . CZ 50
Grandière (R. de la) . . . . BZ
Grégoire-de-Tours (Pl.) . . DY 52
Grosse-Tour (R. de la) . . AY 55
Gutenberg (R.) . . . . . . DYZ
Halles (Pl. des) . . . . . . AZ
Halles (R. des) . . . . . . BY
Herbes (Carroi aux) . . . AY 56
Heurteloup (Bd) . . . . . CDZ
Jacquemin (R. J.-B.) . . . . DZ

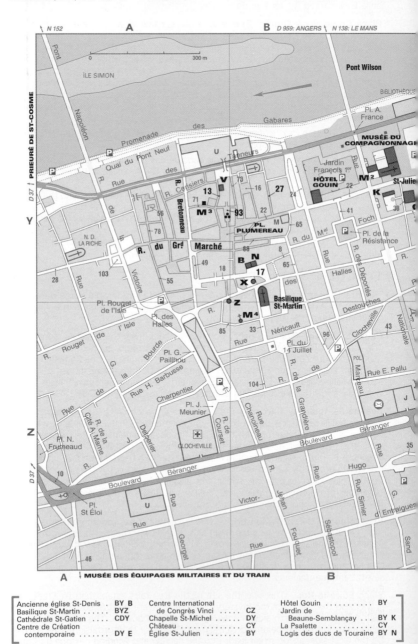

Ancienne église St-Denis . BY B
Basilique St-Martin . . . . . . BYZ
Cathédrale St-Gatien . . . . CDY
Centre de Création
    contemporaine . . . . . . DY E

Centre International
    de Congrès Vinci . . . CZ
Chapelle St-Michel . . . . . DY
Château . . . . CY
Église St-Julien . . . . BY

Hôtel Gouin . . . . BY
Jardin de
    Beaune-Semblançay . . BY K
La Psalette . . . . CY
Logis des ducs de Touraine BY N

Jaurès (Pl. J.)	CZ		Noirmant (R. J.-J.)	DZ		Sébastopol (R.)	BZ
Jehan Fouquet (R.)	BZ		Paillhou (Pl. G.)	AZ		Sicard (Pl. Fr.)	CY
Lavoisier (R.)	CY 60		Paix (R. de la)	BY 73		Simier (R.)	BZ
Leclerc (Pl. du Gén.)	CZ		Palissy			Simon (R. J.)	CDZ
Lobin (R.)	DY		(R. Bernard)	CYZ		Sully (R. de)	BZ 96
Loiseau d'Entraigues			Pallu (R. E.)	BZ		Tanneurs (R. des)	ABY
(Pl.)	DZ		Petit-Cupidon (R. du)	DY 77		Thomas (R. A.)	CDY
Malraux (Av. André)	CDY		Petit-Pré (R. du)	DYZ		Traversière (R.)	DZ
Manceau (R.)	DY 61		Petit-St-Martin (R. du)	AY 78		Tribut (R. M.)	DZ
Marceau (R.)	BYZ		Petites-Boucheries (Pl. des)	DY 80		Truffaut (Pl. F.)	CZ
Maures (R. des)	CDY		Plumereau (Pl.)	ABY		Turones (R. des)	CY
Merville (R. du Prés.)	BY 65		Pont Neuf (Quai du)	AY		Ursulines (R. des)	CDY
Meunier (Pl. J.)	AZ		Préfecture (Pl. de la)	CY		Vaillant (R. Édouard)	CDZ
Meusnier (R. Gén.)	DY 66		Préfecture (R. de la)	CY		Victoire	
Michelet (R.)	CZ		Racine (R.)	DY 84		(Pl. de la)	AY 103
Minimes (R. des)	CZ		Rapin (R.)	AZ 85		Victoire (R. de la)	AY
Mirabeau (R.)	DY		Rempart (R. du)	CDY		Victor-Hugo (R.)	ABZ
Monnaie			Résistance (Pl. de la)	BY		Vinci	
(R. de la)	BY 68		Rouget de l'Isle (Pl.)	AZ		(R. Léonard de)	BZ 104
Mûrier (R. du)	AY 71		Rouget de l'Isle (R.)	AZ		Voltaire (R.)	CY
Nantes (R. de)	CZ		St-Éloi (Pl.)	AZ		Wilson (Pont)	BY
Napoléon (Pont)	AY		St-Pierre-le-Puellier (Pl.)	ABY 93		Zola (R. Émile)	BVY
Nationale (R.)	BYZ		Sand (R. G.)	BZ		14-juillet (Pl.)	BZ
Néricault Destouches (R.)	ABZ		Scellerie (R. de la)	BCY			

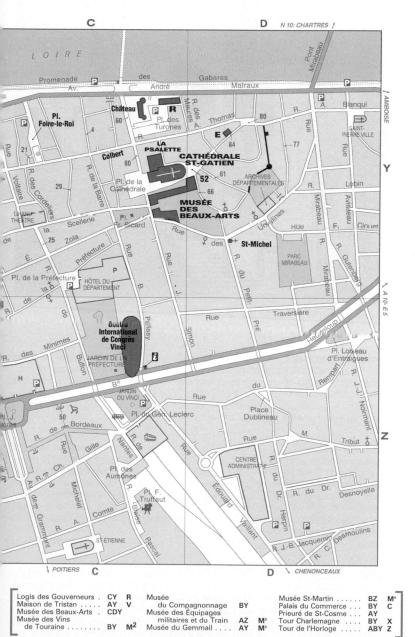

Logis des Gouverneurs	CY R		Musée			Musée St-Martin	BZ M⁴
Maison de Tristan	AY V		du Compagnonnage	BY		Palais du Commerce	BY C
Musée des Beaux-Arts	CDY		Musée des Équipages			Prieuré de St-Cosme	AY
Musée des Vins			militaires et du Train	AZ M³		Tour Charlemagne	BY X
de Touraine	BY M²		Musée du Gemmail	AY M³		Tour de l'Horloge	ABY Z

Tours – Hôtel Gouin

ADDITIONAL SIGHTS

Musée du Gemmail ⊙ – *Entrance at no 7 rue du Mûrier*. The **Hôtel Raimbault** (1835), a beautiful Restoration building with columns, contains a collection of non-leaded stained-glass windows graced with the luminosity of ordinary stained glass and the brilliance of precious stones *(see p 289)*. The 70 pieces on display were executed by master craftsmen whose methods were similar to those of colourists working from cartoons. The 12C underground chapel is decorated with stained glass.

Musée St-Martin ⊙ – This museum in rue Rapin is housed in the 13C Chapel of St-Jean, once an outbuilding of St Martin's cloisters. Texts and engravings evoke crucial events in the life of the saint and his influence on the Christian world, borne out by the many churches dedicated to him not only in France, where about 4 000 carry his name, but throughout Europe. The museum also displays remains from the basilicas built in succession over the saint's tomb. Among them are carved marble items from the one built in about 470 as well as murals and mosaics from the 11C Romanesque basilica.

Before leaving rue Rapin, note the old houses, particularly that at no 6 which is the Centre for Advanced Studies of the Renaissance.

★Hôtel Gouin ⊙ – This mansion, a perfect example of living accommodation during the Renaissance, is one of the most interesting of its kind in Tours. It was burnt out in June 1940, but the **south façade★** with its finely sculpted Renaissance ornamental foliage and the north façade with its fine staircase tower were spared.

It houses the **museum** of the Touraine Archaeological Society which has a very varied collection of exhibits from the prehistoric era through the Gallo-Roman, medieval and Renaissance periods to the 19C. Displayed against a background of 18C panelling are the instruments from the physics study at Chenonceau Château designed by Dupin de Francueil and Jean-Jacques Rousseau as part of the education of Dupin's son. Exhibits include an Archimedes' screw, an inclined plane and a vacuum pump.

★ La Psalette ⊘ **(Cathedral Cloisters)** – This is an elegant Gothic-Renaissance building which once housed the canons and choir, hence the name La Psalette – the place where psalms were sung. The cloisters, which are on the north side of the cathedral, have three ranges: the west range (1460) supports the first-floor library whereas the north and east ranges (1508-24) are almost completely covered by terraces. A graceful Renaissance spiral staircase leads up to the scriptorium (1520) next to the library, a beautiful room with ogive vaulting and an exhibition of the 13C-14C frescoes from the church in Beaumont-Village.

Centre de création contemporaine ⊘ – The centre organises temporary exhibitions of all forms of contemporary art.

Chapelle St-Michel ⊘ – Mary of the Incarnation is remembered in this 17C chapel. Mary was an Ursuline nun who left Tours to spread the Gospel in Canada and founded the first Ursuline convent in Quebec in 1639.

Musée des Vins de Touraine ⊘ – Housed in the huge 12C vaulted cellars of St-Julien Church, this museum illustrates the history of Touraine wines with displays of tools, stills and old winepresses.

★★ Musée du Compagnonnage ⊘ – *Entrance through a porch, 8 rue Nationale, and over a footbridge.* The Trade Guild Museum is housed in the Guest Room (11C) and the **monks' dormitory** (16C) above the chapter-house of the abbey of St-Julien. It traces the history, customs and skills of trade guilds which provided training for their members and protected their interests. Both current and obsolete trades (weavers, ropemakers, woodturners etc) are represented through their tools, historical documents and the many **masterpieces** which the **companions** (derived from *com pani* and meaning someone with whom one shares one's bread) had to produce to receive their official title.

★★ Musée des Beaux-Arts ⊘ – The Fine Arts Museum is housed in the old **Archbishop's Palace** built in the 17C and 18C. Before going in, pause to admire the imposing cedar of Lebanon, perfect in shape, which was planted in the main courtyard around 1804. From the formal garden there is a good **view** of the front of the museum and the cathedral.

The rooms, which are decorated with Louis XVI panelling and silks made in Tours, make a perfect setting for the works of art, some of which used to adorn the châteaux of Richelieu and Chanteloup (now demolished) and the abbeys of Touraine. The walls of the Louis XIII room are hung with a series of highly colourful anonymous paintings, known as the *Five Senses*, executed after engravings by **Abraham Bosse** (1602-76), born in Tours. The work of this artist, who came to master the art of etching by adopting the techniques of Jacques Callot, can be seen in the Abraham Bosse room. His prints depict the different strata of society and thus provide us with an interesting insight into how people lived in the 17C. Among the 14C and 15C paintings are some Italian Primitives and the museum's masterpieces, *Christ in the Garden of Olives* and *The Resurrection*, both by **Mantegna**; both once belonged to the retable of San Zeno Maggiore in Verona *(see The Green Guide Italy)*.

Taste after Abraham Bosse
Musée des Beaux-Arts, Tours

J. Benazet/PIX

The **second floor** is devoted to 19C and 20C work: Delacroix, Chasseriau, Boulanger's portrait of Balzac and a splendid collection of works heavily influenced by Oriental culture, in particular the mysterious and haunting *Femmes d'Alger* by Eugène Giraud. One room is devoted to the contemporary painter Olivier Debré. There is also a display of **ceramics** by Avisseau (19C), from the Touraine: plates decorated with motifs in relief in the style of Bernard Palissy. Note the splendid collections of Langeais faience, highly valued throughout Europe in the 19C: the fine texture of the local clay, combined with kaolin, makes it possible to produce a great variety of shapes and the platinum glaze provides an unusual finishing touch.

Château – A tree-lined walk beside the Loire skirts the heterogeneous buildings of the castle, reminders of past ages. The **Tour de Guise**, with machicolations and a pepper-pot roof, was part of the 13C fortress; the tower owes its name to the young Duke of Guise who was imprisoned in the castle after the assassination of his father and then escaped. Next to it stands the **Pavillon de Mars**, which was built in the reign of Louis XVI and is flanked on the south side by a 13C round tower.

Aquarium tropical – ⊙ Located on the ground floor of the château, the aquarium is home to over 220 marine and freshwater varieties of tropical fish. The tanks, conceived as living tableaux, are in constant evolution thanks to the dedication of the aquarium staff, who endeavour to recreate the natural environment of the fish by carefully selecting suitable flora and fauna species.

On the quay stands the **Logis des Gouverneurs**, a 15C building with gable dormers. At its base and running towards the Tour de Guise is the Gallo-Roman wall, composed of courses of brick alternating with small stones, typical of the period. On the second floor, the **Atelier Histoire de Tours** ⊙ contains archaeological and historical documents as well as models and audio-visual presentations which explain the history of Tours and the development of its townscape. In conjunction with these permanent displays there are temporary exhibitions about living in Tours *(Vivre à Tours)* which highlight its history.

* **Musée des Équipages militaires et du Train** ⊙ – In 1807 Napoleon created the service corps to remedy the problem of insufficient transport means: up to then, the army administration had resorted to using the services of civilian companies, whose efficiency left something to be desired. The museum has been set up in the **Pavillon de Condé** (the only vestiges of the abbey of Ste-Marie in Beaumont). Some 10 carefully laid out rooms retrace the history of the service corps. On the ground floor, the Empire Room explains how the first units of this corps were grouped together to form battalions. The Restauration Room evokes Marshal Bugeaud and his flying columns in Algeria; the 1914-18 Room is a reminder to visitors that the automobile network, functioning on an experimental basis in 1915, became fully operational in 1916, in particular along the Voie Sacrée running between Bar-le-Duc and Verdun *(see The Green Guide Alsace-Lorraine)*. The first floor collections, displayed in rooms bearing the titles Second World War, Indochinese War and Algeria, are concerned with the modern service corps. Three adjoining rooms are devoted to the history of horse-drawn military vehicles, insignia and muleteers who hired out their animals as a public service.

Centre International de Congrès Vinci

Centre international de congrès Vinci – *Not open to the public*. Resembling a gigantic crystal car-ferry, with its stern pointing to the station and its huge elongated hull nudging its way towards the cathedral, this international conference centre (1993), the work of Jean Nouvel, heralds a new architectural style in Tours. The interior features three auditoriums (350, 700 and 2 000 seats) suspended in mid-air – a remarkable technical achievement unique in France. The complex consists of more than 3 500m²/37 670sq ft of exhibition space and 22 meeting rooms.

★ **Prieuré de St-Cosme** ⊘ – *3km/2mi W via quai du Pont-Neuf and avenue Proudhon, then along the riverside embankment*.

A haven of peace set amid well-tended gardens, the priory is the perfect place for a leisurely stroll the gardens, which are ablaze with colour from March to October, boast more than 200 varieties of roses and irises. These form a charming backdrop to the former priory buildings where Pierre de Ronsard stayed between 1565 and 1585. The poet was buried in the chancel; a stone slab with a flowering rose bush marks his tomb.

In the monks' refectory, a large 12C building, note the reader's pulpit decorated with columns and sculptured capitals. The **Prior's Lodging**, where Ronsard lived and died, is a charming little 15C house; in Ronsard's time an outside staircase led to the first floor of the residence, which only had one large room on each level. This staircase was pulled down in the 17C to make way for the inside staircase. The lodging now houses a small **Lapidary Museum**, in which a collection of drawings, plans, photographs, engravings and an audio-visual presentation evoke the poet's life.

Louis XI at Plessis-lès-Tours

Son of Charles VII and Marie of Anjou, **Louis XI** was born in Bourges in 1423 and acceded to the throne in 1461. The new king declared that the sites of Amboise, Loches and Chinon were not to his liking and in 1463 he acquired the Montils estate from the Chamberlain of Maillé. The title was changed to Plessis and Louis XI commissioned the construction of a simple and somewhat austere château consisting of three U-shaped wings. Although its general appearance seemed more fitting for a wealthy patrician than for a king, Louis XI spent the greater part of his life in this residence. Anxious to encourage the economic expansion of his kingdom after the ravages of the Hundred Years War, he made a point of developing industry and trade. He was known to have a nervous disposition and a political rather than military outlook; he succeeded in imposing his authority, ending the Hundred Years War and reviving the national economy. His struggle with the Duke of Burgundy, Charles the Bold, who had designs on the crown, led to the defeat and death of the Duke in 1477, and annexation of part of the duchy in 1482.

Château de Plessis-lès-Tours – *1km/0.6mi from the Prieuré de St-Cosme along avenue du Prieuré*.

This modest brick building *(not open to the public)* is only a small part of the château built by Louis XI in the 15C.

Louis XI's last years were fraught with difficulty; fearing an attack on his life and imagining that he had contracted leprosy, he lived shrouded in mistrust and superstition. The betrayal of Cardinal **Jean Balue** came to light in this context a favourite of Louis XI who showered him with honours, the cardinal secretly conspired with the Duke of Burgundy. He was exposed in 1469 and imprisoned at Loches until 1480.

Louis XI died at the Château de Plessis on 30 August 1483, after having ruled for 22 years.

EXCURSIONS

★ **Grange de Meslay** ⊘ – *10km/6mi NE via N 10 and a road to the right*. This former **fortified tithe farm** belonging to Marmoutier Abbey has a beautiful porch, the remains of a perimeter wall and a remarkable **barn**. The barn is a very good example of 13C secular architecture. The rounded main door is set in a pointed gable and the 15C timber roof is supported by four rows of oak heartwood pillars.

The barn is regularly used as a concert hall and a venue for temporary art exhibitions.

Montbazon – *9km/5.6mi S along N 10.* This is one of the 20 fortresses built by Fulk Nerra; violent storms caused considerable damage to it in 2001. From the ruined **keep** *(private property)* which dominates the village there is a good view. Take rue des Moulins near the town hall and then a path on the right beyond the old gateway.

Dolmen de Mettray – *10km/6.2mi NW along N 138 turning right onto D 76 to Mettray.* In a spinney in St-Antoine-du-Rocher to the north of Mettray on the right bank of the Choisille *(signposted)* stands the beautiful dolmen of the Fairy Grotto, one of the most skilfully constructed megalithic monuments in France; it is 11m/37ft long and 3.7m/12ft high and consists of 12 evenly cut stone slabs.

Luynes – *7km/4.3mi W along N 152 then right.* From the road running along the Loire embankment, there is a pretty view of this charming little town built in tiers up the hillside. Luynes still features numerous cellars hollowed out of the rock face, and a handsome timber-frame covered market hall, the **halles**, dating from the 15C, with a high roof of flat tiles. Visitors should also look out for one or two half-timbered houses, and in particular a house with carved corner pillars opposite the church (in rue Paul-Louis-Courier).

Leaving town on D 49, which climbs through vine-clad hillsides, there is a good view, looking back, of the medieval castle above the town.

★ **Château** ⊙ – This large and austere medieval fortress perched on a rocky spur high above the little town was transformed in the 15C. It belonged to a crony of Louis XI, Hardouin de Maillé. Only three families have lived in the castle since the 11C, the Maillés, the Lavals and the Luynes. The castle is now occupied by the 12th Duc de Luynes. From the delightful inner courtyard there is a fine **panorama** of the Loire Valley. The elegant residential block of the château, in brick and stone, was built during the reign of Louis XI, whereas the two wings date from the 17C. The interior houses sumptuous tapestries, paintings and antique furniture. Well laid out attractive gardens.

★★★DOWNSTREAM TO CHINON

From Tours to Chinon *61km/38mi – about 5hr*

Leave Tours on D 88 going W.

The road runs along the Loire embankment passing gardens and vegetable plots and the **Priory of St-Cosme**★ *(see p 295)*. Fine views of the south bank of the river.

In L'Aireau-des-Bergeons turn left.

The Garden of France

"Are you familiar with the land which has been called The Garden of France, a land where the air is pure and the landscape a tender green, graced by a great and noble river? If, during the summer months, you were given an opportunity to travel through beautiful Touraine, you would follow the lazy meanderings of the Loire with delight, and you would be in a quandary indeed, not knowing which of the two banks to choose as your place of residence, to which you could retreat with your loved one, away from the bustle of mankind."

Alfred de Vigny – *Cinq-Mars* (1826)

Savonnières – The church has a beautiful Romanesque doorway decorated with doves and other animals.

Grottes pétrifiantes ⊙ – *On the western edge of the town on the road to Villandry.* ▣ The petrifying caves were formed in the Secondary Era. In the 12C they were used as quarries and then partially flooded with water. The continuing infiltration of water saturated with limestone is slowly creating stalactites, pools and curtains. There is a reconstruction of prehistoric fauna and a **Musée de la Pétrification** with lithographic stones and 19C copper matrices. There is also the opportunity to indulge in some wine tasting in the caves.

★★★Villandry – *See VILLANDRY.*

After Villandry take the road S (D 39) out of troglodyte country and into the Indre Valley.

***Château d'Azay-le-Rideau** – *See AZAY-LE-RIDEAU.*

The road (D 17) runs W between Chinon Forest (left) and the River Indre, which splits into several channels at this point.

A charming but narrow road winds between hedges and spinneys with occasional glimpses of the river. A bridge spanning the Indre provides one of the best views of the Château d'Ussé.

Château d'Ussé – See Château d'USSÉ.

After Rigny-Ussé, the road crosses the **Véron**, a tongue of highly fertile alluvial soil at the confluence of the Loire and the Vienne. It yields grain, grapes and fruit in abundance; the plums used in the famous *pruneaux de Tours* are grown here.

Drive to Chinon via Huismes.

TROO

Population 301
Michelin map 318: B-5, 232 fold 24 or 238 fold 1
Local map see VENDÔME

The bell-tower of Troo, which is perched on a steep-sided slope, can be seen from a long way off. The village still has numerous troglodyte dwellings. The houses are built in tiers, one above the other up the hillside, and linked by narrow alleys, stairways and mysterious passages. A labyrinth of galleries, called *caforts* (short for *caves fortes*), exists underground in the white-tufa rock. In times of war these *caforts* served as hideouts.

SIGHTS

***La Butte** – This is a feudal mound which provides a splendid **panorama** *(viewing table and telescope)* of the sinuous course of the River Loir and of the small church of St-Jacques-des-Guérets on the far bank.

Ancienne collégiale St-Martin – The collegiate church was built in 1050 and altered one century later. It is dominated by a remarkable square tower pierced by openings; the splays are ornamented with small columns in characteristic Angevin style. The windows in the Romanesque apse are Gothic. The nave and chancel are covered by a convex vault. The historiated capitals at the transept crossing are Romanesque. The choir stalls and Communion table are 15C. The 16C wooden statue is of St Mamès who is invoked against all stomach ailments.

> **ROOMS WITH A VIEW**
>
> **Chambre d'hôte Château de La Voute** – ☏ 02 54 72 52 52 – http://members.aol.com/chatlavout – ✉ – 5 rooms 75/110€. No matter which room you choose in this castle on a magnificent site, you will be thrilled with the view over the Loir Valley. The refined decor and romantic setting cannot fail to please.

Grand Puits – The great well is known also as the talking well because of its excellent echo; it is 45m/148ft deep and covered by a wooden shingle roof.

Maladrerie Ste-Catherine – On the eastern edge of the town on the south side of D 917 stands a 12C building with fine Romanesque blind arcades. Originally it was a hospice for sick pilgrims travelling to Tours and Compostela; there was also a leper house to the west of Troo. When this disappeared the hospice took over its goods and its name.

Fresco depicting the
martyrdom of St James

Grotte pétrifiante ⊘ – The petrifying cave, in which running water is a permanent feature, contains stalactites and lime encrustations.

Église St-Jacques-des-Guérets – *South bank of the Loir*. The services in this church were conducted by the Augustinians from the abbey of St-Georges (St-Martin-des-Bois) south-east of Troo.

The **murals**★ were painted between 1130 and 1170 and reflect Byzantine influence; the draughtsmanship and the freshness of the colours are particularly pleasing. The most beautiful are in the apse: the Crucifixion, in which the half-figures represent the Sun and the Moon, and the Resurrection of the Dead *(left)*; Christ in Majesty, surrounded by the Symbols of the Evangelists; and the Last Supper *(right)*. Statues of St Augustine and St George adorn the embrasure of the central window.

On the right side of the apse appears the Martyrdom of St James who was beheaded by Herod, with Paradise above: the Heavenly Elect shelter in niches like pigeon-holes. High up on the south wall of the nave is St Nicholas performing a miracle the saint is throwing three gold pieces to three sisters whose father was about to sell them because he was too poor to give them a dowry and below is the Resurrection of Lazarus. Further on is a vast composition representing the Descent into Hell; a majestic figure of Jesus is seen delivering Adam and Eve. The left wall of the church was painted at different times from the 12C to 15C; Nativity and Massacre of the Innocents. In the church are two painted wooden statues (16C): in a niche *(left)* St James on a base which bears the arms of Savoy; in the chancel *(left)* St Peter.

Château d'USSÉ★★

Michelin map 317: K-5, 232 fold 34 or 4037 B4 – 14km/9mi NE of Chinon
Local map see TOURS: Excursions

The **château** stands with its back to a cliff on the edge of Chinon Forest, its terraced gardens overlooking the River Indre. Its impressive bulk and fortified towers contrast sharply with the white stone and myriad roofs, turrets, dormers and chimneys rising against a green background. The best view is from the bridge, some 200m/220yd from the château, or from the Loire embankment. Tradition has it that when **Charles Perrault**, the famous French writer of fairy tales, was looking for a setting for *Sleeping Beauty*, he chose Ussé as his model.

Every year, Ussé hosts an **exhibition of historic costumes** (mannequins, fashion accessories).

From the Bueils to the Blacas – Ussé is a very old fortress; in the 15C it became the property of a great family from Touraine, the Bueils, who had distinguished themselves in the Hundred Years War (1337-1453). In 1485, Antoine de Bueil, who had married one of the daughters of Charles VII and Agnès Sorel, sold Ussé to the Espinays, a Breton family who had been chamberlains and cupbearers to the Duke of Brittany and to Louis XI and Charles VIII. It was they who built the courtyard ranges and the chapel in the park. The château frequently changed hands. Among its owners was Vauban's son-in-law, Louis Bernin de Valentinay; the great engineer paid frequent visits to Ussé. Voltaire and Chateaubriand were guests at the château. The estate has belonged to the Blacas family since the late 19C.

TOUR ⊘

Exterior

On the walk up towards the château, a lovely kaleidoscope of roofs and turrets can be glimpsed through the leaves of the stately cedars of Lebanon, said to have been planted by the great French author Chateaubriand.

The outside walls (15C) have a military appearance whereas the buildings overlooking the courtyard are more welcoming and some even carry an elegant Renaissance touch.

The courtyard is enclosed by three heavily restored ranges: the east wing is Gothic, the west wing Renaissance and the south wing a combination of Gothic and Classical styles. As in the case of Chaumont Château, the north wing was pulled down in the 17C to open up the view of the Loire and Indre valleys from the terrace. The west wing is extended by a 17C pavilion.

★ **Chapel** – Standing on its own in the park, the chapel was built from 1520 to 1538 in the pure Renaissance style. The west façade is the most remarkable. The initials C and L, to be found in other parts of the domain, are used as a decorative motif; they refer to the first names of Charles d'Espinay, who built the chapel, and his wife Lucrèce de Pons. The lofty, luminous interior contains fine 16C stalls decorated with carved figures. The south chapel, supported by rib vaulting, houses a pretty Virgin Mary in enamelled earthenware attributed to Luca della Robbia.

Interior

Salle des Gardes – In a corner of the building, the guard-room boasts a superb 17C *trompe-l'œil* ceiling and houses a collection of Oriental weapons. The small adjoining room presents porcelain from China and Japan.

Ancienne chapelle – The old chapel, which has been converted into a salon, has a fine set of furniture, including a Mazarin desk fashioned from lemon-tree wood and three 400-year-old Brussels tapestries, with colours which have remained vivid.

Grande Galerie – Linking the east and west wings of the château, the Great Gallery is hung with **Flemish tapestries★** depicting lively, realistic country scenes inspired by the work of Teniers.

Beyond the room devoted to hunting trophies, the wide 17C staircase (fine wrought-iron banister) leads to the rooms on the first floor: the library and the King's apartment. In the antechamber there is a splendid 16C Italian cabinet with 49 drawers (admire the ebony marquetry inside, inlaid with ivory and mother-of-pearl).

Chambre du Roi – As in all large stately residences, one of the bedrooms was set aside for the king in the event of his paying a visit to the château. This particular

Château d'Ussé – Flemish tapestry after Teniers the Younger

B. Kaufmann/MICHELIN

room was in fact never occupied by the sovereign.

Note the silk furnishings with Chinese motifs, a four-poster bed, a large Venetian mirror and a fine set of Louis XVI furniture.

The top of the **donjon** (keep) houses an extremely interesting **salle de jeux★** (recreation room) with china dinner services, toy trains and miniature furniture items from dolls' houses.

Dotted along the **wall walk**, several display cabinets illustrate the story of Sleeping Beauty: the wicked Fairy, Prince Charming and other popular childhood characters will delight visitors of all ages.

Dried pears, a speciality of Rivarennes

The recipe is virtually identical to that used for making dried apples *(see p 174)*: the pears are peeled whole, then left to dry in a bread oven for four days. During this operation, they lose 70% of their weight. They are then beaten flat *(tapées)* with a spatula in order to remove the remaining air. They can be kept dried or preserved in glass jars.

They provide a perfect accompaniment to game or meat dishes served with gravy, in which case they are simply made to swell by soaking in a good Chinon wine.

EXCURSION

Rivarennes – *5km/3mi from Rigny-Ussé.* Lying on the banks of the River Indre, Rivarennes once boasted some 60 ovens producing the famous dried pears.

La Poire Tapée à l'Ancienne ⊙ – This troglodytic cave contains an old oven where pears are still dried today. Its owners will tell you the story of this delicious regional speciality and explain how it is made. You will then be invited to try the mouthwatering fruit.

Château de VALENÇAY★★★

Michelin map 318: G-9 or 238 fold 16

Geographically speaking, Valençay is in the Berry region but the château can be included with those in the Loire Valley because of the period of its construction and its huge size, in which it resembles Chambord. A *son et lumière* show enhances the château's beautiful setting.

A financier's château – Valençay was built c 1540 by Jacques d'Estampes, the owner of the existing castle. He had married the daughter of a financier, who brought him a large dowry, and he wanted a residence worthy of his new fortune. The 12C castle was demolished and in its place rose the present sumptuous building.

Finance has often been involved in the history of Valençay; among its owners were several Farmers-General and even the famous **John Law** whose dizzy banking career was an early and masterly example of inflation.

Charles-Maurice de Talleyrand-Périgord, who had begun his career under Louis XVI as Bishop of Autun, was Minister of Foreign Affairs when he bought Valençay in 1803 at the request of Napoleon, so that he would have somewhere to receive important foreign visitors. Talleyrand managed his career so skilfully that he did not finally retire until 1834.

TOUR ⊙ *1hr*

The entrance pavilion is a huge building, designed like a keep, but for show not defence, with many windows, harmless turrets and fancy machicolations. The steep roof is pierced with high dormer windows and surmounted by monumental chimneys. Such architecture is also found in the Renaissance châteaux of the Loire Valley but here there are also the first signs of the Classical style: superimposed pilasters with Doric (ground floor), Ionic (first floor) and Corinthian (second floor) capitals.

The Classical style is even more evident in the huge corner towers: domes take the place of the pepper-pot roofs which were the rule on the banks of the Loire in the 16C.

West wing – The west wing was added in the 17C and altered in the 18C. At roof level mansard windows alternate with bulls' eyes (small circular apertures). The tour of the ground floor includes the great Louis XVI vestibule; the gallery devoted to the Talleyrand-Périgord family; the Grand Salon and the Blue Salon which contain many works of art and sumptuous Empire furniture including the famous Congress of Vienna table; and the apartments of the Duchess of Dino.

On the first floor the bedroom of Prince Talleyrand is followed by the room occupied by Ferdinand VII, King of Spain, when he was confined to Valençay by Napoleon from 1808 to 1814; the apartments of the Duke of Dino and those of Mme de Bénévent (portrait of the princess by Élisabeth Vigée-Lebrun); the great gallery (with a *Diana* by Houdon) and the great staircase. Something of the spirit of the festivities organised by Talleyrand and his master chef, **Marie-Antoine Carême**, still lingers in the great dining room and the kitchens beneath.

Park – Black swans, ducks and peacocks strut freely in the formal French gardens near the château. Under the great trees in the park deer, llamas, camels and kangaroos are kept in vast enclosures.

Musée de l'Automobile du Centre ⊙ – *Avenue de la Résistance*. The Car Museum contains the collection of the Guignard brothers, the grandsons of a coachbuilder from Vatan (Indre). There are over

60 vintage cars (the earliest dating from 1898), perfectly maintained in working order, including the 1908 Renault limousine used by presidents Poincaré and Millerand; there are also road documents from the early days of motoring, old Michelin maps and guides predating 1914.

EXCURSION

Chabris – *14km/8.7mi NE along D 4*. This ancient Roman town lying on the south bank of the Cher is renowned for its wines and goat's cheese.

Église – The church is dedicated to St Phalier, a 5C anchorite who died in Chabris and was at the origin of a pilgrimage *(third Sunday in September)*. The 11C **crypt** contains the saint's sarcophagus.

The present building dates from the 15C but there are traces of an earlier church (primitive sculptures of supernatural animals) behind the east end.

An arcaded porch with a gallery stands in front of the Gothic doorway with its remarkable carved door panels. In the chancel, note the two naïve-style panels depicting the life and miracles of St Phalier, who was reputed to make women fertile.

VENDÔME★★

Population 17 707
Michelin map 318: D-5 or 238 fold 2
Local maps see BONNEVAL and Vallée du Loir below

At the foot of a steep bluff, which is crowned by a castle, the River Loir branches out into several channels which flow slowly under a number of bridges. Vendôme, which since 1990 is only 42min away from Paris thanks to the new TGV line, stands on a group of islands dotted with gables and steep slate roofs.

A troubled history – Although the origins of Vendôme can be traced back to the Gaulish, and even as far back as the Neolithic periods, before the town received its name, Vindocenum, in the Gallo-Roman period, it only began to acquire importance under the counts, first the Bouchard family, who were faithful supporters of the Capet dynasty, and particularly under the son of Fulk Nerra, **Geoffrey Martel** (11C), who founded La Trinité Abbey.

In 1371 the royal House of Bourbon inherited Vendôme (by marriage) and in 1515 François I raised it to a duchy. In 1589 the town sided with the League but was captured by its overlord, Henri IV, and suffered for its disloyalty; the town was sacked and only the abbey church was left standing.

Henri IV's son, César – Vendôme was given to César de Bourbon, the eldest son of Henri IV and Gabrielle d'Estrées as a royal prerogative. César de Vendôme was often resident on his feudal estate while he involved himself with conspiracies, first during the minority of Louis XIII and then against Richelieu. He was imprisoned at Vincennes for four years before being exiled. He eventually lent his support to Mazarin's cause, before dying in 1665.

TOWN WALK

A pleasant alternative – In rue du Change, a barge overflowing with flowers marks the starting point of a boat trip down the River Loir, during which you will glide past the Porte d'Eau and the east end of the abbey, basking in delightfully cool and luxuriant surroundings.

Jardin public – Running down to the riverside, the public garden gives a good view over the town, the abbey and the 13C-14C gateway, **Porte d'Eau** or Arche des Grands Prés.

From the open space on the opposite bank, place de la Liberté, there are views of the Porte d'Eau from a different angle as well as of the 13C **Tour de l'Islette**. Together with the **Porte St-Georges** *(see below)* these structures are all that is left of the old ramparts.

Parc Ronsard – Round this shaded park are the Lycée Ronsard (originally the Collège des Oratoriens where Balzac was a pupil and now occupied by the offices of the town hall), the late-15C Hôtel de Saillant (now the Tourist Information Centre) and the municipal library with its important collection of old books including 11 incunabula. A 16C two-storeyed wash-house is sited on the arm of the river running through the park. The *Fallen Warrior* on the lawn is a bronze by Louis Leygue.

Chapelle St-Jacques – Rebuilt in the 15C, and subsequently attached to the Collège des Oratoriens in the 16C, the chapel once served the pilgrims on their way to Compostela. It now houses temporary exhibitions.

Eating out

BUDGET

Auberge de la Madeleine – *Pl. de la Madeleine* – ☎ *02 54 77 20 79* – *closed during Feb school holidays and Wed* – *12.96/33.54€*. There is a real family atmosphere in this town-centre inn, with its smart, split-level dining room. In fine weather eat outside on the lovely terrace by the Loir. Good choice of menus at attractive prices. A few functional, well-soundproofed rooms.

Auberge du Val de Loir – *3 pl. M.-Morand* – *72500 Dissay-sous-Courcillon* – *5km/3mi SE of Château-du-Loir on N 138* – ☎ *02 43 44 09 06* – *closed 23 Dec-8 Jan, Fri and Sun evening out of season* – *reservation required* – *13.57/28.97€*. This simply decorated restaurant with its Virginia creeper-covered façade has a faithful regular clientele. The shady terrace is ideal for hot days. Tasty regional cuisine. Ten fairly spacious rooms.

MODERATE

Le Petit Bilboquet – *On the old Tours road* – ☎ *02 54 77 16 60* – *closed 16 Aug-7 Sep, Thu evening in winter, Sun evening and Mon* – *reservation required for weekends* – *14€ lunch, 19.82/26€*. This little restaurant was once an officers' mess, and its wooden façade dates from the 19C. There are two terraces to enjoy in fine weather, a lively one in front and a quieter one at the back. The cooking is well presented and simple, as is the decor.

Auberge de la Sellerie – *At Les Fontaines* – *41100 Pezou* – *15km/9.3mi N of Vendôme on N 10* – ☎ *02 54 23 41 43* – *closed 5-26 Jan, 9-22 Oct, Mon and Tue* – *22.87/42.69€*. Situated on the main holiday route, this local-style inn is easy to find. Open fireplace or terrace sheltered by a little wood for fine days. Reasonably priced dishes.

Where to stay

BUDGET

Chambre d'hôte Ferme de Crislaine – *41100 Azé* – *11km/6.8mi NW of Vendôme on D 957 towards Épuisay* – ☎ *02 54 72 14 09* – 🖂 – *5 rooms 29/37€* – *evening meal 15.58€*. Staying here is an excellent way to discover an organic farm. If you don't know the region, your hosts will advise you what to see. An ideal stopping place for families and walkers. Bikes and swimming pool for guests' use.

Auberge du Port des Roches – *At Le Port-des-Roches* – *72800 Luché-Pringé* – *2.5km/1.5mi E of Luché-Pringé on D 13 and D 214* – ☎ *02 43 45 44 48* – *closed 29 Jan-6 Mar, Sun evening and Mon* – *12 rooms 36.59/47.26€* – 🍽 *5.34€* – *restaurant 18/31€*. A pleasant, peaceful little hotel. Enjoy a good night's sleep in the functional rooms with their contemporary decor. Terrace and garden on the banks of the Loir.

MODERATE

Chambre d'hôte Château de la Volonière – *49 r. Principale* – *72340 Poncé-sur-le-Loir* – ☎ *02 43 79 68 16* – *closed Feb* – *5 rooms 56/76€* – *evening meal 40€*. Although Ronsard lived near here, Classicism is no longer always the rule! Here, the former troglodytic kitchen has been turned into an exhibition area, the bedrooms combine antique furniture with brilliant colours, and the dining room is a former chapel. The result is an appealing blend that is both bohemian and relaxed.

LUXURY

Chambre d'hôte Château de la Vaudourière – *41360 Lunay* – *14km/8.75mi W of Vendôme on D 5 towards Lunay, and D 53* – ☎ *02 54 72 19 46* – *3 rooms 70/90€*. Alfred de Musset spent his childhood in this small 18C castle, where you will be made to feel like a friend of the family. The drawing room has a spiral staircase and an extremely unusual original painted ceiling. The rooms are opulent. Stroll in the park and appreciate the peaceful surroundings.

Shopping

Glass-blower's workshop – *Verrerie d'art de Poncé-sur-le-Loir* – *daily 9am-noon, 2-6.30pm* – *closed Wed and Sun* – ☎ *02 43 79 05 69*. In his workshop located at the foot of the castle, Gérard Torcheux reveals all the secrets of his craft.

Honoré de Balzac (1799-1850)

On 22 June 1807 the Collège des Oratoriens in Vendôme registered the entry of an eight-year-old boy, Honoré de Balzac. The future historical novelist was an absent-minded and undisciplined pupil. Balzac was to recall the severity of school discipline of those days in his writing. His general clumsiness and ineptitude at standard children's pursuits made him the frequent butt of his fellow pupils' jokes. He regularly got himself put into detention in order to read in peace. The harshness of the school regime eventually undermined his health and his parents had to take him away.

Balzac's early efforts at writing met with minimal success, so he embarked on a career in printing. However, the firm in which he was joint partner went bankrupt, leaving him at the age of 30 with debts which he was to spend the rest of his life attempting to pay off. He returned to writing and over the next 20 years produced a phenomenal number of novels (about 90), a vast collection which constitutes a richly detailed record of contemporary society, covering all walks of life and reflecting what he saw as people's overriding motivations at that time, chiefly money and ambition. Typically, Balzac's novels contain keenly observed settings, peopled by characters exaggerated almost to the point of caricature by their creator's vivid imagination. Balzac's fascination by the contrast between life in the provinces and that in the glittering French capital is also reflected in his work.

Balzac retrospectively attached the label **La Comédie Humaine** to his life's work, giving some indication of the breadth of scope of the world he had tried to evoke – an ambitious project formulated after he had already written many of his most famous novels, but which was to remain uncompleted on his untimely death from overwork, just months after he had finally married Eveline Hanska, the Polish countess with whom he had passionately corresponded for over 18 years.

Église de la Madeleine 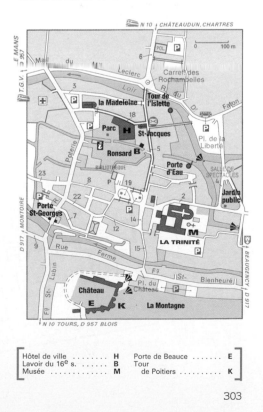 – The church bell-tower, which dates from 1474, is surmounted by an elegant crocketed spire.

Place St-Martin – Until the 19C St Martin's Church (15C-16C) stood here; only the bell-tower remains. There is also a fine 16C timber-framed house called the Grand St-Martin; it is ornamented with figures and coats of arms and has a statue of **Maréchal de Rochambeau** *(see Middle reaches of the Loir below).*

Porte St-Georges – St-Georges gateway was the entrance to the town from the River Loir; it is flanked by towers largely built in the 14C although the front facing the bridge is decorated with machicolations and carvings of dolphins and Renaissance medallions which were added early in the 16C by Marie de Luxembourg, Duchess of Vendôme.

Castle ⊘ – *Access by car via St-Lubin district and Le Temple, a hamlet which grew up round a Templar commandery.* The ruined castle is set on the top of an outcrop – La Montagne – which overlooks the Loir.

VENDÔME

Abbaye (R. de l')	2
Béguinoo (R. doc)	3
Bourbon (R. A.)	4
Change (R. du)	5
Chartrain (Fg)	6
Chevallier (R.)	7
Gaulle (R. du Gén.-de)	8
Grève (R. de la)	9
Guesnault (R.)	12
Poterie (R.)	
République (Pl. de la)	14
St-Bié (R.)	15
St-Jacques (R.)	18
St-Martin (Pl.)	19
Saulnerie (R.)	22
Verdun (Av. de)	23

Hôtel de ville .... H
Lavoir du 16ᵉ s. ...... B
Musée .... M

Porte de Beauce .... E
Tour
  de Poitiers .... K

It consists of an earth wall and ramparts with 13C and 14C machicolated round towers at intervals; the great Poitiers Tower on the east side was reconstructed in the 15C. The early-17C Beauce gate leads into the precinct which is now a huge garden. There are traces of the collegiate church of St-Georges which was founded by Agnès of Burgundy and where the counts of Vendôme were buried. Antoine de Bourbon and Jeanne d'Albret, the parents of Henri IV, were also buried here.

Heavy rains and flooding in the spring of 2001 so engorged the soil that one of the towers collapsed, and the castle is currently off-limits while the authorities verify the condition of the foundations.

Promenade de la Montagne – From the terraces there are panoramic **views**★ of Vendôme and the Loir Valley.

★ANCIENNE ABBAYE DE LA TRINITÉ

One summer night, Geoffrey Martel, Count of Anjou, saw three fiery spears plunge into a fountain and decided to found a monastery which was dedicated to the Holy Trinity on 31 May 1040. Under the Benedictine Order the abbey grew considerably, becoming one of the most powerful religious foundations in France, to the extent that eventually the abbot was automatically made a cardinal. In the late 11C this office was held by the famous Geoffroi of Vendôme, friend of Pope Urban II. Until the Revolution pilgrims flocked to Trinité Abbey to venerate a relic of the Holy Tear (Sainte Larme) – shed by Christ on Lazarus's tomb – which Geoffrey Martel had brought back from Constantinople. The knights of Vendôme would rally to the cry of *"Sainte Larme de Vendôme"*. The relic was venerated on Lazarus' Friday and its curative powers were invoked in the case of eye diseases.

★★ **Abbey Church** – The abbey church is a remarkable example of Flamboyant Gothic architecture. The entrance to the abbey precinct is in rue de l'Abbaye. On either side of the wall stand the Romanesque bays of the abbey granary which have been incorporated into more modern buildings; in fact from the 14C onwards the monks allowed tradesmen to build their shops against the abbey walls.

Exterior – To the right of the west front and set apart from it stands the 12C **bell-tower**, 80m/262ft high. An interesting feature is the way the windows and arcades, which are blind at ground level, grow larger as the embrasures also increase in size. The transition from a square to an octagonal tower is made by means of openwork, mini bell-towers at the corners. The base of the cornices is embellished with grinning masks and animals.

The astonishing Flamboyant **west front**, which is accentuated by a great carved gable, is thought to have been built in the early 16C by Jean de Beauce, who designed the new bell-tower of Chartres Cathedral. The decorative openwork, so delicate it looks like a piece of lace, contrasts with the plainer Romanesque tower.

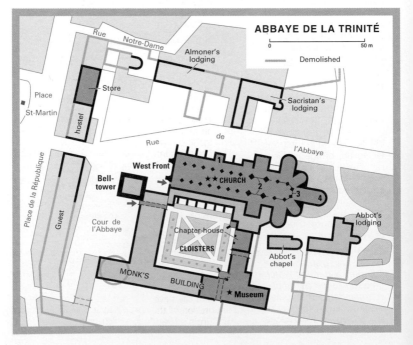

Interior – The nave, which was started at the transept end in the middle of the 14C, was not completed until the early 16C; the transept, all that is left of the 11C building, leads to the chancel and ambulatory with its five radiating chapels.

The baptismal chapel (**1**) in the north aisle contains a beautiful Renaissance font in white marble supported by a carved pedestal from the gardens of Blois Château. The primitive capitals of the transept crossing are surmounted by polychrome statues (13C) of the Virgin Mary with the Archangel Gabriel, St Peter and St Eutropius who was venerated in the abbey church. The transept vaulting with its historiated keystones was altered in the 14C in the Angevin style; in the north transept are statues of St John the Baptist (14C) and the Virgin Mary (16C).

The 14C chancel, which is lit through windows from the same period, is decorated with beautiful late-15C **stalls★** (**2**). The misericords are decorated with naïve scenes illustrating daily life with various trades and zodiac signs. The choir screen (**3**) enclosing the chancel bears the influence of the first Renaissance. To the left of the high altar is the base of the famous monument of the Holy Tear, decorated with tears, with a small aperture through which the relic was displayed to the faithful by one of the monks.

The chapels radiating from the ambulatory are decorated with 14C and 16C stained glass which has been extensively restored: the best section, which depicts the meal in Simon's house, taken from a German engraving, is in the first chapel to the left of the axial chapel. This also contains a **window** dating from 1140 depicting the Virgin and Child (**4**).

14C windows in Trinity Abbey depicting the meal in Simon's house

Conventual buildings – Only the east side of the 16C cloisters exists in its entirety. In the 14C **chapter-house** ⊙ a number of wall paintings have been uncovered, depicting episodes from the Life of Christ. The Classical-style buildings now house a museum. Take the passage through the south range of buildings to admire the monumental south front which was built between 1732 and 1742; the pediments bear the royal fleur-de-lis, the motto (Pax) and the emblem (Lamb) of the Order of St Benedict.

★ Museum ⊙ – The museum collections are displayed in the abbey's monastic buildings which are reached up a majestic stairway.

The most interesting rooms on the ground floor are devoted to **mural painting★** in the Loire Valley and to **religious art★** in the Vendôme area from the Middle Ages to the Renaissance. There are remains of the 16C tomb of Marie de Luxembourg and François de Bourbon-Vendôme, fragments of the funerary sculptures of Catherine and Jean VII de Bourbon, keystones from the cloister vaults, and an octagonal stoup which once formed part of the Holy Tear monument.

On the upper floors are the sections on archaeology and natural history. Certain rooms are devoted to 16C-19C paintings and furniture and to earthenware; there is a superb late-18C **harp★**, the work of Nadermann, Marie-Antoinette's instrument maker, together with contemporary sculptures by the artist **Louis Leygue** (1905-92).

EXCURSIONS

Nourray – *12km/7.5mi S on D 16, then right onto D 64 in Crucheray.* The little **church** ⊙ which stands alone in the square has a row of Romanesque arcades beneath carved corbels on the chevet; note the multilobed arch of the central window. Inside, the oven-vaulted apse is surrounded by arcading with carved capitals.

Villemardy – *14km/9mi SE on D 957; turn left to Périgny and bear right to Villemardy.* The **church** ⊙ dating from the 12C has a simple nave ending in a Gothic chancel. The interior decoration in carved oak is remarkably uniform; the high altar and tabernacle, which are surmounted by an altarpiece, are in the Classical style, as are the two small symmetrical altars in the nave. The left wall of the chancel is decorated with a fresco (16C), the Adoration of the Magi, flanked by columns and a pediment in *trompe-l'œil;* note the Virgin's headdress which helps to determine the date of the work.

Rhodon – *20km/12.5mi SE on D 917 (towards Beaugency), then turn right in Noyers.* The internal walls and Gothic vaulting of the **church** bear traces of 14C and 15C mural paintings: Christ in Majesty in the apse and the Months of the Year on one of the transverse arches of the nave.

★MIDDLE REACHES OF THE LOIR

① From Vendôme to La Chartre

78km/49mi – allow one day

Villiers-sur-Loir – The village overlooks the sloping vineyards opposite Rochambeau Castle. The church is decorated with some very attractive 16C **murals**: on the left wall of the nave there is a huge figure of St Christopher carrying the Child Jesus and the Legend of the Three Living and the Three Dead. The stalls date from the 15C.

Numerous outdoor activities are available: swimming, rambling, fishing, volleyball, *boules*, table tennis, sailing, archery, and more. In Riotte, special courses offer an introduction to the local fauna and flora.

Take the road towards Thoré. Immediately after crossing the Loir turn left.

Rochambeau – The road runs along the foot of the cliff through the semi-troglodyte village up to the castle where **Maréchal de Rochambeau** (1725-1807) was born; he commanded the French expeditionary force in the American War of Independence and was buried in Thoré.

Return to the west bank of the river and turn left onto D 5.

Le Gué-du-Loir – The hamlet was built where the Boulon joins the Loir amid lush meadows and islands ringed by reed-beds, willows, alders and poplars. On leaving the hamlet the road (D 5) skirts the wall of **Manoir de Bonaventure**, which was probably named after a chapel dedicated to St Bonaventure. In the 16C the manor house belonged to Henri IV's father, Antoine de Bourbon-Vendôme who entertained his friends there, including some of the poets of the Pléiade. Later Bonaventure came into the possession of the De Musset family. The poet, **Alfred de Musset**, whose father was born at the manor, used to spend his holidays as a child with his godfather, Louis de Musset, at the Château de Cogners, since the manor had by then been sold.

Continue W on D 5 towards Savigny; then take the second turning to the right (C 13) at a wayside cross.

A wooded valley leads to the picturesque village of **Mazangé** clustered round the pretty church with its Gothic door.

Return to Gué-du-Loir; turn right onto D 24 towards Montoire-sur-le-Loir, then right again onto D 82 to Lunay.

Lunay – Lunay is grouped in a valley round the main square where some old houses have survived. The huge, Flamboyant Gothic **church of St-Martin** presents an attractive doorway. The stones of the arch are carved with ivy and vine ornaments *(pampres)*; in one of the niches which have decorated canopies stands a charming little statue of the Virgin Mary and Child.

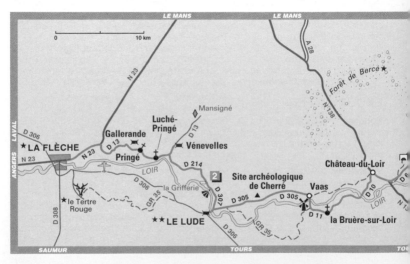

Les Roches-l'Évêque – The village occupies a long narrow site between the river and the cliff. The troglodyte dwellings are a well-known feature of the region, their hen houses and sheds half-concealed by festoons of wistaria and lilac in season.

Cross the Loir (D 917 – follow the signposts); turn right to Lavardin.

★**Lavardin** – *See LAVARDIN.*

Take the pretty minor road along the south bank of the river to Montoire.

Montoire-sur-le-Loir – *See MONTOIRE-SUR-LE-LOIR.*

Soon Troo and its church appear on the skyline.

Troo – *See TROO.*

At Sougé turn left onto the signposted tourist road to Artins.

Vieux-Bourg d'Artins – The village is situated right on the river bank. The **church** has Romanesque walls with Flamboyant Gothic windows and a pointed-arched doorway.

From Artins take D 10 E; then turn right to L'Isle Verte; after 100m/110yd turn left onto a road which runs in front of the Château du Pin.

From the bridge opposite the château **L'Isle Verte** (Green Island) can be seen a little way upstream where the Braye joins the Loir. It was here, where the row of poplars sway in the breeze and the willows mark the edges of the meadows, that the poet Ronsard wanted to be buried; nowhere is more evocative of his genius.

Couture-sur-Loir – The **church** has a Gothic chancel with Angevin vaulting and 17C woodwork in the Rosary Chapel (on right of chancel). The recumbent figures in the nave are Ronsard's parents; note the costume detail.

In Couture-sur-Loir take D 57 S to La Possonnière.

★**Manoir de la Possonnière** ⊙ – When Louis de Ronsard, soldier and man of letters, returned from Italy in the early 16C he undertook to rebuild his country seat in the new Italian style. The result was La Possonnière, characterised by the profusion of mottoes engraved on the walls.

★**Manor** – The name comes from the word *posson* (*poinçon*, a measure of volume) and has sometimes been altered to Poissonnière under the influence of the Ronsard family coat of arms – three silver fishes (*poisson*) on a blue ground – which can be seen on the pediment of the carved dormer window at the top of the turret. The manor house is built against the hillside on the northern fringes of Gâtines Forest and enclosed with a wall. The main façade has mullioned windows in the style of Louis XII on the ground floor but the windows on the first floor are flanked by pilasters with medallions, clearly in the Renaissance style. Projecting from the rear façade is a graceful staircase turret adorned with an elegant doorway capped by a pediment decorated with a bust.

Return to Couture and continue N (D 57), crossing the Loir at the foot of the wooded hill on which Château de la Flotte stands.

Poncé-sur-le-Loir – Beside the road (D 197) leading into Poncé from the east stands a Renaissance château. On the west side of the town, south of the main road and the railway line, is a crafts centre, **Les grès du Loir** ⊙. This is housed in

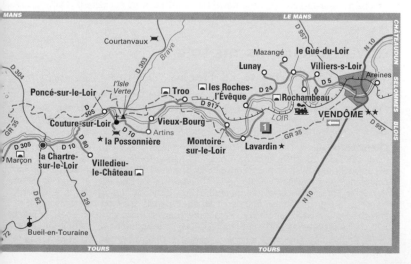

The Prince of Poets

In 1524 **Pierre de Ronsard**, son of Louis, was born at the manor. He was destined to a brilliant future in the army or the diplomatic service and at 12 became a page at the court of François I. At the age of 15, however, an illness left him half deaf and he had to renounce his ambitions. He took holy orders and turned to poetry and the study of the Ancients; Pindar in Greek and Horace in Latin became his models. He excelled in composing sonnets in which he described the beauty of Cassandra Salviati and Marie. He was the leader of the Pléiade group of poets and in 1558 was appointed Poet Laureate. However, he suffered from severe gout so chose to withdraw to his priories at Ste-Madeleine-de-Croixval *(6km/4mi SE of La Possonnière)* and at St-Cosme-lès-Tours where he died in 1585 leaving a considerable body of work, including his famous collection of sonnets *Les Amours*.

---

the 18C buildings of the old Pallard paper mill on the river bank and consists of the studios of several self-employed craftsmen: pottery, glassware, ironwork, weaving, woodwork and candle making.

Château ⊙ – This originally consisted of two pavilions flanking a central staircase tower, one of which was destroyed in the 18C and replaced by a more austere wing. Ionic pilasters flanking the windows and pronounced horizontal cornices give a balanced, geometrical appearance to the façade. The north façade, once the entrance façade, has an elegant Italian-style arcade which forms a terrace at first-floor level.

The stone **Renaissance staircase★★** is one of the most remarkable in France; in front of it are the remains of a loggia. The coffered, white-stone ceilings of the six straight flights are sumptuously sculpted, executed with refinement, fluidity and a mastery of the art of perspective rarely to be found. Over 160 decorative motifs portray real-life, allegorical and mythological subjects.

The well-tended **gardens**, with their highly effective symmetrical layout, make a pleasant place for a stroll: beyond the flower beds prettily edged with boxwood, the arbour leads to several *salles de verdure* (clearings where the leafy branches meet overhead to form a ceiling of foliage), a maze and a long vaulted path. Overlooking the entire scene runs a terrace with an avenue of lime trees.

The dovecot with its 1 800 nesting holes and revolving ladders for gathering the eggs is still intact. The outbuildings house the local folklore museum, the **Musée départemental du Folklore sarthois**.

In Ruillé turn left onto D 80 which crosses the Loir.

The road is very picturesque, particularly south of Tréhet, where it runs along a hillside riddled with caves.

Villedieu-le-Château – This village has a pleasant **setting** in a valley with troglodyte dwellings hollowed out of the valley slopes. Houses, gardens, crumbling remnants of the old town wall and the ruins of the belfry of St-Jean priory all add to the charm of the scene.

Return to Tréhet and turn left onto D 10.

La Chartre-sur-le-Loir – On the north bank of the river, opposite this village, are Bercé Forest and the Jasnières vineyard which produces a white dessert wine which ages well.

★LOWER REACHES OF THE LOIR

② From La Chartre to La Flèche *75km/47mi – allow one day*

The road from La Chartre to **Marçon** (fine wines) passes through peaceful countryside.

In Marçon turn right onto D 61 which cuts across the valley and crosses the river at the foot of the hillside on which the chapel of Ste-Cécile stands. Turn left onto D 64, which skirts the hillside with its numerous troglodyte dwellings.

Château-du-Loir – The keep in the public gardens is all that remains of the medieval castle to which this town owes its name. Underneath it are the old cells occupied briefly by the many convicts who passed through here bound for the penal colony of Cayenne via the ports of Nantes or La Rochelle. In the chancel of the **Église St-Guingalois** is a monumental 17C terracotta *Pietà* and, in the north transept, a pair of Flemish Mannerist wooden panels showing the Nativity (15C) and the Resurrection (late 15C). Below the chancel there is a Romanesque crypt and, in the **presbytery**, a fine wooden group (16C) depicting the Scourging of Christ.

Leave Château-du-Loir on D 10 going S towards Château-la-Vallière. After crossing the bridge in Nogent turn right immediately onto C 2.

La Bruère-sur-Loir – The **church** here contains several interesting statues in the nave: St Fiacre holding his spade, St Roch and St Sebastian. The elegant chancel vaulting is in the Renaissance style and the stained-glass windows date from the 16C.

Leave La Bruère on D 11 towards Vaas and turn right onto D 30.

Vaas – On the left, just before you reach the bridge, stands an old corn mill, the **Moulin à blé de Rotrou** ☉. The riverside, with its houses, tiny garden plots, church and washing place makes a delightful scene.

The road passes through meadows, nursery gardens and evergreen forests with clumps of gorse and broom.

Follow D 305, then turn right to Cherré archaeological site.

Site archéologique de Cherré – The Gallo-Roman settlement dates from the 1C and 2C AD and comprises a temple, baths, two other buildings and a theatre of pointed reddish sandstone which has been completely excavated. During the digs a necropolis from the Hallstatt period (the protohistoric period – 8C to 5C BC) was discovered under the *cavea* (the seating area).

Carry on towards Le Lude along the north bank of the Loir.

★★**Château du Lude** – *See Château du LUDE.*

Follow D 307 towards Pontvallain, then take the first road left to Mansigné.

Soon after the turn and before reaching the Château de la Grifferie there is a view over the valley which is laid out in fruit orchards, asparagus beds, potato fields and maize plantations.

Bear left onto D 214 to Luché-Pringé. After crossing the River Aune, turn right onto D 13 to the Manoir de Vénevelles.

Manoir de Vénevelles – *Not open to the public.* This 15C-17C manor house stands in a quiet valley and is surrounded by a broad moat.

Luché-Pringé – The exterior of the **church** ☉ (13C-16C) is quite unusual in appearance, with its many gables decorated with crockets and the row of tiny musician figures sitting on the edge of the roof on either side of the façade. Above the entrance door is a low-relief sculpture of St Martin on horseback.

The interior contains an early-16C *Pietà (right)* carved in walnut. The wide chancel (13C) ends in a square chevet; the Angevin vaulting is supported on tall slim columns in the traditional Plantagenet style. Next to the church stands an elegant priory (13C-15C) with an octagonal turret.

Pringé – The tiny Romanesque **church** at Pringé was altered in the 15C. The doorway with arch mouldings in the façade is Romanesque. The interior is decorated with 16C murals depicting St Hubert, St George and St Christopher.

Château de Gallerande – *Not open to the public, but visitors can walk up as far as the gateway to the courtyard.* The road (D 13) skirts the moat enclosing the inviting, peaceful park in which huge trees – cedars, limes and oaks – line the edges of the vast lawns. From the courtyard gate there is a fine view of the northeast façade of the château which has four machicolated round towers and an unusual octagonal keep.

Jardins et Château de VILLANDRY★★★

Michelin map 317: M-4, 232 fold 35 or 4037 D3
Local map see TOURS: Excursions

Villandry was one of the last great Renaissance châteaux to be built on the Loire; it has unusual features for Touraine, like rectangular pavilions (instead of round towers) as well as the layout of the esplanade and its moat.

Villandry's international fame is, however, based not so much on its château as on its gardens, which are among the most fascinating in France.

★★★GARDENS ⊘ 1hr

The best overall **view** of the gardens is from the terraces to the rear of the château or from the top of the keep. The Promenade dans les Bois is an itinerary leading to the new belvedere and, from there, to the greenhouses, offering pretty views all along (the path overlooks the 5ha/12.4-acre gardens and the village from a height of 30m/99ft). The tour continues southwards to the water garden, the new maze, the herb garden and the kitchen garden.

The gardens at Villandry are the most complete example in France of the formal Renaissance style adopted under the influence of the Italian gardeners brought into the country by Charles VIII; French traditions nevertheless assert themselves in many of the details.

When the physician Joachim de Carvallo, founder of the French Historic Houses Association, acquired Villandry in 1906, he set about restoring the gardens to their original state, since previous owners had altered them beyond recognition.

Eating out

BUDGET

Domaine de la Giraudière – 37510 Villandry – 1km/0.5mi S of Villandry on D 121 towards Druye – ☎ 02 47 50 08 60 – closed 12 Nov-10 Mar – reservation required for weekends – 11.14/26.06€. This property was formerly a convent, then the castle's home farm; today La Giraudière has become a famous place for gourmets. The magnificent farm is an appropriate setting for fine regional cooking. Shop selling local produce.

Where to stay

MODERATE

Chambre d'hôte La Meulière – 10 r. de la Gare – 37130 Cinq-Mars-la-Pile – ☎ 02 47 96 53 63 – ⧖ – 3 rooms 30.49/39.64€. This 19C town house is conveniently located near the station, yet nice and quiet. Its colourful rooms are reached by a fine wooden staircase. In summer the sunbeds in the lovely garden are an invitation to idleness.

LUXURY

Chambre d'hôte Le Prieuré des Granges – 15 r. des Fontaines – 37510 Savonnières – 2km/1.25mi E of Villandry on D 7 – ☎ 02 47 50 09 67 – closed Dec-Feb – ⧖ – 6 rooms 79.27/89.94€. A dream come true! You are made to feel truly at home, and each of the elegant rooms has its own entrance. Stroll in the park and admire the statues. Swimming pool.

There are three terraces one above the other: the highest, the **water garden**, has a fine sheet of water acting as a reservoir; below it is the **flower garden**, consisting of geometric designs outlined in box, one representing allegories of Love, the other symbolising Music; further designs are based on the Maltese, Languedoc and Basque crosses.

At the lowest level is the fascinating **ornamental kitchen garden**, a multicoloured chequerboard of vegetables and fruit trees arranged in nine squares and enclosed by clipped hedges of box and yew. Between this and the church a herb garden has been laid out; as was the case in the Middle Ages, it is devoted to aromatic herbs and medicinal plants.

Canals, fountains, cascades, vine-covered pergolas, and the Romanesque village church all combine to make a charming background to the scene.

16C gardens

At the time of the Renaissance, the species of flowers, shrubs and fruit trees were more or less the same as today, though the potato had not yet made its appearance (introduced by Parmentier in the 18C). The art of gardening was already well advanced, with pruning, grafting, the use of greenhouses and the raising of early vegetables.

★★CHÂTEAU ⊘

Nothing remains of the early fortress except the keep, a square tower incorporated in the present structure which was built in the 16C by Jean Le Breton, Secretary of State to François I. Three ranges of buildings enclose the courtyard which is open on the north side overlooking the Cher and the Loire in the valley. Joachim Carvallo, a Spaniard, furnished the château with Spanish furniture and an interesting collection of paintings (16C, 17C and 18C Spanish Schools). The great salon and the dining room on the ground floor have Louis XV panelling. The grand staircase with its wrought-iron banister leads to the first floor where visitors will be able to admire a brightly coloured Empire-style bedroom; at the end of the corridor, Madame Carvallo's bedroom commands a fine view of the gardens with the church and the village in the background; note the splendid parquet flooring made from different species of wood.

Return to the staircase; the other wing houses the picture gallery which contains a great deal of Spanish religious painting; note, however, a striking work by Goya depicting a severed head, as well as two 16C Italian paintings on wood *(St Paul and St John)* in lively colours and a portrait of the Infanta by the Velasquez School. An audio-visual display shows the astonishingly varied appearance of the gardens according to the season and the time of day.

At the end of the gallery is the room with the 13C **Mudejar ceiling**★ which came from Toledo; the coffers are painted and gilded with typical Moorish motifs, an unexpected sight under northern skies.

On the second floor, two children's bedrooms have been refurbished.

From the keep there is a splendid **view**★ over the terraces of the gardens towards the River Cher and the River Loire.

The château seen from the kitchen gardens

A.de Valroger/MICHELIN

Admission times and charges

As times and charges for admission are liable to alteration, the information below is given for guidance only. Every sight for which there are times and charges is indicated by the symbol ⊙ in the main part of the guide.

Order: The information is listed in the same order as the entries in the alphabetical section of the guide.

Dates given are inclusive.

Ticket offices usually shut 30min before closing time; exceptions only are mentioned below.

The charge is for an individual adult; the charge for a child is given for places of special interest to younger visitors. Prices are given in euros (€); during the introduction of the euro, prices quoted are approximate conversions from the former currency. In some cases, no price was indicated to our services, but the sight may not necessarily be free of charge.

Sights which have comprehensive facilities for disabled tourists are indicated by the symbol ⅋ below.

Guided tours: The departure time of the last tour of the morning or afternoon will be up to 1hr before the actual closing time. Most tours are conducted by French speaking guides but in some cases the term "guided tours" may cover group visiting with recorded commentaries; some of the larger and more frequented sights may offer guided tours in other languages. Enquire at the ticket office or bookstall. Other aids commonly available for the foreign tourist are notes, pamphlets or audio-guides.

Lecture tours: These are regularly organised during the tourist season in towns of special interest. The information is given under the appropriate heading. In towns and districts labelled Villes et Pays d'Art et d'Histoire, identified by the symbol ⊠, tours are conducted by lecturers or guides approved by the Centre des Monuments Nationaux.

Churches: Admission times are indicated if the interior is of special interest. Churches are usually closed from noon to 2pm. Visitors should refrain from walking about during services. Visitors to chapels are accompanied by the person who keeps the keys. A donation is welcome.

Tourist offices ⬛: The addresses and telephone numbers are given for the local tourist offices, which provide information on local market days, early closing days etc.

A

AMBOISE
⬛ Quai du Général-de-Gaulle, 37400 AMBOISE, ☎ 02 47 57 09 28.

Château – Jul and Aug: 9am-7pm; Apr-Jun: 9am-6.30pm; mid to end Mar, Sep and Oct: 9am-6pm; early to mid-Nov: 9am-5.30pm; mid-Nov to end Jan: 9am-noon, 2-4.45pm; early Feb to mid-Mar: 9am-noon, 1.30-5.30pm. Closed 1 Jan and 25 Dec. 6.50€. ☎ 02 47 57 00 98.

Le Clos-Lucé: Leonardo da Vinci's house – Jul and Aug: 9am-8pm; end Mar to end Jun, Sep and Oct: 9am-7pm; early Feb to end Mar, Nov and Dec: 9am-6pm; Jan: 10am-5pm. Closed 1 Jan and 25 Dec. 6.50€ (children: 3.50€). ☎ 02 47 57 00 73.

Musée de l'Hôtel de ville – Jul and Aug: 2-6pm. No charge. ☎ 02 47 23 47 23.

La Maison enchantée – ⅋ Jul and Aug: 10am-7pm; Apr-Jun, Sep and Oct: daily except Mon 10am-noon, 2-6pm; Nov-Mar: daily except Mon 2-5pm. Closed Jan. 5.40€ (children: 4.30€). ☎ 02 47 23 24 50.

Mini-châteaux – ⅋ Apr-Sep: 10am-6pm (Jun-Aug: 7pm); Oct to mid-Nov: 10.30am-5pm. 10€ (children: 6€). ☎ 02 47 23 44 44.

Le Fou de l'âne – ⅋ Apr-Sep: 10am-6pm (Jul and Aug: 7pm); Oct to mid-Nov: 10.30am-5pm. 4€ (children: 3€). ☎ 02 47 23 44 44.

Excursions

Pagode de Chateloup – Jul and Aug: 9.30am-7.30pm; Jun: 10am-7pm; May and Sep: 10am-6.30pm; Easter Monday to end Apr: 10am-noon, 2-6pm, Sat-Sun 10am-6pm; Oct and Nov: Sat-Sun and public holidays 10am-5pm. Closed Jan to Easter Monday. 6€. ☎ 02 47 57 20 97.

Aquarium de Touraine – ♿ Apr-Sep: 10am-7pm (Jul to early Sep: 8pm; Oct-Mar: 10.30am-6pm. 10€ (children: 6€). ☎ 02 47 23 44 44.

ANGERS

🄵 Pl. du Président Kennedy, 49100 ANGERS, ☎ 02 41 23 50 00.

🄰 discovery tours (2hr). Jul and Aug: daily. 7€. Information at the tourist office. www.vpah.culture.fr

Cathédrale St-Maurice – Jul and Aug: possibility of guided tours. Contact the presbytery. No charge. ☎ 02 41 87 58 45.

Monastey buildings – Daily 9am-5.30pm (except events at the Hôtel du Département). No charge. ☎ 02 41 81 49 49. www.cg49.fr

Église St-Serge – Daily except certain Sun afternoons. ☎ 02 41 43 66 76.

Château – May to early Sep: guided tours (1hr) 9.30am-6.30pm (last admission 45min before closing); early Sep to end Apr: 10am-5.30pm. Closed 1 Jan, 1 May, 1 and 11 Nov, 25 Dec. No charge 1st Sunday in the month from Oct to Mar. 5.50€ (under 17s: no charge). ☎ 02 41 87 43 47.

Galeries David d'Anger – Mid-Jun to mid-Sep: 9.30am-6.30pm; mid-Sep to mid-Jun: daily except Mon 10am-noon, 2-6pm. Closed 1 Jan, 1 and 8 May, 14 Jul, 1 and 11 Nov, 25 Dec. 2€. ☎ 02 41 87 21 03.

Hôtel Pincé – As for the David d'Angers Gallery. 2€. ☎ 02 41 88 94 27.

Musée des Beaux-Arts (Logis Barrault) – Closed for renovation until spring 2004.

Musée régional de l'Air – ♿ Mid-Apr to mid-Oct: 2-6pm (Sat-Sun 3-7pm); mid-Oct to mid-Apr: Sat-Sun 2-6pm. 4€. ☎ 02 41 33 04 10. www.gppa.decollage.org

Musée Jean-Lurçat et de la Tapisserie contemporaine – Mid-Jun to mid-Sep: 9.30am-6.30pm; mid-Sep to mid-Jun: daily except Mon 10am-noon, 2-6pm. Closed 1 Jan, 1 and 8 May, 14 Jul, 1 and 11 Nov, 25 Dec. 3.50€. ☎ 02 41 24 18 45 or 02 41 24 18 48.

Excursions

St-Barthélemy-d'Anjou: Musée Cointreau – May, Jun, Sep and Oct: guided tours (1hr 30min) at 10.30am and 3pm, additional tour Sun at 4.30pm; Jul and Aug: 10.30am, 2.30pm, 3.30pm and 4.30pm; Nov-Apr: 3pm, Sun 3pm and 4.30pm. Closed Jan, 25 Dec and public holidays. 5.50€ (children: 2.60€). ☎ 02 41 31 50 50. www.cointreau.com

Château de Pignerolle: Musée européen de la Communication – Easter to All Saints: 10am-12.30pm, 2.30-6pm, Sat 2.30-6pm. Closed 1 Jan and 25 Dec. 7€ (children: 4€). ☎ 02 41 93 38 38.

St-Sylvain-d'Anjou: Motte-and-bailey – Jun-Sep: daily except Mon 3-7pm; May: Sun and public holidays 3-7pm. 4.50€. ☎ 02 41 76 81 78.

Golf Club d'Angers – Moulin de Pistrait - 49320 St-Jean-des-Mauvrets - ☎ 02 41 91 96 56 - golf.angers@infonie.fr – 9am-7pm.

Trélazé: Musée de l'Ardoise – ♿ Mid-Feb to end Nov: guided tours (1hr 30min) Sun and public holidays 2-6pm (Jul to mid-Sep: daily except Mon). Closed 1 Jan and 25 Dec. 5.34€. ☎ 02 41 69 04 71. www.multimania.com/museeardoise

La Loire Maugeoise

Montjean-sur-Loire: Museum – ♿ Easter to All Saints: daily except Mon 2.30-6.30pm. 4.57€. ☎ 02 41 39 08 48.

St-Florent-le-Vieil: Musée d'Histoire locale et des Guerres de Vendée – Early Apr to end Sep: Sat-Sun and public holidays 2.30-6.30pm (early Jul to mid-Sep: daily). 3€. ☎ 02 41 72 62 32.

St-Florent-le-Vieil: Ferme abbatiale des Coteaux – ♿ Jul and Aug: daily except Mon 2.30-7pm; mid to end Jun: Sat-Sun and public holidays 2.30-7pm; Sep-Oct: Sun and public holidays 2.30-7pm. No charge. ☎ 02 41 71 77 30.

Chapelle de la Bourgonnière – Mid-Jul to mid-Aug: 9am-noon, 2-6pm, Sun and public holidays 2-6pm; Sep to mid-Jul: by appointment. 3€. ☎ 02 40 98 10 18.

Liré: Musée Joachim-du-Bellay – Mid-Jan to Jun and Oct to mid-Dec: daily except Mon and Tue 10.30am-12.30pm, 3-6pm, Sat 3-6pm, guided tours Sun at 11am, 3.30pm and 5.30pm; Jul-Sep: guided tours at 11am, 3.30pm and 5.30pm. Closed mid-Dec to mid-Jan, Easter. 4€. ☎ 02 40 09 04 13. www.musee-du-bellay.fr.st

Oudon: Tower – Apr-Jun and Sep: 10-11am, 2-5.30pm; Jul and Aug: 9.30-11am, 2-6pm; Oct-Mar: Sat-Sun and public holidays 10-11am, 2-5pm. Closed Jan. 4.60€. ☎ 02 40 83 60 00.

AZAY-LE-RIDEAU

🖪 Pl. de l'Europe, 37190 AZAY-LE-RIDEAU, ☎ 02 47 45 44 40.

Château – Apr-Oct: (last admission 45min before closing) 9.30am-6pm (Jul and Aug: 7pm); Nov-Mar: 10am-12.30pm, 2-5.30pm. Closed 1 Jan, 1 May, 1 and 11 Nov, 25 Dec. 5.50€ (children: no charge). ☎ 02 47 45 42 04. www.monum.fr

Jouets d'autrefois, Rêves d'aujourd'hui – ♿ Jun to end Sep: daily except Tue 3-6pm. 5.34€. ☎ 02 47 45 97 65.

Excursions

Marnay: Musée Maurice-Dufresne – ♿ Feb to end Nov: 9.15am-6pm (May-Sep: 9.15am-7pm). 10€ (children: 5€). ☎ 02 47 45 36 18. www.musee-dufresne.com

Vallée de l'Indre

Villaines-les-Rochers: Société coopérative agricole de vannerie – ♿ Apr to mid-Oct: 9am-12.30pm (Sat-Sun and public holidays noon), 2-7pm (Jul and Aug: 9am-7pm); mid-Oct to end Mar: 9am-12.30pm (Sat noon), 2-7pm, Sun and public holidays 2-7pm. Closed 1 Jan and 25 Dec. No charge. ☎ 02 47 45 43 03. www.vannerie.com

Saché: Château – Oct-Mar: 9.30am-12.30pm, 2-5.30pm; Apr-Sep: 9am-7pm. Closed 1 Jan and 25 Dec. 3.80€. ☎ 02 47 26 86 50.

B

BAUGÉ

🖪 Au château, 49150 BAUGÉ, ☎ 02 41 89 18 07.

Château – Mid-Jun to mid-Sep: guided tours (1hr 30min) daily except Mon 2.30-6pm (Jul and Aug: daily 11am-1pm, 3-7pm); Apr to mid-Jun and mid-Sep to Oct: Sat-Sun and public holidays 2.30-6pm. 4€. ☎ 02 41 89 18 07.

Chapelle des Filles-du-Cœur-de-Marie – Guided tours daily except Tue 2.15-4.15pm. Closed 3 days before Whitsun, Whitsun, 1st Sunday in Jul, 24-26 Jul, 11, 12 and 31 Dec. Sister Monique Lourdais. ☎ 02 41 89 12 20.

The Baugeois Region

Parc et château de Lathan – Apr to early Nov: daily except Tue 10am-6pm. 2.50€. ☎ 02 41 82 31 00.

Chapelle Notre-Dame-de-Montplacé – Guided tours by appointment. Tourist office. ☎ 02 41 89 18 07.

BEAUGENCY

🖪 3 pl. Dr-Hyvernaud, BP 44, 45190 BEAUGENCY, ☎ 02 38 44 54 42.

Hôtel de ville – May-Sep: guided tours (15min) Mon-Fri at 11am, 3pm, 4pm and 4.30pm, Sat at 11am; Oct-Apr: Tue-Fri at 3pm, 4pm and 4.30pm. Closed public holidays. 1.50€. ☎ 02 38 44 54 42.

Musée Daniel Vannier – Guided tours (1hr, last admission 1hr before closing time) daily except Tue 10am-noon, 2-5pm (Jun-Aug: 6pm). Closed 1 Jan, 1 May, 24, 25 and 31 Dec. 3.30€. ☎ 02 38 44 55 23.

Château de BEAUREGARD

Château – Apr-Sep: 9.30am-noon, 2-6.30pm (Jul and Aug: 9.30am-6.30pm); Oct-Mar: daily except Wed 9.30am-noon, 2-5pm. Closed early Jan to early Feb, 25 Dec. 6.50€. ☎ 02 54 70 36 74.

Forêt de BERCÉ

Mid-Jul to end Aug: guided tours (2hr), departure from the Chêne Boppe car park. Information available at the ONF. ☎ 02 43 24 44 70.

BLOIS

🖪 3 av. J.-Laigret, 41000 BLOIS, ☎ 02 54 90 41 41.

🅰 discovery tours (2hr). Information at the tourist office or on www.vpah.culture.fr

Château – Mid-Mar to end Oct: 9am-6pm (Jul and Aug: 7.30pm); Nov to mid-Mar: 9am-12.30pm, 2-5.30pm. Closed 1 Jan and 25 Dec. 6€ (children: 4€). ☎ 02 54 90 33 33.

Musée archéologique – Same as for the château. Same ticket. ☎ 02 54 90 33 33.

Musée des Beaux-Arts – Jul and Aug: 9am-7.30pm; mid-Mar to end Jun and Sep-Nov: 9am-6pm; Jan to mid-Mar and Dec: 9am-12.30pm, 2-5.30pm. Closed 1 Jan and 25 Dec. 6€ (children: 4€). ☎ 02 54 90 33 33.

Musée d'Art religieux – ♿ Daily except Mon, Sun and public holidays 2-6pm. No charge. ☎ 02 54 78 17 14.

Muséum d'Histoire naturelle – ♿ Daily except Mon 2-6pm. Closed 1 Jan, 1 May, 1 Nov, 25 Dec. 2.40€. ☎ 02 54 90 21 00. www.ville-blois.com

Hôtel d'Alluye – Daily except Sat-Sun and public holidays 10am-noon, 2-4pm by appointment 4 days in advance, contact Mme Terré, 8 r. St-Honoré, 41000 Blois. No charge. ☎ 02 54 56 38 00.

Tour Beauvoir – Early Apr to mid-Sep: Sat-Sun and public holidays 2.30-7pm (Jul and Aug: daily); rest of the year: by appointment. 2.70€. ☎ 02 54 71 82 77.

Maison de la Magie Robert-Houdin – ♿ Jul and Aug: show (30min) 10am-6.30pm; Apr-Jun and Sep: daily except certain Mondays in May and Jun 10am-noon, 2-6pm. Closed Oct-Mar. 7.50€ (children: 4.50€). ☎ 02 54 55 26 26.

Musée de l'Objet – ♿ Mid-May to mid-Sep: daily except Mon 1.30-6.30pm; mid-Sep to mid-May: daily except Mon 9am-12.30pm, 1.30-6.30pm (Sat-Sun 1.30-6.30pm). Closed 1 Jan, 1 and 8 May, 11 Nov, 25 Dec. 4€. ☎ 02 54 55 37 40.

Haras national – ♿ Jul and Aug: guided tours (1hr 30min) at 10.30am and 3.30pm; Sep-Jun: daily except Sun at 2.30pm. 6€. ☎ 02 54 55 22 82 (Cheval et Culture association).

Cloître St-Saturnin – As for the Musée des Beaux-Arts. ☎ 02 54 90 33 33.

Excursions

Orchaise: Priory Botanical Gardens – Mid-Mar to end Oct: Sun 3-7pm. 5€. ☎ 02 54 70 03 92.

Maves: Windmill – Closed for renovation work. Contact M. Pillot for information. ☎ 02 54 87 31 35.

Mulsans: Church – If closed contact M. Brisset, 4 r. de la Place, opposite the church.

Suèvres: Église St-Lubin – Guided tours by appointment with Mme Claudine Jacqmin. ☎ 02 54 87 80 83.

La Loire Tourangelle

Château de Valmer – May to end Sep: Sat-Sun and public holidays 2-7pm (Jul and Aug: daily except Mon). 7€. ☎ 02 47 52 93 12.

Château de Jallanges – ♿ Mid-Mar to end Oct: 10am-noon, 2-6pm. 6€ (children: 4.50€). ☎ 02 47 52 06 66.

BONNEVAL
🛈 2 pl. de l'Église, 28800 BONNEVAL, ☎ 02 37 47 55 89.

🅰 – Discover tours Tue-Sat 9.30am-noon, 2-6.30pm. No charge (for individual visitors). Contact the tourist office.

Excursions

Alluyes: Church – Apply to the town hall to visit. ☎ 02 37 47 25 09.

Upper Reaches of the Loir

Montigny-le-Gannelon: Church – Closed for restoration work. Shrine transferred temporarily to the château.

Château – ♿ Early Apr to mid-Jun and Oct: guided tours of the château (45min) Sat-Sun and public holidays 2.30-6pm; mid-Jun to end Sep: Mon-Fri 10am-noon, 2.30-6.30pm, Sat-Sun and public holidays 2.30-6.30pm. 7€, 3.80€ (park). ☎ 02 37 98 30 03.

BOURGUEIL
🛈 Pl. de l'Église, 37140 BOURGUEIL, ☎ 02 47 97 91 39.

Church – Daily except Sun afternoon and public holidays.

Abbey – Apr-Oct: guided tours (1hr) Sun and public holidays 2-6pm (Jul and Aug: daily except Tue and Wed). 4.80€. ☎ 02 47 97 72 04.

Musée Van-Oeveren – ♿ Jul and Aug: guided tours (1hr) daily except Mon 2-6pm. 6€ (children: 4.50€). ☎ 02 47 97 98 99.

Moulin bleu – Feb to mid-Dec: guided tours (15min) daily except Tue and Wed. 2.29€. ☎ 02 47 97 73 13.

Cave touristique de la Dive Bouteille – ♿ Apr to end Sep: guided tours (30min) daily except Mon 10am-12.30pm, 2-6pm. 3.30€. ☎ 02 47 97 72 01.

Excursions

Les Réaux: Château – Mar to mid-Nov: 10am-6pm. 3€. ☎ 02 47 95 14 40.

Chouzé-sur-Loire: Musée des Mariniers – Jun to end Aug: Sat-Sun and public holidays 3-5pm. 2€. ☎ 02 47 95 10 10.

Brain-sur-Allonnes: Cave peinte – Mid-Apr to mid-Oct: daily except Mon 10am-noon, 2-6pm. 3.05€. ☎ 02 41 52 87 40.

Museum – Daily except Mon 10am-noon, 2-6pm, Sun 2-5pm, public holidays 10am-noon, 2-5pm. 2.29€. ☎ 02 41 52 87 40.

Château de BRÉZÉ

Château – Mar to mid-Nov: 10am-noon, 1.30-6.30pm (Jun to mid-Sep: 10am-7.30pm). 5.40€ (château and subterranean passages), 9.20€ (combined ticket for château and subterranean passages). ☎ 02 41 51 60 15. www.chateaudebreze.com

BRIARE

🛈 1 pl. Charles-de-Gaulle, 45250 BRIARE, ☎ 02 38 31 24 51.

Musée de la Mosaïque et des Émaux – ♿ Feb-Dec: 2-6pm (Jun-Sep: 6.30pm). Closed Jan and 25 Dec. 4€. ☎ 02 38 31 20 51.

Château de BRISSAC

🛈 8 pl. de la République, 49320 BRISSAC-QUINCÉ, ☎ 02 41 91 21 50.

Château – Apr-Jun and mid-Sep to end Oct: guided tours (1hr) 10am-5.15pm; Jul to mid-Sep: daily except Tue 10am-5.45pm. 7.50€ (children: 6€). ☎ 02 41 91 22 21. www.chateau-brissac.fr

Excursion

Centre de découverte du milieu aquatique et de la pêche – ♿ Jul and Aug: guided tours (2hr) daily except Sat 2-6pm; Apr-Jun, Sep and Oct: 3rd Sunday in the month and public holidays 2-6pm. Closed 1 May and Nov-Mar. 5€. ☎ 02 41 91 24 25.

BROU

🛈 R. de la Chevalerie, 28160 BROU, ☎ 02 37 47 01 12.

Le Perche-Gouet

Frazé: Château – ♿ Easter to end Sep: unaccompanied visits Sun and public holidays 3-6pm. 2.50€. ☎ 02 37 29 56 76.

St-Ulphace: Church – Spring and summer: Sat-Sun 9am-7pm. Guided tours available, contact the town hall, ☎ 02 43 93 27 06.

Courgenard: Church – Apply to the town hall to visit. ☎ 02 43 93 26 02.

Semur-en-Vallon: Tourist train – May-Sep: journeys (45min) Sun and public holidays 2.30-6.30pm. At mid-journey, visit of the museum train. 3€. ☎ 02 43 71 30 36 or 02 43 93 67 86.

Montmirail: Castle – Apr-Sep: guided tours daily except Tue 2.30-6pm. 4.50€. ☎ 02 43 93 72 71.

C

Château de CHAMBORD

Château – Jul and Aug: 9.30am-6.45pm; Apr-Jun and Sep: 9am-6.30pm; Oct-Mar: 9am-5.30pm. Closed 1 Jan, 1 May, 25 Dec. 7€. ☎ 02 54 50 40 00. www.chambord.org

Park – Unaccompanied tours of the national reserve (site equipped for observation), guided tours of the park in tune with each season (call of the wild stag). ☎ 02 54 50 50 00.

Boat rental – Mid-Mar-1 early Nov: boat rental (1hr), 10am-nightfall. 10.67€/2 people, 11.43€/3 people, 15.24€/4 people. Bike rental. ☎ 02 54 33 37 54

Display of horsemanship – Jul and Aug: equestrian show (45min) at 11.45am and 5pm; May, Jun and Sep: at 11.45am, Sat-Sun at 11.45am and 4pm. 7.50€ (children: 5€). ☎ 02 54 20 31 01.

Horse-drawn carriage – May to end Sep: discovery tour of the grounds of Chambord in a horse-drawn carriage (45min) on request. 7.50€ (children: 5€). ☎ 02 54 20 31 01.

Excursion

Château de Villesavin – ♿ Jun-Sep: 10am-7pm; mid-Feb to end May: 10am-noon, 2-7pm; Oct and Nov: 10am-noon, 2-6pm; Dec: Sat-Sun and public holidays 10am-noon, 2-6pm. Closed Jan to mid-Feb and 25 Dec. 7.30€. ☎ 02 54 46 42 88.

CHÂTEAUDUN   🛈 1 r. de Luynes, 28200 CHÂTEAUDUN, ☎ 02 37 45 22 46.

Guided tour of the town – Contact the tourist office.

Église de la Madeleine – Easter to All Saints: 9am-7pm. ☎ 02 37 45 00 09.

Château – Jan-Apr and Sep-Dec: 10am-12.30pm, 2-6pm; May-Aug: 10am-6pm. 5.50€, no charge 1st Sunday in the month. Closed 1 Jan, 1 May, 25 Dec. ☎ 02 37 94 02 90.

Musée des Beaux-Arts et d'Histoire naturelle – Sep-Jun: daily except Tue 9.30am-noon, 1.30-6pm (Oct-Mar: 5pm); Jul and Aug: daily 9.30am-6.30pm. Closed 1 Jan, 1 May and 25 Dec. 3.11€. ☎ 02 37 45 55 36.

Grottes du Foulon – ♿ Jun-Sep: guided tours (1hr) 10am-noon, 2-6pm; Mar-Jun: daily except Mon 10am-noon, 2-6pm; Oct-Feb: Sat-Sun and public holidays 2-6pm. Closed mid-Dec to mid-Jan. 5€. ☎ 02 37 45 19 60.

Excursion

Abbaye du Bois de Nottonville – May to end Oct: guided tours (45min) Sat-Sun and public holidays 2.30-6.30pm (Jul and Aug: daily except Sat-Sun by appointment 2 days in advance). 3.10€. ☎ 02 37 96 91 64.

CHÂTEAU-GONTIER   🛈 Péniche "l'Élan", quai Alsace, BP 402, 53204 CHÂTEAU-GONTIER, ☎ 02 43 70 42 74.

Musée d'Art et d'Archéologie – Jul and Aug: guided tours 2-6pm; early May to end Jun: Sat-Sun and public holidays. No charge. ☎ 02 43 07 26 42.

Église de la Trinité – Daily except Sun afternoon.

Ancienne église Notre-Dame-du-Genêteil – ♿ Guided tours (2hr) daily except Mon and Tue 2-7pm, Sat 10am-noon, 2-7pm, Sun and public holidays 2-7pm. No charge. ☎ 02 43 07 88 96.

Excursions

Refuge de l'Arche – ♿ May-Aug: 9.30am-7pm; Apr and Sep: 10am-7pm; Mar and Oct: 10am-6pm; Nov-Feb: 1.30-6pm. Closed 1 Jan and 25 Dec. 5€ (4-11 years: 3€). ☎ 02 43 07 24 38.

Château de la Maroutière – Mid-Jun to mid-Sep: guided tours (30min, last admission 15min before closing time) Wed and Fri 2-5pm. 3.81€ (children under 8: no charge). ☎ 02 43 07 20 44.

Vallée de la Mayenne

Chenillé-Changé: Fortified watermill – May-Sep: 10am-noon, 2.30-6.30pm, Sun 3-6pm; Oct-Apr: daily except Sun 2.30-6pm. 3€. ☎ 02 41 95 10 83. www.maine-anjou-rivieres.org

Le Lion-d'Angers: Église St-Martin – Contact the parish priest. ☎ 02 41 95 31 02 (late afternoon).

Haras national de l'Isle-Briand – ♿ Easter to mid-Sep: guided tours (1hr 15min) at 11am, 3pm, 4.15pm; mid-Sep to Easter: Sat-Sun and public holidays at 2.45pm and 4pm. Closed Jan. 5.34€. ☎ 02 41 18 05 05.

CHÂTEAU-LA-VALLIÈRE   🛈 Pl. d'Armes, 37330 CHÂTEAU-LA-VALLIÈRE, ☎ 02 47 24 14 31.

CHÂTEAUNEUF-SUR-LOIRE   🛈 Pl. A.-Briand, 45110 CHÂTEAUNEUF-SUR-LOIRE, ☎ 02 38 58 44 79.

Musée de la Marine de Loire – ♿ Apr-Oct: daily except Tue 10am-6pm; Nov-Mar: daily except Tue 2-6pm. Closed 1 Jan, 1 May, 25 Dec. 3.05€. ☎ 02 38 46 84 46. www.coeurdefrance.com

Excursion

Chécy: Musée de la Tonnellerie – ♿ Palm Sunday to All Saints: guided tours (1hr 30min) Sat-Sun and public holidays 3-6.30pm (Jun-Sep: daily except Mon). Closed 1 May. 1.52€. ☎ 02 38 86 95 93.

CHÂTEAU-RENAULT

🏠 32 pl. Jean-Jaurès, BP 60,
37110 CHÂTEAU-RENAULT, ☎ 02 47 56 22 22.

Musée du Cuir et de la Tannerie – Mid-May to mid-Sep: daily except Mon 2-6pm (Jul and Aug: 10am-noon, 2-6pm). 3.05€. ☎ 02 47 56 03 59.

Château de CHAUMONT-SUR-LOIRE

🏠 R. du Maréchal-Leclerc,
41150 CHAUMONT-SUR-LOIRE, ☎ 02 54 20 91 73.

Park – ♿ 9am to dusk. Closed 1 Jan, 1 May, 1 and 11 Nov, 25 Dec. No charge. ☎ 02 54 51 26 26.

Apartments – Early May to mid-Sep: 9.30am-6.30pm; Apr to early May and mid to end Sep: 10.30am-5.30pm; Oct-Mar: 10am-5pm. Closed 1 Jan, 1 May, 1 and 11 Nov, 25 Dec. 5.50€. ☎ 02 54 51 26 23.

Stables – ♿ Same as for the apartments.

Conservatoire international des Parcs et Jardins et du Paysage – ♿ Early Jun to mid-Oct: 9.30am to dusk. 8€ (children: 3.20€). ☎ 02 54 20 99 22.

Château de CHENONCEAU

🏠 1 r. Bretonneau, BP 1, 37150 CHENONCEAUX,
☎ 02 47 23 94 45.

Château – Mid-Mar to mid-Sep: 9am-7pm; mid to end Sep: 9am-6.30pm; early to mid-Mar and early to mid-Oct: 9am-6pm; mid to end Oct and mid to end Feb: 9am-5.30pm; early to mid-Feb and early to mid-Nov: 9am-5pm; mid-Nov to end Jan: 9am-4.30pm. 7.60€ (children: 6.10€). ☎ 02 47 23 90 07. www.chenonceau.com

Musée de Cires – As for the château. 3€. ☎ 02 47 23 90 07. www.chenonceau.com.

The Cher Valley

Prieuré de Saint-Jean-du-Grais – Easter to end Jun: Sun and public holidays 2.30-7pm; Jul and Aug: daily except Mon 2.30-7pm. 4.50€. ☎ 02 47 50 73 00.

Château de Leugny – Apr to end Oct: guided tours (1hr) by appointment. 7.62€. ☎ 02 47 50 45 61.

Montlouis-sur-Loire: Maison de la Loire – Daily except Mon 2-6pm. Closed public holidays. 3€. ☎ 02 47 50 97 52.

Château de la Bourdaisière – ♿ Apr to end Oct: guided tours (45min) 10am-noon, 2-6pm (Jun-Sep: 10am-7pm). 6€ (8€ during the period when shows are given). ☎ 02 47 45 16 31. www.chateaulabourdaisiere.com

Château de CHEVERNY

🏠 4 av. de Cheverny, 41700 COUR-CHEVERNY,
☎ 02 54 79 95 63.

Château – Apr-Sep: 9.15am-6.15pm (Jul and Aug: 6.45pm); Oct-Mar: 9.15am-noon, 2.15-5pm (Mar and Oct: 5.30pm). Apr to mid-Sep: "feeding the dogs" at 5pm; mid-Sep to end Mar: daily except Tue, Sat-Sun and public holidays at 3pm. 5.80€ (château and park), 10€ (château and permanent exhibition), 10.40€ (château and discovery of unusual sights in the park and canal). ☎ 02 54 79 96 29. www.chateau-cheverny.com

Excursions

Château de Troussay – ♿ Jul and Aug: guided tours (30min) 10am-6pm (Tue 10pm); Apr-Jun and Sep: 10.30am-12.30pm, 2-6pm; Oct: Sat-Sun and public holidays 10.30am-12.30pm, 2-5.30pm. Closed Nov-Mar. 4.60€ (children: 3.10€). ☎ 02 54 44 29 07 or ☎ 01 45 04 04 34.

CHINON

🏠 Pl. Hosheim, BP 141, 37501 CHINON, ☎ 02 47 93 17 85.

🅰 discovery tours (1hr 30min). 4.60€. Information at the tourist office or on www.vpah.culture.fr

Bons Entonneurs rabelaissiens – For the schedule and to make a reservation, contact: Secrétariat de la Confrérie, imp. des Caves-Paintes, 37500 Chinon, ☎ 02 47 93 30 44, fax 02 47 93 36 36.

Chapelle Ste-Radegonde – Jul and Aug: 9am-7pm; Sep-Jun: by appointment. 1.50€. ☎ 02 47 93 18 12.

Château – Apr-Sep: 9am-7pm; Oct-Mar: 9.30am-5pm. Closed 1 Jan and 25 Dec. 4.60€. ☎ 02 47 93 13 45.

Musée animé du Vin et de la Tonnellerie – Apr to end Sep: audio-tours (30min) 10.30am-12.30pm, 2-7pm. Closed 1 Jan and 25 Dec. 4€. ☎ 02 47 93 25 63.

Musée du Vieux Chinon – Early Apr to early Oct: 10.30am-12.30pm, 2-6pm; rest of the year: by appointment. 2.30€. ☎ 02 47 93 18 12.

Maison de la Rivière – ♿ Jul and Aug: daily except Mon 10am-12.30pm, 2-6.30pm, Sat-Sun and public holidays 3-6.30pm; Apr to Jun and Sep to early Nov: daily except Mon 10am-12.30pm, 2-5.30pm, Sat-Sun and public holidays 2-5.30pm. 4€. ☎ 02 47 93 21 34. www.cpie-val-de-vienne.org

Excursions

Huisme: Château de la Villaumaire – Jul and Aug: daily except Mon and Tue 2-6pm. 5.50€. ☎ 02 47 95 46 30.

Centre nucléaire de production d'électricité de Chinon – Visitors over 18 must have identity papers with them and a booking must be made with the Public Information Centre. No charge. ☎ 02 47 98 77 77.

Rabelais Country

La Devinière – Apr-Sep: 9.30am-7pm; Oct-Mar: 9.30am-12.30pm, 2-5pm. Closed 1 Jan and 25 Dec. 3.80€. ☎ 02 47 95 91 18.

Vallée de la Vienne

Vieux Bourg de Cravant: Church – ♿ Guided tours (30min). 2.30€. ☎ 02 47 93 20 04.

Parçay-sur-Vienne: Church – Daily except Wed and Sat-Sun 9am-noon, 2-6pm. ☎ 02 47 58 54 57.

Tavant: Church – Visits by request at the town hall. ☎ 02 47 58 58 01.

Château du Rivau – Jun to Sep: daily except Tue 1-7pm; May and Oct: Sat-Sun and public holidays 2-7pm. 6€. ☎ 02 47 95 77 47. www.chateaudurivau.com

La Loire Saumuroise

Montsoreau: Château – ♿ May to mid-Sep: 9.30am-7pm; mid-Sep to Apr: 10am-6pm. Closed mid-Nov to mid-Feb. 7€ (children: 4.40€). ☎ 02 41 67 12 60.

Saut-aux-Loups – ♿ Mar to 11 Nov: guided tours (1hr) 10am-6.30pm. 4.80€. ☎ 02 41 51 70 30.

Turquant: Troglo des pommes tapées – Easter to mid-Nov: Sat-Sun and public holidays 10am-noon, 2.30-6pm (Jul and Aug: daily except Mon 10am-noon, 2.30-6pm); mid-Jun to mid-Sep: daily except Mon 2.30-6pm. 4.60€. ☎ 02 41 51 48 30.

Turquant: Aux mille et un casse-tête du monde entier – Early May to end Sep: Sat-Sun and public holidays 2-7pm, weekdays by appointment. 3.51€ (children under 10: no charge). ☎ 02 41 51 71 91.

Le Parc Naturel Régional: Loire-Anjou-Touraine – Maison du Parc, 7 r. Jehanne-d'Arc, 49730 Montsoreau. ☎ 02 41 53 66 00. www.parc-loire-anjou-touraine.fr

CHOLET
🛈 Pl. de Rougé, BP 636, 49306 CHOLET. ☎ 02 41 49 80 00.

Guided Tour of the town – Contact the tourist office.

Musée d'Art et d'Histoire – ♿ Daily except Tue 10am-noon, 2-6pm. Closed public holidays. 3.10€, no charge Sat from Oct to May. ☎ 02 41 49 29 00. www.ville-cholet.fr

Musée du Textile – ♿ Daily except Tue 2-6pm (Jun-Sep: 6.30pm). Closed public holidays. 1.55€, no charge Sat from Oct to May. ☎ 02 41 75 25 40. www.ville-cholet.fr

Les Mauges

St-Laurent-de-la-Plaine: Cité des métiers de tradition – Apr and Sep: daily except Mon 2-6pm; May-Aug: daily except Sat-Sun and public holidays 10am-12.30pm, 2.30-7pm. 5.50€ (children: 3€). ☎ 02 41 78 24 08.

Maulévrier: Parc oriental – Jul and Aug: daily 10.30am-7.30pm (last admission 1hr before closing time); Mar-Jun and Sep to mid-Dec: daily except Mon 2-6pm, Sun and public holidays 2-7pm. 5€. ☎ 02 41 55 50 14. www.parc-oriental.com

Maulévrier: Ferme de la Goubaudière – Daily except Tue 2-6pm. Closed public holidays. No charge. ☎ 02 41 29 09 07.

Basilique de CLÉRY-SAINT-ANDRÉ
🛈 Pl. de l'Église, 45370 CLÉRY-ST-ANDRÉ. ☎ 02 38 45 94 33.

CRAON

4 r. du Mûrier, 53400 CRAON, ☎ 02 43 06 10 14.

Château – Early Apr to early Nov: unaccompanied tours of the grounds and vegetable garden daily except Tue 1-7pm (Jul and Aug: guided tours of the chateau and chapel 2-6pm). 5€, 7€ (château and park). ☎ 02 43 06 11 02.

Excursions

Cossé-le-Vivien: Musée Robert-Tatin – Apr-Sep: 10am-7pm, Tue 2-7pm; Oct-Mar: daily except Tue 10am-noon, 2-6pm, Sat-Sun and public holidays 2-6pm. Closed first 3 weeks in Jan. 7.20€ (house and museum). ☎ 02 43 78 80 89. www.musee-robert-tatin.org

Renazé: Musée de l'Ardoise – ♿ Mid-May to mid-Oct: Thu and Fri, Sun and public holidays 2-5.30pm (Jul and Aug: daily except Mon and Tue). 4€. Town hall. ☎ 02 43 06 40 14.

Château de Mortiercrolles – End Jul to end Aug: guided tours of the fortifications and the chapel (1hr) at 3.30pm and 4.30pm. 4€.

D

DESCARTES

Mairie, 37160 DESCARTES, ☎ 02 47 92 42 20.

Musée Descartes – Jun to end Sep: daily except Tue 2-6pm. 3.80€. ☎ 02 47 59 79 19.

DOUÉ-LA-FONTAINE

30 pl. du Champ-de-Foire, 49700 DOUÉ-LA-FONTAINE, ☎ 02 41 59 20 49.

Arènes – ♿ Early May to end Sep: guided tours (45min) Thu at 3pm. 1.55€. ☎ 02 41 59 22 28.

Musée des Commerces anciens – ♿ Mar, Apr, Oct and Nov: (last admission 1hr before closing) 9.30am-noon, 2-6pm; May, Jun and Sep: 9.30am-noon, 2-7pm; Jul and Aug: 9am-7pm. 5.50€. ☎ 02 41 59 28 23.

Zoo de Doué – Summer: 9am-7pm; winter: 10am-6pm. Closed early Nov to early Feb. 11.50€ (children under 10: 5.50€). ☎ 02 41 59 18 58. www.zoodoue.fr

La cave aux sarcophages – Apr to mid-Sep: tours (45min) 10am-noon, 2-7pm; low season: by appointment. 3.70€. ☎ 02 41 59 24 95.

Les Chemins de la rose – Mid-May to mid-Sep: 9.30am-7pm. 5.50€. ☎ 02 41 59 95 95.

Excursions

Louresse: Village troglodytique Rochemenier – Apr-Oct: daily 9.30am-7pm; Feb, Mar and Nov: Sat-Sun and public holidays 2-6pm. 4€. ☎ 02 41 59 18 15.

Maisons troglodytes de Forges – Jun-Sep: 9.30am-7pm; Mar-May and Oct: 9.30am-noon, 2-6pm. Closed Nov-Feb. 4.50€. ☎ 02 41 59 00 32.

Caverne sculptée de Dénezé-sous-Doué – Jun-Aug: 10am-7pm; Sep: 10am-6pm; Apr and May: daily except Mon (apart from public holidays) 2-6pm. 3.80€. ☎ 02 41 59 15 40.

F

La FERTÉ-BERNARD

15 pl. de la Lice, 72400 La FERTÉ-BERNARD, ☎ 02 43 71 21 21.

Chapelle St-Lyphard – May-Sep: for exhibitions.

Église N.-D.-des-Marais – Unaccompanied tour of the church. Guided tours available, ask at the tourist office. ☎ 02 43 71 21 21.

La FERTÉ-ST-AUBIN

R. des Jardins, 45240 La FERTÉ-ST-AUBIN, ☎ 02 38 64 67 93.

Château – End Mar to mid-Nov: 10am-7pm. Closed mid-Nov to end Mar. 7€ (children: 4.50€). ☎ 02 38 76 52 72.

La FLÈCHE

Bd. de Montréal, 72200 La FLÈCHE, ☎ 02 43 94 02 53.

Prytanée national militaire – Jul and Aug: guided tours 10am-noon, 2-6pm. 3.50€. ☎ 02 43 48 67 04.

Église St-louis – Closed outside summer school holidays. ☎ 02 43 48 67 04.

Excursions

Parc zoologique du Tertre rouge – &. May-Sep: 9.30am-7pm (last admission 1hr before closing, Jul and Aug: 8pm); Apr: 9.30am-6pm; Oct-Mar: 10am-noon, 1.30-5.30, Sun 10am-5.30pm. 13€ (children: 9.50€). ☎ 02 43 48 19 19. www.zoo-la-fleche.com

Bazouges-sur-le-Loir: Château – Mid-Jun to mid-Sep: guided tours (45min) Thu Sun and public holidays 3-6pm, Tue 10am-noon. 3.05€. ☎ 02 43 45 32 62.

Church – Jul and Aug: daily except Mon, Sat-Sun and public holidays 3-5pm. ☎ 02 43 94 88 44.

Durtal: Château – Apr-Jun and Sep: guided tours (45min) daily except Tue 2-6pm; Jul and Aug: daily 9.30am-12.30pm, 1.30-6.30pm; Nov-Mar: by appointment. Closed in Jan. 3€. ☎ 02 41 76 31 37.

FONTEVRAUD-L'ABBAYE 🖪 Chapelle Ste-Catherine, 49590 FONTEVRAUD-L'ABBAYE, ☎ 02 41 51 79 45.

Abbey – Major works have been undertaken over the years to highlight new aspects of the monument. Jun-Sep: 9am-6.30pm; Oct, Apr and May: 10am-6pm; Nov-Mar: 10am-5.30pm. Closed 1 Jan, 1 and 11 Nov, 25 Dec. 5.50€. ☎ 02 41 51 71 41. www.abbaye-fontevraud.com

Fontevraud-l'Abbaye: Centre culturel de l'ouest – Information on scheduled events: ☎ 02 41 51 73 52.

Château de FOUGÈRES-SUR-BIÈVRE

Château – Apr-Sep: 9.30am-12.30pm, 2-6.30pm; Oct-Mar: daily except Tue 10am-12.30pm, 2-5pm. Closed 1 Jan, 1 May, 1 and 11 Nov, 25 Dec. 3.96€, no charge 1st Sunday in the month. ☎ 02 54 20 27 18.

G

GIEN 🖪 Pl. Jean-Jaurès, 45501 GIEN, ☎ 02 38 67 25 28.

Musée international de la Chasse – Jun-Sep: 9am-6pm; Oct-May: 9am-noon, 2-6pm. Closed 1 Jan and 25 Dec. 5.35€. ☎ 02 38 67 69 69.

Faïencerie – May-Sep: 9am-12.30pm, 1.30-6.30pm, Sun and public holidays 10am-noon, 2-6pm; Oct-Dec, Mar and Apr: 9am-noon, 2-6pm, Sun and public holidays 10am-noon, 2-6pm; Jan and Feb: 2-6pm. Closed 1 Jan, 1 May, 1 and 11 Nov, 25 Dec. 3€. ☎ 02 38 67 89 99. Tours of the factory possible (outside Jul, Aug and Dec) Mon-Thu on request. Closed public holidays. For safety reasons, children under 11 (even if accompanied) are not allowed to visit the workshops. 5.50€ (includes museum visit). Shop (2nd choice and end of line) daily except Sun 9am-noon, 2-6pm, Sat 9am-6pm. Closed public holidays. ☎ 02 38 67 89 92.

Excursions

St-Brisson-sur-Loire: Fortress – First Sat in Apr to mid-Nov: guided tours (45min) daily except Wed 10am-noon, 2-6pm. 3.50€. ☎ 02 38 36 71 29.

Dampierre-en-Burly: Centre nucléaire de production d'électricité CNPE – Application of the «vigipirate» security plan may cause the site to be closed for visits, enquire for information. Guided tours (2hr 30min) at 9am and 2pm, by appointment 1 week in advance. Centrale nucléaire de Dampierre-en-Burly, BP 18, 45570 Ouzouer-sur-Loire. Visitors must have identity papers with them, minimum age: 11 years. Closed 1 Jan, 1 May, 25 Dec. ☎ 02 38 29 70 04.

GIZEUX

Château – May-Sep: guided tours (45min) 10am-6pm, Sun 2-6pm. Tour with a story of the château for children (4-12 years) Jul and Aug: Wed and Sat-Sun 2-6pm; Jun and Sep: Sun 2-6pm. 6€, 4.50€ (tour with story). ☎ 02 47 96 50 92.

Excursion

Parçay-les-Pins: Musée Jules-Desbois – Jul and Aug: 11am-1pm, 3-7pm; mid to end Jun and early to mid-Sep: daily except Mon 2.30-6pm; Apr to mid-Jun and mid-Sep to 1 Nov: Sat-Sun and public holidays. 4€ (under 18s: no charge). ☎ 02 41 82 28 80.

Blou: Church – Key available at the café opposite the church daily except Mon.

Le GRAND-PRESSIGNY

Château – Feb-Dec: 9.30am-12.30pm, 2-5pm (Apr-Sep: 9.30am-7pm). Closed Jan and 25 Dec. 3.80€. ☎ 02 47 94 90 20.

I

L'ÎLE-BOUCHARD

Prieuré St-Léonard – 10am-5pm. Key available at the home of Mme Page, 3 r. de la Vallée-aux-Nains.

Église St-Maurice – This church is closed except for religious services.

Avon-les-Roches: Church – Apply to the town hall to visit. ☎ 02 47 58 54 07.

ILLIERS-COMBRAY 🖪 5 r. Henri-Germond, 28120 ILLIERS-COMBRAY, ☎ 02 37 24 24 00.

Maison de tante Léonie – Mid-Jun to mid-Sep: guided tours (1hr 15min) daily except Mon at 11am, 2.30pm, 3.30pm, 4.30pm; mid-Jan to mid-Jun and mid-Sep to mid-Dec: daily except Mon at 2.30pm and 4pm. 4.57€ (children: no charge). ☎ 02 37 24 30 97.

L

LANGEAIS 🖪 Pl. du 14-Juillet, 37130 LANGEAIS, ☎ 02 47 96 58 22.

Château – Apr to mid-Oct: 9.30am-6.30pm (mid-Jul to end Aug: 8pm); mid-Oct to end Mar: 10am-5.30pm. Closed 25 Dec. 6.50€ (children: 4€). ☎ 02 47 96 72 60.

Excursions

Cinq-Mars-la-Pile: Château – ♿ Jul to mid-Sep: daily except Tue 2-8pm; Apr-Jun and mid-Sep to Oct: Sat-Sun 9am-6pm. Closed Nov-Mar. 3€. ☎ 02 47 96 40 49.

St-Étienne-de-Chigny: Church – Closed except for services.

Château de Champchevrier – Mid-Jun to mid-Sep: unaccompanied tours of the outbuildings, guided tours of the château (45min) 10am-6pm. 7€. ☎ 02 47 24 93 93.

LAVARDIN

Mairie – Tue 8.30am-noon, Wed and Fri 4-7pm. No charge. ☎ 02 54 85 07 74.

Castle – Jun to Heritage days: daily except Mon 11am-noon, 3-6pm. 3€. ☎ 02 54 85 07 74.

Excursion

Parc et jardin du domaine de Sasnières – Easter to All Saints: daily except Tue and Wed 10am-6pm. 6.10€. ☎ 02 54 82 92 34.

Vallée du LAYON

Les Cerqueux-sous-Passavant: Bisonland – ♿ Jul and Aug: guided tours (1hr) 10am-7pm. 5.50€. ☎ 02 41 59 58 02.

Beaulieu-sur-Layon: Caveau du vin – End May to Aug: daily except Tue and Sat 10am-12.30pm, 2.30-6.30pm, Sun 10am-1pm; Sep to end May: daily except Tue and Sat-Sun 2-5pm. Make an appointment at the tourist office. No charge. ☎ 02 41 78 65 07.

St-Lambert-du-Lattay: Musée de la Vigne et du Vin d'Anjou – Jul and Aug: daily 11am-1pm, 3-7pm; Apr-Jun and Sep to end Oct: Sat-Sun and public holidays 2.30-6.30pm. 4.50€. ☎ 02 41 78 42 75.

Château de la Haute-Guerche – Jul and Aug: 9am-noon, 2-6pm. No charge. ☎ 02 41 78 41 48.

LOCHES 🖪 Pl. Wermelskirchen, 37600 LOCHES, ☎ 02 47 91 82 82.

Maison Lansyer – Jul and Aug: 10am-7pm; Jun and Sep: daily except Tue 10am-12.30pm, 1.15-7pm; Apr, May and Oct to mid-Nov: daily except Tue 10am-noon, 1.30-6pm. Closed mid-Nov to early Apr. 4.20€. ☎ 02 47 59 05 45. www.lochesentouraine.com

Château – Apr-Sep: 9am-7pm; Oct-Mar: 9.30am-5pm. Closed 1 Jan and 25 Dec. 3.80€. ☎ 02 47 59 01 32.

Donjon – Apr-Sep: 9am-7pm; Oct-Mar: 9.30am-5pm. Closed 1 Jan and 25 Dec. 3.80€. ☎ 02 47 59 07 86.

Excursions

Vignemont: Carrières troglodytes – Easter school holidays-Nov school holidays: 10am-noon, 2-6pm. 6,25€ (enf. : 4,75€). ☎ 02 47 91 54 54.

Bridoré: Castle – Jun to end Sep: guided tours (1hr) 1-7pm. 4.57€. ☎ 02 47 94 72 63.

Vallée de l'Indre

Cormery: Abbey – Guided tours available, ask at the tourist office. ☎ 02 47 91 82 82.

LORRIS
🖪 2 r. des Halles, 45260 LORRIS, ☎ 02 38 94 81 42.

Musée départemental de la Résistance et de la Déportation – ♿ Daily except Tue 10am-noon, 2-6pm, Sun 2-6pm. Closed 1 Jan, 1 May, 25 Dec. 5€. ☎ 02 38 94 84 19.

Château du LUDE

Tour of château – ♿ Apr-Sep: guided tours of the interior (45min) 2.30-6pm; unaccompanied tours of the outside 9.30am-noon, 2-6pm. Closed Oct-Mar and Wed in Apr, May, Jun and Sep. 6€. ☎ 02 43 94 60 09. www.chateauxcountry.com

Excursion

La Boissère – Easter school holidays and Aug: unaccompanied tours of the chapels and the outside of the building only. Possibility of guided tours, contact M. Pallu de Beaupuy, Château de la Boissière, Noyant, 49490 Deneze-sous-le-Lude. ☎ 02 41 89 55 52.

M

Le MANS
🖪 Hôtel des Ursulines, r. de l'Étoile, 72000 Le MANS, ☎ 02 43 28 17 22.

🅰 Information at the tourist office or on www.vpah.culture.fr

St-Pierre-la-Cour – Jul and Aug: 10.30am-12.30pm, 2-6.30pm; Sep-Jun: 9am-noon, 2-6pm, Sun and public holidays 10am-noon, 2-6pm. Closed some public holidays. No charge (except during temporary exhibitions). ☎ 02 43 47 38 51.

Église N.-D.-du-Pré – Jul-Sep: Sat-Sun 3-6pm; Oct-Jun: Wed-Sat 3-6pm.

Église Ste-Jeanne-d'Arc (ancien hôpital Coëffort) – Easter to All Saints: Sun 3-6pm. ☎ 02 43 84 69 55.

Musée de la Reine-Bérengère – Daily except Mon 10am-12.30pm, 2-6.30pm (Oct-Apr:2-6pm only). Closed 1 Jan, 1 May, 14 Jul, 1 Nov, 25 Dec. 2.80€. ☎ 02 43 47 38 80.

Musée de Tessé – ♿ Jul and Aug: daily except Mon 10am-12.30pm, 2-6.30pm (last admission 45min before closing) ; Sep-Jun: daily except Mon 9am-noon, 2-6pm, Sun and public holidays 10am-noon, 2-6pm. 4€. ☎ 02 43 47 38 51.

Musée Vert Véron de Forbonnais – ♿ Daily except Sat 9am-noon, 2-6pm, Sun 2-6pm. Closed public holidays (variable). 2.80€. ☎ 02 43 47 39 94.

Circuit Bugatti – Mar-Oct: 7.30am-7pm; Nov-Feb: 9am-5pm. Closed on race days. ☎ 02 43 40 24 04.

Musée de l'Automobile de la Sarthe – ♿ Jun-Sep: 10am-7pm ((last admission 1hr before closing); Oct-Dec and Feb-May: 10am-6pm; Jan: Sat-Sun 10am-6pm. Closed 1 Jan and 25 Dec. 6€ (12-18 years: 5€, 7-11 years: 2€). ☎ 02 43 72 72 24. www.sarthe.com/auto/museint.htm

Excursion

Abbaye de l'Épau – 9.30am-noon, 2-6pm. Closed 1 Jan and 25 Dec. 2.30€. ☎ 02 43 84 22 29.

Arche de la Nature – Poney rides available Apr-Oct. Many activities in the summer months. Information from: ☎ 02 43 50 38 45. www.arche-nature.org

Les jardins du manoir de la Massonière – Jun-Sep: Fri, Sat, Sun 2-6pm. 4€. ☎ 02 43 88 61 26.

Meandering down the Sarthe Valley

Parc ornithologique de Spay – ☎ 02 43 21 33 02 - 6,10€.

Fillé: Church – Tours possible by appointment. ☎ 02 43 87 14 10.

Malicorne Espace faïence – AprOct 10am-7pm; Feb-Mar and Nov-Dec: daily except Mon 10am-12.30pm, 2.30-6.30pm. 6€ (child: 3€). ☏ 02 43 48 07 17.

Malicorne-sur-Sarthe: Espace faïence – ♿ Apr to end Sep: guided tours of the workshops and museum (1hr 15min) daily except Mon 9-11am, 2-4.15pm. Closed Sun and public holidays. 3.05€. ☏ 02 43 94 81 18.

MEUNG-SUR-LOIRE

🛈 42 r. Jehan-de-Meung, 45130 MEUNG-SUR-LOIRE, ☏ 02 38 44 32 28.

MONDOUBLEAU

🛈 2 r. Brizieux, 41170 MONDOUBLEAU, ☏ 02 54 80 77 08.

Fortress – Easter to end Sep: guided tours Sat at 3pm (Jul and Aug: Wed at 3pm). Departure from the Maison du Perche, place du Marché near the fountain. ☏ 02 54 80 77 08.

Excursions

Château de St-Agil – Tours of the outside only: daily except Sun and public holidays 9am-noon, 2-6pm. 3.50€. ☏ 02 54 80 94 02.

Commanderie d'Arville – Mid-Feb to mid-Dec: guided tours of the outside and tours of the Centre d'Histoire des Ordres de Chevalerie (Order of the Templars History Centre) (2hr) daily except Tue 10am-noon, 2-6pm (Jun-Sep: 7pm). 7.70€. ☏ 02 54 80 75 41.

Souday: Church – Guided tours possible by appointment. ☏ 02 54 80 93 18.

Sargé-sur-Braye: Church of St-Martin – May-Sep: 8am-6pm.

Baillou: Church – Apply to the Maison du Perche for a guided tour. ☏ 02 54 80 77 08.

MONTOIRE-SUR-LE-LOIR

🛈 16 pl. Clemenceau, 41800 MONTOIRE-SUR-LE-LOIR, ☏ 02 54 85 23 30.

Castle – To visit, contact the tourist office in Pithiviers, ☏ 02 38 30 50 02.

Station – Visits can be made when the Vallée du Loir tourist train passes through or by request at the tourist office, 16 pl. Clemenceau. ☏ 02 54 85 23 30.

Musikenfête – Mar-Sep: daily except Mon 10am-noon, 2-4pm; Oct-Dec: daily except Mon 2-6pm. Closed Jan and Feb. ☏ 02 54 85 28 95.

MONTRÉSOR

🛈 Mairie, 37460 MONTRÉSOR, ☏ 02 47 91 43 00.

Château – Apr to early Nov: guided tours (45min) 10am-noon, 2-6pm (early Jul to early Sep: 10am-6pm). 6€ (children: 3.50€). ☏ 02 47 92 60 04.

Excursions

Chartreuse du Liget: Charter house – 9am-noon, 2-6pm. 0.50€. ☏ 02 47 92 60 02.

Chapelle St-Jean-du-Liget – Visits by appointment with Mme Arnould at La Chartreuse. ☏ 02 47 92 60 02.

MONTREUIL-BELLAY

🛈 Pl. du Concorde, 49260 MONTREUIL-BELLAY, ☏ 02 41 52 32 39.

Château – Apr to end Oct: guided tours (1hr) daily except Tue 10am-noon, 2-5.30pm. 7€. ☏ 02 41 52 33 06.

Musée de la Soie vivante – ♿ Mid-May to end Oct: daily except Mon 10am-noon, 1.30-6pm. 4€ (children: 2.50€). ☏ 02 41 38 72 58.

Excursion

Ancienne abbaye d'Asnières – Jul to end Aug: guided tours (30min) daily except Tue 2-6.30pm. Town hall. ☏ 02 41 67 04 70.

MONTRICHARD

🛈 1 r. du Pont, 41400 MONTRICHARD, ☏ 02 54 32 05 10.

Donjon: Museums – May-Sep: 10am-noon, 2-6pm (mid-Jul to mid-Aug: visits of the keep with sound effects 2.30pm and 4.30pm); Apr: Sat-Sun and feast days 2-6pm. Closed Oct-Mar. 5€. ☏ 02 54 32 05 10.

Caves Monmousseau – ♿ Apr to mid-Nov: guided tours (1hr) 10am-6pm; mid-Nov-Mar: daily except Sat-Sun and public holidays 10am-noon, 2-5pm. 2.75€. ☏ 02 54 32 35 15. www.monmousseau.com

Excursions

Chissay-en-Touraine: Distillerie Fraise-Or – Easter to end Sep: guided tours (45min) daily except Mon 3-6pm. 4€. ☎ 02 54 32 32 05.

Bourré: Caves champignonnières des Roches – ♿ Jul and Aug: guided tours (1hr) at 10am, 11am, 1pm, 2pm, 3pm, 4pm, 5pm; Palm Sunday to end Jun: at 10am, 11am, 2pm, 3pm, 4pm, 5pm, early Sep to mid-Nov. at 11am, 3pm, 4pm. Closed mid Nov to Palm Sunday. 5.50€ (under 14s: 3.60€). ☎ 02 54 32 95 33. Make sure that anyone confined to a wheelchair has a warm rug or blanket, the temperature is between 10 and 12°.

Champignonnières des Roches: La Ville souterraine – Same as for the Caves champignonnières des Roches.

Thésée: Musée archéologique – Jul and Aug: guided tours daily except Tue 2-6.30pm; Easter to end Jun: Sat-Sun and public holidays 2-6pm. 3€. ☎ 02 54 71 00 88.

Château du Gué-Péan – Jul to end Aug: guided tours (45min) 10.30am-12.30pm, 2-6pm. 4€. ☎ 02 54 71 37 10.

Château de Montpoupon – Jul and Aug: guided tours (1hr) 10am-6pm; Apr-Jun and Sep: 10am-noon, 2-6pm; Oct-Dec, Feb and Mar: Sat-Sun and public holidays 10am-noon, 2-4pm (Oct: 5pm). Closed in Jan. 6.50€. ☎ 02 47 94 21 15. www.montpoupon.com

○

ORLÉANS
🛈 6 r. Albert-Ier, 45000 ORLÉANS, ☎ 02 38 24 05 05.

Tourist train – Runs through the centre of the town (45min). Call for information. ☎ 02 38 24 05 05.

Crypte de St-Aignan – Mid-Jun to mid-Sep: daily except Mon 1-5.15pm. Contact the tourist office, ☎ 02 38 24 05 05.

Cathédrale Ste-Croix: Crypt – Work in progress.

Musée des Beaux-Arts – ♿ Daily except Mon 10am-12.15pm, 1.30-6pm, Sun and public holidays 1.30-6pm. Closed 1 Jan, 1 and 8 May, 1 Nov, 25 Dec. 4€, no charge 1st Sunday in the month. ☎ 02 38 79 21 55.

Musée historique et archéologique – Jul and Aug: daily except Mon 10am-6pm; May, Jun and Sep: daily except Mon 2-6pm; Oct-Apr: Wed, Sat-Sun 2-6pm. Closed 1 Jan, 1 and 8 May, 1 Nov, 25 Dec. 2.29€. ☎ 02 38 79 21 55.

Centre Charles-Péguy – Museum and interior courtyard: May-Sep: 2-6pm; Oct-Apr: daily except Sat-Sun 2-6pm. Closed public holidays. 2€ (museum + the house of Joan of Arc), no charge (interior courtyard and temporary exhibitions). ☎ 02 38 53 20 23.

Maison de Jeanne d'Arc – May-Oct: daily except Mon 10am-12.15pm, 1.30-6pm; Nov-Apr: daily except Mon 1.30-6pm. Closed 1 Jan, 1 and 8 May (afternoon), 25 Dec. 2€, no charge 2nd Sunday in the month. ☎ 02 38 52 99 89.

Centre Jeanne-d'Arc – Guided tours (30min) daily except Sat-Sun 9am-12.15pm, 2-6pm, Fri 9am-12.15pm, 2-4.30pm. No charge. ☎ 02 38 79 24 92.

Museum – ♿ 2-6pm. Closed 1 Jan, 1 and 8 May, 1 Nov, 25 Dec. 3.05€. ☎ 02 38 54 61 05.

Hôtel Toutin – Daily except Sun and Mon 10am-12.30pm, 2-6.30pm. Closed Aug and public holidays. No charge.

Collégiale St-Pierre-le-Puellier – ♿ Daily except Mon 10am-12.30pm, 1.30-6pm, Sat-Sun 2-6pm. Closed public holidays. No charge. ☎ 02 38 79 24 85.

Excursions

Gidy: Géodrome – ♿ Apr-Sep: daily except Wed and Thu noon-7pm; Oct to mid-Nov: Sat-Sun noon-5pm. Closed mid-Nov to end Mar. 2€. ☎ 02 38 64 47 06.

Artenay: Musée du Théâtre forain – ♿ Jun-Sep: daily except Tue 10am-noon, 2-6pm; Oct-May: daily except Tue 2-5.30pm. Closed 1 Jan, 1 May, 1 Nov, 25 Dec. 3.05€, no charge 1st Sunday in the month. ☎ 02 38 80 09 73. www.cœur-de-france.com

La Loire Blésoise

Parc floral de la Source – Apr to mid-Nov: 9am-7pm (last admission 1hr before closing); mid-Nov to Mar: 2-5pm. Closed 25 Dec. 3.50€, park and butterfly glasshouse 5.95€ (children: 1.98€, park and glasshouse 3.80€). ☎ 02 38 49 30 00. www.parfloral-lasource.fr

St-Laurent-des-Eaux: Centre nucléaire de production d'électricité (CNPE) – For information, contact the Communications Dept., BP 42, 41220 St-Laurent-Nouan (2 days in advance). ☎ 02 54 44 84 09.

St-Dyé-sur-Loire: Church – For guided tours, ask at the tourist office. ☎ 02 54 81 65 45.

Maison de la Loire – Mar-Jun, Sep and Oct: by appointment; Jul and Aug: at 10am. Closed 1 May and 11 Nov. 3.05€. ☎ 02 54 81 65 45.

P

PITHIVIERS
🛈 Mail Ouest, Gare routière, 45300 PITHIVIERS, ☎ 02 38 30 50 02.

Musée des Transports – May to mid-Oct: Sun and public holidays 2-6pm (Jul and Aug: Sat 2-6pm). 6€.

Musée municipal – Closed for renovation work. Call for information, ☎ 02 38 30 00 64.

Excursion

Malesherbes: Château – Mid-Mar to mid-Nov: guided tours (45min) Wed and Sat-Sun at 3pm, 4pm, 5pm and 6pm. Closed 1 May. 7€. ☎ 02 38 34 41 02.

Le Pithiverais

Yèvre-le-Châtel: Château fort – Apr-Oct: 2-6pm; Nov-Mar: by appointment. 3€. ☎ 02 38 34 25 91.

Boynes: Maison du Safran – Apr to 1 Nov: guided tours (1hr 30min) Sat-Sun and public holidays 2.30-6pm. 2.50€. ☎ 02 38 33 13 05 or ☎ 02 38 33 10 09.

Bellegarde: Hôtel de ville – Daily except Sun 8.30am-noon, 1.15-4pm (Mon 5pm), Sat 9am-noon. Closed public holidays. No charge. ☎ 02 38 90 10 03.

Château de Chamerolles – Feb-Dec: daily except Tue 10am-noon, 2-5pm (Apr-Sep: daily 10am-6pm). Closed Jan and 25 Dec. 4.90€. ☎ 02 38 39 84 66.

Château du PLESSIS-BOURRÉ

Château – Apr-Sep: guided tours (1hr) daily except Wed 10am-noon, 2-6pm, Thu 2-6pm (Jul and Aug: daily 10am-6pm); Oct-Mar: daily except Wed 2-6pm. Closed Dec to mid-Feb. 8€. ☎ 02 41 32 06 01. www.plessis-bourre.com

Excursion

Manoir de la Hamonnière – Tours by appointment. 1.50€. ☎ 02 41 42 01 38.

Château du PLESSIS-MACÉ

Château – Spring school holidays to end Jun and Sep to November school holidays: guided tours (1hr) daily except Mon and Tue 1.30-5.30pm (Jul and Aug: daily 10.30am-6.30pm). Closed Dec-Feb. 4.60€ (children 12 to 18: 2.80€). ☎ 02 41 32 67 93. www.cg49.fr

PONTLEVOY
🛈 5 pl. du Collège, 41400 PONTLEVOY, ☎ 02 54 80 60 80.

Musée municipal – Closed during 2002.

POUANCÉ
🛈 2 bis r. Porte-Angevine, 49420 POUANCÉ, ☎ 02 41 92 45 86.

Castle – Mid-Jun to mid-Sep: guided tours (1hr 15min) by appointment daily except Mon 10am-noon, 2-6.30pm, Tue 2-6.30pm, Sat 1.30-7pm, Sun and public holidays 2-7.30pm. 2€. ☎ 02 41 92 41 08.

Excursion

Château de la Motte-Glain – Mid-Jun to mid-Sep: guided tours (45min) daily except Tue 2-6.30pm. By appointment (3 days in advance). 5.50€ (children: 4€). ☎ 01 40 55 52 01. www.uehha.org

R

RICHELIEU
8 6 Grande-Rue, 37120 RICHELIEU, ☎ 02 47 58 13 62.

Hôtel de ville – Jul and Aug: guided tours (30min) 10am-noon, 2-6pm; Sep-Jun: daily except Tue, Sat-Sun and public holidays 10am-noon, 2-6pm. 2€ museum and park. ☎ 02 47 58 10 13.

Parc du château – Daily 10am-6pm. Closed 1 May. 1.50€. ☎ 02 47 58 10 09.

Steam train of Touraine – Call for information on times and prices. ☎ 02 47 58 12 97.

Excursions

Champigny-sur-Veude: Sainte-Chapelle – Call for information. ☎ 02 47 95 71 46.

Faye-la-Vineuse: Église St-Georges – ☎ 02 47 95 63 29.

Abbaye de Bois-Aubry – 9am-noon, 2-5.30pm. No charge. ☎ 02 47 58 34 48.

ROMORANTIN-LANTHENAY
8 32 pl. de la Paix, 41200 ROMORANTIN-LANTHENAY, ☎ 02 54 76 43 89.

Guided tour of the town – Contact the tourist office.

Maison du Carroir doré – ♿ Mid-May to end Sep: daily except Thu and Sun 2.30-6pm. Closed Whitsun, 14 Jul and 15 Aug. 2€. ☎ 02 54 76 22 06.

Espace automobile Matra – ♿ Daily except Tue 9am-noon, 2-6pm, Sun and public holidays 10am-noon, 2-5pm. Closed 1 Jan, 1 May, 25 Dec. 4.57€. ☎ 02 54 94 55 55.

Musée de Sologne – ♿ Jun-Aug: daily except Tue 10am-6pm, Sun and public holidays 2-6pm; Sep-May: daily except Tue 10am-noon, 2-6pm, Sun and public holidays 2-6pm. Closed 1 Jan, 1 May, 25 Dec. 4.50€. ☎ 02 54 95 33 66.

S

SABLÉ-SUR-SARTHE
8 Pl. Raphaël-Élize, BP 127, 72305 SABLÉ-SUR-SARTHE, ☎ 02 43 95 00 60.

Boat trips: Anjou Navigation – Quai National, 72300 Sablé-sur-Sarthe. ☎ 02 43 95 14 42.
Les Croisières Saboliennes – Quai National, 72300 Sablé-sur-Sarthe. ☎ 02 43 95 93 13.

Excursions

Asnières-sur-Vègre: Church – Easter to last Sunday in Sep: guided tours (1hr) Sun at 4.30pm (Jul and Aug: daily except Mon). Meeting point: place de l'Église. ☎ 02 43 92 40 47.

Chapelle de Varennes-Bourreau – Apr-Sep: guided tours available by appointment with the tourist office. ☎ 02 43 70 69 09.

Château de Vaux – The château is undergoing restoration. Unaccompanied tours of the surrounding areas.

ST-AIGNAN
8 Mairie, 41110 ST-AIGNAN, ☎ 02 54 75 22 85.

Maison de la Prévôté – Mid-May to end Sep: daily except Mon 10am-12.30pm, 4-7pm, Sat-Sun and public holidays 10am-noon, 3-6pm. No charge. ☎ 02 54 71 22 18.

Zoo-parc de Beauval – ♿ Apr to early Nov: 9am to dusk; Nov to end Mar: 10am-6pm. 13€ (children: 8€). ☎ 02 54 75 50 00. www.zoobeauval.com

Château de Chémery – Mar-Nov 11am-6pm; Dec-Feb: by appointment. 5€. ☎ 02 54 71 82 77.

ST-BENOÎT-SUR-LOIRE
8 44 r. Orléanaise, 45730 ST-BENOÎT-SUR-LOIRE, ☎ 02 38 35 79 00.

Basilica – Unaccompanied tours daily and guided tours available from Easter to All saints by appointment. 3€. ☎ 02 38 35 72 43.

ST-CALAIS
8 Pl. de l'Hôtel-de-Ville, 72120 ST-CALAIS, ☎ 02 43 35 82 95.

Excursion

Château de Courtanvaux – Easter to mid-Oct: guided tours (1hr) daily except Tue at 10am, 11am, 3pm, 4pm and 5pm. No visits when receptions are being held (it is advisable to call for information). 2.80€. ☎ 02 43 35 34 43.

ST-PATERNE-RACAN

Excursion

Château de la Roche-Racan – Early Aug to mid-Sep: guided tours (45min) 10am-noon, 3-5pm. 4.50€. ☎ 02 47 29 20 02.

STE-MAURE-DE-TOURAINE   🖪 R. du Château, 37800 STE-MAURE-DE-TOURAINE,
☎ 02 47 65 66 20.

SAUMUR   🖪 Pl. de la Bilange, BP 241, 49418 SAUMUR, ☎ 02 41 40 20 60.

Petit train touristique – Mid-Apr-Sep tours (45min) depart from the Tourist office ☎ 02 41 40 20 60.

Château – Jun-Sep: guided tours (45min) 9.30am-6pm (Jul and Aug: evening visits Wed and Sat 8.30-10.30pm); Oct-May: 9.30am-noon, 2-5.30pm (Oct to end Mar: daily except Tue). Closed 1 Jan and 25 Dec. 6€. ☎ 02 41 40 24 40.

Musée des Arts décoratifs – As for the château.

Musée du Cheval – As for the château.

Musée de l'École de Cavalerie – No individual unaccompanied tours. Guided tours possible by appointment. 2.50€. Av. du Maréchal-Foch, 49409 Saumur Cedex. ☎ 02 41 83 69 99.

Musée des Blindés – ♿ May-Sep: 9.30am-6.30pm; Oct-Apr: 10am-5pm. Closed 1 Jan and 25 Dec. 5.50€. ☎ 02 41 53 06 99. www.musee-des-blindes.asso.fr

Excursions

Bagneux: Musée du Moteur – Daily except Thu 9am-noon, 2-6pm, Sun and public holidays 2-6pm (mid-Nov to mid-May: daily except Thu, Sun and Public holidays 1.30-5.30pm). 4€. ☎ 02 41 50 26 10.

Bagneux: Le Grand Dolmen – ♿ Daily except Wed 9am-7pm (Jul and Aug: daily). 3€. ☎ 02 41 50 23 02. www.saumur-dolmen.com

Château de Boumois – Mid-Jun to mid-Aug: guided tours (45min) daily except Tue 10am-noon, 2-6pm. 6€. ☎ 02 41 38 43 16.

St-Cyr-en-Bourg: Cave des vignerons de Saumur – May-Sep: guided tours (1hr) 9.30am-12.30pm, 2.30-6.30pm (Jul and Aug: 9.30am-6.30pm); Oct-Apr: daily except Sun 9.30am-noon, 2-6pm. Closed 1 Jan, 1 and 11 Nov, 25 Dec. 2.30€. ☎ 02 41 53 06 18.

La Loire Angevine

St-Hilaire-St-Florent: Caves Bouvet-Ladubay – ♿ Jun-Sep: guided tours (1hr) 9am-7pm (Sun 9.30am); Oct-May: 9am-noon, 2-6pm, Sat 10am-noon, 2-6pm, Sun and public holidays 10am-12.30pm, 2.30-6pm. Closed 1 Jan and 25 Dec. 0.76€. ☎ 02 41 83 83 83. www.bouvet-ladubay.fr

St-Hilaire-St-Florent: Galerie d'Art contemporain Bouvet-Ladubay – ♿ Apr to Dec: daily except Mon and Tue 10am-noon, 2-6pm, Sat 2-6pm, Sun and public holidays 2.30-6pm. Closed 1 Jan and 25 Dec. ☎ 02 41 83 83 82. www.bouvet-ladubay.fr

École nationale d'équitation – ♿ Apr-Sep: guided tours (1hr) daily except Sun and Mon 9.30-11am, 2-4pm and riders' training session (30min) at 9.30am. 6.50€ (installations and training session), 4.50€ (afternoon). Closed public holidays. Service des visites (Dept. which deals with visits), ENE, BP 207, 49411 Saumur Cédex. ☎ 02 41 53 50 60.

Musée du Champignon – ♿ Early Feb to mid-Nov: 10am-7pm. 6.50€. ☎ 02 41 50 31 55.

Parc miniature Pierre et Lumière – Early Feb to mid-Nov: 10am-7pm. 6.50€. ☎ 02 41 50 70 04.

Gennes: Amphithéâtre – Jul and Aug: guided tours (45min) 10am-12.30pm, 3-6.30pm; Apr-Jun and Sep: Sun and public holidays 3-6.30pm. 2.70€. ☎ 02 41 51 55 04.

Église St-Eusèbe – Closed for renovation work.

Château de Montgeoffroy – End Mar to mid-Nov: guided tours (1hr) 9.30am-noon, 2.30-6.30pm (mid-Jun to mid-Sep: 9.30am-6.30pm). 8.50€. ☎ 02 41 80 60 02.

SEGRÉ   🖪 5 r. David-d'Angers, 49500 SEGRÉ, ☎ 02 41 92 86 83.

Guided tour of the town – Contact the tourist office.

Château de la Lorie – ♿ Early Jul to mid-Sep: daily except Tue 3-6pm. 3.80€. ☎ 02 41 92 10 04.

Château de Raguin – Jul and Aug: guided tours (45min) 2-6pm. 5.35€ (children: 3€). ☎ 02 41 61 40 20.

Nyoiseau: Domaine de la Petite Couère – Mar to mid-Nov: Sun and public holidays 10am-7pm (May to mid-Sep: daily). 10€ (children: 4.50€). ☎ 02 41 61 06 31.

SELLES-SUR-CHER 🛈 Pl. Charles-de-Gaulle, 41100 SELLES SUR CHER, ☎ 02 54 95 25 44.

Musée du Val-de-Cher – ♿ Jun to end Aug: daily except Mon 10am-noon, 2.30-6pm. Closed 14 Jul and 15 Aug. 3.10€. ☎ 02 54 95 25 40.

Excursions

Châtillon-sur-Cher: Église St-Blaise – The keys are available at the home of Mme and M. Bouquet, 2 r. de l'Église.

Meusnes: Musée de la Pierre à fusil – ♿ Daily except Sat-Sun and Mon 9am-1pm. Closed public holidays. 0.76€. ☎ 02 54 71 00 23.

Château de SERRANT

Château – Apr to mid-Nov: guided tours (1hr) daily except Mon and Tue 10am-noon, 2-5.15pm (Jul and Aug: daily 10am-5.15pm). Closed mid-nov to end Mar. 9€. ☎ 02 41 39 13 01.

Excursion

St-Georges-sur-Loire: former abbey – Jul and Aug: daily except Sat-Sun 11.30am-12.30pm, 2.30-6pm. ☎ 02 41 72 14 80.

La SOLOGNE

Ligny-le-Ribault: Maison du Cerf – ♿ Jun-mid-Sep: Wed, Sat, Sun and holidays 3pm-7pm (school holidays: daily except Mon); Mid-Sep-May: 2-6.30pm. Closed 1 Jan and 25 Dec. 3€. ☎ 02 38 45 45 44.

Neuvy: Church – Apply to the town hall to visit. ☎ 02 54 46 42 69.

Ménestreau-en-Villette: Domaine du Ciran – ♿ Apr-Sep: 10am-noon, 2-6pm; Oct-Mar: daily except Tue 10am-noon, 2-5pm. Closed 1 Jan and 25 Dec. 4.60€. ☎ 02 38 76 90 93. www.domaineduciran.com

Villeherviers: Church – Weekdays: ask at the administration office at the town hall to visit. ☎ 02 54 76 07 92.

Aliotis, les poissons du monde entier – ♿ Apr-Sep: 10am-6.30pm (Jul and Aug: 7.30pm); Jan-Mar and Oct-Dec: 11am-5.30pm. 10€, 9€ low season (children: 7€, 6.20€ low season). ☎ 02 54 95 26 26.

Gy-en-Sologne: Locature de la Straize – ♿ Apr to end Oct: guided tours (1hr) by appointment 2 weeks in advance with M. Picard, daily except Tue 10-11.30am, 3-6pm. Closed All Saints and Palm Sunday. 4€. ☎ 02 54 83 82 89.

Lassay-sur-Croisne: Église St-Denis – Daily. The key is available at the town hall. ☎ 02 54 83 87 64.

Château du Moulin – Apr-Sep: guided tours (1hr) daily except Wed 9-11.30am, 2-6.30pm. Closed Oct-Mar. 6.10€. ☎ 02 54 83 83 51.

SULLY-SUR-LOIRE 🛈 Pl. du Général-de-Gaulle, BP 12, 45600 SULLY-SUR-LOIRE, ☎ 02 38 36 23 70.

Église St-Germain – Tours of the outside only.

Château – Apr-Sep: 10am-6pm; Feb, Mar and Oct-Dec: 10am-noon, 2-5pm. Closed Jan and 25 Dec. 4.90€. ☎ 02 38 36 36 86. www.loiret.com

T

Château de TALCY

Château – ♿ May-Aug: 9.30am-noon, 2-6pm; Apr and Sep: 10am-noon, 2-5.30pm; Oct-Mar: daily except Tue 10am-noon, 2-4.30pm. Closed 1 Jan, 1 May, 1 and 11 Nov, 25 Dec. 4€ (under 18s: no charge). ☎ 02 54 81 03 01.

TOURS

🅱 78 r. Bernard-Palissy, 37000 TOURS, ☏ 02 47 70 37 37.

🅰 discovery tours. Information at the tourist office or on www.vpah.culture.fr

Musée du Gemmail – Daily except Mon 10am-noon, 2-6.30pm (mid-Nov to end Mar: Sat-Sun and public holidays). 4.57€. ☏ 02 47 61 01 19.

Musée St-Martin – Mid-Mar to mid-Nov: daily except Mon and Tue 9.30am-12.30pm, 2-5.30pm. Closed 1 May and 14 Jul. 2€. ☏ 02 47 64 48 87.

Hôtel Gouin – Apr-Sep: 9.30am-noon, 1.15-6.30pm; Oct-Mar: 9.30am-12.30pm, 2-5.30pm. Closed 1 Jan and 25 Dec. 3.50€. ☏ 02 47 66 22 32.

La Psalette – Apr and May: guided tours (30min) 10am-12.30pm, 2-5.30pm, Sun morning on request; May-Sep: 9.45am-1pm, 2-6pm, Sun morning on request; Oct-Mar: daily except Mon and Tue 9.30am-12.30pm, 2-5pm, Sun 2-5pm (Mar: 5.30pm). Closed 1 Jan, 1 May, 25 Dec. 2.50€. ☏ 02 47 47 05 19.

Centre de création contemporaine – ♿ Daily except Mon and Tue 2-6pm. Closed 1 Jan and 25 Dec. No charge. ☏ 02 47 66 50 00.

Chapelle St-Michel – Summer: 3-6pm; winter: Wed. Outside these periods, visits can be arranged by contacting Mme de Sinçay, 79 r. Blanqui, 37000 Tours. ☏ 02 47 66 65 95.

Musée des Vins de Touraine – Mid-Jun to mid-Sep: 9am-12.30pm, 2-6pm; mid-Sep to mid-Jun: daily except Tue 9am-noon, 2-6pm. Closed 1 Jan, 1 May, 14 Jul, 1 and 11 Nov, 25 Dec. 4€. ☏ 02 47 61 07 93.

Musée du Compagnonnage – ♿ Mid-Jun to mid-Sep: 9am-12.30pm, 2-6pm; mid-Sep to mid-Jun: daily except Tue 9am-noon, 2-6pm. Closed 1 Jan, 1 May, 14 Jul, 1 and 11 Nov, 25 Dec. 4€. ☏ 02 47 61 07 93.

Musée des Beaux-Arts – Daily except Tue 9am-12.45pm, 2-6pm. Closed 1 Jan, 1 May, 14 Jul, 1 and 11 Nov, 25 Dec. 4€. ☏ 02 47 05 68 73.

Atelier Histoire de Tours – Wed and Sat 3-6.30pm. No charge. ☏ 02 47 64 90 52.

Musée des Équipages militaires et du Train – Wed and Thu 2-5pm (last admission 1hr before closing). Closed Aug, school and public holidays. No charge. ☏ 02 47 77 33 07.

Prieuré de St-Cosme – ♿ Apr-Sep: 9am-7pm; Oct-Mar: 9.30am-12.30pm, 2-5pm. Closed 1 Jan and 25 Dec. 3.80€. ☏ 02 47 37 32 70.

Excursions

Grange de Meslay – ♿ Easter to All Saints: Sat-Sun and public holidays 3-6.30pm. 4€. ☏ 02 47 29 19 29. www.meslay.com

Luynes: Château – Apr to end Sep: guided tours (45min) 10am-6pm. 6.90€ (children: 3€). ☏ 02 47 55 67 55.

Savonnières: Grottes pétrifiantes – Feb to mid-Dec: guided tours (1hr 15min) 9.30am-noon, 2-6pm (Apr-Sep: 9am-6.30pm). Closed Thu from mid-Nov to mid-Dec. 5€. ☏ 02 47 50 00 09.

TROO

🅱 41800 TROO, ☏ 02 54 72 58 74.

Grotte pétrifiante – 10am-8pm. 1€. ☏ 02 54 72 52 04.

U

Château d'USSÉ

Château – Apr-Sep: guided tours (45min) 9.30am-6.30pm; mid-Feb to end Mar and end Sep to mid-Nov: 10am-noon, 2-5.30pm. Closed mid-Nov to mid-Feb. 9.80€. ☏ 02 47 95 54 05.

Rivarennes: La Poire Tapée à l'Ancienne – Daily 10am-noon, 2-7pm. ☏ 02 47 95 49 19

V

Château de VALENÇAY

Château – Apr to early Nov: 9.30am-6pm (Jul and Aug: 7.30pm). Closed early Nov to end Mar. 8.50€ château and show (children: 4.50€). ☏ 02 54 00 10 66. www.chateau-valencay.com

Musée de l'Automobile du Centre – ♿ Apr-Oct: 10am-12.30pm, 1.30-6pm (Jul and Aug: 7.30pm). Closed 1 Jan and 25 Dec. 4€. ☏ 02 54 00 07 74.

VENDÔME

🅱 Hôtel du Saillant, Parc Ronsard, 41100 VENDÔME, ☎ 02 54 77 05 07.

🅰 discovery tours. May-Oct: guided tours at 3pm or 4pm. 4.70€. Information at the tourist office.

Église de la Madeleine – Closed Sun afternoon.

Castle – Jun-Sep: 9am-8pm; Oct-May: 9am-7pm. No charge. Theme visits in high season (1hr 15min). 3.90€. ☎ 02 54 77 05 07.

Chapter-house – Daily except Tue 10am-noon, 2-6pm. Closed 1 Jan, 1 May, 25 Dec and Sun (Nov-Mar). No charge. ☎ 02 54 77 26 13.

Museum – Daily except Tue 10am-noon, 2-6pm. Closed 1 Jan, 1 May, 25 Dec and Sun (Nov-Mar). 2.65€. ☎ 02 54 77 26 13.

Nourray: Church – Apply to the town hall to visit (Tue and Thu morning, Fri afternoon). ☎ 02 54 77 05 38.

Villemardy: Church – Guided tours by appointment with M. Foucher, 15 rue des Peziers, 41100 Villemardy, ☎ 02 54 23 80 02.

Manoir de la Possonnière – 🕭 Mid-Jun to mid-Sep: guided tours (45min, last admission 6.30pm) daily except Tue 2-7pm, unaccompanied tours 10am-2pm (mid-Jun to mid-Aug: evening tours Fri and Sat 7-9pm); end of Mar to mid-Jun and mid-Sep to mid-Nov: Mon, Fri, Sat-Sun and public holidays 2-6pm (last admission 5.30pm). Closed mid-Nov to end Mar. 5€ (guided tours), 3.50€ (unaccompanied and evening tours). ☎ 02 54 85 23 30.

Poncé-sur-le-Loir: Les grès du Loir – 🕭 Daily except Mon 10am-noon, 2-6pm, Sun and public holidays 2.30-6.30pm. Closed 31 Dec. 4.60€. ☎ 02 43 44 45 31.
Château – Apr-Oct: 10am-noon, 2-6pm, Sun 2-6pm. 5.30€. ☎ 02 43 44 45 39.

Vaas: Moulin à blé de Rotrou – Jul and Aug: guided tours (1hr 30min) 2.30-5.30pm; Apr-Jun, Sep and Oct: Sun and public holidays 2.30-5.30pm. 3.20€. ☎ 02 43 46 70 22.

Pringé: Eglise – If closed, contact Mme Doyen, 1 place de l'Église.

Château de VILLANDRY

🅱 Le Potager, 37510 Château de VILLANDRY, ☎ 02 47 50 12 66.

Gardens – Nov-Feb: 9am-5.30pm; Mar: 9am-6pm; Apr and mid-Sep to mid Oct: 9am-7pm; May to mid-Sep: 9am-7.30pm; mid to end Oct: 9am-6.30pm. 5€, 7.50€ château and gardens (children: 3.50€/5€). ☎ 02 47 50 02 09. www.chateauvillandry.com

Château – Jul and Aug: 9am-6.30pm; Feb and end Oct to mid-Nov: 9am-5pm; Mar: 9am-5.30pm; Apr-Jun, Sep and Oct: 9am-6pm. Closed mid-Nov to early Feb. 7.50€ (château and gardens). ☎ 02 47 50 02 09.

Index

Tours *Indre-et-Loire* . . . . Towns, sights and tourist regions followed by the name of the departement.

Balzac, Honoré de . . . . People, historical events, artistic styles and local terms mentioned in the guide.

A

Abbo 259
Accomodation 26
The Affair of the White Flag 141
Agriculture 52, 56
Alain-Fournier 52, 73
Alcuin 52, 63, 72, 285
Alluyes *Eure-et-Loir* 132
Amboise *Indre-et-Loire* 90
Ancenis Loire-Atlantique 109
The Amboise Conspiracy . . .52, 65, 90
Ancenis *Loire-Atlantique* 109
Angers *Maine-et-Loire* 96
Angevin style 52, 81
Anjou 52, 56
Anjou, Charles of 97
Antin, Duc d' 247
Aquitaine, Eleonor of 117
Arbrissel, Robert d' 190
Arche de la Nature *Sarthe* 224
Arche (Refuge) *Mayenne* 150
Architecture, religious 52, 81
Architecture, secular 52, 80
Areines *Loir-et-Cher* 134
Artenay *Loiret* 242
Arville (Commanderie) *Loir-et-Cher* .226
Asnières (Ancienne Abbaye)
    Maine-et-Loire 232
Asnières-sur-Vègre *Sarthe* 256
Aubigné, Françoise d' 213
Aubigné-sur-Layon *Maine-et-Loire* . .204
Aurelle de Paladines, General . . .52, 66
Auvers-le-Hamon *Sarthe* 256
Avon-les-Roches *Indre-et-Loire* 198
Azay-le-Rideau *Indre-et-Loire* 110
Azay-sur-Indre *Indre-et-Loire* 209

B

Babou family 161
Bagneux *Maine-et-Loire* 269
Baïf, Jean-Antoine de 52, 73
Baillou *Loir-et-Cher* 227
Balue, Jean 208, 295
Balzac, Honoré de 52, 73,
                                    113, 131, 303
Bas-Maine 52, 56
Bastarnay, Imbert de 229
Baugé *Maine-et-Loire* 114
Baugeois 52, 56
Bazin, Hervé 52, 73
Bazin, René 52, 73
Bazouges-sur-le-Loir *Sarthe* 189
Beauce 52, 55
Beaufort-en-Vallée *Maine-et-Loire* . .271
Beaugency *Loiret* 117

Beaujeu, Anne de 193
Beaulieu-lès-Loches *Indre-et-Loire* . .209
Beaulieu-sur-Layon *Maine-et-Loire* . .204
Beaune-la-Rolande *Loiret* 246
Beaupréau *Maine-et-Loire* 178
Beauregard (Château) *Loir-et-Cher* .120
Beauval (Zoo-parc) *Loir-et-Cher* . .258
Becket, Thomas 140
Bed and Breakfast 27
Béhuard *Maine-et-Loire* 107
Bellay, Joachim du 52, 73, 109
Bellegarde *Loiret* 247
Benedict, Saint 258
Benjamin, René 52, 73
Béranger, Pierre-Jean de 52, 73
Bercé (Forêt) *Sarthe* 120
Berengaria, Queen 212
Berthelot, Gilles 110
Béthune, Maximilien de 281
Birds and birdwatching 36
The Black Death 285
Bléré *Indre-et-Loire* 161
Blésois 52, 55
Blois *Loir-et-Cher* 121
Blou *Maine-et-Loire* 196
Bocage 52, 54
Boësse *Loiret* 246
Bohier, Thomas 158
Boires 52, 55
Les Bois (Étang) *Loiret* 210
Bois-Aubry (Abbaye) *Indre-et-Loire* .253
Boiscommun *Loiret* 246
Bois-Montbourcher *Maine-et-Loire* .151
La Boissière *Maine-et-Loire* 212
Bollée, Amédée 213
Bonaventure (Manoir) *Loir-et-Cher* .306
Bonchamps, Charles de 108
Bonneval *Eure-et-Loir* 132
Bosse, Abraham 293
Bouër *Sarthe* 140
Boumois (Château) *Maine-et-Loire* .269
The Bourbons 52, 61
La Bourdaisière *Indre-et-Loire* 161
Le Bourg-d'Iré *Maine-et-Loire* 273
La Bourgonnière (Château)
    Loire-Atlantique 109
Bourgueil *Indre-et-Loire* 134
Bourgueil, Baudri de 52, 72
Bournan *Indre-et-Loire* 263
Bourré *Loir-et-Cher* 234
Bourré, Jean 248, 257
Boussay *Indre-et-Loire* 251
Boynes *Loiret* 246
Bracieux *Loir-et-Cher* 279
Brain-sur-Allonnes *Maine-et-Loire* . .135
Branicki, Count Xavier 229
Breil *Maine-et-Loire* 116
Brézé (Château) *Maine-et-Loire* . . .136
Briare *Loiret* 136
Briçonnet, Catherine 158

Bridoré *Indre-et-Loire* 209
Brissac (Centre de découverte
du milieu aquatique
et de la pêche) *Maine-et-Loire* . . .138
Brissac (Château) *Maine-et-Loire* . .137
Brittany, Anne of 52, 71, 122
Broc *Maine-et-Loire* 212
Brou *Eure-et-Loir* 138
La Bruère-sur-Loir *Sarthe* 309
Budget .22
Bueil-en-Touraine *Indre-et-Loire* . . .262
La Bussière *Loiret* 195

C

Cabernet de Saumur 174
Cadre Noir 265
Calder, Alexander 113
Calendar of events 47
Calvin, Jean 52, 65, 239
Camping 27
Candes-St-Martin *Indre-et-Loire* . . .172
Canoeing 41
The Capets 52, 60, 284
Carème, Marie-Antoine 300
Carmet, Jean 134
Carnutes 52, 63
Car rental 26
Castles 52, 67
La Celle-Guenand *Indre-et-Loire* . . .196
Cenomanni 52, 63
Les Cerqueux-sous-Passavant
Maine-et-Loire 203
Ceton *Sarthe* 140
Chabris *Indre* 301
Chalonnes-sur-Loire *Maine-et-Loire* .107
Chambiers (Forest) *Maine-et-Loire* .189
Chambon-la-Forêt *Loiret* 247
Chambord (Château) *Loir-et-Cher* . .141
Chamerolles (Château) *Loiret* 247
Champagnes 52, 54
Champchevrier (Château)
Indre-et-Loire 201
Champigny wine 174
Champigny-sur-Veude
Indre-et-Loire 252
Champtocé-sur-Loire *Maine-et-Loire* 108
Champtoceaux *Maine-et-Loire* 110
Chandelais (Forêt) *Maine-et-Loire* . .115
Chanteloup (Pagode) 94
Chanzy, General 52, 67
Charlemagne 285
Charles, Jacques 119
Charles V 141
Charles VII 212
Charles VIII 52, 64, 166, 236
La Chartre-sur-le-Loir *Sarthe* 308
Château-du-Loir *Sarthe* 308
Châteaudun *Eure-et-Loir* 145
Château-Gontier *Mayenne* 148
Château-la-Vallière *Indre-et-Loire* . .153
Château-la-Vallière (Forêt)
Indre-et-Loire 153
Chateauneuf-sur-Loire *Loiret* 153
Château-Renault *Indre-et-Loire* 155
Châteaux 52, 67
Le Châtelier (Château) *Indre-et-Loire*182
Châtillon-sur-Cher *Loir-et-Cher* 274
Chaumont-sur-Loire (Château)
Loir-et-Cher 156
Chaumont-sur-Tharonne *Loir-et-Cher* .277
Chécy *Loiret* 154
Chemazé *Mayenne* 150
Chémery (Château) *Loir-et-Cher* . . .258

Chemillé *Maine-et-Loire* 178
Chênehutte-les-Tuffeaux
Maine-et-Loire 270
Chenillé-Changé *Maine-et-Loire* 151
Chenonceau (Château)
Indre-et-Loire 156, 158
Cherré (Site Archéologique) *Sarthe* .309
Cheverny (Château) *Loir-et-Cher* . .162
Chigné *Maine-et-Loire* 212
Children 39
Children's Crusade 133
Chinon (Château) *Indre-et-Loire* . . .164
Chissay-en-Touraine *Loir-et-Cher* . . .234
Choiseul, Duke of 94
Cholet *Maine-et-Loire* 175
Cholet handkerchiefs 177
Chouans 66
Chouzé-sur-Loire *Indre-et-Loire* . . .135
Christopher, Saint 91
Cinq-Mars-la-Pile *Indre-et-Loire* . . .200
Ciran (Domaine) *Loir-et-Cher* 278
Classical style 52, 81
Cléry-St-André (Basilique) *Loiret* . .180
Les Clos (Futaie) *Sarthe* 121
Clovis .284
Cloyes-sur-le-Loir *Eure-et-Loir* 133
Combreux *Loiret* 154
Conie *Eure-et-Loir* 132
Connerré *Sarthe* 224
Cormery *Indre-et-Loire* 209
Corniche Angevine 107
Cossé, Charles de 137
Cossé-le-Vivien *Mayenne* 181
Cottereau, Jean 52, 66
Le Coudray-Montbault (Château)
Maine-et-Loire 178
Le Coudray-Montpensier (Château)
Indre-et-Loire 171
La Coudre (Fontaine) *Sarthe* 121
Coulangé *Indre-et-Loire* 230
Courgenard *Sarthe* 140
Courier, Paul-Louis 52, 73, 161
Courtangis (Château) *Sarthe* 140
Courtanvaux (Château) *Sarthe* 262
Courteline, Georges 52, 73
Courtineau (Route) 198
Court life 52, 70
Couture-sur-Loir *Loir-et-Cher* 307
Craon *Mayenne* 181
Crissay-sur-Manse *Indre-et-Loire* . . .198
Cross of Anjou 114, 212
Crotti, Jean 52, 83
Crouzilles *Indre-et-Loire* 171
Cunault (Église) *Maine-et-Loire* 270
Cuon *Maine-et-Loire* 116
Currency 22
Customs 21
Cycling 43

D

Dampierre-en-Burly *Loiret* 195
Dangeau *Eure-et-Loir* 132
Daon *Mayenne* 151
Dénezé-sous-Doué (Caverne sculptée)
Maine-et-Loire 184
Denier tournois 285
Descartes *Indre-et-Loire* 182
Descartes, René 52, 73, 182
Desportes, François 194
La Devinière *Indre-et-Loire* 170
Disabled travellers 20
Discounts (student, youth, teacher) .23
Dodun .145

Dolet, Étienne 52, 73
Doué-la-Fontaine *Maine-et-Loire* . .182
Dovalle, Charles 231
Dried apples 174
Dried pears 299
Driving tours 33
Dunois, Bastard of Orléans 145
Dupetit-Thouars, Aristide 269
Duplessis-Mornay 265
Durtal *Maine-et-Loire* 189

E

Edict of Nantes 52, 66
Electricity 30
Embassies and consulates in France .19
Enamels 137
L'Épau (Abbaye) *Sarthe* 223
Esves-le-Moutier *Indre-et-Loire* . . .264
Étampes, Duchess of 52, 72
Les Étilleux *Eure-et-Loir* 140
Euro (currency) 22

F

Falunières 52, 54
Faluns Sea 52, 54
Fay-aux-Loges *Loiret* 154
Faye-la-Vineuse *Indre-et-Loire* 253
Fercé-sur-Sarthe *Sarthe* 224
Ferrière-Larçon *Indre-et-Loire* 182
Ferté, Maréchal de la 187
La Ferté-Beauharnais *Loir-et-Cher* . .277
La Ferté-Bernard *Sarthe* 184
La Ferté-St-Aubin *Loiret* 186
Fiefs 52, 64
Fillé *Sarthe* 224
Fishing 41
Flamboyant style 52, 81
La Flèche *Sarthe* 187
The Flying Squad 52, 71
Fontaine-Guérin *Maine-et-Loire* . . .116
Fontaines-en-Sologne *Loir-et-Cher* . .280
Fontevraud-l'Abbaye *Maine-et-Loire* 190
Food and wine 52, 84
Forests 120
Forges (Maisons troglodytes)
    Maine-et-Loire 184
Le Fou de l'Âne 94
Fougères-sur-Bièvres (Château)
    Loir-et-Cher 193
Fouquet, Jean 99, 285
François I 52, 64, 122, 253
Frazé *Eure-et-Loir* 139
Frescoes 52, 82
Fréteval *Loir-et-Cher* 134
Fruit 52, 56
Le Fuilet *Maine-et-Loire* 178
Fulk IV 117
Fulk Nerra 52, 60, 63, 96,
                    114, 148, 179, 231
Fulk V the Younger 96

G

Gallerande (Château) *Sarthe* 309
Garnier, Robert 184
Gâtines 52, 54
Gaucourt, Raoul de 235
Gauzlin 259

Gemmail 52, 83
Genevoix, Maurice 52, 73
Genillé *Indre-et-Loire* 230
Gennes *Maine-et-Loire* 271
Genneteil *Maine-et-Loire* 212
Geoffrey V 97
Germigny-des-Près (Église) *Loiret* . .260
Gidy *Loiret* 242
Gien *Loiret* 193
Gizeux *Indre-et-Loire* 195
Glossary of French terms 50
Golf 44
Goubaudière (Ferme) *Maine-et-Loire* .180
Gouet, William 139
Le Grand-Pressigny *Indre-et-Loire* . .196
Gresset, Jean-Baptiste 188
Grez-Neuville *Maine-et-Loire* 152
Grignon *Loiret* 210
Grillemont (Château) *Indre-et-Loire* .264
Grottes Pétrifiantes *Indre-et-Loire* . .296
Le Gué-du-Loir *Loir-et-Cher* 306
Gué-Péan (Château) *Loir-et-Cher* . .234
Guise, Henri de 122
Gy-en-Sologne *Loir-et-Cher* 280

H

La Haie-Longue *Maine-et-Loire* 107
La Hamonnière (Manoir)
    Maine-et-Loire 248
La Haute-Guerche (Château)
    Maine-et-Loire 204
Haut-Maine 52, 56
Health 21
Henri III 52, 65, 122
Henri IV 97
Henri V 141
Henry II 212
L'Hermitière (Sources) *Sarthe* 121
La Herpinière (Moulin)
    Maine-et-Loire 173
Highway code 25
Historical table and notes 60
Historical tourist routes 35
Hoche, General 52, 66
Hostels 27
Hot-air balloons 39
Hotels 26
House of Anjou 96, 265
House of Blois 121
Hubert, Saint 91
Humanists 52, 72
Hunting 44

I

L'Île-Bouchard *Indre-et-Loire* 197
Illiers-Combray *Eure-et-Loir* 199
Indre (Vallée) 209
Indrois (Vallée) 230
Ingrandes *Maine-et-Loire* 108
Ingrand, Max 52, 82
L'Isle-Briand (Haras National)
    Maine-et-Loire 152
L'Isle Verte *Loir-et-Cher* 307
Jacob, Max 52, 73, 259
La Jaille-Yvon *Maine-et-Loire* 151
Jallanges (Château) *Indre-et-Loire* . .131
Jarzé *Maine-et-Loire* 116
Joan of Arc 165, 235
Juigné-sur-Sarthe *Sarthe* 225

L

Lackland, John 52, 64, 165
Lamotte-Beuvron *Loir-et-Cher* 278
Landscape 54
Langeais *Indre-et-Loire* 199
Lanoyer, Emmanuel 205
Lanthenay *Loir-et-Cher* 255
Lassay-sur-Croisne *Loir-et-Cher* 280
Lathan (Château) *Maine-et-Loire* . .116
Lavardin *Loir-et-Cher* 201
Law, John 300
Layes 52, 55
Layon (Vallée) 203
Lerné *Indre-et-Loire* 171
Leugny (Château) *Indre-et-Loire* . . .161
Lévis-Mirepoix family 133
Leygue, Louis 305
Le Liget (Chartreuse) *Indre-et-Loire* 229
Ligny-le-Ribault *Loir-et-Cher* 277
Ligueil *Indre-et-Loire* 263
Linières-Bouton *Maine-et-Loire* 116
Le Lion-d'Angers *Maine-et-Loire* . . .151
Liré *Maine-et-Loire* 109
Livestock 52, 57
Local industry 35
Loches *Indre-et-Loire* 205
Loire (Vallée) 52, 55
La Lorie (Château) *Maine-et-Loire* . .272
Lorraine, Louise de 159
Lorris *Loiret* 210
Lorris, Guillaume de 52, 72
Loudon (Bois) *Sarthe* 224
Louis XI 199, 295
Louis XII 52, 64
Louis XIV 141
Louresse (Village troglodytique)
    Maine-et-Loire 184
Louvois, Marquis de 262
Luché-Pringé *Sarthe* 309
Le Lude (Château) *Sarthe* 211
Lunay *Loir-et-Cher* 306
Lurçat, Jean 52, 83, 103
Luther 52, 65
Lutz-en-Dunois *Eure-et-Loir* 148
Luynes *Indre-et-Loire* 306

M

Maine 52, 56
Malesherbes *Loiret* 245
Malicorne-sur-Sarthe *Sarthe* 225
Manessier, Alfred 52, 82
Le Mans *Sarthe* 212
Manse (Vallée) 198
Marboué *Eure-et-Loir* 132
Marcel, Alexandre 179
Marçon *Sarthe* 308
Mardelles 52, 55
Marmoutier (Abbaye) *Indre-et-Loire* 131
Maroutière (Château) *Mayenne* 150
Martel, Geoffroy 301
Martigné-Briand *Maine-et-Loire* . .204
Martin, Saint 52, 63, 284
Maulévrier *Maine-et-Loire* 179
Maulévrier (Forêt) *Maine-et-Loire* . .178
Maves *Loir-et-Cher* 130
Mayenne (Vallée) 151
Mazangé *Loir-et-Cher* 306
Medical treatment 21
Medici, Catherine de 52, 72, 159
Medici, Marie de 124

Ménars Loir-et-Cher 130
Ménestreau-en-Villette *Loiret* 278
Mennetou-sur-Cher *Loir-et-Cher* . . .255
Mercier, Pierre-Mathurin 148
Mercogliano, Pacello de 52, 80
Meslay (Grange) *Indre-et-Loire* 295
Mettray (Dolmen) *Indre-et-Loire* . . .296
Meung, Jean de 52, 72
Meung-sur-Loire, *Loiret* 225
Michel, Jean 52, 72
Miré *Maine-et-Loire* 257
Le Moal, Jean 52, 82
Moléans *Eure-et-Loir* 132
Molière 141
Mondoubleau *Loir-et-Cher* 226
Monmousseau (Caves) *Loir-et-Cher* .233
Montayer (Étang) *Maine-et-Loire* . .138
Montbazon *Indre-et-Loire* 296
Montfort-le-Gesnois *Sarthe* 224
Montgeoffroy (Château)
    Maine-et-Loire 272
Montigny-le-Gannelon *Eure-et-Loire* 133
Montjean-sur-Loire *Maine-et-Loire* . .108
Montlouis-sur-Loire *Indre-et-Loire* . .161
Montmirail *Sarthe* 140
Montmorency-Laval, François de . .188
Montoire-sur-le-Loir *Loir-et-Cher* . .228
Montpoupon (Château) *Loir-et-Cher* 234
Montrésor *Indre-et-Loire* 229
Montreuil-Bellay *Maine-et-Loire* . .230
Montrichard *Loir-et-Cher* 232
Montsoreau *Maine-et-Loire* 172
Mortiercrolles *Mayenne* 182
Mosnier, Jean 164
Motoring 25
Motor racing circuits 222
La Motte-Glain (Château)
    Maine-et-Loire 250
Mouliherne *Maine-et-Loire* 116
Le Moulin (Château) *Loir-et-Cher* . .280
Moulin, Philippe du 280
Mulsans *Loir-et-Cher* 130
Mushrooms 173, 270
Musset, Alfred de 283, 306

N

Négron *Indre-et-Loire* 131
Néricault-Destouches 52, 73
Neuvy *Loir-et-Cher* 277
Neuvy-le-Roi *Indre-et-Loire* 262
Notre-Dame-des-Ardilliers (Église)
    Maine-et-Loire 269
Notre-Dame-de-Lorette (Chapelle)
    Indre-et-Loire 198
Notre-Dame-de-Montplacé (Chapelle)
    Maine-et-Loire 116
Nouans-les-Fontaines *Indre-et-Loire* .230
Nourray *Loir-et-Cher* 305
Noyen-sur-Sarthe *Sarthe* 224
Nyoiseau *Maine-et-Loire* 273

O

Odo .259
Olivet *Loiret* 243
Orchaise *Loir-et-Cher* 130
Orléanais 52, 55
Orléans *Loiret* 235
Orléans (Canal) 154
Orléans (Forest) 52, 55
Orléans, Charles of 52, 72, 122

Orléans, Gaston of 124
Oudon (Vallée) 273
Oudon *Loire-Atlantique* 110
Oudry, Jean-Baptiste 194

P

Papin, Denis 127
Parçay-les-Pins *Maine-et-Loire* 196
Parçay-sur-Vienne *Indre-et-Loire* . . .172
Parcé-sur-Sarthe *Sarthe* 225
Parks and gardens 35
Passavant-sur-Layon *Maine-et-Loire* .203
Passport and visa regulations 21
Pays Fort 52, 55
Peguy, Charles 52, 73
Le Perche-Gouet 139
Perrault, Charles 298
Petite Couère (Domaine)
    Maine-et-Loire 273
Philippe Auguste 285
Pierre Couverte (Dolmen)
    Maine-et-Loire 115
Pierre Frite (Menhir) *Maine-et-Loire* 250
Pignerolle (Château) *Maine-et-Loire* .105
Pirmil *Sarthe* 224
Pithiviers *Loiret* 245
Plantagenet, Henry 97, 117
Plantagenets 97, 190, 212
Plantagenet style 52, 81
The Pléiade 52, 64, 73
Plessis, Armand du 251
Le Plessis-Bourré (Château)
    Maine-et-Loire 248
Le Plessis-Macé (Château)
    Maine-et-Loire 249
Poitiers, Diane de . . .52, 72, 156, 158
Poncé-sur-le-Loir *Sarthe* 307
Pont-de-Ruan *Indre-et-Loire* 113
Pontigné *Maine-et-Loire* 115
Pontlevoy *Loir-et-Cher* 249
Les Ponts-de-Cé *Maine-et-Loire* . . .106
La Possonnière (Manoir)
    Loir-et-Cher 307
Post offices 30
Pouancé *Maine-et-Loire* 250
Poulain, Auguste 250
Practical information 16
Preuilly-sur-Claise *Indre-et-Loire* . . .251
Le Prieuré *Maine-et-Loire* 271
Pringé *Sarthe* 309
Proust, Marcel 52, 73, 199
Public holidays 31
Puiseaux *Loiret* 246
Le Puy-Notre-Dame *Maine-et-Loire* .232

Q – R

Quarts de chaume 107
Rabelais, François . . .52, 73, 165, 170
Rablay-sur-Layon *Maine-et-Loire* . .204
Racan, Marquis de 52, 73, 262
Radegund, Saint 168
Raguin (Château) *Maine-et-Loire* . .273
Rais, Gilles de 108
Rambling 44
Les Réaux *Indre-et-Loire* 135
The Reformation 285
Reignac-sur-Indre *Indre-et-Loire* . . .209
Renaissance style 52, 81
La Renaudie 285
Renazé *Mayenne* 181
René, King of Anjou 52, 64, 97

Restaurants 28
Restigné *Indre-et-Loire* 135
The Revolution 52, 66
Rhodon *Loir-et-Cher* 306
Ribou (Lac) *Maine-et-Loire* 180
Richelieu *Indre-et-Loire* 251
Richelieu, Cardinal de 251
Riding 44
Rivarennes *Indre-et-Loire* 300
Le Rivau (Château) *Indre-et-Loire* . .172
River cruising 40
Robertet, Florimond 127
Robert-Houdin, Jean Eugène 129
Rochambeau *Loir-et-Cher* 306
Rochambeau, Maréchal de . . .303, 306
Rochechouart de Mortemart,
    Gabrielle de 190
Roche-Clermault (Château)
    Indre-et-Loire 171
Rochecorbon *Indre-et-Loire* 131
Rochefort-sur-Loire *Maine-et-Loire* .107
La Roche-Racan (Château)
    Indre-et-Loire 262
Les Roches-l'Évêque *Loir-et-Cher* . .307
Les Roches-Tranchelion (Collégiale)
    Indre-et-Loire 198
Rohan-Guéménée, Pierre de 250
Rollo, M 52, 82
Romilly-sur-Aigre *Eure-et-Loir* 133
Romorantin-Lanthenay *Loir-et-Cher* 253
Ronsard, Pierre de 52, 73,
                                134, 283, 308
Les Rosiers-sur-Loire *Maine-et-Loire* 271
Rougemont (Ferme) *Eure-et-Loir* . . .140
Rousseau, Jean-Jacques 159
Le Royer de la Dauversière, Jérôme 188
Ruggieri, Cosimo 156

S

Sablé-sur-Sarthe *Sarthe* 255
Saché *Indre-et-Loire* 113
St-Agil (Château) *Loir-et-Cher* 226
St-Aignan *Loir-et-Cher* 257
St-Barthélemy-d'Anjou
    Maine-et-Loire 104
St Bartholomew's Massacre . . .52, 65
St-Benoît-sur-Loire *Loiret* 258
St-Brisson-sur-Loire *Loiret* 195
St-Calais *Sarthe* 261
St-Christophe *Eure-et-Loir* 132
St-Christophe-sur-le-Nais
    Indre-et-Loire 262
St-Claude *Loir-et-Cher* 133
St-Cyr-en-Bourg *Maine-et-Loire* . . .269
St-Denis-d'Anjou *Mayenne* 257
St-Dyé-sur-Loire *Loir-et-Cher* 244
St-Épain *Indre-et-Loire* 198
St-Étienne-de-Chigny *Indre-et-Loire* .200
St-Florent-le-Vieil *Maine-et-Loire* . .108
St-Georges-sur-Loire *Maine-et-Loire* 275
St-Hilaire-St-Florent *Maine-et-Loire* .269
St-Jean-du-Grais (Prieuré)
    Indre-et-Loire 161
St-Jean-Froidmentel *Loir-et-Cher* . .133
St-Lambert-du-Lattay *Maine-et-Loire* 204
St-Laurent-de-la-Plaine
    Maine-et-Loire 178
St-Laurent-des-Eaux (CNPE)
    Loir-et-Cher 244
St-Laurent-en-Gâtines *Indre-et-Loire* 155
St-Lazare (Chapelle) *Loir-et-Cher* . .258
St-Martin-le-Beau *Indre-et-Loire* . . .161
St-Maur-de-Glanfeuil (Abbaye)
    Maine-et-Loire 271

St-Ouen (Château) *Mayenne* 150
St-Paterne-Racan *Indre-et-Loire* . . .262
St-Quentin-sur-Indrois
  Indre-et-Loire 230
St-Sylvain-d'Anjou *Maine-et-Loire* . .106
St-Ulphace *Eure-et-Loir* 140
St-Viâtre *Loir-et-Cher* 279
Ste-Catherine-de-Fierbois
  Indre-et-Loire 264
Ste-Maure-de-Touraine
  Indre-et-Loire 263
Salbris *Loir-et-Cher* 279
Salisbury, Earl of 236
Sargé-sur-Braye *Loir-et-Cher* 227
Sarthe (Vallée) 224
Sasnières (Domaine) *Loir-et-Cher* . .202
Saumur *Maine-et-Loire* 265
Saumurois 52, 56
Sautret (Château) *Maine-et-Loire* . .152
Savennières *Maine-et-Loire* 107
Savennières *Indre-et-Loire* 296
Savoy, Louise of 52, 71
Saxe, Maréchal de 143
Say, Mademoiselle 156
Scarron, Paul 213
Segré *Maine-et-Loire* 272
Selles-St-Denis *Loir-et-Cher* 279
Selles-sur-Cher *Loir-et-Cher* 273
Semur-en-Vallon *Sarthe* 140
Serrant (Château) 274
Seuilly-Côteaux *Indre-et-Loire* 171
Shopping 33
Siege of 1428-1429 235
Siege warfare 52, 68
Solesmes *Sarthe* 256
Son et lumière shows 49
Sorel, Agnès 52, 71, 207
Souday *Loir-et-Cher* 227
Souvigny-en-Sologne *Loir-et-Cher* . .278
Spay *Sarthe* 224
Sports 41
Staël, Madame de 156
Stained glass 52, 81
Stuart, Mary 52, 72
Sue, Eugène 119
Suèvres *Loir-et-Cher* 130
Sully-sur-Loire *Loiret* 281

T

Talcy *Loir-et-Cher* 283
Talleyrand-Périgord,
  Charles-Maurice de 300
Tapestries 52, 83
Tatin, Robert 181
Tavant *Indre-et-Loire* 172
Tax, recovery of cost 33
Telephoning 30
Templars 227
Le Temple *Loir-et-Cher* 227
Le Tertre Rouge
  (Parc Zoologique) *Sarthe* 189
Thematic Itineraries 35
Theodulf 52, 63, 258-259
Thésée *Loir-et-Cher* 234
Thiron-Gardais *Eure-et-Loir* 140
Le Thoureil *Maine-et-Loire* 271
Time 31
Tipping .22
Le Tort, Lambert 145
Touraine 52, 55
Touraine (Aquarium) 95
Tourist offices
  inside France 19
  outside France 18

Tourist trains 37
Tours *Indre-et-Loire* 283
Tours, Gregory of 52, 72, 284
Travelling to France 24
Trélazé *Maine-et-Loire* 107
Trèves-Cunault *Maine-et-Loire* 270
Troo *Loir-et-Cher* 297
Troussay (Château) *Indre-et-Loire* . .164
Tufa 52, 54
Turpin-de-Crissé, Lancelot-Théodore 103
Turquant *Maine-et-Loire* 173-174

U - V

Ussé (Château) 298
Vaas *Sarthe* 309
Valençay (Château) *Indre* 300
Vallée (Étang) Loiret 154
Valmer (Château) *Indre-et-Loire* . . .131
Vallée (Étang) Loiret 154
Valmer (Château) *Indre-et-Loire* . . .131
The Valois 52, 60
Valois, Marguerite of 52, 72
Varennes 52, 54
Varennes-Bourreau (Chapelle)
  Mayenne 257
Varennes-sur-Loire *Indre-et-Loire* . .135
Vaujours (Château) *Indre-et-Loire* . .153
Vaux (Château) *Maine-et-Loire* 257
Vegetables 52, 56
Vendée War 52, 66
Vendôme *Loir-et-Cher* 301
Vénevelles (Manoir) *Sarthe* 309
Verdon (Lac) *Maine-et-Loire* 179
Véretz *Indre-et-Loire* 161
Vernantes *Maine-et-Loire* 196
Vernoil *Maine-et-Loire* 196
Vernou-sur-Brenne *Indre-et-Loire* . .131
Véron (River) 52, 55, 297
Le Vieil-Baugé *Maine-et-Loire* 117
Vieux-Bourg d'Artins *Loir-et-Cher* . .307
Vieux Bourg de Cravant
  Indre-et-Loire 171
Vigny, Alfred de 52, 73, 205
Villaines-les-Rochers *Indre-et-Loire* .113
Villandry (Château) 310
Villedieu-le-Château *Loir-et-Cher* . . .308
Villeherviers *Loir-et-Cher* 278
Villemardy *Loir-et-Cher* 305
Villeneuve-la-Barre *Maine-et-Loire* . .204
Villesavin (Château) 144
Villiers-sur-Loir *Loir-et-Cher* 306
Villon, François 52, 72
Vinci, Leonardo da 93, 95
Visconti, Valentina 145
Volney, Comte de 181
Voltaire 282
Vouvray *Indre-et-Loire* 131
Vouvray wines 131

W - Y - Z

Wars of Religion 285
Weather 20
Windmills 52, 57
Wine 49
Wine country 36
Wright, Wilbur 213
Yèvre-le-Châtel *Loiret* 245
Yèvres (Église) *Eure-et-Loir* 139
Yron (Chapelle) *Eure-et-Loir* 133
Zola, Émile 133

Notes

Notes

Notes